WINDOWING SYSTEM API REFERENCE

UNIX SVR4.2

Edited by Lynda Feng

UNIX
Press

Published by Prentice-Hall, Inc.
A Simon & Schuster Company
Englewood Cliffs, New Jersey 07632

TRADEMARKS

Helvetica, Times is a registered trademark of Linotype Co.
PostScript is a registered trademark of Adobe Systems, Inc.
MoOLIT is a trademark of UNIX System Laboratories, Inc. in the USA and other countries.
Motif is a trademark of the Open Software Foundation, Inc.
OPEN LOOK is a registered trademark of UNIX System Laboratories, Inc. in the USA and other countries.
UNIX is a registered trademark of UNIX System Laboratories, Inc. in the USA and other countries.
WE is a registered trademark of AT&T.
X Window System is a trademark of Massachusetts Institute of Technology.
XENIX is a registered trademark of Microsoft Corporation.
XWIN is a registered trademark of UNIX System Laboratories, Inc. in the USA and other countries.

10 9 8 7 6 5 4 3 2 1

ISBN 0-13-017716-4

UNIX
PRESS
A Prentice Hall Title

PRENTICE HALL

ORDERING INFORMATION

UNIX® SYSTEM V RELEASE 4.2 DOCUMENTATION

To order single copies of UNIX® SYSTEM V Release 4.2 documentation, please call (515) 284-6761.

ATTENTION DOCUMENTATION MANAGERS AND TRAINING DIRECTORS:

For bulk purchases in excess of 30 copies, please write to:

Corporate Sales Department
PTR Prentice Hall
113 Sylvan Avenue
Englewood Cliffs, N.J. 07632

or

Phone: (201) 592-2863
FAX: (201) 592-2249

ATTENTION GOVERNMENT CUSTOMERS:

For GSA and other pricing information, please call (201) 461-7107.

Prentice-Hall International (UK) Limited, *London*
Prentice-Hall of Australia Pty. Limited, *Sydney*
Prentice-Hall Canada Inc., *Toronto*
Prentice-Hall Hispanoamericana, S.A., *Mexico*
Prentice-Hall of India Private Limited, *New Delhi*
Prentice-Hall of Japan, Inc., *Tokyo*
Simon & Schuster Asia Pte. Ltd., *Singapore*
Editora Prentice-Hall do Brasil, Ltda., *Rio de Janeiro*

Table of Contents

Introduction

Section 3 - Library Functions

Table of Contents   **vii**

Table of Contents

Section 3 - Widgets

Permuted Index

Introduction

This reference manual describes the C programming interface of windowing library functions on the UNIX system.

The *Programmer's Reference Manual: Windowing System API* includes a detailed description of the various MoOLIT™ widgets and convenience routines, UNIX Desktop functions, Drag and Drop functions, curses and Extended Terminal Interface (ETI) functions available to programmers writing windowing applications.

The first three sets of functions pertain to graphical based applications. MoOLIT, an Intrinsics-based toolkit, provides support for both the MOTIF™ Graphical User Interface (GUI) and the OPEN LOOK® Graphical User Interface.

 NOTE — MOTIF is a trademark of Open Software Foundation, Inc. The MOTIF GUI will be referred to as MOTIF "look," "feel" or "look and feel," as appropriate.

OPEN LOOK is a registered trademark of UNIX System Laboratories, Inc. The OPEN LOOK GUI will be referred to as OPEN LOOK "look," "feel" or "look and feel," as appropriate.

The curses and ETI functions apply to character based applications.

This reference manual differs from the other Reference Manuals in the UNIX System V Release 4 set in that the widget manual pages are sorted separately rather than together. This manual contains

Section	Component Type
3DnD	Drag and Drop Functions
3Dt	UNIX Desktop Functions
3Olit	Convenience Routines
3curses	curses and ETI Functions
3Olit	Widgets

Organization of this Reference Manual

This reference manual has 3 sections:

- this introduction, including discussion about **wksh**, widgets, gadgets, and convenience routines,

  □ introduces the graphical windowing widgets and functions available to the application programmer, manual page formats, and **wksh**. Key differences between the widget manual pages from the rest of the UNIX System V Release 4 Reference Manual set are highlighted. Translating from C language interfaces to **wksh** interfaces [see **wksh**(1)] allows all manual pages to be used with **wksh** rather than in C programs.

  □ introduces general resources. Resources are the visual and functional characteristics of a particular widget or gadget. Widgets inherit resources from common classes: standard Intrinsics classes such as **Core** and **Shell**, and MoOLIT specific classes such as **Flat**, **Manager**, and **Primitive**.

    The frequently used resources are grouped as follows:

      - Application Resources
      - Core Resources
      - Common Flat Container Resources
      - Manager Widget Resources
      - Primitive Widget Resources
      - Shell Resources

  □ lists convenience routines and other functions by functional groups, making it easier to find those routines which perform specific functions, or work together as a functional group.

  □ lists the widgets, gizmos and gadgets (hereafter referred to as widgets) by functional groups.

- Sections 3Olit convenience routines, 3DnD, 3Dt, and 3curses function manual pages, sorted alphabetically,

- Section 3Olit widget manual pages, sorted alphabetically.

Manual Page Format

All manual page entries use a common format, not all of whose parts always appear:

- The **NAME** section gives the name(s) of the entry and briefly states its purpose.

- The **SYNOPSIS** section summarizes the component interface by compactly representing the order of any arguments for the component, the type of each argument (if any) and the type of value the component returns. A few conventions are used:

  - `Constant width typeface` strings are literals and are to be typed just as they appear.

  - *Italic* strings usually represent substitutable argument prototypes and functions.

  - Ellipses **. . .** are used to show that the previous argument prototype may be repeated.

  - Function prototype format is used.

  For widget manual pages, the conventions are slightly different:

  - Rather than a declaration in function prototype format, the `XtCreateWidget` function call is presented with the correct widget class.

  - Substitutable `XtCreateWidget` arguments are in *italic*. Ellipses **. . .** are used to show that the standard `XtCreateWidget` arguments follow.

- The **DESCRIPTION** section describes the function. Unlike other UNIX System V Release 4 manual pages, most widget manual pages have several subsections, each with a separate heading.

  The **CONSTRAINT RESOURCES** subsection defining constraining resources on the widget.

  The **SUBSTRUCTURE** subsection is included if the widget is automatically built up from other widgets. The application and end-user interfaces to this substructure are detailed.

  The **RESOURCES** is a complete alphabetical listing of resources available for the widget is provided. Resources are not broken into class groupings as the class hierarchy is implementation dependent. (Of course, some of the hierarchy is built into the "X Toolkit Intrinsics.") Many of the resources listed are part of the superclasses (see "General Resources"). All widgets are subclasses of a superclass.

 NOTE Do not use a general resource for the widget if that resource is not listed for the widget.

Each resource entry has six attributes:

- the resource name;

- the class to which the resource belongs;

- the type of values handled by the resource;

- the default value given to the resource by the widget if no or an invalid value is set by the application;

- the allowed access to the base window:

  I   the value can be set at initialization time;

  S   the value can be set with a call to **XtSetValues**;

  G   the value can be read with a call to **XtGetValues**;

  *   the value is set by other methods — see the description of the resource for further information;

  †   the access is conditional — see the description of the resource for further information.

- the superclass from which the resources are inherited

In addition, the following footnotes are used in the resource tables:

1. Use **XtSetSensitive** to set this resource.

2. Not used in the OPEN LOOK look and feel.

3. **"2 points"** in the MOTIF look and feel.

4. **TRUE** in the MOTIF look and feel.

5. **OL_RIGHT** in the MOTIF look and feel.

6. 250 msec. in the MOTIF look and feel.

7. 50 msec. in the MOTIF look and feel.

8. **OL_SHADOW_IN** in the MOTIF look and feel.

9. Default is combination of **OL_WM_DELETE_WINDOW** and **OL_WM_TAKE_FOCUS**.

10. 500 msec. in the MOTIF look and feel.

11. **FALSE** in the MOTIF look and feel.

12. Not available in the gadget version.

As defined in the "X Toolkit Intrinsics," each resource is referred to in resource files by stripping off the **XtN** prefix from the name for direct reference, or the **XtC** prefix from the class name for reference by class.

The resources that are unique to a widget are described in detail after the list of resources.

The range of values that a unique resource can take are given after the resource name, if the resource can be set or initialized by an application. Exceptions are resources that take pointer values: the pointer cannot be validated, so no range is given.

The values are listed using C language bindings (for example, a variable or macro name like **OL_LEFT**). If the resource file bindings differ, they follow the C bindings, separated with a slash and enclosed in double quotes (for example, **OL_LEFT**/"**left**").

■ The **USAGE** section discussing issues in using the function. Many widget manual pages have several subsections, each with a separate heading.

The **SUBCLASSING** subsection discusses information needed to subclass from the function.

The **EXAMPLES** subsection gives example(s) of usage, where appropriate.

The **FILES** subsection lists files specifically related to the function or built into the program.

■ The **RETURN VALUES** section discusses the return values of the function(s) and related diagnostic indications, if any [see **intro**(2) for a full discussion of **errno** values].

■ The **NOTES** section gives generally helpful hints about the use of the utility.

■ The **SEE ALSO** section gives pointers to related information. Reference to manual pages with section numbers other than those in this book can be found in other reference manuals, as listed above.

wksh and the Widget Manual Pages

There are two ways to use the widgets, the C programming language and the **wksh** shell programming languague. The manual pages present the information needed in C, to use **wksh**, the **SYNOPSIS** of the manual pages should be translated from C into **wksh**. This section describes that translation. For information on using **wksh**, see **wksh**(1).

The general form of the **SYNOPSIS** of the widget manual pages, in C language form, is

> `#include` <*header_file.h*>
>
> *widget* = `XtCreateWidget(`*name,* *wtype*`WidgetClass, . . .);`

where the *header_file.h, widget* and *wtype* are specific to the particular widget in question. Note that the "`. . .`" in the C SYNOPSIS shows standard `XtCreateWidget` arguments follow.

Translating that general form to a general **wksh** command line for creating a widget results in

> `XtCreateManagedWidget` *EVAR name wtype $WPAR* [*res:value*]

where:

EVAR	identifier to reference this widget, an environment variable
name	name of the widget, same as the C language substitutable
wtype	kind of widget (for example, `flatList`), same as the C language substitutable
WPAR	identifier of the widget's parent, an environment variable
res:value	resource and associated value for *name*

The [*res:value*] in the **wksh** command line can be repeated as many times as necessary. (By convention, optional command line arguments are shown within brackets, [ ], and there can be an arbitrary number of them.)

General Resources

The general resources, in the form or superclasses, are listed below.

- `Application`
- `Core`
- `Flat`
- `Manager`
- `Primitive`
- `Shell`
- `VendorShell`

Convenience Routines and Other Functions

General Functions

```
Error
Flattened Widget Utilities
OlCallAcceptFocus
OlCanAcceptFocus
OlFindHelpFile
OlGetCurrentFocusWidget
OlGetGui
OlGetMessage
OlHasFocus
OlMoveFocus
OlSetGui
OlSetInputFocus
OlQueryAcceleratorDisplay
```

```
OlQueryMnemonicDisplay
OlGetApplicationValues
OlRegisterHelp
OlSetApplicationValues
OlToolkitInitialize
OlWMProtocolAction
OlWidgetToClassName
OlWidgetClassToClassName
OlUpdateDisplay
Packed Widgets
Pixel Conversion
Widget Activation/Association
```

Buffer and Text Buffer Utilities

AllocateBuffer
AllocateTextBuffer
BackwardScanTextBuffer
Buffer Macros
CopyBuffer
CopyTextBufferBlock
EndCurrentTextBufferWord
ForwardScanTextBuffer
FreeBuffer
FreeTextBuffer
GetTextBufferBlock
GetTextBufferBuffer
GetTextBufferChar
GetTextBufferLine
GetTextBufferLocation
GrowBuffer
IncrementTextBufferLocation
InsertIntoBuffer
LastTextBufferLocation
LastTextBufferPosition
LineOfPosition
LocationOfPosition
NextLocation

NextTextBufferWord
PositionOfLine
PositionOfLocation
PreviousLocation
PreviousTextBufferWord
ReadFileIntoBuffer
ReadFileIntoTextBuffer
ReadPipeIntoTextBuffer
ReadStringIntoBuffer
ReadStringIntoTextBuffer
RegisterTextBufferScanFunctions
RegisterTextBufferUpdate
RegisterTextBufferWordDefinition
ReplaceCharInTextBuffer
ReplaceBlockInTextBuffer
SaveTextBuffer
StartCurrentTextBufferWord
stropen
strgetc
strclose
TextBuffer Macros
WriteTextBuffer
UnregisterTextBufferUpdate

Converters

Converters
OlCvtFontGroupToFontStructList

Database Routines

OlClassSearchIEDB
OlClassSearchTextDB
OlClassUnsearchIEDB
OlCloseDatabase
OlOpenDatabase
OlCreateInputEventDB
OlDestroyInputEventDB

OlGetApplicationValues
OlLookupInputEvent
OlSetApplicationValues
OlWidgetSearchIEDB
OlWidgetSearchTextDB
OlWidgetUnsearchIEDB
OlUpdateDisplay

Drag And Drop

OlDnDAllocTransientAtom
OlDnDBeginSelectionTransaction
OlDnDChangeDropSitePreviewHints
OlDnDClearDragState
OlDnDDeliverPreviewMessage
OlDnDDeliverTriggerMessage
OlDnDDestroyDropSite
OlDnDDisownSelection
OlDnDDragAndDrop
OlDnDDragNDropDone
OlDnDEndSelectionTransaction
OlDnDErrorDuringSelectionTransaction
OlDnDFreeTransientAtom
OlDnDGetCurrentSelectionsForWidget
OlDnDGetDropSitesOfWidget
OlDnDGetDropSitesOfWindow
OlDnDGetWidgetOfDropSite
OlDnDGetWindowOfDropSite

OlDnDGrabDragCursor
OlDnDInitializeDragState
OlDnDOwnSelection
OlDnDOwnSelectionIncremental
OlDnDQueryDropSiteInfo
OlDnDRegisterDDI
OlDnDRegisterDragKeyProc
OlDnDRegisterWidgetDropSite
OlDnDRegisterWindowDropSite
OlDnDSendTriggerMessage
OlDnDSetDropSiteInterest
OlDnDSetInterestInWidgetHier
OlDnDTrackDragCursor
OlDnDUngrabDragCursor
OlDnDUpdateDropSiteGeometry
OlDnDVCXInitialize
OlDnDWidgetConfiguredInHier

Dynamic Settings Utilities

GetOlMoveCursor
GetOlDuplicateCursor
GetOlBusyCursor
GetOlMoveCursor
GetOlPanCursor
GetOlQuestionCursor
GetOlStandardCursor
GetOlTargetCursor
OlCallDynamicCallbacks
OlGet50PercentGrey

OlGet75PercentGrey
OlGetBusyCursor
OlGetDuplicateCursor
OlGetMoveCursor
OlGetPanCursor
OlGetQuestionCursor
OlGetStandardCursor
OlGetTargetCursor
OlRegisterDynamicCallback
OlUnregisterDynamicCallback

Input Method Support Routines

OlResetIc
OlCloseIm
OlCreateIc
OlDestroyIc
OlDisplayOfIm
OlGetIcValues
OlGetImValues

OlImOfIc
OlLookUpImString
OlLocaleOfIm
OlOpenIm
OlSetIcFocus
OlSetIcValues
OlUnSetIcFocus

Regular Expression Utilities

strexp
streexp
strrexp

Text Handling Utilities

OlCtToEuc
OlDrawImageString
OlDrawString
OlEucToCt

OlGetNextStrSegment
OlMaxFontInfo
OlTextWidth

Gauge Widget Routines

OlSetGaugeValue

PopupMenuShell Widget Routines

OlAddDefaultPopupMenuEH
OlPostPopupMenu
OlUnpostPopupMenu

TextEdit Widget Routines

OlTextEditClearBuffer
OlTextEditCopyBuffer
OlTextEditCopySelection
OlTextEditGetCursorPosition
OlTextEditGetLastPosition
OlTextEditInsert

OlTextEditPaste
OlTextEditReadSubString
OlTextEditRedraw
OlTextEditSetCursorPosition
OlTextEditTextBuffer
OlTextEditUpdate

TextField Widget Routines

OlTextFieldCopyString
OlTextFieldGetString

UNIX Desktop Routines

DtAcceptReply
DtEnqueueRequest
DtGetAppId
DtGetFileNames

DtInitialize
DtNewDnDTransaction
DtSetAppId

Widget Manual Pages

The following is a list of all widgets available to the application programmer.

Action Widgets

AbbrevBtn
AbbreviatedMenuBtn
CheckBox
Gauge
MenuButton
Nonexclusives
OblongButton
RectButton
Scrollbar
Slider
Stub

Text Control Widgets	`IntegerField`
	`StaticText`
	`StepField`
	`TextEdit`
	`TextField`
Manager Widgets	`Bulletinboard`
	`ControlArea`
	`Footer`
	`FooterPanel`
	`Form`
	`Panes`
	`RubberTile`
Container Widgets	`Caption`
	`Category`
	`Exclusives`
	`FlatButtons`
	`FlatCheckBox`
	`FlatExclusives`
	`FlatList`
	`FlatNonexclusives`
	`ScrolledWindow`
	`ScrollingList`
Popup Choices	`MenuShell`
	`ModalShell`
	`Notice`
	`PopMenuShell`
	`PopWindowShell`

NAME

AllocateBuffer – allocate a buffer

SYNOPSIS

```
#include <Xol/buffutil.h>
```

`Buffer *AllocateBuffer(int` *element_size,* `int` *initial_size);`

DESCRIPTION

The **AllocateBuffer** function allocates a **Buffer** for elements of the given **element_size**. The **Buffer** structure includes the following members:

```
int size;            /* the size of the Buffer */
int used;            /* the amount of the Buffer currently used */
int esize;           /* the size of each element in the Buffer */
BufferElement *p;    /* pointer to the Buffer */
```

The *used* member of the **Buffer** is set to zero and the *size* member is set to the value of **initial_size**. If **initial_size** is zero the **Buffer** member pointer *p* is set to NULL, otherwise the amount of space required (**initial_size** * **element_size**) is allocated and the pointer *p* is set to point to this space. The function returns the pointer to the allocated Buffer.

SEE ALSO

Buffer_Macros(3Olit), **CopyBuffer**(3Olit), **FreeBuffer**(3Olit), **GetTextBufferBuffer**(3Olit), **GrowBuffer**(3Olit), **InsertIntoBuffer**(3Olit), **ReadFileIntoBuffer**(3Olit), **ReadStringIntoBuffer**(3Olit), **TextBuffer_Macros**(3Olit)

AllocateTextBuffer (3Olit)

NAME

AllocateTextBuffer – allocate a `TextBuffer`

SYNOPSIS

```
#include <Xol/textbuff.h>
. . .
TextBuffer *AllocateTextBuffer(
    char *filename,
    TextUpdateFunction func,
    caddr_t data
);
```

DESCRIPTION

The `AllocateTextBuffer` function is used to allocate a new `TextBuffer`. After it allocates the structure itself, it initializes the members of the structure, allocating storage, setting initial values, and so on. The routine also registers the update function provided by the caller. This function normally need not be called by an application developer since the `ReadFileIntoTextBuffer` and `ReadStringIntoTextBuffer` functions call this routine before starting their operation. The routine returns a pointer to the allocated `TextBuffer`.

The `FreeTextBuffer` function should be used to deallocate the storage allocated by this routine.

SEE ALSO

`FreeTextBuffer`(3Olit), `ReadFileIntoTextBuffer`(3Olit),
`ReadStringIntoTextBuffer`(3Olit)

NAME

BackwardScanTextBuffer – scan a TextBuffer backwards

SYNOPSIS

```
#include <Xol/textbuff.h>

ScanResult BackwardScanTextBuffer(
    TextBuffer *text,
    char *exp,
    TextLocation *location
);
```

DESCRIPTION

The BackwardScanTextBuffer function is used to scan, towards the beginning of the buffer, for a given expression, *exp*, in the TextBuffer starting at *location*. A ScanResult is returned which indicates

SCAN_NOTFOUND	the scan wrapped without finding a match
SCAN_WRAPPED	a match was found at a location after the start location
SCAN_FOUND	a match was found at a location before the start location
SCAN_INVALID	either the location or the expression was invalid

SEE ALSO

ForwardScanTextBuffer(3Olit)

Buffer_Macros (3Olit)

NAME

NAME

Buffer_Macros: `BufferFilled`, `BufferLeft`, `BufferEmpty` – get information on a `Buffer`

SYNOPSIS

`#include <Xol/buffutil.h>`

`BufferFilled(Buffer *buffer);`
`BufferLeft(Buffer *buffer);`
`BufferEmpty(Buffer *buffer);`

DESCRIPTION

These macros are provided for use with the Buffer Utilities.

`BufferFilled`	returns a flag indicating whether *buffer* is filled
`BufferLeft`	returns the number of unused elements in *buffer*
`BufferEmpty`	returns a flag indicating whether *buffer* is empty

SEE ALSO

`GetTextBufferBuffer`(3Olit)

NAME

　　`Converters` – resource converters

SYNOPSIS

　　`#include <Xol/OpenLook.h>`

DESCRIPTION

　　The following converters are registered by MoOLIT. They are called by an application via the **`XtConvertAndStore`** or **`XtCallConverter`** functions. All of these converters are "new-style" converters, are registered with **`XtSetTypeConverter`**, and are automatically registered when an application initializes the toolkit. Converters may require additional arguments and these are noted in the description of each of the converters below.

MoOLIT Registered Converters

Target Representation	Converter Name	Additional Arguments
`XtRFont`	`OlCvtStringToFont`	`char *` `Screen *`
`XtRFontStruct`	`OlCvtStringToFontStruct`	`char *` `Screen *`
`XtRDimension`	`OlCvtStringToDimension`	`char *` `Screen *`
`XtRPixmap`	`OlCvtStringToPixmap`	`Screen *`
`XtRPointer`	`OlCvtStringToImage`	`Screen *`
`XtRPosition`	`OlCvtStringToPosition`	`char *` `Screen *`
`XtRGravity`	`OlCvtStringToGravity`	
`XtRCardinal`	`OlCvtStringToCardinal`	`char *`
`XtROlDefine`	`OlCvtStringToOlDefine`	
`XtRModifiers`	`OlCvtStringToModifiers`	
`XtRCursor`	`OlCvtStringToCursor`	`Screen *`

OlCvtStringToFont

　　The converter **`OlCvtStringToFont`** is registered by MoOLIT to convert a string to a **`XFont`** pointer, **`XFont *`**. This converter goes beyond the standard Intrinsics **`XtCvtStringToFont`** in two ways: it provides a best fit mapping to all available XLFD fonts, and it allows for GUI-dependent default fonts.

　　The best fit mechanism allows a user to specify an XLFD font name that will match the closest font based on the desired font family and specified attributes. Typically, when the wild card is used for an XLFD attribute, the first font to match in the server is returned. The best fit mechanism fills in the default point size and the resolution of the screen before attempting to find the font. If the point size cannot be found in the current resolution, other available resolutions are used with an adjusted point size. For example, if a 12 point lucida font can not be found for the current 75x75dpi resolution, a 10 point lucida font for the 100x100dpi resolution will be returned. The actual display of the 10 point 100x100dpi resolution on the 75x75dpi display will appear to be a 12 point lucida font.

`OlCvtStringToFont` recognizes the resources listed below and maps them to GUI-dependent fonts. These resources can be set to any valid XLFD name to override the default value. Note that the value set to these resources will be used for both Motif and OPEN LOOK modes. To set these resources in a way that allows a different font for each GUI mode, use a customized resource file for each GUI mode. Note that the `XtDefaultFont` resource is not GUI-dependent and is subject to the font mapping mechanism described above.

Resource name:	`olDefaultFont`
Resource class:	`OlDefaultFont`
Motif Default:	`-*-helvetica-medium-r-*-*-*-*-*-*-*-iso8859-1`
OPEN LOOK Default:	`-*-lucida-medium-r-*-*-*-*-*-*-*-iso8859-1`

Resource name:	`olDefaultBoldFont`
Resource class:	`OlDefaultBoldFont`
Motif Default:	`-*-helvetica-bold-r-*-*-*-*-*-*-*-iso8859-1`
OPEN LOOK Default:	`-*-lucida-bold-r-*-*-*-*-*-*-*-iso8859-1`

Resource name:	`olDefaultFixedFont`
Resource class:	`OlDefaultFixedFont`
Motif Default:	`-*-courier-medium-r-*-*-*-*-*-*-*-iso8859-1`
OPEN LOOK Default:	`-*-lucidatypewriter-medium-r-*-*-*-*-*-*-*-iso8859-1`

Resource name:	`olDefaultItailicFont`
Resource class:	`OlDefaultItailicFont`
Motif Default:	`-*-helvetica-medium-o-*-*-*-*-*-*-*-iso8859-1`
OPEN LOOK Default:	`-*-lucida-medium-i-*-*-*-*-*-*-*-iso8859-1`

Resource name:	`olDefaultBoldItailicFont`
Resource class:	`OlDefaultBoldItailicFont`
Motif Default:	`-*-helvetica-bold-o-*-*-*-*-*-*-*-iso8859-1`
OPEN LOOK Default:	`-*-lucida-bold-i-*-*-*-*-*-*-*-iso8859-1`

Resource name:	`olDefaultNoticeFont`
Resource class:	`OlDefaultNoticeFont`
Motif Default:	`-*-helvetica-medium-r-*-*-*-*-*-*-*-iso8859-1`
OPEN LOOK Default:	`-*-lucida-bold-r-*-*-*-140-*-*-*-*-iso8859-1`

Resource name:	`xtDefaultFont`
Resource class:	`XtDefaultFont`
Default:	`-*-*-*-R-*-*-*-120-*-*-*-*-iso8859-1`

OlCvtStringToFontStruct

The converter `OlCvtStringToFontStruct` uses the same method as the `OlCvtStringToFont`. Rather than converting to an `XFont` *, this converter converts the given string to an `XFontStruct` *.

OlCvtStringToDimension

The converter `OlCvtStringToDimension` converts a number followed by a unit to a `Dimension` type. The default unit is pixels, and the case of the string does not matter. The following units are recognized:

```
i                   c
in                  cent
inch                centimeter
inches              centimeters
m                   p
meter               pt
meters              point
mm                  points
millimeter          pixel
millimeters         pixels
```

By default, the units are converted based on the size of a horizontal pixel for the given screen. The following key words can be combined with a unit to specify the orientation of the measure. This is necessary for displays that do not have square pixels.

```
hor         ver
horz        vert
horizontal  vertical
```

OlCvtStringToPixmap

The converter **OlCvtStringToPixmap** converts a string to a filename, searches for the file, and if found, reads it in as a pixmap or bitmap. It accepts pathnames and, in order, searches:

the path as an absolute if it begins with **/** or **./**

default desktop locations for pixmaps and bitmaps (**/usr/X/lib/pixmaps** and **/usr/X/lib/bitmaps**)

in typical **XtResolvePathname** places for a pixmaps or bitmaps directory with the specified file in it

in typical **XtResolvePathname** places for the file with a **.xpm** or **.xbm** suffix (note, not in additional pixmaps or bitmaps directories like the other search), assuming there is no such suffix already

in the current directory

Pixmaps are found before bitmaps when there are both of the same base name (that is, **/usr/X/lib/pixmaps/dtclock.32** is used instead of **/usr/X/lib/bitmaps/dtclock.32** if **dtclock.32** is specified as the resource value).

OlCvtStringToImage

The converter **OlCvtStringToImage** converts a string to a pixmap using the same methods as **OlCvtStringToPixmap** and then creates an **XImage** out of the pixmap.

OlCvtStringToPosition

The converter **OlCvtStringToPosition** converts a string to type **Position** using the units and axis described above in **OlCvtStringToDimension**. In addition, a **Position** can be preceded with **+** or **-** to indicated a signed value. The case of the string does not matter.

Converters (3Olit)

OlCvtStringToGravity

The converter `OlCvtStringToGravity` has no additional arguments. The follow-ing strings are valid gravity values:

forget	north	south	east
center	northeast	southeast	west
all	northwest	southwest	eastwest
static	northeastwest	southeastwest	northsouthwest
unmap	northsouth	northsoutheast	northsoutheastwest

These strings are converted to an **XtGravity** enumeration type. The case of the string does not matter.

OlCvtStringToCardinal

The converter `OlCvtStringToCardinal` converts a string to type **Cardinal**. The string must represent a positive integer.

OlCvtStringToOlDefine

The converter `OlCvtStringToOlDefine` converts a string to type **Modifiers**. The case of the string does not matter.

OlCvtStringToModifiers

The converter `OlCvtStringToModifiers` converts a string to type **Modifiers**. The case of the string does not matter.

OlCvtStringToCursor

The converter `OlCvtStringToCursor` converts a string to type **Cursor**. The case of the string does not matter. The following strings are converted to the equivalent OPEN LOOK or standard X cursors:

OLmove_cursor	double_arrow	right_tee
OLduplicate_cursor	draft_large	rightbutton
OLbusy_cursor	draft_small	rtl_logo
OLpan_cursor	draped_box	sailboat
OLquestion_cursor	exchange	sb_down_arrow
OLtarget_cursor	fleur	sb_h_double_arrow
OLstandard_cursor	gobbler	sb_left_arrow
X_cursor	gumby	sb_right_arrow
arrow	hand1	sb_up_arrow
based_arrow_down	hand2	sb_v_double_arrow
based_arrow_up	heart	shuttle
boat	icon	sizing
bogosity	iron_cross	spider
bottom_left_corner	left_ptr	spraycan
bottom_right_corner	left_side	star
bottom_side	left_tee	target
bottom_tee	leftbutton	tcross
box_spiral	ll_angle	top_left_arrow
center_ptr	lr_angle	top_left_corner
circle	man	top_right_corner
clock	middlebutton	top_side

coffee_mug	mouse	top_tee
cross	pencil	trek
cross_reverse	pirate	ul_angle
crosshair	plus	umbrella
diamond_cross	question_arrow	ur_angle
dot	right_ptr	watch
dotbox	right_side	xterm

EXAMPLES

Using **XtConvertAndStore** to call a converter:

```
XrmValue                from, to;
XFontStruct             *newfont;

/* Call the string to font converter to get the default font */
from.addr = OlDefaultFont;
from.size = strlen(from.addr)+1;
to.addr = (char *)&newfont;
to.size = sizeof(XFontStruct);

if (XtConvertAndStore(w, XtRString, &from, XtRFontStruct, &to) == False) {
                    /*  The conversion failed  */
                    }
                    else {
                    /* The to.addr contains the FontStruct *  */
                    XtSetArg(arg[0], XtNfont, newfont);
                    ...
}
```

Examples of strings that **OlCvtStringToDimension** recognizes:

> 10 vertical points
> 2.5mm
> 30 (no units defaults to pixels)

CopyBuffer (3Olit)

NAME

    `CopyBuffer` – allocate and copy a `Buffer`

SYNOPSIS

    `#include <Xol/buffutil.h>`

    `Buffer *CopyBuffer(Buffer *`*buffer*`);`

DESCRIPTION

    The `CopyBuffer` function is used to allocate a new `Buffer` with the same attributes as the given *buffer* and to copy the data associated with the given *buffer* into the new `Buffer`. A pointer to the newly allocated and initialized `Buffer` is returned. It is the responsibility of the caller to free this storage when appropriate.

SEE ALSO

    `AllocateBuffer`(3Olit), `FreeBuffer`(3Olit), `GetTextBufferBuffer`(3Olit), `InsertIntoBuffer`(3Olit)

NAME

CopyTextBufferBlock – get a text block from a TextBuffer

SYNOPSIS

```
#include <Xol/textbuff.h>

int CopyTextBufferBlock(
    TextBuffer *text,
    char *buffer,
    TextPosition start_position,
    TextPosition end_position
);
```

DESCRIPTION

The CopyTextBufferBlock function is used to retrieve a text block from the *text* TextBuffer. The block is defined as the characters between *start_position* and *end_position* inclusive.

RETURN VALUES

On success, CopyTextBufferBlock returns the number of bytes copied. On failure, if the parameters are invalid, CopyTextBufferBlock returns 0.

NOTES

The storage for the copy is allocated by the caller. It is the responsibility of the caller to ensure that enough storage is allocated to copy at least *end_position - start_position* + 1 bytes. The actual storage required will depend on the width of the characters retrieved. Non-ASCII characters are represented in multibyte EUC form. An upper limit on the amount of memory required is 4 * (*end_position - start_position*) + 1 bytes.

SEE ALSO

GetTextBufferChar(3Olit), GetTextBufferLine(3Olit),
GetTextBufferLocation(3Olit)

curs_addch(3curses)

NAME

curs_addch: addch, waddch, mvaddch, mvwaddch, echochar, wechochar – add a character (with attributes) to a **curses** window and advance cursor

SYNOPSIS

```
#include <curses.h>

int addch(chtype ch);
int waddch(WINDOW *win, chtype ch);
int mvaddch(int y, int x, chtype ch);
int mvwaddch(WINDOW *win, int y, int x, chtype ch);
int echochar(chtype ch);
int wechochar(WINDOW *win, chtype ch);
```

DESCRIPTION

The **addch**, **waddch**, **mvaddch**, and **mvwaddch** routines put the character *ch* into the window at the current cursor position of the window and advance the position of the window cursor. Their function is similar to that of **putchar**. At the right margin, an automatic newline is performed. At the bottom of the scrolling region, if **scrollok** is enabled, the scrolling region is scrolled up one line.

If *ch* is a tab, newline, or backspace, the cursor is moved appropriately within the window. A newline also does a **clrtoeol** before moving. Tabs are considered to be at every eighth column. If *ch* is another control character, it is drawn in the ^X notation. Calling **winch** after adding a control character does not return the control character, but instead returns the representation of the control character.

Video attributes can be combined with a character by OR-ing them into the parameter. This results in these attributes also being set. (The intent here is that text, including attributes, can be copied from one place to another using **inch** and **addch**.) [see **standout**, predefined video attribute constants, on the **curs_attr**(3curses) page].

The **echochar** and **wechochar** routines are functionally equivalent to a call to **addch** followed by a call to **refresh**, or a call to **waddch** followed by a call to **wrefresh**. The knowledge that only a single character is being output is taken into consideration and, for non-control characters, a considerable performance gain might be seen by using these routines instead of their equivalents.

Line Graphics

The following variables may be used to add line drawing characters to the screen with routines of the **addch** family. When variables are defined for the terminal, the **A_ALTCHARSET** bit is turned on [see **curs_attr**(3curses)]. Otherwise, the default character listed below is stored in the variable. The names chosen are consistent with the VT100 nomenclature.

Name	Default	Glyph Description
ACS_ULCORNER	+	upper left-hand corner
ACS_LLCORNER	+	lower left-hand corner
ACS_URCORNER	+	upper right-hand corner
ACS_LRCORNER	+	lower right-hand corner
ACS_RTEE	+	right tee (–|)
ACS_LTEE	+	left tee (|–)
ACS_BTEE	+	bottom tee (|_)
ACS_TTEE	+	top tee (|⌐)
ACS_HLINE	–	horizontal line
ACS_VLINE	|	vertical line
ACS_PLUS	+	plus
ACS_S1	–	scan line 1
ACS_S9	_	scan line 9
ACS_DIAMOND	+	diamond
ACS_CKBOARD	:	checker board (stipple)
ACS_DEGREE	'	degree symbol
ACS_PLMINUS	#	plus/minus
ACS_BULLET	o	bullet
ACS_LARROW	<	arrow pointing left
ACS_RARROW	>	arrow pointing right
ACS_DARROW	v	arrow pointing down
ACS_UARROW	^	arrow pointing up
ACS_BOARD	#	board of squares
ACS_LANTERN	#	lantern symbol
ACS_BLOCK	#	solid square block

RETURN VALUE

All routines return the integer **ERR** upon failure and an integer value other than **ERR** upon successful completion, unless otherwise noted in the preceding routine descriptions.

NOTES

The header file **curses.h** automatically includes the header files **stdio.h** and **unctrl.h**.

Note that **addch**, **mvaddch**, **mvwaddch**, and **echochar** may be macros.

SEE ALSO

curses(3curses), **curs_attr**(3curses), **curs_clear**(3curses), **curs_inch**(3curses), **curs_outopts**(3curses), **curs_refresh**(3curses) **putc**(3S)

curs_addchstr (3curses)

NAME

curs_addchstr: addchstr, addchnstr, waddchstr, waddchnstr, mvaddchstr, mvaddchnstr, mvwaddchstr, mvwaddchnstr – add string of characters (and attributes) to a **curses** window

SYNOPSIS

```
#include <curses.h>
```

```
int addchstr(chtype *chstr);
int addchnstr(chtype *chstr, int n);
int waddchstr(WINDOW *win, chtype *chstr);
int waddchnstr(WINDOW *win, chtype *chstr, int n);
int mvaddchstr(int y, int x, chtype *chstr);
int mvaddchnstr(int y, int x, chtype *chstr, int n);
int mvwaddchstr(WINDOW *win, int y, int x, chtype *chstr);
int mvwaddchnstr(WINDOW *win, int y, int x, chtype *chstr, int n);
```

DESCRIPTION

All of these routines copy *chstr* directly into the window image structure starting at the current cursor position. The four routines with *n* as the last argument copy at most *n* elements, but no more than will fit on the line. If *n*=**-1** then the whole string is copied, to the maximum number that fit on the line.

The position of the window cursor is not advanced. These routines work faster than **waddnstr** because they merely copy *chstr* into the window image structure. On the other hand, care must be taken when using these functions because they don't perform any kind of checking (such as for the newline character), they don't advance the current cursor position, and they truncate the string, rather then wrapping it around to the new line.

RETURN VALUE

All routines return the integer **ERR** upon failure and an integer value other than **ERR** upon successful completion, unless otherwise noted in the preceding routine descriptions.

NOTES

The header file **curses.h** automatically includes the header files **stdio.h** and **unctrl.h**.

Note that all routines except **waddchnstr** may be macros.

SEE ALSO

curses(3curses)

NAME

curs_addstr: addstr, addnstr, waddstr, waddnstr, mvaddstr, mvaddnstr, mvwaddstr, mvwaddnstr – add a string of characters to a **curses** window and advance cursor

SYNOPSIS

```
#include <curses.h>

int addstr(char *str);
int addnstr(char *str, int n);
int waddstr(WINDOW *win, char *str);
int waddnstr(WINDOW *win, char *str, int n);
int mvaddstr(int y, int x, char *str);
int mvaddnstr(int y, int x, char *str, int n);
int mvwaddstr(WINDOW *win, int y, int x, char *str);
int mvwaddnstr(WINDOW *win, int y, int x, char *str, int n);
```

DESCRIPTION

All of these routines write all the characters of the null-terminated character string *str* on the given window. The effect is similar to calling **waddch** once for each character in the string. The four routines with *n* as the last argument write at most *n* characters. If *n* is negative, then the entire string will be added.

RETURN VALUE

All routines return the integer **ERR** upon failure and an integer value other than **ERR** upon successful completion.

NOTES

The header file **curses.h** automatically includes the header files **stdio.h** and **unctrl.h**.

Note that all of these routines except **waddstr** and **waddnstr** may be macros.

SEE ALSO

curses(3curses), **curs_addch**(3curses)

curs_addwch(3curses)

NAME
NAME

curs_addwch: **addwch**, **waddwch**, **mvaddwch**, **mvwaddwch**, **echowchar**, **wechowchar** – add a **wchar_t** character (with attributes) to a **curses** window and advance cursor

SYNOPSIS

```
#include <curses.h>

int addwch(chtype wch);
int waddwch(WINDOW *win, chtype wch);
int mvaddwch(int y, int x, chtype wch);
int mvwaddwch(WINDOW *win, int y, int x, chtype wch);
int echowchar(chtype wch);
int wechowchar(WINDOW *win, chtype wch);
```

DESCRIPTION

The **addwch**, **waddwch**, **mvaddwch**, and **mvwaddwch** routines put the character *wch*, holding a **wchar_t** character, into the window at the current cursor position of the window and advance the position of the window cursor. Their function is similar to that of **putwchar** in the C multibyte library. At the right margin, an automatic newline is performed. At the bottom of the scrolling region, if **scrollok** is enabled, the scrolling region is scrolled up one line.

If *wch* is a tab, newline, or backspace, the cursor is moved appropriately within the window. A newline also does a **clrtoeol** before moving. Tabs are considered to be at every eighth column. If *wch* is another control character, it is drawn in the ^*X* notation. Calling **winwch** after adding a control character does not return the control character, but instead returns the representation of the control character.

Video attributes can be combined with a **wchar_t** character by OR-ing them into the parameter. This results in these attributes also being set. (The intent here is that text, including attributes, can be copied from one place to another using **inwch** and **addwch**.) [see **standout**, predefined video attribute constants, on the curs_attr(3curses) page].

The **echowchar** and **wechowchar** routines are functionally equivalent to a call to **addwch** followed by a call to **refresh**, or a call to **waddwch** followed by a call to **wrefresh**. The knowledge that only a single character is being output is taken into consideration and, for non-control characters, a considerable performance gain might be seen by using these routines instead of their equivalents.

Line Graphics

The following variables may be used to add line drawing characters to the screen with routines of the **addwch** family. When variables are defined for the terminal, the **A_ALTCHARSET** bit is turned on [see **curs_attr**(3curses)]. Otherwise, the default character listed below is stored in the variable. The names chosen are consistent with the VT100 nomenclature.

Name	Default	Glyph Description
ACS_ULCORNER	+	upper left-hand corner
ACS_LLCORNER	+	lower left-hand corner
ACS_URCORNER	+	upper right-hand corner
ACS_LRCORNER	+	lower right-hand corner
ACS_RTEE	+	right tee (–|)
ACS_LTEE	+	left tee (⊢)
ACS_BTEE	+	bottom tee (|_)
ACS_TTEE	+	top tee (|¯)
ACS_HLINE	–	horizontal line
ACS_VLINE	|	vertical line
ACS_PLUS	+	plus
ACS_S1	–	scan line 1
ACS_S9	_	scan line 9
ACS_DIAMOND	+	diamond
ACS_CKBOARD	:	checker board (stipple)
ACS_DEGREE	'	degree symbol
ACS_PLMINUS	#	plus/minus
ACS_BULLET	o	bullet
ACS_LARROW	<	arrow pointing left
ACS_RARROW	>	arrow pointing right
ACS_DARROW	v	arrow pointing down
ACS_UARROW	^	arrow pointing up
ACS_BOARD	#	board of squares
ACS_LANTERN	#	lantern symbol
ACS_BLOCK	#	solid square block

RETURN VALUE

All routines return the integer **ERR** upon failure and an integer value other than **ERR** upon successful completion, unless otherwise noted in the preceding routine descriptions.

NOTES

The header file **curses.h** automatically includes the header files **stdio.h** and **unctrl.h**.

Note that **addwch**, **mvaddwch**, **mvwaddwch**, and **echowchar** may be macros.

SEE ALSO

curses(3curses), **curs_attr**(3curses), **curs_clear**(3curses), **curs_inch**(3curses), **curs_outopts**(3curses), **curs_refresh**(3curses), **putwc**(3W)

curs_addwchstr (3curses)

NAME

curs_addwchstr: addwchstr, addwchnstr, waddwchstr, waddwchnstr, mvaddwchstr, mvaddwchnstr, mvwaddwchstr, mvwaddwchnstr – add string of wchar_t characters (and attributes) to a **curses** window

SYNOPSIS

```
#include <curses.h>

int addwchstr(chtype *wchstr);
int addwchnstr(chtype *wchstr, int n);
int waddwchstr(WINDOW *win, chtype *wchstr);
int waddwchnstr(WINDOW *win, chtype *wchstr, int n);
int mvaddwchstr(int y, int x, chtype *wchstr);
int mvaddwchnstr(int y, int x, chtype *wchstr, int n);
int mvwaddwchstr(WINDOW *win, int y, int x, chtype *wchstr);
int mvwaddwchnstr(WINDOW *win, int y, int x, chtype *wchstr, int n);
```

DESCRIPTION

All of these routines copy *wchstr*, which points to a string of **wchar_t** characters, directly into the window image structure starting at the current cursor position. The four routines with *n* as the last argument copy at most *n* elements, but no more than will fit on the line. If *n*=**-1** then the whole string is copied, to the maximum number that fit on the line.

The position of the window cursor is not advanced. These routines work faster than **waddnwstr** because they merely copy *wchstr* into the window image structure. On the other hand, care must be taken when using these functions because they don't perform any kind of checking (such as for the newline character), they don't advance the current cursor position, and they truncate the string, rather then wrapping it around to the new line.

RETURN VALUE

All routines return the integer **ERR** upon failure and an integer value other than **ERR** upon successful completion, unless otherwise noted in the preceding routine descriptions.

NOTES

The header file **curses.h** automatically includes the header files **stdio.h** and **unctrl.h**.

Note that all routines except **waddwchnstr** may be macros.

SEE ALSO

curses(3curses)

NAME

curs_addwstr: addwstr, addnwstr, waddwstr, waddnwstr, mvaddwstr, mvaddnwstr, mvwaddwstr, mvwaddnwstr – add a string of wchar_t characters to a curses window and advance cursor

SYNOPSIS

```
#include <curses.h>

int addwstr(wchar_t *wstr);
int addnwstr(wchar_t *wstr, int n);
int waddwstr(WINDOW *win, wchar_t *wstr);
int waddnwstr(WINDOW *win, wchar_t *wstr, int n);
int mvaddwstr(int y, int x, wchar_t *wstr);
int mvaddnwstr(int y, int x, wchar_t *wstr, int n);
int mvwaddwstr(WINDOW *win, int y, int x, wchar_t *wstr);
int mvwaddnwstr(WINDOW *win, int y, int x, wchar_t *wstr, int n);
```

DESCRIPTION

All of these routines write all the characters of the null-terminated wchar_t character string str on the given window. The effect is similar to calling waddwch once for each wchar_t character in the string. The four routines with n as the last argument write at most n wchar_t characters. If n is negative, then the entire string will be added.

RETURN VALUE

All routines return the integer ERR upon failure and an integer value other than ERR upon successful completion.

NOTES

The header file curses.h automatically includes the header files stdio.h and unctrl.h.

Note that all of these routines except waddwstr and waddnwstr may be macros.

SEE ALSO

curses(3curses), curs_addwch(3curses).

curs_attr (3curses)

NAME

curs_attr: attroff, wattroff, attron, wattron, attrset, wattrset, standend, wstandend, standout, wstandout – curses character and window attribute control routines

SYNOPSIS

```
#include <curses.h>
```

```
int attroff(chtype attrs);
int wattroff(WINDOW *win, chtype attrs);
int attron(chtype attrs);
int wattron(WINDOW *win, chtype attrs);
int attrset(chtype attrs);
int wattrset(WINDOW *win, chtype attrs);
int standend(void);
int wstandend(WINDOW *win);
int standout(void);
int wstandout(WINDOW *win);
```

DESCRIPTION

All of these routines manipulate the current attributes of the named window. The current attributes of a window are applied to all characters that are written into the window with **waddch**, **waddstr** and **wprintw**. Attributes are a property of the character, and move with the character through any scrolling and insert/delete line/character operations. To the extent possible on the particular terminal, they are displayed as the graphic rendition of characters put on the screen.

The routine **attrset** sets the current attributes of the given window to *attrs*. The routine **attroff** turns off the named attributes without turning any other attributes on or off. The routine **attron** turns on the named attributes without affecting any others. The routine **standout** is the same as **attron(A_STANDOUT)**. The routine **standend** is the same as **attrset(0)**, that is, it turns off all attributes.

Attributes

The following video attributes, defined in **curses.h**, can be passed to the routines **attron**, **attroff**, and **attrset**, or ORed with the characters passed to **addch**.

A_STANDOUT	Best highlighting mode of the terminal.
A_UNDERLINE	Underlining
A_REVERSE	Reverse video
A_BLINK	Blinking
A_DIM	Half bright
A_BOLD	Extra bright or bold
A_ALTCHARSET	Alternate character set
A_CHARTEXT	Bit-mask to extract a character
COLOR_PAIR(n)	Color-pair number n

The following macro is the reverse of **COLOR_PAIR(n)**:

PAIR_NUMBER(*attrs*)	Returns the pair number associated with the **COLOR_PAIR(n)** attribute.

RETURN VALUE

These routines always return 1.

NOTES

The header file **curses.h** automatically includes the header files **stdio.h** and **unctrl.h**.

Note that **attroff, wattroff, attron, wattron, attrset, wattrset, standend** and **standout** may be macros.

SEE ALSO

curses(3curses), **curs_addch**(3curses), **curs_addstr**(3curses), **curs_printw**(3curses)

curs_beep (3curses)

NAME

curs_beep: **beep**, **flash** – **curses** bell and screen flash routines

SYNOPSIS

```
#include <curses.h>

int beep(void);
int flash(void);
```

DESCRIPTION

The **beep** and **flash** routines are used to signal the terminal user. The routine **beep** sounds the audible alarm on the terminal, if possible; if that is not possible, it flashes the screen (visible bell), if that is possible. The routine **flash** flashes the screen, and if that is not possible, sounds the audible signal. If neither signal is possible, nothing happens. Nearly all terminals have an audible signal (bell or beep), but only some can flash the screen.

RETURN VALUE

These routines always return **OK**.

NOTES

The header file **curses.h** automatically includes the header files **stdio.h** and **unctrl.h**.

SEE ALSO

curses(3curses)

NAME

curs_bkgd: **bkgdset, wbkgdset, bkgd, wbkgd** – **curses** window background manipulation routines

SYNOPSIS

```
#include <curses.h>

void bkgdset(chtype ch);
void wbkgdset(WINDOW *win, chtype ch);
int bkgd(chtype ch);
int wbkgd(WINDOW *win, chtype ch);
```

DESCRIPTION

The **bkgdset** and **wbkgdset** routines manipulate the background of the named window. Background is a **chtype** consisting of any combination of attributes and a character. The attribute part of the background is combined (ORed) with all non-blank characters that are written into the window with **waddch**. Both the character and attribute parts of the background are combined with the blank characters. The background becomes a property of the character and moves with the character through any scrolling and insert/delete line/character operations. To the extent possible on a particular terminal, the attribute part of the background is displayed as the graphic rendition of the character put on the screen.

The **bkgd** and **wbkgd** routines combine the new background with every position in the window. Background is any combination of attributes and a character. Only the attribute part is used to set the background of non-blank characters, while both character and attributes are used for blank positions. To the extent possible on a particular terminal, the attribute part of the background is displayed as the graphic rendition of the character put on the screen.

RETURN VALUE

bkgd and **wbkgd** return the integer **OK**, or a non-negative integer, if **immedok** is set.

NOTES

The header file **curses.h** automatically includes the header files **stdio.h** and **unctrl.h**.

Note that **bkgdset** and **bkgd** may be macros.

SEE ALSO

curses(3curses), **curs_addch**(3curses), **curs_outopts**(3curses)

curs_border(3curses)

NAME

curs_border: **border**, **wborder**, **box**, **hline**, **whline**, **vline**, **wvline** – create **curses** borders, horizontal and vertical lines

SYNOPSIS

```
#include <curses.h>

int border(chtype ls, chtype rs, chtype ts, chtype bs, chtype tl,
    chtype tr, chtype bl, chtype br);
int wborder(WINDOW *win, chtype ls, chtype rs, chtype ts, chtype bs,
    chtype tl, chtype tr, chtype bl, chtype br);
int box(WINDOW *win, chtype verch, chtype horch);
int hline(chtype ch, int n);
int whline(WINDOW *win, chtype ch, int n);
int vline(chtype ch, int n);
int wvline(WINDOW *win, chtype ch, int n);
```

DESCRIPTION

With the **border, wborder** and **box** routines, a border is drawn around the edges of the window. The argument *ls* is a character and attributes used for the left side of the border, *rs* - right side, *ts* - top side, *bs* - bottom side, *tl* - top left-hand corner, *tr* - top right-hand corner, *bl* - bottom left-hand corner, and *br* - bottom right-hand corner. If any of these arguments is zero, then the following default values (defined in **curses.h**) are used instead: ACS_VLINE, ACS_VLINE, ACS_HLINE, ACS_HLINE, ACS_ULCORNER, ACS_URCORNER, ACS_LLCORNER, ACS_LRCORNER.

box(*win, verch, horch*) is a shorthand for the following call:

```
wborder(win, verch, verch, horch, horch, 0, 0, 0, 0)
```

hline and **whline** draw a horizontal (left to right) line using *ch* starting at the current cursor position in the window. The current cursor position is not changed. The line is at most *n* characters long, or as many as fit into the window.

vline and **wvline** draw a vertical (top to bottom) line using *ch* starting at the current cursor position in the window. The current cursor position is not changed. The line is at most *n* characters long, or as many as fit into the window.

RETURN VALUE

All routines return the integer OK, or a non-negative integer if **immedok** is set.

NOTES

The header file **curses.h** automatically includes the header files **stdio.h** and **unctrl.h**.

Note that **border** and **box** may be macros.

SEE ALSO

curses(3curses), **curs_outopts**(3curses)

NAME

curs_clear: erase, werase, clear, wclear, clrtobot, wclrtobot, clrtoeol, wclrtoeol – clear all or part of a **curses** window

SYNOPSIS

```
# include <curses.h>

int erase(void);
int werase(WINDOW *win);
int clear(void);
int wclear(WINDOW *win);
int clrtobot(void);
int wclrtobot(WINDOW *win);
int clrtoeol(void);
int wclrtoeol(WINDOW *win);
```

DESCRIPTION

The **erase** and **werase** routines copy blanks to every position in the window.

The **clear** and **wclear** routines are like **erase** and **werase**, but they also call **clearok**, so that the screen is cleared completely on the next call to **wrefresh** for that window and repainted from scratch.

The **clrtobot** and **wclrtobot** routines erase all lines below the cursor in the window. Also, the current line to the right of the cursor, inclusive, is erased.

The **clrtoeol** and **wclrtoeol** routines erase the current line to the right of the cursor, inclusive.

RETURN VALUE

All routines return the integer OK, or a non-negative integer if **immedok** is set.

NOTES

The header file **curses.h** automatically includes the header files **stdio.h** and **unctrl.h**.

Note that **erase, werase, clear, wclear, clrtobot,** and **clrtoeol** may be macros.

SEE ALSO

curses(3curses), **curs_outopts**(3curses), **curs_refresh**(3curses)

curs_color(3curses)

NAME

NAME

curs_color: start_color, init_pair, init_color, has_colors, can_change_color, color_content, pair_content – **curses** color manipulation routines

SYNOPSIS

```
# include <curses.h>

int start_color(void);
int init_pair(short pair, short f, short b);
int init_color(short color, short r, short g, short b);
bool has_colors(void);
bool can_change_color(void);
int color_content(short color, short *r, short *g, short *b);
int pair_content(short pair, short *f, short *b);
```

DESCRIPTION

Overview

curses provides routines that manipulate color on color alphanumeric terminals. To use these routines **start_color** must be called, usually right after **initscr**. Colors are always used in pairs (referred to as color-pairs). A color-pair consists of a foreground color (for characters) and a background color (for the field on which the characters are displayed). A programmer initializes a color-pair with the routine **init_pair**. After it has been initialized, **COLOR_PAIR**(n), a macro defined in **curses.h**, can be used in the same ways other video attributes can be used. If a terminal is capable of redefining colors, the programmer can use the routine **init_color** to change the definition of a color. The routines **has_colors** and **can_change_color** return **TRUE** or **FALSE**, depending on whether the terminal has color capabilities and whether the programmer can change the colors. The routine **color_content** allows a programmer to identify the amounts of red, green, and blue components in an initialized color. The routine **pair_content** allows a programmer to find out how a given color-pair is currently defined.

Routine Descriptions

The **start_color** routine requires no arguments. It must be called if the programmer wants to use colors, and before any other color manipulation routine is called. It is good practice to call this routine right after **initscr**. **start_color** initializes eight basic colors (black, red, green, yellow, blue, magenta, cyan, and white), and two global variables, **COLORS** and **COLOR_PAIRS** (respectively defining the maximum number of colors and color-pairs the terminal can support). It also restores the colors on the terminal to the values they had when the terminal was just turned on.

The **init_pair** routine changes the definition of a color-pair. It takes three arguments: the number of the color-pair to be changed, the foreground color number, and the background color number. The value of the first argument must be between 1 and **COLOR_PAIRS-1**. The value of the second and third arguments must be between 0 and **COLORS**. If the color-pair was previously initialized, the screen is refreshed and all occurrences of that color-pair is changed to the new definition.

The **init_color** routine changes the definition of a color. It takes four arguments: the number of the color to be changed followed by three RGB values (for the amounts of red, green, and blue components). The value of the first argument must be between **0** and **COLORS**. (See the subsection Colors for the default color index.) Each of the last three arguments must be a value between 0 and 1000. When **init_color** is used, all occurrences of that color on the screen immediately change to the new definition.

The **has_colors** routine requires no arguments. It returns **TRUE** if the terminal can manipulate colors; otherwise, it returns **FALSE**. This routine facilitates writing terminal-independent programs. For example, a programmer can use it to decide whether to use color or some other video attribute.

The **can_change_color** routine requires no arguments. It returns **TRUE** if the terminal supports colors and can change their definitions; other, it returns **FALSE**. This routine facilitates writing terminal-independent programs.

The **color_content** routine gives users a way to find the intensity of the red, green, and blue (RGB) components in a color. It requires four arguments: the color number, and three addresses of **short**s for storing the information about the amounts of red, green, and blue components in the given color. The value of the first argument must be between 0 and **COLORS**. The values that are stored at the addresses pointed to by the last three arguments are between 0 (no component) and 1000 (maximum amount of component).

The **pair_content** routine allows users to find out what colors a given color-pair consists of. It requires three arguments: the color-pair number, and two addresses of **short**s for storing the foreground and the background color numbers. The value of the first argument must be between 1 and **COLOR_PAIRS-1**. The values that are stored at the addresses pointed to by the second and third arguments are between 0 and **COLORS**.

Colors

In **curses.h** the following macros are defined. These are the default colors. **curses** also assumes that **COLOR_BLACK** is the default background color for all terminals.

    COLOR_BLACK
    COLOR_RED
    COLOR_GREEN
    COLOR_YELLOW
    COLOR_BLUE
    COLOR_MAGENTA
    COLOR_CYAN
    COLOR_WHITE

RETURN VALUE

All routines that return an integer return **ERR** upon failure and **OK** upon successful completion.

curs_color(3curses)

NOTES

The header file **curses.h** automatically includes the header files **stdio.h** and **unctrl.h**.

SEE ALSO

curses(3curses), **curs_initscr**(3curses), **curs_attr**(3curses)

NAME

curs_delch: delch, wdelch, mvdelch, mvwdelch – delete character under cursor in a **curses** window

SYNOPSIS

```
#include <curses.h>
```

```
int delch(void);
int wdelch(WINDOW *win);
int mvdelch(int y, int x);
int mvwdelch(WINDOW *win, int y, int x);
```

DESCRIPTION

With these routines the character under the cursor in the window is deleted; all characters to the right of the cursor on the same line are moved to the left one position and the last character on the line is filled with a blank. The cursor position does not change (after moving to *y*, *x*, if specified). (This does not imply use of the hardware delete character feature.)

RETURN VALUE

All routines return the integer **ERR** upon failure and an integer value other than **ERR** upon successful completion.

NOTES

The header file **curses.h** automatically includes the header files **stdio.h** and **unctrl.h**.

Note that **delch**, **mvdelch**, and **mvwdelch** may be macros.

SEE ALSO

curses(3curses)

curs_deleteln (3curses)

NAME

curs_deleteln: deleteln, wdeleteln, insdelln, winsdelln, insertln, winsertln – delete and insert lines in a **curses** window

SYNOPSIS

```
#include <curses.h>

int deleteln(void);
int wdeleteln(WINDOW *win);
int insdelln(int n);
int winsdelln(WINDOW *win, int n);
int insertln(void);
int winsertln(WINDOW *win);
```

DESCRIPTION

With the **deleteln** and **wdeleteln** routines, the line under the cursor in the window is deleted; all lines below the current line are moved up one line. The bottom line of the window is cleared. The cursor position does not change. (This does not imply use of a hardware delete line feature.)

With the **insdelln** and **winsdelln** routines, for positive n, insert n lines into the specified window above the current line. The n bottom lines are lost. For negative n, delete n lines (starting with the one under the cursor), and move the remaining lines up. The bottom n lines are cleared. The current cursor position remains the same.

With the **insertln** and **insertln** routines, a blank line is inserted above the current line and the bottom line is lost. (This does not imply use of a hardware insert line feature.)

RETURN VALUE

All routines return the integer **ERR** upon failure and an integer value other than **ERR** upon successful completion.

NOTES

The header file **curses.h** automatically includes the header files **stdio.h** and **unctrl.h**.

Note that all but **winsdelln** may be a macros.

SEE ALSO

curses(3curses)

NAME

curs_getch: **getch**, **wgetch**, **mvgetch**, **mvwgetch**, **ungetch** – get (or push back) characters from **curses** terminal keyboard

SYNOPSIS

```
#include <curses.h>

int getch(void);
int wgetch(WINDOW *win);
int mvgetch(int y, int x);
int mvwgetch(WINDOW *win, int y, int x);
int ungetch(int ch);
```

DESCRIPTION

The **getch**, **wgetch**, **mvgetch**, and **mvwgetch** routines read a character from the terminal associated with the window. In no-delay mode, if no input is waiting, the value **ERR** is returned. In delay mode, the program waits until the system passes text through to the program. Depending on the setting of **cbreak**, this is after one character (**cbreak** mode), or after the first newline (**nocbreak** mode). In half-delay mode, the program waits until a character is typed or the specified timeout has been reached. Unless **noecho** has been set, the character will also be echoed into the designated window.

If the window is not a pad, and it has been moved or modified since the last call to **wrefresh**, **wrefresh** will be called before another character is read.

If **keypad** is **TRUE**, and a function key is pressed, the token for that function key is returned instead of the raw characters. Possible function keys are defined in **curses.h** with integers beginning with **0401**, whose names begin with **KEY_**. If a character that could be the beginning of a function key (such as escape) is received, **curses** sets a timer. If the remainder of the sequence does not come in within the designated time, the character is passed through; otherwise, the function key value is returned. For this reason, many terminals experience a delay between the time a user presses the escape key and the escape is returned to the program. Since tokens returned by these routines are outside the ASCII range, they are not printable.

The **ungetch** routine places *ch* back onto the input queue to be returned by the next call to **wgetch**.

Function Keys

The following function keys, defined in **curses.h**, might be returned by **getch** if **keypad** has been enabled. Note that not all of these may be supported on a particular terminal if the terminal does not transmit a unique code when the key is pressed or if the definition for the key is not present in the **terminfo** database.

Name	Key name
KEY_BREAK	Break key
KEY_DOWN	The four arrow keys ...
KEY_UP	
KEY_LEFT	
KEY_RIGHT	
KEY_HOME	Home key (upward+left arrow)
KEY_BACKSPACE	Backspace
KEY_F0	Function keys; space for 64 keys is reserved.
KEY_F(n)	For $0 \leq n \leq 63$
KEY_DL	Delete line
KEY_IL	Insert line
KEY_DC	Delete character
KEY_IC	Insert char or enter insert mode
KEY_EIC	Exit insert char mode
KEY_CLEAR	Clear screen
KEY_EOS	Clear to end of screen
KEY_EOL	Clear to end of line
KEY_SF	Scroll 1 line forward
KEY_SR	Scroll 1 line backward (reverse)
KEY_NPAGE	Next page
KEY_PPAGE	Previous page
KEY_STAB	Set tab
KEY_CTAB	Clear tab
KEY_CATAB	Clear all tabs
KEY_ENTER	Enter or send
KEY_SRESET	Soft (partial) reset
KEY_RESET	Reset or hard reset
KEY_PRINT	Print or copy
KEY_LL	Home down or bottom (lower left). Keypad is arranged like this:

```
     A1     up     A3
     left   B2     right
     C1     down   C3
```

Name	Key name
KEY_A1	Upper left of keypad
KEY_A3	Upper right of keypad
KEY_B2	Center of keypad
KEY_C1	Lower left of keypad
KEY_C3	Lower right of keypad
KEY_BTAB	Back tab key
KEY_BEG	Beg(inning) key
KEY_CANCEL	Cancel key
KEY_CLOSE	Close key
KEY_COMMAND	Cmd (command) key
KEY_COPY	Copy key
KEY_CREATE	Create key

Name	Key name
KEY_END	End key
KEY_EXIT	Exit key
KEY_FIND	Find key
KEY_HELP	Help key
KEY_MARK	Mark key
KEY_MESSAGE	Message key
KEY_MOVE	Move key
KEY_NEXT	Next object key
KEY_OPEN	Open key
KEY_OPTIONS	Options key
KEY_PREVIOUS	Previous object key
KEY_REDO	Redo key
KEY_REFERENCE	Ref(erence) key
KEY_REFRESH	Refresh key
KEY_REPLACE	Replace key
KEY_RESTART	Restart key
KEY_RESUME	Resume key
KEY_SAVE	Save key
KEY_SBEG	Shifted beginning key
KEY_SCANCEL	Shifted cancel key
KEY_SCOMMAND	Shifted command key
KEY_SCOPY	Shifted copy key
KEY_SCREATE	Shifted create key
KEY_SDC	Shifted delete char key
KEY_SDL	Shifted delete line key
KEY_SELECT	Select key
KEY_SEND	Shifted end key
KEY_SEOL	Shifted clear line key
KEY_SEXIT	Shifted exit key
KEY_SFIND	Shifted find key
KEY_SHELP	Shifted help key
KEY_SHOME	Shifted home key
KEY_SIC	Shifted input key
KEY_SLEFT	Shifted left arrow key
KEY_SMESSAGE	Shifted message key
KEY_SMOVE	Shifted move key
KEY_SNEXT	Shifted next key
KEY_SOPTIONS	Shifted options key
KEY_SPREVIOUS	Shifted prev key
KEY_SPRINT	Shifted print key
KEY_SREDO	Shifted redo key
KEY_SREPLACE	Shifted replace key
KEY_SRIGHT	Shifted right arrow
KEY_SRSUME	Shifted resume key
KEY_SSAVE	Shifted save key
KEY_SSUSPEND	Shifted suspend key

Name	Key name
KEY_SUNDO	Shifted undo key
KEY_SUSPEND	Suspend key
KEY_UNDO	Undo key

RETURN VALUE

All routines return the integer **ERR** upon failure and an integer value other than **ERR** upon successful completion.

NOTES

The header file **curses.h** automatically includes the header files **stdio.h** and **unctrl.h**.

Use of the escape key by a programmer for a single character function is discouraged.

When using **getch**, **wgetch**, **mvgetch**, or **mvwgetch**, **nocbreak** mode and **echo** mode should not be used at the same time. Depending on the state of the tty driver when each character is typed, the program may produce undesirable results.

Note that **getch**, **mvgetch**, and **mvwgetch** may be macros.

SEE ALSO

curses(3curses), **curs_inopts**(3curses), **curs_move**(3curses), **curs_refresh**(3curses)

NAME

curs_getstr: **getstr**, **wgetstr**, **mvgetstr**, **mvwgetstr**, **wgetnstr** – get character strings from **curses** terminal keyboard

SYNOPSIS

```
#include <curses.h>
```

```
int getstr(char *str);
int wgetstr(WINDOW *win, char *str);
int mvgetstr(int y, int x, char *str);
int mvwgetstr(WINDOW *win, int y, int x, char *str);
int wgetnstr(WINDOW *win, char *str, int n);
```

DESCRIPTION

The effect of **getstr** is as though a series of calls to **getch** were made, until a new-line or carriage return is received. The resulting value is placed in the area pointed to by the character pointer *str*. **wgetnstr** reads at most *n* characters, thus preventing a possible overflow of the input buffer. The user's erase and kill characters are interpreted, as well as any special keys (such as function keys, "home" key, "clear" key, and so on).

RETURN VALUE

All routines return the integer **ERR** upon failure and an integer value other than **ERR** upon successful completion.

NOTES

The header file **curses.h** automatically includes the header files **stdio.h** and **unctrl.h**.

Note that **getstr**, **mvgetstr**, and **mvwgetstr** may be macros.

SEE ALSO

curses(3curses), **curs_getch**(3curses)

curs_getwch (3curses)

NAME

curs_getwch: getwch, wgetwch, mvgetwch, mvwgetwch, ungetwch – get (or push back) wchar_t characters from **curses** terminal keyboard

SYNOPSIS

```
#include <curses.h>

int getwch(void);
int wgetwch(WINDOW *win);
int mvgetwch(int y, int x);
int mvwgetwch(WINDOW *win, int y, int x);
int ungetwch(int wch);
```

DESCRIPTION

The **getwch**, **wgetwch**, **mvgetwch**, and **mvwgetwch** routines read an *EUC* character from the terminal associated with the window, transform it into a **wchar_t** character, and return a **wchar_t** character. In no-delay mode, if no input is waiting, the value **ERR** is returned. In delay mode, the program waits until the system passes text through to the program. Depending on the setting of **cbreak**, this is after one character (**cbreak** mode), or after the first newline (**nocbreak** mode). In half-delay mode, the program waits until a character is typed or the specified timeout has been reached. Unless **noecho** has been set, the character will also be echoed into the designated window.

If the window is not a pad, and it has been moved or modified since the last call to **wrefresh**, **wrefresh** will be called before another character is read.

If **keypad** is **TRUE**, and a function key is pressed, the token for that function key is returned instead of the raw characters. Possible function keys are defined in **curses.h** with integers beginning with **0401**, whose names begin with **KEY_**. If a character that could be the beginning of a function key (such as escape) is received, **curses** sets a timer. If the remainder of the sequence does not come in within the designated time, the character is passed through; otherwise, the function key value is returned. For this reason, many terminals experience a delay between the time a user presses the escape key and the escape is returned to the program.

The **ungetwch** routine places *wch* back onto the input queue to be returned by the next call to **wgetwch**.

Function Keys

The following function keys, defined in **curses.h**, might be returned by **getwch** if **keypad** has been enabled. Note that not all of these may be supported on a particular terminal if the terminal does not transmit a unique code when the key is pressed or if the definition for the key is not present in the **terminfo** database.

Name	Key name
`KEY_BREAK`	Break key
`KEY_DOWN`	The four arrow keys ...
`KEY_UP`	
`KEY_LEFT`	
`KEY_RIGHT`	
`KEY_HOME`	Home key (upward+left arrow)
`KEY_BACKSPACE`	Backspace
`KEY_F0`	Function keys; space for 64 keys is reserved.
`KEY_F(n)`	For $0 \leq n \leq 63$
`KEY_DL`	Delete line
`KEY_IL`	Insert line
`KEY_DC`	Delete character
`KEY_IC`	Insert char or enter insert mode
`KEY_EIC`	Exit insert char mode
`KEY_CLEAR`	Clear screen
`KEY_EOS`	Clear to end of screen
`KEY_EOL`	Clear to end of line
`KEY_SF`	Scroll 1 line forward
`KEY_SR`	Scroll 1 line backward (reverse)
`KEY_NPAGE`	Next page
`KEY_PPAGE`	Previous page
`KEY_STAB`	Set tab
`KEY_CTAB`	Clear tab
`KEY_CATAB`	Clear all tabs
`KEY_ENTER`	Enter or send
`KEY_SRESET`	Soft (partial) reset
`KEY_RESET`	Reset or hard reset
`KEY_PRINT`	Print or copy
`KEY_LL`	Home down or bottom (lower left).

Keypad is arranged like this:

```
A1     up     A3
left   B2     right
C1     down   C3
```

Name	Key name
`KEY_A1`	Upper left of keypad
`KEY_A3`	Upper right of keypad
`KEY_B2`	Center of keypad
`KEY_C1`	Lower left of keypad
`KEY_C3`	Lower right of keypad
`KEY_BTAB`	Back tab key
`KEY_BEG`	Beg(inning) key
`KEY_CANCEL`	Cancel key
`KEY_CLOSE`	Close key
`KEY_COMMAND`	Cmd (command) key
`KEY_COPY`	Copy key
`KEY_CREATE`	Create key

Name	Key name
KEY_END	End key
KEY_EXIT	Exit key
KEY_FIND	Find key
KEY_HELP	Help key
KEY_MARK	Mark key
KEY_MESSAGE	Message key
KEY_MOVE	Move key
KEY_NEXT	Next object key
KEY_OPEN	Open key
KEY_OPTIONS	Options key
KEY_PREVIOUS	Previous object key
KEY_REDO	Redo key
KEY_REFERENCE	Ref(erence) key
KEY_REFRESH	Refresh key
KEY_REPLACE	Replace key
KEY_RESTART	Restart key
KEY_RESUME	Resume key
KEY_SAVE	Save key
KEY_SBEG	Shifted beginning key
KEY_SCANCEL	Shifted cancel key
KEY_SCOMMAND	Shifted command key
KEY_SCOPY	Shifted copy key
KEY_SCREATE	Shifted create key
KEY_SDC	Shifted delete char key
KEY_SDL	Shifted delete line key
KEY_SELECT	Select key
KEY_SEND	Shifted end key
KEY_SEOL	Shifted clear line key
KEY_SEXIT	Shifted exit key
KEY_SFIND	Shifted find key
KEY_SHELP	Shifted help key
KEY_SHOME	Shifted home key
KEY_SIC	Shifted input key
KEY_SLEFT	Shifted left arrow key
KEY_SMESSAGE	Shifted message key
KEY_SMOVE	Shifted move key
KEY_SNEXT	Shifted next key
KEY_SOPTIONS	Shifted options key
KEY_SPREVIOUS	Shifted prev key
KEY_SPRINT	Shifted print key
KEY_SREDO	Shifted redo key
KEY_SREPLACE	Shifted replace key
KEY_SRIGHT	Shifted right arrow
KEY_SRSUME	Shifted resume key
KEY_SSAVE	Shifted save key
KEY_SSUSPEND	Shifted suspend key

Name	Key name
KEY_SUNDO	Shifted undo key
KEY_SUSPEND	Suspend key
KEY_UNDO	Undo key

RETURN VALUE

All routines return the integer **ERR** upon failure and an integer value other than **ERR** upon successful completion.

NOTES

The header file **curses.h** automatically includes the header files **stdio.h** and **unctrl.h**.

Use of the escape key by a programmer for a single character function is discouraged.

When using **getwch, wgetwch, mvgetwch,** or **mvwgetwch, nocbreak** mode and **echo** mode should not be used at the same time. Depending on the state of the tty driver when each character is typed, the program may produce undesirable results.

Note that **getwch, mvgetwch,** and **mvwgetwch** may be macros.

SEE ALSO

curses(3curses), **curs_inopts**(3curses), **curs_move**(3curses), **curs_refresh**(3curses).

curs_getwstr (3curses)

NAME

curs_getwstr: getwstr, getnwstr, wgetwstr, wgetnwstr, mvgetwstr, mvgetnwstr, mvwgetwstr, mvwgetnwstr – get **wchar_t** character strings from **curses** terminal keyboard

SYNOPSIS

```
#include <curses.h>
```

int getwstr(wchar_t *wstr);
int getnwstr(wchar_t *wstr, int n);
int wgetwstr(WINDOW *win, wchar_t *wstr);
int wgetnwstr(WINDOW *win, wchar_t *wstr, int n);
int mvgetwstr(int y, int x, wchar_t *wstr);
int mvgetnwstr(int y, int x, wchar_t *wstr, int n);
int mvwgetwstr(WINDOW *win, int y, int x, wchar_t *wstr);
int mvwgetnwstr(WINDOW *win, int y, int x, wchar_t *wstr, int n);

DESCRIPTION

The effect of **getwstr** is as though a series of calls to **getwch** were made, until a newline and carriage return is received. The resulting value is placed in the area pointed to by the **wchar_t** pointer *str*. **getnwstr** reads at most *n* **wchar_t** characters, thus preventing a possible overflow of the input buffer. The user's erase and kill characters are interpreted, as well as any special keys (such as function keys, "home" key, "clear" key, and so on).

RETURN VALUE

All routines return the integer **ERR** upon failure and an integer value other than **ERR** upon successful completion.

NOTES

The header file **curses.h** automatically includes the header files **stdio.h** and **unctrl.h**.

Note that all routines except **wgetnwstr** may be macros.

SEE ALSO

curses(3curses), curs_getwch(3curses).

NAME

curs_getyx: getyx, getparyx, getbegyx, getmaxyx – get **curses** cursor and window coordinates

SYNOPSIS

```
#include <curses.h>

void getyx(WINDOW *win, int y, int x);
void getparyx(WINDOW *win, int y, int x);
void getbegyx(WINDOW *win, int y, int x);
void getmaxyx(WINDOW *win, int y, int x);
```

DESCRIPTION

With the **getyx** macro, the cursor position of the window is placed in the two integer variables y and x.

With the **getparyx** macro, if *win* is a subwindow, the beginning coordinates of the subwindow relative to the parent window are placed into two integer variables, y and x. Otherwise, **–1** is placed into y and x.

Like **getyx**, the **getbegyx** and **getmaxyx** macros store the current beginning coordinates and size of the specified window.

RETURN VALUE

The return values of these macros are undefined (that is, they should not be used as the right-hand side of assignment statements).

NOTES

The header file **curses.h** automatically includes the header files **stdio.h** and **unctrl.h**.

Note that all of these interfaces are macros and that ''**&**'' is not necessary before the variables y and x.

SEE ALSO

curses(3curses)

curs_inch (3curses)

NAME

curs_inch: **inch**, **winch**, **mvinch**, **mvwinch** – get a character and its attributes from a **curses** window

SYNOPSIS

```
#include <curses.h>

chtype inch(void);
chtype winch(WINDOW *win);
chtype mvinch(int y, int x);
chtype mvwinch(WINDOW *win, int y, int x);
```

DESCRIPTION

These routines return the character, of type **chtype**, at the current position in the named window. If any attributes are set for that position, their values are OR-ed into the value returned. Constants defined in **curses.h** can be used with the **&** (logical AND) operator to extract the character or attributes alone.

Attributes

The following bit-masks may be AND-ed with characters returned by **winch**.

A_CHARTEXT	Bit-mask to extract character
A_ATTRIBUTES	Bit-mask to extract attributes
A_COLOR	Bit-mask to extract color-pair field information

NOTES

The header file **curses.h** automatically includes the header files **stdio.h** and **unctrl.h**.

Note that all of these routines may be macros.

SEE ALSO

curses(3curses)

NAME

curs_inchstr: inchstr, inchnstr, winchstr, winchnstr, mvinchstr, mvinchnstr, mvwinchstr, mvwinchnstr – get a string of characters (and attributes) from a **curses** window

SYNOPSIS

```
#include <curses.h>
```

int inchstr(chtype *chstr);
int inchnstr(chtype *chstr, int n);
int winchstr(WINDOW *win, chtype *chstr);
int winchnstr(WINDOW *win, chtype *chstr, int n);
int mvinchstr(int y, int x, chtype *chstr);
int mvinchnstr(int y, int x, chtype *chstr, int n);
int mvwinchstr(WINDOW *win, int y, int x, chtype *chstr);
int mvwinchnstr(WINDOW *win, int y, int x, chtype *chstr, int n);

DESCRIPTION

These routines return a string of type **chtype**, starting at the current cursor position in the named window and ending at the right margin of the window. The four functions with *n* as the last argument, return the string at most *n* characters long. Constants defined in **curses.h** can be used with the **&** (logical AND) operator to extract the character or the attribute alone from any position in the *chstr* [see curs_inch(3curses)].

RETURN VALUE

All routines return the integer **ERR** upon failure and an integer value other than **ERR** upon successful completion.

NOTES

The header file **curses.h** automatically includes the header files **stdio.h** and **unctrl.h**.

Note that all routines except **winchnstr** may be macros.

SEE ALSO

curses(3curses), **curs_inch**(3curses)

curs_initscr (3curses)

NAME

curs_initscr: initscr, newterm, endwin, isendwin, set_term, delscreen –
curses screen initialization and manipulation routines

SYNOPSIS

```
#include <curses.h>
```

```
WINDOW *initscr(void);
int endwin(void);
int isendwin(void);
SCREEN *newterm(char *type, FILE *outfd, FILE *infd);
SCREEN *set_term(SCREEN *new);
void delscreen(SCREEN *sp);
```

DESCRIPTION

initscr is almost always the first routine that should be called (the exceptions are **slk_init**, **filter**, **ripoffline**, **use_env** and, for multiple-terminal applications, **newterm**.) This determines the terminal type and initializes all **curses** data structures. **initscr** also causes the first call to **refresh** to clear the screen. If errors occur, **initscr** writes an appropriate error message to standard error and exits; otherwise, a pointer is returned to **stdscr**. If the program needs an indication of error conditions, **newterm** should be used instead of **initscr**; **initscr** should only be called once per application.

A program that outputs to more than one terminal should use the **newterm** routine for each terminal instead of **initscr**. A program that needs an indication of error conditions, so it can continue to run in a line-oriented mode if the terminal cannot support a screen-oriented program, would also use this routine. The routine **newterm** should be called once for each terminal. It returns a variable of type **SCREEN** * which should be saved as a reference to that terminal. The arguments are the *type* of the terminal to be used in place of **$TERM**, a file pointer for output to the terminal, and another file pointer for input from the terminal (if *type* is **NULL**, **$TERM** will be used). The program must also call **endwin** for each terminal being used before exiting from curses. If **newterm** is called more than once for the same terminal, the first terminal referred to must be the last one for which **endwin** is called.

A program should always call **endwin** before exiting or escaping from **curses** mode temporarily. This routine restores tty modes, moves the cursor to the lower left-hand corner of the screen and resets the terminal into the proper non-visual mode. Calling **refresh** or **doupdate** after a temporary escape causes the program to resume visual mode.

The **isendwin** routine returns **TRUE** if **endwin** has been called without any subsequent calls to **wrefresh**, and **FALSE** otherwise.

The **set_term** routine is used to switch between different terminals. The screen reference **new** becomes the new current terminal. The previous terminal is returned by the routine. This is the only routine which manipulates **SCREEN** pointers; all other routines affect only the current terminal.

The **delscreen** routine frees storage associated with the **SCREEN** data structure. The **endwin** routine does not do this, so **delscreen** should be called after **endwin** if a particular **SCREEN** is no longer needed. The file pointers passed to **newterm** must also be closed.

RETURN VALUE

endwin returns the integer **ERR** upon failure and **OK** upon successful completion.

Routines that return pointers always return **NULL** on error.

NOTES

The header file **curses.h** automatically includes the header files **stdio.h** and **unctrl.h**.

Note that **initscr** and **newterm** may be macros.

SEE ALSO

curses(3curses), **curs_kernel**(3curses), **curs_refresh**(3curses), **curs_slk**(3curses), **curs_util**(3curses)

curs_inopts(3curses)

NAME

curs_inopts: **cbreak, nocbreak, echo, noecho, halfdelay, intrflush, keypad, meta, nodelay, notimeout, raw, noraw, noqiflush, qiflush, timeout, wtimeout, typeahead** – **curses** terminal input option control routines

SYNOPSIS

```
#include <curses.h>

int cbreak(void);
int nocbreak(void);
int echo(void);
int noecho(void);
int halfdelay(int tenths);
int intrflush(WINDOW *win, bool bf);
int keypad(WINDOW *win, bool bf);
int meta(WINDOW *win, bool bf);
int nodelay(WINDOW *win, bool bf);
int notimeout(WINDOW *win, bool bf);
int raw(void);
int noraw(void);
void noqiflush(void);
void qiflush(void);
void timeout(int delay);
void wtimeout(WINDOW *win, int delay);
int typeahead(int fd);
```

DESCRIPTION

The **cbreak** and **nocbreak** routines put the terminal into and out of **cbreak** mode, respectively. In this mode, characters typed by the user are immediately available to the program, and erase/kill character-processing is not performed. When out of this mode, the tty driver buffers the typed characters until a newline or carriage return is typed. Interrupt and flow control characters are unaffected by this mode. Initially the terminal may or may not be in **cbreak** mode, as the mode is inherited; therefore, a program should call **cbreak** or **nocbreak** explicitly. Most interactive programs using **curses** set the **cbreak** mode.

Note that **cbreak** overrides **raw**. [See **curs_getch**(3curses) for a discussion of how these routines interact with **echo** and **noecho**.]

The **echo** and **noecho** routines control whether characters typed by the user are echoed by **getch** as they are typed. Echoing by the tty driver is always disabled, but initially **getch** is in echo mode, so characters typed are echoed. Authors of most interactive programs prefer to do their own echoing in a controlled area of the screen, or not to echo at all, so they disable echoing by calling **noecho**. [See **curs_getch**(3curses) for a discussion of how these routines interact with **cbreak** and **nocbreak**.]

The **halfdelay** routine is used for half-delay mode, which is similar to **cbreak** mode in that characters typed by the user are immediately available to the program. However, after blocking for *tenths* tenths of seconds, **ERR** is returned if nothing has been typed. The value of **tenths** must be a number between 1 and 255. Use **nocbreak** to leave half-delay mode.

If the **intrflush** option is enabled, (*bf* is **TRUE**), when an interrupt key is pressed on the keyboard (interrupt, break, quit) all output in the tty driver queue will be flushed, giving the effect of faster response to the interrupt, but causing **curses** to have the wrong idea of what is on the screen. Disabling (*bf* is **FALSE**), the option prevents the flush. The default for the option is inherited from the tty driver settings. The window argument is ignored.

The **keypad** option enables the keypad of the user's terminal. If enabled (*bf* is **TRUE**), the user can press a function key (such as an arrow key) and **wgetch** returns a single value representing the function key, as in **KEY_LEFT**. If disabled (*bf* is **FALSE**), **curses** does not treat function keys specially and the program has to interpret the escape sequences itself. If the keypad in the terminal can be turned on (made to transmit) and off (made to work locally), turning on this option causes the terminal keypad to be turned on when **wgetch** is called. The default value for keypad is false.

Initially, whether the terminal returns 7 or 8 significant bits on input depends on the control mode of the tty driver [see **termio**(7)]. To force 8 bits to be returned, invoke **meta**(*win,* **TRUE**). To force 7 bits to be returned, invoke **meta**(*win,* **FALSE**). The window argument, *win*, is always ignored. If the terminfo capabilities **smm** (meta_on) and **rmm** (meta_off) are defined for the terminal, **smm** is sent to the terminal when **meta**(*win,* **TRUE**) is called and **rmm** is sent when **meta**(*win,* **FALSE**) is called.

The **nodelay** option causes **getch** to be a non-blocking call. If no input is ready, **getch** returns **ERR**. If disabled (*bf* is **FALSE**), **getch** waits until a key is pressed.

While interpreting an input escape sequence, **wgetch** sets a timer while waiting for the next character. If **notimeout**(*win,* **TRUE**) is called, then **wgetch** does not set a timer. The purpose of the timeout is to differentiate between sequences received from a function key and those typed by a user.

With the **raw** and **noraw** routines, the terminal is placed into or out of raw mode. Raw mode is similar to **cbreak** mode, in that characters typed are immediately passed through to the user program. The differences are that in raw mode, the interrupt, quit, suspend, and flow control characters are all passed through uninterpreted, instead of generating a signal. The behavior of the BREAK key depends on other bits in the tty driver that are not set by **curses**.

When the **noqiflush** routine is used, normal flush of input and output queues associated with the **INTR**, **QUIT** and **SUSP** characters will not be done [see **termio**(7)]. When **qiflush** is called, the queues will be flushed when these control characters are read.

The **timeout** and **wtimeout** routines set blocking or non-blocking read for a given window. If *delay* is negative, blocking read is used (that is, waits indefinitely for input). If *delay* is zero, then non-blocking read is used (that is, read returns **ERR** if no input is waiting). If *delay* is positive, then read blocks for *delay* milliseconds, and returns **ERR** if there is still no input. Hence, these routines provide the same functionality as **nodelay**, plus the additional capability of being able to block for only *delay* milliseconds (where *delay* is positive).

curses does "line-breakout optimization" by looking for typeahead periodically while updating the screen. If input is found, and it is coming from a tty, the current update is postponed until **refresh** or **doupdate** is called again. This allows faster response to commands typed in advance. Normally, the input FILE pointer passed to **newterm**, or **stdin** in the case that **initscr** was used, will be used to do this typeahead checking. The **typeahead** routine specifies that the file descriptor *fd* is to be used to check for typeahead instead. If *fd* is –1, then no typeahead checking is done.

RETURN VALUE

All routines that return an integer return **ERR** upon failure and an integer value other than **ERR** upon successful completion, unless otherwise noted in the preceding routine descriptions.

NOTES

The header file **curses.h** automatically includes the header files **stdio.h** and **unctrl.h**.

Note that **echo**, **noecho**, **halfdelay**, **intrflush**, **meta**, **nodelay**, **notimeout**, **noqiflush**, **qiflush**, **timeout**, and **wtimeout** may be macros.

SEE ALSO

curses(3curses), **curs_getch**(3curses), **curs_initscr**(3curses), **termio**(7)

NAME

curs_insch: **insch, winsch, mvinsch, mvwinsch** – insert a character before the character under the cursor in a **curses** window

SYNOPSIS

#include <curses.h>

int insch(chtype *ch***);**
int winsch(WINDOW **win***, chtype** *ch***);**
int mvinsch(int *y***, int** *x***, chtype** *ch***);**
int mvwinsch(WINDOW **win***, int** *y***, int** *x***, chtype** *ch***);**

DESCRIPTION

These routines insert the character *ch* before the character under the cursor. All characters to the right of the cursor are moved one space to the right, with the possibility of the rightmost character on the line being lost. The cursor position does not change (after moving to *y, x,* if specified). (This does not imply use of the hardware insert character feature.)

RETURN VALUE

All routines return the integer **ERR** upon failure and an integer value other than **ERR** upon successful completion.

NOTES

The header file **curses.h** automatically includes the header files **stdio.h** and **unctrl.h**.

Note that **insch, mvinsch,** and **mvwinsch** may be macros.

SEE ALSO

curses(3curses)

curs_insstr (3curses)

NAME

curs_insstr: insstr, insnstr, winsstr, winsnstr, mvinsstr, mvinsnstr, mvwinsstr, mvwinsnstr – insert string before character under the cursor in a curses window

SYNOPSIS

```
#include <curses.h>

int insstr(char *str);
int insnstr(char *str, int n);
int winsstr(WINDOW *win, char *str);
int winsnstr(WINDOW *win, char *str, int n);
int mvinsstr(int y, int x, char *str);
int mvinsnstr(int y, int x, char *str, int n);
int mvwinsstr(WINDOW *win, int y, int x, char *str);
int mvwinsnstr(WINDOW *win, int y, int x, char *str, int n);
```

DESCRIPTION

These routines insert a character string (as many characters as will fit on the line) before the character under the cursor. All characters to the right of the cursor are moved to the right, with the possibility of the rightmost characters on the line being lost. The cursor position does not change (after moving to y, x, if specified). (This does not imply use of the hardware insert character feature.) The four routines with n as the last argument insert at most n characters. If $n<=0$, then the entire string is inserted.

If a character in *str* is a tab, newline, carriage return, or backspace, the cursor is moved appropriately within the window. A newline also does a **clrtoeol** before moving. Tabs are considered to be at every eighth column. If a character in *str* is another control character, it is drawn in the ^X notation. Calling **winch** after adding a control character (and moving to it, if necessary) does not return the control character, but instead returns the representation of the control character.

RETURN VALUE

All routines return the integer **ERR** upon failure and an integer value other than **ERR** upon successful completion.

NOTES

The header file **curses.h** automatically includes the header files **stdio.h** and **unctrl.h**.

Note that all but **winsnstr** may be macros.

SEE ALSO

curses(3curses), **curs_clear**(3curses), **curs_inch**(3curses)

NAME

curs_instr: **instr, innstr, winstr, winnstr, mvinstr, mvinnstr, mvwinstr, mvwinnstr** – get a string of characters from a **curses** window

SYNOPSIS

```
#include <curses.h>
```

int **instr**(char *str*);
int **innstr**(char *str*, int *n*);
int **winstr**(WINDOW *win*, char *str*);
int **winnstr**(WINDOW *win*, char *str*, int *n*);
int **mvinstr**(int *y*, int *x*, char *str*);
int **mvinnstr**(int *y*, int *x*, char *str*, int *n*);
int **mvwinstr**(WINDOW *win*, int *y*, int *x*, char *str*);
int **mvwinnstr**(WINDOW *win*, int *y*, int *x*, char *str*, int *n*);

DESCRIPTION

These routines return the string of characters in *str* starting at the current cursor position in the named window and ending at the right margin of the window. Attributes are stripped from the characters. The four functions with *n* as the last argument return the string at most *n* characters long.

RETURN VALUE

All routines return the integer **ERR** upon failure and an integer value other than **ERR** upon successful completion.

NOTES

The header file **curses.h** automatically includes the header files **stdio.h** and **unctrl.h**.

Note that all routines except **winnstr** may be macros.

SEE ALSO

curses(3curses)

curs_inswch (3curses)

NAME
curs_inswch: **inswch, winswch, mvinswch, mvwinswch** – insert a **wchar_t** character before the character under the cursor in a **curses** window

SYNOPSIS
`#include <curses.h>`

`int inswch(chtype` *wch*`);`
`int winswch(WINDOW` *`*win`*`, chtype` *wch*`);`
`int mvinswch(int` *y*`, int` *x*`, chtype` *wch*`);`
`int mvwinswch(WINDOW` *`*win`*`, int` *y*`, int` *x*`, chtype` *wch*`);`

DESCRIPTION
These routines insert the character *wch*, holding a **wchar_t** character, before the character under the cursor. All characters to the right of the cursor are moved one space to the right, with the possibility of the rightmost character on the line being lost. The cursor position does not change (after moving to *y*, *x*, if specified). (This does not imply use of the hardware insert character feature.)

RETURN VALUE
All routines return the integer **ERR** upon failure and an integer value other than **ERR** upon successful completion.

NOTES
The header file **curses.h** automatically includes the header files **stdio.h** and **unctrl.h**.

Note that **inswch, mvinswch,** and **mvwinswch** may be macros.

SEE ALSO
curses(3curses).

NAME

curs_inswstr: **inswstr**, **insnwstr**, **winswstr**, **winsnwstr**, **mvinswstr**, **mvinsnwstr**, **mvwinswstr**, **mvwinsnwstr** – insert **wchar_t** string before character under the cursor in a **curses** window

SYNOPSIS

```
#include <curses.h>

int inswstr(char *wstr);
int insnwstr(char *wstr, int n);
int winswstr(WINDOW *win, char *wstr);
int winsnwstr(WINDOW *win, char *wstr, int n);
int mvinswstr(int y, int x, char *wstr);
int mvinsnwstr(int y, int x, char *wstr, int n);
int mvwinswstr(WINDOW *win, int y, int x, char *wstr);
int mvwinsnwstr(WINDOW *win, int y, int x, char *wstr, int n);
```

DESCRIPTION

These routines insert a **wchar_t** character string (as many **wchar_t** characters as will fit on the line) before the character under the cursor. All characters to the right of the cursor are moved to the right, with the possibility of the rightmost characters on the line being lost. The cursor position does not change (after moving to y, x, if specified). (This does not imply use of the hardware insert character feature.) The four routines with n as the last argument insert at most n **wchar_t** characters. If $n<=0$, then the entire string is inserted.

If a character in *wstr* is a tab, newline, carriage return, or backspace, the cursor is moved appropriately within the window. A newline also does a **clrtoeol** before moving. Tabs are considered to be at every eighth column. If a character in *wstr* is another control character, it is drawn in the ^X notation. Calling **winch** after adding a control character (and moving to it, if necessary) does not return the control character, but instead returns the representation of the control character.

RETURN VALUE

All routines return the integer **ERR** upon failure and an integer value other than **ERR** upon successful completion.

NOTES

The header file **curses.h** automatically includes the header files **stdio.h** and **unctrl.h**.

Note that all but **winsnwstr** may be macros.

SEE ALSO

curses(3curses), **curs_clear**(3curses), **curs_inwch**(3curses).

curs_inwch (3curses)

NAME
curs_inwch: inwch, winwch, mvinwch, mvwinwch – get a wchar_t character and its attributes from a **curses** window

SYNOPSIS
```
#include <curses.h>

chtype inwch(void);
chtype winwch(WINDOW *win);
chtype mvinwch(int y, int x);
chtype mvwinwch(WINDOW *win, int y, int x);
```

DESCRIPTION
These routines return the **wchar_t** character, of type **chtype**, at the current position in the named window. If any attributes are set for that position, their values are OR-ed into the value returned. Constants defined in **curses.h** can be used with the **&** (logical AND) operator to extract the character or attributes alone.

Attributes
The following bit-masks may be AND-ed with characters returned by **winwch**.

A_CHARTEXT	Bit-mask to extract character
A_ATTRIBUTES	Bit-mask to extract attributes
A_COLOR	Bit-mask to extract color-pair field information

NOTES
The header file **curses.h** automatically includes the header files **stdio.h** and **unctrl.h**.

Note that all of these routines may be macros.

SEE ALSO
curses(3curses).

NAME

curs_inwchstr: inwchstr, inwchnstr, winwchstr, winwchnstr, mvinwchstr, mvinwchnstr, mvwinwchstr, mvwinwchnstr – get a string of **wchar_t** characters (and attributes) from a **curses** window

SYNOPSIS

```
#include <curses.h>
```

int inwchstr(chtype *wchstr);
int inwchnstr(chtype *wchstr, int n);
int winwchstr(WINDOW *win, chtype *wchstr);
int winwchnstr(WINDOW *win, chtype *wchstr, int n);
int mvinwchstr(int y, int x, chtype *wchstr);
int mvinwchnstr(int y, int x, chtype *wchstr, int n);
int mvwinwchstr(WINDOW *win, int y, int x, chtype *wchstr);
int mvwinwchnstr(WINDOW *win, int y, int x, chtype *wchstr, int n);

DESCRIPTION

These routines return a string of type **chtype**, holding **wchar_t** characters, starting at the current cursor position in the named window and ending at the right margin of the window. The four functions with n as the last argument, return the string at most n **wchar_t** characters long. Constants defined in **curses.h** can be used with the **&** (logical AND) operator to extract the **wchar_t** character or the attribute alone from any position in the *chstr* [see **curs_inwch**(3curses)].

RETURN VALUE

All routines return the integer **ERR** upon failure and an integer value other than **ERR** upon successful completion.

NOTES

The header file **curses.h** automatically includes the header files **stdio.h** and **unctrl.h**.

Note that all routines except **winwchnstr** may be macros.

SEE ALSO

curses(3curses), **curs_inwch**(3curses).

curs_inwstr(3curses)

NAME

curs_inwstr: inwstr, innwstr, winwstr, winnwstr, mvinwstr, mvinnwstr, mvwinwstr, mvwinnwstr – get a string of **wchar_t** characters from a **curses** window

SYNOPSIS

```
#include <curses.h>

int inwstr(char *str);
int innwstr(char *str, int n);
int winwstr(WINDOW *win, char *str);
int winnwstr(WINDOW *win, char *str, int n);
int mvinwstr(int y, int x, char *str);
int mvinnwstr(int y, int x, char *str, int n);
int mvwinwstr(WINDOW *win, int y, int x, char *str);
int mvwinnwstr(WINDOW *win, int y, int x, char *str, int n);
```

DESCRIPTION

These routines return the string of **wchar_t** characters in *str* starting at the current cursor position in the named window and ending at the right margin of the window. Attributes are stripped from the characters. The four functions with *n* as the last argument return the string at most *n* **wchar_t** characters long.

RETURN VALUE

All routines return the integer **ERR** upon failure and an integer value other than **ERR** upon successful completion.

NOTES

The header file **curses.h** automatically includes the header files **stdio.h** and **unctrl.h**.

Note that all routines except **winnwstr** may be macros.

SEE ALSO

curses(3curses).

NAME

curs_kernel: def_prog_mode, def_shell_mode, reset_prog_mode, reset_shell_mode, resetty, savetty, getsyx, setsyx, ripoffline, curs_set, napms – low-level **curses** routines

SYNOPSIS

```
#include <curses.h>

int def_prog_mode(void);
int def_shell_mode(void);
int reset_prog_mode(void);
int reset_shell_mode(void);
int resetty(void);
int savetty(void);
int getsyx(int y, int x);
int setsyx(int y, int x);
int ripoffline(int line, int (*init)(WINDOW *, int));
int curs_set(int visibility);
int napms(int ms);
```

DESCRIPTION

The following routines give low-level access to various **curses** functionality. Theses routines typically are used inside library routines.

The **def_prog_mode** and **def_shell_mode** routines save the current terminal modes as the "program" (in **curses**) or "shell" (not in **curses**) state for use by the **reset_prog_mode** and **reset_shell_mode** routines. This is done automatically by **initscr**.

The **reset_prog_mode** and **reset_shell_mode** routines restore the terminal to "program" (in **curses**) or "shell" (out of **curses**) state. These are done automatically by **endwin** and, after an **endwin**, by **doupdate**, so they normally are not called.

The **resetty** and **savetty** routines save and restore the state of the terminal modes. **savetty** saves the current state in a buffer and **resetty** restores the state to what it was at the last call to **savetty**.

With the **getsyx** routine, the current coordinates of the virtual screen cursor are returned in y and x. If **leaveok** is currently **TRUE**, then –1,–1 is returned. If lines have been removed from the top of the screen, using **ripoffline**, y and x include these lines; therefore, y and x should be used only as arguments for **setsyx**.

With the **setsyx** routine, the virtual screen cursor is set to y, x. *If y and x are both –1, then* **leaveok** *is set. The two routines* **getsyx** *and* **setsyx** *are designed to be used by a library routine, which manipulates* **curses** *windows but does not want to change the current position of the program's cursor. The library routine would call* **getsyx** *at the beginning, do its manipulation of its own windows, do a* **wnoutrefresh** *on its windows, call* **setsyx**, *and then call* **doupdate**.

The **ripoffline** routine provides access to the same facility that **slk_init** [see curs_slk(3curses)] uses to reduce the size of the screen. **ripoffline** must be called before **initscr** or **newterm** is called. If *line* is positive, a line is removed from the top of **stdscr**; if *line* is negative, a line is removed from the bottom. When this is done inside **initscr**, the routine **init** (supplied by the user) is called with two arguments: a window pointer to the one-line window that has been allocated and an integer with the number of columns in the window. Inside this initialization routine, the integer variables **LINES** and **COLS** (defined in **curses.h**) are not guaranteed to be accurate and **wrefresh** or **doupdate** must not be called. It is allowable to call **wnoutrefresh** during the initialization routine.

ripoffline can be called up to five times before calling **initscr** or **newterm**.

With the **curs_set** routine, the cursor state is set to invisible, normal, or very visible for **visibility** equal to **0**, **1**, or **2** respectively. If the terminal supports the *visibility* requested, the previous *cursor* state is returned; otherwise, **ERR** is returned.

The **napms** routine is used to sleep for *ms* milliseconds.

RETURN VALUE

Except for **curs_set**, these routines always return **OK**. **curs_set** returns the previous cursor state, or **ERR** if the requested *visibility* is not supported.

NOTES

The header file **curses.h** automatically includes the header files **stdio.h** and **unctrl.h**.

Note that **getsyx** is a macro, so **&** is not necessary before the variables *y* and *x*.

SEE ALSO

curses(3curses), **curs_initscr**(3curses), **curs_outopts**(3curses), **curs_refresh**(3curses), **curs_scr_dump**(3curses), **curs_slk**(3curses)

NAME

curs_move: **move, wmove** – move **curses** window cursor

SYNOPSIS

```
#include <curses.h>

int move(int y, int x);
int wmove(WINDOW *win, int y, int x);
```

DESCRIPTION

With these routines, the cursor associated with the window is moved to line y and column x. This routine does not move the physical cursor of the terminal until **refresh** is called. The position specified is relative to the upper left-hand corner of the window, which is (0,0).

RETURN VALUE

These routines return the integer **ERR** upon failure and an integer value other than **ERR** upon successful completion.

NOTES

The header file **curses.h** automatically includes the header files **stdio.h** and **unctrl.h**.

Note that **move** may be a macro.

SEE ALSO

curses(3curses), **curs_refresh**(3curses)

curs_outopts(3curses)

NAME

curs_outopts: clearok, idlok, idcok, immedok, leaveok, setscrreg, wsetscrreg, scrollok, nl, nonl – **curses** terminal output option control routines

SYNOPSIS

```
#include <curses.h>

int clearok(WINDOW *win, bool bf);
int idlok(WINDOW *win, bool bf);
void idcok(WINDOW *win, bool bf);
void immedok(WINDOW *win, bool bf);
int leaveok(WINDOW *win, bool bf);
int setscrreg(int top, int bot);
int wsetscrreg(WINDOW *win, int top, int bot);
int scrollok(WINDOW *win, bool bf);
int nl(void);
int nonl(void);
```

DESCRIPTION

These routines set options that deal with output within **curses**. All options are initially **FALSE**, unless otherwise stated. It is not necessary to turn these options off before calling **endwin**.

With the **clearok** routine, if enabled (*bf* is **TRUE**), the next call to **wrefresh** with this window will clear the screen completely and redraw the entire screen from scratch. This is useful when the contents of the screen are uncertain, or in some cases for a more pleasing visual effect. If the *win* argument to **clearok** is the global variable **curscr**, the next call to **wrefresh** with any window causes the screen to be cleared and repainted from scratch.

With the **idlok** routine, if enabled (*bf* is **TRUE**), **curses** considers using the hardware insert/delete line feature of terminals so equipped. If disabled (*bf* is **FALSE**), **curses** very seldom uses this feature. (The insert/delete character feature is always considered.) This option should be enabled only if the application needs insert/delete line, for example, for a screen editor. It is disabled by default because insert/delete line tends to be visually annoying when used in applications where it isn't really needed. If insert/delete line cannot be used, **curses** redraws the changed portions of all lines.

With the **idcok** routine, if enabled (*bf* is **TRUE**), **curses** considers using the hardware insert/delete character feature of terminals so equipped. This is enabled by default.

With the **immedok** routine, if enabled (*bf* is **TRUE**), any change in the window image, such as the ones caused by **waddch, wclrtobot, wscrl**, and so on, automatically cause a call to **wrefresh**. However, it may degrade the performance considerably, due to repeated calls to **wrefresh**. It is disabled by default.

Normally, the hardware cursor is left at the location of the window cursor being refreshed. The **leaveok** option allows the cursor to be left wherever the update happens to leave it. It is useful for applications where the cursor is not used, since it reduces the need for cursor motions. If possible, the cursor is made invisible when this option is enabled.

The **setscrreg** and **wsetscrreg** routines allow the application programmer to set a software scrolling region in a window. *top* and *bot* are the line numbers of the top and bottom margin of the scrolling region. (Line 0 is the top line of the window.) If this option and **scrollok** are enabled, an attempt to move off the bottom margin line causes all lines in the scrolling region to scroll up one line. Only the text of the window is scrolled. (Note that this has nothing to do with the use of a physical scrolling region capability in the terminal, like that in the VT100. If **idlok** is enabled and the terminal has either a scrolling region or insert/delete line capability, they will probably be used by the output routines.)

The **scrollok** option controls what happens when the cursor of a window is moved off the edge of the window or scrolling region, either as a result of a newline action on the bottom line, or typing the last character of the last line. If disabled, (*bf* is **FALSE**), the cursor is left on the bottom line. If enabled, (*bf* is **TRUE**), **wrefresh** is called on the window, and the physical terminal and window are scrolled up one line. [Note that in order to get the physical scrolling effect on the terminal, it is also necessary to call **idlok**.]

The **nl** and **nonl** routines control whether newline is translated into carriage return and linefeed on output, and whether return is translated into newline on input. Initially, the translations do occur. By disabling these translations using **nonl**, **curses** is able to make better use of the linefeed capability, resulting in faster cursor motion.

RETURN VALUE

setscrreg and **wsetscrreg** return **OK** upon success and **ERR** upon failure. All other routines that return an integer always return **OK**.

NOTES

The header file **curses.h** automatically includes the header files **stdio.h** and **unctrl.h**.

Note that **clearok, leaveok, scrollok, idcok, nl, nonl** and **setscrreg** may be macros.

The **immedok** routine is useful for windows that are used as terminal emulators.

SEE ALSO

curses(3curses), **curs_addch**(3curses), **curs_clear**(3curses), **curs_initscr**(3curses), **curs_scroll**(3curses), **curs_refresh**(3curses)

curs_overlay (3curses)

NAME

curs_overlay: overlay, overwrite, copywin – overlap and manipulate overlapped **curses** windows

SYNOPSIS

#include <curses.h>

int overlay(WINDOW *srcwin, WINDOW *dstwin);
int overwrite(WINDOW *srcwin, WINDOW *dstwin);
int copywin(WINDOW *srcwin, WINDOW *dstwin, int sminrow,
    int smincol, int dminrow, int dmincol, int dmaxrow,
    int dmaxcol, int overlay);

DESCRIPTION

The **overlay** and **overwrite** routines overlay srcwin on top of dstwin. scrwin and
dstwin are not required to be the same size; only text where the two windows overlap is copied. The difference is that **overlay** is non-destructive (blanks are not
copied) whereas **overwrite** is destructive.

The **copywin** routine provides a finer granularity of control over the **overlay** and
overwrite routines. Like in the **prefresh** routine, a rectangle is specified in the
destination window, (dminrow, dmincol) and (dmaxrow, dmaxcol), and the upper-left-
corner coordinates of the source window, (sminrow, smincol). If the argument overlay is **true**, then copying is non-destructive, as in **overlay**.

RETURN VALUE

Routines that return an integer return **ERR** upon failure and an integer value other
than **ERR** upon successful completion.

NOTES

The header file **curses.h** automatically includes the header files **stdio.h** and
unctrl.h.

Note that **overlay** and **overwrite** may be macros.

SEE ALSO

curses(3curses), **curs_pad**(3curses), **curs_refresh**(3curses)

NAME

curs_pad: **newpad, subpad, prefresh, pnoutrefresh, pechochar, pechowchar** –
create and display **curses** pads

SYNOPSIS

```
#include <curses.h>

WINDOW *newpad(int nlines, int ncols);
WINDOW *subpad(WINDOW *orig, int nlines, int ncols,
    int begin_y, int begin_x);
int prefresh(WINDOW *pad, int pminrow, int pmincol,
    int sminrow, int smincol, int smaxrow, int smaxcol);
int pnoutrefresh(WINDOW *pad, int pminrow, int pmincol,
    int sminrow, int smincol, int smaxrow, int smaxcol);
int pechochar(WINDOW *pad, chtype ch);
int pechowchar(WINDOW *pad, chtype wch);
```

DESCRIPTION

The **newpad** routine creates and returns a pointer to a new pad data structure with
the given number of lines, *nlines,* and columns, *ncols.* A pad is like a window,
except that it is not necessarily associated with a viewable part of the screen.
Automatic refreshes of pads (for example, from scrolling or echoing of input) do
not occur. It is not legal to call **wrefresh** with a *pad* as an argument; the routines
prefresh or **pnoutrefresh** should be called instead. Note that these routines
require additional parameters to specify the part of the pad to be displayed and the
location on the screen to be used for the display.

The **subpad** routine creates and returns a pointer to a subwindow within a pad
with the given number of lines, *nlines,* and columns, *ncols.* Unlike **subwin,** which
uses screen coordinates, the window is at position (*begin_x, begin_y*) **on the pad.**
The window is made in the middle of the window *orig,* **so that changes
made to one window affect both windows. During the use of this
routine, it will often be necessary to call touchwin or touchline
on** *orig* **before calling prefresh.**

The **prefresh** and **pnoutrefresh** routines are analogous to **wrefresh** and
wnoutrefresh except that they relate to pads instead of windows. The additional
parameters are needed to indicate what part of the pad and screen are involved.
pminrow and *pmincol* specify the upper left-hand corner of the rectangle to be
displayed in the pad. *sminrow, smincol, smaxrow,* and *smaxcol* specify the edges of
the rectangle to be displayed on the screen. The lower right-hand corner of the rectangle to be displayed in the pad is calculated from the screen coordinates, since the
rectangles must be the same size. Both rectangles must be entirely contained within
their respective structures. Negative values of *pminrow, pmincol, sminrow,* or *smincol*
are treated as if they were zero.

The **pechochar** routine is functionally equivalent to a call to **addch** followed by a
call to **refresh,** a call to **waddch** followed by a call to **wrefresh,** or a call to **waddch**
followed by a call to **prefresh.** The knowledge that only a single character is
being output is taken into consideration and, for non-control characters, a considerable performance gain might be seen by using these routines instead of their
equivalents. In the case of **pechochar,** the last location of the pad on the screen is
reused for the arguments to **prefresh.**

The **pechowchar** routine is functionally equivalent to a call to **addwch** followed by a call to **refresh**, a call to **waddwch** followed by a call to **wrefresh**, or a call to **waddwch** followed by a call to **prefresh.**

RETURN VALUE

Routines that return an integer return **ERR** upon failure and an integer value other than **ERR** upon successful completion.

Routines that return pointers return **NULL** on error.

NOTES

The header file **curses.h** automatically includes the header files **stdio.h** and **unctrl.h**.

Note that **pechochar** may be a macro.

SEE ALSO

curses(3curses), **curs_refresh**(3curses), **curs_touch**(3curses), **curs_addch**(3curses), **curs_addwch**(3curses)

NAME

curs_printw: printw, wprintw, mvprintw, mvwprintw, vwprintw – print formatted output in **curses** windows

SYNOPSIS

```
#include <curses.h>
```

int **printw**(char *fmt [, arg] . . .);
int **wprintw**(WINDOW *win, char *fmt [, arg] . . .);
int **mvprintw**(int y, int x, char *fmt [, arg] . . .);
int **mvwprintw**(WINDOW *win, int y, int x, char *fmt [, arg] . . .);

```
#include <varargs.h>
```

int **vwprintw**(WINDOW *win, char *fmt, va_list varglist);

DESCRIPTION

The **printw**, **wprintw**, **mvprintw** and **mvwprintw** routines are analogous to **printf** [see **printf**(3S)]. In effect, the string that would be output by **printf** is output instead as though **waddstr** was used on the given window.

The **vwprintw** routine is analogous to **vprintf** [see **vprintf**(3S)] and performs a **wprintw** using a variable argument list. The third argument is a **va_list**, a pointer to a list of arguments, as defined in **varargs.h**.

RETURN VALUE

All routines return the integer **ERR** upon failure and an integer value other than **ERR** upon successful completion.

NOTES

The header file **curses.h** automatically includes the header files **stdio.h** and **unctrl.h**.

SEE ALSO

curses(3curses), **printf**(3S), **vprintf**(3S)

curs_refresh (3curses)

NAME

curs_refresh: refresh, wrefresh, wnoutrefresh, doupdate, redrawwin, wredrawln – refresh **curses** windows and lines

SYNOPSIS

```
#include <curses.h>

int refresh(void);
int wrefresh(WINDOW *win);
int wnoutrefresh(WINDOW *win);
int doupdate(void);
int redrawwin(WINDOW *win);
int wredrawln(WINDOW *win, int beg_line, int num_lines);
```

DESCRIPTION

The **refresh** and **wrefresh** routines (or **wnoutrefresh** and **doupdate**) must be called to get any output on the terminal, as other routines merely manipulate data structures. The routine **wrefresh** copies the named window to the physical terminal screen, taking into account what is already there in order to do optimizations. The **refresh** routine is the same, using **stdscr** as the default window. Unless **leaveok** has been enabled, the physical cursor of the terminal is left at the location of the cursor for that window.

The **wnoutrefresh** and **doupdate** routines allow multiple updates with more efficiency than **wrefresh** alone. In addition to all the window structures, **curses** keeps two data structures representing the terminal screen: a physical screen, describing what is actually on the screen, and a virtual screen, describing what the programmer wants to have on the screen.

The routine **wrefresh** works by first calling **wnoutrefresh**, which copies the named window to the virtual screen, and then calling **doupdate**, which compares the virtual screen to the physical screen and does the actual update. If the programmer wishes to output several windows at once, a series of calls to **wrefresh** results in alternating calls to **wnoutrefresh** and **doupdate**, causing several bursts of output to the screen. By first calling **wnoutrefresh** for each window, it is then possible to call **doupdate** once, resulting in only one burst of output, with fewer total characters transmitted and less CPU time used. If the *win* argument to **wrefresh** is the global variable **curscr**, the screen is immediately cleared and repainted from scratch.

The **redrawwin** routine indicates to **curses** that some screen lines are corrupted and should be thrown away before anything is written over them. These routines could be used for programs such as editors, which want a command to redraw some part of the screen or the entire screen. The routine **redrawln** is preferred over **redrawwin** where a noisy communication line exists and redrawing the entire window could be subject to even more communication noise. Just redrawing several lines offers the possibility that they would show up unblemished.

RETURN VALUE

All routines return the integer **ERR** upon failure and an integer value other than **ERR** upon successful completion.

NOTES

The header file **curses.h** automatically includes the header files **stdio.h** and **unctrl.h**.

Note that **refresh** and **redrawwin** may be macros.

SEE ALSO

curses(3curses), **curs_outopts**(3curses)

NAME

curs_scanw: scanw, wscanw, mvscanw, mvwscanw, vwscanw – convert formatted input from a **curses** widow

SYNOPSIS

```
#include <curses.h>

int scanw(char *fmt [, arg] . . .);
int wscanw(WINDOW *win, char *fmt [, arg] . . .);
int mvscanw(int y, int x, char *fmt [, arg] . . .);
int mvwscanw(WINDOW *win, int y, int x, char *fmt [, arg] . . .);
int vwscanw(WINDOW *win, char *fmt, va_list varglist);
```

DESCRIPTION

The **scanw**, **wscanw** and **mvscanw** routines correspond to **scanf** [see **scanf**(3S)]. The effect of these routines is as though **wgetstr** were called on the window, and the resulting line used as input for the scan. Fields which do not map to a variable in the *fmt* field are lost.

The **vwscanw** routine is similar to **vwprintw** in that it performs a **wscanw** using a variable argument list. The third argument is a *va_list*, a pointer to a list of arguments, as defined in **varargs.h**.

RETURN VALUE

vwscanw returns **ERR** on failure and an integer equal to the number of fields scanned on success.

Applications may interrogate the return value from the **scanw**, **wscanw**, **mvscanw** and **mvwscanw** routines to determine the number of fields which were mapped in the call.

NOTES

The header file **curses.h** automatically includes the header files **stdio.h** and **unctrl.h**.

SEE ALSO

curses(3curses), **curs_getstr**, **curs_printw**, **scanf**(3S)

NAME

curs_scr_dump: scr_dump, scr_restore, scr_init, scr_set – read (write) a curses screen from (to) a file

SYNOPSIS

```
#include <curses.h>
```

int scr_dump(char *filename);
int scr_restore(char *filename);
int scr_init(char *filename);
int scr_set(char *filename);

DESCRIPTION

With the **scr_dump** routine, the current contents of the virtual screen are written to the file *filename*.

With the **scr_restore** routine, the virtual screen is set to the contents of *filename*, which must have been written using **scr_dump**. The next call to **doupdate** restores the screen to the way it looked in the dump file.

With the **scr_init** routine, the contents of *filename* are read in and used to initialize the **curses** data structures about what the terminal currently has on its screen. If the data is determined to be valid, **curses** bases its next update of the screen on this information rather than clearing the screen and starting from scratch. **scr_init** is used after **initscr** or a **system** [see **system**(3S)] call to share the screen with another process which has done a **scr_dump** after its **endwin** call. The data is declared invalid if the time-stamp of the tty is old or the terminfo capabilities **rmcup** and **nrrmc** exist.

The **scr_set** routine is a combination of **scr_restore** and **scr_init**. It tells the program that the information in *filename* is what is currently on the screen, and also what the program wants on the screen. This can be thought of as a screen inheritance function.

To read (write) a window from (to) a file, use the **getwin** and **putwin** routines [see curs_util(3curses)].

RETURN VALUE

All routines return the integer **ERR** upon failure and **OK** upon success.

NOTES

The header file **curses.h** automatically includes the header files **stdio.h** and **unctrl.h**.

Note that **scr_init**, **scr_set**, and **scr_restore** may be macros.

SEE ALSO

curses(3curses), curs_initscr(3curses), curs_refresh(3curses), curs_util(3curses), system(3S)

curs_scroll(3curses)

NAME
curs_scroll: **scroll**, **srcl**, **wscrl** – scroll a **curses** window

SYNOPSIS
```
#include <curses.h>

int scroll(WINDOW *win);
int scrl(int n);
int wscrl(WINDOW *win, int n);
```

DESCRIPTION
With the **scroll** routine, the window is scrolled up one line. This involves moving the lines in the window data structure. As an optimization, if the scrolling region of the window is the entire screen, the physical screen is scrolled at the same time.

With the **scrl** and **wscrl** routines, for positive n scroll the window up n lines (line $i+n$ becomes i); otherwise scroll the window down n lines. This involves moving the lines in the window character image structure. The current cursor position is not changed.

For these functions to work, scrolling must be enabled via **scrollok**.

RETURN VALUE
All routines return the integer **ERR** upon failure and an integer value other than **ERR** upon successful completion.

NOTES
The header file **curses.h** automatically includes the header files **stdio.h** and **unctrl.h**.

Note that **scrl** and **scroll** may be macros.

SEE ALSO
curses(3curses), **curs_outopts**(3curses)

NAME

curs_slk: slk_init, slk_set, slk_refresh, slk_noutrefresh, slk_label, slk_clear, slk_restore, slk_touch, slk_attron, slk_attrset, slk_attroff – curses soft label routines

SYNOPSIS

```
#include <curses.h>

int slk_init(int fmt);
int slk_set(int labnum, char *label, int fmt);
int slk_refresh(void);
int slk_noutrefresh(void);
char *slk_label(int labnum);
int slk_clear(void);
int slk_restore(void);
int slk_touch(void);
int slk_attron(chtype attrs);
int slk_attrset(chtype attrs);
int slk_attroff(chtype attrs);
```

DESCRIPTION

curses manipulates the set of soft function-key labels that exist on many terminals. For those terminals that do not have soft labels, **curses** takes over the bottom line of **stdscr**, reducing the size of **stdscr** and the variable **LINES**. **curses** standardizes on eight labels of up to eight characters each.

To use soft labels, the **slk_init** routine must be called before **initscr** or **newterm** is called. If **initscr** eventually uses a line from **stdscr** to emulate the soft labels, then *fmt* determines how the labels are arranged on the screen. Setting *fmt* to **0** indicates a 3-2-3 arrangement of the labels; **1** indicates a 4-4 arrangement.

With the **slk_set** routine, *labnum* is the label number, from **1** to **8**. *label* is the string to be put on the label, up to eight characters in length. A null string or a null pointer sets up a blank label. *fmt* is either **0**, **1**, or **2**, indicating whether the label is to be left-justified, centered, or right-justified, respectively, within the label.

The **slk_refresh** and **slk_noutrefresh** routines correspond to the **wrefresh** and **wnoutrefresh** routines.

With the **slk_label** routine, the current label for label number *labnum* is returned with leading and trailing blanks stripped.

With the **slk_clear** routine, the soft labels are cleared from the screen.

With the **slk_restore** routine, the soft labels are restored to the screen after a **slk_clear** is performed.

With the **slk_touch** routine, all the soft labels are forced to be output the next time a **slk_noutrefresh** is performed.

The **slk_attron**, **slk_attrset** and **slk_attroff** routines correspond to **attron**, **attrset**, and **attroff**. They have an effect only if soft labels are simulated on the bottom line of the screen.

curs_slk (3curses)

RETURN VALUE

Routines that return an integer return **ERR** upon failure and an integer value other than **ERR** upon successful completion.

`slk_label` returns **NULL** on error.

NOTES

The header file **curses.h** automatically includes the header files **stdio.h** and **unctrl.h**.

Most applications would use **slk_noutrefresh** because a **wrefresh** is likely to follow soon.

SEE ALSO

curses(3curses), **curs_attr**(3curses), **curs_initscr**(3curses), **curs_refresh**(3curses)

NAME

curs_termattrs: baudrate, erasechar, has_ic, has_il, killchar, longname, termattrs, termname – curses environment query routines

SYNOPSIS

```
#include <curses.h>

int baudrate(void);
char erasechar(void);
int has_ic(void);
int has_il(void);
char killchar(void);
char *longname(void);
chtype termattrs(void);
char *termname(void);
```

DESCRIPTION

The **baudrate** routine returns the output speed of the terminal. The number returned is in bits per second, for example **9600**, and is an integer.

With the **erasechar** routine, the user's current erase character is returned.

The **has_ic** routine is true if the terminal has insert- and delete-character capabilities.

The **has_il** routine is true if the terminal has insert- and delete-line capabilities, or can simulate them using scrolling regions. This might be used to determine if it would be appropriate to turn on physical scrolling using **scrollok**.

With the **killchar** routine, the user's current line kill character is returned.

The **longname** routine returns a pointer to a static area containing a verbose description of the current terminal. The maximum length of a verbose description is 128 characters. It is defined only after the call to **initscr** or **newterm**. The area is overwritten by each call to **newterm** and is not restored by **set_term**, so the value should be saved between calls to **newterm** if **longname** is going to be used with multiple terminals.

If a given terminal doesn't support a video attribute that an application program is trying to use, **curses** may substitute a different video attribute for it. The **termattrs** function returns a logical **OR** of all video attributes supported by the terminal. This information is useful when a **curses** program needs complete control over the appearance of the screen.

The **termname** routine returns the value of the environmental variable **TERM** (truncated to 14 characters).

RETURN VALUE

longname and **termname** return **NULL** on error.

Routines that return an integer return **ERR** upon failure and an integer value other than **ERR** upon successful completion.

NOTES

The header file **curses.h** automatically includes the header files **stdio.h** and **unctrl.h**.

Note that **termattrs** may be a macro.

curs_termattrs(3curses)

SEE ALSO

      curses(3curses), **curs_initscr**(3curses), **curs_outopts**(3curses)

NAME

curs_termcap: **tgetent, tgetflag, tgetnum, tgetstr, tgoto, tputs** – curses interfaces (emulated) to the termcap library

SYNOPSIS

```
#include <curses.h>
#include <term.h>

int tgetent(char *bp, char *name);
int tgetflag(char id[2]);
int tgetnum(char id[2]);
char *tgetstr(char id[2], char **area);
char *tgoto(char *cap, int col, int row);
int tputs(char *str, int affcnt, int (*putc)(void));
```

DESCRIPTION

These routines are included as a conversion aid for programs that use the *termcap* library. Their parameters are the same and the routines are emulated using the **terminfo** database. These routines are supported at Level 2 and should not be used in new applications.

The **tgetent** routine looks up the termcap entry for *name*. The emulation ignores the buffer pointer *bp*.

The **tgetflag** routine gets the boolean entry for *id*.

The **tgetnum** routine gets the numeric entry for *id*.

The **tgetstr** routine returns the string entry for *id*. Use **tputs** to output the returned string.

The **tgoto** routine instantiates the parameters into the given capability. The output from this routine is to be passed to **tputs**.

The **tputs** routine is described in the **curs_terminfo**(3curses) manual page.

RETURN VALUE

Routines that return an integer return **ERR** upon failure and an integer value other than **ERR** upon successful completion.

Routines that return pointers return **NULL** on error.

NOTES

The header file **curses.h** automatically includes the header files **stdio.h** and **unctrl.h**.

SEE ALSO

curses(3curses), **curs_terminfo**(3curses), **putc**(3S)

curs_terminfo(3curses)

NAME

curs_terminfo: setupterm, setterm, set_curterm, del_curterm, restartterm, tparm, tputs, putp, vidputs, vidattr, mvcur, tigetflag, tigetnum, tigetstr – curses interfaces to terminfo database

SYNOPSIS

```
#include <curses.h>
#include <term.h>

int setupterm(char *term, int fildes, int *errret);
int setterm(char *term);
TERMINAL *set_curterm(TERMINAL *nterm);
int del_curterm(TERMINAL *oterm);
int restartterm(char *term, int fildes, int *errret);
char *tparm(char *str, long int p1, long int p2, long int p3,
      long int p4, long int p5, long int p6, long int p7,
      long int p8, long int p9);
int tputs(char *str, int affcnt, int (*putc)(int));
int putp(char *str);
int vidputs(chtype attrs, int (*putc)(int));
int vidattr(chtype attrs);
int mvcur(int oldrow, int oldcol, int newrow, int newcol);
int tigetflag(char *capname);
int tigetnum(char *capname);
int tigetstr(char *capname);
```

DESCRIPTION

These low-level routines must be called by programs that have to deal directly with the **terminfo** database to handle certain terminal capabilities, such as programming function keys. For all other functionality, **curses** routines are more suitable and their use is recommended.

Initially, **setupterm** should be called. Note that **setupterm** is automatically called by **initscr** and **newterm**. This defines the set of terminal-dependent variables [listed in **terminfo**(4)]. The **terminfo** variables **lines** and **columns** are initialized by **setupterm** as follows: If **use_env(FALSE)** has been called, values for **lines** and **columns** specified in **terminfo** are used. Otherwise, if the environment variables **LINES** and **COLUMNS** exist, their values are used. If these environment variables do not exist and the program is running in a window, the current window size is used. Otherwise, if the environment variables do not exist, the values for **lines** and **columns** specified in the **terminfo** database are used.

The header files **curses.h** and **term.h** should be included (in this order) to get the definitions for these strings, numbers, and flags. Parameterized strings should be passed through **tparm** to instantiate them. All **terminfo** strings [including the output of **tparm**] should be printed with **tputs** or **putp**. Call the **reset_shell_mode** to restore the tty modes before exiting [see **curs_kernel**(3curses)]. Programs which use cursor addressing should output **enter_ca_mode** upon startup and should output **exit_ca_mode** before exiting. Programs desiring shell escapes should call **reset_shell_mode** and output **exit_ca_mode** before the shell is called and should output **enter_ca_mode** and call **reset_prog_mode** after returning from the shell.

The **setupterm** routine reads in the **terminfo** database, initializing the **terminfo** structures, but does not set up the output virtualization structures used by **curses**. The terminal type is the character string *term*; if *term* is null, the environment variable **TERM** is used. All output is to file descriptor **fildes** which is initialized for output. If **errret** is not null, then **setupterm** returns **OK** or **ERR** and stores a status value in the integer pointed to by **errret**. A status of **1** in **errret** is normal, **0** means that the terminal could not be found, and **−1** means that the **terminfo** database could not be found. If **errret** is null, **setupterm** prints an error message upon finding an error and exits. Thus, the simplest call is:

        setupterm((char *)0, 1, (int *)0);,

which uses all the defaults and sends the output to **stdout**.

The **setterm** routine is being replaced by **setupterm**. The call:

        setupterm(*term*, 1, (int *)0)

provides the same functionality as **setterm**(*term*). The **setterm** routine is included here for compatibility and is supported at Level 2.

The **set_curterm** routine sets the variable **cur_term** to *nterm*, and makes all of the **terminfo** boolean, numeric, and string variables use the values from *nterm*.

The **del_curterm** routine frees the space pointed to by *oterm* and makes it available for further use. If *oterm* is the same as **cur_term**, references to any of the **terminfo** boolean, numeric, and string variables thereafter may refer to invalid memory locations until another **setupterm** has been called.

The **restartterm** routine is similar to **setupterm** and **initscr**, except that it is called after restoring memory to a previous state. It assumes that the windows and the input and output options are the same as when memory was saved, but the terminal type and baud rate may be different.

The **tparm** routine instantiates the string *str* with parameters *pi*. A pointer is returned to the result of *str* with the parameters applied.

The **tputs** routine applies padding information to the string *str* and outputs it. The *str* must be a terminfo string variable or the return value from **tparm**, **tgetstr**, or **tgoto**. *affcnt* is the number of lines affected, or 1 if not applicable. *putc* is a **putchar**-like routine to which the characters are passed, one at a time.

The **putp** routine calls **tputs**(*str*, 1, **putchar**). Note that the output of **putp** always goes to **stdout**, not to the *fildes* specified in **setupterm**.

The **vidputs** routine displays the string on the terminal in the video attribute mode *attrs*, which is any combination of the attributes listed in **curses**(3curses). The characters are passed to the **putchar**-like routine *putc*.

The **vidattr** routine is like the **vidputs** routine, except that it outputs through **putchar**.

The **mvcur** routine provides low-level cursor motion.

The **tigetflag**, **tigetnum** and **tigetstr** routines return the value of the capability corresponding to the **terminfo** *capname* passed to them, such as **xenl**.

With the **tigetflag** routine, the value **−1** is returned if *capname* is not a boolean capability.

With the **tigetnum** routine, the value **−2** is returned if *capname* is not a numeric capability.

With the **tigetstr** routine, the value **(char *)−1** is returned if *capname* is not a string capability.

The *capname* for each capability is given in the table column entitled *capname* code in the capabilities section of **terminfo**(4).

char *boolnames, *boolcodes, *boolfnames

char *numnames, *numcodes, *numfnames

char *strnames, *strcodes, *strfnames

These null-terminated arrays contain the *capnames*, the **termcap** codes, and the full C names, for each of the **terminfo** variables.

RETURN VALUE

All routines return the integer **ERR** upon failure and an integer value other than **ERR** upon successful completion, unless otherwise noted in the preceding routine descriptions.

Routines that return pointers always return **NULL** on error.

NOTES

The header file **curses.h** automatically includes the header files **stdio.h** and **unctrl.h**.

The **setupterm** routine should be used in place of **setterm**.

Note that **vidattr** and **vidputs** may be macros.

SEE ALSO

curses(3curses), **curs_initscr**(3curses), **curs_kernel**(3curses), **curs_termcap**(3curses), **putc**(3S), **terminfo**(4)

NAME

curs_touch: touchwin, touchline, untouchwin, wtouchln, is_linetouched, is_wintouched – **curses** refresh control routines

SYNOPSIS

`#include <curses.h>`

`int touchwin(WINDOW *win);`
`int touchline(WINDOW *win, int start, int count);`
`int untouchwin(WINDOW *win);`
`int wtouchln(WINDOW *win, int y, int n, int changed);`
`int is_linetouched(WINDOW *win, int line);`
`int is_wintouched(WINDOW *win);`

DESCRIPTION

The **touchwin** and **touchline** routines throw away all optimization information about which parts of the window have been touched, by pretending that the entire window has been drawn on. This is sometimes necessary when using overlapping windows, since a change to one window affects the other window, but the records of which lines have been changed in the other window do not reflect the change. The routine **touchline** only pretends that *count* lines have been changed, beginning with line *start*.

The **untouchwin** routine marks all lines in the window as unchanged since the last call to **wrefresh**.

The **wtouchln** routine makes *n* lines in the window, starting at line *y*, look as if they have (*changed*=**1**) or have not (*changed*=**0**) been changed since the last call to **wrefresh**.

The **is_linetouched** and **is_wintouched** routines return **TRUE** if the specified line/window was modified since the last call to **wrefresh**; otherwise they return **FALSE**. In addition, **is_linetouched** returns **ERR** if *line* is not valid for the given window.

RETURN VALUE

All routines return the integer **ERR** upon failure and an integer value other than **ERR** upon successful completion, unless otherwise noted in the preceding routine descriptions.

NOTES

The header file **curses.h** automatically includes the header files **stdio.h** and **unctrl.h**.

Note that all routines except **wtouchln** may be macros.

SEE ALSO

curses(3curses), **curs_refresh**(3curses)

curs_util(3curses)

NAME

curs_util: **unctrl**, **keyname**, **filter**, **use_env**, **putwin**, **getwin**, **delay_output**, **draino**, **flushinp** – miscellaneous **curses** utility routines

SYNOPSIS

```
#include <curses.h>

char *unctrl(chtype c);
char *keyname(int c);
void filter(void);
void use_env(char bool);
int putwin(WINDOW *win, FILE *filep);
WINDOW *getwin(FILE *filep);
int delay_output(int ms);
int draino(int ms);
int flushinp(void);
```

DESCRIPTION

The **unctrl** macro expands to a character string which is a printable representation of the character *c*. Control characters are displayed in the ^X notation. Printing characters are displayed as is.

With the **keyname** routine, a character string corresponding to the key *c* is returned.

The **filter** routine, if used, is called before **initscr** or **newterm** are called. It makes **curses** think that there is a one-line screen. **curses** does not use any terminal capabilities that assume that they know on what line of the screen the cursor is positioned.

The **use_env** routine, if used, is called before **initscr** or **newterm** are called. When called with **FALSE** as an argument, the values of **lines** and **columns** specified in the **terminfo** database will be used, even if environment variables **LINES** and **COLUMNS** (used by default) are set, or if **curses** is running in a window (in which case default behavior would be to use the window size if **LINES** and **COLUMNS** are not set).

With the **putwin** routine, all data associated with window *win* is written into the file to which *filep* points. This information can be later retrieved using the **getwin** function.

The **getwin** routine reads window related data stored in the file by **putwin**. The routine then creates and initializes a new window using that data. It returns a pointer to the new window.

The **delay_output** routine inserts an *ms* millisecond pause in output. This routine should not be used extensively because padding characters are used rather than a CPU pause.

The **draino** routine returns when *ms* are needed to clear the output completely. Current valid value for *ms* is 0.

The **flushinp** routine throws away any typeahead that has been typed by the user and has not yet been read by the program.

RETURN VALUE

Except for **flushinp**, routines that return an integer return **ERR** upon failure and an integer value other than **ERR** upon successful completion.

flushinp always returns **OK**.

Routines that return pointers return **NULL** on error.

NOTES

The header file **curses.h** automatically includes the header files **stdio.h** and **unctrl.h**.

Note that **unctrl** is a macro, which is defined in **unctrl.h**.

SEE ALSO

curses(3curses), **curs_initscr**(3curses), **curs_scr_dump**(3curses)

curs_window (3curses)

NAME

curs_window: newwin, delwin, mvwin, subwin, derwin, mvderwin, dupwin, wsyncup, syncok, wcursyncup, wsyncdown – create **curses** windows

SYNOPSIS

```
#include <curses.h>
```

WINDOW *newwin(int *nlines*, int *ncols*, int *begin_y*, int *begin_x*);
int delwin(WINDOW *win*);
int mvwin(WINDOW *win*, int *y*, int *x*);
WINDOW *subwin(WINDOW *orig*, int *nlines*, int *ncols*, int *begin_y*,
    int *begin_x*);
WINDOW *derwin(WINDOW *orig*, int *nlines*, int *ncols*, int *begin_y*,
    int *begin_x*);
int mvderwin(WINDOW *win*, int *par_y*, int *par_x*);
WINDOW *dupwin(WINDOW *win*);
void wsyncup(WINDOW *win*);
int syncok(WINDOW *win*, bool *bf*);
void wcursyncup(WINDOW *win*);
void wsyncdown(WINDOW *win*);

DESCRIPTION

The **newwin** routine creates and returns a pointer to a new window with the given number of lines, *nlines*, and columns, *ncols*. The upper left-hand corner of the window is at line *begin_y*, column *begin_x*. If either *nlines* or *ncols* is zero, they default to `LINES − `*begin_y*` and COLS − `*begin_x*`. A new full-screen window is created by calling newwin(0,0,0,0).`

The **delwin** routine deletes the named window, freeing all memory associated with it. Subwindows must be deleted before the main window can be deleted.

The **mvwin** routine moves the window so that the upper left-hand corner is at position (*x, y*). If the move would cause the window to be off the screen, it is an error and the window is not moved. Moving subwindows is allowed, but should be avoided.

The **subwin** routine creates and returns a pointer to a new window with the given number of lines, *nlines*, and columns, *ncols*. The window is at position (*begin_y*, *begin_x*) on the screen. (This position is relative to the screen, and not to the window *orig*.) The window is made in the middle of the window *orig*, so that changes made to one window will affect both windows. The subwindow shares memory with the window *orig*. When using this routine, it is necessary to call **touchwin** or **touchline** on *orig* before calling **wrefresh** on the subwindow.

The **derwin** routine is the same as **subwin**, except that *begin_y* and *begin_x* are relative to the origin of the window *orig* rather than the screen. There is no difference between the subwindows and the derived windows.

The **mvderwin** routine moves a derived window (or subwindow) inside its parent window. The screen-relative parameters of the window are not changed. This routine is used to display different parts of the parent window at the same physical position on the screen.

The **dupwin** routine creates an exact duplicate of the window *win*.

Each **curses** window maintains two data structures: the character image structure and the status structure. The character image structure is shared among all windows in the window hierarchy (that is, the window with all subwindows). The status structure, which contains information about individual line changes in the window, is private to each window. The routine **wrefresh** uses the status data structure when performing screen updating. Since status structures are not shared, changes made to one window in the hierarchy may not be properly reflected on the screen.

The routine **wsyncup** causes the changes in the status structure of a window to be reflected in the status structures of its ancestors. If **syncok** is called with second argument **TRUE** then **wsyncup** is called automatically whenever there is a change in the window.

The routine **wcursyncup** updates the current cursor position of all the ancestors of the window to reflect the current cursor position of the window.

The routine **wsyncdown** updates the status structure of the window to reflect the changes in the status structures of its ancestors. Applications seldom call this routine because it is called automatically by **wrefresh**.

RETURN VALUE

Routines that return an integer return the integer **ERR** upon failure and an integer value other than **ERR** upon successful completion.

delwin returns the integer **ERR** upon failure and **OK** upon successful completion.

Routines that return pointers return **NULL** on error.

NOTES

The header file **curses.h** automatically includes the header files **stdio.h** and **unctrl.h**.

If many small changes are made to the window, the **wsyncup** option could degrade performance.

Note that **syncok** may be a macro.

SEE ALSO

curses(3curses), **curs_refresh**(3curses), **curs_touch**(3curses)

curses (3curses)

NAME

`curses` – CRT screen handling and optimization package

SYNOPSIS

`#include <curses.h>`

DESCRIPTION

The **curses** library routines give the user a terminal-independent method of updating character screens with reasonable optimization. A program using these routines must be compiled with the **−lcurses** option of **cc**.

The **curses** package allows: overall screen, window and pad manipulation; output to windows and pads; reading terminal input; control over terminal and **curses** input and output options; environment query routines; color manipulation; use of soft label keys; terminfo access; and access to low-level **curses** routines.

To initialize the routines, the routine **initscr** or **newterm** must be called before any of the other routines that deal with windows and screens are used. The routine **endwin** must be called before exiting. To get character-at-a-time input without echoing (most interactive, screen-oriented programs want this), the following sequence should be used:

> `initscr,cbreak,noecho;`

Most programs would additionally use the sequence:

> `nonl,intrflush(stdscr,FALSE),keypad(stdscr,TRUE);`

Before a **curses** program is run, the tab stops of the terminal should be set and its initialization strings, if defined, must be output. This can be done by executing the **tput init** command after the shell environment variable **TERM** has been exported. [See **terminfo**(4) for further details.]

The **curses** library permits manipulation of data structures, called *windows*, which can be thought of as two-dimensional arrays of characters. A default window called **stdscr**, which is the size of the terminal screen, is supplied. Others may be created with **newwin()**.

Windows are referred to by variables declared as **WINDOW ***. These data structures are manipulated with routines described on 3curses pages (whose names begin ''**curs_**''). Among the most basic routines are **move** and **addch**. More general versions of these routines are included that allow the user to specify a window.

After using routines to manipulate a window, **refresh** is called, telling **curses** to make the user's CRT screen look like **stdscr**. The characters in a window are actually of type **chtype** (character and attribute data) so that other information about the character may also be stored with each character.

Special windows called *pads* may also be manipulated. These are windows that are not necessarily associated with a viewable part of the screen. See **curs_pad**(3curses) for more information.

In addition to drawing characters on the screen, video attributes and colors may be included, causing the characters to show up in such modes as underlined, reverse video or color on terminals that support such display enhancements. Line drawing characters may be specified to be output. On input, **curses** is also able to translate arrow and function keys that transmit escape sequences into single values. The video attributes, line drawing characters and input values use names, defined in `curses.h`, such as `A_REVERSE`, `ACS_HLINE`, and `KEY_LEFT`.

If the environment variables `LINES` and `COLUMNS` are set, or if the program is executing in a window environment, line and column information in the environment will override information read by `terminfo`. This would affect a program running in a window environment, for example, where the size of a screen is changeable.

If the environment variable `TERMINFO` is defined, any program using `curses` checks for a local terminal definition before checking in the standard place. For example, if `TERM` is set to `wyse150`, then the compiled terminal definition is found in

> `/usr/share/lib/terminfo/w/wyse150`.

(The `w` is copied from the first letter of `wyse150` to avoid creation of huge directories.) However, if `TERMINFO` is set to `$HOME/myterms`, `curses` first checks

> `$HOME/myterms/w/wyse150`,

and if that fails, it then checks

> `/usr/share/lib/terminfo/w/wyse150`.

This is useful for developing experimental definitions or when write permission in `/usr/share/lib/terminfo` is not available.

The integer variables `LINES` and `COLS` are defined in `curses.h` and will be filled in by `initscr` with the size of the screen. The constants `TRUE` and `FALSE` have the values `1` and `0`, respectively.

`curses` routines also define the `WINDOW *` variable `curscr` which is used for certain low-level operations like clearing and redrawing a screen containing garbage. `curscr` can be used in only a few routines.

International Functions

The number of bytes and the number of columns to hold a character from the supplementary character set is locale-specific (locale category `LC_CTYPE`) and can be specified in the character class table.

For editing, operating at the character level is entirely appropriate. For screen formatting, arbitrary movement of characters on screen is not desirable.

Overwriting characters (`addch`, for example) operates on a screen level. Overwriting a character by a character that requires a different number of columns may produce *orphaned columns*. These orphaned columns are filled with background characters.

Inserting characters (`insch`, for example) operates on a character level (that is, at the character boundaries). The specified character is inserted right before the character, regardless of which column of a character the cursor points to. Before insertion, the cursor position is adjusted to the first column of the character.

As with inserting characters, deleting characters (`delch`, for example) operates on a character level (that is, at the character boundaries). The character at the cursor is deleted whichever column of the character the cursor points to. Before deletion, the cursor position is adjusted to the first column of the character.

A *multi-column* character cannot be put on the last column of a line. When such attempts are made, the last column is set to the background character. In addition, when such an operation creates orphaned columns, the orphaned columns are filled with background characters.

Overlapping and overwriting a window follows the operation of overwriting characters around its edge. The orphaned columns, if any, are handled as in the character operations.

The cursor is allowed to be placed anywhere in a window. If the insertion or deletion is made when the cursor points to the second or later column position of a character that holds multiple columns, the cursor is adjusted to the first column of the character before the insertion or deletion.

Routine and Argument Names

Many **curses** routines have two or more versions. Routines prefixed with **p** require a pad argument. Routines whose names contain a **w** generally require either a window argument or a wide-character argument. If **w** appears twice in a routine name, the routine usually requires both a window and a wide-character argument. Routines that do not require a pad or window argument generally use **stdscr**.

The routines prefixed with **mv** require an *x* and *y* coordinate to move to before performing the appropriate action. The **mv** routines imply a call to **move** before the call to the other routine. The coordinate *y* always refers to the row (of the window), and *x* always refers to the column. The upper left-hand corner is always (0,0), not (1,1).

The routines prefixed with **mvw** take both a window argument and *x* and *y* coordinates. The window argument is always specified before the coordinates.

In each case, *win* is the window affected, and *pad* is the pad affected; *win* and *pad* are always pointers to type **WINDOW**.

Option setting routines require a Boolean flag *bf* with the value **TRUE** or **FALSE**; *bf* is always of type **bool**. The variables *ch* and *attrs* are always of type **chtype**. The types **WINDOW**, **SCREEN**, **bool**, and **chtype** are defined in **curses.h**. The type **TERMINAL** is defined in **term.h**. All other arguments are integers.

Routine Name Index

The following table lists each **curses** routine and the name of the manual page on which it is described.

curses Routine Name	Manual Page Name
addch	curs_addch(3curses)
addchnstr	curs_addchstr(3curses)
addchstr	curs_addchstr(3curses)
addnstr	curs_addstr(3curses)
addnwstr	curs_addwstr(3curses)
addstr	curs_addstr(3curses)
addwch	curs_addwch(3curses)
addwchnstr	curs_addwchstr(3curses)
addwchstr	curs_addwchstr(3curses)

curses Routine Name	Manual Page Name
addwstr	curs_addwstr(3curses)
attroff	curs_attr(3curses)
attron	curs_attr(3curses)
attrset	curs_attr(3curses)
baudrate	curs_termattrs(3curses)
beep	curs_beep(3curses)
bkgd	curs_bkgd(3curses)
bkgdset	curs_bkgd(3curses)
border	curs_border(3curses)
box	curs_border(3curses)
can_change_color	curs_color(3curses)
cbreak	curs_inopts(3curses)
clear	curs_clear(3curses)
clearok	curs_outopts(3curses)
clrtobot	curs_clear(3curses)
clrtoeol	curs_clear(3curses)
color_content	curs_color(3curses)
copywin	curs_overlay(3curses)
curs_set	curs_kernel(3curses)
def_prog_mode	curs_kernel(3curses)
def_shell_mode	curs_kernel(3curses)
del_curterm	curs_terminfo(3curses)
delay_output	curs_util(3curses)
delch	curs_delch(3curses)
deleteln	curs_deleteln(3curses)
delscreen	curs_initscr(3curses)
delwin	curs_window(3curses)
derwin	curs_window(3curses)
doupdate	curs_refresh(3curses)
draino	curs_util(3curses)
dupwin	curs_window(3curses)
echo	curs_inopts(3curses)
echochar	curs_addch(3curses)
echowchar	curs_addwch(3curses)
endwin	curs_initscr(3curses)
erase	curs_clear(3curses)
erasechar	curs_termattrs(3curses)
filter	curs_util(3curses)
flash	curs_beep(3curses)
flushinp	curs_util(3curses)
getbegyx	curs_getyx(3curses)
getch	curs_getch(3curses)
getmaxyx	curs_getyx(3curses)
getnwstr	curs_getwstr(3curses)
getparyx	curs_getyx(3curses)
getstr	curs_getstr(3curses)

curses Routine Name	Manual Page Name
getsyx	curs_kernel(3curses)
getwch	curs_getwch(3curses)
getwin	curs_util(3curses)
getwstr	curs_getwstr(3curses)
getyx	curs_getyx(3curses)
halfdelay	curs_inopts(3curses)
has_colors	curs_color(3curses)
has_ic	curs_termattrs(3curses)
has_il	curs_termattrs(3curses)
hline	curs_border(3curses)
idcok	curs_outopts(3curses)
idlok	curs_outopts(3curses)
immedok	curs_outopts(3curses)
inch	curs_inch(3curses)
inchnstr	curs_inchstr(3curses)
inchstr	curs_inchstr(3curses)
init_color	curs_color(3curses)
init_pair	curs_color(3curses)
initscr	curs_initscr(3curses)
innstr	curs_instr(3curses)
innwstr	curs_inwstr(3curses)
insch	curs_insch(3curses)
insdelln	curs_deleteln(3curses)
insertln	curs_deleteln(3curses)
insnstr	curs_insstr(3curses)
insnwstr	curs_inswstr(3curses)
insstr	curs_insstr(3curses)
instr	curs_instr(3curses)
inswch	curs_inswch(3curses)
inswstr	curs_inswstr(3curses)
intrflush	curs_inopts(3curses)
inwch	curs_inwch(3curses)
inwchnstr	curs_inwchstr(3curses)
inwchstr	curs_inwchstr(3curses)
inwstr	curs_inwstr(3curses)
is_linetouched	curs_touch(3curses)
is_wintouched	curs_touch(3curses)
isendwin	curs_initscr(3curses)
keyname	curs_util(3curses)
keypad	curs_inopts(3curses)
killchar	curs_termattrs(3curses)
leaveok	curs_outopts(3curses)
longname	curs_termattrs(3curses)
meta	curs_inopts(3curses)
move	curs_move(3curses)
mvaddch	curs_addch(3curses)

curses Routine Name	Manual Page Name
mvaddchnstr	curs_addchstr(3curses)
mvaddchstr	curs_addchstr(3curses)
mvaddnstr	curs_addstr(3curses)
mvaddnwstr	curs_addwstr(3curses)
mvaddstr	curs_addstr(3curses)
mvaddwch	curs_addwch(3curses)
mvaddwchnstr	curs_addwchstr(3curses)
mvaddwchstr	curs_addwchstr(3curses)
mvaddwstr	curs_addwstr(3curses)
mvcur	curs_terminfo(3curses)
mvdelch	curs_delch(3curses)
mvderwin	curs_window(3curses)
mvgetch	curs_getch(3curses)
mvgetnwstr	curs_getwstr(3curses)
mvgetstr	curs_getstr(3curses)
mvgetwch	curs_getwch(3curses)
mvgetwstr	curs_getwstr(3curses)
mvinch	curs_inch(3curses)
mvinchnstr	curs_inchstr(3curses)
mvinchstr	curs_inchstr(3curses)
mvinnstr	curs_instr(3curses)
mvinnwstr	curs_inwstr(3curses)
mvinsch	curs_insch(3curses)
mvinsnstr	curs_insstr(3curses)
mvinsnwstr	curs_inswstr(3curses)
mvinsstr	curs_insstr(3curses)
mvinstr	curs_instr(3curses)
mvinswch	curs_inswch(3curses)
mvinswstr	curs_inswstr(3curses)
mvinwch	curs_inwch(3curses)
mvinwchnstr	curs_inwchstr(3curses)
mvinwchstr	curs_inwchstr(3curses)
mvinwstr	curs_inwstr(3curses)
mvprintw	curs_printw(3curses)
mvscanw	curs_scanw(3curses)
mvwaddch	curs_addch(3curses)
mvwaddchnstr	curs_addchstr(3curses)
mvwaddchstr	curs_addchstr(3curses)
mvwaddnstr	curs_addstr(3curses)
mvwaddnwstr	curs_addwstr(3curses)
mvwaddstr	curs_addstr(3curses)
mvwaddwch	curs_addwch(3curses)
mvwaddwchnstr	curs_addwchstr(3curses)
mvwaddwchstr	curs_addwchstr(3curses)
mvwaddwstr	curs_addwstr(3curses)
mvwdelch	curs_delch(3curses)

curses (3curses)

curses Routine Name	Manual Page Name
mvwgetch	curs_getch(3curses)
mvwgetnwstr	curs_getwstr(3curses)
mvwgetstr	curs_getstr(3curses)
mvwgetwch	curs_getwch(3curses)
mvwgetwstr	curs_getwstr(3curses)
mvwin	curs_window(3curses)
mvwinch	curs_inch(3curses)
mvwinchnstr	curs_inchstr(3curses)
mvwinchstr	curs_inchstr(3curses)
mvwinnstr	curs_instr(3curses)
mvwinnwstr	curs_inwstr(3curses)
mvwinsch	curs_insch(3curses)
mvwinsnstr	curs_insstr(3curses)
mvwinsstr	curs_insstr(3curses)
mvwinstr	curs_instr(3curses)
mvwinswch	curs_inswch(3curses)
mvwinswstr	curs_inswstr(3curses)
mvwinwch	curs_inwch(3curses)
mvwinwchnstr	curs_inwchstr(3curses)
mvwinwchstr	curs_inwchstr(3curses)
mvwinwstr	curs_inwstr(3curses)
mvwprintw	curs_printw(3curses)
mvwscanw	curs_scanw(3curses)
napms	curs_kernel(3curses)
newpad	curs_pad(3curses)
newterm	curs_initscr(3curses)
newwin	curs_window(3curses)
nl	curs_outopts(3curses)
nocbreak	curs_inopts(3curses)
nodelay	curs_inopts(3curses)
noecho	curs_inopts(3curses)
nonl	curs_outopts(3curses)
noqiflush	curs_inopts(3curses)
noraw	curs_inopts(3curses)
notimeout	curs_inopts(3curses)
overlay	curs_overlay(3curses)
overwrite	curs_overlay(3curses)
pair_content	curs_color(3curses)
pechochar	curs_pad(3curses)
pechowchar	curs_pad(3curses)
pnoutrefresh	curs_pad(3curses)
prefresh	curs_pad(3curses)
printw	curs_printw(3curses)
putp	curs_terminfo(3curses)
putwin	curs_util(3curses)
qiflush	curs_inopts(3curses)

curses Routine Name	Manual Page Name
raw	curs_inopts(3curses)
redrawwin	curs_refresh(3curses)
refresh	curs_refresh(3curses)
reset_prog_mode	curs_kernel(3curses)
reset_shell_mode	curs_kernel(3curses)
resetty	curs_kernel(3curses)
restartterm	curs_terminfo(3curses)
ripoffline	curs_kernel(3curses)
savetty	curs_kernel(3curses)
scanw	curs_scanw(3curses)
scr_dump	curs_scr_dump(3curses)
scr_init	curs_scr_dump(3curses)
scr_restore	curs_scr_dump(3curses)
scr_set	curs_scr_dump(3curses)
scrl	curs_scroll(3curses)
scroll	curs_scroll(3curses)
scrollok	curs_outopts(3curses)
set_curterm	curs_terminfo(3curses)
set_term	curs_initscr(3curses)
setscrreg	curs_outopts(3curses)
setsyx	curs_kernel(3curses)
setterm	curs_terminfo(3curses)
setupterm	curs_terminfo(3curses)
slk_attroff	curs_slk(3curses)
slk_attron	curs_slk(3curses)
slk_attrset	curs_slk(3curses)
slk_clear	curs_slk(3curses)
slk_init	curs_slk(3curses)
slk_label	curs_slk(3curses)
slk_noutrefresh	curs_slk(3curses)
slk_refresh	curs_slk(3curses)
slk_restore	curs_slk(3curses)
slk_set	curs_slk(3curses)
slk_touch	curs_slk(3curses)
standend	curs_attr(3curses)
standout	curs_attr(3curses)
start_color	curs_color(3curses)
subpad	curs_pad(3curses)
subwin	curs_window(3curses)
syncok	curs_window(3curses)
termattrs	curs_termattrs(3curses)
termname	curs_termattrs(3curses)
tgetent	curs_termcap(3curses)
tgetflag	curs_termcap(3curses)
tgetnum	curs_termcap(3curses)
tgetstr	curs_termcap(3curses)

curses (3curses)

curses Routine Name	Manual Page Name
tgoto	curs_termcap(3curses)
tigetflag	curs_terminfo(3curses)
tigetnum	curs_terminfo(3curses)
tigetstr	curs_terminfo(3curses)
timeout	curs_inopts(3curses)
touchline	curs_touch(3curses)
touchwin	curs_touch(3curses)
tparm	curs_terminfo(3curses)
tputs	curs_termcap(3curses)
tputs	curs_terminfo(3curses)
typeahead	curs_inopts(3curses)
unctrl	curs_util(3curses)
ungetch	curs_getch(3curses)
ungetwch	curs_getwch(3curses)
untouchwin	curs_touch(3curses)
use_env	curs_util(3curses)
vidattr	curs_terminfo(3curses)
vidputs	curs_terminfo(3curses)
vline	curs_border(3curses)
vwprintw	curs_printw(3curses)
vwscanw	curs_scanw(3curses)
waddch	curs_addch(3curses)
waddchnstr	curs_addchstr(3curses)
waddchstr	curs_addchstr(3curses)
waddnstr	curs_addstr(3curses)
waddnwstr	curs_addwstr(3curses)
waddstr	curs_addstr(3curses)
waddwch	curs_addwch(3curses)
waddwchnstr	curs_addwchstr(3curses)
waddwchstr	curs_addwchstr(3curses)
waddwstr	curs_addwstr(3curses)
wattroff	curs_attr(3curses)
wattron	curs_attr(3curses)
wattrset	curs_attr(3curses)
wbkgd	curs_bkgd(3curses)
wbkgdset	curs_bkgd(3curses)
wborder	curs_border(3curses)
wclear	curs_clear(3curses)
wclrtobot	curs_clear(3curses)
wclrtoeol	curs_clear(3curses)
wcursyncup	curs_window(3curses)
wdelch	curs_delch(3curses)
wdeleteln	curs_deleteln(3curses)
wechochar	curs_addch(3curses)
wechowchar	curs_addwch(3curses)
werase	curs_clear(3curses)

curses Routine Name	Manual Page Name
wgetch	curs_getch(3curses)
wgetnstr	curs_getstr(3curses)
wgetnwstr	curs_getwstr(3curses)
wgetstr	curs_getstr(3curses)
wgetwch	curs_getwch(3curses)
wgetwstr	curs_getwstr(3curses)
whline	curs_border(3curses)
winch	curs_inch(3curses)
winchnstr	curs_inchstr(3curses)
winchstr	curs_inchstr(3curses)
winnstr	curs_instr(3curses)
winnwstr	curs_inwstr(3curses)
winsch	curs_insch(3curses)
winsdelln	curs_deleteln(3curses)
winsertln	curs_deleteln(3curses)
winsnstr	curs_insstr(3curses)
winsnwstr	curs_inswstr(3curses)
winsstr	curs_insstr(3curses)
winstr	curs_instr(3curses)
winswch	curs_inswch(3curses)
winswstr	curs_inswstr(3curses)
winwch	curs_inwch(3curses)
winwchnstr	curs_inwchstr(3curses)
winwchstr	curs_inwchstr(3curses)
winwstr	curs_inwstr(3curses)
wmove	curs_move(3curses)
wnoutrefresh	curs_refresh(3curses)
wprintw	curs_printw(3curses)
wredrawln	curs_refresh(3curses)
wrefresh	curs_refresh(3curses)
wscanw	curs_scanw(3curses)
wscrl	curs_scroll(3curses)
wsetscrreg	curs_outopts(3curses)
wstandend	curs_attr(3curses)
wstandout	curs_attr(3curses)
wsyncdown	curs_window(3curses)
wsyncup	curs_window(3curses)
wtimeout	curs_inopts(3curses)
wtouchln	curs_touch(3curses)
wvline	curs_border(3curses)

RETURN VALUE

Routines that return an integer return **ERR** upon failure and an integer value other than **ERR** upon successful completion, unless otherwise noted in the routine descriptions.

All macros return the value of the window version, except **setscrreg**, **wsetscrreg**, **getyx**, **getbegyx** and **getmaxyx**. The return values of **setscrreg**, **wsetscrreg**, **getyx**, **getbegyx** and **getmaxyx** are undefined (that is, these should not be used as the right-hand side of assignment statements).

Routines that return pointers return **NULL** on error.

NOTES

The header file **curses.h** automatically includes the header files **stdio.h** and **unctrl.h**.

SEE ALSO

terminfo(4) and 3curses pages whose names begin "**curs_**" for detailed routine descriptions

NAME

DtAcceptReply – accept a Desktop Metaphor reply

SYNOPSIS

#include <Dt/Desktop.h>

```
int DtAcceptReply(Screen *scrn, Atom queue, Window client,
    DtReply *reply);
```

DESCRIPTION

The DtAcceptReply function accepts a Desktop Metaphor reply, where:

scrn   is the Screen pointer

queue   is the queue name

client is the window ID of the sender

reply   is a pointer to the *DtReply* structure

For each client reply, DtReplyHeader, the standard header structure, is prefixed to each reply specific structure:

```
DtReplyType rtype;         /* integer including all reply type */
unsigned long serial;      /* serial number of related request */
unsigned short version;    /* version number */
int status;                /* reply specific status info */
```

The DtReply structure is a union of all structures related to each request type, where **version** can take the values:

DT_ADD_TO_HELPDESK	DT_OPEN_FOLDER
DT_DEL_FROM_HELPDESK	DT_QUERY_FILE_CLASS
DT_MOVE_TO_WB	DT_CREATE_FILE_CLASS
DT_MOVE_FROM_WB	DT_DELETE_FILE_CLASS
	DT_GET_DESKTOP_PROPERTY

serial can take the values:

DT_BAD_INPUT   some of the input in the request structure were invalid

DT_FAILED   the request failed

DT_OK   completed successfully

DT_DUP   a resource of the specified name already exists

DT_NOENT   the specified resource does not exist

and **status** can take values described in DtEnqueueRequest(3Dt).

DtAcceptReply returns a reply structure in response to certain requests, as defined below.

DtAddToHelpDeskReply

structure includes the following members:

```
char *app_name;        /* name of executable */
char *icon_label;      /* icon label, used as app. title */
char *icon_file;       /* icon pixmap file */
char *help_file;       /* help file name */
char *help_dir;        /* help directory */
```

DtAcceptReply (3Dt)

DtDelFromHelpDeskReply
>>structure includes the following members:

```
char *app_name;      /* application name */
char *icon_label;    /* icon label */
```

DtMoveToWBReply
>>structure includes the following members:

DtMoveFromWBReply
>>structure includes the following members:

DtCreateFclassReply
>>structure includes the following members:

```
char *file_name;     /* name of the class file */
DtAttrs options;     /* options */
```
`options` may be one of:

>>**DT_DUP**
>>>file name already exists in class database

>>**DT_FAILED**
>>>unable to process the specified file

>>**DT_OK** success

DtDeleteFclassReply
>>structure includes the following member:

```
char *file_name;     /* name of the class file */
```

DtQueryFclassReply
>>structure includes the following members:

```
char *class_name;    /* name of the file class */
DtAttrs options;     /* options */
```

DtGetDesktopPropertyReply
>>structure includes the following members:

```
char *value;         /* property value */
DtAttrs attrs;       /* attributes */
```

RETURN VALUES
>On success, **DtAcceptReply** returns 0.

>On failure, **DtAcceptReply** returns −1.

SEE ALSO
>**DtEnqueueRequest**(3Dt), **DtInitialize**(3Dt)

NAME

DtEnqueueRequest – queue a Desktop Metaphor request

SYNOPSIS

```
#include <Dt/Desktop.h>

int DtEnqueueRequest( Screen *scrn, Atom queue, Atom my_queue,
    Window client, DtRequest *request);
```

DESCRIPTION

The DtEnqueueRequest function queues a Desktop Metaphor request, where:

scrn   is the Screen pointer

queue   is the destination queue name

my_queue is the queue for storing the request and reply, if any. If a client does not send multiple requests simultaneously, *my_queue* can be the same as *queue*.

client   is the window ID of the sender

request   is a pointer to the DtRequest structure

For each client request, DtRequestHeader, a standard header structure, is prefixed to each request specific structure and includes the following members:

```
DtRequestType rqtype;        /* integer request type */
unsigned long serial;        /* serial number */
unsigned short version;      /* version number */
Window client;               /* sender's window ID */
char *node_name;             /* system node name of requestor */
```

The client supplies rqtype, all other members are supplied automatically.

The DtRequest structure is a union of all structures related to each type where DtRequestType can take the values:

DT_DISPLAY_HELP

        display help in a help window. The DtDisplayHelpRequest structure includes the following members:

```
unsigned long source_type; /* source type */
char *app_title;           /* application title */
char *app_name;            /* application name */
char *title;               /* title in help window */
char *help_dir;            /* help directory */
char *icon_file;           /* icon file */
char *string;              /* help string */
char *file_name;           /* help file name */
char *sect_tag;            /* section tag/name */
```

        source_type

            the type of help requested, one of the following:

                DT_OPEN_HELPDESK

                    open the help desk

DT_SECTION_HELP
> display a specified section or the first section of a help file if section name/tag is not provided

DT_STRING_HELP
> display the specified string in the help window pane

DT_TOC_HELP
> display the table of contents of a help file

app_title
> the help window title. The title is of the format *app_title* **Help:** *topic*. If not specified, *app_name* is used instead.

app_name
> is the application name, an executable, and must be specified

title used in the help window, instead of, or if no section name is available, as in the case of **DT_STRING_HELP**

help_dir
> help directory where the help file resides. This is used if the help file is not located in a standard path.

icon_file
> name of the application's icon file, displayed in the magnifying glass in the help window. If not specified, a default icon is used.

string
> string to be displayed in the help window pane, and must be specified if **source_type** is **DT_STRING_HELP**

file_name
> name of a help file, full or relative path name. If **file_name** is a relative path name and a help directory is not specified, **XtResolvePathname** is used to locate it in the standard paths. Note that only **string** or **file_name** may be specified, not both. This member must be specified is **source_type** is **DT_DISPLAY_HELP** or **DT_TOC_HELP**.

sect_tag
> section tag or name. If not specified, the first section is displayed. This only has an effect if **source_type** is **DT_DISPLAY_HELP**.

DT_ADD_TO_HELPDESK
> add a new application to the help desk. The **DtAddToHelpDesk-Request** structure includes the following members:

```
char *app_name;     /* application name */
char *icon_label;   /* icon label, also in help win title*/
char *icon_file;    /* icon file */
char *help_file;    /* help file name */
char *help_dir;     /* help directory */
```

DT_DEL_FROM_HELPDESK
> remove an application from the help desk. The **DtDelFromHelp-DeskRequest** structure includes the following members:

```
char *app_name;    /* application name */
char *icon_lable;  /* icon label */
```

DT_MOVE_TO_WB
> move a file to the wastebasket. The **DtMoveToWB** structure includes the following members:

```
char *pathname;    /* full pathname */
```

DT_MOVE_FROM_WB
> move a file from the wastebasket. The **DtMoveFromWB** structure includes the following members:

```
char *pathname;    /* full pathname */
```

DT_OPEN_FOLDER
> present the user with a folder window associated with the specified directory. If the window does not already exist, create it. If the window is already on the screen, raise it to the top of the window stack, set focus to it, and do not use the title, if provided.

> The **DtOpenFolderRequest** structure includes the following members:

```
char *title;       /* title of folder window */
char *path;        /* full path of the diretory */
DtAttrs options;   /* options */
```

> Where **options** is an unsigned long used as a bit field to store option flags, and **options** can take the following values:

DT_NOTIFY_ON_CLOSE
> > notify requestor when specified folder window is closed

DT_SYNC_FOLDER
> update the folder window directory information. The desktop manager first checks if the specified folder is open. This request should be issued after modifying contents of a directory.

> The **DtSyncFolderRequest** structure includes the following members:

```
char *path;        /* full path of the directory */
```

DT_CREATE_FILE_CLASS
> add a new file class to the file database. The new file class is appended to the end of the list; if a file class of the same name exists, the new file class replaces the existing one.

```
char *file_name;   /* name of the class file */
DtAttrs options;   /* options */
```

> **options** can have the value **DT_APPEND**, causing the file to be appended to the end of the file rather than added at the beginning.

DT_DELETE_FILE_CLASS
> delete the specified file class from the file database. The deleted file class will not be used for new icons thereafter, and existing icons will be reclassified immediately.

```
char *file_name;     /* file name class */
```

DT_QUERY_FILE_CLASS
> query an existing file class. A client should use this to validate an existing file class created by the same application before replacing it with a new file class. The **DtQueryFclass** structure initiates the query and includes the following members:

```
char *class_name;    /* name of the file class */
DtAttrs options;     /* options */
```

> Where **options** can take the value **DT_GET_PROPERTIES**, which gets a list of all properties.

DT_GET_DESKTOP_PROPERTY
> gets the value of a desktop property. The **DtGetDesktopPropertyRequest** structure specified the desktop property to query and includes the following members:

```
char *name;          /* property name */
```

DT_SET_DESKTOP_PROPERTY
> sets the value of a desktop property and includes the following members (attrs is 0):

```
char *name;          /* property name */
char *value;         /* property value */
DtAttrs attrs;       /* attributes */
```

RETURN VALUES

On success, **DtEnqueueRequest** returns the serial number of the request, a non-negative number.

On failure, **DtEnqueueRequest** returns -1.

NOTES

The following request structures have corresponding reply structures [see DtAcceptReply(3Dt)]:

DT_ADD_TO_HELPDESK,
DT_DEL_FROM_HELPDESK,
DT_MOVE_TO_WB,
DT_MOVE_FROM_WB,
DT_OPEN_FOLDER,
DT_CREATE_FILE_CLASS,
DT_DELETE_FILE_CLASS,
DT_QUERY_FILE_CLASS, and
DT_GET_DESKTOP_PROPERTY.

SEE ALSO

DtAcceptReply(3Dt), DtInitialize(3Dt), DtToolkitInitialize(3Olit)

NAME

DtGetAppId – get the current owner of ID

SYNOPSIS

```
#include <Dt/Desktop.h>
```

```
Window DtGetAppId(Display *dpy, Atom id);
```

DESCRIPTION

The DtGetAppId gets the current owner of a named ID, where

dpy   is the Display pointer

id   is the named ID.

RETURN VALUES

DtGetAppId returns the current owner of the ID.

SEE ALSO

DtSetAppId(3Dt)

DtGetFileNames (3Dt)

NAME

        DtGetFileNames – get list of filenames

SYNOPSIS

        `#include <Dt/Desktop.h>`

        DtDnDInfoPtr DtGetFileNames(
            Widget *w*,
            Atom *selection*,
            Time *timestamp*,
            Boolean *send_done*,
            void (*proc*)(Widget, XtPointer, XtPointer),
            XtPointer *client_data*
        );

DESCRIPTION

The **DtGetFileNames** function requests the list of filenames from the sender of the trigger message, upon receiving a drag and drop trigger message.

The **DtDnDInfo** structure, and the associated pointer to the structure, **DtDnDInfoPtr**, includes the following members:

```
char **files;      /* list of file names */
DtAttrs attrs;     /* reserved for future use */
Boolean error;     /* error */
int nitems;        /* number of filenames received */
Time timestamp;    /* timestamp of trigger message */
```

By default, the files list in the **DtDnDInfo** structure is freed upon returning from the *proc* callback. If the application wants to keep the list of files and free it later, the application should set files to NULL before returning from the callback.

NAME

DtInitialize – initialize widget for Desktop Metaphor

SYNOPSIS

#include <Dt/Desktop.h>

void DtInitialize(Widget *wid*);

DESCRIPTION

The DtInitialize function initializes a widget for the Desktop Metaphor. This function must be called before any other functions in libDt are referenced.

wid   the widget ID, typically returned from the toolkit initialization routine [see OlToolkitInitialize(3Olit)].

RETURN VALUES

DtInitialize has no return value.

SEE ALSO

DtAcceptReply(3Dt), DtEnqueueRequest(3Dt), OlToolkitInitialize(3Olit)

DtLockCursor (3Dt)

NAME
DtLockCursor – lock the cursor for an interval

SYNOPSIS

```
#include <Dt/DtLock.h>

DtCallbackInfo *DtLockCursor(
        Widget w,
        unsigned long interval,
        void (*f)(),
        XtPointer client_data,
        Cursor cursor
);
```

DESCRIPTION

The **DtLockCursor** function is used to lock a display pointer for a specified amount of time. This function can be used, for example, to indicate that an operation is in progress, where:

w	is the widget on the display
interval	is the amount of time in milliseconds to lock the pointer
f	is the function to invoke when the pointer is unlocked
client_data	is the input to *f*
cursor	is the locked cursor

During the lock, *cursor* replaces the current mouse pointer cursor on the display associated with *w*. When the lock is cleared, the function *f* is called with the single argument *client_data*.

The **DtCallbackInfo** structure includes the following members:

```
void        (*f)();
Display *   display;
XtPointer   client_data;
XtIntervalId timer_id;
```

RETURN VALUES

On success, **DtLockCursor** returns a pointer to the **DtCallbackInfo** structure.

On failure, **DtLockCursor** returns NULL.

SEE ALSO

DtUnlockCursor(3Dt)

NAME

`DtNewDnDTransaction` – initiate a drag and drop transaction

SYNOPSIS

```
#include <Dt/Desktop.h>

DtDnDSendPtr DtNewDnDTransaction(
        Widget w,
        char **files,
        DtAttrs options,
        Position root_x,
        Position root_y,
        Time timestamp,
        Window dst_window,
        int dnd_hint,
        XtCallbackProc del_proc,
        XtCallbackProc done_proc,
        XtPointer client_data
);
```

DESCRIPTION

The **DtNewDnDTransaction** function initiates a drag and drop transaction with a drop site, and transmits a list of filenames to the drop site. Typically, this routine is called from within a **XtNdropProc** callback [see **FlatList**(3Olit)].

w	widget ID of the widget initiating the drag and drop transaction
files	a NULL terminated list of filenames.
options	two options are currently supported:

    DT_B_STATIC_LIST
        the files is a static list. Thus it should not be freed after the completion of the transaction.
        If this option is not used, then the list will be freed automatically upon returning from the *done_proc* callback.

    DT_B_SEND_EVENT
        perform a "simulated" drop on a drop site.

root_x	x coordinate, relative to the root window, of the drop point. This value is ignored if **DT_SEND_EVENT** option is set.
root_y	y coordinate, relative to the root window, of the drop point. This value is ignored if **DT_SEND_EVENT** option is set.
timestamp	time stamp of the event that triggers the drag and drop transaction.
dst_window	destination window. This is only used if **DT_SEND_EVENT** option is set.
dnd_hint	The are possible values: **DT_COPY_OP**, **DT_MOVE_OP**, and **DT_LINK_OP**. These values correspond to values of **OlDnDTriggerOperation**.
del_proc	invoke this callback on receiving a DELETE conversion request within the drag and drop transaction. The call data is the name of the file being deleted.

DtNewDnDTransaction (3Dt)

done_proc   invoke this callback when the transaction is terminated. The call data is a pointer to a **DtDnDSendInfo** structure. If the **DT_B_STATIC_LIST** option is not set, then the files list will be freed upon returning from the callback.

client_data   client data for the *del_proc* and *done_proc* callbacks.

The **DtDnDSend** structure, and the associated **DtDnDSendPtr** pointer, includes the following members:

```
char **files;        /* accumulated list of file names */
DtAttrs attrs;       /* attributes */
Widget widget;       /* owner widget */
Atom selection;      /* DnD transaction ID */
char **fp;           /* current file name */
Time drop_timestamp; /* timestamp of drop action */
int hint;            /* DnD hint */
```

RETURN VALUES

On success, **DtNewDnDTransaction** returns a **DtDnDSendPtr**.

On failure, **DtNewDnDTransaction** returns NULL.

SEE ALSO

FlatList(3Olit), OlDnDTriggerOperation(3DnD)

NAME

    `DtSetAppId` – establish an ID for an application

SYNOPSIS

    `#include <Dt/Desktop.h>`

    `Window DtSetAppId(Display *dpy, Window owner, char *id);`

DESCRIPTION

    The `DtSetAppId` function establishes and ID for an application, where

    dpy   is the Display pointer

    owner is the intended owner of the ID, and

    id   is the named ID.

    `DtSetAppId` first checks if an owner already exists for the named ID. Note that the check and ownership assertion is performed as one atomic operation.

    Once an ownership is asserted, other clients can communicate with the owner by performing a Selection conversion on the ID [see `XtGetSelectionValue`(Xt)] or send a simulated drop message [see `DtNewDnDTransaction`(3Dt)].

RETURN VALUES

    `DtSetAppId` returns

        the window ID of the current owner if an owner already exists for the named ID, or

        ''None'' and ownership of the named ID is ensured.

SEE ALSO

    `DtGetAppId`(3Dt), `DtNewDnDTransaction`(3Dt)

DtUnlockCursor (3Dt)

NAME

DtUnlockCursor – unlock a cursor locked with DtLockCursor

SYNOPSIS

#include <Dt/DtLock.h>

void DtUnlockCursor(XtPointer *client_data*, XtIntervalId *timer_id*);

DESCRIPTION

The DtUnlockCursor function removes a lock created with DtLockCursor.

client_data   DtCallbackInfo * from the DtLockCursor function

timer_id   reserved parameter

This function is automatically invoked when the lock interval has elapsed [see DtLockCursor(3Dt)]. It may also be invoked by an application to prematurely remove the lock.

RETURN VALUES

DtUnlockCursor has no return values.

SEE ALSO

DtLockCursor(3Dt)

NAME

EndCurrentTextBufferWord – find the end of a word in a **TextBuffer**

SYNOPSIS

#include <Xol/textbuff.h>

TextLocation EndCurrentTextBufferWord(
    TextBuffer *textBuffer*,
    TextLocation *current*
);

DESCRIPTION

The **EndCurrentTextBufferWord** function is used to locate the end of a word in the **TextBuffer** relative to a given *current* location. The function returns the location of the end of the current word. This return value will equal the given *current* value if the current location is already at the end of a word.

SEE ALSO

NextTextBufferWord(3Olit), PreviousTextBufferWord(3Olit)

Error (3Olit)

NAME

NAME

Error: OlError, OlWarning, OlVaDisplayErrorMsg, OlVaDisplayWarningMsg, OlSetErrorHandler, OlSetWarningHandler, OlSetVaDisplayErrorMsg-Handler, OlSetVaDisplayWarningMsgHandler – error and warning message handling

SYNOPSIS

```
#include <Xol/OpenLook.h>
#include <varargs.h>

void OlVaDisplayErrorMsg(
    Display *dpy,           /* Display pointer or NULL  */
    String name,           /* message name             */
    String type,           /* message type             */
    String class,          /* message class            */
    String default_msg     /* message format string    */
    . . .                  /* variable arguments for   */
                           /* the message format string */
);

void OlVaDisplayWarningMsg(
    Display *dpy,           /* Display pointer or NULL  */
    String name,           /* message name             */
    String type,           /* message type             */
    String class,          /* message class            */
    String default_msg     /* message format string    */
    . . .                  /* variable arguments for   */
                           /* the message format string */
);

void OlError(String msg);

void OlWarning(String msg);

OlErrorHandler OlSetErrorHandler(OlErrorHandler handler);

OlWarningHandler OlSetWarningHandler(OlWarningHandler handler);

OlVaDisplayErrorMsgHandler OlSetVaDisplayErrorMsgHandler(
    OlVaDisplayErrorMsgHandler handler
);

OlVaDisplayWarningMsgHandler OlSetVaDisplayWarningMsgHandler(
    OlVaDisplayWarningMsgHandler handler
);

typedef void (*OlErrorHandler)(
    String msg              /* error message string */
);

typedef void (*OlWarningHandler)(
    String msg              /* warning message string */
);

typedef void (*OlVaDisplayErrorMsgHandler)(
    Display *dpy,           /* Display pointer or NULL  */
```

```
        String name,              /* message name             */
        String type,              /* message type             */
        String class,             /* message class            */
        String default_msg,       /* message format string     */
        va_list ap                /* variable arguments for    */
                                  /* the message format string */
);
typedef void (*OlVaDisplayWarningMsgHandler)(
        Display *dpy,             /* Display pointer or NULL   */
        String name,              /* message name             */
        String type,              /* message type             */
        String class,             /* message class            */
        String default_msg,       /* message format string     */
        va_list ap                /* variable arguments for    */
                                  /* the message format string */
);
```

DESCRIPTION
OlVaDisplayErrorMsg

OlVaDisplayErrorMsg writes an error to stderr and exits. The error message is looked up in the error database by calling XtAppGetErrorDatabaseText using the *name*, *type*, and *class* arguments. If no message is found in the error database, the default_msg string is used. The application context is determined by calling XtDisplayToApplicationContext with the supplied Display pointer. If the display pointer is NULL, the display created at application startup is used to determine the application context.

An application programmer can choose to customize the text in an error message prefix. The following example shows the standard prefix:

> "*application class*" OPEN LOOK Toolkit Error: *message*

To customize the prefix, put the following line in the client's *client*_msgs file, where *client* is the name of the client:

> *message.prefix: t e x t %s t e x t %s t e x t

where the first %s will be the application name and the second will be the content of the message.

If the prefix is not customized, the current prefix will be supplied as the default.

To silence any toolkit error, put a corresponding NULL message in the client app-defaults/*client*_msgs file:

For example, to silence:

> *invalidResource.setValues: SetValues: widget

Put the line

> *invalidResource.setValues:

in the *client*_msgs file.

Note that OlVaDisplayErrorMsg will still cause the client application to exit.

Error (3Olit)

OlVaDisplayWarningMsg

`OlVaDisplayWarningMsg` has the same semantics as `OlVaDisplayErrorMsg` except it returns instead of exiting.

An application programmer can choose to customize the text in a warning message prefix. The following example shows the prefix in a sample warning message:

"application class" **OPEN LOOK Toolkit Warning:** *m e s s a g e*

To customize the prefix, put the following line in the client's *client_msgs* file:

`*message.prefix: t e x t %s t e x t %s t e x t`

where the first %s will be the application name and the second will be the type of message.

If the prefix is not customized, the current prefix will be supplied as the default.

To silence any toolkit warning, put a corresponding NULL message in the client **app-defaults/***client_msgs* file:

For example, to silence:

`*invalidResource.setValues: SetValues: widget`

Put the line

`*invalidResource.setValues:`

in the *client_msgs* file.

OlError

`OlError` writes a simple string to **stderr** and then exits.

OlWarning

`OlWarning` writes a simple string to **stderr** and then returns.

Others

`OlSetErrorHandler`, `OlSetWarningHandler`, `OlSetVaDisplayErrorMsg-Handler`, and `OlSetVaDisplayWarningMsgHandler` allow an application to override the various warning and error handlers. These routines return a pointer to the previous handler. If NULL is supplied to any of these routines, the default handler will be used.

Since the error routines normally exit the program, application-supplied error handlers should do the same since continuation of an application will result in undefined behavior.

NOTES

Most programs should not use `OlError` and `OlWarning` since they don't allow for customization and internationalization.

Since **OpenLook.h** does not include **stdarg.h** (or **varargs.h**), an application using `OlSetVaDisplayErrorMsgHandler` or `OlSetVaDisplayWarningMsgHandler` should include one of these two headers before including **OpenLook.h** to insure the correct function prototype will be used for the application's error/warning handler.

SEE ALSO

OlGetMessage(3Olit)

NAME

Flattened_Widget_Utilities: `OlFlatCallAcceptFocus`, `OlFlatGetFocus-Item`, `OlFlatGetItemIndex`, `OlFlatGetItemGeometry`, `OlFlatGetValues`, `OlFlatSetValues`, `OlVaFlatGetValues`, `OlVaFlatSetValues` – queries and manipulates flattened widget attributes

SYNOPSIS

```
#include <Xol/OpenLook.h>
#include <Xol/Flat.h>

Boolean OlFlatCallAcceptFocus(
      Widget widget,            /* Flattened widget ID */
      Cardinal index,           /* Item's index        */
      Time time                 /* time of request     */
);

Cardinal OlFlatGetFocusItem(Widget widget);

Cardinal OlFlatGetItemIndex(
      Widget widget,            /* Flattened widget ID   */
      Position x,               /* x location within widget */
      Position y                /* y location within widget */
);

void OlFlatGetItemGeometry(
      Widget widget,            /* Flattened widget ID   */
      Cardinal index,           /* Item's index          */
      Position *x_ret,          /* returned x coordinate */
      Position *y_ret,          /* returned y coordinate */
      Dimension w_ret,          /* returned width        */
      Dimension *h_ret          /* returned height       */
);
```

Getting and Setting Flattened Widget Item State

```
void OlFlatGetValues(
      Widget widget,            /* Flattened widget ID   */
      Cardinal index,           /* Item's index          */
      ArgList args,             /* attributes to query   */
      Cardinal num_args         /* number of args        */
);

void OlFlatSetValues(
      Widget widget,            /* Flattened widget ID   */
      Cardinal index,           /* Item's index          */
      ArgList args,             /* attributes to set     */
      Cardinal num_args         /* number of args        */
);

void OlVaFlatGetValues(
      Widget widget,            /* Flattened widget ID   */
      Cardinal index,           /* Item's index          */
      . . .                     /* resource name/variable address pairs */
);
```

Flattened_Widget_Utilities (3Olit)

```
void OlVaFlatSetValues(
     Widget widget,            /* Flattened widget ID      */
     Cardinal index,           /* Item's index             */
     . . .                     /* resource name/value pairs */
);
void OlFlatChangeManagedItems(
     Widget wid,               /* Flattened widget ID */
     Cardinal *managed,        /* indexes of items to manage */
     Cardinal num_managed,     /* number of managed indexes */
     Cardinal *unmanaged,      /* indexes of items to unmanage */
     Cardinal num_unmanaged    /* number of unmanaged indexes */
);
void OlFlatRefreshItem(
     Widget wid,               /* Flattened widget ID */
     Cardinal item_index,      /* index of item to refresh */
     Boolean clear_area        /* clear area first flag */
);
```

DESCRIPTION

These convenience routines query or manipulate flattened widget attributes. All of these routines issue a warning if the widget ID is not a subclass of a flattened widget.

OlFlatCallAcceptFocus

If specified item is capable of accepting input focus, focus is assigned to the item and function returns **TRUE**; otherwise, **FALSE** is returned.

OlFlatGetFocusItem

Returns the item within the flattened widget which has focus. **OL_NO_ITEM** is returned if no item within the widget has focus.

OlFlatGetItemIndex

Returns the item that contains the given **x** and **y** coordinates. **OL_NO_ITEM** is returned otherwise if no item contains the coordinate pair.

OlFlatGetItemGeometry

Returns the location and width/height of an item with respect to its flattened widget container. If the supplied item index is invalid, a warning is issued and the return values are set to zero.

OlFlatGetValues

Queries attributes of an item. This routine is very similar to **XtGetValues**. Applications can query any attribute of an item even if the attribute was not specified in the **XtNitemFields** resource of the flat widget container. [See **OlVaFlatGetValues**.]

OlFlatSetValues

Sets attributes of an item. This routine is very similar to **XtSetValues**. Applications can set values of item attributes only if the attribute name was specified in the **XtNitemFields** resource of the flat widget container or if the item's attribute is always maintained (that is, implicitly) by the flat widget container regardless of the **XtNitemFields** entries. For example, the **FlatExclusives** Widget always maintains the value of an item's **XtNset** attribute even if **XtNset** was not in the

XtNitemFields resource [see **FlatExclusives**(3Olit)]. Therefore, an application can set the value of **XtNset** even though **XtNset** was not specified explicitly in the **XtNitemFields** resource for the widget. **XtNfont**, on the other hand, is not implicitly maintained by the **FlatExclusives** Widget, so an application must specify **XtNfont** in the **XtNitemFields** resource if that application wants to change the font value via **OlFlatSetValues**. [See **OlVaFlatSetValues**.]

OlVaFlatGetValues

Variable argument interface to **OlFlatGetValues**. The variable length list of resource name/value pairs is terminated by a NULL resource name.

OlVaFlatSetValues

Variable argument interface to **OlFlatSetValues**. The variable length list of resource name/value pairs is terminated by a NULL resource name.

OlFlatChangeManagedItems

Manages a set of items and unmanages a set of items simultaneously.

OlFlatRefreshItem

Refreshes a specific item. This function calls **XClearArea** first if *clear_crea* is **TRUE**.

SEE ALSO

FlatExclusives(3Olit)

form_cursor (3curses)

NAME

form_cursor: **pos_form_cursor** – position **forms** window cursor

SYNOPSIS

#include <form.h>

int **pos_form_cursor**(FORM *form*);

DESCRIPTION

pos_form_cursor moves the form window cursor to the location required by the form driver to resume form processing. This may be needed after the application calls a **curses** library I/O routine.

RETURN VALUE

pos_form_cursor returns one of the following:

E_OK	– The function returned successfully.
E_SYSTEM_ERROR	– System error.
E_BAD_ARGUMENT	– An argument is incorrect.
E_NOT_POSTED	– The form is not posted.

NOTES

The header file **form.h** automatically includes the header files **eti.h** and **curses.h**.

SEE ALSO

curses(3curses), **forms**(3curses)

NAME

form_data: data_ahead, data_behind – tell if **forms** field has off-screen data ahead or behind

SYNOPSIS

#include <form.h>

int data_ahead(FORM *form);
int data_behind(FORM *form);

DESCRIPTION

data_ahead returns **TRUE** (1) if the current field has more off-screen data ahead; otherwise it returns **FALSE** (0).

data_behind returns **TRUE** (1) if the current field has more off-screen data behind; otherwise it returns **FALSE** (0).

NOTES

The header file **form.h** automatically includes the header files **eti.h** and **curses.h**.

SEE ALSO

curses(3curses), **forms**(3curses)

form_driver (3curses)

NAME

form_driver – command processor for the **forms** subsystem

SYNOPSIS

```
#include <form.h>
```

int form_driver(FORM *form*, int *c*);

DESCRIPTION

form_driver is the workhorse of the **forms** subsystem; it checks to determine whether the character *c* is a **forms** request or data. If it is a request, the form driver executes the request and reports the result. If it is data (a printable ASCII character), it enters the data into the current position in the current field. If it is not recognized, the form driver assumes it is an application-defined command and returns **E_UNKNOWN_COMMAND**. Application defined commands should be defined relative to **MAX_COMMAND**, the maximum value of a request listed below.

Form driver requests:

REQ_NEXT_PAGE	Move to the next page.
REQ_PREV_PAGE	Move to the previous page.
REQ_FIRST_PAGE	Move to the first page.
REQ_LAST_PAGE	Move to the last page.
REQ_NEXT_FIELD	Move to the next field.
REQ_PREV_FIELD	Move to the previous field.
REQ_FIRST_FIELD	Move to the first field.
REQ_LAST_FIELD	Move to the last field.
REQ_SNEXT_FIELD	Move to the sorted next field.
REQ_SPREV_FIELD	Move to the sorted prev field.
REQ_SFIRST_FIELD	Move to the sorted first field.
REQ_SLAST_FIELD	Move to the sorted last field.
REQ_LEFT_FIELD	Move left to field.
REQ_RIGHT_FIELD	Move right to field.
REQ_UP_FIELD	Move up to field.
REQ_DOWN_FIELD	Move down to field.
REQ_NEXT_CHAR	Move to the next character in the field.
REQ_PREV_CHAR	Move to the previous character in the field.
REQ_NEXT_LINE	Move to the next line in the field.
REQ_PREV_LINE	Move to the previous line in the field.
REQ_NEXT_WORD	Move to the next word in the field.
REQ_PREV_WORD	Move to the previous word in the field.
REQ_BEG_FIELD	Move to the first char in the field.
REQ_END_FIELD	Move after the last char in the field.
REQ_BEG_LINE	Move to the beginning of the line.
REQ_END_LINE	Move after the last char in the line.
REQ_LEFT_CHAR	Move left in the field.
REQ_RIGHT_CHAR	Move right in the field.
REQ_UP_CHAR	Move up in the field.
REQ_DOWN_CHAR	Move down in the field.
REQ_NEW_LINE	Insert/overlay a new line.

REQ_INS_CHAR	Insert the blank character at the cursor.
REQ_INS_LINE	Insert a blank line at the cursor.
REQ_DEL_CHAR	Delete the character at the cursor.
REQ_DEL_PREV	Delete the character before the cursor.
REQ_DEL_LINE	Delete the line at the cursor.
REQ_DEL_WORD	Delete the word at the cursor.
REQ_CLR_EOL	Clear to the end of the line.
REQ_CLR_EOF	Clear to the end of the field.
REQ_CLR_FIELD	Clear the entire field.
REQ_OVL_MODE	Enter overlay mode.
REQ_INS_MODE	Enter insert mode.
REQ_SCR_FLINE	Scroll the field forward a line.
REQ_SCR_BLINE	Scroll the field backward a line.
REQ_SCR_FPAGE	Scroll the field forward a page.
REQ_SCR_BPAGE	Scroll the field backward a page.
REQ_SCR_FHPAGE	Scroll the field forward half a page.
REQ_SCR_BHPAGE	Scroll the field backward half a page.
REQ_SCR_FCHAR	Horizontal scroll forward a character.
REQ_SCR_BCHAR	Horizontal scroll backward a character.
REQ_SCR_HFLINE	Horizontal scroll forward a line.
REQ_SCR_HBLINE	Horizontal scroll backward a line.
REQ_SCR_HFHALF	Horizontal scroll forward half a line.
REQ_SCR_HBHALF	Horizontal scroll backward half a line.
REQ_VALIDATION	Validate field.
REQ_PREV_CHOICE	Display the previous field choice.
REQ_NEXT_CHOICE	Display the next field choice.

RETURN VALUE

form_driver returns one of the following:

E_OK	– The function returned successfully.
E_SYSTEM_ERROR	– System error.
E_BAD_ARGUMENT	– An argument is incorrect.
E_NOT_POSTED	– The form is not posted.
E_INVALID_FIELD	– The field contents are invalid.
E_BAD_STATE	– The routine was called from an initialization or termination function.
E_REQUEST_DENIED	– The form driver request failed.
E_UNKNOWN_COMMAND	– An unknown request was passed to the the form driver.

NOTES

The header file **form.h** automatically includes the header files **eti.h** and **curses.h**.

SEE ALSO

curses(3curses), **forms**(3curses)

form_field (3curses)

NAME

form_field: set_form_fields, form_fields, field_count, move_field – connect fields to forms

SYNOPSIS

#include <form.h>

int set_form_fields(FORM *form, FIELD **field);
FIELD **form_fields(FORM *form);
int field_count(FORM *form);
int move_field(FIELD *field, int frow, int fcol);

DESCRIPTION

set_form_fields changes the fields connected to *form* to *fields*. The original fields are disconnected.

form_fields returns a pointer to the field pointer array connected to *form*.

field_count returns the number of fields connected to *form*.

move_field moves the disconnected *field* to the location *frow, fcol* in the forms subwindow.

RETURN VALUE

form_fields returns NULL on error.

field_count returns -1 on error.

set_form_fields and move_field return one of the following:

E_OK	– The function returned successfully.
E_CONNECTED	– The field is already connected to a form.
E_SYSTEM_ERROR	– System error.
E_BAD_ARGUMENT	– An argument is incorrect.
E_POSTED	– The form is posted.

NOTES

The header file form.h automatically includes the header files eti.h and curses.h.

SEE ALSO

curses(3curses), forms(3curses)

NAME

form_field_attributes: set_field_fore, field_fore, set_field_back, field_back, set_field_pad, field_pad – format the general display attributes of forms

SYNOPSIS

```
#include <form.h>

int set_field_fore(FIELD *field, chtype attr);
chtype field_fore(FIELD *field);
int set_field_back(FIELD *field, chtype attr);
chtype field_back(FIELD *field);
int set_field_pad(FIELD *field, int pad);
int field_pad(FIELD *field);
```

DESCRIPTION

set_field_fore sets the foreground attribute of *field*. The foreground attribute is the low-level **curses** display attribute used to display the field contents. field_fore returns the foreground attribute of *field*.

set_field_back sets the background attribute of *field*. The background attribute is the low-level **curses** display attribute used to display the extent of the field. field_back returns the background attribute of *field*.

set_field_pad sets the pad character of *field* to *pad*. The pad character is the character used to fill within the field. field_pad returns the pad character of *field*.

RETURN VALUE

field_fore, field_back and **field_pad** return default values if *field* is **NULL**. If *field* is not **NULL** and is not a valid **FIELD** pointer, the return value from these routines is undefined.

set_field_fore, set_field_back and **set_field_pad** return one of the following:

E_OK	– The function returned successfully.
E_SYSTEM_ERROR	– System error.
E_BAD_ARGUMENT	– An argument is incorrect.

NOTES

The header file **form.h** automatically includes the header files **eti.h** and **curses.h**.

SEE ALSO

curses(3curses), forms(3curses)

form_field_buffer(3curses)

NAME

form_field_buffer: set_field_buffer, field_buffer, set_field_status, field_status, set_max_field – set and get **forms** field attributes

SYNOPSIS

```
#include <form.h>

int set_field_buffer(FIELD *field, int buf, char *value);
char *field_buffer(FIELD *field, int buf);
int set_field_status(FIELD *field, int status);
int field_status(FIELD *field);
int set_max_field(FIELD *field, int max);
```

DESCRIPTION

set_field_buffer sets buffer *buf* of *field* to *value*. Buffer 0 stores the displayed contents of the field. Buffers other than 0 are application specific and not used by the **forms** library routines. **field_buffer** returns the value of *field* buffer *buf*.

Every field has an associated status flag that is set whenever the contents of field buffer 0 changes. **set_field_status** sets the status flag of *field* to *status*. field_status returns the status of *field*.

set_max_field sets a maximum growth on a dynamic field, or if *max=0* turns off any maximum growth.

RETURN VALUE

field_buffer returns **NULL** on error.

field_status returns **TRUE** or **FALSE**.

set_field_buffer, set_field_status and **set_max_field** return one of the following:

E_OK	– The function returned successfully.
E_SYSTEM_ERROR	– System error.
E_BAD_ARGUMENT	– An argument is incorrect.

NOTES

The header file **form.h** automatically includes the header files **eti.h** and **curses.h**.

SEE ALSO

curses(3curses), **forms**(3curses)

NAME

form_field_info: field_info, dynamic_field_info – get forms field characteristics

SYNOPSIS

```
#include <form.h>

int field_info(FIELD field, int rows, int cols, int frow, int fcol,
    int nrow, int nbuf);
int dynamic_field_info(FIELD field, int drows, int dcols, int max);
```

DESCRIPTION

field_info returns the size, position, and other named field characteristics, as defined in the original call to new_field, to the locations pointed to by the arguments *rows, cols, frow, fcol, nrow,* and *nbuf.*

dynamic_field_info returns the actual size of the *field* in the pointer arguments *drows, dcols* and returns the maximum growth allowed for *field* in *max.* If no maximum growth limit is specified for *field, max* will contain 0. A field can be made dynamic by turning off the field option O_STATIC.

RETURN VALUE

These routines return one of the following:

E_OK	– The function returned successfully.
E_SYSTEM_ERROR	– System error.
E_BAD_ARGUMENT	– An argument is incorrect.

NOTES

The header file **form.h** automatically includes the header files **eti.h** and **curses.h**.

SEE ALSO

curses(3curses), **forms**(3curses)

form_field_just(3curses)

NAME
form_field_just: set_field_just, field_just – format the general appearance of forms

SYNOPSIS
#include <form.h>

int set_field_just(FIELD *field, int justification);
int field_just(FIELD *field);

DESCRIPTION
set_field_just sets the justification for field. Justification may be one of:

NO_JUSTIFICATION, JUSTIFY_RIGHT, JUSTIFY_LEFT, or JUSTIFY_CENTER.

The field justification will be ignored if field is a dynamic field.

Field justification will not be allowed for a non-editable field. However, if the field was already justified before making it non-editable, it will remain justified.

field_just returns the type of justification assigned to field.

RETURN VALUE
field_just returns the one of:

NO_JUSTIFICATION, JUSTIFY_RIGHT, JUSTIFY_LEFT, or JUSTIFY_CENTER.

set_field_just returns one of the following:

E_OK	– The function returned successfully.
E_SYSTEM_ERROR	– System error.
E_BAD_ARGUMENT	– An argument is incorrect.
E_REQUEST_DENIED	– Justification request denied.

NOTES
The header file form.h automatically includes the header files eti.h and curses.h.

SEE ALSO
curses(3curses), forms(3curses)

NAME

form_field_new: new_field, dup_field, link_field, free_field, – create and
destroy forms fields

SYNOPSIS

```
#include <form.h>
```

FIELD *new_field(int *r*, int *c*, int *frow*, int *fcol*, int *nrow*, int *ncol*);
FIELD *dup_field(FIELD *field*, int *frow*, int *fcol*);
FIELD *link_field(FIELD *field*, int *frow*, int *fcol*);
int free_field(FIELD *field*);

DESCRIPTION

new_field creates a new field with *r* rows and *c* columns, starting at *frow*, *fcol*, in
the subwindow of a form. *nrow* is the number of off-screen rows and *nbuf* is the
number of additional working buffers. This routine returns a pointer to the new
field.

dup_field duplicates *field* at the specified location. All field attributes are dupli-
cated, including the current contents of the field buffers.

link_field also duplicates *field* at the specified location. However, unlike
dup_field, the new field shares the field buffers with the original field. After creation, the attributes of the new field can be changed without affecting the original
field.

free_field frees the storage allocated for *field*.

RETURN VALUE

Routines that return pointers return **NULL** on error. free_field returns one of the
following:

E_OK	– The function returned successfully.
E_CONNECTED	– The field is already connected to a form.
E_SYSTEM_ERROR	– System error.
E_BAD_ARGUMENT	– An argument is incorrect.

NOTES

The header file **form.h** automatically includes the header files **eti.h** and
curses.h.

SEE ALSO

forms(3curses)

form_field_opts (3curses)

NAME

form_field_opts: set_field_opts, field_opts_on, field_opts_off, field_opts – forms field option routines

SYNOPSIS

#include <form.h>

int set_field_opts(FIELD *field, OPTIONS opts);
int field_opts_on(FIELD *field, OPTIONS opts);
int field_opts_off(FIELD *field, OPTIONS opts);
OPTIONS field_opts(FIELD *field);

DESCRIPTION

set_field_opts turns on the named options of *field* and turns off all remaining options. Options are boolean values that can be OR-ed together.

field_opts_on turns on the named options; no other options are changed.

field_opts_off turns off the named options; no other options are changed.

field_opts returns the options set for *field*.

Field Options:

O_VISIBLE	The field is displayed.
O_ACTIVE	The field is visited during processing.
O_PUBLIC	The field contents are displayed as data is entered.
O_EDIT	The field can be edited.
O_WRAP	Words not fitting on a line are wrapped to the next line.
O_BLANK	The whole field is cleared if a character is entered in the first position.
O_AUTOSKIP	Skip to the next field when the current field becomes full.
O_NULLOK	A blank field is considered valid.
O_STATIC	The field buffers are fixed in size.
O_PASSOK	Validate field only if modified by user.

RETURN VALUE

set_field_opts, field_opts_on and field_opts_off return one of the following:

E_OK	– The function returned successfully.
E_SYSTEM_ERROR	– System error.
E_CURRENT	– The field is the current field.

NOTES

The header file **form.h** automatically includes the header files **eti.h** and **curses.h**.

SEE ALSO

curses(3curses), forms(3curses)

NAME

form_field_userptr: **set_field_userptr**, **field_userptr** – associate application data with **forms**

SYNOPSIS

#include <form.h>

int set_field_userptr(FIELD *field, char *ptr);
char *field_userptr(FIELD *field);

DESCRIPTION

Every field has an associated user pointer that can be used to store pertinent data. **set_field_userptr** sets the user pointer of *field*. **field_userptr** returns the user pointer of *field*.

RETURN VALUE

field_userptr returns **NULL** on error. **set_field_userptr** returns one of the following:

E_OK   – The function returned successfully.
E_SYSTEM_ERROR   – System error.

NOTES

The header file **form.h** automatically includes the header files **eti.h** and **curses.h**.

SEE ALSO

curses(3curses), **forms**(3curses)

form_field_validation (3curses)

NAME

form_field_validation: set_field_type, field_type, field_arg – forms
field data type validation

SYNOPSIS

#include <form.h>

int set_field_type(FIELD *field, FIELDTYPE *type, . . .);
FIELDTYPE *field_type(FIELD *field);
char *field_arg(FIELD *field);

DESCRIPTION

set_field_type associates the specified field type with *field*. Certain field types take additional arguments. **TYPE_ALNUM**, for instance, requires one, the minimum width specification for the field. The other predefined field types are: **TYPE_ALPHA**, **TYPE_ENUM**, **TYPE_INTEGER**, **TYPE_NUMERIC**, **TYPE_REGEXP**.

field_type returns a pointer to the field type of *field*. **NULL** is returned if no field type is assigned.

field_arg returns a pointer to the field arguments associated with the field type of *field*. **NULL** is returned if no field type is assigned.

RETURN VALUE

field_type and field_arg return **NULL** on error.

set_field_type returns one of the following:

E_OK	– The function returned successfully.
E_SYSTEM_ERROR	– System error.

NOTES

The header file **form.h** automatically includes the header files **eti.h** and **curses.h**.

SEE ALSO

curses(3curses), forms(3curses)

NAME

form_fieldtype: new_fieldtype, free_fieldtype, set_fieldtype_arg, set_fieldtype_choice, link_fieldtype – forms fieldtype routines

SYNOPSIS

```
#include <form.h>

FIELDTYPE *new_fieldtype(int (* field_check)(FIELD *, char *),
     int (* char_check)(int, char *));
int free_fieldtype(FIELDTYPE *fieldtype);
int set_fieldtype_arg(FIELDTYPE *fieldtype,
     char *(* mak_arg)(va_list *),
     char *(* copy_arg)(char *), void (* free_arg)(char *));
int set_fieldtype_choice(FIELDTYPE *fieldtype,
     int (* next_choice)(FIELD *, char *),
     int (* prev_choice)(FIELD *, char *));
FIELDTYPE *link_fieldtype(FIELDTYPE *type1, FIELDTYPE *type2);
```

DESCRIPTION

new_fieldtype creates a new field type. The application programmer must write the function *field_check*, which validates the field value, and the function *char_check*, which validates each character. **free_fieldtype** frees the space allocated for the field type.

By associating function pointers with a field type, **set_fieldtype_arg** connects to the field type additional arguments necessary for a **set_field_type** call. Function *mak_arg* allocates a structure for the field specific parameters to **set_field_type** and returns a pointer to the saved data. Function *copy_arg* duplicates the structure created by *mak_arg*. Function *free_arg* frees any storage allocated by *mak_arg* or *copy_arg*.

The **form_driver** requests **REQ_NEXT_CHOICE** and **REQ_PREV_CHOICE** let the user request the next or previous value of a field type comprising an ordered set of values. **set_fieldtype_choice** allows the application programmer to implement these requests for the given field type. It associates with the given field type those application-defined functions that return pointers to the next or previous choice for the field.

link_fieldtype returns a pointer to the field type built from the two given types. The constituent types may be any application-defined or pre-defined types.

RETURN VALUE

Routines that return pointers always return **NULL** on error. Routines that return an integer return one of the following:

E_OK	– The function returned successfully.
E_SYSTEM_ERROR	– System error.
E_BAD_ARGUMENT	– An argument is incorrect.
E_CONNECTED	– Type is connected to one or more fields.

NOTES

The header file **form.h** automatically includes the header files **eti.h** and **curses.h**.

form_fieldtype (3curses)

SEE ALSO
curses(3curses), forms(3curses)

NAME

form_hook: set_form_init, form_init, set_form_term, form_term, set_field_init, field_init, set_field_term, field_term – assign application-specific routines for invocation by **forms**

SYNOPSIS

```
#include <form.h>

int set_form_init(FORM *form, void (*func)(FORM *));
void (*)(FORM *) form_init(FORM *form);
int set_form_term(FORM *form, void (*func)(FORM *));
void (*)(FORM *) form_term(FORM *form);
int set_field_init(FORM *form, void (*func)(FORM *));
void (*)(FORM *) field_init(FORM *form);
int set_field_term(FORM *form, void (*func)(FORM *));
void (*)(FORM *) field_term(FORM *form);
```

DESCRIPTION

These routines allow the programmer to assign application specific routines to be executed automatically at initialization and termination points in the **forms** application. The user need not specify any application-defined initialization or termination routines at all, but they may be helpful for displaying messages or page numbers and other chores.

set_form_init assigns an application-defined initialization function to be called when the *form* is posted and just after a page change. **form_init** returns a pointer to the initialization function, if any.

set_form_term assigns an application-defined function to be called when the *form* is unposted and just before a page change. **form_term** returns a pointer to the function, if any.

set_field_init assigns an application-defined function to be called when the *form* is posted and just after the current field changes. **field_init** returns a pointer to the function, if any.

set_field_term assigns an application-defined function to be called when the *form* is unposted and just before the current field changes. **field_term** returns a pointer to the function, if any.

RETURN VALUE

Routines that return pointers always return **NULL** on error. Routines that return an integer return one of the following:

E_OK	– The function returned successfully.
E_SYSTEM_ERROR	– System error.

NOTES

The header file **form.h** automatically includes the header files **eti.h** and **curses.h**.

SEE ALSO

curses(3curses), **forms**(3curses)

form_new (3curses)

NAME

form_new: new_form, free_form – create and destroy **forms**

SYNOPSIS

```
#include <form.h>
```

```
FORM *new_form(FIELD **fields);
int free_form(FORM *form);
```

DESCRIPTION

new_form creates a new form connected to the designated fields and returns a pointer to the form.

free_form disconnects the *form* from its associated field pointer array and deallocates the space for the form.

RETURN VALUE

new_form always returns **NULL** on error. **free_form** returns one of the following:

E_OK	– The function returned successfully.
E_BAD_ARGUMENT	– An argument is incorrect.
E_POSTED	– The form is posted.

NOTES

The header file **form.h** automatically includes the header files **eti.h** and **curses.h**.

SEE ALSO

curses(3curses), **forms**(3curses)

NAME

form_new_page: set_new_page, new_page – forms pagination

SYNOPSIS

#include <form.h>

int set_new_page(FIELD *field, int bool);
int new_page(FIELD *field);

DESCRIPTION

set_new_page marks *field* as the beginning of a new page on the form.

new_page returns a boolean value indicating whether or not *field* begins a new page of the form.

RETURN VALUE

new_page returns TRUE or FALSE.

set_new_page returns one of the following:

E_OK	– The function returned successfully.
E_CONNECTED	– The field is already connected to a form.
E_SYSTEM_ERROR	– System error.

NOTES

The header file **form.h** automatically includes the header files **eti.h** and **curses.h**.

SEE ALSO

curses(3curses), forms(3curses)

form_opts (3curses)

NAME

form_opts: set_form_opts, form_opts_on, form_opts_off, form_opts – forms
option routines

SYNOPSIS

```
#include <form.h>

int set_form_opts(FORM *form, OPTIONS opts);
int form_opts_on(FORM *form, OPTIONS opts);
int form_opts_off(FORM *form, OPTIONS opts);
OPTIONS form_opts(FORM *form);
```

DESCRIPTION

set_form_opts turns on the named options for *form* and turns off all remaining
options. Options are boolean values which can be OR-ed together.

form_opts_on turns on the named options; no other options are changed.

form_opts_off turns off the named options; no other options are changed.

form_opts returns the options set for *form*.

Form Options:

O_NL_OVERLOAD	Overload the REQ_NEW_LINE form driver request.
O_BS_OVERLOAD	Overload the REQ_DEL_PREV form driver request.

RETURN VALUE

set_form_opts, form_opts_on and form_opts_off return one of the following:

E_OK	– The function returned successfully.
E_SYSTEM_ERROR	– System error.

NOTES

The header file form.h automatically includes the header files eti.h and
curses.h.

SEE ALSO

curses(3curses), forms(3curses)

NAME

form_page: set_form_page, form_page, set_current_field, current_field, field_index – set forms current page and field

SYNOPSIS

#include <form.h>

int set_form_page(FORM *form, int *page*);
int form_page(FORM *form);
int set_current_field(FORM *form, FIELD *field);
FIELD *current_field(FORM *form);
int field_index(FIELD *field);

DESCRIPTION

set_form_page sets the page number of *form* to *page*. form_page returns the current page number of *form*.

set_current_field sets the current field of *form* to *field*. current_field returns a pointer to the current field of *form*.

field_index returns the index in the field pointer array of *field*.

RETURN VALUE

form_page returns -1 on error.

current_field returns NULL on error.

field_index returns -1 on error.

set_form_page and set_current_field return one of the following:

E_OK	– The function returned successfully.
E_SYSTEM_ERROR	– System error.
E_BAD_ARGUMENT	– An argument is incorrect.
E_BAD_STATE	– The routine was called from an initialization or termination function.
E_INVALID_FIELD	– The field contents are invalid.
E_REQUEST_DENIED	– The form driver request failed.

NOTES

The header file form.h automatically includes the header files eti.h and curses.h.

SEE ALSO

curses(3curses), forms(3curses)

form_post(3curses)

NAME

form_post: post_form, unpost_form – write or erase **forms** from associated subwindows

SYNOPSIS

```
#include <form.h>
```

```
int post_form(FORM *form);
int unpost_form(FORM *form);
```

DESCRIPTION

post_form writes *form* into its associated subwindow. The application programmer must use **curses** library routines to display the form on the physical screen or call **update_panels** if the **panels** library is being used.

unpost_form erases *form* from its associated subwindow.

RETURN VALUE

These routines return one of the following:

E_OK	– The function returned successfully.
E_SYSTEM_ERROR	– System error.
E_BAD_ARGUMENT	– An argument is incorrect.
E_POSTED	– The form is posted.
E_NOT_POSTED	– The form is not posted.
E_NO_ROOM	– The form does not fit in the subwindow.
E_BAD_STATE	– The routine was called from an initialization or termination function.
E_NOT_CONNECTED	– The field is not connected to a form.

NOTES

The header file **form.h** automatically includes the header files **eti.h** and **curses.h**.

SEE ALSO

curses(3curses), forms(3curses), panels(3curses), panel_update(3curses)

NAME

form_userptr: set_form_userptr, form_userptr – associate application data with **forms**

SYNOPSIS

```
#include <form.h>

int set_form_userptr(FORM *form, char *ptr);
char *form_userptr(FORM *form);
```

DESCRIPTION

Every form has an associated user pointer that can be used to store pertinent data. **set_form_userptr** sets the user pointer of *form*. **form_userptr** returns the user pointer of *form*.

RETURN VALUE

form_userptr returns **NULL** on error. **set_form_userptr** returns one of the following:

E_OK	– The function returned successfully.
E_SYSTEM_ERROR	– System error.

NOTES

The header file **form.h** automatically includes the header files **eti.h** and **curses.h**.

SEE ALSO

curses(3curses), **forms**(3curses)

form_win (3curses)

NAME

form_win: **set_form_win**, **form_win**, **set_form_sub**, **form_sub**, **scale_form** —
forms window and subwindow association routines

SYNOPSIS

```
#include <form.h>

int set_form_win(FORM *form, WINDOW *win);
WINDOW *form_win(FORM *form);
int set_form_sub(FORM *form, WINDOW *sub);
WINDOW *form_sub(FORM *form);
int scale_form(FORM *form, int *rows, int *cols);
```

DESCRIPTION

set_form_win sets the window of *form* to *win*. **form_win** returns a pointer to the window associated with *form*.

set_form_sub sets the subwindow of *form* to *sub*. **form_sub** returns a pointer to the subwindow associated with *form*.

scale_form returns the smallest window size necessary for the subwindow of *form*. *rows* and *cols* are pointers to the locations used to return the number of rows and columns for the form.

RETURN VALUE

Routines that return pointers always return **NULL** on error. Routines that return an integer return one of the following:

E_OK	– The function returned successfully.
E_SYSTEM_ERROR	– System error.
E_BAD_ARGUMENT	– An argument is incorrect.
E_NOT_CONNECTED	– The field is not connected to a form.
E_POSTED	– The form is posted.

NOTES

The header file **form.h** automatically includes the header files **eti.h** and **curses.h**.

SEE ALSO

curses(3curses), **forms**(3curses)

NAME

forms – character based forms package

SYNOPSIS

```
#include <form.h>
```

DESCRIPTION

The **form** library is built using the **curses** library, and any program using **forms** routines must call one of the **curses** initialization routines such as **initscr**. A program using these routines must be compiled with **−lform** and **−lcurses** on the **cc** command line.

The **forms** package gives the applications programmer a terminal-independent method of creating and customizing forms for user-interaction. The **forms** package includes: field routines, which are used to create and customize fields, link fields and assign field types; fieldtype routines, which are used to create new field types for validating fields; and form routines, which are used to create and customize forms, assign pre/post processing functions, and display and interact with forms.

Current Default Values for Field Attributes

The **forms** package establishes initial current default values for field attributes. During field initialization, each field attribute is assigned the current default value for that attribute. An application can change or retrieve a current default attribute value by calling the appropriate set or retrieve routine with a **NULL** field pointer. If an application changes a current default field attribute value, subsequent fields created using **new_field** will have the new default attribute value. (The attributes of previously created fields are not changed if a current default attribute value is changed.)

Routine Name Index

The following table lists each **forms** routine and the name of the manual page on which it is described.

forms Routine Name	Manual Page Name
current_field	form_page(3curses)
data_ahead	form_data(3curses)
data_behind	form_data(3curses)
dup_field	form_field_new(3curses)
dynamic_field_info	form_field_info(3curses)
field_arg	form_field_validation(3curses)
field_back	form_field_attributes(3curses)
field_buffer	form_field_buffer(3curses)
field_count	form_field(3curses)
field_fore	form_field_attributes(3curses)
field_index	form_page(3curses)
field_info	form_field_info(3curses)
field_init	form_hook(3curses)
field_just	form_field_just(3curses)
field_opts	form_field_opts(3curses)
field_opts_off	form_field_opts(3curses)

forms (3curses)

forms Routine Name	Manual Page Name
field_opts_on	form_field_opts(3curses)
field_pad	form_field_attributes(3curses)
field_status	form_field_buffer(3curses)
field_term	form_hook(3curses)
field_type	form_field_validation(3curses)
field_userptr	form_field_userptr(3curses)
form_driver	form_driver(3curses)
form_fields	form_field(3curses)
form_init	form_hook(3curses)
form_opts	form_opts(3curses)
form_opts_off	form_opts(3curses)
form_opts_on	form_opts(3curses)
form_page	form_page(3curses)
form_sub	form_win(3curses)
form_term	form_hook(3curses)
form_userptr	form_userptr(3curses)
form_win	form_win(3curses)
free_field	form_field_new(3curses)
free_fieldtype	form_fieldtype(3curses)
free_form	form_new(3curses)
link_field	form_field_new(3curses)
link_fieldtype	form_fieldtype(3curses)
move_field	form_field(3curses)
new_field	form_field_new(3curses)
new_fieldtype	form_fieldtype(3curses)
new_form	form_new(3curses)
new_page	form_new_page(3curses)
pos_form_cursor	form_cursor(3curses)
post_form	form_post(3curses)
scale_form	form_win(3curses)
set_current_field	form_page(3curses)
set_field_back	form_field_attributes(3curses)
set_field_buffer	form_field_buffer(3curses)
set_field_fore	form_field_attributes(3curses)
set_field_init	form_hook(3curses)
set_field_just	form_field_just(3curses)
set_field_opts	form_field_opts(3curses)
set_field_pad	form_field_attributes(3curses)
set_field_status	form_field_buffer(3curses)
set_field_term	form_hook(3curses)
set_field_type	form_field_validation(3curses)
set_field_userptr	form_field_userptr(3curses)
set_fieldtype_arg	form_fieldtype(3curses)
set_fieldtype_choice	form_fieldtype(3curses)
set_form_fields	form_field(3curses)
set_form_init	form_hook(3curses)

forms Routine Name	Manual Page Name
set_form_opts	form_opts(3curses)
set_form_page	form_page(3curses)
set_form_sub	form_win(3curses)
set_form_term	form_hook(3curses)
set_form_userptr	form_userptr(3curses)
set_form_win	form_win(3curses)
set_max_field	form_field_buffer(3curses)
set_new_page	form_new_page(3curses)
unpost_form	form_post(3curses)

RETURN VALUE

Routines that return a pointer always return **NULL** on error. Routines that return an integer return one of the following:

E_OK	–	The function returned successfully.
E_CONNECTED	–	The field is already connected to a form.
E_SYSTEM_ERROR	–	System error.
E_BAD_ARGUMENT	–	An argument is incorrect.
E_CURRENT	–	The field is the current field.
E_POSTED	–	The form is posted.
E_NOT_POSTED	–	The form is not posted.
E_INVALID_FIELD	–	The field contents are invalid.
E_NOT_CONNECTED	–	The field is not connected to a form.
E_NO_ROOM	–	The form does not fit in the subwindow.
E_BAD_STATE	–	The routine was called from an initialization or termination function.
E_REQUEST_DENIED	–	The form driver request failed.
E_UNKNOWN_COMMAND	–	An unknown request was passed to the the form driver.

NOTES

The header file **form.h** automatically includes the header files **eti.h** and **curses.h**.

SEE ALSO

curses(3curses), and 3curses pages whose names begin "**form_**" for detailed routine descriptions

ForwardScanTextBuffer (3Olit)

NAME

ForwardScanTextBuffer – forward scan a **TextBuffer**

SYNOPSIS

```
#include <Xol/textbuff.h>

ScanResult ForwardScanTextBuffer(
    TextBuffer *text,
    char *exp,
    TextLocation *location
);
```

DESCRIPTION

The **ForwardScanTextBuffer** function is used to scan, towards the end of the buffer, for a given **exp**ression in the **TextBuffer** starting at *location*. A **ScanResult** is returned which indicates

SCAN_NOTFOUND	The scan wrapped without finding a match.
SCAN_WRAPPED	A match was found at a location before the start location.
SCAN_FOUND	A match was found at a location after the start location.
SCAN_INVALID	Either the location or the expression was invalid.

SEE ALSO

BackwardScanTextBuffer(3Olit)

154

NAME

FreeBuffer – free a Buffer

SYNOPSIS

#include <Xol/buffutil.h>

void FreeBuffer(Buffer *buffer);

DESCRIPTION

The FreeBuffer procedure is used to deallocate (free) storage associated with the given *buffer* pointer.

SEE ALSO

AllocateBuffer(3Olit), GetTextBufferBuffer(3Olit)

FreeTextBuffer (3Olit)

NAME

       FreeTextBuffer – free a TextBuffer

SYNOPSIS

       #include <Xol/textbuff.h>

       void FreeTextBuffer(TextBuffer *text, TextUpdateFunction func,
          caddr_t data);

DESCRIPTION

       The **FreeTextBuffer** procedure is used to deallocate storage associated with a
       given **TextBuffer**. Note that the storage is not actually freed if the **TextBuffer** is
       still associated with other update function/data pairs.

SEE ALSO

       AllocateTextBuffer(3Olit), RegisterTextBufferUpdate(3Olit)

NAME

GetOlBusyCursor – get the cursor ID for a Busy cursor

SYNOPSIS

#include <Xol/OlCursors.h>

Cursor GetOlBusyCursor(Screen *screen);

DESCRIPTION

The GetOlBusyCursor function is used to retrieve the Cursor ID for *screen* that complies with the Busy cursor.

RETURN VALUE

In the OPEN LOOK look and feel, the Cursor ID of an OPEN LOOK compliant Busy cursor is returned.

In the Motif look and feel, the XC_watch from the standard cursor font is returned.

SEE ALSO

GetOlDuplicateCursor(3Olit), GetOlMoveCursor(3Olit), GetOlPanCursor(3Olit), GetOlQuestionCursor(3Olit), GetOlStandardCursor(3Olit), GetOlTargetCursor(3Olit), OlGetGui(3Olit)

GetOlDuplicateCursor (3Olit)

NAME

GetOlDuplicateCursor – get the cursor ID for a Duplicate cursor

SYNOPSIS

```
#include <Xol/OlCursors.h>
```

```
Cursor GetOlDuplicateCursor(Screen *screen);
```

DESCRIPTION

The `GetOlDuplicateCursor` function is used to retrieve the Cursor ID for *screen* that complies with the specification of the Duplicate cursor in either Motif or OPEN LOOK look and feel.

RETURN VALUE

The Cursor ID is returned.

SEE ALSO

GetOlBusyCursor(3Olit), GetOlMoveCursor(3Olit), GetOlPanCursor(3Olit), GetOlQuestionCursor(3Olit), GetOlStandardCursor(3Olit), GetOlTargetCursor(3Olit), OlGetGui(3Olit)

NAME

GetOlMoveCursor – get the cursor ID for a Move cursor

SYNOPSIS

#include <Xol/OlCursors.h>

Cursor GetOlMoveCursor(Screen *screen);

DESCRIPTION

The **GetOlMoveCursor** function is used to retrieve the Cursor ID for *screen* that complies with the Move cursor.

RETURN VALUE

In the OPEN LOOK look and feel, the Cursor ID of an OPEN LOOK compliant Move cursor is returned.

In the Motif look and feel, the **XC_fleur** from the standard cursor font is returned.

SEE ALSO

GetOlBusyCursor(3Olit), GetOlDuplicateCursor(3Olit), GetOlPanCursor(3Olit), GetOlQuestionCursor(3Olit), GetOlStandardCursor(3Olit), GetOlTargetCursor(3Olit), OlGetGui(3Olit)

GetOlPanCursor (3Olit)

NAME

GetOlPanCursor – get the cursor ID for a Pan cursor

SYNOPSIS

```
#include <Xol/OlCursors.h>
```

`Cursor GetOlPanCursor(Screen *screen);`

DESCRIPTION

The `GetOlPanCursor` function is used to retrieve the Cursor ID for *screen* that complies with the specification of the Pan cursor in either Motif or OPEN LOOK look and feel.

RETURN VALUE

The Cursor ID is returned.

SEE ALSO

GetOlBusyCursor(3Olit), GetOlDuplicateCursor(3Olit), GetOlMoveCursor(3Olit), GetOlQuestionCursor(3Olit), GetOlStandardCursor(3Olit), GetOlTargetCursor(3Olit), OlGetGui(3Olit)

NAME

GetOlQuestionCursor – get the cursor ID for a Question cursor

SYNOPSIS

```
#include <Xol/OlCursors.h>
```

```
Cursor GetOlQuestionCursor(Screen *screen);
```

DESCRIPTION

The GetOlQuestionCursor function is used to retrieve the Cursor ID for *screen* that complies with the Question cursor.

RETURN VALUE

In the OPEN LOOK look and feel, the Cursor ID of an OPEN LOOK compliant Question cursor is returned.

In the Motif look and feel, the XC_question_arrow from the standard cursor font is returned.

SEE ALSO

GetOlBusyCursor(3Olit), GetOlDuplicateCursor(3Olit), GetOlMoveCursor(3Olit), GetOlPanCursor(3Olit), GetOlStandardCursor(3Olit), GetOlTargetCursor(3Olit), OlGetGui(3Olit)

GetOlStandardCursor (3Olit)

NAME

    `GetOlStandardCursor` – get the cursor ID for a Standard cursor

SYNOPSIS

    `#include <Xol/OlCursors.h>`

    `Cursor GetOlStandardCursor(Screen *screen);`

DESCRIPTION

    The `GetOlStandardCursor` function is used to retrieve the Cursor ID for *screen* that complies with the Standard cursor.

RETURN VALUE

    In the OPEN LOOK look and feel, the Cursor ID of an OPEN LOOK compliant Standard cursor is returned.

    In the Motif look and feel, the `XC_left_ptr` from the standard cursor font is returned.

SEE ALSO

    GetOlBusyCursor(3Olit), GetOlDuplicateCursor(3Olit),
GetOlMoveCursor(3Olit), GetOlPanCursor(3Olit), GetOlQuestionCursor(3Olit),
GetOlTargetCursor(3Olit), OlGetGui(3Olit)

NAME

GetOlTargetCursor – get the cursor ID for a Target cursor

SYNOPSIS

```
#include <Xol/OlCursors.h>
```

```
Cursor GetOlTargetCursor(Screen *screen);
```

DESCRIPTION

The GetOlTargetCursor function is used to retrieve the Cursor ID for *screen* that complies with the Target cursor.

RETURN VALUE

In the OPEN LOOK look and feel, the Cursor ID of an OPEN LOOK compliant Target cursor is returned.

In the Motif look and feel, the **XC_crosshair** from the standard cursor font is returned.

SEE ALSO

GetOlBusyCursor(3Olit), GetOlDuplicateCursor(3Olit),
GetOlMoveCursor(3Olit), GetOlPanCursor(3Olit), GetOlQuestionCursor(3Olit),
GetOlStandardCursor(3Olit), OlGetGui(3Olit)

GetTextBufferBlock (3Olit)

NAME

GetTextBufferBlock – retrieve a text block from a **TextBuffer**

SYNOPSIS

```
#include <Xol/textbuff.h>

char *GetTextBufferBlock(
    TextBuffer *text,
    TextLocation start_location,
    TextLocation end_location
);
```

DESCRIPTION

The **GetTextBufferBlock** function is used to retrieve a text block from the *text* **TextBuffer**. The block is defined as the characters between **start_location** and **end_location** inclusive. It returns a pointer to a string containing the copy. If the parameters are invalid NULL is returned.

NOTES

The storage for the copy is allocated by this routine. It is the responsibility of the caller to free this storage when it becomes dispensable.

SEE ALSO

GetTextBufferChar(3Olit), GetTextBufferLine(3Olit),
GetTextBufferLocation(3Olit)

NAME

GetTextBufferBuffer – retrieve a pointer to a buffer in **TextBuffer**

SYNOPSIS

```
#include <Xol/textbuff.h>
```

Buffer *GetTextBufferBuffer(TextBuffer *text, TextLine line);

DESCRIPTION

The **GetTextBufferBuffer** function is used to retrieve a pointer to the **Buffer** stored in **TextBuffer** *text* for *line*. This pointer is volatile; subsequent calls to any **TextBuffer** routine may make it invalid. If a more permanent copy of this **Buffer** is required the Buffer Utility **CopyBuffer** can be used to create a private copy of it.

The Buffer Utilities are general purpose routines to create and manipulate buffers of characters. The **TextEdit** widget and its subclasses provide applications access to a **TextBuffer** structure which contains a **Buffer** structure. The **Buffer** or **TextBuffer** is accessed through **GetTextBufferBuffer**. The **TextBuffer** in a **TextEdit** widget or subclass is accessed through **XtGetValues** on **XtNsource** or **OlTextEdit** [see **TextBuffer_Macros**(3Olit)].

SEE ALSO

GetTextBufferBlock(3Olit), **GetTextBufferLocation**(3Olit), **TextBuffer**(3Olit), **TextEdit**(3Olit)

GetTextBufferChar (3Olit)

NAME
NAME

GetTextBufferChar – get a character in a **TextBuffer**

SYNOPSIS

```
#include <Xol/textbuff.h>
```

int GetTextBufferChar(**TextBuffer** *text*, **TextLocation** *location*);

DESCRIPTION

The **GetTextBufferChar** function is used to retrieve a character stored in the *text* **TextBuffer** at *location*.

RETURN VALUES

This function returns either a character representation or EOF if the location is outside the range of valid locations within the **TextBuffer**. To convert the return value to an actual multibyte character, use **wctomb** [see **mbchar**(3W)].

NOTES

The **GetTextBufferChar** function returns a **BufferElement** (that is, a **wchar_t**) cast to an **int**, or EOF. If comparing the return value against EOF, EOF should not be cast to BufferElement; this comparison may fail.

SEE ALSO

GetTextBufferBlock(3Olit), **GetTextBufferLine**(3Olit), **GetTextBufferLocation**(3Olit), **mbchar**(3W)

NAME

GetTextBufferLine – get a line from TextBuffer

SYNOPSIS

#include <Xol/textbuff.h>

char *GetTextBufferLine(TextBuffer *text, TextLine lineindex);

DESCRIPTION

The GetTextBufferLine function is used to retrieve the contents of line from the text TextBuffer.

RETURN VALUES

On success, GetTextBufferLine returns a pointer to a string containing the copy of the contents of the line, or NULL if the line is outside the range of valid lines in text.

NOTES

The storage for the copy is allocated by this routine. It is the responsibility of the caller to free this storage when it becomes dispensable.

SEE ALSO

GetTextBufferBlock(3Olit), GetTextBufferChar(3Olit), GetTextBufferLocation(3Olit)

GetTextBufferLocation (3Olit)

NAME

GetTextBufferLocation – get a location in a **TextBuffer**

SYNOPSIS

```
#include <Xol/textbuff.h>

char *GetTextBufferLocation(
    TextBuffer *text,
    TextLine line_number,
    TextLocation *location
);
```

DESCRIPTION

The `GetTextBufferLocation` function is used to retrieve the contents of the given line within the **TextBuffer**. The contents of this string are only valid until the next call to `GetTextBufferLocation`. If the contents must be preserved across calls, use `GetTextBufferLine`.

If a non-NULL **TextLocation** pointer is supplied in the argument list the contents of this structure are modified to reflect the values corresponding to the given line.

RETURN VALUES

On success, `GetTextBufferLocation` returns a pointer to the character string. On failure, if the line number is invalid, **GetTextBufferLocation** returns a NULL pointer.

SEE ALSO

GetTextBufferBlock(3Olit), **GetTextBufferLine**(3Olit)

NAME

GrowBuffer – expand a `Buffer`

SYNOPSIS

`#include <Xol/buffutil.h>`

`void GrowBuffer(Buffer *buffer, int increment);`

DESCRIPTION

The `GrowBuffer` procedure is used to expand (or compress) a given *buffer* size by *increment* elements. If the increment is negative the operation results in a reduction in the size of the `Buffer`.

SEE ALSO

`AllocateBuffer`(3Olit), `GetTextBufferBuffer`(3Olit)

IncrementTextBufferLocation (3Olit)

NAME

IncrementTextBufferLocation – increment the location in a **TextBuffer**

SYNOPSIS

```
#include <Xol/textbuff.h>

TextLocation IncrementTextBufferLocation(
    TextBuffer *text,
    TextLocation location,
    TextLine line,
    TextPosition offset
);
```

DESCRIPTION

The **IncrementTextBufferLocation** function is used to increment a *location* by either *line* lines and/or *offset* characters.

Note that if *line* or *offset* are negative the function performs a decrement operation. If the starting location or the resulting location is invalid the starting location is returned without modification; otherwise the new location is returned.

RETURN VALUES

On success, **IncrementTextBufferLocation** returns the new location.

SEE ALSO

NextLocation(3Olit), PreviousLocation(3Olit)

NAME

InsertIntoBuffer – put an element into a Buffer

SYNOPSIS

#include <Xol/buffutil.h>

int InsertIntoBuffer(Buffer *target, Buffer *source, int offset);

DESCRIPTION

The **InsertIntoBuffer** function is used to insert the elements stored in the *source* buffer into the *target* buffer *before* the element stored at *offset*. If the **offset** is invalid or if the *source* buffer is empty the function returns **0**; otherwise it returns **1** after completing the insertion.

SEE ALSO

BufferMacros(3Olit), ReadFileIntoBuffer(3Olit), ReadStringIntoBuffer(3Olit)

LastTextBufferLocation (3Olit)

NAME

LastTextBufferLocation – find the last valid `TextLocation` in a `TextBuffer`

SYNOPSIS

```
#include <Xol/textbuff.h>

TextLocation LastTextBufferLocation(TextBuffer *text);
```

DESCRIPTION

The `LastTextBufferLocation` function returns the last valid `TextLocation` in the `TextBuffer` associated with *text*.

SEE ALSO

`FirstTextBufferLocation`(3Olit), `LastTextBufferPosition`(3Olit)

NAME

LastTextBufferPosition – return the last **TextPosition** in a **TextBuffer**

SYNOPSIS

    #include <Xol/textbuff.h>

    TextPosition LastTextBufferPosition(TextBuffer *text);

DESCRIPTION

The **LastTextBufferPosition** function returns the last valid **TextPosition** in the **TextBuffer** associated with *text*.

SEE ALSO

FirstTextBufferLocation(3Olit), LastTextBufferLocation(3Olit)

LineOfPosition (3Olit)

NAME

  LineOfPosition – translate a position to a line index in a `TextBuffer`

SYNOPSIS

  `#include <textbuff.h>`

  `extern int LineOfPosition(TextBuffer *text, TextPosition position);`

DESCRIPTION

  The `LineOfPosition` function is used to translate a *position* in the *text* `TextBuffer` to a line index. It returns the translated line index or EOF if the *position* is invalid.

SEE ALSO

  `LineOfPosition`(3Olit), `LocationOfPosition`(3Olit),
  `PositionOfLocation`(3Olit)

NAME

LocationOfPosition – translate a position to a **TextLocation** in a **TextBuffer**

SYNOPSIS

```
#include <textbuff.h>
```

```
TextLocation LocationOfPosition(TextBuffer *text,
    TextPosition position);
```

DESCRIPTION

The **LocationOfPosition** function is used to translate a *position* in the *text* **TextBuffer** to a **TextLocation**. It returns the translated **TextLocation**. If the **position** is invalid the **Buffer** pointer *buffer* of the returned **TextLocation** is set to NULL and the line and offset members are set the last valid location in the **TextBuffer**; otherwise *buffer* is set to a non-NULL (though useless) value.

SEE ALSO

LineOfPosition(3Olit), LocationOfPosition(3Olit),
PositionOfLocation(3Olit)

menu_attributes (3curses)

NAME

menu_attributes: set_menu_fore, menu_fore, set_menu_back, menu_back, set_menu_grey, menu_grey, set_menu_pad, menu_pad – control **menus** display attributes

SYNOPSIS

```
#include <menu.h>
```

int set_menu_fore(MENU *menu, chtype attr);
chtype menu_fore(MENU *menu);
int set_menu_back(MENU *menu, chtype attr);
chtype menu_back(MENU *menu);
int set_menu_grey(MENU *menu, chtype attr);
chtype menu_grey(MENU *menu);
int set_menu_pad(MENU *menu, int pad);
int menu_pad(MENU *menu);

DESCRIPTION

set_menu_fore sets the foreground attribute of *menu* — the display attribute for the current item (if selectable) on single-valued menus and for selected items on multi-valued menus. This display attribute is a **curses** library visual attribute. **menu_fore** returns the foreground attribute of *menu*.

set_menu_back sets the background attribute of **menu** — the display attribute for unselected, yet selectable, items. This display attribute is a **curses** library visual attribute.

set_menu_grey sets the grey attribute of *menu* — the display attribute for non-selectable items in multi-valued menus. This display attribute is a **curses** library visual attribute. **menu_grey** returns the grey attribute of *menu*.

The pad character is the character that fills the space between the name and description of an item. **set_menu_pad** sets the pad character for *menu* to *pad*. **menu_pad** returns the pad character of *menu*.

RETURN VALUE

These routines return one of the following:

E_OK	– The routine returned successfully.
E_SYSTEM_ERROR	– System error.
E_BAD_ARGUMENT	– An incorrect argument was passed to the routine.

NOTES

The header file **menu.h** automatically includes the header files **eti.h** and **curses.h**.

SEE ALSO

curses(3curses), **menus**(3curses)

NAME

menu_cursor: pos_menu_cursor – correctly position a **menus** cursor

SYNOPSIS

```
#include <menu.h>

int pos_menu_cursor(MENU *menu);
```

DESCRIPTION

pos_menu_cursor moves the cursor in the window of *menu* to the correct position to resume menu processing. This is needed after the application calls a **curses** library I/O routine.

RETURN VALUE

This routine returns one of the following:

E_OK	– The routine returned successfully.
E_SYSTEM_ERROR	– System error.
E_BAD_ARGUMENT	– An incorrect argument was passed to the routine.
E_NOT_POSTED	– The menu has not been posted.

NOTES

The header file **menu.h** automatically includes the header files **eti.h** and **curses.h**.

SEE ALSO

curses(3curses), **menus**(3curses), **panels**(3curses), **panel_update**(3curses)

menu_driver (3curses)

NAME

menu_driver – command processor for the **menus** subsystem

SYNOPSIS

```
#include <menu.h>

int menu_driver(MENU *menu, int c);
```

DESCRIPTION

menu_driver is the workhorse of the **menus** subsystem. It checks to determine whether the character *c* is a menu request or data. If *c* is a request, the menu driver executes the request and reports the result. If *c* is data (a printable ASCII character), it enters the data into the pattern buffer and tries to find a matching item. If no match is found, the menu driver deletes the character from the pattern buffer and returns **E_NO_MATCH**. If the character is not recognized, the menu driver assumes it is an application-defined command and returns **E_UNKNOWN_COMMAND**.

Menu driver requests:

REQ_LEFT_ITEM	Move left to an item.
REQ_RIGHT_ITEM	Move right to an item.
REQ_UP_ITEM	Move up to an item.
REQ_DOWN_ITEM	Move down to an item.
REQ_SCR_ULINE	Scroll up a line.
REQ_SCR_DLINE	Scroll down a line.
REQ_SCR_DPAGE	Scroll up a page.
REQ_SCR_UPAGE	Scroll down a page.
REQ_FIRST_ITEM	Move to the first item.
REQ_LAST_ITEM	Move to the last item.
REQ_NEXT_ITEM	Move to the next item.
REQ_PREV_ITEM	Move to the previous item.
REQ_TOGGLE_ITEM	Select/de-select an item.
REQ_CLEAR_PATTERN	Clear the menu pattern buffer.
REQ_BACK_PATTERN	Delete the previous character from pattern buffer.
REQ_NEXT_MATCH	Move the next matching item.
REQ_PREV_MATCH	Move to the previous matching item.

RETURN VALUE

menu_driver returns one of the following:

E_OK	– The routine returned successfully.
E_SYSTEM_ERROR	– System error.
E_BAD_ARGUMENT	– An incorrect argument was passed to the routine.
E_BAD_STATE	– The routine was called from an initialization or termination function.
E_NOT_POSTED	– The menu has not been posted.

E_UNKNOWN_COMMAND	– An unknown request was passed to the menu driver.
E_NO_MATCH	– The character failed to match.
E_NOT_SELECTABLE	– The item cannot be selected.
E_REQUEST_DENIED	– The menu driver could not process the request.

NOTES

Application defined commands should be defined relative to (greater than) **MAX_COMMAND**, the maximum value of a request listed above.

The header file **menu.h** automatically includes the header files **eti.h** and **curses.h**.

SEE ALSO

curses(3curses), **menus**(3curses)

menu_format (3curses)

NAME

`menu_format`: `set_menu_format`, `menu_format` – set and get maximum numbers of rows and columns in **menus**

SYNOPSIS

```
#include <menu.h>
```

```
int set_menu_format(MENU *menu, int rows, int cols);
void menu_format(MENU *menu, int *rows, int *cols);
```

DESCRIPTION

`set_menu_format` sets the maximum number of rows and columns of items that may be displayed at one time on a menu. If the menu contains more items than can be displayed at once, the menu will be scrollable.

`menu_format` returns the maximum number of rows and columns that may be displayed at one time on *menu*. *rows* and *cols* are pointers to the variables used to return these values.

RETURN VALUE

`set_menu_format` returns one of the following:

E_OK	– The routine returned successfully.
E_SYSTEM_ERROR	– System error.
E_BAD_ARGUMENT	– An incorrect argument was passed to the routine.
E_POSTED	– The menu is already posted.

NOTES

The header file **menu.h** automatically includes the header files **eti.h** and **curses.h**.

SEE ALSO

curses(3curses), **menus**(3curses)

NAME

menu_hook: set_item_init, item_init, set_item_term, item_term, set_menu_init, menu_init, set_menu_term, menu_term – assign application-specific routines for automatic invocation by **menus**

SYNOPSIS

```
#include <menu.h>

int set_item_init(MENU *menu, void (*func)(MENU *));
void (*)(MENU *) item_init(MENU *menu);
int set_item_term(MENU *menu, void (*func)(MENU *));
void (*)(MENU *) item_term(MENU *menu);
int set_menu_init(MENU *menu, void (*func)(MENU *));
void (*)(MENU *) menu_init(MENU *menu);
int set_menu_term(MENU *menu, void (*func)(MENU *));
void (*)(MENU *) menu_term(MENU *menu);
```

DESCRIPTION

set_item_init assigns the application-defined function to be called when the *menu* is posted and just after the current item changes. **item_init** returns a pointer to the item initialization routine, if any, called when the *menu* is posted and just after the current item changes.

set_item_term assigns an application-defined function to be called when the *menu* is unposted and just before the current item changes. **item_term** returns a pointer to the termination function, if any, called when the *menu* is unposted and just before the current item changes.

set_menu_init assigns an application-defined function to be called when the *menu* is posted and just after the top row changes on a posted menu. **menu_init** returns a pointer to the menu initialization routine, if any, called when the *menu* is posted and just after the top row changes on a posted menu.

set_menu_term assigns an application-defined function to be called when the *menu* is unposted and just before the top row changes on a posted menu. **menu_term** returns a pointer to the menu termination routine, if any, called when the *menu* is unposted and just before the top row changes on a posted menu.

RETURN VALUE

Routines that return pointers always return **NULL** on error. Routines that return an integer return one of the following:

E_OK	– The routine returned successfully.
E_SYSTEM_ERROR	– System error.

NOTES

The header file **menu.h** automatically includes the header files **eti.h** and **curses.h**.

SEE ALSO

curses(3curses), **menus**(3curses)

menu_item_current (3curses)

NAME

menu_item_current: set_current_item, current_item, set_top_row, top_row, item_index – set and get current **menus** items

SYNOPSIS

#include <menu.h>

int set_current_item(MENU *menu, ITEM *item);
ITEM *current_item(MENU *menu);
int set_top_row(MENU *menu, int row);
int top_row(MENU *menu);
int item_index(ITEM *item);

DESCRIPTION

The current item of a menu is the item where the cursor is currently positioned. **set_current_item** sets the current item of *menu* to *item*. **current_item** returns a pointer to the the current item in *menu*.

set_top_row sets the top row of *menu* to *row*. The left-most item on the new top row becomes the current item. **top_row** returns the number of the menu row currently displayed at the top of *menu*.

item_index returns the index to the *item* in the item pointer array. The value of this index ranges from **0** through $N-1$, where N is the total number of items connected to the menu.

RETURN VALUE

current_item returns **NULL** on error.

top_row and **index_item** return **–1** on error.

set_current_item and **set_top_row** return one of the following:

E_OK	– The routine returned successfully.
E_SYSTEM_ERROR	– System error.
E_BAD_ARGUMENT	– An incorrect argument was passed to the routine.
E_BAD_STATE	– The routine was called from an initialization or termination function.
E_NOT_CONNECTED	– No items are connected to the menu.

NOTES

The header file **menu.h** automatically includes the header files **eti.h** and **curses.h**.

SEE ALSO

curses(3curses), **menus**(3curses)

NAME

menu_item_name: item_name, item_description – get menus item name and description

SYNOPSIS

#include <menu.h>

char *item_name(ITEM *item);
char *item_description(ITEM *item);

DESCRIPTION

item_name returns a pointer to the name of item.

item_description returns a pointer to the description of item.

RETURN VALUE

These routines return NULL on error.

NOTES

The header file menu.h automatically includes the header files eti.h and curses.h.

SEE ALSO

curses(3curses), menus(3curses), menu_new(3curses)

menu_item_new (3curses)

NAME

menu_item_new: new_item, free_item – create and destroy **menus** items

SYNOPSIS

```
#include <menu.h>

ITEM *new_item(char *name, char *desc);
int free_item(ITEM *item);
```

DESCRIPTION

new_item creates a new item from *name* and *description*, and returns a pointer to the new item.

free_item frees the storage allocated for *item*. Once an item is freed, the user can no longer connect it to a menu.

RETURN VALUE

new_item returns NULL on error.

free_item returns one of the following:

E_OK	– The routine returned successfully.
E_SYSTEM_ERROR	– System error.
E_BAD_ARGUMENT	– An incorrect argument was passed to the routine.
E_CONNECTED	– One or more items are already connected to another menu.

NOTES

The header file **menu.h** automatically includes the header files **eti.h** and **curses.h**.

SEE ALSO

curses(3curses), **menus**(3curses)

NAME

menu_item_opts: set_item_opts, item_opts_on, item_opts_off, item_opts – menus item option routines

SYNOPSIS

```
#include <menu.h>

int set_item_opts(ITEM *item, OPTIONS opts);
int item_opts_on(ITEM *item, OPTIONS opts);
int item_opts_off(ITEM *item, OPTIONS opts);
OPTIONS item_opts(ITEM *item);
```

DESCRIPTION

set_item_opts turns on the named options for *item* and turns off all other options. Options are boolean values that can be OR-ed together.

item_opts_on turns on the named options for *item*; no other option is changed.

item_opts_off turns off the named options for *item*; no other option is changed.

item_opts returns the current options of *item*.

Item Options:

O_SELECTABLE   The item can be selected during menu processing.

RETURN VALUE

Except for item_opts, these routines return one of the following:

E_OK   – The routine returned successfully.
E_SYSTEM_ERROR   – System error.

NOTES

The header file **menu.h** automatically includes the header files **eti.h** and **curses.h**.

SEE ALSO

curses(3curses), menus(3curses)

menu_item_userptr (3curses)

NAME

menu_item_userptr: set_item_userptr, item_userptr – associate application data with menus items

SYNOPSIS

```
#include <menu.h>
```

```
int set_item_userptr(ITEM *item, char *userptr);
char *item_userptr(ITEM *item);
```

DESCRIPTION

Every item has an associated user pointer that can be used to store relevant information. set_item_userptr sets the user pointer of *item*. item_userptr returns the user pointer of *item*.

RETURN VALUE

item_userptr returns NULL on error. set_item_userptr returns one of the following:

E_OK	– The routine returned successfully.
E_SYSTEM_ERROR	– System error.

NOTES

The header file menu.h automatically includes the header files eti.h and curses.h.

SEE ALSO

curses(3curses), menus(3curses)

NAME
menu_item_value: set_item_value, item_value – set and get **menus** item values

SYNOPSIS
#include <menu.h>

int set_item_value(ITEM *item, int bool);
int item_value(ITEM *item);

DESCRIPTION
Unlike single-valued menus, multi-valued menus enable the end-user to select one or more items from a menu. **set_item_value** sets the selected value of the *item* — **TRUE** (selected) or **FALSE** (not selected). **set_item_value** may be used only with multi-valued menus. To make a menu multi-valued, use **set_menu_opts** or **menu_opts_off** to turn off the option O_ONEVALUE. [see **menu_opts**(3curses)].

item_value returns the select value of *item*, either **TRUE** (selected) or **FALSE** (unselected).

RETURN VALUE
set_item_value returns one of the following:

E_OK	– The routine returned successfully.
E_SYSTEM_ERROR	– System error.
E_REQUEST_DENIED	– The menu driver could not process the request.

NOTES
The header file **menu.h** automatically includes the header files **eti.h** and **curses.h**.

SEE ALSO
curses(3curses), **menus**(3curses), **menu_opts**(3curses)

menu_item_visible (3curses)

NAME

menu_item_visible: item_visible – tell if menus item is visible

SYNOPSIS

```
#include <menu.h>
```

```
int item_visible(ITEM *item);
```

DESCRIPTION

A menu item is visible if it currently appears in the subwindow of a posted menu. item_visible returns **TRUE** if *item* is visible, otherwise it returns **FALSE**.

NOTES

The header file **menu.h** automatically includes the header files **eti.h** and **curses.h**.

SEE ALSO

curses(3curses), menus(3curses), menu_new(3curses)

NAME

menu_items: set_menu_items, menu_items, item_count – connect and disconnect items to and from **menus**

SYNOPSIS

```
#include <menu.h>

int set_menu_items(MENU *menu, ITEM **items);
ITEM **menu_items(MENU *menu);
int item_count(MENU *menu);
```

DESCRIPTION

set_menu_items changes the item pointer array connected to *menu* to the item pointer array *items*.

menu_items returns a pointer to the item pointer array connected to *menu*.

item_count returns the number of items in *menu*.

RETURN VALUE

menu_items returns **NULL** on error.

item_count returns -1 on error.

set_menu_items returns one of the following:

E_OK	– The routine returned successfully.
E_SYSTEM_ERROR	– System error.
E_BAD_ARGUMENT	– An incorrect argument was passed to the routine.
E_POSTED	– The menu is already posted.
E_CONNECTED	– One or more items are already connected to another menu.

NOTES

The header file **menu.h** automatically includes the header files **eti.h** and **curses.h**.

SEE ALSO

curses(3curses), **menus**(3curses)

menu_mark (3curses)

NAME

menu_mark: set_menu_mark, menu_mark – **menus** mark string routines

SYNOPSIS

```
#include <menu.h>
```

```
int set_menu_mark(MENU *menu, char *mark);
char *menu_mark(MENU *menu);
```

DESCRIPTION

menus displays mark strings to distinguish selected items in a menu (or the current item in a single-valued menu). **set_menu_mark** sets the mark string of *menu* to *mark*. **menu_mark** returns a pointer to the mark string of *menu*.

RETURN VALUE

menu_mark returns **NULL** on error. **set_menu_mark** returns one of the following:

E_OK	– The routine returned successfully.
E_SYSTEM_ERROR	– System error.
E_BAD_ARGUMENT	– An incorrect argument was passed to the routine.

NOTES

The header file **menu.h** automatically includes the header files **eti.h** and **curses.h**.

The mark string cannot be **NULL**.

SEE ALSO

curses(3curses), **menus**(3curses)

NAME
menu_new: new_menu, free_menu – create and destroy menus

SYNOPSIS
```
#include <menu.h>

MENU *new_menu(ITEM **items);
int free_menu(MENU *menu);
```

DESCRIPTION
new_menu creates a new menu connected to the item pointer array *items* and returns a pointer to the new menu.

free_menu disconnects *menu* from its associated item pointer array and frees the storage allocated for the menu.

RETURN VALUE
new_menu returns NULL on error.

free_menu returns one of the following:

E_OK	– The routine returned successfully.
E_SYSTEM_ERROR	– System error.
E_BAD_ARGUMENT	– An incorrect argument was passed to the routine.
E_POSTED	– The menu is already posted.

NOTES
The header file **menu.h** automatically includes the header files **eti.h** and **curses.h**.

SEE ALSO
curses(3curses), menus(3curses)

menu_opts (3curses)

NAME

menu_opts: set_menu_opts, menu_opts_on, menu_opts_off, menu_opts – menus option routines

SYNOPSIS

```
#include <menu.h>

int set_menu_opts(MENU *menu, OPTIONS opts);
int menu_opts_on(MENU *menu, OPTIONS opts);
int menu_opts_off(MENU *menu, OPTIONS opts);
OPTIONS menu_opts(MENU *menu);
```

DESCRIPTION

set_menu_opts turns on the named options for *menu* and turns off all other options. Options are boolean values that can be OR-ed together.

menu_opts_on turns on the named options for *menu*; no other option is changed.

menu_opts_off turns off the named options for *menu*; no other option is changed.

menu_opts returns the current options of *menu*.

Menu Options

O_ONEVALUE	Only one item can be selected from the menu.
O_SHOWDESC	Display the description of the items.
O_ROWMAJOR	Display the menu in row major order.
O_IGNORECASE	Ignore the case when pattern matching.
O_SHOWMATCH	Place the cursor within the item name when pattern matching.
O_NONCYCLIC	Make certain menu driver requests non-cyclic.

RETURN VALUE

Except for menu_opts, these routines return one of the following:

E_OK	– The routine returned successfully.
E_SYSTEM_ERROR	– System error.
E_POSTED	– The menu is already posted.

NOTES

The header file **menu.h** automatically includes the header files **eti.h** and **curses.h**.

SEE ALSO

curses(3curses), **menus**(3curses)

NAME

menu_pattern: set_menu_pattern, menu_pattern – set and get **menus** pattern match buffer

SYNOPSIS

```
#include <menu.h>

int set_menu_pattern(MENU *menu, char *pat);
char *menu_pattern(MENU *menu);
```

DESCRIPTION

Every menu has a pattern buffer to match entered data with menu items. **set_menu_pattern** sets the pattern buffer to *pat* and tries to find the first item that matches the pattern. If it does, the matching item becomes the current item. If not, the current item does not change. **menu_pattern** returns the string in the pattern buffer of *menu*.

RETURN VALUE

menu_pattern returns **NULL** on error. **set_menu_pattern** returns one of the following:

E_OK	– The routine returned successfully.
E_SYSTEM_ERROR	– System error.
E_BAD_ARGUMENT	– An incorrect argument was passed to the routine.
E_NO_MATCH	– The character failed to match.

NOTES

The header file **menu.h** automatically includes the header files **eti.h** and **curses.h**.

SEE ALSO

curses(3curses), **menus**(3curses)

menu_post(3curses)

NAME

menu_post: post_menu, unpost_menu – write or erase **menus** from associated subwindows

SYNOPSIS

```
#include <menu.h>

int post_menu(MENU *menu);
int unpost_menu(MENU *menu);
```

DESCRIPTION

post_menu writes *menu* to the subwindow. The application programmer must use **curses** library routines to display the menu on the physical screen or call **update_panels** if the **panels** library is being used.

unpost_menu erases *menu* from its associated subwindow.

RETURN VALUE

These routines return one of the following:

E_OK	– The routine returned successfully.
E_SYSTEM_ERROR	– System error.
E_BAD_ARGUMENT	– An incorrect argument was passed to the routine.
E_POSTED	– The menu is already posted.
E_BAD_STATE	– The routine was called from an initialization or termination function.
E_NO_ROOM	– The menu does not fit within its subwindow.
E_NOT_POSTED	– The menu has not been posted.
E_NOT_CONNECTED	– No items are connected to the menu.

NOTES

The header file **menu.h** automatically includes the header files **eti.h** and **curses.h**.

SEE ALSO

curses(3curses), **menus**(3curses), **panels**(3curses)

NAME

menu_userptr: set_menu_userptr, menu_userptr – associate application data with **menus**

SYNOPSIS

```
#include <menu.h>
```

```
int set_menu_userptr(MENU *menu, char *userptr);
char *menu_userptr(MENU *menu);
```

DESCRIPTION

Every menu has an associated user pointer that can be used to store relevant information. **set_menu_userptr** sets the user pointer of *menu*. **menu_userptr** returns the user pointer of *menu*.

RETURN VALUE

menu_userptr returns **NULL** on error.

set_menu_userptr returns one of the following:

E_OK	– The routine returned successfully.
E_SYSTEM_ERROR	– System error.

NOTES

The header file **menu.h** automatically includes the header files **eti.h** and **curses.h**.

SEE ALSO

curses(3curses), **menus**(3curses)

menu_win (3curses)

NAME

menu_win: set_menu_win, menu_win, set_menu_sub, menu_sub, scale_menu –
menus window and subwindow association routines

SYNOPSIS

```
#include <menu.h>

int set_menu_win(MENU *menu, WINDOW *win);
WINDOW *menu_win(MENU **menu);
int set_menu_sub(MENU *menu, WINDOW *sub);
WINDOW *menu_sub(MENU *menu);
int scale_window(MENU *menu, int *rows, int *cols);
```

DESCRIPTION

set_menu_win sets the window of *menu* to *win*. menu_win returns a pointer to the window of *menu*.

set_menu_sub sets the subwindow of *menu* to *sub*. menu_sub returns a pointer to the subwindow of *menu*.

scale_window returns the minimum window size necessary for the subwindow of *menu*. *rows* and *cols* are pointers to the locations used to return the values.

RETURN VALUE

Routines that return pointers always return **NULL** on error. Routines that return an integer return one of the following:

E_OK	– The routine returned successfully.
E_SYSTEM_ERROR	– System error.
E_BAD_ARGUMENT	– An incorrect argument was passed to the routine.
E_POSTED	– The menu is already posted.
E_NOT_CONNECTED	– No items are connected to the menu.

NOTES

The header file **menu.h** automatically includes the header files **eti.h** and **curses.h**.

SEE ALSO

curses(3curses), menus(3curses)

NAME

menus – character based menus package

SYNOPSIS

```
#include <menu.h>
```

DESCRIPTION

The **menu** library is built using the **curses** library, and any program using **menus** routines must call one of the **curses** initialization routines, such as **initscr**. A program using these routines must be compiled with **–lmenu** and **–lcurses** on the **cc** command line.

The **menus** package gives the applications programmer a terminal-independent method of creating and customizing menus for user interaction. The **menus** package includes: item routines, which are used to create and customize menu items; and menu routines, which are used to create and customize menus, assign pre- and post-processing routines, and display and interact with menus.

Current Default Values for Item Attributes

The **menus** package establishes initial current default values for item attributes. During item initialization, each item attribute is assigned the current default value for that attribute. An application can change or retrieve a current default attribute value by calling the appropriate set or retrieve routine with a **NULL** item pointer. If an application changes a current default item attribute value, subsequent items created using **new_item** will have the new default attribute value. (The attributes of previously created items are not changed if a current default attribute value is changed.)

Routine Name Index

The following table lists each **menus** routine and the name of the manual page on which it is described.

menus Routine Name	Manual Page Name
current_item	menu_item_current(3curses)
free_item	menu_item_new(3curses)
free_menu	menu_new(3curses)
item_count	menu_items(3curses)
item_description	menu_item_name(3curses)
item_index	menu_item_current(3curses)
item_init	menu_hook(3curses)
item_name	menu_item_name(3curses)
item_opts	menu_item_opts(3curses)
item_opts_off	menu_item_opts(3curses)
item_opts_on	menu_item_opts(3curses)
item_term	menu_hook(3curses)
item_userptr	menu_item_userptr(3curses)
item_value	menu_item_value(3curses)
item_visible	menu_item_visible(3curses)
menu_back	menu_attributes(3curses)
menu_driver	menu_driver(3curses)

menus (3curses)

RETURN VALUE

Routines that return pointers always return **NULL** on error. Routines that return an integer return one of the following:

E_OK	– The routine returned successfully.
E_SYSTEM_ERROR	– System error.
E_BAD_ARGUMENT	– An incorrect argument was passed to the routine.
E_POSTED	– The menu is already posted.
E_CONNECTED	– One or more items are already connected to another menu.
E_BAD_STATE	– The routine was called from an initialization or termination function.
E_NO_ROOM	– The menu does not fit within its subwindow.
E_NOT_POSTED	– The menu has not been posted.
E_UNKNOWN_COMMAND	– An unknown request was passed to the menu driver.
E_NO_MATCH	– The character failed to match.
E_NOT_SELECTABLE	– The item cannot be selected.
E_NOT_CONNECTED	– No items are connected to the menu.
E_REQUEST_DENIED	– The menu driver could not process the request.

NOTES

The header file **menu.h** automatically includes the header files **eti.h** and **curses.h**.

SEE ALSO

curses(3curses), and 3curses pages whose names begin ''**menu_**'' for detailed routine descriptions

NextLocation (3Olit)

NAME

NextLocation – return the next TextLocation in a TextBuffer

SYNOPSIS

#include <Xol/textbuff.h>

TextLocation NextLocation(TextBuffer *textBuffer, TextLocation current);

DESCRIPTION

The NextLocation function returns the TextLocation which follows the given current location in a TextBuffer. If the current location points to the end of the TextBuffer this function wraps.

SEE ALSO

PreviousLocation(3Olit)

NAME

NextTextBufferWord – get the start of the next word in a `TextBuffer`

SYNOPSIS

`#include <Xol/textbuff.h>`

`TextLocation NextTextBufferWord(TextBuffer *textBuffer,`
`        TextLocation current);`

DESCRIPTION

The `NextTextBufferWord` function is used to locate the beginning of the next word from a given *current* location in a `TextBuffer`. If the current location is within the last word in the `TextBuffer` the function wraps to the beginning of the `TextBuffer`.

SEE ALSO

`PreviousTextBufferWord`(3Olit), `StartCurrentTextBufferWord`(3Olit)

OlAddDefaultPopupMenuEH (3Olit)

NAME

OlAddDefaultPopupMenuEH – add a system default event handler

SYNOPSIS

```
#include <Xol/OpenLook.h>
#include <Xol/PopupMenu.h>

void OlAddDefaultPopupMenuEH(Widget menu_owner, Widget popup_menu);
```

DESCRIPTION

This function is used to add a system default event handler.

menu_owner   specifies the object that the *popup_menu* is currently associated with

popup_menu   a **PopupMenuShell** widget ID obtained by creating it explicitly. It will be the *client_data* of **XtAddEventHandler**.

The **PopupMenuShell** widget does not automatically attach an event handler to its parent. Applications need to do this, otherwise **PopupMenuShell** will not show when **OL_MENU** is pressed.

Note that this default event handler can only deal with ButtonPress events (that is, **OL_MENU**). Applications can supply their own event handler(s) by invoking:

```
XtAddEventHandler(
    menu_owner,
    ButtonPressMask,
    False,
    YourEH,
    (XtPointer)popup_menu        /* client_data  */
);
```

SEE ALSO

OlPostPopupMenu(3Olit), OlUnpostPopupMenu(3Olit), PopupMenuShell(3Olit)

NAME

OlCallAcceptFocus – accept input focus

SYNOPSIS

```
#include <Xol/OpenLook.h>

Boolean OlCallAcceptFocus(Widget wid, Time time);
```

DESCRIPTION

The OlCallAcceptFocus function accepts an input focus. If widget *wid* currently is capable of accepting input focus, focus is assigned to *wid*. *time* specifies the X server time of the event that initiated this accept focus request.

RETURN VALUES

On success, OlCallAcceptFocus returns TRUE. On failure, FALSE is returned.

NOTES

OlCallAcceptFocus is obsolete, and simply calls XtCallAccpetFocus. Use XtCallAccpetFocus, which has the function prototype

```
Boolean XtCallAccpetFocus(
    Widget wid,
    Time *time );
```

instead.

SEE ALSO

Flattened_Widget_Utilities(3Olit), OlCanAcceptFocus(3Olit), OlGetCurrentFocusWidget(3Olit), OlHasFocus(3Olit), OlMoveFocus(3Olit), OlSetInputFocus(3Olit)

OlCallDynamicCallbacks (3Olit)

NAME

OlCallDynamicCallbacks – start the dynamic callback procedure

SYNOPSIS

```
#include <Xol/OpenLook.h>

void OlCallDynamicCallbacks(void);
```

DESCRIPTION

The OlCallDynamicCallbacks procedure is used to trigger the calling of the functions registered on the dynamic callback list. This procedure is called automatically whenever the RESOURCE_MANAGER property of the RootWindow is updated. It may also be called to force a synchronization of the dynamic settings, though applications rarely need to do this explicitly.

SEE ALSO

OlRegisterDynamicCallback(3Olit), OlUnregisterDynamicCallback(3Olit)

NAME

OlCanAcceptFocus – determine if input focus can be accepted

SYNOPSIS

`#include <Xol/OpenLook.h>`

`Boolean OlCanAcceptFocus(Widget` *wid*`, Time` *time*`);`

DESCRIPTION

The `OlCanAcceptFocus` function determines if a widget can accept input focus. Acceptance of focus is determined by the following:

the widget is not being destroyed

the widget is managed

the widget is mapped when managed (if it's not a gadget)

the widget is realized, or for a gadget, the gadget's parent must be realized

the widget and its ancestors are sensitive

a query window attributes is successful and the widget's window is viewable (that is, the window and all its ancestor windows are mapped)

RETURN VALUES

If the widget can accept focus, `OlCanAcceptFocus` returns **TRUE**. If not, it returns **FALSE**.

SEE ALSO

`Flattened_Widget_Utilities`(3Olit), `OlCallAccpetFocus`(3Olit), `OlGetCurrentFocusWidget`(3Olit), `OlHasFocus`(3Olit), `OlMoveFocus`(3Olit), `OlSetInputFocus`(3Olit)

OlClassSearchIEDB (3Olit)

NAME

OlClassSearchIEDB – register a given database on a specific widget class

SYNOPSIS

```
#include <Xol/OpenLook.h>

void OlClassSearchIEDB(WidgetClass wc, OlVirtualEventTable db);
```

DESCRIPTION

The OlClassSearchIEDB procedure is used to register a given database on a specific widget class. The db value was returned from a call to OlCreate-InputEventDB.

Once a database is registered with a given widget class, the OlLookupInputEvent procedure (if db_flag is OL_DEFAULT_IE or db) will include this database in the search stack if the given widget ID is a subclass of this widget class.

NOTES

The registering order determines the searching order when doing a lookup.

EXAMPLE

```
/* To create a client application database */
#include <Xol/OpenLook.h>
#include <Xol/Stub.h>
     /* start with a big value to avoid */
     /* the "virtual_name" collision    */
#define OL_MY_BASE              1000
#define OL_MY_DRAWLINEBTN       OL_MY_BASE+0
#define OL_MY_DRAWARCBTN        OL_MY_BASE+1
#define OL_MY_REDISPLAYKEY      OL_MY_BASE+2
#define OL_MY_SAVEPARTKEY       OL_MY_BASE+3

#define XtNmyDrawLineBtn        "myDrawLineBtn"
#define XtNmyDrawArcBtn         "myDrawArcBtn"
#define XtNmyRedisplayKey       "myRedisplayKey"
#define XtNmySavePartKey        "mySavePartKey"

static OlKeyOrBtnRec    OlMyBtnInfo[] = {
    /*name           default_value     virtual_name         */

    { XtNmyDrawLineBtn, "c<Button1>",         OL_MY_DRAWLINEBTN  },
    { XtNmyDrawArcBtn,  "s<myDrawLineBtn>", OL_MY_DRAWARCBTN   },
};

static OlKeyOrBtnRec    OlMyKeyInfo[] = {
    /*name              default_value     virtual_name         */

    { XtNmyRedisplayKey, "c<F5>",             OL_MY_REDISPLAYKEY },
    { XtNmySavePartKey,  "c<F5>",             OL_MY_SAVEPARTKEY  },
};

static OlVirtualEventTable      OlMyDB;
```

```
OlMyDB = OlCreateInputEventDB(
                w,
                OlMyKeyInfo, XtNumber(OlMyKeyInfo),
                OlMyBtnInfo, XtNumber(OlMyBtnInfo)
        );
        /* assume: all stub widgets are interested in OlMyDB */
OlClassSearchIEDB(stubWidgetClass, OlMyDB);
        /* once this step is done, all stub widget instances */
        /* will receive the OlMyDB commands after a call to  */
        /* OlLookupInputEvent(), or in the XtNconsumeEvent    */
        /* callback's OlVirtualEvent structure supplied with */
        /* the call_data field.                              */
```

SEE ALSO

OlClassSearchTextDB(3Olit), OlClassUnsearchDB(3Olit),
OlCreateInputEventDB(3Olit), OlDestroyInputEventDB(3Olit),
OlLookupInputEvent(3Olit), OlWidgetSearchIEDB(3Olit),
OlWidgetSearchTextDB(3Olit), OlWidgetUnsearchIEDB(3Olit)

OlClassSearchTextDB (3Olit)

NAME

    `OlClassSearchTextDB` – register an OPEN LOOK TEXT database

SYNOPSIS

    `#include <Xol/OpenLook.h>`

    `void OlClassSearchTextDB(WidgetClass` *wc*`);`

DESCRIPTION

    The `OlClassSearchTextDB` procedure is used to register the OPEN LOOK TEXT database on a specific widget class.

    Once the OPEN LOOK TEXT database is registered with a given widget class, the `OlLookupInputEvent` procedure (if *db_flag* is `OL_DEFAULT_IE` or `OL_TEXT_IE`) will include this database in the search stack if the given widget ID is a subclass of this widget class.

NOTES

    The registering order determines the searching order when doing a lookup.

EXAMPLE

```
    ...
#include <Xol/OpenLook.h>
#include <Xol/Stub.h>
    ...

    /* assume: all stub widgets are interested in the   */
    /*             OPEN LOOK TEXT database               */
OlClassSearchTextDB(stubWidgetClass);
    /* once this step is done, all stub widget instances */
    /* will receive OPEN LOOK TEXT commands after a      */
    /* call to OlLookupInputEvent(), or in the          */
    /* XtNconsumeEvent callback's OlVirtualEvent         */
    /* structure supplied with the call_data field.     */
    ...
```

SEE ALSO

    `OlClassSearchIEDB`(3Olit), `OlClassUnsearchIEDB`(3Olit), `OlCreateInputEventDB`(3Olit), `OlDestroyInputEventDB`(3Olit), `OlLookupInputEvent`(3Olit), `OlWidgetSearchIEDB`(3Olit), `OlWidgetSearchTextDB`(3Olit), `OlWidgetUnsearchIEDB`(3Olit)

NAME

OlClassUnsearchIEDB – unregister a database on a specific widget class

SYNOPSIS

#include <Xol/OpenLook.h>

void OlClassUnsearchIEDB(WidgetClass *wc*, OlVirtualEventTable *db*);

DESCRIPTION

The OlClassUnsearchIEDB procedure is used to unregister a given database on a specific widget class. All widget classes that have the reference of *db* will be removed from the list of registered databases if the *wc* value is NULL.

The *db* value can be either OL_TEXT_IE or a value that was returned from a call to OlCreateInputEventDB.

SEE ALSO

OlClassSearchIEDB(3Olit), OlClassSearchTextDB(3Olit), OlClassUnsearchIEDB(3Olit), OlCreateInputEventDB(3Olit), OlDestroyInputEventDB(3Olit), OlLookupInputEvent(3Olit), OlWidgetSearchIEDB(3Olit), OlWidgetSearchTextDB(3Olit), OlWidgetUnsearchIEDB(3Olit)

OlCloseDatabase (3Olit)

NAME

OlCloseDatabase – close a database opened with OlOpenDatabase

SYNOPSIS

#include <Xol/OpenLook.h>

void OlCloseDatabase(XrmDatabase *database*);

DESCRIPTION

This function is responsible for closing a database opened by OlOpenDatabase. Both functions expect the database to be in **XrmDatabase** format.

The function will resolve the pathname of the database according to the current locale.

SEE ALSO

OlGetMessage(3Olit), OlOpenDatabase(3Olit)

NAME

OlCloseIm – close the Input Method

SYNOPSIS

`#include <Xol/OpenLook.h>`

`void OlCloseIm(OlIm` *im*`);`

DESCRIPTION

This function is responsible for closing the Input Method (IM). Its functionality is implementation dependent. Some common steps that are performed by all implementations include:

Destroying all ICs (Input Contexts) associated with the IM and de-allocating storage used by these ICs.

De-allocating storage used by the `OlIm` structure.

SEE ALSO

`OlDisplayOfIm`(3Olit), `OlGetImValues`(3Olit), `OlImOfIc`(3Olit), `OlLocaleOfIm`(3Olit), `OlOpenIm`(3Olit)

OlCvtFontGroupToFontStructList (3Olit)

NAME

OlCvtFontGroupToFontStructList – convert a **fontGroup** string into a font_list

SYNOPSIS

```
#include <Xol/OpenLook.h>
#include <Xol/OlStrings.h>
#include <Xol/Converters.h>

OlFontList *font_list;

static XtResource resources[] =
    {
      { XtNfontGroup, XtCFontGroup, OlROlFontList,
        sizeof(OlFontList *), &font_list, XtRString, (XtPointer)NULL
      },
        .
        .
        .
    }

static Boolean CvtFontGroupToFontStrucList(
    Display display,
    XrmValuePtr args = NULL,
    Cardinal num_args = 0,
    XrmValue from,
    XrmValue to,
    XtCacheRef *cache_ref_return = NULL
)
    char *fontGroup;
    Cardinal num_args=0;

from.addr = (XtPointer) fontGroup;
from.size = strlen(fontGroup);
to.addr = (XtPointer) &font_list;
to.size = sizeof(OlFontList *);

XtCallConverter(
    Display display,
    OlCvtFontGroupToFontStruct,
    XrmValuePtr args,
    Cardinal num_args,
    XrmValue &from,
    XrmValue &to,
    XtCacheRef cache_ref_return
);
```

DESCRIPTION

The **OlCvtFontGroupToFontStructList** OPEN LOOK converter converts a **font-Group** string into corresponding **OlFontList**P for use with internationalized text drawing.

The converter can be invoked in two ways:

1. By specifying the source type of a **fontGroup** as a string and destination type as **OlFontList (OlROlFontList)** in the **XtResource** array. The converter, in this case is automatically invoked and, if successful, a pointer to the **OlFontList** structure is returned in *font_list*.

2. The converter can be directly invoked by the application to obtain a pointer to **OlFontList** by calling the Xt Intrinsics function **XtCallConverter** as shown above.

The *font_list* returned in either case can then be passed to text drawing utilities **OlDrawString**, **OlDrawImageString**, **OlTextWidth**, **OlGetNextStrSegment**.

NOTES

The storage for the **OlFontList** is allocated by the converter in both cases. Invocation by specifying different *source* and *destination* types in the **XtResource** array will cause Intrinsics to keep track of reference count and manage the cache. Hence the user does not need to free storage explicitly. However, in case of direct invocation via **XtCallConverter**, it is the caller's responsibility to free the storage for **OlFontList**.

SEE ALSO

OlDrawImageString(3Olit), **OlDrawString**(3Olit), **OlGetNextStrSegment**(3Olit), **OlTextWidth**(3Olit)

OlCtToEuc (3Olit)

NAME

`OlCtToEuc` – returns a null-terminated string

SYNOPSIS

```
#include <Xol/OpenLook.h>

int OlCtToEuc(XctString ctstr, XctString eucstr, int euc_len,
    OlFontList *fontl);
```

DESCRIPTION

Given a null-terminated compound text encoded string in the **ctstr** argument, this function returns a semantically equivalent null-terminated string in the *eucstr* argument that conforms to the EUC syntax. Equivalence implies that the characters in both strings are the same and are stored in the same logical order. The code set scheme syntax is the only difference in the two strings. The *fontl* argument provides this function with information about supplemental EUC code set support in the current locale. If during the conversion **OlCtToEuc** encounters a character from an unsupported code set, it generates an error by returning −1. Optional directional information provided in the compound text encoded string is ignored as EUC does not support directional rendering.

The memory for storing the EUC encoded string must be pre-allocated prior to the function call. Doing this, rather than making the function allocate the memory every time it is called, results in better performance, because pre-allocated memory could be easily re-used in case of repeated calls to **OlCtToEuc**. The *euc_len* argument specifies the length of the *eucstr* and is required to prevent buffer overflow. If the number of bytes indicated by **euc_len** is too small to store the converted string, −1 is returned.

This function returns the length, in bytes (not counting the terminating null character), of the EUC encoded string on success, or −1 on failure.

SEE ALSO

`OlEucToCt`(3Olit)

NAME

OlCreateIc – create an Input Context to register a text insertion window

SYNOPSIS

```
#include <Xol/OpenLook.h>

OlIc *OlCreateIc(OlIm *im, OlIcValues icvalues);
```

DESCRIPTION

The **OlCreateIc** function creates an Input Context for the client's text insertion window with an Input Method. *im* is a pointer to the **OlIm** structure returned by the function **OlOpenIm**. *icvalues* points to a variable list of attribute (name, value) pairs to be associated with the Input Context. One attribute, **XtNclientWindow** must always be specified at creation time.

The function creates and initializes the **OlIc** structure, containing the context information about a particular text area. This includes information about client and focus windows, pre-edit and status areas, pre-edit and status attributes, a pointer to the **OlIm** structure associated with the Input Context, and a pointer to the next Input Context associated with the same Input Method. The function returns a pointer to this structure.

If for any reason the function fails to create an Input Context, it should return a NULL value. The *ictype* field in the **OlIc** structure is a hook for attaching implementation dependent data structures.

The **OlIcWindowAttr** structure contains the following members:

```
Pixel           background;
Pixel           foreground;
Colormap        colormap;
Colormap        std_colormap;
Pixmap          back_pixmap;
OlFontList      fontlist;
int             spacing;
Cursor          cursor;
OlImCallback    callback[NUM_IM_CALLBACKS];
```

The **OlIc** structure contains the following members:

```
Window          cl_win;
XRectangle      cl_area;
Window          focus_win;
OlIcWindowAttr  s_attr;
XRectangle      s_area;
OlIcWindwoAttr  pre_attr;
XRectangle      pre_area;
OlImStyle       style;
XPoint          spot;
struct _OlIm    *im;
struct _OlIc    *nextic;
void            *ictype;
```

The `OlIcValues` structure contains a list of Input Context attribute names and value pairs, and includes the following members:

```
String attr_name;
void *attr_value;
```

The `OlImValues` structure contains a list of Input Method attribute names and value pairs, and includes the following members:

```
String attr_name;
void attr_value;
```

The `OlImCallback` structure includes the following members:

```
OlImValues   client_data;
OlImProc     callback;
```

where

```
typedef OlIcValues * OlIcValuesList;
typedef void  (*OlImProc)();
typedef OlImValues *OlImValuesList;
```

`OlIcValuesList` contains a list of Input Context attribute names and value pairs. It is used for getting and setting various Input Context attributes. The supported Input Context attributes are shown in the table below. The end of the list is indicated by a NULL value in the attribute name.

Input Context Attributes

Attribute Name	Attribute Value Type
OlNclientWindow	Window*
OlNClientArea	XRectangle*
OlNinputStyle	OlImStyle*
OlNfocusWindow	Window*
OlNpreeditArea	XRectangle*
OlNstatusArea	XRectangle*
OlNspotLocation	XPoint*
OlNresourceDatabse	XrmDatabase*
OlNpreeditAttributes	OlIcWindowAttr*
OlNstatusAttributes	OlIcWindowAttr*

Attributes for Preedit and Status Windows

Attribute Name	Attribute Value Type
OlNcolormap	Colormap
OlNstdColormap	Colormap
OlNbackground	Pixel
OlNforeground	Pixel
OlNbackgroundPixmap	Pixmap
OlNfontset	OlFontList

Attributes for Preedit and Status Windows

Attribute Name	Attribute Value Type
OlNlineSpacing	int
OlNcursor	Cursor
Callbacks	OlImCallback

OlNclientWindow

specifies the client window in which the Input Method may display data or create subwindows. Dynamic changes of client window are not supported; this argument must be set at the Input Context creation time and cannot be changed later. It is a static attribute that is required by OlCreateIc. The value is a pointer to a window.

OlNClientArea

specifies the client area in which Input Method may display data or create subwindows. Input Method will establish its own pre-edit and status geometry accordingly. When this attribute is left unspecified, Input Method will default usable client area to actual client window geometry. It is a dynamic attribute that can be modified via calls to OlSetIcValues. The value is a pointer to an **XRectangle**.

OlNinputStyle

specifies the input style to be used. The value of this argument must be one of the supported styles returned by the **OlGetImValues** function, otherwise **OlCreatIc** will fail. If you do not specify this attribute, Input Method will use an implementation defined default style. OPEN LOOK does not support Dynamic changes of Input Method style. This argument must be set at the Input Context creation time and cannot be changed later. The value is a pointer to **OlImStyle**.

OlNfocusWindow

specifies to Input Method the window XID of the focus window. The input method may possibly affect that window: select events on it, send events to it, modify its properties, and grab the keyboard within that window.

When this attribute is left unspecified, Input Method will default from the focus window to the client window. Setting this attribute explicitly to NULL has a specific meaning: when the focus window is set explicitly from a non NULL value to NULL, the Input Method is required to clear any displayed data in the status area corresponding to the focus window. It is a dynamic attribute that can be modified via calls to **OlSetIcValues**. The value is a pointer to a window.

OlNpreeditArea

the area where pre-edit data should be displayed. The value of this argument is a pointer to **XRectangle**, relative to the client window. Input Method may or not create a preedit window in this area, using the specified geometry, as a child of a client window.

When you leave **OlNpreeditArea** unspecified, Input Method will default from the preedit area to an implementation defined area. This area shall be contained within the client area.

If you specify this attribute for root or **XimPreEditCallbacks** Input Method, it is ignored.

If you specify this attribute for an **XimPreEditArea** Input Method, the width and height determine the size of the area within the "over-the-spot" window that is now available for pre-edit.

OlNstatusArea

specifies to the Input Method the usable area to display Input Context state information. The value of this argument is a pointer to **XRectangle**, relative to the client window.

The Input Method may or may not create a status window in this area, using the specified geometry, as a child of the client window.

When **OlNstatusArea** is left unspecified, The Input Method defaults to the status area defined by the Input Method implementation. This area is contained within the client area. This is a dynamic attribute that can be modified via calls to **OlSetIcValues**.

It is important to note that if a client leaves all areas unspecified, the Input Method may not be able to run properly. Some implementations will generate errors if none of the focus window, focus area, client area, preedit area, and status area are defined. At best, it may behave randomly using any area in the client window, possibly clearing the whole window or erasing any region.

OlNspotLocation

specifies to Input Method the coordinates of the "spot" (the current cursor position in the text insertion window), to be used by the "over-the-spot" or "on-the-spot" Input Methods. The type is a pointer to **Xpoint**. The x coordinate specifies the position where the next character would be inserted. The y coordinate is the position of the baseline used by current text line in the focus window.

SEE ALSO

OlCreateIc(3Olit), OlDestroyIc(3Olit), OlGetIcValues(3Olit), OlIcValues(4), OlImOfIc(3Olit), OlReSetIc(3Olit), OlSetIcFocus(3Olit), OlSetIcValues(3Olit), OlUnSetIcFocus(3Olit)

NAME

OlCreateInputEventDB – create client specific Key and/or Button database

SYNOPSIS

```
#include <Xol/OpenLook.h>

OlVirtualEventTable OlCreateInputEventDB(
    Widget w,
    OlKeyOrBtnInfo key_info,
    int num_key_info,
    OlKeyBtnInfo btn_info,
    int num_btn_info
);
```

DESCRIPTION

The OlCreateInputEventDB function is used to create a client specific Key and/or Button database. This function returns a database pointer if the call to this function is successful otherwise a NULL pointer is returned.

Mapping for a new virtual command can be composed from the mappings of a previously defined virtual command.

The returned value from this function is an opaque pointer (OlVirtualEvent-Table). A client application should use this pointer when registering and/or looking up this database.

```
typedef struct _OlVirtualEventInfo *OlVirtualEventTable;
```

The *key_info* and *btn_info* parameters are a pointer to an OlKeyOrBtnRec structure, or pointer to that structure, *OlKeyOrBtnInfo, which contains the following members:

```
String          name;
String          default_value;    /* "," separate string */
OlVirtualName   virtual_name;
```

EXAMPLE

```
/* To create a client application database */
...
#include <Xol/OpenLook.h>
...
    /* start with a big value to avoid */
    /* the "virtual_name" collision     */
#define OL_MY_BASE          1000
#define OL_MY_DRAWLINEBTN   OL_MY_BASE+0
#define OL_MY_DRAWARCBTN    OL_MY_BASE+1
#define OL_MY_REDISPLAYKEY  OL_MY_BASE+2
#define OL_MY_SAVEPARTKEY   OL_MY_BASE+3

#define XtNmyDrawLineBtn    "myDrawLineBtn"
#define XtNmyDrawArcBtn     "myDrawArcBtn"
#define XtNmyRedisplayKey   "myRedisplayKey"
#define XtNmySavePartKey    "mySavePartKey"

static OlKeyOrBtnRec    OlMyBtnInfo[] = {
```

OlCreateInputEventDB (3Olit)

```
      /*name              default_value      virtual_name          */

      { XtNmyDrawLineBtn,  "c<Button1>",         OL_MY_DRAWLINEBTN  },
      { XtNmyDrawArcBtn,   "s<myDrawLineBtn>", OL_MY_DRAWARCBTN     },
};

static OlKeyOrBtnRec      OlMyKeyInfo[] = {
    /*name                default_value        virtual_name          */

      { XtNmyRedisplayKey, "c<F5>",              OL_MY_REDISPLAYKEY },
      { XtNmySavePartKey,  "c<F5>",              OL_MY_SAVEPARTKEY  },
};

static OlVirtualEventTable      OlMyDB;


    ...
OlMyDB = OlCreateInputEventDB(
            w,
            OlMyKeyInfo, XtNumber(OlMyKeyInfo),
            OlMyBtnInfo, XtNumber(OlMyBtnInfo)
    );
    ...
```

NOTES

A client application can create a Key only database by having the NULL *btn_info*. The same applies to a Button only database.

Each virtual command can have two different bindings because the OPEN LOOK toolkit allows the alternate key or button sequence.

The OPEN LOOK toolkit already has a set of predefined OPEN LOOK virtual names. It is important that the *virtual_name* value of a client application database starts with a big value to avoid the *virtual_name* collision.

SEE ALSO

OlClassSearchIEDB(3Olit), OlClassSearchTextDB(3Olit),
OlClassUnsearchIEDB(3Olit), OlDestroyInputEventDB(3Olit),
OlLookupInputEvent(3Olit), OlWidgetSearchIEDB(3Olit),
OlWidgetSearchTextDB(3Olit), OlWidgetUnsearchIEDB(3Olit)

NAME

OlCreatePackedWidgetList – create a widget tree or subtree in one call

SYNOPSIS

```
#include <Xol/OpenLook.h>
```

```
Widget OlCreatePackedWidgetList(OlPackedWidget *pw_list,
    Cardinal num_pw);
```

DESCRIPTION

The `OlCreatePackedWidgetList` routine and its associated `OlPackedWidget` structure allow an application to create a widget tree or subtree in one call.

The tree points to *pw_list*. Each element in this array is of the type `OlPackedWidget`. This structure gives all the information needed to create a new widget, and includes the following members:

```
Widget widget_returned;
String name;
WidgetClass *class_ptr;
Widget *parent_ptr;
String descendant;
ArgList resources;
Cardinal num_resources;
Boolean managed;
```

where:

`widget_returned`
> newly created widget ID

`name`   newly created widget name

`class_ptr`
> *pointer* to the `WidgetClass` pointer for the new widget. This gives the class of widget to create. It is a pointer to the pointer because typically the pointer itself is an external value that is not suitable for using in an array initialization; the pointer to the pointer is.

`parent_ptr`
> pointer to the widget ID of the intended parent of the new widget or the ID of an indirect widget that "knows who the parent is" (see below). This value may point to a `.widget` member in another `PackedWidget` item; if the parent is an indirect widget, it must appear earlier in the list.

`descendant`
> name of a resource available in the widget identified by `parent_ptr`. The value of this resource is the ID of the real parent for the new widget.
>
> If the `.descendant` value is not zero, `.parent` is expected to identify an indirect parent that is interrogated for the ID of the real parent. If this value is zero, `.parent` is expected to identify the real parent.

`resources`
> resource array to use when creating the new widget.

OlCreatePackedWidgetList (3Olit)

num_resources
>
> number of resources in the array.

managed
>
> **TRUE** if the new widget should be managed when created, **FALSE** other-
> wise.

The **OlCreatePackedWidgetList** is passed a pointer to an **OlPackedWidget** array and the number of elements in the array. It creates widgets starting from the first element in the array, and returns the ID of the topmost widget.

NAME

OlDestroyIc – destroy a specified IC

SYNOPSIS

`#include <Xol/OpenLook.h>`

`void OlDestroyIc(OlIc *ic);`

DESCRIPTION

This function will destroy the specified Input Context (IC). It will remove it from the `ic_list` maintained by the Input Method (IM), and then de-allocate memory used by the `OlIc` structure.

SEE ALSO

OlCreateIc(3Olit), OlIcValues(3Olit), OlImOfIc(3Olit), OlSetIcFocus(3Olit), OlSetIcValues(3Olit), OlUnSetIcFocus(3Olit)

OlDestroyInputEventDB (3Olit)

NAME

OlDestroyInputEventDB – destroy a specific Key and/or Button database

SYNOPSIS

#include <Xol/OpenLook.h>

void OlDestroyInputEventDB(OlVirtualEventTable *db*);

DESCRIPTION

The OlDestroyInputEventDB procedure is used to destroy a client specific Key and/or Button database. All widget classes and widget instances with the reference *db* are also removed from the list of registered databases.

The *db* value is returned from a call to OlCreateInputEventDB.

SEE ALSO

OlClassSearchIEDB(3Olit), OlClassSearchTextDB(3Olit),
OlClassUnsearchIEDB(3Olit), OlCreateInputEventDB(3Olit),
OlWidgetSearchIEDB(3Olit), OlWidgetSearchTextDB(3Olit),
OlWidgetUnsearchIEDB(3Olit)

NAME

OlDisplayOfIm – query a display associated with an IM

SYNOPSIS

#include <Xol/OpenLook.h>

Display *OlDisplayOfIm(OlIm *im);

DESCRIPTION

This function returns a pointer to the **Display** corresponding to the given Input Method.

SEE ALSO

OlOpenIm(3Olit), XOpenDisplay(3X)

OlDnDAllocTransientAtom (3DnD)

NAME

OlDnDAllocTransientAtom – allocate a transient atom

SYNOPSIS

#include <DnD/OlDnDVCX.h>

Atom OlDnDAllocTransientAtom(Widget *wid*);

DESCRIPTION

The OlDnDAllocTransientAtom function allocates a reusable transient atom suitable for use in a drag and drop selection transaction to the widget *wid*.

SEE ALSO

OlDnDDisownSelection(3DnD),
OlDnDGetCurrentSelectionsForWidget(3DnD), OlDnDOwnSelection(3DnD),
OlDnDOwnSelectionIncremental(3DnD)

OlDnDBeginSelectionTransaction (3DnD)

NAME

OlDnDBeginSelectionTransaction – provide positive handshake

SYNOPSIS

```
#include <DnD/OlDnDVCX.h>

void OlDnDBeginSelectionTransaction(
    Widget wid,
    Atom select,
    Time time,
    OlDnDProtocolActionCallbackProc callproc,
    XtPointer data
);
```

DESCRIPTION

The OlDnDBeginSelectionTransaction function provides a positive handshake showing a selection transaction.

The parameters are

wid	the initiating widget or drop site owner,
select	the selection atom passed in the trigger notify procedure,
time	the server's current time
callproc	the callback procedure to notify requestor that holder received begin notification
data	user data to pass to the callback procedure

The callback procedure, *callproc*, notifies the requestor that the holder received the begin notification (OlDnDSelectionTransactionBegins).

OlDnDProtocolActionCallbackProc has the following function prototype:

```
typedef void (*OlDnDProtocolActionCallbackProc)(
    Widget wid,
    Atom select,
    OlDnDProtocolAction proto_act,
    Boolean flag,
    XtPointer data,
);
```

Where OlDnDProtocolAction is a **enum** including the following elements:

```
OlDnDSelectionTransactionBegins;
OlDnDSelectionTransactionEnds;
OlDnDSelectionTransactionError;
OlDnDDragNDropTransactionDone;
```

If specified, the OlDnDTransactionCallbackProc procedure will be invoked in the holder side with a state parameter of OlDnDTransactionBegins. This procedure is specified on OlDnDOwnSelection(3DnD) and OlDnDOwnSelectionIncremental(3DnD).

OlDnDBeginSelectionTransaction (3DnD)

SEE ALSO

OlDnDDragNDropDone(3DnD), OlDnDEndSelectionTransaction(3DnD),
OlDnDErrorDuringSelectionTransaction(3DnD), OlDnDOwnSelection(3DnD),
OlDnDOwnSelectionIncremental(3DnD),

OlDnDChangeDropSitePreviewHints (3DnD)

NAME

`OlDnDChangeDropSitePreviewHints` – change a drop site's preview hints

SYNOPSIS

```
#include <DnD/OlDnDVCX.h>

Boolean OlDnDChangeDropSitePreviewHints(
    OlDnDDropSiteID dsiteid,
    OlDnDSitePreviewHints preview_hints
);
```

DESCRIPTION

During the lifetime of a drop site, it may be necessary to alter the nature of its previewing interest. The `OlDnDChangeDropSitePreviewHints` function overwrites the existing preview hints for a drop site, *dsiteid*, with *preview_hints*.

preview_hints specifies the conditions under which the drop site is interested in receiving notification through its preview callback, The `OlDnDSitePreviewHints` **enum** includes the following members:

```
OlDnDSitePreviewNone,        /* specifies no previewing */
OlDnDSitePreviewEnterLeave,  /* Enter/Leave event previewing */
OlDnDSitePreviewMotion,      /* Motion event previewing */
OlDnDSitePreviewBoth,        /* Enter/Leave/Motion previewing */
OlDnDSitePreviewDefaultSite, /* default site */
OlDnDSitePreviewForwarded,   /* shows that previews and/or */
                             /* drops occur on ''forwarded'' */
                             /* drop sites */
OlDnDSitePreviewInsensitive, /* shows that the drop site is */
                             /* currently not able to accept */
                             /* drops */
```

where

`OlDnDSitePreviewDefaultSite`

specifies that the drop site is the default site for drop site forwarding on this application shell

`OlDnDSitePreviewForwarded`

shows that previews and/or drops occur on "forwarded" drop sites. For example, process icons, window decorations, borders, and so on, are "forwarded" drop sites. Note that a window manager needs to precipitate the drag and drop protocol, otherwise, an application will not see the hint.

`OlDnDSitePreviewInsensitive`

shows that the drop site is currently not able to accept drops

SEE ALSO

`OlDnDDestroyDropSite`(3DnD), `OlDnDGetDropSitesOfWidget`(3DnD), `OlDnDGetDropSitesOfWindow`(3DnD), `OlDnDGetWidgetOfDropSite`(3DnD), `OlDnDGetWindowOfDropSite`(3DnD), `OlDnDQueryDropSiteInfo`(3DnD), `OlDnDRegisterWidgetDropSite`(3DnD), `OlDnDRegisterWindowDropSite`(3DnD)

OlDnDClearDragState (3DnD)

NAME

OlDnDClearDragState – clear drag and drop internal state

SYNOPSIS

#include <DnD/OlDnDVCX.h>

void OlDnDClearDragState(Widget *wid*);

DESCRIPTION

The OlDnDClearDragState function clears the internal state withing the drag and drop system and must be called on completion of a drag and drop gesture. *wid* is the selection holder widget ID.

SEE ALSO

OlDnDInitializeDragState(3DnD)

NAME

> OlDnDDeliverPreviewMessage – deliver enter, leave and motion events to drop sites

SYNOPSIS

> #include <DnD/OlDnDVCX.h>
>
> Boolean OlDnDDeliverPreviewMessage(
>   Widget *wid*,
>   Window *root*,
>   Position *root_x*,
>   Position *root_y*,
>   Time *time*
>);

DESCRIPTION

> The **OlDnDDeliverPreviewMessage** function delivers Enter, Leave and Motion events to any drop sites currently under the (*root_x*,*root_y*) location on the *root* window specified, where

>> *wid*   is the selection holder widget ID,

>> *root*   is the root window,

>> *root_x* is the horizontal coordinate at which the drop occurred, relative to the *root* window,

>> *root_y* is the vertical coordinate at which the drop occurred, relative to the *root* window.

To preview drop sites, the Drop Site Database Manager (dsdm) [see dsdm(1)] client must be running in order to provide the source client with up-to-date drop site information.

The drop site preview message notifier, the **OlDnDPreviewMessageNotifyProc** function, is associated with a particular drop site at registration. It is invoked when a drop operation in progress either enters, leaves, or moves across the drop site. Which of these actions invokes the notifier depends on the current value of the drop site's *preview_hints* [see **OlDnDChangeDropSitePreviewHints**(3DnD)]. This function has the function prototype

> typedef void (*OlDnDPreviewMessageNotifyProc *)(
>   Widget *wid*,
>   Window *wind*,
>   Position *root_x*,
>   Position *root_y*,
>   int *event_code*,
>   Time *time*,
>   OlDnDDropSiteID *dsiteid*,
>   Boolean *forward*,
>   XtPointer *data*
>);

OlDnDDeliverPreviewMessage (3DnD)

where

root_x
root_y   are the root-relative x and y coordinates of the preview event, respectively

event_code
       is **EnterNotify**, **LeaveNotify**, or **MotionNotify**

time   is the time of the preview event, and

dsiteid   is the drop site ID on which the preview occurred.

RETURN VALUES

If an event delivery drop site exists, the function returns **TRUE**. Otherwise, it returns **FALSE**.

SEE ALSO

dsdm1(1), **OlDnDChangeDropSitePreviewHints**(3DnD),
OlDnDDeliverTriggerMessage(3DnD), **OlDnDPreviewAndAnimate**(3DnD),
OlDnDRegisterWidgetDropSite(3DnD), **OlDnDRegisterWindowDropSite**(3DnD)

NAME

OlDnDDeliverTriggerMessage – deliver trigger message to drop sites

SYNOPSIS

```
#include <DnD/OlDnDVCX.h>

Boolean OlDnDDeliverTriggerMessage(
    Widget wid,
    Window root,
    Position root_x,
    Position root_y,
    Atom select,
    OlDnDTriggerOperation op,
    Time time
);
```

DESCRIPTION

The OlDnDDeliverTriggerMessage function is invoked by the dragging client to deliver a trigger message to any drop sites currently at the (*root_x,root_y*) location on the *root* window specified, where:

wid	is the selection holder widget ID,
root	is the root window,
root_x *root_y*	are the location of the drop site relative to the *root* window,
select	is the selection atom passed in the trigger notify procedure,
op	is the trigger operation, and
time	is the current server time.

The calling client must establish a timeout period. If the drop target doesn't send selection conversion requests during this period, the calling client should take appropriate action.

The drop site trigger message notifier, the OlDnDTriggerMessageNotifyProc function is associated with a particular drop site at registration. It is invoked when a drag-and-drop operation is completed. This function has the following function prototype:

```
typedef Boolean (*OlDnDTriggerMessageNotifyProc)(
    Widget wid,
    Window window,
    Position root_x,
    Position root_y,
    Atom select
    Time time
    OlDnDDropSiteID dsiteid
    OlDnDTriggerOperation op,
    Boolean send_done,
    Boolean forwarded,
    XtPosition data
);
```

OlDnDDeliverTriggerMessage (3DnD)

The **enum OlDnDTriggerOperation** includes the following members:

```
OlDnDTriggerCopyOp;
OlDnDTriggerMoveOp;
OlDnDTriggerLinkOp;
```

RETURN VALUES

If a drop site exists, the function returns **TRUE**. Otherwise, it returns **FALSE**.

SEE ALSO

OlDnDRegisterWidgetDropSite(3DnD), **OlDnDRegisterWindowDropSite**(3DnD)

OlDnDDestroyDropSite (3DnD)

NAME

OlDnDDestroyDropSite – destroy a drop site

SYNOPSIS

    #include <DnD/OlDnDVCX.h>

    void OlDnDDestroyDropSite(OlDnDDropSiteID *dsiteid*);

DESCRIPTION

The **OlDnDDestroyDropSite** function explicitly destroys the drop site, *dsiteid*. When a drop site's widget or window is destroyed, all drop sites associated with that widget or window are automatically destroyed.

SEE ALSO

OlDnDGetDropSitesOfWidget(3DnD), OlDnDGetDropSitesOfWindow(3DnD), OlDnDRegisterWidgetDropSite(3DnD), OlDnDRegisterWindowDropSite(3DnD)

OlDnDDisownSelection (3DnD)

NAME

OlDnDDisownSelection – disown a selection

SYNOPSIS

#include <DnD/OlDnDVCX.h>

Boolean OlDnDDisownSelection(Widget *wid*, Atom *select*, Time *time*);

DESCRIPTION

The OlDnDDisownSelection function relinquishes ownership of the *select* of the specified *wid*.

This function is identical in semantics to the Xt function XtDisownSelection.

SEE ALSO

OlDnDOwnSelection(3DnD), OlDnDOwnSelectionIncremental(3DnD)

NAME

OlDnDDragAndDrop – mouse and keyboard events processing interface

SYNOPSIS

```
#include <DnD/OlDnDVCX.h>

void OlDnDDragAndDrop(
    Widget wid,
    Window *dst_win,
    Position *dst_x,
    Position *dst_y,
    OlDnDDragDropInfoPtr drop_info,
    OlDnDPreviewAnimateCallbackProc animate,
    XtPointer data
);
```

DESCRIPTION

The **OlDnDDragAndDrop** function provides a simple mouse and keyboard event processing interface during drag and drop operations.

The parameters are

wid	the selection holder widget ID
dst_win	the destination window ID
dst_x *dst_y*	the location of the drop relative to *dst_win*
drop_info	pointer to structure containing the location of the drop
animate	the animate procedure called when the cursor enters the drop site

Before calling this function, you should call **OlGrabDragCursor** or **OlDnDGrab-DragCursor** to effectively grab pointer events. It inserts a raw event handler on the widget specified for the pointer and key events and initializes the drag and drop system with **OlDnDInitializeDragState**. Then it proceeds to process the event stream, delivering preview messages where appropriate via **OlDnDDeliverPreviewMessage** until the drag completes or is aborted.

OlDnDDragDropInfoPtr is a pointer to a **OlDnDDragDropInfo** structure which includes the following members:

```
Window root_wid;        /* root window of drop */
Position root_x;        /* x coordinate of drop occurred */
Position root_y;        /* y coordinate of drop occurred */
Time drop_time;         /* time when drop occurred */
```

OlDnDDragAndDrop (3DnD)

The **OlDnDPreviewAnimateCallbackProc** function has the following function prototype definition:

```
typedef void (*OlDnDPrevewAnimateCallbackProc)(
    Widget wid,
    int event_type,
    Time time,
    Boolean insensitivity,
    XtPointer data
);
```

where the *event_type* is a **EnterNotify**, **LeaveNotify** or **MotionNotify** event.

RETURN VALUES

The function returns the *root_x, root_y* location and the window that the pointer was in when the operation completed. It also returns the necessary root information.

SEE ALSO

OlDnDTrackDragCursor(3DnD)

OlDnDDragNDropDone (3DnD)

NAME

OlDnDDragNDropDone – send drag and drop done notification

SYNOPSIS

```
#include <DnD/OlDnDVCX.h>

void OlDnDDragNDropDone(
    Widget wid,
    Atom select,
    Time time,
    OlDnDProtocolActionCallbackProc callproc,
    XtPointer data
);
```

DESCRIPTION

The **OlDnDDragNDropDone** function sends a notification that the drag and drop is done, where:

wid	is the initiating widget ID or drop site owner,
select	is the selection atom,
time	is the current server time,
callproc	is the callback procedure to notify the requestor that the holder received a done notification,
data	is the user data to pass to *callproc*.

callproc notifies the requestor that the holder received the done notification (**OlDnD-DragNDropTransactionDone**).

If specified, the **OlDnDTransactionStateCallback** procedure will be invoked in the holder site with a state parameter of **OlDnDTransactionDone**. This procedure is specified in **OlDnDOwnSelection** and **OlDnDOwnSelectionIncremental**.

SEE ALSO

OlDnDBeginSelectionTransaction(3DnD),
OlDnDEndSelectionTransaction(3DnD),
OlDnDErrorDuringSelectionTransaction(3DnD), OlDnDOwnSelection(3DnD),
OlDnDOwnSelectionIncremental(3DnD)

OlDnDEndSelectionTransaction (3DnD)

NAME

OlDnDEndSelectionTransaction – provide a positive handshake

SYNOPSIS

```
#include <DnD/OlDnDVCX.h>

void OlDnDEndSelectionTransaction(
    Widget wid,
    Atom select,
    Time time,
    OlDnDProtocolActionCallbackProc callproc,
    XtPointer data
);
```

DESCRIPTION

The OlDnDEndSelectionTransaction function sends an end notification, where:

wid	is the initiating widget ID or drop site owner,
select	is the selection atom,
time	is the current server time,
callproc	is the callback procedure to notify the requestor that the holder received a end notification,
data	is the user data to pass to *callproc*.

callproc notifies the requestor that the holder received the end notification (OlDnDSelectionTransactionEnds).

If specified, the OlDnDTransactionStateCallback procedure will be invoked in the holder site with a state parameter of OlDnDTransactionEnds. This procedure is specified on OlDnDOwnSelection and OlDnDOwnSelectionIncremental.

SEE ALSO

OlDnDDragNDropDone(3DnD), OlDnDEndSelectionTransaction(3DnD), OlDnDErrorDuringSelectionTransaction(3DnD), OlDnDOwnSelection(3DnD), OlDnDOwnSelectionIncremental(3DnD)

OlDnDErrorDuringSelectionTransaction (3DnD)

NAME

OlDnDErrorDuringSelectionTransaction – notify selection holder of an error

SYNOPSIS

```
#include <DnD/OlDnDVCX.h>

void OlDnDErrorDuringSelectionTransaction(
    Widget wid,
    Atom select,
    Time time,
    OlDnDProtocolActionCallbackProc callproc,
    XtPointer data
);
```

DESCRIPTION

The **OlDnDErrorDuringSelectionTransaction** function sends a notification that the drag and drop has an error. Where:

wid	is the initiating widget ID or drop site owner,
select	is the selection atom,
time	is the current server time,
callproc	is the callback procedure to notify the requestor that the holder received a done notification,
data	is the user data to pass to *callproc*.

callproc notifies the requestor that the holder received the error notification (**OlDnDSelectionTransactionError**).

If specified, the **OlDnDTransactionStateCallback** procedure will be invoked in the holder site with a state parameter of **OlDnDTransactionRequestorError**. This procedure is specified on **OlDnDOwnSelection** and **OlDnDOwnSelection-Incremental**.

SEE ALSO

OlDnDBeginSelectionTransaction(3DnD),
OlDnDEndSelectionTransaction(3DnD), OlDnDDragNDropDone(3DnD),
OlDnDOwnSelection(3DnD), OlDnDOwnSelectionIncremental(3DnD)

OlDnDFreeTransientAtom (3DnD)

NAME

    `OlDnDFreeTransientAtom` – free a transient atom

SYNOPSIS

    `#include <DnD/OlDnDVCX.h>`

    `void OlDnDFreeTransientAtom(Widget` *wid*`, Atom` *tran_atom*`);`

DESCRIPTION

    The `OlDnDFreeTransientAtom` function frees the transient atom, *tran_atom*, associated with *wid* for use in a drag and drop selection transaction.

SEE ALSO

    `OlDnDAllocTransientAtom`(3DnD)

OlDnDGetCurrentSelectionsForWidget (3DnD)

NAME

OlDnDGetCurrentSelectionsForWidget – list current atoms for widget

SYNOPSIS

```
#include <DnD/OlDnDVCX.h>

Boolean OlDnDGetCurrentSelectionsForWidget(
    Widget wid,
    Atom **arr_atom,
    Cardinal *num_atom
);
```

DESCRIPTION

The OlDnDGetCurrentSelectionsForWidget function finds all atoms currently held by the widget *wid*. *arr_atom* points to an array of the currently held atoms, and *num_atom* points to the number of currently held atoms.

The caller must call **XtFree** on the pointer returned in the atom's parameter to free the store allocated when no longer needed.

RETURN VALUES

If any atoms are found, the function returns **TRUE**. Otherwise, it returns **FALSE**.

SEE ALSO

OlDnDAllocTransientAtom(3DnD), OlDnDDisownSelection(3DnD), OlDnDOwnSelection(3DnD), OlDnDOwnSelectionIncremental(3DnD)

OlDnDGetDropSitesOfWidget (3DnD)

NAME

OlDnDGetDropSitesOfWidget – list currently registered widget drop sites

SYNOPSIS

```
#include <DnD/OlDnDVCX.h>

OlDnDDropSiteID *OlDnDGetDropSitesOfWidget(
    Widget wid,
    Cardinal *num_sites
);
```

DESCRIPTION

The OlDnDGetDropSitesOfWidget function gets the currently registered list of drop sites for the widget *wid*.

The caller must call **XtFree** on the return value to deallocate the array when it is no longer needed.

RETURN VALUES

The function returns a pointer to an array enumeration of the currently registered drop sites. If the function fails or there are no drop sites, the return value is NULL.

SEE ALSO

OlDnDChangeDropSitePreviewHints(3DnD), OlDnDDestroyDropSite(3DnD), OlDnDGetDropSitesOfWindow(3DnD), OlDnDGetWidgetOfDropSite(3DnD), OlDnDGetWindowOfDropSite(3DnD), OlDnDQueryDropSiteInfo(3DnD), OlDnDRegisterWidgetDropSite(3DnD), OlDnDRegisterWindowDropSite(3DnD), OlDnDUpdateDropSiteGeometry(3DnD)

OlDnDGetDropSitesOfWindow (3DnD)

NAME

OlDnDGetDropSitesOfWindow – list currently registered window drop sites

SYNOPSIS

```
#include <DnD/OlDnDVCX.h>

OlDnDDropSiteID *OlDnDGetDropSitesOfWindow(
    Display *dspy,
    Window win,
    Cardinal *num_sites
);
```

DESCRIPTION

The OlDnDGetDropSitesOfWindow function gets the currently registered list of drop sites for the window *win*.

The caller must call XtFree on the return value to deallocate the array when it is no longer needed.

RETURN VALUES

The function returns a pointer to an array enumeration of the currently registered drop sites. If the function fails or there are no drop sites, the return value is NULL.

SEE ALSO

OlDnDChangeDropSitePreviewHints(3DnD), OlDnDDestroyDropSite(3DnD), OlDnDGetDropSitesOfWindow(3DnD), OlDnDGetWindowOfDropSite(3DnD), OlDnDQueryDropSiteInfo(3DnD), OlDnDRegisterWidgetDropSite(3DnD), OlDnDUpdateDropSiteGeometry(3DnD)

OlDnDGetWidgetOfDropSite (3DnD)

NAME

OlDnDGetWidgetOfDropSite – get widget associated with drop site

SYNOPSIS

```
#include <DnD/OlDnDVCX.h>
```

Widget OlDnDGetWidgetOfDropSite(OlDnDDropSiteID *dsiteid*);

DESCRIPTION

The OlDnDGetWidgetOfDropSite function returns the widget ID associated with the drop site *dsiteid*.

SEE ALSO

OlDnDChangeDropSitePreviewHints(3DnD), OlDnDDestroyDropSite(3DnD), OlDnDGetDropSitesOfWidget(3DnD), OlDnDGetDropSitesOfWindow(3DnD), OlDnDGetWindowOfDropSite(3DnD), OlDnDQueryDropSiteInfo(3DnD), OlDnDRegisterWidgetDropSite(3DnD), OlDnDRegisterWindowDropSite(3DnD), OlDnDUpdateDropSiteGeometry(3DnD)

NAME

OlDnDGetWindowOfDropSite – get window associated with drop site

SYNOPSIS

```
#include <DnD/OlDnDVCX.h>

Window OlDnDGetWindowOfDropSite(OlDnDDropSiteID dsiteid);
```

DESCRIPTION

The OlDnDGetWindowOfDropSite function returns the window associated with the drop site *dsiteid*. If the drop site was registered with a gadget, then the window ID is the gadget's windowed parent.

SEE ALSO

OlDnDChangeDropSitePreviewHints(3DnD), OlDnDDestroyDropSite(3DnD),
OlDnDGetDropSitesOfWidget(3DnD), OlDnDGetDropSitesOfWindow(3DnD),
OlDnDGetWidgetOfDropSite(3DnD), OlDnDQueryDropSiteInfo(3DnD),
OlDnDRegisterWidgetDropSite(3DnD),
OlDnDRegisterWindowDropSite(3DnD), OlDnDUpdateDropSiteGeometry(3DnD)

OlDnDGrabDragCursor (3DnD)

NAME

OlDnDGrabDragCursor – grab the mouse pointer and keyboard if necessary

SYNOPSIS

```
#include <DnD/OlDnDVCX.h>
```

void OlDnDGrabDragCursor(Widget *wid*, Cursor *cursor*, Window *win*);

DESCRIPTION

The OlDnDGrabDragCursor function is used to effect an active grab of the mouse pointer and the keyboard if a OlDnDDragKeyProc function is registered, where:

wid is the widget that initiates the drag and drop operation

cursor is the cursor displayed with the pointer during the grab. The cursor will not change if the value is **None**.

win is the window to confine the pointer. The pointer is not confined to any window if the value is **None**.

This function is normally called after a mouse drag operation occurs and prior to calling the OlDragAndDrop or OlDnDDragAndDrop function which are used to monitor a drag operation.

SEE ALSO

OlDnDRegisterDragKeyProc(3DnD), OlDnDTrackDragCursor(3DnD), OlDnDUngrabDragCursor(3DnD)

NAME

OlDnDInitializeDragState – initialize drag and drop internal state

SYNOPSIS

#include <DnD/OlDnDVCX.h>

Boolean OlDnDInitializeDragState(Widget *wid*);

DESCRIPTION

The OlDnDInitializeDragState function downloads drop site previewing infor-mation for *wid* from the DSDM. It is called prior to a drag-and-drop gesture.

RETURN VALUES

The function returns **TRUE** for successful downloads. Otherwise, it returns **FALSE**.

SEE ALSO

OlDnDClearDragState(3DnD)

OlDnDOwnSelection (3DnD)

NAME

OlDnDOwnSelection – become selection owner

SYNOPSIS

```
#include <DnD/OlDnDVCX.h>

Boolean OlDnDOwnSelection(
    Widget wid,
    Atom select,
    Time time,
    XtConvertSelectionProc conv_sproc,
    XtLoseSelectionProc lose_sproc,
    XtSelectionDoneProc done_sproc,
    OlDnDTransactionStateCallback tstate_cb,
    XtPointer data
);
```

DESCRIPTION

The OlDnDOwnSelection functions acquires the *select* ownership.

Except for the additional parameter *tstate_cb*, this function is semantically identical to the Xt function **XtOwnSelection**. [See **OlDnDOwnSelection-Incremental**(3DnD)]

The **OlDnDTransactionStateCallback** function has the following function prototype:

```
typedef void (*OlDnDTransactionStateCallback)(
    Widget wid,
    Atom select,
    OlDnDTransactionState state,
    Time time,
    XtPointer data,
);
```

Where the **enum** OlDnDTransactionState includes the following members:

```
OlDnDTransactionBegins;
OlDnDTransactionEnds;
OlDnDTransactionDone;
OlDnDTransactionRequestorError;
OlDnDTransactionRequestorWindowDeath;
OnDnDTransactionTimeout;
```

RETURN VALUES

It returns **TRUE** if the specified widget, *wid*, successfully becomes the selection owner, and **FALSE** otherwise.

SEE ALSO

OlDnDAllocTransientAtom(3DnD), OlDnDDisownSelection(3DnD),
OlDnDGetCurrentSelectionsForWidget(3DnD),
OlDnDOwnSelectionIncremental(3DnD)

NAME

OlDnDOwnSelectionIncremental – become selection owner

SYNOPSIS

```
#include <DnD/OlDnDVCX.h>

Boolean OlDnDOwnSelectionIncremental(
    Widget wid,
    Atom select,
    Time time,
    XtConvertSelectionIncrProc conv_sproc,
    XtLoseSelectionIncrProc lose_sproc,
    XtSelectionDoneIncrProc done_sproc,
    XtCancelConvertSelectionProc cncl_sproc,
    XtPointer data,
    OlDnDTransactionStateCallback tstate_cb
);
```

DESCRIPTION

The OlDnDOwnSelectionIncremental function acquires the *select* ownership.

Except for the additional parameter *tstate_cb*, this function is semantically identical the the Xt function XtOwnSelectionIncremental.

RETURN VALUES

If the specified widget, *wid*, successfully becomes the selection owner, **TRUE** is returned. Otherwise, **FALSE** is returned.

SEE ALSO

OlDnDAllocTransientAtom(3DnD), OlDnDDisownSelection(3DnD), OlDnDGetCurrentSelectionsForWidget(3DnD), OlDnDOwnSelection(3DnD)

OlDnDQueryDropSiteInfo (3DnD)

NAME

OlDnDQueryDropSiteInfo – get drop site information

SYNOPSIS

```
#include <DnD/OlDnDVCX.h>

Boolean OlDnDQueryDropSiteInfo(
    OlDnDDropSiteID dsiteid,
    Widget *wid,
    Window *win,
    OlDnDSitePreviewHints *prev_hint,
    OlDnDSiteRectPtr *site_rect,
    unsigned int *num_rects,
    Boolean *on_int
);
```

DESCRIPTION

The **OlDnDQueryDropSiteInfo** function gets information about a drop site *dsiteid*.

The function parameters are

wid	the widget associated with the owner of the drop site
win	the variable type **Window** returning the ID of the window owner of the drop site. This is the windowed ancestor ID for gadgets. If NULL, no query will be made for window ID.
prev_hint	the current hints for the drop site. If NULL, no query will be made for current hints.
site_rect	the array containing the current geometry of the drop site. If NULL, no query will be made for current geometry. Callers must use **XtFree** to free memory used by the array when it is no longer needed.
num_rects	the number of **OlDnDSiteRect** structures specified for the drop site. If *site_rect* is non-NULL, *num_rects* must be non-NULL.
on_int	specifies whether the DSDM should contain this drop site information

RETURN VALUES

The function returns **TRUE** if the query was successful. Otherwise, it returns **FALSE**.

SEE ALSO

OlDnDChangeDropSitePreviewHints(3DnD), OlDnDDestroyDropSite(3DnD),
OlDnDGetWidgetOfDropSite(3DnD), OlDnDGetWindowOfDropSite(3DnD),
OlDnDGetDropSitesOfWidget(3DnD), OlDnDGetDropSitesOfWindow(3DnD),
OlDnDRegisterWidgetDropSite(3DnD),
OlDnDRegisterWindowDropSite(3DnD), OlDnDUpdateDropSiteGeometry(3DnD)

NAME

OlDnDRegisterDDI – register the Desktop drag-and-drop

SYNOPSIS

```
#include <DnD/OlDnDVCX.h>

void OlDnDRegisterDDI(
    Widget wid,
    OlDnDSitePreviewHints preview_hints,
    OlDnDTriggerMessageNotifyProc tm_proc,
    OlDnDPreviewMessageNotifyProc pm_proc,
    Boolean on_interest,
    XtPointer data
);
```

DESCRIPTION

The OlDnDRegisterDDI procedure registers the Desktop drag-and-drop from desktop applications, where

> *on_interest*   is a flag which activates or inactivates the existence of a drop site. The drop sites are made active if *on_interest* is set to **TRUE** otherwise the drop sites are made inactive. Active drop sites respond to drops. Inactive drop sites do not respond to drops.

> *data*   this is a user defined parameter which is passed to the *tm_proc* and *pm_proc* procedures when they are called.

This procedure assumes that the whole window can take the drop and the widget/window does not overlap with any sibling widget/window. It is not necessary to realize *wid* when invoking this routine. However, *wid* must be realized before using OlDnDGetDropSitesOfWidget to obtain *dsiteid*. The registration is automatically removed when *wid* is destroyed.

SEE ALSO

OlDnDChangeDropSitePreviewHints(3DnD),
OlDnDGetDropSitesOfWidget(3DnD), OlDnDRegisterWidgetDropSite(3DnD),
OlDnDSetDropSiteInterest(3DnD)

OlDnDRegisterDragKeyProc (3DnD)

NAME
OlDnDRegisterDragKeyProc – register a OlDnDDragKeyProc procedure

SYNOPSIS
```
#include <DnD/OlDnDVCX.h>

void OlDnDRegisterDragKeyProc(OlDnDDragKeyProc drag_key_proc);
```

DESCRIPTION
The OlDnDRegisterDragKeyProc function registers a OlDnDDragKeyProc function. This function is called in a drag-and-drop operation when a KeyPress event is generated.

To unregister OlDnDDragKeyProc, simply pass NULL to the procedure.

Note that this routine is meant for Xt Intrinsics based toolkits other than MooLIT. For MooLIT users, a default OlDnDDragKeyProc is used and this call will be made automatically in OlToolkitInitialize.

The *drag_key_proc* function handles the mouseless drag-and-drop, where OlDnDDragKeyProc is defined as:

```
typedef OlDnDDragKeyStatus (*OlDnDDragKeyProc)(
    Widget wid,        /* drag-and-drop initiating widget */
    XEvent *xevent     /* KeyPress event */
);
```

RETURN VALUES
The return value is an **enum** which includes the following members:

OlDnDCanceled
> The operation is aborted. In MooLIT, this means that **OL_CANCEL** is pressed.

OlDnDDropped
> The operation is completed. In MooLIT, this means that **OL_DROP** is pressed.

OlDnDStillDragging
> The operation is in progress.

SEE ALSO
OlDnDGrabDragCursor(3DnD), OlDnDUngrabDragCursor(3DnD), OlToolkitInitialize(3Olit)

NAME

OlDnDRegisterWidgetDropSite – create a widget associated drop site

SYNOPSIS

```
#include <DnD/OlDnDVCX.h>

OlDnDDropSiteID OlDnDRegisterWidgetDropSite(
    Widget wid,
    OlDnDSitePreviewHints prev_hint,
    OlDnDSiteRectPtr site_rect,
    unsigned int num_site,
    OlDnDTriggerMessageNotifyProc tmn_proc,
    OlDnDPreviewMessageNotifyProc pmn_proc,
    Boolean on_int,
    XtPointer data
);
```

DESCRIPTION

The **OlDnDRegisterWidgetDropSite** function creates a drop site associated with *wid*. A widget must have a window associated with it before you can create the drop site. Gadgets use their windowed ancestor's window in association with the registered drop site.

The parameters are

wid	the widget associated with the owner of the drop site
prev_hint	the current hints for the drop site
site_rect	the array containing the current geometry of the drop site, where

typedef XRectangle OlDnDSiteRect, *OlDnDSiteRectPtr;

num_site	the number of **OlDnDSiteRect** structures specified for the drop site
tmn_proc	trigger message notify procedure
pmn_proc	preview message notify procedure
on_int	specifies whether DSDM should contain the drop site information
data	the user data passed to both *tmn_proc* and *pmn_proc* when they are invoked

Drop sites are automatically destroyed when the owning widget dies.

SEE ALSO

OlDnDChangeDropSitePreviewHints(3DnD),
OlDnDDeliverPreviewMessage(3DnD), OlDnDDeliverTriggerMessage(3DnD),
OlDnDDestroyDropSite(3DnD), OlDnDGetWidgetOfDropSite(3DnD),
OlDnDGetWindowOfDropSite(3DnD), OlDnDGetDropSitesOfWidget(3DnD),
OlDnDGetDropSitesOfWindow(3DnD), OlDnDQueryDropSiteInfo(3DnD),
OlDnDRegisterWindowDropSite(3DnD), OlDnDUpdateDropSiteGeometry(3DnD)

OlDnDRegisterWindowDropSite (3DnD)

NAME

OlDnDRegisterWindowDropSite – create a window associated drop site

SYNOPSIS

`#include <DnD/OlDnDVCX.h>`

```
OlDnDDropSiteID OlDnDRegisterWindowDropSite(
    Display *disp,
    Window win,
    OlDnDSitePreviewHints prev_hint,
    OlDnDSiteRectPtr site_rect,
    unsigned int num_site,
    OlDnDTriggerMessageNotifyProc tmn_proc,
    OlDnDPreviewMessageNotifyProc pmn_proc,
    Boolean on_int,
    XtPointer data
);
```

DESCRIPTION

The `OlDnDRegisterWindowDropSite` function creates a drop site associated with *win* [see `OlDnDRegisterWidgetDropSite`(3DnD)].

Drop sites are automatically destroyed when the owning window dies.

NOTES

The drop site created is associated with an X window. This is useful for toolkit applications that mix raw X windows with widgets.

SEE ALSO

`OlDnDChangeDropSitePreviewHints`(3DnD),
`OlDnDDeliverPreviewMessage`(3DnD), `OlDnDDeliverTriggerMessage`(3DnD),
`OlDnDDestroyDropSite`(3DnD), `OlDnDGetWidgetOfDropSite`(3DnD),
`OlDnDGetWindowOfDropSite`(3DnD), `OlDnDGetDropSitesOfWidget`(3DnD),
`OlDnDGetDropSitesOfWindow`(3DnD), `OlDnDQueryDropSiteInfo`(3DnD),
`OlDnDRegisterWidgetDropSite`(3DnD), `OlDnDUpdateDropSiteGeometry`(3DnD)

NAME

OlDnDSendTriggerMessage – simulate a Desktop drag-and-drop trigger message

SYNOPSIS

```
#include <DnD/OlDnDVCX.h>

Boolean OlDnDSendTriggerMessage(
    Widget wid,
    Window root,
    Window dst_win,
    Atom     select,
    OlDnDTriggerOperation op,
    Time     time
);
```

DESCRIPTION

The **OlDnDSendTriggerMessage** function simulates a Desktop drag-and-drop trigger message, where:

wid	is the drop site owner widget
root	is the root window ID
dst_win	is the destination window ID
select	is the selection atom used to transfer the data
op	is the trigger operation used (either **OlDnDTriggerCopyOp** or **OlDnDTriggerMoveOp**)
time	is the current server time

This trigger message is forwarded to *dst_win* if the Desktop drag-and-drop has been registered by *dst_win*. The (**-1, -1**) coordinates are used in the trigger message to indicate this is a simulated trigger message because Desktop drag-and-drop protocol uses root window coordinates.

RETURN VALUES

This function returns **TRUE** if it can dispatch a trigger message to *dst_win*. Otherwise it returns **FALSE**.

SEE ALSO

OlDnDDeliverTriggerMessage(3DnD)

OlDnDSetDropSiteInterest (3DnD)

NAME

OlDnDSetDropSiteInterest – activate or inactivate a drop site

SYNOPSIS

#include <DnD/OlDnDVCX.h>

void OlDnDSetDropSiteInterest(OlDnDDropSiteID *dsiteid*, Boolean *int_flag*);

DESCRIPTION

The **OlDnDSetDropSiteInterest** function activates or inactivates a drop site, *dsiteid*, by exporting its existence. Active drop sites respond to drops, inactive ones do not respond.

Setting *int_flag* to **TRUE** or **FALSE** activates or deactivates the drop site, respectively.

OlDnDDropSiteId is an opaque pointer with the following definition:

typedef oldnd_drop_site OlDnDDropSiteID;

SEE ALSO

OlDnDRegisterWidgetDropSite(3DnD), **OlDnDRegisterWindowDropSite**(3DnD)

OlDnDSetInterestInWidgetHier (3DnD)

NAME

    `OlDnDSetInterestInWidgetHier` – activate or inactivate widgets drop sites

SYNOPSIS

    `#include <DnD/OlDnDVCX.h>`

    `void OlDnDSetInterestInWidgetHier(Widget` *wid*`, Boolean` *int_flag*`);`

DESCRIPTION

    The `OlDnDSetInterestInWidgetHier` function activates or inactivates all drop sites associated with *wid*.

    Setting *int_flag* to **TRUE** or **FALSE** activates or deactivates the drop sites, respectively.

SEE ALSO

    `OlDnDSetDropSiteInterest`(3DnD)

OlDnDTrackDragCursor (3DnD)

NAME

`OlDnDTrackDragCursor` – track drag cursor from pointer and keyboard devices

SYNOPSIS

```
#include <DnD/OlDnDVCX.h>

OlDnDDropStatus OlDnDTrackDragCursor(
    Widget wid,
    OlDnDAnimateCursorsPtr cursors,
    OlDnDDestinationInfoPtr dst_info,
    OlDnDDragDropInfoPtr root_info
);
```

DESCRIPTION

The `OlDnDTrackDragCursor` function tracks a drag cursor from a pointer and keyboard devices in the drag-and-drop operation, where:

 wid is the drag-and-drop operation initiating widget

 cursors are the two cursors used in the drag-and-drop operation. The `OlDnDAnimateCursorsPtr` is a pointer to a `OlDnDAnimateCursors` structure that includes the following members:

```
Cursor yes_cursor; /* dragged object over valid area */
Cursor no_cursor;  /* ... over an invalid area */
```

where a valid area means a potential drop site has registered the Desktop drag-and-drop.

The drag-and-drop user feedback is disabled if the value is NULL.

 dst_info contains the destination window ID and location of the drop that is relative to the destination window. The `OlDnDDestinationInfoPtr` is a pointer to a `OlDnDDestinationInfo` structure that includes the following members:

```
Window wind;   /* the destination window ID */
Position x;    /* location of drop relative to wind */
Position y;    /* location of drop relative to wind */
```

 root_info is the pointer to the structure containing the location of the drop

This routine will first grab mouse pointer and then the keyboard if a `OlDnDDragKeyProc` is registered and will relinquish the active pointer and keyboard grabs at end. This routine will register a default `OlDnDPreviewAnimateCallbackProc` procedure if *cursors* is not NULL.

Note that the contents of *dst_info* and *root_info* are not guaranteed if the return status is `OlDnDDropCanceled`.

RETURN VALUES

The return value, `OlDnDDropStatus`, is an **enum** which includes the following members:

 `OlDnDDropSucceeded`
    shows that the destination client has registered the Desktop drag-and-drop

OlDnDDropFailed
> not registered

OlDnDCanceled
> shows the operation was aborted. In MooLIT, this means **OL_CANCEL** was pressed.

SEE ALSO

OlDnDDragAndDrop(3DnD), OlDnDGrabDragCursor(3DnD),
OlDnDUngrabDragCursor(3DnD), OlDnDRegisterDragKeyProc(3DnD)

OlDnDUngrabDragCursor (3DnD)

NAME

    `OlDnDUngrabDragCursor` – relinquish pointer and keyboard grabs

SYNOPSIS

    `#include <DnD/OlDnDVCX.h>`

    `void OlDnDUngrabDragCursor(Widget` *wid*`);`

DESCRIPTION

    The `OlDnDUngrabDragCursor` function relinquishs the active pointer and keyboard grabs initiated by `OlDnDGrabDragCursor` for *wid*, the drag-and-drop initiating widget. This procedure simply ungrabs the pointer and the keyboard if a `OlDnD-DragKeyProc` function is registered.

SEE ALSO

    `OlDnDGrabDragCursor`(3DnD), `OlDnDRegisterDragKeyProc`(3DnD),
    `OlDnDTrackDragCursor`(3DnD)

OlDnDUpdateDropSiteGeometry (3DnD)

NAME

OlDnDUpdateDropSiteGeometry – change geometry of a drop site

SYNOPSIS

```
#include <DnD/OlDnDVCX.h>

Boolean OlDnDUpdateDropSiteGeometry(
    OlDnDDropSiteID dsiteid,
    OlDnDSiteRectPtr site_rect,
    unsigned int num_site
);
```

DESCRIPTION

The OlDnDUpdateDropSiteGeometry function changes the geometry of a drop site, *dsiteid*, to *site_rect*.

These changes are caused by change in the geometry of the owning widget or window.

NOTES

To reduce client-server traffic, changes in the owning window are not automatically tracked. The creator of the drop site is responsible for maintaining the geometry of the site to reflect any changes in the owner.

SEE ALSO

OlDnDRegisterWidgetDropSite(3DnD), OlDnDRegisterWindowDropSite(3DnD)

OlDnDVCXInitialize (3DnD)

NAME

OlDnDVCXInitialize – attach Desktop drag and drop class extension record to vendor class record

SYNOPSIS

```
#include <DnD/OlDnDVCX.h>
```

```
void OlDnDVCXInitialize(void);
```

DESCRIPTION

The OlDnDVCXInitialize procedure is used to attach Desktop drag-and-drop class extension record to the *vendor* class record (see "Shell Resources" in the Introduction). This procedure has to be called before calling any Xt functions.

Note that this routine is meant for Xt Intrinsics based toolkits other than MooLIT. For MooLIT users, this call will be made automatically in **OlToolkitInitialize**.

SEE ALSO

OlToolkitInitialize(3Olit)

NAME

OlDnDWidgetConfiguredInHier – find drop site clipping regions

SYNOPSIS

`#include <DnD/OlDnDVCX.h>`

`void OlDnDWidgetConfiguredInHier(Widget` *wid*`);`

DESCRIPTION

The `OlDnDWidgetConfiguredInHier` function recalculates the clipping region(s) of any drop sites under the configuring widget, *wid*, in the widget hierarchy. This is particularly useful in developing composite widgets.

Because drop sites are separate from the servers window hierarchy, drop site owners must attempt to maintain their drop sites clipped to the visible regions. These visible regions are defined by the server window hierarchy of the widget hierarchy containing the drop sites.

In order to achieve this clipping, widgets and their subclasses must inform the drag and drop system that they have configured some widgets in their subtree, as a result of a call to that **Composite** widgets **ChangeManaged** or **GeometryManager** methods, hence Potentially changing the visible regions of drop sites in that subtree.

In order to eliminate multiple recalculations of drop site clipping regions due to configures propagation down a widget hierarchy a mechanism exists to suppress such multiple calculations, developers should take advantage of this in order to optimize for performance.

EXAMPLES

This is an example of a simple geometry_manager:

```
static XtGeometryResult
GeometryManager()
Widget       requestor;
XtWidgetGeometry *request,
XtWidgetGeometry *reply);
     {
CompositeWidget comp = requestor->core.parent;

Widget       vendor = comp;
Arg   args[2];
Boolean      configured_others = False;

XtSetArg(args[0], XtNconfiguringWidget, (XtPointer)requestor);
XtSetArg(args[1], XtNdisableDSClipping, True);

while(!XtIsVendorShell(w))vendor = vendor->core.parent;
XtSetValues(vendor, args, XtNumber(args));
/* disable clipping in my subtree while I configure */

/* consider the geometry request received and then maybe
 * configure one or more of the managed set and/or perhaps
 * request that my parent reconfigure me as a result of the
 * request being made by the requestor widget.
```

OlDnDWidgetConfiguredInHier(3DnD)

```
        *
        * set configured_others True if the Composite made a successful
        * geometry request to its parent, or it is moved siblings of
        * the requestor .....
        */

        if ((request->request_mode & CWX) == CWX)
           requestor->core.x = request->x;

        if ((request->request_mode & CWY) == CWY)
           requestor->core.y = request->y;

        if ((request->request_mode & CWWidth) == CWWidth)
           requestor->core.width = request->width;

        if ((request->request_mode & CWHeight) == CWHeight)
           requestor->core.height = request->height;

           XtSetArg(args[1], XtNdisableDSClipping, False);
           XtSetValues(vendor, args, XtNumber(args));
        /* enable clipping again */

        /* inform the drag and drop system to clip any drop sites in
         * the widget hierarchy under the configuring widget
        */

        if (configured_others)
           OlDnDWidgetConfiguredInHier((Widget)comp);
        else
           OlDnDWidgetConfiguredInHier(requestor);
        return XtGeometryYes;
}
```

SEE ALSO

OlDnDUpdateDropSiteGeometry(3DnD)

NAME

    `OlDrawImageString` – draw EUC encoded text

SYNOPSIS

    `int OlDrawImageString(Display *display, Drawable drawable,`
        `OlFontList *fontlist, GC gc, int x, int y,`
        `unsigned char *string, int len);`

DESCRIPTION

    `OlDrawImageString` is a general purpose text drawing utility to draw an internationalized string which may be composed of characters from different code sets. It replaces the Xlib function `XDrawImageString`. The argument list is the same as `XDrawImageString` with one additional argument called *fontlist*. The *fontlist* specifies a list of `XFontStructs`. The string is composed of several segments in which characters within a segment belong to the same code set. Each string segment is drawn using the appropriate `XFontStruct` from the *fontlist*. Although, the font information in the *gc* is not used by the function, the *gc* should contain font information for default fonts or ASCII fonts to preserve backward compatibility and to optimize drawing for LATIN-1 characters.

NOTES

    The *len* argument specifies the length of *string* in bytes (not characters) as returned by `strlen`.

    This function assumes the string passed to it is a multibyte string.

    This function will update the font stored in the *gc* argument and will not restore the font before returning. If a client relies on a particular font being present in a *gc*, it must restore the font in the *gc* after calling `OlDrawImageString`.

SEE ALSO

    `OlDrawString`(3Olit), `OlGetNextStrSegment`(3Olit)

OlDrawString (3Olit)

NAME

`OlDrawString` – draw EUC encoded text

SYNOPSIS

```
int OlDrawString(Display *display, Drawable drawable,
     OlFontList *fontlist, GC gc, int x, int y,
     unsigned char *string, int len);
```

DESCRIPTION

`OlDrawString` is a general purpose text drawing utility to draw an internationalized string which may be composed of characters from different code sets. It replaces the Xlib function **XDrawString**. The argument list is the same as **XDrawString** with one additional argument called *fontlist*. The *fontlist* specifies a list of **XFontStructs**. The string is composed of several segments in which characters in a segment belong to the same code set. Each string segment is drawn using the appropriate **XFontStruct** from the *fontlist*. Although, the font information in *gc* is not used by the function, *gc* should contain font information for default fonts or ASCII fonts to preserve backward compatibility and to optimize drawing for LAT!N-1 characters.

NOTES

The *len* argument specifies the length of *string* in bytes (not characters) as returned by **rstrlen**.

This function assumes that the string passed to it is a multibyte string and not a wide character.

This function will update the font stored in the *gc* argument and will not restore the font before returning. If a client relies on a particular font being present in a *gc*, it must restore the font in the *gc* after calling **OlDrawString**.

SEE ALSO

`OlDrawString`(3Olit), `OlGetNextStrSegment`(3Olit)

NAME

OlEucToCt – return a null-terminated string

SYNOPSIS

int OlEucToCt(XctString *eucstr,* XctString *ctstr,* int *ct_len,*
OlFontList **fontl*);

DESCRIPTION

Given a null-terminated EUC encoded string in the argument *eucstr,* this function returns a semantically equivalent null-terminated string in the argument *ctstr* that conforms to the compound text syntax. Equivalence implies that the characters in both strings are the same and are stored in the same logical order. The code set scheme syntax is the only difference in the two strings. OlEucToCt will retrieve necessary EUC code set mapping information from the *fontl* structure.

The memory for storing the *ctstr* string must be pre-allocated prior to the function call. Doing this, rather than making the function allocate the memory every time it is called, will result in a better performance, because pre-allocated memory could be easily re-used in case of repeated calls to OlEucToCt. The *ct_len* argument specifies the length of the *ctstr* and is required to prevent buffer overflow. If the number of bytes indicated by ct_len is too small to store the converted string, -1 is returned.

This function returns the length, in bytes (not counting the terminating null character), of the Compound Text encoded string on success, -1 on failure.

SEE ALSO

OlCtToEuc(3Olit)

OlFetchMneOrAccOwner (3Olit)

NAME

OlFetchMneOrAccOwner – get the owner of a mnemonic or accelerator key

SYNOPSIS

```
#include <Xol/OpenLook.h>
```

Widget OlFetchMneOrAccOwner(Widget *widget*, OlVirtualEvent *ve*);

DESCRIPTION

The function, **OlFetchMneOrAccOwner**, finds the owner of the mnemonic key or accelerator key based on *ve*, where

> *widget* is the owner of the virtual event
>
> *ve*   is the virtual event

If an owner is found, two fields, **virtual_name** and **item_index**, will be changed in *ve*. Where necessary, applications should save these values before invoking **OlFetchMneOrAccOwner**.

> **virtual_name**   is set to **OL_MNEMONICKEY** or **OL_ACCELERATORKEY**
>
> **item_index**   shows which sub-item (for example, flat widgets) owns the mnemonic or accelerator key

RETURN VALUE

On success, **OlFetchMneOrAccOwner** returns the owner ID.

On failure, **OlFetchMneOrAccOwner** returns NULL.

NAME

OlFindHelpFile – find the locale-specific help file

SYNOPSIS

```
#include <Xol/OpenLook.h>

String OlFindHelpFile(
        Widget widget,      /* for getting display info */
        char *filename      /* file to retrieve          */
);
```

DESCRIPTION

The OlFindHelpFile procedure is used to retrieve the full name of the passed in base filename in the current locale. It accesses the application's help directory resource to create the full name. The help directory resource is created using the XFILESEARCHPATH environment variable.

OlFlatGetValues (3Olit)

NAME

OlFlatGetValues – get the values associated with a Flat widget

SYNOPSIS

```
#include <Xol/OpenLook.h>
#include <Xol/Flat.h>

int OlFlatGetValues(Widget fwidget, Cardinal item_index, ArgList args,
    Cardinal num_args);
```

DESCRIPTION

The OlFlatGetValues function gets the values associated with a Flat widget, where

fwidget	is the ID of the widget
item_index	is the item to be queryed
args	is the query resources
num_args	is the number of query resources

SEE ALSO

FlatCheckBox(3Olit), FlatExclusives(3Olit), FlatList(3Olit),
FlatNonexclusives(3Olit), Flattened_Widgets(3Olit), OlFlatSetValues(3Olit)

NAME

    `OlFlatSetValues` – set the values associated with a Flat widget

SYNOPSIS

    `#include <Xol/OpenLook.h>`
    `#include <Xol/Flat.h>`

    `int OlFlatSetValues(Widget` *fwidget*`, Cardinal` *item_index*`, ArgList` *args*`,`
        `Cardinal` *num_args*`);`

DESCRIPTION

    The `OlFlatSetValues` function sets the values associated with a Flat widget, where

fwidget	is the ID of the widget
item_index	is the item to be modified
args	is the new resources
num_args	is the number of new resources

SEE ALSO

    `FlatCheckBox`(3Olit), `FlatExclusives`(3Olit), `FlatList`(3Olit),
    `FlatNonexclusives`(3Olit), `Flattened_Widgets`(3Olit), `OlFlatGetValues`(3Olit)

OlGet50PercentGrey (3Olit)

NAME

    `OlGet50PercentGrey` – get ID of a 50 percent grey pixmap

SYNOPSIS

    `#include <Xol/OlCursors.h>`
    `#include <Xol/OpenLook.h>`

    `Pixmap OlGet50PercentGrey(Screen *screen);`

DESCRIPTION

    The `OlGet50PercentGrey` function is used to retrieve the ID of a 50 percent grey Pixmap for *screen*.

RETURN VALUE

    The Pixmap ID is returned.

NAME

OlGet75PercentGrey – get ID of a 75 percent grey pixmap

SYNOPSIS

```
#include <Xol/OlCursors.h>
#include <Xol/OpenLook.h>
```

Pixmap OlGet75PercentGrey(Screen *screen);

DESCRIPTION

The OlGet75PercentGrey function is used to retrieve the ID of a 75 percent grey Pixmap for *screen*.

RETURN VALUE

The Pixmap ID is returned.

OlGetApplicationValues (3Olit)

NAME

    `OlGetApplicationValues` – retrieve application resources

SYNOPSIS

    `#include <Xol/OpenLook.h>`

    ```
void OlGetApplicationValues(
    Widget widget,          /* for getting display info */
    ArgList args,           /* args to query             */
    Cardinal num_args       /* number of args            */
);
```

DESCRIPTION

    The `OlGetApplicationValues` procedure is used to retrieve the application resources that are accessible from the OPEN LOOK toolkit. The semantics is similar to the `XtGetValues` call.

    Application resources are resources that all OPEN LOOK applications have in common. Their values are updated dynamically by changing preferences in the WorkSpace Manager's property sheets. Therefore, it's recommended that an application query the values each time it needs them.

SEE ALSO

    Application Resources in the "Introduction"

NAME

OlGetBusyCursor – get Busy Cursor ID

SYNOPSIS

```
#include <Xol/OlCursors.h>
#include <Xol/OpenLook.h>

Cursor OlGetBusyCursor(Widget x);
```

DESCRIPTION

The **OlGetBusyCursor** macro is equivalent to

```
Cursor GetOlBusyCursor(XtScreenOfObject(Widget x));
```

RETURN VALUES

In the OPEN LOOK look and feel, **OlGetBusyCursor** returns a Cursor ID for widget x which complies with the specification of the Busy cursor.

In the Motif look and feel, **OlGetBusyCursor** returns the **XC_watch** cursor.

SEE ALSO

GetOlDuplicateCursor(3Olit), GetOlMoveCursor(3Olit), GetOlPanCursor(3Olit), GetOlQuestionCursor(3Olit), GetOlStandardCursor(3Olit), GetOlTargetCursor(3Olit), OlGetDuplicateCursor(3Olit), OlGetMoveCursor(3Olit), OlGetPanCursor(3Olit), OlGetQuestionCursor(3Olit), OlGetStandardCursor(3Olit), OlGetTargetCursor(3Olit)

OlGetCurrentFocusWidget (3Olit)

NAME

OlGetCurrentFocusWidget – get widget with current focus

SYNOPSIS

```
#include <Xol/OpenLook.h>

Widget OlGetCurrentFocusWidget(Widget wid);
```

DESCRIPTION

The OlGetCurrentFocusWidget function returns the ID of the widget which currently has focus in the window group of the specified widget.

RETURN VALUES

On success, OlGetCurrentFocusWidget returns the widget ID. If no widget in the window group has focus, it returns NULL.

SEE ALSO

Flattened_Widget_Utilities(3Olit), OlCallAcceptFocus(3Olit), OlCanAcceptFocus(3Olit), OlHasFocus(3Olit), OlMoveFocus(3Olit), OlSetInputFocus(3Olit)

NAME

OlGetDuplicateCursor – get Duplicate Cursor ID

SYNOPSIS

```
#include <Xol/OlCursors.h>
#include <Xol/OpenLook.h>

Cursor OlGetDuplicateCursor(Widget x);
```

DESCRIPTION

The OlGetDuplicateCursor macro is equivalent to

```
Cursor GetOlDuplicateCursor(XtScreenOfObject(Widget x));
```

RETURN VALUES

OlGetDuplicateCursor returns the Cursor ID of widget x which complies with the specification of the Duplicate cursor, in either the OPEN LOOK or Motif look and feel,

SEE ALSO

GetOlBusyCursor(3Olit), GetOlMoveCursor(3Olit), GetOlPanCursor(3Olit), GetOlQuestionCursor(3Olit), GetOlStandardCursor(3Olit), GetOlTargetCursor(3Olit), OlGetBusyCursor(3Olit), OlGetMoveCursor(3Olit), OlGetPanCursor(3Olit), OlGetQuestionCursor(3Olit), OlGetStandardCursor(3Olit), OlGetTargetCursor(3Olit)

OlGetGui (3Olit)

NAME

       OlGetGui – get current look and feel

SYNOPSIS

       `#include <Xol/OpenLook.h>`

       `OlDefine OlGetGui(void);`

DESCRIPTION

       The `OlGetGui` function returns the GUI mode. `OlToolkitInitialize` must be called before `OlGetGui`.

RETURN VALUES

       `OlGetGui` returns `OL_OPENLOOK_GUI` or `OL_MOTIF_GUI`.

SEE ALSO

       `OlSetGui`(3Olit), `OlToolkitInitialize`(3Olit)

NAME

    `OlGetIcValues` – read Input Context (IC) attributes

SYNOPSIS

    `#include <Xol/OpenLook.h>`

    `String OlGetIcValues(OlIc *ic, OlIcValues *icvalues);`

DESCRIPTION

    This function is used for reading IC attributes. *icvalues* must point to a location where the values will be stored. The function returns NULL if no error occurs; otherwise it returns the name of the first argument that could not be obtained. The end of the *icvalues* list must be indicated by a NULL value for the attribute name. This function will allocate memory to store the values and it is the caller's responsibility to free the storage.

SEE ALSO

    `OlCreateIc`(3Olit), `OlDestroyIc`(3Olit), `OlIcValues`(4), `OlImOfIc`(3Olit), `OlSetIcFocus`(3Olit), `OlSetIcValues`(3Olit), `OlUnSetIcFocus`(3Olit)

OlGetImValues (3Olit)

NAME

OlGetImValues – return list of IM supported properties and features

SYNOPSIS

#include <Xol/OpenLook.h>

void OlGetImValues(OlIm *im, OlImValues *imvalues);

DESCRIPTION

This function returns a list of properties and features supported by the IM. The end of the list is indicated by a NULL value for the attribute name in the *imvalues* list. Only one attribute, **XtNQueryInputStyle**, is defined at this time It is used to query input styles supported by the IM.

A client should always query the IM to find out what styles are supported, to determine if they match the styles that the clients intend to support. If there are no matches, the client should either chose another IM or terminate the execution.

The *imvalues* **attr_value** field must be a pointer to the **OlImStyles** structure, which contains a count and an array of supported styles. The *imvalues* **attr_name** field should contain the string **XtNQueryInputStyle**. Each element in that array is a bitmask in which IM indicates its requirements should a particular style to be selected.

Clients are responsible for freeing **OlImStyles** using **XFree**.

```
#define OlImNeedNothing        000
#define OlImPreEditArea        001
#define OlImPreEditCallbacks   002
#define OlImPreEditPosition    004
#define OlImStatusArea         010
#define OlImStatusCallbacks    020
#define OlImFocusTracks        040

typedef unsigned short OlImStyle;
```

The structure **OlImStyles** includes the following members:

```
short styles_count; OlImStyle        *supported_styles;
```

NOTES

Not all style combinations are allowed.

SEE ALSO

OlImValues(4), OlOpenIm(3Olit)

NAME

OlGetMoveCursor – get Move Cursor ID

SYNOPSIS

```
#include <Xol/OlCursors.h>
#include <Xol/OpenLook.h>

Cursor OlGetMoveCursor(Widget x);
```

DESCRIPTION

The OlGetMoveCursor macro is equivalent to

```
Cursor GetOlMoveCursor(XtScreenOfObject(Widget x));
```

RETURN VALUES

In the OPEN LOOK look and feel, OlGetMoveCursor returns the Cursor ID for widget *x* which complies with the specification of the Move cursor.

In the Motif look and feel, OlGetMoveCursor returns XC_fleur.

SEE ALSO

GetOlBusyCursor(3Olit), GetOlDuplicateCursor(3Olit), GetOlPanCursor(3Olit), GetOlQuestionCursor(3Olit), GetOlStandardCursor(3Olit), GetOlTargetCursor(3Olit), OlGetBusyCursor(3Olit), OlGetDuplicateCursor(3Olit), OlGetPanCursor(3Olit), OlGetQuestionCursor(3Olit), OlGetStandardCursor(3Olit), OlGetTargetCursor(3Olit)

OlGetMessage (3Olit)

NAME

OlGetMessage – provide a localized or default message

SYNOPSIS

#include <Xol/OpenLook.h>

String OlGetMessage(Display *display, String *buf,
    int buf_size, String name, String type, String class,
    String default_msg, XrmDatabase database);

DESCRIPTION

OlGetMessage will get a unique localized message where the class of the message corresponds to the filename and the name and type of message map to a unique message in that **XrmDatabase** format file.

If a message is found and a buffer is supplied, the message is copied into the buffer and the pointer to this buffer returned.

If a message is found and a buffer is not supplied, the pointer returned is the Xt pointer to that message and should not be freed.

If a message is not found and a buffer is supplied, the pointer to that buffer is returned, with the default message copied into it.

If a message is not found and a buffer is not supplied, the pointer returned is a toolkit pointer to the default message and should not be freed.

SEE ALSO

Error(3Olit), OlCloseDatabase(3Olit), OlOpenDatabase(3Olit)

NAME

OlGetNextStrSegment – obtain string segments of same code set characters

SYNOPSIS

```
#include <Xol/OpenLook.h>

int OlGetNextStrSegment(FontList *fontlist, OlStrSegment *segment,
    unsigned char **str, int *len);
```

DESCRIPTION

This function identifies the code set to which the first character (not byte) of the string belongs and copies all subsequent contiguous characters in this string that belong to the same code set into the *segment* field of the **OlStrSegment** structure, until a character belonging to another code set is identified. The auxiliary characters such as single shift two and single shift three (SS2 and SS3) that identify the code set of a character in the EUC scheme are not copied. Sufficient space to store a string segment into the *segment* field must be allocated by the caller. The *fontlist* contains information about the code sets being used. *str* points to the original string that must be parsed; this argument is updated to point to the first character belonging to a different code set. *len* points to an integer for length (in bytes) of the *str*. It is also modified to reflect the length of the remaining part of the string.

The structure **OlStrSegement** includes the following members:

```
unsigned short  code_set;    /* EUC code set number */
int             len;         /* length of the string segment */
unsigned char   *str;        /* string segment */
```

RETURN VALUES

The function returns −1 if an error occurs, 0 otherwise.

EXAMPLES

The following example shows how one could obtain string segments from a *string* using this function.

```
char *str;    /*a string is parsed into segment */
int  len;     /*holds limited length of string  */
OlFontList *fontlist;  /*see CvtOlGetFontGroupToFontStringList */
OlStrSegment *parse;    /* Large enough must have been pre-allocated */
while (len > 0)
   {
     OlGetNextStrSegment (fontlist, parse, &str, &len)
     . . .
     do something useful with parse -> str - it points to string
segment
     }
```

SEE ALSO

OlCvtGetFontGroupToFontStringList(3Olit)

OlGetPanCursor (3Olit)

NAME

OlGetPanCursor – get Pan Cursor ID

SYNOPSIS

```
#include <Xol/OlCursors.h>
#include <Xol/OpenLook.h>
```

Cursor OlGetPanCursor(Widget x);

DESCRIPTION

The OlGetPanCursor macro is equivalent to

Cursor GetOlPanCursor(XtScreenOfObject(Widget x));

RETURN VALUES

OlGetPanCursor returns the Cursor ID for widget x which complies with the specification of the Pan cursor, in either Motif or OPEN LOOK look and feel.

SEE ALSO

GetOlBusyCursor(3Olit), GetOlMoveCursor(3Olit), GetOlPanCursor(3Olit), GetOlQuestionCursor(3Olit), GetOlStandardCursor(3Olit), GetOlTargetCursor(3Olit), OlGetBusyCursor(3Olit), OlGetMoveCursor(3Olit), OlGetPanCursor(3Olit), OlGetQuestionCursor(3Olit), OlGetStandardCursor(3Olit), OlGetTargetCursor(3Olit)

NAME

OlGetQuestionCursor – get Question Cursor ID

SYNOPSIS

```
#include <Xol/OlCursors.h>
#include <Xol/OpenLook.h>

Cursor OlGetQuestionCursor(Widget x);
```

DESCRIPTION

The OlGetQuestionCursor macro is equivalent to

```
Cursor GetOlQuestionCursor(XtScreenOfObject(Widget x));
```

RETURN VALUES

In the OPEN LOOK look and feel, OlGetQuestionCursor returns the Cursor ID for widget x which complies with the specification of the Question cursor.

In the Motif look and feel, OlGetQuestionCursor returns the XC_question_arrow cursor.

SEE ALSO

GetOlBusyCursor(3Olit), GetOlDuplicateCursor(3Olit), GetOlMoveCursor(3Olit), GetOlQuestionCursor(3Olit), GetOlStandardCursor(3Olit), GetOlTargetCursor(3Olit), OlGetBusyCursor(3Olit), OlGetDuplicateCursor(3Olit), OlGetMoveCursor(3Olit), OlGetQuestionCursor(3Olit), OlGetStandardCursor(3Olit), OlGetTargetCursor(3Olit)

OlGetStandardCursor (3Olit)

NAME

OlGetStandardCursor – get Standard Cursor ID

SYNOPSIS

```
#include <Xol/OlCursors.h>
#include <Xol/OpenLook.h>
```

Cursor OlGetStandardCursor(Widget *x*);

DESCRIPTION

The OlGetStandardCursor macro is equivalent to

Cursor GetOlStandardCursor(XtScreenOfObject(Widget *x*));

RETURN VALUES

In the OPEN LOOK look and feel, OlGetStandardCursor returns the Cursor ID for widget *x* which complies with the specification of the Standard cursor.

In the Motif look and feel, OlGetStandardCursor returns the XC_left_ptr cursor.

SEE ALSO

GetOlBusyCursor(3Olit), GetOlDuplicateCursor(3Olit), GetOlMoveCursor(3Olit), GetOlPanCursor(3Olit), GetOlQuestionCursor(3Olit), GetOlTargetCursor(3Olit)

NAME

OlGetTargetCursor – get Target Cursor ID

SYNOPSIS

```
#include <Xol/OlCursors.h>
#include <Xol/OpenLook.h>
```

Cursor OlGetTargetCursor(Widget *x*);

DESCRIPTION

The OlGetTargetCursor macro is equivalent to

Cursor GetOlTargetCursor(XtScreenOfObject(Widget *x*));

RETURN VALUES

In the OPEN LOOK look and feel, OlGetTargetCursor returns the Cursor ID for widget *x* which complies with the specification of the Target cursor.

In the Motif look and feel, OlGetTargetCursor returns the XC_crosshair cursor.

SEE ALSO

GetOlBusyCursor(3Olit), GetOlDuplicateCursor(3Olit), GetOlMoveCursor(3Olit), GetOlPanCursor(3Olit), GetOlQuestionCursor(3Olit), GetOlStandardCursor(3Olit), OlGetBusyCursor(3Olit), OlGetDuplicateCursor(3Olit), OlGetMoveCursor(3Olit), OlGetPanCursor(3Olit), OlGetQuestionCursor(3Olit), OlGetStandardCursor(3Olit)

OlGrabDragPointer (3Olit)

NAME

OlGrabDragPointer – grab the mouse pointer and keyboard

SYNOPSIS

`#include <Xol/OpenLook.h>`

`void OlGrabDragPointer(Widget` *w,* `Cursor` *cursor,* `Window` *window);*

DESCRIPTION

The **OlGrabDragPointer** procedure is used to effect an active grab of the mouse pointer and the keyboard, if necessary. This function is normally called after a mouse drag operation is experienced and prior to calling the **OlDragAndDrop** procedure [see **OlDnDGrabDragPointer**(3DnD)], which monitors a drag operation.

SEE ALSO

OlDragAndDrop(3Olit), OlUngrabDragPointer(3Olit)

NAME

OlHasFocus – check if a widget has input focus

SYNOPSIS

`#include <Xol/OpenLook.h>`

`Boolean OlHasFocus(Widget` *wid*`);`

DESCRIPTION

The `OlHasFocus` function simply calls `OlGetCurrentFocusWidget` and compares the result of that call to the supplied widget ID.

NOTES

`OlHasFocus` is obsolete. Use `OlGetCurrentFocusWidget`(3Olit).

SEE ALSO

`Flattened_Widget_Utilities`(3Olit), `OlCallAcceptFocus`(3Olit), `OlCanAcceptFocus`(3Olit), `OlGetCurrentFocusWidget`(3Olit), `OlMoveFocus`(3Olit), `OlSetInputFocus`(3Olit)

OlImOfIc (3Olit)

NAME

> OlImOfIc – get a pointer to OlIm

SYNOPSIS

> `#include <Xol/OpenLook.h>`
>
> `OlIm *OlImOfIc(OlIc *ic);`

DESCRIPTION

> The `OlImOfIc` gets a pointer to a specific `OlIm`.

RETURN VALUES

> On success, `OlImOfIc` returns a pointer to the `OlIm` structure associated with the specified Input Context.
>
> A NULL value is returned if an invalid *ic* is specified.

SEE ALSO

> OlCreateIc(3Olit)

NAME

OlLocaleOfIm – query locale for the Input Method

SYNOPSIS

```
#include <Xol/OpenLook.h>
```

String OlLocaleOfIm(OlIm *im);

DESCRIPTION

This function returns a locale name string under which the specified Input Method is running.

OlLookUpImString (3Olit)

NAME

`OlLookupImString` – internationalized version of Xlib `XLookupString`

SYNOPSIS

`#include <Xol/OpenLook.h>`

`int OlLookupImString(KeyEvent *event, OlIc *ic, String buffer_return,`
    `int buf_len, KeySym *keysym_return, OlImStatus *status_return);`

DESCRIPTION

This function is similar to Xlib function **XLookupString** except that it takes an extra *ic* argument and may or may not return any string for a key press event. Instead, it will return a composed character when one is available. If an existing program that uses **XLookupString** is modified to use **OlLookupImString**, the program should check for any string that has been returned by the function. The value returned in the *status_return* value indicates what has been returned in the other arguments. The return value is the length, in bytes, of the string returned in *buffer_return* if a string has been returned.

The **enum OlImStatus** has the following possible values:

XBufferOverflow
> means that the input string to be returned is too large for the supplied *buffer_return*. The required size is returned as the value of the function, and the contents of *buffer_return* and *keysym_return* are not modified. The client should call the function again with the same event and a buffer of adequate size in order to obtain the string.

XLookupNone
> means that no consistent input has been composed so far. The contents of *buffer_return* and *keysym_return* are not modified, and the function returns zero as a value.

XStringReturned
> means some input string has been composed. It is placed in *buffer_return* and the string length is returned as the value of the function. The string is encoded in the locale bound to the Input Context. The contents of *keysym_return* is not modified.

XLookupKeySym
> means a **KeySym** has been returned instead of a string. The **KeySym** is returned in *keysym_return*. The contents of *buffer_return* is not modified, and the function returns zero.

XLookupBoth
> means that both a **KeySym** and a string are returned, in *buffer_return* and *keysym_return* respectively.

It is not necessary for the Input Context passed as an argument to **OlLookupImString** to have focus. Input can be composed within this Input Context before it loses focus and that input is returned by the function even though it no longer has keyboard focus. This result is dependent on the IM implementation and may not be true in all cases.

SEE ALSO

OlDrawImString(3Olit)

OlLookupInputEvent (3Olit)

NAME

OlLookupInputEvent – translate an X event to an OPEN LOOK virtual event

SYNOPSIS

```
#include <Xol/OpenLook.h>
```

void OlLookupInputEvent(Widget *w*, XEvent *xevent*,
    OlVirtualEvent *virtual_event_ret*, XtPointer *db_flag*);

DESCRIPTION

The OlLookupInputEvent procedure is used to translate an X event to a Motif or OPEN LOOK virtual event. The X event (*xevent*) could be a KeyPress, ButtonPress, ButtonRelease, EnterNotify, LeaveNotify, or MotionNotify event. The procedure attempts to translate this event based on the setting of the Motif or OPEN LOOK defined dynamic databases.

The *virtual_event_ret* parameter is a pointer to an OlVirtualEventRec structure which includes the following members:

```
Boolean        consumed;
XEvent *       xevent;
Modifiers      dont_care;
OlVirtualName  virtual_name;
KeySym         keysym;
String         buffer;
Cardinal       length;
Cardinal       item_index;
```

If the X event is a KeyPress, the keysym, buffer, and length, information will be included in *virtual_event_ret*. The information was returned from a call to XLookup-String.

The *db_flag* parameter is an XtPointer type. The valid values are OL_DEFAULT_IE, OL_CORE_IE, OL_TEXT_IE, or the return value from a OlCreateInputEventDB call.

The (*w*, *db_flag*) pair determines the searching database(s). If the *db_flag* value is not OL_DEFAULT_IE then only the given database (for example, OL_TEXT_IE means: search the TEXT database) will be searched, otherwise a search stack will be built. This stack is based on the widget information (*w*) and the registering order to determine the searching database(s) (see the input event database and text database convenience routines listed under SEE ALSO for details). Once this stack is built, the procedure uses the LIFO (Last In First Out) fashion to perform the search.

All widgets have an XtNconsumeEvent callback. When this callback is invoked, the *call_data* field is a pointer to an OlVirtualEventRec structure which is filled in with the results of calling OlLookupInputEvent with the *db_flag* set to OL_DEFAULT_IE.

Defined Databases

NOTE: For readability, we have abbreviated the following keys in the Default Bindings column:

Key	Abbreviation
Shift key	s
Alt key	a
Ctrl key	c

Core Database (Key, `OL_CORE_IE`)				
Virtual Expression	OPEN LOOK Virtual Event	Motif Virtual Event	Default	Note
adjustKey	`OL_ADJUSTKEY`	n/a	c s\<ampersand>	
cancelKey	`OL_CANCEL`	`OLM_KCancel`	\<Escape>	
clearKey	n/a	`OLM_KClear`	\<F8>	
copyKey	`OL_COPY`	`OLM_KCopy`	c\<Insert>	
cutKey	`OL_CUT`	`OLM_KCut`	s\<Delete>	
defaultActionKey	`OL_DEFAULTACTION`	`OLM_KActivate`	\<Return> c\<Return>	
deselectAllKey	n/a	`OLM_KDeselectAll`	c\<backslash>	
docEndKey	`OL_DOCEND`	`OLM_KEndData`	c\<End>	(2)
docStartKey	`OL_DOCSTART`	`OLM_KBeginData`	c\<Home>	(2)
downKey	`OL_MOVEDOWN`	`OLM_KDown`	\<Down>	
dragKey	`OL_DRAG`	n/a	\<F5>	
dropKey	`OL_DROP`	n/a	\<F2>	
duplicateKey	`OL_DUPLICATEKEY`	n/a	a\<space>	(3a)
extendKey	n/a	`OLM_KExtend`	s\<space>	
helpKey	`OL_HELP`	`OLM_KHelp`	\<F1>	
horizSBMenuKey	`OL_HSBMENU`	n/a	a c\<r>	
leftKey	`OL_LEFT`	`OLM_KLeft`	\<Left>	
lineEndKey	`OL_LINEEND`	`OLM_KEndLine`	\<End>	(2)
lineStartKey	`OL_LINESTART`	`OLM_KBeginLine`	\<Home>	(2)
menuKey	`OL_MENUKEY`	`OLM_KMenu`	c\<m> \<F4>	
menubarKey	`OL_MENUBARKEY`	`OLM_KMenuBar`	\<F10>	
menuDefaultKey	`OL_MENUDEFAULTKEY`	n/a	c s\<m> s\<F4>	
multiDownKey	`OL_MULTIDOWN`	`OLM_KNextMenuDown`	c\<Down>	(5a)
multiLeftKey	`OL_MULTILEFT`	`OLM_KPrevMenuLeft`	c\<Left>	(5b)
multiRightKey	`OL_MULTIRIGHT`	`OLM_KNextMenuRight`	c\<Right>	(5c)
multiUpKey	`OL_MULTIUP`	`OLM_KPrevMenuUp`	c\<Up>	(5d)
nextAppKey	`OL_NEXTAPP`	`OLM_KNextFamilyWindow`	a\<Escape> a\<Tab>	(1)
nextFieldKey	`OL_NEXT_FIELD`	`OLM_KNextField`	\<Tab>	

OlLookupInputEvent (3Olit)

Core Database (Key, `OL_CORE_IE`)				
Virtual Expression	OPEN LOOK Virtual Event	Motif Virtual Event	Default	Note
			c<Tab>	
nextPaneKey	n/a	`OLM_KNextPane`	<F6>	
nextWinKey	`OL_NEXTWINDOW`	`OLM_KNextWindow`	a<F6>	
pageDownKey	`OL_PAGEDOWN`	`OLM_KPageDown`	<Next>	(3b)
pageLeftKey	`OL_PAGELEFT`	`OLM_KPageLeft`	c<Prior>	(3c)
pageRightKey	`OL_PAGERIGHT`	`OLM_KPageRight`	c<Next>	(3d)
pageUpKey	`OL_PAGEUP`	`OLM_KPageUp`	<Prior>	(3e)
pasteKey	`OL_PASTE`	`OLM_KPaste`	s<Insert>	
prevAppKey	`OL_PREVAPP`	`OLM_KPrevFamilyWindow`	a s<Escape> a s<Tab>	(1)
prevFieldKey	`OL_PREV_FIELD`	`OLM_KPrevField`	s<Tab> c s<Tab>	
prevPaneKey	n/a	`OLM_KPrevPane`	s<F6>	
prevWinKey	`OL_PREVWINDOW`	`OLM_KPrevWindow`	a s<F6>	
propertiesKey	`OL_PROPERTY`	n/a	c<p>	
reselectKey	n/a	`OLM_KReselect`	c s<space>	
restoreKey	n/a	`OLM_KRestore`	c s<Insert>	
rightKey	`OL_MOVERIGHT`	`OLM_KRight`	<Right>	
scrollBottomKey	`OL_SCROLLBOTTOM`	n/a	a<Next>	(5e)
scrollDownKey	`OL_SCROLLDOWN`	n/a	c<bracketleft>	(3f)(4a)
scrollLeftKey	`OL_SCROLLLEFT`	n/a	a<bracketleft>	(4b)
scrollLeftEdgeKey	`OL_SCROLLLEFTEDGE`	n/a	a s<braceleft>	(5f)
scrollRightKey	`OL_SCROLLRIGHT`	n/a	a<bracketright>	(4c)
scrollRightEdgeKey	`OL_SCROLLRIGHTEDGE`	n/a	a s<braceright>	(5g)
scrollTopKey	`OL_SCROLLTOP`	n/a	a<Prior>	(5h)
scrollUpKey	`OL_SCROLLUP`	n/a	c<bracketright>	(3g)(4d)
selectKey	`OL_SELECTKEY`	`OLM_KSelect`	<space> c<space>	
selectAllKey	n/a	`OLM_KSelectAll`	c<slash>	
selCharBakKey	`OL_SELCHARBAK`	n/a	s<Left>	
selCharFwdKey	`OL_SELCHARFWD`	n/a	s<Right>	
selFlipEndsKey	`OL_SELFLIPENDS`	n/a	a<Insert>	
selLineKey	`OL_SELLINE`	n/a	c a<Left>	
selLineBakKey	`OL_SELLINEBAK`	n/a	s<Home>	
selLineFwdKey	`OL_SELLINEFWD`	n/a	s<End>	
selWordBakKey	`OL_SELWORDBAK`	n/a	c s<Left>	
selWordFwdKey	`OL_SELWORDFWD`	n/a	c s<Right>	
stopKey	`OL_STOP`	n/a	c<s>	
togglePushpinKey	`OL_TOGGLEPUSHPIN`	n/a	c<t>	
upKey	`OL_MOVEUP`	`OLM_KUp`	<Up>	

Core Database (Key, `OL_CORE_IE`)				
Virtual Expression	OPEN LOOK Virtual Event	Motif Virtual Event	Default	Note
undoKey	`OL_UNDO`	`OLM_KUndo`	a<BackSpace>	
vertSBMenuKey	`OL_VSBMENU`	n/a	c<r>	
windowMenuKey	`OL_WINDOWMENU`	`OLM_KWindowMenu`	s<Escape>	
workspaceMenuKey	`OL_WORKSPACEMENU`	n/a	c<w>	

Notes to the Core Database(Key, `OL_CORE_IE`):

(1)   Motif binding. Alternate key sequence is added for Motif binding.

(2)   Moved from `OL_TEXT_IE`

(3)   The old binding was:

      a   s<space>

      b   c<Next>

      c   c<bracketleft>

      d   c<bracketright>

      e   c<Prior>

      f   <Next>

      g   <Prior>

(4)   To get the same functionality, the Motif scrollbar should look for

      a   `OLM_KDown`

      b   `OLM_KLeft`

      c   `OLM_KRight`

      d   `OLM_KUp`

(5)   Same as

      a   `KNextMenu` if it is a pull down menu.

      b   `KPrevMenu` if it is a pull right menu.

      c   `KNextMenu` if it is a pull right menu.

      d   `KPrevMenu` if it is a pull down menu.

      e   `OLM_KEndData` if it is a horizontal scrollbar.

      f   `OLM_KBeginLine` if it is a vertical scrollbar.

      g   `OLM_KEndLine` if it is a vertical scrollbar.

      h   `OLM_KBeginData` if it is a horizontal scrollbar.

OlLookupInputEvent (3Olit)

Core Database (Button, OL_CORE_IE)					
Virtual Expression	OPEN LOOK Virtual Event	Motif Virtual Event	Two Button Default	Three Button Default	Note
adjustBtn	OL_ADJUST	OLM_BToggle	c<Button1>	c<Button1>	(a)
constrainBtn	OL_CONSTRAIN	n/a	a s<Button1>	a s<Button1>	(b)
copyBtn	n/a	OLM_BPrimaryCopy OLM_BQuickCopy	c<Button2>	c<Button2>	
cutBtn	n/a	OLM_BPrimaryCut OLM_BQuickCut	a<Button2>	a<Button2>	
duplicateBtn	OL_DUPLICATE	n/a	a<Button1>	a<Button1>	
extendBtn	n/a	OLM_BExtend	s<Button1>	s<Button1>	
linkBtn	OL_LINK	n/a	a c<Button1>	a c<Button1>	
menuDefaultBtn	OL_MENUDEFAULT	n/a	a c s<Button1>	a<Button3>	(c)
menuBtn	OL_MENU	OLM_BMenu	c s<Button1>	<Button3>	(d)
panBtn	OL_PAN	n/a	s<Button2>	s<Button2>	(e)
pasteBtn	n/a	OLM_BPrimaryPaste OLM_BQuickPaste OLM_BDrag	<Button2>	<Button2>	
selectBtn	OL_SELECT	OLM_BSelect	<Button1>	<Button1>	

Notes to the Core Database(Button, OL_CORE_IE):

The old binding was:

a. Two Button: s<Button1>   Three Button: <Button2>

b. Two Button: c<Button1>   Three Button: c<Button1>

c. Two Button: c<Button2>   Three Button: c<Button3>

d. Two Button: <Button2>

e. Two Button: a s<Button1>

Text Database (Key, `OL_TEXT_IE`)				
Virtual Expression	OPEN LOOK Virtual Event	Motif Virtual Event	Default	Same As
addModeKey	n/a	`OLM_KAddMode`	`s<F8>`	
charBakKey	`OL_CHARBAK`	n/a	`<Left>`	`OLM_KLeft`
charFwdKey	`OL_CHARFWD`	n/a	`<Right>`	`OLM_KRight`
delCharBakKey	`OL_DELCHARBAK`	`OLM_KBackSpace`	`<BackSpace>`	
delCharFwdKey	`OL_DELCHARFWD`	`OLM_KDelete`	`<Delete>`	
delLineKey	`OL_DELLINE`	n/a	`a s<Delete>`	
delLineFwdKey	`OL_DELLINEFWD`	`OLM_KEraseEndLine`	`c<Delete>`	
delLineBakKey	`OL_DELLINEBAK`	n/a	`c<BackSpace>`	
delWordBakKey	`OL_DELWORDBAK`	n/a	`c s<BackSpace>`	
delWordFwdKey	`OL_DELWORDFWD`	n/a	`c s<Delete>`	
nextParaKey	n/a	`OLM_KNextPara`	`c<Down>`	
paneEndKey	`OL_PANEEND`	n/a	`c s<End>`	
paneStartKey	`OL_PANESTART`	n/a	`c s<Home>`	
prevParaKey	n/a	`OLM_KPrevPara`	`c<Up>`	
primaryCopyKey	n/a	`OLM_KPrimaryCopy`	`a c<Insert>` `c<F11>`	
primaryCutKey	n/a	`OLM_KPrimaryCut`	`a<F11>`	
primaryPasteKey	n/a	`OLM_KPrimaryPaste`	`<F11>`	
quickCopyKey	n/a	`OLM_KQuickCopy`	`c<F12>`	
quickCutKey	n/a	`OLM_KQuickCut`	`a<F12>`	
quickExtendKey	n/a	`OLM_KQuickExtend`	`s<F12>`	
quickPasteKey	n/a	`OLM_KQuickPaste`	`<F12>`	
returnKey	`OL_RETURN`	`OLM_KEnter`	`<Return>`	
rowDownKey	`OL_ROWDOWN`	n/a	`<Down>`	`OLM_KDown`
rowUpKey	`OL_ROWUP`	n/a	`<Up>`	`OLM_KUp`
wordBakKey	`OL_WORDBAK`	`OLM_KPrevWord`	`c<Left>`	
wordFwdKey	`OL_WORDFWD`	`OLM_KNextWord`	`c<Right>`	

EXAMPLE

```
      ...
#include <Xol/OpenLook.h>
      ...
OlVirtualEventRec    ve;

    /* To look up the OPEN LOOK CORE database */
OlLookupInputEvent(w, xevent, &ve, OL_CORE_IE);
switch (ve.virtual_name)
{
    case OL_UNKNOWN_INPUT:
        ...
        break;
    case OL_UNKNOWN_BTN_INPUT:
        ...
```

```
          break;
      case OL_UNKNOW_KEY_INPUT:
          ...
          break;
      case OL_ADJUST:
          printf ("pressed the adjustBtn\n");
          ...
          break;
      case OL_ADJUSTKEY:
          printf ("pressed the adjustKey\n");
          ...
          break;
          ...
  }
          ...
          ...
  #include <Xol/OpenLook.h>
          ...
  OlVirtualEventRec      ve;
      /* To look up the OPEN LOOK TEXT database */
  OlLookupInputEvent(w, xevent, &ve, OL_TEXT_IE);
  switch (ve.virtual_name)
  {
          ...
      case OL_DOCEND:
          printf ("pressed the docEndKey\n");
          ...
          break;
      case OL_LINEEND:
          printf ("pressed the lineEndKey\n");
          ...
          break;
          ...
  }
          ...
  #include <Xol/OpenLook.h>
          ...
  OlVirtualEventRec      ve;
      /* To look up all possible databases */
      /* assume: "w" is a textfield widget */
  OlLookupInputEvent(w, xevent, &ve, OL_DEFAULT_IE);
  switch (ve.virtual_name)
  {
          ...
  case OL_ADJUST:
      printf ("pressed the adjustBtn\n");
          ...
          break;
      case OL_ADJUSTKEY:
```

```
        printf ("pressed the adjustKey\n");
    ...
        break;
    ...
case OL_DOCEND:
        printf ("pressed the docEndKey\n");
    ...
        break;
case OL_LINEEND:
        printf ("pressed the lineEndKey\n");
    ...
        break;
    ...
}
```

SEE ALSO

EventObj(3Olit), Manager(3Olit), OlClassSearchIEDB(3Olit),
OlClassSearchTextDB(3Olit), OlClassUnsearchIEDB(3Olit),
OlCreateInputEventDB(3Olit), OlDestroyInputEventDB(3Olit),
OlWidgetSearchIEDB(3Olit), OlWidgetSearchTextDB(3Olit),
OlWidgetUnsearchIEDB(3Olit) Primitive(3Olit), Vendor(3Olit),

OlMoveFocus (3Olit)

NAME

OlMoveFocus – move the input focus

SYNOPSIS

`#include <Xol/OpenLook.h>`

`Widget OlMoveFocus(Widget` *wid*`, OlDefine` *direction*`, Time` *time*`);`

DESCRIPTION

The **OlMoveFocus** function moves the input focus from one widget to another and returns the ID of the new focus widget. The routine **OlCallAcceptFocus** is used to move the input focus.

When moving input focus between widgets contained within an exclusives or non-exclusives widget, valid values for *direction* are:

OL_IMMEDIATE

Set focus to the next widget that will accept it, starting with *wid*.

OL_MOVERIGHT

Set focus to the widget in the next column (and same row) that will accept it, starting with the first column after *wid*'s column. If *wid* is located in the extreme right column, focus is set to the widget in the extreme left column of the same row.

OL_MOVELEFT

Set focus to the widget in the previous column (and same row) that will accept it, starting with the first column before *wid*'s column. If *wid* is located on the extreme left column, focus is set to the widget in the extreme right column of the same row. (The widget columns are searched in reverse order.)

OL_MOVEUP

Set focus to the widget in the next row (and same column) that will accept it, starting with the first row after *wid*'s row. If *wid* is located in the top row, focus is set to the widget in the bottom row of the same column. (The widget rows are searched in reverse order.)

OL_MOVEDOWN

Set focus to the widget in the previous row (and same column) that will accept it, starting with the first row before *wid*'s row. If *wid* is located in the bottom row, focus is set to the widget in the top row of the same column.

OL_MULTIRIGHT

Set focus to the widget in the next column (and same row) that will accept it, starting with the first column *m* columns after *wid*' s column. If *m* is greater than the number of objects between *wid* and the extreme right column, focus is set to the widget in the extreme left column of the same row.

Note that for **OL_MULTIRIGHT**, **OL_MULTILEFT**, **OL_MULTIUP**, and **OL_MULTIDOWN** directions, the value of *m* is the value of the application resource **XtNmultiObjectCount**.

OL_MULTILEFT

> Set focus to the widget in the next column (and same row) that will accept it, starting with the first column *m* columns before *wid*'s column. If *m* is greater than the number of objects between *wid* and the extreme left column, focus is set to the widget in the extreme right column of the same row. (The widget columns are searched in reverse order.)

OL_MULTIUP

> Set focus to the widget in the next row (and same column) that will accept it, starting with the first row *m* rows after *wid*'s row. If *m* is greater than the number of objects between *wid* and the extreme bottom row, focus is set to the widget in the extreme top row of the same column. (The widget rows are searched in reverse order.)

OL_MULTIDOWN

> Set focus to the widget in the next row (and same column) that will accept it, starting with the first row *m* rows before *wid*'s row. If *m* is greater than the number of objects between *wid* and the extreme bottom row, focus is set to the widget in the extreme bottom row of the same column.

When moving between widgets in a base window or popup window, valid values for *direction* are:

OL_IMMEDIATE

> Set focus to the next object that will accept it, starting with *wid*.

OL_NEXTFIELD

> Set focus to the next object that will accept it, starting with the first object after *wid*.

OL_PREVFIELD

> Set focus to the next object that will accept it, starting with the first object before *wid*. (The list is searched in reverse order.)

OL_MOVERIGHT

> Behaves like **OL_NEXTFIELD** direction.

OL_MOVELEFT

> Behaves like **OL_PREVFIELD** direction.

OL_MOVEUP

> Behaves like **OL_PREVFIELD** direction.

OL_MOVEDOWN

> Behaves like **OL_NEXTFIELD** direction.

OL_MULTIRIGHT

> Set focus to the next object that will accept it, starting with the first object *m* objects after *wid*.

OL_MULTILEFT

> Set focus to the next object that will accept it, starting with the first object *m* objects before *wid*. (The list is searched in reverse order.)

OlMoveFocus (3Olit)

OL_MULTIUP
    Behaves like `OL_MULTILEFT` direction.

OL_MULTIDOWN
    Behaves like `OL_MULTIRIGHT` direction.

RETURN VALUES
    On success, `OlMoveFocus` returns the widget ID. On failure, if the function is unable to move input focus, it returns NULL.

SEE ALSO
    `Flattened_Widget_Utilities`(3Olit) `OlCallAcceptFocus`(3Olit), `OlCanAcceptFocus`(3Olit), `OlGetCurrentFocusWidget`(3Olit), `OlHasFocus`(3Olit), `OlSetInputFocus`(3Olit)

NAME

OlOpenDatabase – open a localized **Xrmdatabase** format database

SYNOPSIS

#include <Xol/OpenLook.h>

XrmDatabase OlOpenDatabase(Display *display, String *filename*);

DESCRIPTION

This function is responsible for opening a localized version of a database in **XrmDatabase** format. The function will resolve the pathname according to the current locale.

If the function call is successful, the **XrmDatabase** pointer will be returned; if unsuccessful, (**XrmDatabase**) NULL is returned.

If the database has already been opened by **OlOpenDatabase**, the cached **XrmDatabase** pointer is returned.

SEE ALSO

OlCloseDatabase(3Olit), OlGetMessage(3Olit)

OlOpenlm (3Olit)

NAME

OlOpenIm – open a connection to the Input Method

SYNOPSIS

```
#include <Xol/OpenLook.h>

OlIm *OlOpenIm(Display *dpy, XrmDatabase rdb, String res_name,
    String res_class);
```

DESCRIPTION

This is an Input Method dependent function responsible for opening a connection to the Input Method. Depending on a particular implementation it may have to start an Input Method server, establish a connection with an already running server, set up a STREAMS connection, or simply create an **OlIm** structure.

The structure, **OlIm**, includes the following members:

```
OlIc *iclist;              /* input context list */
OlImStyles im_styles;      /* supported re-edit types */
OlImValuesList imvalues;   /* current Input Method attributes */
String appl_name;          /* application name */
String appl_class;         /* application class */
long version;              /* OPEN LOOK version */
void *imtype;              /* hook for Input Method specific data*/
```

where

```
typedef OlImValues *OlImValuesList;
```

The **imtype** field is a hook for attaching implementation dependent data structures.

The structure, **OlImValues**, contains a list of Input Method values or attributes returned by the **OlImStyles** structure which includes the following members:

```
String attr_name;
void  *attr_value;
```

The **OlImStyles** structure includes the following members:

```
short styles_count;
OlImStyle *supported_styles;
```

The **OlImStyles** structure contains in its field **styles_count** the number of input styles supported. This is also the size of the array in the field **supported_styles**. Each element in the array represents a different input style supported by this Input Method. It is a bitmask in which the Input Method indicates its requirements, should this style be selected. These requirements fall into the following categories:

OlImPreEditArea

If chosen the Input Method requires the client to provide some area values for preediting. Refer to the Input Context Attribute **OlNpreeditArea**.

OlIMPreditPosition

If chosen, the Input Method requires the client to provide positional values. Refer to Input Context attributes **OlNspotLocation** and **OlNfocusWindow**.

OlImPreEditCallbacks
> If chosen, the Input Method requires the client to define the set of preedit callbacks. Refer to Input Context values **OlNPreEditStartCallback**, **OlNPreEditDoneCallback**, **OlNPreEditDrawCallback**, **OlNPreEditCaretCallback**.

OlImNeedNothing
> If chosen, the Input Method can function without any PreEdit values.

OlIMStatusArea
> The input method requires the client to provide some area values for it to do its Status feedback. Refer to **OlNArea** and **OlNAreaNeeded**.

OlIMStatusCallbacks
> The Input Method requires the client to define the set of status callbacks.

OlImStatusArea
> The Input Method requires the client to provide some area values for it to do its Status feedback. Refer to **OlNArea** and **OlNAreaNeeded**.

RETURN VALUES

On success, **OlOpenIm** returns a pointer to the **OlIm** structure, a pointer to a list of **OlIc** structures, information about supported Input Method styles, and the Toolkit's version number (to be used by some Input Methods).

SEE ALSO

OlCloseIm(3Olit), **OlDisplayOfIm**(3Olit), **OlGetImValues**(3Olit), **OlImOfIc**(3Olit), **OlImValues**(4), **OlLocaleOfIm**(3Olit)

OlPostPopupMenu (3Olit)

NAME

OlPostPopupMenu – post a **popupMenuShell** widget

SYNOPSIS

```
#include <Xol/OpenLook.h>
#include <Xol/PopupMenu.h>

void OlPostPopupMenu(
    Widget menu_owner,
    Widget popup_menu,
    OlDefine activation_type,
    OlPopupMenuCallbackProc popdown_cb,
    Position root_x,
    Position root_y,
    Position init_x,
    Position init_y
);
```

DESCRIPTION

This routine posts a **popupMenuShell** widget.

menu_owner   This is the object that the *popup_menu* is currently associated with and is supplied to the *popdown_cb* procedure when unposting the *popup_menu*.

popup_menu   A **popupMenuShellWidget** ID obtained by creating it explicitly.

activation_type   This specifies how a **popupMenuShell** widget is posted. The valid values are **OL_MENU** and **OL_MENUKEY**.

popdown_cb   This callback procedure is invoked when unposting this menu widget. The type of this callback procedure is:

typedef void (*OlPopupMenuCallbackProc)(Widget *menu_owner***);**

root_x
root_y   These coordinates are relative to the **RootWindow** and are used to position the *popup_menu*. They are usually obtained from a ButtonPress event (that is, **xevent->xbutton.x_root** and **xevent->xbutton.y_root**) or a KeyPress event (that is, **xevent->xkey.x_root** and **xevent->xkey.y_root**).

init_x
init_y   These coordinates are relative to the *menu_owner* and usually are obtained from a ButtonPress event (that is, **xevent->xbutton.x** and **xevent->xbutton.y**) or a KeyPress event (that is, **xevent->xkey.x** and **xevent->xkey.y**).

Note that the only difference between (*root_x*, *root_y*) and (*init_x*, *init_y*) is that the former is relative to the RootWindow and the latter is relative to the *menu_owner*.

SEE ALSO

OlUnpostPopupMenu(3Olit), **PopupMenuShell**(3Olit)

OlQueryAcceleratorDisplay (3Olit)

NAME

OlQueryAcceleratorDisplay – control accelerator displays

SYNOPSIS

```
#include <Xol/OpenLook.h>

OlDefine OlQueryAcceleratorDisplay(Widget wid);
```

DESCRIPTION

The OlQueryAcceleratorDisplay function queries how the accelerators should be displayed.

RETURN VALUES

OlQueryAcceleratorDisplay returns one of

OL_DISPLAY	the keyboard accelerators should be displayed
OL_NONE	the keyboard accelerators should not be displayed
OL_INACTIVE	the keyboard accelerators should not be displayed and the controls should ignore the accelerator action

SEE ALSO

OlQueryMnemonicDisplay(3Olit)

OlQueryMnemonicDisplay (3Olit)

NAME

OlQueryMnemonicDisplay – control mnemonic displays

SYNOPSIS

#include <Xol/OpenLook.h>

OlDefine OlQueryMnemonicDisplay(Widget *wid*);

DESCRIPTION

The OlQueryMnemonicDisplay function queries how the keyboard mnemonics on the controls should be displayed.

RETURN VALUES

OlQueryMnemonicDisplay returns one of

OL_UNDERLINE   this is the default value. The mnemonics should be displayed in the Primitive controls by drawing a line under the character in the font color.

OL_HIGHLIGHT   display the mnemonic character with the background and foreground colors reversed. When highlighting a character that is displayed on a pixmap background, the mnemonic character will be drawn in a solid color.

OL_NONE

OL_INACTIVE   the mnemonic accelerator will not be displayed and will not activate the control

SEE ALSO

OlQueryAcceleratorDisplay(3Olit)

Dynamic Settings

NAME

OlRegisterDynamicCallback – add a function to the callback list

SYNOPSIS

```
#include <Xol/OpenLook.h>

extern void OlRegisterDynamicCallback(
    OlDynamicCallbackProc   CB,
    XtPointer data
);
```

DESCRIPTION

The OlRegisterDynamicCallback procedure is used to add a function to the list of registered callbacks to be called whenever the procedure OlCallDynamicCallbacks is invoked. The OlCallDynamicCallback procedure is invoked whenever the RESOURCE_MANAGER property of the Root Window is updated. The OlCallDynamicCallback procedure may also be called directly by either the application or other routines in the widget libraries. The callbacks registered are guaranteed to be called in FIFO order of registration and will be called as

```
(*CB)(data);
```

SEE ALSO

OlCallDynamicCallbacks(3Olit), OlUnregisterDynamicCallback(3Olit)

OlRegisterHelp (3Olit)

NAME

OlRegisterHelp – associate help information with a widget instance or class

SYNOPSIS

```
#include <Intrinsic.h>
#include <OpenLook.h>

void OlRegisterHelp(
    OlDefine id_type,
    XtPointer id,
    String tag,
    OlDefine source_type,
    XtPointer source
);
```

DESCRIPTION

The `OlRegisterHelp` function associates help information with a specific widget instance or widget class. These resources define the look of the Help window.

Default Window Decorations

Resource	Type	Default
XtNmenuButton	Boolean	FALSE
XtNpushpin	OlDefine	OL_IN
XtNresizeCorners	Boolean	FALSE
XtNwindowHeader	Boolean	TRUE

Associating Help with Widgets or Gadgets

The `OlRegisterHelp` routine associates help information with either a widget instance or a widget class. The widget ID or widget class pointer is given in *id*, and *id_type* identifies whether it is a widget or a widget class using one of the values **OL_WIDGET_HELP**, **OL_CLASS_HELP**, or **OL_FLAT_HELP**, respectively. Use **OL_WIDGET_HELP** to register help on gadgets.

The *tag* value is shown in the title of the help window, as suggested below:

> *app-name*: *tag* Help

where *app-name* is the name of the application. More than one help message can be registered with the same *tag*. Note that *tag* can be null, in which case only

> *app-name*: Help

is printed.

Help for Flat Widgets

To set the same help message for all items in a flat widget container, use the **OlRegisterHelp** routine with *id_type* set to **OL_WIDGET_HELP**.

To register help for individual items in a flat widget container, use **OlRegisterHelp** with *id_type* set to **OL_FLAT_HELP**. Use the **OlFlatHelpId** structure to specify an object that gets the help message. The **OlFlatHelpId** structure includes the following members:

```
Widget widget;
Cardinal item_index;
```

314

Format of the Help

The help message is identified in *source*; *source_type* identifies the form of the help message:

OL_STRING_SOURCE

>The *source* is of type **String** and contains simple text with embedded newlines. The **OlRegisterHelp** function does not copy this source; the application is expected to maintain the original as long as it is registered with a *tag*.

OL_DISK_SOURCE

>The *source* is also of type **String**, but contains the name of a file that contains the text. The **OlRegisterHelp** function does not copy this filename; the application is expected to maintain the original as long as it is registered. The file content is considered to be simple text with embedded newlines.

OL_INDIRECT_SOURCE

>The *source* is of type **void(*)** and is a pointer to an application defined routine. The function is called after HELP has been clicked. The application is expected to define the type of source in the routine. After the function has returned, the help information is displayed.

>The routine is called as follows:

>>(***source**)(*id_type*, *id*, *src_x*, *src_y*, &*source_type*, &*source*);

>*id_type*
>*id*   are the values for the widget class or widget instance that was under the pointer when HELP was pressed. These are the same values registered with the *tag*.

>*src_x*
>*src_y*   are the coordinates of the pointer when HELP was pressed. These are relative to the upper-left corner of the window.

>*source_type*
>*source*   are pointers to values the application's routine should set for the help source it wants to display. The only *source_type* values accepted are **OL_STRING_SOURCE** and **OL_DISK_SOURCE**.

OL_TRANSPARENT_SOURCE

>The *source* is of type **void(*)** and is a pointer to an application defined routine. The routine is called after HELP has been invoked. The application is expected to handle the HELP event completely. This might be used by an application that does not want the standard help window (for example, **xterm** simply generates an escape sequence).

>The routine is called as follows:

>>(***source**)(*id_type*, *id*, *src_x*, *src_y*);

>*id_type*
>*id*   are the values for the widget class or widget instance that was under the pointer when HELP was pressed. These are the same values registered with the **tag**.

315

OlResetIc (3Olit)

NAME

OlResetIc – reset the state of an Input Context to the initial state

SYNOPSIS

#include <Xol/OpenLook.h>

String OlResetIc(OlIc *ic);

DESCRIPTION

OlResetIc resets the input context to its initial state. Any input pending on that context is deleted. The Input Method is required to clear the pre-edit area, if any, and update the status accordingly. Calling OlResetIc does not change the focus.

SEE ALSO

OlCreateIc(3Olit), OlDestroyIc(3Olit), OlGetIcValues(3Olit), OlImOfIc(3Olit), OlSetIcFocus(3Olit), OlSetIcValues(3Olit), OlUnSetIcFocus(3Olit)

NAME

OlSetApplicationValues – set application resources

SYNOPSIS

```
#include <Xol/OpenLook.h>

void OlSetApplicationValues(
    Widget      widget,      /* for getting display info */
    ArgList     args,        /* args to query            */
    Cardinal    num_args     /* number of args           */
);
```

DESCRIPTION

The **OlSetApplicationValues** function is used to set the application resources that are accessible from the OPEN LOOK toolkit. The semantics is similar to the **XtSetValues** call.

Application resources are resources that all OPEN LOOK applications have in common. Their values are updated dynamically by changing preferences in the WorkSpace Manager's property sheets.

OlSetGaugeValue (3Olit)

NAME

    `OlSetGaugeValue` – set the slider value on a gauge widget

SYNOPSIS

    `#include <Xol/OpenLook.h>`
    `#include <Xol/Gauge.h>`

    `void OlSetGaugeValue(Widget` *w*`, int` *value*`);`

DESCRIPTION

    This function is an alternate and faster way of setting the slider value of a gauge widget.

SEE ALSO

    Gauge(3Olit)

NAME

     `OlSetGui` – set current look and feel

SYNOPSIS

     `#include <Xol/OpenLook.h>`

     . . .

     `void OlSetGui(OlDefine` *mode*`);`

DESCRIPTION

     The `OlSetGui` function is used to set the GUI mode. *mode* can be either `OL_OPENLOOK_GUI` or `OL_MOTIF_GUI`. This can be useful if the application has no intention of supporting multiple GUI modes. In this case, `OlSetGui` should be called after `OlToolkitInitialize`.

     `OlSetGui` must be invoked before `XtInitialize` (any Xt functions) so that the correct set of library routines will be used. Invoking it after causes unpredictable results such as incorrect layout of widgets, different widgets appearing in different GUIs in the same base window, and so on.

SEE ALSO

     `OlGetGui`(3Olit), `OlToolkitInitialize`(3Olit)

OlSetIcFocus (3Olit)

NAME

OlSetIcFocus – notify Input Method that window received keyboard focus

SYNOPSIS

```
#include <Xol/OpenLook.h>

void OlSetIcFocus(OlIc *ic);
```

DESCRIPTION

This function informs the Input Method that the text area associated with a particular Input Context now has the input focus and should receive all the keyboard events. Its implementation depends on the Input Method. Depending on the implementation, this function may update the status information and provide appropriate feedback. For an input method style that includes the OlImFocus-Tracks mask, the client must call OlSetIcFocus(ic) in response to a FocusOut event on the widget associated with the Input Context.

SEE ALSO

OlGetImValues(3Olit), OlUnsetIcFocus(3Olit)

NAME

OlSetIcValues – set Input Context attributes

SYNOPSIS

#include <Xol/OpenLook.h>

String OlSetIcValues(OlIc *ic, OlIcValues *icvalues);

DESCRIPTION

The OlSetIcValues function sets Input Context attributes.

ic specifies the input context to be changed

icvalues is a pointer to a list of attribute names and new value pairs

All values must be of the appropriate data type [see OlIcValues(4)]

The end of the icvalues list will be indicated by a NULL value for the attribute name.

RETURN VALUES

On success, if all arguments can be set, OlSetIcValues returns NULL. On failure, OlSetIcValues returns the name of the first argument that can not be set.

SEE ALSO

OlCreateIc(3Olit), OlDestroyIc(3Olit), OlGetIcValues(3Olit), OlIcValues(4)

OlSetInputFocus (3Olit)

NAME

OlSetInputFocus – set the input focus

SYNOPSIS

#include <Xol/OpenLook.h>

void OlSetInputFocus(Widget *wid*, int *revert_to*, Time *time*);

DESCRIPTION

The OlSetInputFocus function sets focus to a widget. Applications should use this function rather than XSetInputFocus because this function checks the current focus model before setting focus.

SEE ALSO

Flattened_Widge_Utilities(3Olit), OlCallAcceptFocus(3Olit), OlCanAcceptFocus(3Olit), OlGetCurrentFocusWidget(3Olit), OlHasFocus(3Olit), OlMoveFocus(3Olit)

NAME

OlTextEditClearBuffer – clear a **TextEdit** widget

SYNOPSIS

```
#include <Xol/OpenLook.h>
#include <Xol/TextEdit.h>

Boolean OlTextEditClearBuffer(TextEditWidget ctx);
```

DESCRIPTION

The **OlTextEditClearBuffer** function is used to delete all of the text associated with the **TextEdit** widget *ctx*.

RETURN VALUE

On success, **OlTextEditClearBuffer** returns **TRUE**.

On failure, if the widget supplied is not a **TextEdit** widget, or a subclass of **TextEdit**, or if the clear operation fails, **OlTextEditClearBuffer** returns **FALSE**.

SEE ALSO

OlTextEditUpdate(3Olit), **TextEdit**(3Olit)

OlTextEditCopyBuffer (3Olit)

NAME

NAME

OlTextEditCopyBuffer – get a copy of a **TextEdit** widget's **TextBuffer**

SYNOPSIS

```
#include <Xol/OpenLook.h>
#include <Xol/TextEdit.h>

Boolean OlTextEditCopyBuffer(TextEditWidget ctx, char **buffer);
```

DESCRIPTION

The **OlTextEditCopyBuffer** function is used to retrieve a copy of the **TextBuffer** associated with the **TextEdit** Widget *ctx*. The storage required for the copy is allocated by this routine; it is the responsibility of the caller to free this storage when appropriate.

RETURN VALUE

On success, **OlTextEditCopyBuffer** returns **TRUE**.

On failure, if the widget supplied is not a **TextEdit** widget, or a subclass of **TextEdit**, or if the buffer cannot be read, **OlTextEditCopyBuffer** returns **FALSE**.

SEE ALSO

OlTextEditReadSubString(3Olit), **TextEdit**(3Olit)

NAME

OlTextEditCopySelection – copy the **TextEdit** selection to the CLIPBOARD

SYNOPSIS

#include <Xol/OpenLook.h>
#include <Xol/TextEdit.h>

Boolean OlTextEditCopySelection(TextEditWidget *ctx*, int *delete*);

DESCRIPTION

The **OlTextEditCopySelection** function is used to Copy or Cut the current selection in the **TextEdit** *ctx*. The selection is copied to the CLIPBOARD then, if the *delete* flag is non-zero, the text is then deleted from the **TextBuffer** associated with the **TextEdit** widget (that is, a Cut operation is performed).

RETURN VALUE

On success, **OlTextEditCopySelection** returns **TRUE**.

On failure,

if no selection exists,

if the **TextEdit** cannot acquire the CLIPBOARD

if the widget supplied is not a **TextEdit** widget, or a subclass of **TextEdit**, or

if the operation fails,

OlTextEditCopySelection returns **FALSE**.

SEE ALSO

OlTextEditUpdate(3Olit), **OlTextEditGetCursorPosition**(3Olit), **OlTextEditSetCursorPosition**(3Olit), **OlTextEditReadSubString**(3Olit), **OlTextEditCopyBuffer**(3Olit), **TextEdit**(3Olit)

OlTextEditGetCursorPosition (3Olit)

NAME

OlTextEditGetCursorPosition – get cursor position and selection boundaries

SYNOPSIS

```
#include <Xol/OpenLook.h>
#include <Xol/TextEdit.h>

Boolean OlTextEditGetCursorPosition(
    TextEditWidget ctx,
    TextPosition *start,
    TextPosition *end,
    TextPosition *cursorPosition
);
```

DESCRIPTION

The **OlTextEditGetCursorPosition** function is used to retrieve the current selection *start* and *end* and *cursorPosition*. If there is no current selection *start* and *end* will both be equal to *cursorPosition*.

RETURN VALUE

On success, **OlTextEditGetCursorPosition** returns **TRUE**.

On failure, if the widget supplied is not a **TextEdit** widget, or a subclass of **TextEdit**, **OlTextEditGetCursorPosition** returns **FALSE**.

SEE ALSO

OlTextEditSetCursorPosition(3Olit), **TextEdit**(3Olit)

NAME

`OlTextEditGetLastPosition` – get last position in `TextBuffer`

SYNOPSIS

```
#include <Xol/OpenLook.h>
#include <Xol/TextEdit.h>

Boolean OlTextEditGetLastPosition(
    TextEditWidget ctx,
    TextPosition *position
);
```

DESCRIPTION

The `OlTextEditGetLastPosition` function is used to retrieve the *position* of the last character in the `TextBuffer` associated with the `TextEdit` widget *ctx*.

RETURN VALUE

On success, `OlTextEditGetLastPosition` returns `TRUE`.

On failure, if the widget supplied is not a `TextEdit` widget, or a subclass of `TextEdit`, `OlTextEditGetLastPosition` returns `FALSE`.

SEE ALSO

`OlTextEditGetCursorPosition`(3Olit), `TextEdit`(3Olit)

OlTextEditInsert (3Olit)

NAME
OlTextEditInsert – insert a string in a **TextBuffer**

SYNOPSIS
```
#include <Xol/OpenLook.h>
#include <Xol/TextEdit.h>

Boolean OlTextEditInsert(TextEditWidget ctx, String buffer, int length);
```

DESCRIPTION
The **OlTextEditInsert** function is used to insert a NULL-terminated *buffer* containing *length* bytes in the **TextBuffer** associated with the **TextEdit** widget *ctx*. The inserted text replaces the current (if any) selection.

Note that the value of *length* is not used internally, but is passed on as the length field in the **XtNmodifyVerification** callback.

RETURN VALUE
On success, **OlTextEditInsert** returns **TRUE**.

On failure, if the widget supplied is not a **TextEdit** widget, or a subclass of **TextEdit**, or if the insert operation fails, **OlTextEditInsert** returns **FALSE**.

SEE ALSO
OlTextEditGetCursorPosition(3Olit), **TextEdit**(3Olit)

NAME

OlTextEditPaste – paste CLIPBOARD selection into a **TextEdit** widget

SYNOPSIS

```
#include <Xol/OpenLook.h>
#include <Xol/TextEdit.h>

Boolean OlTextEditPaste(TextEditWidget ctx);
```

DESCRIPTION

The **OlTextEditPaste** function is used to paste the contents of the CLIPBOARD into the **TextEdit** widget *ctx*. The current (if any) selection is replaced by the contents of the CLIPBOARD.

RETURN VALUE

On success, **OlTextEditPaste** returns **TRUE**.

On failure, if the widget supplied is not a **TextEdit** widget, or a subclass **TextEdit**, **OlTextEditPaste** returns **FALSE**.

SEE ALSO

OlTextEditCopySelection(3Olit), **TextEdit**(3Olit)

OlTextEditReadSubString (3Olit)

NAME

OlTextEditReadSubString – get a substring of a **TextBuffer**

SYNOPSIS

```
#include <Xol/OpenLook.h>
#include <Xol/TextEdit.h>

Boolean OlTextEditReadSubString(
    TextEditWidget ctx,
    char **buffer,
    TextPosition start,
    TextPosition end
);
```

DESCRIPTION

The **OlTextEditReadSubString** function is used to retrieve a copy of a substring from the **TextBuffer** associated with the **TextEdit** widget *ctx* between positions *start* through *end* inclusive. The storage required for the copy is allocated by this routine; it is the responsibility of the caller to free this storage when appropriate.

RETURN VALUE

On success, **OlTextEditReadSubString** returns **TRUE**.

On failure, if the widget supplied is not a **TextEdit** widget, or a subclass of **TextEdit**, or if the operation fails, **OlTextEditReadSubString** returns **FALSE**.

SEE ALSO

OlTextEditCopyBuffer(3Olit), **TextEdit**(3Olit)

NAME

OlTextEditRedraw – force a refresh of a **TextEdit** display

SYNOPSIS

```
#include <Xol/OpenLook.h>
#include <Xol/TextEdit.h>

Boolean OlTextEditRedraw(TextEditWidget ctx);
```

DESCRIPTION

The **OlTextEditRedraw** function is used to force a complete refresh of the **TextEdit** widget display. This routine does nothing if the **TextEdit** widget is not realized or if the update state is set to **FALSE**.

RETURN VALUE

On success, **OlTextEditRedraw** returns **TRUE**.

On failure,

if the widget supplied is not a **TextEdit** widget, or a subclass of **TextEdit**,

if the widget is not realized or

if the update state is **FALSE**; **OlTextEditRedraw** returns **FALSE**.

SEE ALSO

OlTextEditUpdate(3Olit), **TextEdit**(3Olit)

OlTextEditResize (3Olit)

NAME

    `OlTextEditResize` – resize a `TextEdit` widget

SYNOPSIS

```
#include <Xol/textbuff.h>
#include <Xol/TextEdit.h>

void OlTextEditResize(
    Widget w,
    int request_linesVisible,
    int request_charsVisible
);
```

DESCRIPTION

    The `OlTextEditResize` function requests a size change of a `TextEdit` widget, w, to display *request_linesVisible* lines and *request_charsVisible* characters per line.

    The calculated width will be an approximation based on the width of the character 'n' from the `TextEdit` font. For a constant-width font, this approximation will be accurate; for a non-constant-width font, it may not be accurate. (The actual number of characters displayed will depend on the characters displayed.)

    After calculating the appropriate geometry the widget then requests a resize of its parent. Note that the new size may or may not be honored by the widget's parent, therefore the outcome is non-deterministic.

RETURN VALUES

    The `OlTextEditResize` function returns no value.

SEE ALSO

    `TextEdit`(3Olit)

NAME

OlTextEditSetCursorPosition – modify the start, end, and position of cursor

SYNOPSIS

```
#include <Xol/OpenLook.h>
#include <Xol/TextEdit.h>

OlTextEditSetCursorPosition(
    TextEditWidget ctx,
    TextPosition start,
    TextPosition end,
    TextPosition cursorPosition
);
```

DESCRIPTION

The OlTextEditSetCursorPosition function is used to change the current selection *start* and *end* and *cursorPosition*. The function does not check (for efficiency) the validity of the positions. If invalid values are given results are unpredictable. The function attempts to ensure that the cursorPosition is visible by scrolling the display.

RETURN VALUE

On success, OlTextEditSetCursorPosition returns TRUE. On failure, if the widget supplied is not a TextEdit Widget, OlTextEditSetCursorPosition returns FALSE.

SEE ALSO

OlTextEditGetCursorPosition(3Olit), TextEdit(3Olit)

OlTextEditTextBuffer (3Olit)

NAME

OlTextEditTextBuffer – get TextBuffer pointer

SYNOPSIS

#include <Xol/OpenLook.h>
#include <Xol/TextEdit.h>

TextBuffer *OlTextEditTextBuffer(TextEditWidget *ctx*);

DESCRIPTION

The OlTextEditTextBuffer function is used to retrieve the TextBuffer pointer associated with the TextEdit widget *ctx*. This pointer can be used to access the facilities provided by the Text Buffer Utilities module.

SEE ALSO

TextBuffer_Macros(3Olit), TextEdit(3Olit)

NAME

OlTextEditUpdate – set update state of a **TextEdit** widget

SYNOPSIS

```
#include <Xol/OpenLook.h>
#include <Xol/TextEdit.h>

Boolean OlTextEditUpdate(TextEditWidget ctx, Boolean state);
```

DESCRIPTION

The **OlTextEditUpdate** function is used to set the **updateState** of a **TextEdit** widget. Setting the state to **FALSE** turns screen update off; setting the state to **TRUE** turns screen updates on and refreshes the display.

RETURN VALUE

On success, **OlTextEditUpdate** returns **TRUE**.

On failure, if the widget supplied is not a **TextEdit** widget, or a subclass of **TextEdit**, **OlTextEditUpdate** returns **FALSE**.

SEE ALSO

OlTextEditRedraw(3Olit), **TextEdit**(3Olit)

OlTextFieldCopyString (3Olit)

NAME

OlTextFieldCopyString – copy a **TextField** string

SYNOPSIS

#include <Xol/OpenLook.h>
#include <Xol/TextField.h>

int OlTextFieldCopyString(Widget *tfw*, String *string*);

DESCRIPTION

The OlTextFieldCopyString function is used to copy the string associated with the **TextField** widget *tfw* into the user supplied area pointed to by *string*.

RETURN VALUES

On success, OlTextFieldCopyString returns the length (in bytes) of this string.

SEE ALSO

OlTextFieldGetString(3Olit), **TextField**(3Olit)

NAME

OlTextFieldGetString – get a **TextField** string

SYNOPSIS

#include <Xol/OpenLook.h>
#include <Xol/TextField.h>

char * OlTextFieldGetString(TextFieldWidget *tfw*, Cardinal *∗size*);

DESCRIPTION

The OlTextFieldGetString function is used to retrieve a new copy of the string associated with the **TextField** Widget *tfw*.

RETURN VALUES

The function returns a pointer to the newly allocated string copy. Optionally, if *size* is not NULL, the function returns in *size* the length of the string.

SEE ALSO

OlTextFieldCopyString(3Olit), **TextField**(3Olit)

OlTextWidth (3Olit)

NAME

NAME

       `OlTextWidth` – get a localized string's width in pixels

SYNOPSIS

       `#include <Xol/OpenLook.h>`

       `int OlTextWidth(OlFontList *fontlist, unsigned char *string, int len);`

DESCRIPTION

       The `OlTextWidth` function returns the width of an EUC string in pixels and as such replaces the Xlib function `TextWidth`.

       fontlist   is a pointer to a list of `XFontStruct`

       string   specifies a string whose width in pixels is to be computed

       len   specifies the length of *string* in bytes (not characters)

RETURN VALUES

       On success, the function returns the width of the *string* in pixels. On failure, it returns 0.

NAME

OlToolkitInitialize – initialize OPEN LOOK toolkit

SYNOPSIS

```
#include <Xol/OpenLook.h>
. . .

void OlToolkitInitialize(int *argc, char **argv, XtPointer closure);
```

DESCRIPTION

The **OlToolkitInitialize** procedure determines the GUI mode and initializes the OPEN LOOK toolkit internals. This routine must be called by each application before initializing the Xt Intrinsics and the widget creations.

> *argc*   specifies a pointer to the number of command line parameters
>
> *argv*   specifies the command line parameters
>
> *closure*   is reserved for future extensions

For determining the GUI mode, the following steps are taken:

1. set the GUI mode to **OL_OPENLOOK_GUI** initially,

2. look for the environment variable, **XGUI**, and if non-null, then set the appropriate GUI mode, that is, **OL_OPENLOOK_GUI** if **XGUI=OPEN_LOOK** or **OL_MOTIF_GUI** if **XGUI=MOTIF**,

3. parse the command line for **–openlook** or **–motif**, and if found, remove the option from **argv** and **argc** and set the GUI mode to **OL_OPENLOOK_GUI** or **OL_MOTIF_GUI**.

EXAMPLES

```
OlToolkitInitialize(...);
toplevel = XtInitialize(...);
. . .
XtMainLoop();
```

OR

```
OlToolkitInitialize(...);
toplevel = XtAppInitialize(&app_context, ...);
. . .
XtAppMainLoop(app_context);
```

OR

```
OlToolkitInitialize(...);
XtToolkitInitialize(...);
app_context = XtCreateApplicationContext();
dpy = XtOpenDisplay(...);
/* or dpy = XOpenDisplay(...);
 * XtDisplayInitialize(app_context, dpy, ...);
 */
toplevel = XtAppCreateShell(..., applicationShellWidgetClass, ...);
. . .
XtAppMainLoop(app_context);
```

OlToolkitInitialize (3Olit)

You should refer to "X Toolkit Intrinsics - C Language Interface" for other information.

SEE ALSO

OlGetGui(3Olit), OlInitialize(3Olit), OlSetGui(3Olit)

NAME

    OlUngrabDragPointer – release an active pointer grab

SYNOPSIS

    #include <Xol/OpenLook.h>

    void OlUngrabDragPointer(Widget w);

DESCRIPTION

    The **OlUngrabDragPointer** procedure is used to relinquish the active pointer grab which was initiated by the **OlGrabDragPointer** procedure. This function simply ungrabs the pointer.

NOTES

    The **OlUngrabDragPointer** function is obsolete. Use **OlDnDUngrabDragCursor** instead.

SEE ALSO

    OlDnDUngrabDragCursor(3DnD)

OlUnpostPopupMenu (3Olit)

NAME

    `OlUnpostPopupMenu` – unpost a **popupMenuShell** widget

SYNOPSIS

    `void OlUnpostPopupMenu(Widget` *popup_menu*`);`

DESCRIPTION

    This routine unposts a **popupMenuShell** widget.

SEE ALSO

    `PopupMenuShell`(3Olit)

NAME

OlUnregisterDynamicCallback – remove function from callback list

SYNOPSIS

```
#include <Xol/OpenLook.h>

int OlUnregisterDynamicCallback(
    OlDynamicCallbackProc CB,
    XtPointer data
);
```

DESCRIPTION

The OlUnregisterDynamicCallback procedure is used to remove a function from the list of registered callbacks to be called whenever the procedure OlCallDynamic-Callbacks is invoked.

RETURN VALUE

Zero (0) is returned if the dynamic callback cannot be removed; otherwise one (1) is returned.

SEE ALSO

OlCallDynamicCallbacks(3Olit), OlRegisterDynamicCallback(3Olit)

OlUnsetIcFocus (3Olit)

NAME

NAME

OlUnsetIcFocus – notify Input Method a window has lost focus

SYNOPSIS

`#include <Xol/OpenLook.h>`

`void OlUnsetIcFocus(OlIc *ic);`

DESCRIPTION

The `OlUnsetIcFocus` function informs the Input Method that the text insertion window associated with a particular Input Context no longer has the input focus and should not receive the keyboard events. Its implementation depends on the Input Method. The Input Method may choose to give some visual feedback to indicate loss of focus (for example, change color of cursor in pre-edit text).

SEE ALSO

`OlIcValues`(4), `OlSetIcFocus`(3Olit)

NAME

OlUpdateDisplay – process all pending exposure events immediately

SYNOPSIS

```
#include <Xol/OpenLook.h>

void OlUpdateDisplay(Widget w);
```

DESCRIPTION

The OlUpdateDisplay procedure is used to process all pending exposure events so that the appearance of a given widget can be updated right away.

Normally, an operation is accomplished by a set of callback functions. If one of the callback functions performs a time-consuming action, it is possible that the portion of an application window will not be redrawn right away after a XtSetValues call. This is because the normal exposure processing does not occur until all callback functions have been invoked. This situation can be resolved by calling this function before starting a time-consuming action.

EXAMPLE

```
    ...
#include <Xol/OpenLook.h>
    ...
extern Widget     status_area;      /* a staticText widget */
    ...
void
fooCB(w, client_data, call_data)
    Widget    w;
    XtPointer  client_data;
    XtPointer  call_data;
    {
        ...
        Arg     args[5];

            /* display the status in the footer area     */
            /* before the actual operation               */
        XtSetArg(args[0], XtNstring,
                    "Start the operation, please wait ...");
        XtSetValues(status_area, args, 1);
            /* show the status in the footer area right away*/
        OlUpdateDisplay(status_area);

            /* now we can start the actual operation      */
        ...
        return;
    }
```

OlWidgetClassToClassName (3Olit)

NAME

OlWidgetClassToClassName – find the classname for a widget class

SYNOPSIS

`#include <Xol/OpenLook.h>`

`String OlWidgetClassToClassName(WidgetClass wc);`

DESCRIPTION

Given a widget class, the function returns the classname of the widget.

SEE ALSO

OlWidgetToClassName(3Olit)

NAME

`OlWidgetSearchIEDB` – register a given database on a specific widget instance

SYNOPSIS

```
#include <Xol/OpenLook.h>

void OlWidgetSearchIEDB(Widget w, OlVirtualEventTable db);
```

DESCRIPTION

The `OlWidgetSearchIEDB` procedure is used to register a given database on a specific widget instance. The *db* value was returned from a call to `OlCreateInputEventDB`.

Once a database is registered with a given widget instance, the `OlLookupInputEvent`(3Olit) procedure (if *db_flag* is `OL_DEFAULT_IE` or *db*) will include this database in the search stack if the given widget ID is this widget instance.

NOTES

The registering order determines the searching order when doing a lookup.

EXAMPLE

```
        /* To create a client application database */
    ...
#include <Xol/OpenLook.h>
    ...
        /* start with a big value to avoid */
        /* the "virtual_name" collision   */
#define OL_MY_BASE              1000
#define OL_MY_DRAWLINEBTN       OL_MY_BASE+0
#define OL_MY_DRAWARCBTN        OL_MY_BASE+1
#define OL_MY_REDISPLAYKEY      OL_MY_BASE+2
#define OL_MY_SAVEPARTKEY       OL_MY_BASE+3

#define XtNmyDrawLineBtn        "myDrawLineBtn"
#define XtNmyDrawArcBtn         "myDrawArcBtn"
#define XtNmyRedisplayKey       "myRedisplayKey"
#define XtNmySavePartKey        "mySavePartKey"

static OlKeyOrBtnRec    OlMyBtnInfo[] = {
    /*name              default_value       virtual_name        */

    { XtNmyDrawLineBtn,  "c<Button1>",          OL_MY_DRAWLINEBTN  },
    { XtNmyDrawArcBtn,   "s<myDrawLineBtn>", OL_MY_DRAWARCBTN   },
};
static OlKeyOrBtnRec    OlMyKeyInfo[] = {
    /*name              default_value       virtual_name        */

    { XtNmyRedisplayKey, "c<F5>",               OL_MY_REDISPLAYKEY },
    { XtNmySavePartKey,  "c<F5>",               OL_MY_SAVEPARTKEY  },
};

static OlVirtualEventTable      OlMyDB;
```

OlWidgetSearchlEDB (3Olit)

```
      ...
    OlMyDB = OlCreateInputEventDB(
                 w,
                 OlMyKeyInfo, XtNumber(OlMyKeyInfo),
                 OlMyBtnInfo, XtNumber(OlMyBtnInfo)
         );
         ...
         /* assume: "w" is a stub widget that is interested in */
         /*           OlMyDB                                    */
    OlWidgetSearchIEDB(w, OlMyDB);
         /* once this step is done, this widget instance will  */
         /* receive OlMyDB commands after a call to             */
         /* OlLookupInputEvent(), or in the XtNconsumeEvent     */
         /* callback's OlVirtualEvent structure supplied with   */
         /* the call_data field.                                */
         ...
```

SEE ALSO

OlClassSearchIEDB(3Olit), OlClassSearchTextDB(3Olit),
OlClassUnsearchIEDB(3Olit), OlCreateInputEventDB(3Olit),
OlDestroyInputEventDB(3Olit), OlLookupInputEvent(3Olit),
OlWidgetSearchTextDB(3Olit), OlWidgetUnsearchIEDB(3Olit)

NAME

`OlWidgetSearchTextDB` – register the OPEN LOOK TEXT database on a specific widget instance

SYNOPSIS

`#include <Xol/OpenLook.h>`

`void OlWidgetSearchTextDB(Widget` *w*`);`

DESCRIPTION

The `OlWidgetSearchTextDB` procedure is used to register the OPEN LOOK TEXT database on a specific widget instance.

Once the OPEN LOOK TEXT database is registered with a given widget instance, the `OlLookupInputEvent` function (if *db_flag* is `OL_DEFAULT_IE` or `OL_TEXT_IE`) will include this database in the search stack if the given widget ID is this widget instance.

NOTES

The registering order determines the searching order when doing a lookup.

EXAMPLE

```
    ...
#include <Xol/OpenLook.h>
    ...

        /* assume: "w" is a stub widget that is interested in */
        /*           the OPEN LOOK TEXT database               */
OlWidgetSearchTextDB(w);
        /* once this step is done, this widget instance will  */
        /* receive OPEN LOOK TEXT commands after a call       */
        /* to OlLookupInputEvent(), or in the XtNconsumeEvent */
        /* callback's OlVirtualEvent structure supplied with  */
        /* the call_data field.                               */
    ...
```

SEE ALSO

`OlClassSearchIEDB`(3Olit), `OlClassSearchTextDB`(3Olit), `OlCreateInputEventDB`(3Olit), `OlLookupInputEvent`(3Olit), `OlWidgetSearchIEDB`(3Olit)

OlWidgetToClassName (3Olit)

NAME

OlWidgetToClassName – find the class name for a widget

SYNOPSIS

`#include <Xol/OpenLook.h>`

`String OlWidgetToClassName(Widget` w`);`

DESCRIPTION

Given a widget, the function returns the classname of the widget.

SEE ALSO

OlWidgetClassToClassName(3Olit)

NAME

OlWidgetUnsearchIEDB – unregister a database on a widget instance

SYNOPSIS

#include <Xol/OpenLook.h>

void OlWidgetUnsearchIEDB(Widget *widget*, OlVirtualEventTable *db*);

DESCRIPTION

The OlWidgetUnsearchIEDB procedure is used to unregister a given database on a specific widget instance. All widget instances with the reference *db* will be removed from the list of registered databases if the *widget* value is NULL.

The *db* value can be either OL_TEXT_IE or a value that was returned from a call to OlCreateInputEventDB.

SEE ALSO

OlClassSearchIEDB(3Olit), OlClassSearchTextDB(3Olit), OlClassUnsearchIEDB(3Olit), OlCreateInputEventDB(3Olit), OlDestroyInputEventDB(3Olit), OlWidgetSearchIEDB(3Olit), OlWidgetSearchTextDB(3Olit)

panel_above (3curses)

NAME

panel_above: panel_above, panel_below – panels deck traversal primitives

SYNOPSIS

#include <panel.h>

PANEL *panel_above(PANEL *panel);
PANEL *panel_below(PANEL *panel);

DESCRIPTION

panel_above returns a pointer to the panel just above *panel*, or **NULL** if *panel* is the top panel. **panel_below** returns a pointer to the panel just below *panel*, or **NULL** if *panel* is the bottom panel.

If **NULL** is passed for *panel*, **panel_above** returns a pointer to the bottom panel in the deck, and **panel_below** returns a pointer to the top panel in the deck.

RETURN VALUE

NULL is returned if an error occurs.

NOTES

These routines allow traversal of the deck of currently visible panels.

The header file **panel.h** automatically includes the header file **curses.h**.

SEE ALSO

curses(3curses), **panels**(3curses)

NAME

panel_move: move_panel – move a **panels** window on the virtual screen

SYNOPSIS

#include <panel.h>

int move_panel(PANEL *panel, int *starty*, int *startx*);

DESCRIPTION

move_panel moves the **curses** window associated with *panel* so that its upper left-hand corner is at *starty, startx*. See NOTES, below.

RETURN VALUE

OK is returned if the routine completes successfully, otherwise **ERR** is returned.

NOTES

For **panels** windows, use **move_panel** instead of the **mvwin curses** routine. Otherwise, **update_panels** will not properly update the virtual screen.

The header file **panel.h** automatically includes the header file **curses.h**.

SEE ALSO

curses(3curses), **panels**(3curses), **panel_update**(3curses)

panel_new (3curses)

NAME

panel_new: **new_panel**, **del_panel** – create and destroy **panels**

SYNOPSIS

#include <panel.h>

PANEL *new_panel(WINDOW *win);
int del_panel(PANEL *panel);

DESCRIPTION

new_panel creates a new panel associated with *win* and returns the panel pointer. The new panel is placed on top of the panel deck.

del_panel destroys *panel*, but not its associated window.

RETURN VALUE

new_panel returns **NULL** if an error occurs.

del_win returns **OK** if successful, **ERR** otherwise.

NOTES

The header file **panel.h** automatically includes the header file **curses.h**.

SEE ALSO

curses(3curses), **panels**(3curses), **panel_update**(3curses)

NAME

panel_show: show_panel, hide_panel, panel_hidden – panels deck manipulation routines

SYNOPSIS

```
#include <panel.h>
```

```
int show_panel(PANEL *panel);
int hide_panel(PANEL *panel);
int panel_hidden(PANEL *panel);
```

DESCRIPTION

show_panel makes *panel*, previously hidden, visible and places it on top of the deck of panels.

hide_panel removes *panel* from the panel deck and, thus, hides it from view. The internal data structure of the panel is retained.

panel_hidden returns TRUE (1) or FALSE (0) indicating whether or not *panel* is in the deck of panels.

RETURN VALUE

show_panel and hide_panel return the integer OK upon successful completion or ERR upon error.

NOTES

The header file panel.h automatically includes the header file curses.h.

SEE ALSO

curses(3curses), panels(3curses), panel_update(3curses)

panel_top(3curses)

NAME

panel_top: top_panel, bottom_panel – panels deck manipulation routines

SYNOPSIS

#include <panel.h>

int top_panel(PANEL *panel);
int bottom_panel(PANEL *panel);

DESCRIPTION

top_panel pulls *panel* to the top of the desk of panels. It leaves the size, location, and contents of its associated window unchanged.

bottom_panel puts *panel* at the bottom of the deck of panels. It leaves the size, location, and contents of its associated window unchanged.

RETURN VALUE

All of these routines return the integer OK upon successful completion or ERR upon error.

NOTES

The header file panel.h automatically includes the header file curses.h.

SEE ALSO

curses(3curses), panels(3curses), panel_update(3curses)

NAME

panel_update: update_panels – panels virtual screen refresh routine

SYNOPSIS

```
#include <panel.h>
```

```
void update_panels(void);
```

DESCRIPTION

update_panels refreshes the virtual screen to reflect the depth relationships between the panels in the deck. The user must use the curses library call **doupdate** [see **curs_refresh**(3curses)] to refresh the physical screen.

NOTES

The header file **panel.h** automatically includes the header file **curses.h**.

SEE ALSO

curses(3curses), **curs_refresh**(3curses), **panels**(3curses)

panel_userptr (3curses)

NAME

panel_userptr: set_panel_userptr, **panel_userptr** – associate application data with a **panels** panel

SYNOPSIS

```
#include <panel.h>

int set_panel_userptr(PANEL *panel, char *ptr);
char *panel_userptr(PANEL *panel);
```

DESCRIPTION

Each panel has a user pointer available for maintaining relevant information.

set_panel_userptr sets the user pointer of *panel* to *ptr*.

panel_userptr returns the user pointer of *panel*.

RETURN VALUE

set_panel_userptr returns OK if successful, ERR otherwise.

panel_userptr returns NULL if there is no user pointer assigned to *panel*.

NOTES

The header file **panel.h** automatically includes the header file **curses.h**.

SEE ALSO

curses(3curses), **panels**(3curses)

NAME

panel_window: **panel_window**, **replace_panel** – get or set the current window of a **panels** panel

SYNOPSIS

```
#include <panel.h>
```

```
WINDOW *panel_window(PANEL *panel);
int replace_panel(PANEL *panel, WINDOW *win);
```

DESCRIPTION

panel_window returns a pointer to the window of *panel*.

replace_panel replaces the current window of *panel* with *win*.

RETURN VALUE

panel_window returns **NULL** on failure.

replace_panel returns **OK** on successful completion, **ERR** otherwise.

NOTES

The header file **panel.h** automatically includes the header file **curses.h**.

SEE ALSO

curses(3curses), **panels**(3curses)

panels (3curses)

NAME

`panels` – character based panels package

SYNOPSIS

`#include <panel.h>`

DESCRIPTION

The **panel** library is built using the **curses** library, and any program using **panels** routines must call one of the **curses** initialization routines such as **initscr**. A program using these routines must be compiled with **–lpanel** and **–lcurses** on the **cc** command line.

The **panels** package gives the applications programmer a way to have depth relationships between **curses** windows; a **curses** window is associated with every panel. The **panels** routines allow **curses** windows to overlap without making visible the overlapped portions of underlying windows. The initial **curses** window, **stdscr**, lies beneath all panels. The set of currently visible panels is the *deck* of panels.

The **panels** package allows the applications programmer to create panels, fetch and set their associated windows, shuffle panels in the deck, and manipulate panels in other ways.

Routine Name Index

The following table lists each **panels** routine and the name of the manual page on which it is described.

panels Routine Name	Manual Page Name
bottom_panel	panel_top(3curses)
del_panel	panel_new(3curses)
hide_panel	panel_show(3curses)
move_panel	panel_move(3curses)
new_panel	panel_new(3curses)
panel_above	panel_above(3curses)
panel_below	panel_above(3curses)
panel_hidden	panel_show(3curses)
panel_userptr	panel_userptr(3curses)
panel_window	panel_window(3curses)
replace_panel	panel_window(3curses)
set_panel_userptr	panel_userptr(3curses)
show_panel	panel_show(3curses)
top_panel	panel_top(3curses)
update_panels	panel_update(3curses)

RETURN VALUE

Each **panels** routine that returns a pointer to an object returns **NULL** if an error occurs. Each panel routine that returns an integer, returns **OK** if it executes successfully and **ERR** if it does not.

NOTES

The header file **panel.h** automatically includes the header file **curses.h**.

SEE ALSO

curses(3curses), and 3curses pages whose names begin with **panel_** , for detailed routine descriptions

Pixel_Conversion (3Olit)

NAME

Pixel_Conversion: OlMMToPixel, OlPointToPixel, OlScreenMMToPixel, OlScreenPointToPixel, OlPixelToMM, OlPixedToPoint, OlScreenPixelToPoint, OlScreenPixeltoMM – examine physical dimensions and pixel resolution of a screen

SYNOPSIS

```
#include <Xol/OpenLook.h>

Screen *OlDefaultScreen;
Display *OlDefaultDisplay;

OlDefine axis;
Screen *screen;

OlMMToPixel(axis, millimeters);
Ol_MMToPixel(axis, millimeters);

OlPointToPixel(axis, points);
Ol_PointToPixel(axis, points);

OlScreenMMToPixel(axis, millimeters, screen);
Ol_ScreenMMToPixel(axis, millimeters, screen);

OlScreenPointToPixel(axis, points, screen);
Ol_ScreenPointToPixel(axis, points, screen);

OlPixelToMM(axis, pixels);
Ol_PixelToMM(axis, pixels);

OlPixelToPoint(axis, pixels);
Ol_PixelToPoint(axis, pixels);

OlScreenPixelToPoint(axis, pixels, screen);
Ol_ScreenPixelToPoint(axis, pixels, screen);

OlScreenPixelToMM(axis, pixels, screen);
Ol_ScreenPixelToMM(axis, pixels, screen);
```

DESCRIPTION

All the X-based OPEN LOOK widgets refer to pixels in coordinates and dimensions for compatibility with other X Window System widgets. However, this puts the burden on the application programmer to convert between externally useful measures, such as points or millimeters, and pixels as applied to the screen at hand. These routines examine the data structures that describe the physical dimensions and the pixel resolution of a screen and convert among millimeters, points, and pixels for that screen.

Which Screen?

The shorter forms of these routines (the ones without the word **Screen** in their names) work for the default screen. This is the screen that is active when the X Toolkit Intrinsics are started. The longer forms of these routines take a **Screen *** type argument that refers to a particular screen.

The macros **OlDefaultScreen** and **OlDefaultDisplay** identify the current screen and display being used by the Intrinsics. Although the SYNOPSIS above implies these are variables of type **Screen *** and **Display ***, respectively, they are really macros that produce values of these types.

Note: Use After Toolkit Initialization

These routines make use of data structures that are initialized when the Toolkit is initialized (see `OlInitialize` later in this document). Therefore, using them before Toolkit initilization (for example, as an initial value to a statically defined variable) will result in a *run time* error.

Axis Argument

The first argument of all the routines is the direction in which the measurement is made. This is necessary because not all screens have equivalent resolution in the horizontal and vertical axes. The **axis** argument can take one of the two values: **OL_HORIZONTAL** or **OL_VERTICAL**. These routines are not directly usable in computing a diagonal measure. (Find the diagonal with the Pythagorean Theorem: $a^2 + b^2 = c^2$)

Implemented as Macros

All these routines are implemented as macros, so they can take any reasonable type value for the **millimeters**, **points**, and **pixels**. The macros cast the values into the proper type needed for the conversion. However, only a single type value can be "returned". The routines without an underscore in their names produce values of type **int** (the values are rounded to the nearest integer). The routines with an underscore in their names produce values of type **double** (these values have not been rounded, leaving it up to the application to round up, round down, or truncate as needed). Given the small size of the units involved, the integer returning routines should be sufficient for many applications.

Because these routines are implemented as macros, there are no function addresses available.

PositionOfLine (3Olit)

NAME

PositionOfLine – convert a `TextLine` into a `TextPosition`

SYNOPSIS

`#include <Xol/textbuff.h>`

`TextPosition PositionOfLine(TextBuffer *text, TextLine lineindex);`

DESCRIPTION

The `PositionOfLine` function is used to translate a *lineindex* in the *text* `TextBuffer` to a `TextPosition`.

RETURN VALUES

On success, `PositionOfLine` returns the translated `TextPosition` or EOF if the `lineindex` is invalid.

SEE ALSO

LineOfPosition(3Olit), LocationOfPosition(3Olit), PositionOfLocation(3Olit)

NAME

PositionOfLocation – convert a TextLocation into a TextPosition

SYNOPSIS

#include <Xol/textbuff.h>

TextPosition PositionOfLocation(TextBuffer *text,
    TextLocation *location*);

DESCRIPTION

The PositionOfLocation function is used to translate a *location* in the *text* TextBuffer to a TextPosition.

RETURN VALUES

PositionOfLocation returns the translated TextPosition or EOF if the *location* is invalid.

SEE ALSO

PositionOfLine(3Olit), LocationOfPosition(3Olit)

PreviousLocation (3Olit)

NAME

      PreviousLocation – return the previous location in a **TextBuffer**

SYNOPSIS

      `#include <Xol/textbuff.h>`

      `TextLocation PreviousLocation(`
          `TextBuffer` *textBuffer*,
          `TextLocation` *current*
      `);`

DESCRIPTION

      The **PreviousLocation** function returns the location which precedes the given *current* location in a **TextBuffer**. If the current location points to the beginning of the **TextBuffer** this function wraps.

SEE ALSO

      NextLocation(3Olit)

NAME

PreviousTextBufferWord – find the beginning of a word in a `TextBuffer`

SYNOPSIS

```
#include <Xol/textbuff.h>

TextLocation PreviousTextBufferWord(
    TextBuffer *textBuffer,
    TextLocation current
);
```

DESCRIPTION

The `PreviousTextBufferWord` function is used to locate the beginning of a word in a `TextBuffer` relative to a given *current* location. It returns the location of the beginning of the word which precedes the given current location. If the current location is within a word this function will skip over the current word. If the current word is the first word in the `TextBuffer` the function wraps to the end of the buffer.

SEE ALSO

PreviousTextBufferWord(3Olit)

ReadFileIntoBuffer (3Olit)

NAME

ReadFileIntoBuffer – read a file into a `Buffer`

SYNOPSIS

`#include <Xol/buffutil.h>`

`int ReadFileIntoBuffer(FILE *fp, Buffer *buffer);`

DESCRIPTION

The `ReadFileIntoBuffer` function reads the file associated with *fp* and inserts the characters read into the *buffer*. The read operation terminates when either EOF is returned when reading the file or when a NEWLINE is encountered. The function returns the last character read to the caller (either EOF or NEWLINE).

SEE ALSO

ReadStringIntoBuffer(3Olit)

NAME

ReadFileIntoTextBuffer – read a file into a TextBuffer

SYNOPSIS

```
#include <Xol/textbuff.h>

TextBuffer *ReadFileIntoTextBuffer(
    char *filename,
    TextUpdateFunction f,
    caddr_t d
);
```

DESCRIPTION

The ReadFileIntoTextBuffer function is used to read the given file, *filename*, into a newly allocated TextBuffer. The supplied TextUpdateFunction, *f*, and data pointer, *d*, are associated with this TextBuffer.

SEE ALSO

AllocateTextBuffer(3Olit), ReadPipeIntoTextBuffer(3Olit), ReadStringIntoTextBuffer(3Olit), RegisterTextBufferUpdate(3Olit)

ReadPipeIntoTextBuffer (3Olit)

NAME

ReadPipeIntoTextBuffer – read a pipe into a `TextBuffer`

SYNOPSIS

```
#include <Xol/textbuff.h>

TextBuffer *ReadPipeIntoTextBuffer(
    FILE *fp,
    TextUpdateFunction f,
    caddr_t d
);
```

DESCRIPTION

The `ReadPipeIntoTextBuffer` function is used to read the given pipe, *fp*, into a newly allocated `TextBuffer`. The supplied `TextUpdateFunction`, *f*, and data pointer, *d*, are associated with this `TextBuffer`.

SEE ALSO

AllocateTextBuffer(3Olit), ReadFileIntoTextBuffer(3Olit), ReadStringIntoTextBuffer(3Olit), RegisterTextBufferUpdate(3Olit)

NAME

      `ReadStringIntoBuffer` – read a string into a `Buffer`

SYNOPSIS

      `#include <Xol/buffutil.h>`

      `int ReadStringIntoBuffer(Buffer *sp, Buffer *buffer);`

DESCRIPTION

      The `ReadStringIntoBuffer` function reads the buffer associated with *sp* and inserts the characters read into *buffer*. The read operation terminates when either EOF is returned when reading the buffer or when a NEWLINE is encountered. The function returns the last character read to the caller (either EOF or NEWLINE).

SEE ALSO

      `ReadFileIntoBuffer`(3Olit)

ReadStringIntoTextBuffer (3Olit)

NAME

    `ReadStringIntoTextBuffer` – read a string into a `TextBuffer`

SYNOPSIS

    `#include <Xol/textbuff.h>`

```
TextBuffer *ReadStringIntoTextBuffer(
    char *string,
    TextUpdateFunction f,
    caddr_t d
);
```

DESCRIPTION

    The `ReadStringIntoTextBuffer` function is used to copy the given *string* into a newly allocated `TextBuffer`. The supplied `TextUpdateFunction`, *f*, and data pointer, *d*, are associated with this `TextBuffer`.

SEE ALSO

    `AllocateTextBuffer`(3Olit), `ReadFileIntoTextBuffer`(3Olit), `ReadPipeIntoTextBuffer`(3Olit), `RegisterTextBufferUpdate`(3Olit)

NAME

RegisterTextBufferScanFunctions – replace functions for scanning TextBuffer

SYNOPSIS

```
#include <Xol/textbuff.h>

void RegisterTextBufferScanFunctions(
        char *(*forward)(char *string, char *curp, char *expression),
        char *(*backward)(char *string, char *curp, char *expression)
);
```

DESCRIPTION

The **RegisterTextBufferScanFunctions** function provides the capability to replace the scan functions used by the **ForwardScanTextBuffer** and **BackwardScanTextBuffer** functions, and are responsible for returning either a pointer to the beginning of a match for the expression or NULL.

Calling this procedure with NULL function pointers reinstates the default regular expression facility.

SEE ALSO

BackwardScanTextBuffer(3Olit), ForwardScanTextBuffer(3Olit), strexp(3Olit), strrexp(3Olit)

RegisterTextBufferUpdate (3Olit)

NAME

RegisterTextBufferUpdate – assign **TextBuffer** an update function and pointer

SYNOPSIS

```
#include <Xol/textbuff.h>
```

void RegisterTextBufferUpdate(TextBuffer *text, TextUpdateFunction *f*,
    caddr_t *d*);

DESCRIPTION

The **RegisterTextBufferUpdate** procedure associates the **TextUpdateFunction** *f* and data pointer *d* with the given **TextBuffer** *text*. This update function will be called whenever an update operation is performed on the **TextBuffer**. See **ReplaceBlockInTextBuffer** for more details.

NOTES

Calling this function increments a reference count mechanism used to determine when to actually free the **TextBuffer**. Calling the function with a NULL value for the function circumvents this mechanism.

SEE ALSO

ReadFileIntoTextBuffer(3Olit), ReadStringIntoTextBuffer(3Olit),
ReplaceBlockInTextBuffer(3Olit), UnregisterTextBufferUpdate(3Olit)

NAME

    `RegisterTextBufferWordDefinition` – replace word definition

SYNOPSIS

    `#include <Xol/textbuff.h>`

    `void RegisterTextBufferWordDefinition(*word_definition(int c));`

DESCRIPTION

    The `RegisterTextBufferWordDefinition` function provides the capability to replace the word definition function used by the Text Buffer Utilities.

    Calling this function with NULL reinstates the default word definition which allows the following set of characters: a-zA-Z0-9_

RETURN VALUES

    On success, if the character c is considered a character that can occur in a word, `RegisterTextBufferWordDefinition` returns non-zero. On failure, `RegisterTextBufferWordDefinition` returns zero.

SEE ALSO

    `TextBuffer_Macros`(3Olit)

ReplaceBlockInTextBuffer (3Olit)

NAME

ReplaceBlockInTextBuffer – update a block of data in a **TextBuffer**

SYNOPSIS

```
#include <Xol/textbuff.h>

EditResult ReplaceBlockInTextBuffer(TextBuffer *text,
    TextLocation *startloc, TextLocation *endloc, char *string,
    TextUpdateFunction f, caddr_t d);
```

DESCRIPTION

The **ReplaceBlockInTextBuffer** function is used to update the contents of the **TextBuffer** associated with *text*. The characters stored between *startloc* and *endloc* are deleted and the *string* is inserted after *startloc*. If the edit succeeds the **TextUpdateFunction** *f* is called with the parameters: *d, text*, and **1**; then any other different update functions associated with the **TextBuffer** are called with their associated data pointer, *text*, and 0.

This function records the operation performed in **TextUndoItem** structures. The contents of these structures can be used to implement an undo function. The contents can also be used to determine the type of operation performed. A structure is allocated for both the delete and insert information.

The hints provided in these structures is the inclusive OR of:

```
TEXT_BUFFER_NOP
TEXT_BUFFER_INSERT_LINE
TEXT_BUFFER_INSERT_SPLIT_LINE
TEXT_BUFFER_INSERT_CHARS
TEXT_BUFFER_DELETE_START_LINE
TEXT_BUFFER_DELETE_END_LINE
TEXT_BUFFER_DELETE_START_CHARS
TEXT_BUFFER_DELETE_END_CHARS
TEXT_BUFFER_DELETE_JOIN_LINE
TEXT_BUFFER_DELETE_SIMPLE
```

SEE ALSO

ReplaceCharInTextBuffer(3Olit)

NAME

ReplaceCharInTextBuffer – replace a character in a **TextBuffer**

SYNOPSIS

```
#include <Xol/textbuff.h>

EditResult ReplaceCharInTextBuffer(TextBuffer *text,
    TextLocation *location, int c, TextUpdateFunction f,
    caddr_t d);
```

DESCRIPTION

The **ReplaceCharInTextBuffer** function is used to replace the character in the **TextBuffer** *text* at *location* with the character *c*.

SEE ALSO

ReplaceBlockInTextBuffer(3Olit)

SaveTextBuffer (3Olit)

NAME

SaveTextBuffer – write a **TextBuffer** to a file

SYNOPSIS

```
#include <Xol/textbuff.h>
```

SaveResult SaveTextBuffer(TextBuffer *text, char *filename);

DESCRIPTION

The **SaveTextBuffer** function is used to write the contents of the *text* **TextBuffer** to the file *filename*. The contents are written in multibyte format.

RETURN VALUES

On success, **SaveResult** returns **SAVE_SUCCESS**.

On failure, **SaveResult** returns **SAVE_FAILURE**.

NAME

StartCurrentTextBufferWord – find beginning of a word in a **TextBuffer**

SYNOPSIS

```
#include <Xol/textbuff.h>

TextLocation StartCurrentTextBufferWord(
    TextBuffer *textBuffer,
    TextLocation current
);
```

DESCRIPTION

The **StartCurrentTextBufferWord** function is used to locate the beginning of a word in the **TextBuffer** relative to a given *current* location. The function returns the location of the beginning of the current word.

NOTES

The return value will equal the given current value if the current location is the beginning of a word.

SEE ALSO

NextTextBufferWord(3Olit), **PreviousTextBufferWord**(3Olit)

strclose (3Olit)

NAME

strclose – close a string `Buffer`

SYNOPSIS

```
#include <Xol/buffutil.h>
```

```
void strclose(Buffer *sp);
```

DESCRIPTION

The **strclose** procedure is used to close a string `Buffer` which was opened using the **stropen** function.

SEE ALSO

strgetc(3Olit), stropen(3Olit)

NAME

streexp – get pointer to last matching character

SYNOPSIS

```
#include <Xol/regexp.h>

extern char *streexp(void);
```

DESCRIPTION

The streexp function is used to retrieve the pointer of the last character in a match found following a strexp/strrexp function call.

SEE ALSO

strexp(3Olit), strrexp(3Olit)

strexp (3Olit)

NAME

strexp – forward scan a regular expression

SYNOPSIS

#include <Xol/regexp.h>

char *strexp(char *string, char *curp, char *expression);

DESCRIPTION

The strexp function is used to perform a regular expression forward scan of *string* for *expression* starting at *curp*.

The regular expression language used is

```
        c - match c
[<set>] - match any character in <set>
[!<set>] - match any character not in <set>
      * - match any character(s)
      ^ - match must start at curp
```

RETURN VALUES

NULL is returned if expression cannot be found in string; otherwise a pointer to the first character in the substring which matches expression is returned. The function streexp(3Olit) can be used to get the pointer to the last character in the match.

SEE ALSO

streexp(3Olit), strrexp(3Olit)

NAME

`strgetc` – read the next character in a `Buffer`

SYNOPSIS

`#include <Xol/buffutil.h>`

`extern int strgetc(Buffer *buffer);`

DESCRIPTION

The `strgetc` function is used to read the next character stored in the string *buffer*. The function returns the next character in the `Buffer`. When no characters remain the routine returns EOF.

SEE ALSO

`strclose`(3Olit), `stropen`(3Olit)

stropen (3Olit)

NAME

    stropen – copy a string into a `Buffer`

SYNOPSIS

    `#include <Xol/buffutil.h>`

    `Buffer *stropen(char *string);`

DESCRIPTION

    The **stropen** function copies the *string* into a newly allocated Buffer. This string buffer can be *read* using the **strgetc** function and *closed* using the **strclose** procedure. The **strclose** function frees the buffer allocated by **stropen**.

SEE ALSO

    strclose(3Olit), **strgetc**(3Olit)

NAME

strrexp – backward scan a string

SYNOPSIS

```
#include <Xol/regexp.h>
```

`char *strrexp(char *string, char *curp, char *expression);`

DESCRIPTION

The **strrexp** function is used to perform a regular expression backward scan of *string* for *expression* starting at *curp*.

The regular expression language used is

```
        c - match c
 [<set>] - match any character in <set>
[!<set>] - match any character not in <set>
       * - match any character(s)
       ^ - match must start at curp
```

RETURN VALUE

NULL is returned if expression cannot be found in string; otherwise a pointer to the first character in the substring which matches expression is returned. The function **streexp** can be used to get the pointer to the last character in the match.

SEE ALSO

streexp(3Olit), **strexp**(3Olit)

NAME

tam – TAM transition libraries

SYNOPSIS

```
#include <tam.h>

cc -I /usr/include/tam [flags] files -ltam -lcurses [libraries]
```

DESCRIPTION

These routines are used to port UNIX PC character-based TAM programs to any machine so that they will run using any terminal supported by **curses**(3curses), the low-level ETI library. Once a TAM program has been changed to remove machine-specific code, it can be recompiled with the standard TAM header file **<tam.h>** and linked with the TAM transition and **curses**(3curses) libraries.

FUNCTIONS

The following is a list of TAM routines supplied in the transition library. Those routines marked with a dagger (†) are macros and do not return a value. For a complete description of each routine, see the references below.

Routines	Description
addch†, addstr†	see **curses**(3curses)
adf_gttok	converts word to token
adf_gtwrd	Gets next word from string and copies it to buffer
adf_gtxcd	gets next text code from string and copies it to buffer
attroff, attron, baudrate, beep, cbreak, clear, clearok†, clrtobot, clrtoeol, delch, deleteln, echo, endwin, erase†,	see **curses**(3curses)
exhelp	see **message**(1F)
fixterm, flash†, flushinp	see **curses**(3curses)
form	see **forms**(3curses)
getch, getyx†, initscr, insch, insertln	see **curses**(3curses)
iswind	always returns 0
kcodemap, keypad, leaveok†	see **curses**(3curses)
menu	see **menus**(3curses)
message, mtype	see **message**(1F)

Routines	Description
move†, mvaddch†, mvaddstr†, mvinch	see **curses**(3curses)
nl†, nocbreak, nodelay, noecho	not supported
nonl†	not supported
pb_check	Checks whether paste buffer is empty or not
pb_empty	Clears out the paste buffer and closes it
pb_gbuf	Reads pate buffer file into buffer
pb_gets	Reads paste buffer file, converts it to text
pb_name	Gets name of paste buffer file
pb_open	Opens/creates the paste buffer file
pb_puts	Outputs the string to the paste buffer in ADF format
pb_seek	Seeks to end of paste buffer file and sets for append
pb_weof	Outputs "EOF" string to paste buffer and closes the file
printw, refresh†, resetterm, resetty, savetty	see **curses**(3curses)
track, track_t	maps to **wgetc** in the current window
wcmd	Outputs a null- terminated string to the entry/echo line.
wcreate	creates a window
wdelete	deletes the specified window
wexit	deletes all windows and exits
wgetc	gets the keyboard input
wgetmouse	no-op; returns 0
wgetpos	Gets the current position (row, column) of the cursor in the specified window (*wn*).
wgetsel	returns the currently selected window

Routines	Description
`wgetstat`	returns the information in WSTAT for a window
`wgoto`	moves the window's cursor to a specified row, column
`wicoff`	no-op; returns 0
`wicon`	no-op; returns 0
`wind`	creates a window of specific height and width and loads it with the specified fonts
`winit`	Sets up the process for window access
`wlabel, wndelay, wnl`	outputs a null-terminated string to the window label area
`wpostwait`	Reverses the effects of **wprexec**.
`wprexec`	Performs the appropriate actions for passing a window to a child process.
`wprintf, wprompt`	Outputs a null-terminated string to the prompt line.
`wputc`	Outputs a character to a window.
`wputs`	Outputs a character string to a window.
`wrastop`	not supported
`wreadmouse`	no-op; returns 0
`wrefresh`	Flushes all output to the window.
`wselect`	Selects the specified window as the current or active one.
`wsetmouse`	no-op; returns 0
`wsetstat`	Sets the status for a window.
`wslk`	Writes a null-terminated string to a set of screen-labeled keys.
`wslk`	Writes a null-terminated string to a screen-labeled key. The alternate form writes all the screen-labeled keys at once more efficiently.
`wuser`	not supported

NAME

TextBuffer Macros: `TextBufferUserData`, `TextBufferName`, `TextBuffer-Modified`, `TextBufferEmpty`, `TextBufferNamed`, `LinesInTextBuffer`, `Last-TextBufferLine`, `LastCharacterInTextBufferLine`, `LengthOfTextBuffer-Line`, `SameTextLocation` – Text Buffer Macros

SYNOPSIS

```
#include <Xol/textbuff.h>
```

`TextBufferUserData(TextBuffer` *text*, `TextLine` *line*`);`

`TextBufferName(TextBuffer` *text*`);`

`TextBufferModified(TextBuffer` *text*`);`

`TextBufferEmpty(TextBuffer` *text*`);`

`TextBufferNamed(TextBuffer` *text*`);`

`LinesInTextBuffer(TextBuffer` *text*`);`

`LastTextBufferLine(TextBuffer` *text*`);`

`LastCharacterInTextBufferLine(TextBuffer` *text*, `TextLine` *line*`);`

`LengthOfTextBufferLine(TextBuffer` *text*, `TextLine` *line*`);`

`SameTextLocation(TextLocation` *x*, `TextLocation` *y*`);`

DESCRIPTION

These macros are provided for use with the Text Buffer Utilities.

`TextBufferUserData`	used to access the per-line user data.
`TextBufferName`	returns the filename associated with *text*.
`TextBufferModified`	returns a flag indicating whether *text* has been modified since last saved.
`TextBufferEmpty`	returns a flag indicating whether *text* is empty.
`TextBufferNamed`	returns a flag indicating whether *text* is associated with a filename.
`LinesInTextBuffer`	returns the number of lines in *text*.
`LastTextBufferLine`	returns the line number of the last line in *text*.
`LastCharacterInTextBufferLine`	returns the offset of the last character in *text* on *line*.
`LengthOfTextBufferLine`	returns the length of *line* in *text*.
`SameTextLocation`	returns a flag indicating whether location *x* and *y* are the same.

UnregisterTextBufferUpdate (3Olit)

NAME

UnregisterTextBufferUpdate – remove `TextBuffer` update function and pointer

SYNOPSIS

```
#include <Xol/textbuff.h>
```

```
int UnregisterTextBufferUpdate(TextBuffer *text,
    TextUpdateFunction f, caddr_t d);
```

DESCRIPTION

The `UnregisterTextBufferUpdate` function disassociates the `TextUpdateFunction` f and data pointer d with the given `TextBufferfP` *text*.

RETURN VALUES

On success, `UnregisterTextBufferUpdate` returns 0 and the association is dissolved.

On failure, if the function/data pointer pair is not associated with the given `TextBuffer`, `UnregisterTextBufferUpdate` returns 0.

SEE ALSO

FreeTextBuffer(3Olit), RegisterTextBufferUpdate(3Olit)

NAME

OlActivateWidget, OlAssociateWidget, OlUnassociateWidget – activate widget based on widget type

SYNOPSIS

#include <Xol/OpenLook.h>

Boolean OlActivateWidget(Widget *widget*, OlVirtualName *activation_type*, XtPointer *data*);

Boolean OlAssociateWidget(Widget *leader*, Widget *follower*, Boolean *disable_traversal*);

void OlUnassociateWidget(Widget *follower*);

DESCRIPTION

OlActivateWidget programmatically activates a widget using the specified type. (See the widget manual pages for valid activation types.) The function returns **TRUE** if the activation type was accepted by the supplied widget or one of its associated followers; otherwise, **FALSE** is returned. When activating a widget, if the initially-supplied widget does not accept the activation request, **OlActivateWidget** recursively attempts to activate all associated follower widgets until one of them accepts the activation type.

OlAssociateWidget associates a widget (the *follower*) with another widget (the *leader*). Associating a widget with a lead widget effectively expands the number of ways the lead widget can be activated since **OlActivateWidget** automatically activates any *follower* widgets if the lead widget does not accept the supplied activation type. This routine returns **TRUE** if the association was successful; otherwise **FALSE** is returned. Attempts to create an association-cycle is illegal and produces a warning. It's typically desirable to prevent keyboard traversal into widgets which are associated with other widgets. The *disable_traversal* parameter is a convenient interface to setting the *follower* widget's **XtNtraversalOn** resource to **FALSE**.

OlUnassociateWidget removes a *follower* widget from a previous association with another lead widget. No warning is generated if the supplied widget was not previously associated with another widget.

NOTES

The above routines accept gadget arguments also.

WriteTextBuffer (3Olit)

NAME

WriteTextBuffer – write to a **TextBuffer**

SYNOPSIS

`#include <Xol/textbuff.h>`

`WriteResult WriteTextBuffer(TextBuffer *text, FILE *fp);`

DESCRIPTION

The **WriteTextBuffer** function is used to write the contents of a given **TextBuffer**, *text,* to the file pointed to by *fp.* The contents are written in multibyte form.

RETURN VALUES

The function returns a **WriteResult** which can be **WRITE_FAILURE** or **WRITE_SUCCESS**.

SEE ALSO

SaveTextBuffer(3Olit)

NAME

AbbreviatedButton – create a small button to pop up a menu or window

SYNOPSIS

```
#include <X11/Intrinsic.h>
#include <X11/StringDefs.h>
#include <Xol/OpenLook.h>
#include <Xol/AbbrevButt.h>
```

Widget abbrev;

abbrev = XtCreateWidget (*name*, abbreviatedButtonWidgetClass, . . .);

DESCRIPTION

The **AbbreviatedButton** widget is similar to the **AbbreviatedMenuButton** in appearance and features, but **AbbreviatedButton** is designed to work with the **PopupMenuShell** [see **PopupMenuShell**(3Olit)]. The **AbbreviatedButton** widget supports both the MOTIF and the OPEN LOOK look and feel.

Unlike **AbbreviatedMenuButton**, **AbbreviatedButton** does not create a menu-pane that applications use as the parent for adding button widgets and gadgets. Instead, applications create a **PopupMenuShell** widget with a **FlatButtons** widget as its child to define the menu. This shell is then given as the **XtNpopupWidget** resource of the **AbbreviatedButton** to associate the menu with the Abbreviated Button. The Current Selection widget, or preview widget, is programmed identically for both styles of Abbreviated Button.

AbbreviatedButton Components

Each abbreviated button has a popup widget, either a **PopupMenuShell** or a **PopupWindowShell**. An application typically identifies an additional component, the Current Selection widget, where previewing of the default menu choice can be done.

AbbreviatedButton Sensitive Area

While on the abbreviated button and the power-user option is on:

– Pressing SELECT previews the default menu item (if a preview widget exists) and releasing it will activate the default menu item.

– Clicking SELECT previews the default menu item briefly (if a preview widget exists) and then activates the default menu item.

– Pressing MENU brings up a pop-up menu.

– Clicking MENU produces a stayup menu.

If the power-user option is off:

– Pressing SELECT or MENU brings up a pop-up menu.

– Clicking SELECT or MENU produces a stayup menu.

(The power-user option is set in the Miscellaneous property sheet of the desktop manager.)

Current Selection Widget

The Current Selection widget is created by the application. Typically, the Current Selection widget and the **AbbreviatedButton** widget are placed together in a composite widget that manages their side-by-side placement. The **AbbreviatedButton** widget uses the Current Selection widget only for previewing the default item in the menu. The application is responsible for using it to implement the OPEN LOOK user interface needs of showing the current menu selection and acquiring a new item to add to the menu, as appropriate.

AbbreviatedButton Coloration

The abbreviated button shows it has focus differently in different look and feel.

In the MOTIF look and feel, the abbreviated button shows it has focus by drawing a border of `XtNhighlightThickness` in the `XtNinputFocusColor`.

In the OPEN LOOK look and feel. on a monochrome display, the abbreviated button shows it has input focus by inverting the foreground and background colors of the control. On color displays, when the abbreviated button receives input focus, the background color is changed to the input focus color set in the `XtNinputFocusColor` resource.

Note that if the input focus color is the same as the window background color, then the widget inverts the foreground and background colors when it has input focus.

Keyboard Traversal

The default value of the `XtNtraversalOn` resource is `TRUE`.

The action of the SELECTKEY depends on whether the user has selected the power-user option. (The power-user option is set in the property sheet of the desktop manager.) While on the `AbbreviatedButton` and the power-user option is on, clicking the SELECTKEY activates the default menu item. If the power-user option is off, pressing the SELECTKEY posts the stayup menu.

The `AbbreviatedButton` does not control the keyboard traversal between the abbreviated button widget and the Current Selection widget. The Current Selection widget's traversal resources can be set up to allow for traversal between it and the abbreviated button, but it is recommended that the `XtNtraversalOn` resource on the Current Selection widget be `FALSE`. Normal menu traversal can always be used to access the Current Selection widget.

The DEFAULTACTION key will activate the default control in the `Abbreviated-Button` widget as if the user clicked the SELECT button on the control.

Abbreviated Button Activation Types

Activation Type	Expected Results
`OL_SELECTKEY`	see discussion above
`OL_MENUKEY`	popup the abbreviated button's submenu

Display of Keyboard Mnemonic

The `AbbreviatedButton` does not display the mnemonic accelerator. If the `AbbreviatedButton` is the child of a `Caption` widget, the `Caption` widget can be used to display the mnemonic.

RESOURCES

AbbreviatedButton Resource Set					
Name	Class	Type	Default	Acc	Inherit
XtNaccelerator	XtCAccelerator	String	NULL	SGI	Primitive
XtNacceleratorText	XtCAcceleratorText	String	(calculated)	SGI	Primitive
XtNancestorSensitive	XtCSensitive	Boolean	(calculated)	G[1]	Core
XtNbackground	XtCBackground	Pixel	"XtDefaultBackground"	SGI	Core
XtNbackgroundPixmap	XtCPixmap	Pixmap	XtUnspecifiedPixmap	SGI	Core
XtNborderColor	XtCBorderColor	Pixel	"XtDefaultForeground"	SGI	Core
XtNborderPixmap	XtCPixmap	Pixmap	XtUnspecifiedPixmap	SGI	Core
XtNborderWidth	XtCBorderWidth	Dimension	0	SGI	Core
XtNbuttonType	XtCButtonType	OlDefine	OL_MENU_BTN	SGI	
XtNcolormap	XtCColormap	Colormap	(parent's)	GI	Core
XtNconsumeEvent	XtCCallback	XtCallbackList	NULL	SGI	Primitive
XtNdepth	XtCDepth	Cardinal	(parent's)	GI	Core
XtNdestroyCallback	XtCCallback	XtCallbackList	NULL	SGI	Object
XtNfont	XtCFont	XFontStruct *	"OlDefaultFont"	SGI	Primitive
XtNfontColor	XtCFontColor	Pixel	"XtDefaultForeground"	SGI	Primitive
XtNfontGroup	XtCFontGroup	OlFontList *	NULL	SGI	Primitive
XtNforeground	XtCForeground	Pixel	"XtDefaultForeground"	SGI	Primitive
XtNheight	XtCHeight	Dimension	(calculated)	SGI	Core
XtNhighlightThickness	XtCHighlightThickness	Dimension	"2 points"[2]	SGI	Primitive
XtNinputFocusColor	XtCInputFocusColor	Pixel	"Red"	SGI	Primitive
XtNmappedWhenManaged	XtCMappedWhenManaged	Boolean	TRUE	SGI	Core
XtNmnemonic	XtCMnemonic	char	NULL	SGI	Primitive
XtNpopupWidget	XtCPopupWidget	Widget	NULL	SGI	
XtNpreviewWidget	XtCPreviewWidget	Widget	NULL	SGI	
XtNreferenceName	XtCReferenceName	String	NULL	SGI	Primitive
XtNreferenceWidget	XtCReferenceWidget	Widget	NULL	SGI	Primitive
XtNscreen	XtCScreen	Screen *	(parent's)	GI	Core
XtNsensitive	XtCSensitive	Boolean	TRUE	G[1]	Core
XtNshadowThickness	XtCShadowThickness	Dimension	"0 points"[3]	SGI	Primitive
XtNshadowType	XtCShadowType	OlDefine	OL_SHADOW_IN	SGI	Primitive
XtNtranslations	XtCTranslations	XtTranslations	NULL	SGI	Core
XtNtraversalOn	XtCTraversalOn	Boolean	TRUE	SGI	Primitive
XtNuserData	XtCUserData	XtPointer	NULL	SGI	Primitive
XtNwidth	XtCWidth	Dimension	(calculated)	SGI	Core
XtNx	XtCPosition	Position	0	SGI	Core
XtNy	XtCPosition	Position	0	SGI	Core

[1] Use XtSetSensitive to set this resource.
[2] Not used in OPEN LOOK look and feel.
[3] "2 points" in MOTIF look and feel.

AbbreviatedButton (3Olit)

XtNbuttonType
Range of values:

       OL_MENU_BTN/''menubtn''
       OL_WINDOW_BTN/''windowbtn''

This resource defines the look of the abbreviated button.

Setting this resource to **OL_MENU_BTN** will have the look of the abbreviated menu button and a menu pops up when **OL_MENU** or **OL_MENUKEY** is pressed. Setting this resource to **OL_WINDOW_BTN** will give the look of an abbreviated window button with the components indicating a window will pop up from the button.

XtNpopupWidget
Range of values:

       valid widget ID

This resource contains the ID of the popup widget.

A popup widget that is a subclass of **PopupMenuShellClass** must be used if **XtNbuttonType** is set to **OL_MENU_BTN** and **OlPostPopupMenu** function will be used to popup this menu widget.

A popup widget that is a subclass of **TransientShellClass** must be used if **XtNbuttonType** is set to **OL_WINDOW_BTN** and **XtPopup** will be used to popup this popup widget.

Note that the popup behaviors are not guaranteed if the given popup widget is not a subclass of **PopupMenuShellClass**, **PopupWindowShellClass**, or **TransientShellClass**.

XtNpreviewWidget
This resource identifies the widget whose window is used when previewing. When Select-Does-Preview mode is in effect and the user presses the SELECT button in the **AbbreviatedButton**, the default menu item is displayed in the preview widget's window, and drawn using the preview widget's size and location. If the **XtNpreviewWidget** resource is not set, or if the preview widget is not mapped, previewing does not take place.

SEE ALSO
AbbrevMenuButton(3Olit), **Primitive**(3Olit), **PopupMenuShell**(3Olit)

NAME

AbbrevMenuButton – create a button with a menu mark and menu

SYNOPSIS

```
#include <X11/Intrinsic.h>
#include <X11/StringDefs.h>
#include <Xol/OpenLook.h>
#include <Xol/AbbrevMenu.h>

static Widget stack, menupane, w;

Arg args[1];

stack = XtCreateWidget(name, abbrevMenuButtonWidgetClass, . . .);
XtSetArg(args[0], XtNmenuPane, &menupane);
XtGetValues(stack, args, 1);

w = XtCreateWidget(name, widget-class, menupane, . . .);
```

DESCRIPTION

The **AbbrevMenuButton** widget provides the end user the same features as the **MenuButton** widget (menu default selection, menu previewing, menu selection), plus current selection viewing, and the ability to add a new selection by typing in its name. The **AbbrevMenuButton** only supports the OPEN LOOK look and feel.

AbbrevMenuButton Components

Each abbreviated menu button has a menu. An application typically identifies an additional component, the Current Selection widget, where previewing of the default menu choice can be done.

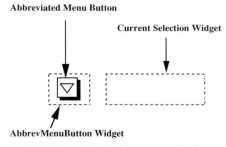

Figure 1. OPEN LOOK 2D Abbreviated Menu Button

Each abbreviated menu button also has the components of a **Menu** widget. These are not shown in Figure 1.

AbbrevMenuButton Sensitive Area

While on the Abbreviated Menu Button and the power-user option is on:

–   Pressing SELECT previews the default menu item (if a preview widget exists) and releasing it will activate the default menu item.

- Clicking SELECT previews the default menu item briefly (if a preview widget exists) and then activates the default menu item.
- Pressing MENU brings up a pop-up menu.
- Clicking MENU produces a stayup menu.

If the power-user option is off:

- Pressing SELECT or MENU brings up a pop-up menu.
- Clicking SELECT or MENU produces a stayup menu.

(The power-user option is set in the Miscellaneous property sheet of the desktop manager.)

All Features of Menu Button Widget

The **AbbrevMenuButton** widget includes all the features of the **MenuButton** widget, except for the previewing (done instead in the Current Selection widget) and the behavior in a menu (the **AbbrevMenuButton** widget cannot be used in a menu). The features of the **MenuButton** widget apply here.

Current Selection Widget

The Current Selection widget is created by the application. Typically, the Current Selection widget and the **AbbrevMenuButton** widget are placed together in a composite widget that manages their side-by-side placement. The **AbbrevMenuButton** widget uses the Current Selection widget only for previewing the default item in the menu. The application is responsible for using it to implement the OPEN LOOK user interface needs of showing the current menu selection and acquiring a new item to add to the menu, as appropriate.

AbbrevMenuButton Coloration

On a monochrome display, the **AbbrevMenuButton** widget indicates it has input focus by inverting the foreground and background colors of the control.

On color displays, when the **AbbrevMenuButton** widget receives the input focus, the background color is changed to the input focus color set in the **XtNinputFocusColor** resource.

EXCEPTION:

- If the input focus color is the same as the window background color, then the **AbbrevMenuButton** widget inverts the foreground and background colors when it has input focus.

Figure 2 illustrates the resources that affect the coloration of the **AbbrevMenuButton** widget.

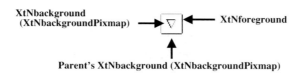

Figure 2. OPEN LOOK 3D Abbreviated Menu Button Coloration

Keyboard Traversal

The default value of the **XtNtraversalOn** resource is **TRUE**.

The action of the SELECTKEY depends on whether the user has selected the power-user option. (The power-user option is set in the property sheet of the desktop manager.) While on the **AbbrevMenuButton** and the power-user option is on, clicking the SELECTKEY activates the default menu item. If the power-user option is off, pressing the SELECTKEY posts the stayup menu.

The **AbbrevMenuButton** does not control the keyboard traversal between the **AbbrevMenuButton** widget and the Current Selection widget. The Current Selection widget's traversal resources can be set up to allow for traversal between it and the **AbbrevMenuButton**, but it is recommended that the **XtNtraversalOn** resource on the Current Selection widget be **FALSE**. Normal menu traversal can always be used to access the Current Selection widget.

Keyboard traversal within a menu can be done using the PREV_FIELD, NEXT_FIELD, MOVEUP, MOVEDOWN, MOVELEFT, and MOVERIGHT keys. The semantics of these keys depends on the position of input focus within the menu pane.

The PREV_FIELD and MOVEUP keys move the input focus to the previous menu item with keyboard traversal enabled. If the input focus is on the first item of the menu, then pressing one of these keys wraps to the last item of the menu with keyboard traversal enabled. The NEXT_FIELD, MOVEDOWN, and MOVERIGHT keys move the input focus to the next menu item with keyboard traversal enabled. If the input focus is on the last item of the menu, then pressing one of these keys wraps to the first item of the menu with keyboard traversal enabled. One exception to the action of MOVERIGHT is when input focus is on a MenuButton with **XtNmenuMark** **OL_RIGHT**. In this case, the MOVERIGHT key posts the MenuButton's menu. One exception to the action of MOVEDOWN is when input focus is on a MenuButton with **XtNmenuMark OL_DOWN**. In this case, the MOVEDOWN key posts the MenuButton's menu.

To traverse out of the menu, the following keys can be used:

MOVELEFT   Unpost menu and traverse to originating abbreviated menu button

CANCEL   Unpost entire cascading menu tree, and traverse to originating abbreviated menu button.

NEXTWINDOW   moves to the next window in the application

PREVWINDOW   moves to the previous window in the application

NEXTAPP   moves to the first window in the next application

PREVAPP   moves to the first window in the previous application

The DEFAULTACTION key will activate the default control in the **AbbrevMenuButton** widget as if the user clicked the SELECT button on the control.

The MENUDEFAULTKEY can be used by the user to change the default control in the **AbbrevMenuButton** widget. When the user presses the MENUDEFAULTKEY, the control which has input focus will become the default control.

AbbrevMenuButton Activation Types

Activation Type	Expected Results
OL_SELECTKEY	see discussion above
OL_MENUKEY	popup the **AbbrevMenuButton**'s submenu

Display of Keyboard Mnemonic

The **AbbrevMenuButton** does not display the mnemonic accelerator. If the **AbbrevMenuButton** is the child of a **Caption** widget, the **Caption** widget can be used to display the mnemonic.

SUBSTRUCTURE

Application Resources				
Name	Class	Type	Default	Access
XtNcenter*	XtCCenter	Boolean	TRUE	I
XtNhPad*	XtCHPad	Dimension	4	I
XtNhSpace*	XtCHSpace	Dimension	4	I
XtNlayoutType*	XtCLayoutType	OlDefine	OL_FIXEDROWS	I
XtNmeasure*	XtCMeasure	int	1	I
XtNpushpin	XtCPushpin	OlDefine	OL_NONE	I
XtNpushpinDefault	XtCPushpinDefault	Boolean	FALSE	I
XtNsameSize*	XtCSameSize	OlDefine	OL_COLUMNS	I
XtNtitle	XtCTitle	String	(widget's name)	I
XtNvPad*	XtCVPad	Dimension	4	I
XtNvSpace*	XtCVSpace	Dimension	4	I

* See the **Menu** and **ControlArea** widgets for more information on these resources.

RESOURCES

<table>
<tr><th colspan="6">AbbrevMenuButton Resource Set</th></tr>
<tr><th>Name</th><th>Class</th><th>Type</th><th>Default</th><th>Acc</th><th>Inherit</th></tr>
<tr><td>XtNaccelerator</td><td>XtCAccelerator</td><td>String</td><td>NULL</td><td>SGI</td><td>Primitive</td></tr>
<tr><td>XtNacceleratorText</td><td>XtCAcceleratorText</td><td>String</td><td>(calculated)</td><td>SGI</td><td>Primitive</td></tr>
<tr><td>XtNancestorSensitive</td><td>XtCSensitive</td><td>Boolean</td><td>(calculated)</td><td>G[1]</td><td>Core</td></tr>
<tr><td>XtNbackground</td><td>XtCBackground</td><td>Pixel</td><td>"XtDefaultBackground"</td><td>SGI</td><td>Core</td></tr>
<tr><td>XtNbackgroundPixmap</td><td>XtCPixmap</td><td>Pixmap</td><td>XtUnspecifiedPixmap</td><td>SGI</td><td>Core</td></tr>
<tr><td>XtNcolormap</td><td>XtCColormap</td><td>Colormap</td><td>(parent's)</td><td>GI</td><td>Core</td></tr>
<tr><td>XtNconsumeEvent</td><td>XtCCallback</td><td>XtCallbackList</td><td>NULL</td><td>SGI</td><td>Primitive</td></tr>
<tr><td>XtNdepth</td><td>XtCDepth</td><td>Cardinal</td><td>(parent's)</td><td>GI</td><td>Core</td></tr>
<tr><td>XtNdestroyCallback</td><td>XtCCallback</td><td>XtCallbackList</td><td>NULL</td><td>SGI</td><td>Object</td></tr>
<tr><td>XtNforeground</td><td>XtCForeground</td><td>Pixel</td><td>"XtDefaultForeground"</td><td>SGI</td><td>Primitive</td></tr>
<tr><td>XtNheight</td><td>XtCHeight</td><td>Dimension</td><td>(calculated)</td><td>SGI</td><td>Core</td></tr>
<tr><td>XtNinputFocusColor</td><td>XtCInputFocusColor</td><td>Pixel</td><td>"Red"</td><td>SGI</td><td>Primitive</td></tr>
<tr><td>XtNmappedWhenManaged</td><td>XtCMappedWhenManaged</td><td>Boolean</td><td>TRUE</td><td>SGI</td><td>Core</td></tr>
<tr><td>XtNmenuPane</td><td>XtNMenuPane</td><td>Widget</td><td>(n/a)</td><td>G</td><td></td></tr>
<tr><td>XtNmnemonic</td><td>XtCMnemonic</td><td>char</td><td>NULL</td><td>SGI</td><td>Primitive</td></tr>
<tr><td>XtNpreviewWidget</td><td>XtCPreviewWidget</td><td>Widget</td><td>NULL</td><td>SGI</td><td></td></tr>
<tr><td>XtNreferenceName</td><td>XtCReferenceName</td><td>String</td><td>NULL</td><td>SGI</td><td>Primitive</td></tr>
<tr><td>XtNreferenceWidget</td><td>XtCReferenceWidget</td><td>Widget</td><td>NULL</td><td>SGI</td><td>Primitive</td></tr>
<tr><td>XtNscreen</td><td>XtCScreen</td><td>Screen *</td><td>(parent's)</td><td>GI</td><td>Core</td></tr>
<tr><td>XtNsensitive</td><td>XtCSensitive</td><td>Boolean</td><td>TRUE</td><td>G[1]</td><td>Core</td></tr>
<tr><td>XtNtranslations</td><td>XtCTranslations</td><td>XtTranslations</td><td>NULL</td><td>SGI</td><td>Core</td></tr>
<tr><td>XtNtraversalOn</td><td>XtCTraversalOn</td><td>Boolean</td><td>TRUE</td><td>SGI</td><td>Primitive</td></tr>
<tr><td>XtNuserData</td><td>XtCUserData</td><td>XtPointer</td><td>NULL</td><td>SGI</td><td>Primitive</td></tr>
<tr><td>XtNwidth</td><td>XtCWidth</td><td>Dimension</td><td>(calculated)</td><td>SGI</td><td>Core</td></tr>
<tr><td>XtNx</td><td>XtCPosition</td><td>Position</td><td>0</td><td>SGI</td><td>Core</td></tr>
<tr><td>XtNy</td><td>XtCPosition</td><td>Position</td><td>0</td><td>SGI</td><td>Core</td></tr>
</table>

[1] Use **XtSetSensitive** to set this resource.

XtNmenuPane

This is the widget where menu items can be attached; its value is available once the **AbbrevMenuButton** widget has been created.

XtNpreviewWidget

Range of values:

(ID of existing widget)

This resource identifies the Current Selection widget that the **AbbrevMenuButton** can use for previewing the Default Item.

When the end user presses SELECT over the **AbbrevMenuButton** widget, the **AbbrevMenuButton** widget uses the location and size of the Current Selection widget to display the label of the Default Item. The preview is constrained to be within the height and width of the Current Selection widget.

If the Current Selection widget is not defined or is not mapped, previewing does not take place.

The previewing feature is not accessible with keyboard only operation.

NOTES

Use **AbbreviatedButton** to get an **AbbrevMenuButton** button with a MOTIF look and feel.

SEE ALSO

AbbreviatedButton(3Olit), **Caption**(3Olit), **ControlArea**(3Olit), **Core**(3Olit), **MenuShell**(3Olit)

NAME

`Application` – `Application` widget superclass

SYNOPSIS

```
#include <X11/Intrinsic.h>
#include <X11/StringDefs.h>
#include <Xol/OpenLook.h>
```

DESCRIPTION

MoOLIT uses several resources to determine the state of an application. These can be accessed using the `OlGetApplicationValues` function [see `OlGetApplicationValues`(3Olit)]. In order to maintain a consistent look and feel between applications running simultaneously on the same display device, applications do not set these resources directly since the desktop manager preference property sheets are responsible for maintaining their values by updating the appropriate resource files.

RESOURCES

<table>
<tr><th colspan="5">`Application` Resource Set</th></tr>
<tr><th>Name</th><th>Class</th><th>Type</th><th>Default</th><th>Access</th></tr>
<tr><td>XtNbeep</td><td>XtCBeep</td><td>OlDefine</td><td>OL_BEEP_ALWAYS</td><td>G</td></tr>
<tr><td>XtNbeepVolume</td><td>XtCBeepVolume</td><td>int</td><td>0</td><td>G</td></tr>
<tr><td>XtNColorTupleList</td><td>XtCColorTupleList</td><td>OlColorTupleList</td><td>NULL</td><td>G</td></tr>
<tr><td>XtNcontrolName</td><td>XtCControlName</td><td>String</td><td>"Ctrl"</td><td>G</td></tr>
<tr><td>XtNdontCare</td><td>XtCDontCare</td><td>OlBitMask</td><td>LockMask|Mod2Mask</td><td>G</td></tr>
<tr><td>XtNdragRightDistance</td><td>XtCDragRightDistance</td><td>Dimension</td><td>20 (pixels)</td><td>G</td></tr>
<tr><td>XtNhelpDirectory</td><td>XtCHelpDirectory</td><td>String</td><td>(calculated)</td><td>G</td></tr>
<tr><td>XtNhelpModel</td><td>XtCHelpModel</td><td>OlDefine</td><td>OL_POINTER</td><td>G</td></tr>
<tr><td>XtNkeyDontCare</td><td>XtCDontCare</td><td>OlBitMask</td><td>LockMask</td><td>G</td></tr>
<tr><td>XtNkeyRemapTimeOut</td><td>XtCKeyRemapTimeOut</td><td>Cardinal</td><td>2 (msec)</td><td>G</td></tr>
<tr><td>XtNlockName</td><td>XtCLockName</td><td>String</td><td>"Lock"</td><td>G</td></tr>
<tr><td>XtNmenuMarkRegion</td><td>XtCMenuMarkRegion</td><td>Dimension</td><td>10 (pixels)</td><td>G</td></tr>
<tr><td>XtNmnemonicPrefix</td><td>XtCMnemonicPrefix</td><td>Modifiers</td><td>Alt</td><td>G</td></tr>
<tr><td>XtNmod1Name</td><td>XtCMod1Name</td><td>String</td><td>"Alt"</td><td>G</td></tr>
<tr><td>XtNmod2Name</td><td>XtCMod2Name</td><td>String</td><td>"Mod2"</td><td>G</td></tr>
<tr><td>XtNmod3Name</td><td>XtCMod3Name</td><td>String</td><td>"Mod3"</td><td>G</td></tr>
<tr><td>XtNmod4Name</td><td>XtCMod4Name</td><td>String</td><td>"Mod4"</td><td>G</td></tr>
<tr><td>XtNmod5Name</td><td>XtCMod5Name</td><td>String</td><td>"Mod5"</td><td>G</td></tr>
<tr><td>XtNmouseDampingFactor</td><td>XtNmouseDampingFactor</td><td>Cardinal</td><td>8 (points)</td><td>G</td></tr>
<tr><td>XtNmouseStatus</td><td>XtCMouseStatus</td><td>Boolean</td><td>True</td><td>G</td></tr>
<tr><td>XtNmultiClickTimeout</td><td>XtCMultiClickTimeout</td><td>Cardinal</td><td>500 (msec)</td><td>G</td></tr>
<tr><td>XtNmultiObjectCount</td><td>XtCMultiObjectCount</td><td>Cardinal</td><td>3</td><td>G</td></tr>
<tr><td>XtNscaleMap</td><td>XtCScaleMap</td><td>String</td><td>(calculated)</td><td>G</td></tr>
<tr><td>XtNselectDoesPreview</td><td>XtCNSelectDoesPreview</td><td>Boolean</td><td>FALSE</td><td>G</td></tr>
<tr><td>XtNshiftName</td><td>XtCShiftName</td><td>string</td><td>"Shift"</td><td>G</td></tr>
</table>

Application Resource Set (cont'd)				
Name	Class	Type	Default	Access
XtNshowAccelerators	XtCShowAccelerators	OlDefine	OL_DISPLAY	G
XtNshowMnemonics	XtCShowMnemonics	OlDefine	OL_UNDERLINE	G
XtNthreeD	XtCThreeD	Boolean	TRUE	G
XtNuseColorTupleList	XtCuseColorTupleList	Boolean	XtUnspecifiedBoolean	G
XtNuseShortOLWinAttr	XtCUseShortOLWinAttr	Boolean	FALSE	G

XtNbeep

Range of values:

        OL_BEEP_NEVER/"never"
        OL_BEEP_ALWAYS/"always"
        OL_BEEP_NOTICES/"notices"

This resource determines the type of objects that can generate audible warnings to the user. **OL_BEEP_NEVER** implies no objects should generate audible warnings. **OL_BEEP_ALWAYS** implies any object can generate audible warnings. **OL_BEEP_NOTICES** implies only Notices should generate audible warnings.

XtNbeepVolume

Range of values:

        $-100 \leq$ XtNbeepVolume $\leq +100$

This resource specifies a percentage of the keyboard's normal beep that should be used when generating audible warnings to the user.

XtNColorTupleList

This resource specifies the color tuple list. On color-rich devices, when a button is pressed, it is drawn slightly darker then when it is not pressed. On devices with few colors, this is usually not possible, but a reasonable effect can sometimes be forced by specifying colors via the color tuple list. The **OlColorTuple** structure includes the following members:

        Pixel bg0;   /* emphasis is highlight color */
        Pixel bg1;   /* normal background */
        Pixel bg2;   /* indent and menu choice background */
        Pixel bg3;   /* 3D shadow color */

If the **XtNuseColorTupleList** resource indicates the color tuple list should be used, a widget that would normally use **bg1** as the background color will use **bg0**, **bg2**, and **bg3** for highlight, indent, and shadow, respectively.

The **OlColorTupleList** structure includes the following members:

        OlColorTuple *list;
        Cardinal size;

bg2 and **bg3** should be derived from **bg1**, by the addition of gray, if applications need to conform to the OPEN LOOK specification.

XtNcontrolName
XtNlockName
XtNmod1Name
XtNmod2Name
XtNmod3Name
XtNmod4Name
XtNmod5Name
XtNshiftName

These resources define the names used to display the accelerator in buttons and labels. They are provided as resources so they can be easily changed for a particular keyboard. For example, the `mod1Name` is usually "Alt," but on some keyboards it may be labeled "Meta."

XtNdontCare

Range of values are determined by ORing the following bit masks:

`LockMask` (typically the mask associated with the CAPS LOCK key)
`Mod1Mask`
`Mod2Mask` (typically the mask associated with the NUM LOCK key)
`Mod3Mask`
`Mod4Mask`
`Mod5Mask`
`ShiftMask`
`ControlMask`

This resource specifies the modifier bits that are ignored when processing mouse button events. For example, assume the `Mod2Mask` bit is in the `XtNdontCare` bits. Now if the NUM LOCK key is in a set state and the user presses the SELECT mouse button, the press is interpreted as a SELECT button press because the `Mod2Mask` bit is ignored. But if the `Mod2Mask` bit is not in the `XtNdontCare` bits, the press is not interpreted as a SELECT button press because the internal event handling routine honors the `Mod2Mask` bit in the `XEvent`.

XtNdragRightDistance

This resource represents the number of pixels the pointer must be dragged over a MenuButton with the `MENU` mouse button depressed to post the MenuButton's submenu. The direction of the drag is to the right. This resource only applies to MenuButtons on press-drag-release menus.

XtNhelpDirectory

This resource specifies the directory in which all help files for an application are located. It is locale-specific. The default value depends on the user's `XFILESEAR-CHPATH` environment variable and system configuration, but a typical value is `/usr/X/lib/locale/C/help/app-classname`, where everything before "C" is hardcoded somewhere in the `XFILESEARCHPATHDEFAULT` variable.

This resource is used by the `OlFindHelpFile` call and should normally only be set once per application instance [see `OlFindHelpFile`(3Olit)].

XtNhelpModel

Range of values:

`OL_POINTER`/"`pointer`"
`OL_INPUTFOCUS`/"`inputfocus`"

Application (3Olit)

The MoOLIT help model defaults to follow the mouse pointer. So, when the **HELP** key is pressed, the item under the pointer is the subject of the help message. When this resource is set to **OL_INPUT_FOCUS**, the subject of the help message follows input focus.

XtNkeyDontCare

Range of values are determined by ORing the following bit masks:

```
LockMask
Mod1Mask
Mod2Mask
Mod3Mask
Mod4Mask
Mod5Mask
ShiftMask
ControlMask
```

This resource specifies the modifier bits that are ignored when processing keyboard events. (See **XtNdontCare** above.) For example, assume the **LockMask** bit is in the **XtNkeyDontCare** bits. Now if the CAPS LOCK key is in a set state and the user presses the DRAG key, the press is interpreted as a DRAG key press because the **LockMask** bit is ignored. But if the **LockMask** bit is not in the **XtNkeyDontCare** bits, the press is not interpreted as a DRAG key press because the internal event handling routine honors the **LockMask** bit in the **XEvent**.

XtNkeyRemapTimeOut
XtNmenuMarkRegion

This resource represents the width (in pixels) of the MenuButton's "menu mark region." If the pointer is moved into this region with the **MENU** mouse button depressed, the MenuButton's submenu is posted.

XtNmnemonicPrefix

This resource specifies the modifier key that must accompany the mnemonic character when activating an object from the keyboard if that object is not on a menu.

XtNmouseDampingFactor

Range of values:

```
TRUE/"true"
FALSE/"false"
```

This resource specifies the number of pixels the pointer can be moved before a drag operation is initiated.

XtNmouseStatus

This Boolean resource indicates whether there is a mouse on the server.

XtNmultiClickTimeout

This resource specifies the number of milliseconds that determines when two mouse button clicks are considered a multi-click, provided the pointer does not move beyond the **XtNmouseDampingFactor** value.

XtNmultiObjectCount

This resource determines the number of times the **OL_MULTIRIGHT**, **OL_MULTILEFT**, **OL_MULTIUP** and **OL_MULTIDOWN** keys repeat the **OL_MOVERIGHT**, **OL_MOVELEFT**, **OL_MOVEUP** and **OL_MOVEDOWN** keys, respectively.

XtNscaleMap

This resource names a custom scale-map file. A scale-map file contains encoded descriptions of the various graphical elements of the OPEN LOOK or MOTIF look and feel. By default, the MoOLIT drawing routines pick a file using the current screen resolution (that is, the scale-map file for a 76 DPI screen is named `/usr/X/lib/Xol/76x76.arc`).

XtNselectDoesPreview

Range of values:

        `TRUE`/"`true`"
        `FALSE`/"`false`"

This `Boolean` resource reflects the behavior of the SELECT mouse button when it is pressed over a MenuButton, AbbreviatedMenuButton, or AbbreviatedButton. If its value is `TRUE`, pressing SELECT will cause the MenuButton to preview the submenu's default item and releasing the SELECT button will activate the default item. If its value is `FALSE`, pressing SELECT will post the submenu.

XtNshowAccelerators

Range of values:

        `OL_DISPLAY`/"`display`"
        `OL_INACTIVE`/"`inactive`"
        `OL_NONE`/"`none`"

When this resource is set to `OL_DISPLAY`, the keyboard accelerators on the controls will be displayed. When this resource is set to `OL_NONE`, the keyboard accelerators on the controls will not be displayed. Setting this resource to `OL_INACTIVE` will cause the keyboard accelerators to not be displayed and will cause the controls to ignore the accelerator action.

XtNshowMnemonics

Range of values:

        `OL_HIGHLIGHT`/"`highlight`"
        `OL_UNDERLINE`/"`underline`"
        `OL_INACTIVE`/"`inactive`"
        `OL_NONE`/"`none`"

This resource determines if the keyboard mnemonics on the controls should be displayed. Setting it to `OL_UNDERLINE` will cause the mnemonics to be displayed in the primitive children by drawing a line under the character in the font color. Setting it to `OL_HIGHLIGHT` will display the mnemonic character with the background and foreground colors reversed. When highlighting a character that is displayed on a pixmap background, the mnemonic character will be drawn in a solid color. The mnemonic accelerator will not be displayed if this resource is set to `OL_NONE`. The resource set to `OL_INACTIVE` turns off the mnemonic display as well as making the mnemonic key inactive.

XtNthreeD

Range of values:

        `TRUE`/"`true`"
        `FALSE`/"`false`"

Application (3Olit)

This resource determines how the visuals are rendered. The default value, **TRUE**, displays the visuals with a three dimensional look. Setting this resource to **FALSE** will cause the visuals to have a two dimensional appearance.

XtNuseColorTupleList
Range of values:

        TRUE/''true''
        FALSE/''false''

This resource determines whether the **XtNcolorTupleList** resource should be used. If **XtNuseColorTupleList** is **TRUE**, the color-tuple list is always used. If the resource is **FALSE**, the color-tuple list is never used. If the resource is **XtUnspecifiedBoolean**, the color-tuple list is only used on color-poor systems. **XtUnspecifiedBoolean** is the default value. A client that needs this value should simply not set the resource, it cannot be directly set by a client

XtNuseShortOLWinAttr
Range of values:

        TRUE/''true''
        FALSE/''false''

This resource specified the OPEN LOOK window manager. Most OPEN LOOK window managers use the standard ''five-element window attributes protocol.'' However, certain versions of Sun's Open Windows window manager use a ''three-element'' version. This resource is **FALSE** if a ''five-element'' window manager is being used.

SEE ALSO
Core(3Olit), OlFindHelpFile(3Olit), OlGetApplicationValues(3Olit)

NAME

BulletinBoard – create a simple manager widget

SYNOPSIS

```
#include <X11/Intrinsic.h>
#include <X11/StringDefs.h>
#include <Xol/OpenLook.h>
#include <Xol/BulletinBo.h>

widget = XtCreateWidget(name, bulletinBoardWidgetClass, . . .);
```

DESCRIPTION

The **BulletinBoard** widget puts up a bulletin board in either the MOTIF or OPEN LOOK look and feel.

Simple Composite Widget

The **BulletinBoard** widget is a composite widget that enforces no ordering on its children. It is up to the application to specify the x- and y-coordinates of each child inserted; otherwise, it will be placed in the upper left corner of the **BulletinBoard** widget.

No Children

The **BulletinBoard** can be mapped with no children. It displays an empty space, possibly surrounded by a border.

BulletinBoard Border

The **BulletinBoard** widget has the ability to draw a border that appears to stand out or push in the surface, as specified by the **XtNshadowType** resource. This border uses space within the bulletin board as determined by the value of the **XtNshadowThickness** resource.

BulletinBoard Coloration

Figure 1 illustrates the resources that affect the coloration of the **BulletinBoard** widget without a shadowed border. If a shadowed border is used, the shadow color is calculated from **XtNbackground**.

BulletinBoard (3Olit)

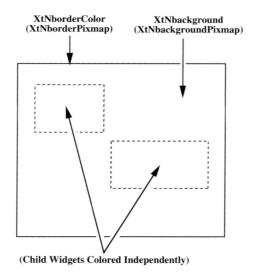

(Child Widgets Colored Independently)

Figure 1. Bulletin Board Coloration

Keyboard Traversal

The `BulletinBoard` widget is a composite widget and cannot be accessed via keyboard traversal. Input focus moves between the Primitive children of this widget.

RESOURCES

BulletinBoard Resource Set					
Name	Class	Type	Default	Acc	Inherit
XtNancestorSensitive	XtCSensitive	Boolean	(calculated)	G[1]	Core
XtNbackground	XtCBackground	Pixel	"XtDefaultBackground"	SGI	Core
XtNbackgroundPixmap	XtCPixmap	Pixmap	XtUnspecifiedPixmap	SGI	Core
XtNborderColor	XtCBorderColor	Pixel	"XtDefaultForeground"	SGI	Core
XtNborderPixmap	XtCPixmap	Pixmap	XtUnspecifiedPixmap	SGI	Core
XtNborderWidth	XtCBorderWidth	Dimension	0	SGI	Core
XtNchildren	XtCReadOnly	WidgetList	NULL	G	Composite
XtNcolormap	XtCColormap	Colormap	(parent's)	GI	Core
XtNconsumeEvent	XtCCallback	XtCallbackList	NULL	SGI	Manager
XtNdepth	XtCDepth	Cardinal	(parent's)	GI	Core
XtNdestroyCallback	XtCCallback	XtCallbackList	NULL	SGI	Object
XtNheight	XtCHeight	Dimension	(calculated)	SGI	Core
XtNinsertPosition	XtCInsertPosition	XtWidgetProc	NULL	SGI	Composite

BulletinBoard Resource Set (cont'd)					
Name	Class	Type	Default	Acc	Inherit
XtNlayoutHeight	XtCLayout	OlDefine	OL_MINIMIZE	SGI	
XtNlayoutWidth	XtCLayout	OlDefine	OL_MINIMIZE	SGI	
XtNmappedWhenManaged	XtCMappedWhenManaged	Boolean	TRUE	SGI	Core
XtNnumChildren	XtCReadOnly	Cardinal	0	G	Composite
XtNreferenceName	XtCReferenceName	String	NULL	SGI	Manager
XtNreferenceWidget	XtCReferenceWidget	Widget	NULL	SGI	Manager
XtNscreen	XtCScreen	Screen*	(parent's)	GI	Core
XtNsensitive	XtCSensitive	Boolean	TRUE	G[1]	Core
XtNshadowThickness	XtCShadowThickness	Dimension	"0 points"[3]	SGI	Manager
XtNshadowType	XtCShadowType	OlDefine	OL_SHADOW_OUT	SGI	Manager
XtNtranslations	XtCTranslations	XtTranslations	NULL	SGI	Core
XtNtraversalOn	XtCTraversalOn	Boolean	TRUE	SGI	Manager
XtNuserData	XtCUserData	XtPointer	NULL	SGI	Manager
XtNwidth	XtCWidth	Dimension	(calculated)	SGI	Core
XtNx	XtCPosition	Position	0	SGI	Core
XtNy	XtCPosition	Position	0	SGI	Core

[1]   Use XtSetSensitive to set this resource.

[3]   "2 points" in MOTIF look and feel.

XtNlayoutHeight
XtNlayoutWidth

Range of values:

OL_MINIMIZE/"minimize"
OL_MAXIMIZE/"maximize"
OL_IGNORE/"ignore"

These resources identify the layout policy the BulletinBoard widget as follows:

OL_MINIMIZE

The BulletinBoard widget will always be just large enough to contain all its children, regardless of any provided width and height values. Thus the BulletinBoard widget will grow and shrink depending on the size needs of its children.

OL_IGNORE

The BulletinBoard widget will honor the width and height as set by the client. It will not grow or shrink in response to the addition, deletion, or altering of its children. If the client does not set an initial size, the fixed size is computed when the widget is realized.

OL_MAXIMIZE

The BulletinBoard widget will ask for additional space when it needs it for new or altered children, but will not give up extra space.

SEE ALSO

Manager(3Olit)

Caption (3Olit)

NAME

Caption – create a caption or label for any widget

SYNOPSIS

```
#include <X11/Intrinsic.h>
#include <X11/StringDefs.h>
#include <Xol/OpenLook.h>
#include <Xol/Caption.h>

widget = XtCreateWidget(name, captionWidgetClass, . . .);
```

DESCRIPTION

The **Caption** composite widget provides a convenient way to label an arbitrary widget. This widget supports both the MOTIF and the OPEN LOOK look and feel. The difference between the MOTIF and the OPEN LOOK look and feel is the default font.

Caption Components

A **Caption** widget has two parts: the Label and the Child widget.

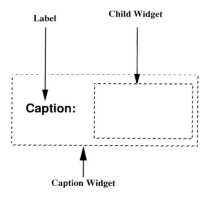

Figure 1. Caption Widget

Layout Control

The application can determine how the Label is placed next to the Child widget (by specifying that it goes above, below, to the left, or to the right), and by specifying how far away the Label is to be placed.

Child Constraints

The **Caption** composite allows at most one managed child; attempts to manage more than one are refused with a warning. Any number of unmanaged children are allowed. If the **Caption** widget is mapped without a Child widget, or if no Child widget is managed, only the Label is shown.

Geometry Management

The **Caption** widget will attempt to pass on to its Child any geometry changes made to the **Caption**. However, if the Child refuses some or all of the geometry changes, the **Caption** absorbs the remaining ones by shrinking or enlarging the Label. If the Label is made small, an arrow is displayed to indicated part of the

Label is not shown.

Caption Coloration

Figure 2 illustrates the resources that affect the coloration of the **Caption** widget.

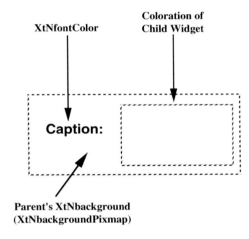

Figure 2. Caption Coloration

Keyboard Traversal

The **Caption** widget is a composite widget and cannot be accessed via keyboard traversal. Input focus will move to the **Caption**'s child.

Display of Keyboard Mnemonic

The **Caption** widget displays the mnemonic for its child as part of its label. If the mnemonic character is in the label, then that character is highlighted according to the value of the application resource **XtNshowMneumonics**. If the mnemonic character is not in the label, it is displayed to the right of the label in parenthesis and highlighted according to the value of the application resource **XtNshowMneumonics**.

If truncation is necessary, the mnemonic displayed in parenthesis is truncated as a unit.

RESOURCES

Name	Class	Type	Default	Acc	Inherit
			Caption Resource Set		
XtNalignment	XtCAlignment	OlDefine	OL_CENTER	SGI	
XtNancestorSensitive	XtCSensitive	Boolean	(calculated)	G[I]	Core
XtNbackground	XtCBackground	Pixel	"XtDefaultBackground"	SGI	Core
XtNbackgroundPixmap	XtCPixmap	Pixmap	XtUnspecifiedPixmap	SGI	Core
XtNborderColor	XtCBorderColor	Pixel	"XtDefaultForeground"	SGI	Core
XtNborderPixmap	XtCPixmap	Pixmap	XtUnspecifiedPixmap	SGI	Core

Caption (3Olit)

Caption Resource Set (cont'd)					
Name	Class	Type	Default	Acc	Inherit
XtNborderWidth	XtCBorderWidth	Dimension	0	SGI	Core
XtNchildren	XtCReadOnly	WidgetList	NULL	G	Composite
XtNcolormap	XtCColormap	Colormap	(parent's)	GI	Core
XtNconsumeEvent	XtCCallback	XtCallbackList	NULL	SGI	Manager
XtNdepth	XtCDepth	Cardinal	(parent's)	GI	Core
XtNdestroyCallback	XtCCallback	XtCallbackList	NULL	SGI	Object
XtNfont	XtCFont	XFontStruct *	"OlDefaultBoldFont"	SGI	
XtNfontColor	XtCFontColor	Pixel	"XtDefaultForeground"	SGI	
XtNfontGroup	XtCFontGroup	OlFontList *	NULL	SGI	
XtNheight	XtCHeight	Dimension	(calculated)	SGI	Core
XtNinsertPosition	XtCInsertPosition	XtWidgetProc	NULL	SGI	Composite
XtNlabel	XtCLabel	String	(widget name)	SGI	
XtNlayoutHeight	XtCLayout	OlDefine	OL_MINIMIZE	SGI	
XtNlayoutWidth	XtCLayout	OlDefine	OL_MINIMIZE	SGI	
XtNmappedWhenManaged	XtCMappedWhenManaged	Boolean	TRUE	SGI	Core
XtNmnemonic	XtCMnemonic	char	NULL	SGI	
XtNnumChildren	XtCReadOnly	Cardinal	0	G	Composite
XtNposition	XtCPosition	OlDefine	OL_LEFT	SGI	
XtNreferenceName	XtCReferenceName	String	NULL	SGI	Manager
XtNreferenceWidget	XtCReferenceWidget	Widget	NULL	SGI	Manager
XtNscreen	XtCScreen	Screen *	(parent's)	GI	Core
XtNsensitive	XtCSensitive	Boolean	TRUE	G[1]	Core
XtNshadowThickness	XtCShadowThickness	Dimension	0	SGI	Manager
XtNshadowType	XtCShadowType	OlDefine	OL_SHADOW_OUT[8]	SGI	Manager
XtNspace	XtCSpace	Dimension	4	SGI	
XtNtranslations	XtCTranslations	XtTranslations	NULL	SGI	Core
XtNtraversalOn	XtCTraversalOn	Boolean	TRUE	SGI	Manager
XtNuserData	XtCUserData	XtPointer	NULL	SGI	Manager
XtNwidth	XtCWidth	Dimension	(calculated)	SGI	Core
XtNx	XtCPosition	Position	0	SGI	Core
XtNy	XtCPosition	Position	0	SGI	Core

[1] Use XtSetSensitive to set this resource.

[8] OL_SHADOW_IN in the MOTIF look and feel.

XtNalignment

Range of values:

If XtNposition is OL_TOP or OL_BOTTOM:

OL_LEFT/"left"
OL_CENTER/"center"
OL_RIGHT/"right"

If `XtNposition` is `OL_LEFT` or `OL_RIGHT`:

`OL_TOP`/"top"
`OL_CENTER`/"center"
`OL_BOTTOM`/"bottom"

This specifies how the Label is to be aligned relative to the Child widget, as described below:

`OL_LEFT`	The left edge of the Label is aligned with the left edge of the Child widget.
`OL_TOP`	The top edge of the Label is aligned with the top edge of the Child widget.
`OL_CENTER`	The center of the Label is aligned with the center of the Child widget.
`OL_RIGHT`	The right edge of the Label is aligned with the right edge of the Child widget.
`OL_BOTTOM`	The bottom edge of the Label is aligned with the bottom edge of the Child widget.

XtNlabel

This resource gives the string to use for the Label. If NULL, the size of the **Caption** widget will be identical to the size of the Child widget.

Note that the Label is displayed as given; no punctuation (such as a colon) is added.

Control characters (other than spaces) are ignored without warning. For example, embedded newlines do not cause line breaks.

XtNlayoutHeight
XtNlayoutWidth

Range of values:

`OL_MINIMIZE`/"minimize"
`OL_MAXIMIZE`/"maximize"
`OL_IGNORE`/"ignore"

These resources identify the layout policy the **Caption** widget as follows:

`OL_MINIMIZE`

The **Caption** widget will always be just large enough to contain the Label and Child, regardless of any provided width and height values. Thus the -**Caption** widget will grow and shrink depending on the size needs of its Child.

`OL_IGNORE`

The **Caption** widget will honor the width and height as set by the client. It will not grow or shrink in response to the addition, deletion, or altering of its Label or Child. If the client does not set an initial size, the fixed size is computed when the widget is realized.

`OL_MAXIMIZE`

The **Caption** widget will ask for additional space when it needs it for a new or altered Label or Child, but will not give up extra space.

XtNposition
Range of values:
```
OL_LEFT/"left"
OL_RIGHT/"right"
OL_TOP/"top"
OL_BOTTOM/"bottom"
```

This resource determines on which side of the Child widget the Label is to be placed. The value may be one of `OL_LEFT`, `OL_RIGHT`, `OL_TOP`, or `OL_BOTTOM` to indicate the Label is to be placed to the left, to the right, above, or below the Child widget, respectively.

XtNspace
Range of values:
```
0 ≤ XtNspace
```

This resource gives the separation of the Label from the Child widget, in pixels, as suggested by Figure 3.

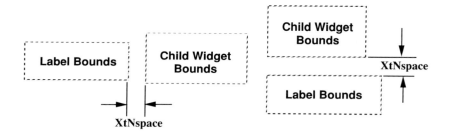

Figure 3. Label and Child Widget Spacing

SEE ALSO
> `Manager`(3Olit)

NAME

Category – create and manage multiple category property windows

SYNOPSIS

```
#include <X11/Intrinsic.h>
#include <X11/StringDefs.h>
#include <Xol/OpenLook.h>
#include <Xol/Category.h>

widget = XtCreateWidget(name, categoryWidgetClass, . . .);
```

DESCRIPTION

The **Category** widget provides a convenient way of creating and managing multiple-category property windows, in both the OPEN LOOK and the MOTIF look and feel.

Components

Each **Category** widget has the following parts:

Category Label

Abbreviated Menu Button

Menu

Page Label

Pane

Lower Control Area

Left and Right Footers

The Category Label can be set by the client to indicate the class of panes or pages that the user can choose. The Menu lists the panes or pages to choose from, and is accessed via the Abbreviated Menu Button. The Page Label identifies the page currently displayed in the Pane; as the user selects other pages to view, they are shown in the Pane, one at a time. The Lower Control Area is a place for controls (typically buttons) that allow the user to act on the page or pages.

Children as Pages

Each widget added by a client as a child of a **Category** widget is considered to be a page. Typically a page is a composite widget that contains several controls. Associated with each page is its Page Label. This label is used to identify the page in the Menu, and is displayed next to the Abbreviated Menu Button when the page is selected. The **Category** widget builds the Menu from the Page Labels provided by the client.

Automatic Mapping/Unmapping of Pages

The **Category** widget will ensure that only one page is displayed to the user at a time, by unmapping the old page and mapping the new page that the user has selected from the Menu. Thus the normal **XtNmappedWhenManaged** resource is ignored by the **Category** widget.

Callback When Switching Pages

The **Category** widget can tell the client when the user has switched to a new page. The client can use this callback to clean up the previous page and initialize the new page.

Category (3Olit)

Page Changes

The **Category** widget helps a client keep track of which pages have changes on them, via a constraint resource for each page. The client can mark a page as having changes, then be informed in the page change callback when there are changes pending on other pages. The **Category** widget will also show a change bar next to the Category Label when pages other than the one visible have changes, and will ask the window manager to display the Cancel button instead of the Dismiss button in its window menu (as appropriate in the look and feel at hand), when one or more pages have changes.

Substructure
Lower Control Area

Name: **lowerControlArea**
Class: **ControlArea**

Name: **footer**
Class: **Footer**

Additional Routines

```
Boolean OlCategorySetPage(
    CategoryWidget    w,
    Widget            child
);
```

A client can change to a new page by calling the **OlCategorySetPage** routine. The page is identified by *child*, which must be a child of the **Category** widget *w*. **OlCategorySetPage** returns **TRUE** if, on switching to the new page, unseen pages have changes in them (see the **XtNchanged** constraint resource).

RESOURCES

Category Resource Set					
Name	Class	Type	Default	Acc	Inherit
XtNancestorSensitive	XtCSensitive	Boolean	(calculated)	G[1]	Core
XtNbackground	XtCBackground	Pixel	"XtDefaultBackground"	SGI	Core
XtNbackgroundPixmap	XtCPixmap	Pixmap	XtUnspecifiedPixmap	SGI	Core
XtNborderColor	XtCBorderColor	Pixel	"XtDefaultForeground"	SGI	Core
XtNborderPixmap	XtCPixmap	Pixmap	XtUnspecifiedPixmap	SGI	Core
XtNborderWidth	XtCBorderWidth	Dimension	0	SGI	Core
XtNcategoryFont	XtCFont	XFontStruct *	"OlDefaultBoldFont"	SGI	
XtNcategoryLabel	XtCCategoryLabel	String	"CATEGORY:"	SGI	
XtNchildren	XtCReadOnly	WidgetList	NULL	G	Composite
XtNcolormap	XtCColormap	Colormap	(parent's)	GI	Core
XtNconsumeEvent	XtCCallback	XtCallbackList	NULL	SGI	Manager
XtNdepth	XtCDepth	Cardinal	(parent's)	GI	Core
XtNdestroyCallback	XtCCallback	XtCallbackList	NULL	SGI	Object
XtNfont	XtCFont	XFontStruct *	"OlDefaultFont"	SGI	
XtNfontColor	XtCFontColor	Pixel	"XtDefaultForeground"	SGI	
XtNfontGroup	XtCFontGroup	OlFontList *	NULL	SGI	

Category Resource Set (cont'd)					
Name	Class	Type	Default	Acc	Inherit
XtNfooter	XtCReadOnly	Widget	(n/a)	G	
XtNheight	XtCHeight	Dimension	(calculated)	SGI	Core
XtNinsertPosition	XtCInsertPosition	XtWidgetProc	NULL	SGI	Composite
XtNlayoutHeight	XtCLayout	OlDefine	OL_MINIMIZE	SGI	
XtNlayoutWidth	XtCLayout	OlDefine	OL_MINIMIZE	SGI	
XtNleftFoot	XtCFoot	String	NULL	SGI	
XtNlowerControlArea	XtCReadOnly	Widget	(n/a)	G	
XtNmappedWhenManaged	XtCMappedWhenManaged	Boolean	TRUE	SGI	Core
XtNnewPage	XtCCallback	XtCallbackList	NULL	SGI	
XtNnumChildren	XtCReadOnly	Cardinal	0	G	Composite
XtNpageHeight	XtCPageHeight	Dimension	0	SGI	
XtNpageWidth	XtCPageWidth	Dimension	0	SGI	
XtNreferenceName	XtCReferenceName	String	NULL	SGI	Manager
XtNreferenceWidget	XtCReferenceWidget	Widget	NULL	SGI	Manager
XtNrightFoot	XtCFoot	String	NULL	SGI	
XtNscreen	XtCScreen	Screen *	(parent's)	GI	Core
XtNsensitive	XtCSensitive	Boolean	TRUE	G[1]	Core
XtNshadowThickness	XtCShadowThickness	Dimension	"2 points"	SGI	Manager
XtNshadowType	XtCShadowType	OlDefine	OL_SHADOW_ETCHED_IN	SGI	Manager
XtNshowFooter	XtCShowFooter	Boolean	FALSE	SGI	
XtNtranslations	XtCTranslations	XtTranslations	NULL	SGI	Core
XtNtraversalOn	XtCTraversalOn	Boolean	TRUE	SGI	Manager
XtNuserData	XtCUserData	XtPointer	NULL	SGI	Manager
XtNwidth	XtCWidth	Dimension	(calculated)	SGI	Core
XtNx	XtCPosition	Position	0	SGI	Core
XtNy	XtCPosition	Position	0	SGI	Core

[1]   Use XtSetSensitive to set this resource.

XtNcategoryLabel
This resource provides the value for the Category Label.

XtNcategoryFont
This resource controls the font to use for the Category Label.

XtNfont
This resource controls the font to use for the Page Label

XtNfontColor
This resource gives the color for the Category and Page Labels and the Left and Right Footers.

XtNfooter
This resource is the widget ID of the footer.

XtNlayoutWidth
XtNlayoutHeight
> Range of values:
>> OL_MINIMIZE/"minimize"
>> OL_MAXIMIZE/"maximize"
>> OL_IGNORE/"ignore"

These resources identify the layout policy for each of the horizontal (width) and vertical (height) dimensions:

OL_MINIMIZE
> The **Category** widget will always be just large enough to contain the current page and Category Label, Abbreviated Menu Button, Page Label, and Lower Control Area, regardless of any dimension set by the client. Thus the **Category** widget will grow and shrink depending on the size of the current page (and perhaps the size of the Page Label or the content of the Lower Control Area).

OL_MAXIMIZE
> The **Category** widget will grow as needed to accommodate each page but will not try to shrink.

OL_IGNORE
> The **Category** widget will honor its set width or height and will not try to grow or shrink when switching pages. When the width or height is not set by the client, the size will be large enough to exactly fit the first page displayed (though see the **XtNpageWidth** and **XtNpageHeight** resources).

For the **OL_MAXIMIZE** and **OL_MINIMIZE** layout policies the **Category** widget will always go through its parent to negotiate a new size.

XtNpageWidth
XtNpageHeight
> For **OL_IGNORE** layout policies, these resources provide the fixed size that should be used for each page. These resources are ignored if the **XtNwidth** or **XtNheight** resources (respectively) are given, and are ignored for policies other than **OL_IGNORE**.

XtNleftFoot
XtNrightFoot
> These resources are used to control the information shown in the Left and Right Footers (respectively). The footers are displayed at the bottom of the **Category** widget, with 3/4 of the width used for the Left Footer and 1/4 of the width for the Right Footer. If a Footer cannot be fully displayed in the space available, it is truncated and an arrow is displayed to the right of the Footer to let the user know of the truncation.

XtNlowerControlArea
> This is the widget ID of the Lower Control Area.

XtNnewPage
> This callback list can be used by the client to learn when the user has selected a new page. The *call_data* parameter is a pointer to an **OlCategoryNewPage** structure, which includes the following members:

```
Widget     new;
Widget     old;
Boolean    other_changes;
```

new
old   identify the new and old pages, respectively.

other_changes
          notes whether pages other than **new** have changes.

XtNshowFooter
Range of values:
```
TRUE/"true"
FALSE/"false"
```

This resource controls whether the Left and Right Footers are shown. If **TRUE**, the footer, identified by **XtNfooter**, is managed (displayed) or — if the footer is blank — vertical space is left where the footer would normally appear. If **FALSE**, the footer is unmanaged.

Constraint Resources

Category Constraint Resources				
Name	Class	Type	Default	Access
XtNchanged	XtCChanged	Boolean	FALSE	SGI
XtNdefault	XtCDefault	Boolean	FALSE	SGI
XtNpageLabel	XtCPageLabel	String	NULL	SGI
XtNpaneGravity	XtCGravity	int	CenterGravity	SGI

XtNchanged
Range of values:
```
TRUE/"true"
FALSE/"false"
```

This resource marks a page as having changes. It is only used to control the window manager's window menu choice (Dismiss vs Cancel), to control when a changebar is shown next to the Category Label, and to tell the client when a switch to a new page leaves other pages with changes pending (see the **XtNnewPage** callback and the **OlCategorySetPage** routine). Other than this, what it means for a page to "have changes" is left for the client to interpret.

XtNdefault
Range of values:
```
TRUE/"true"
FALSE/"false"
```

This resource marks the child that should be made the default page. The Menu will reflect this default choice, and the default page will be the page displayed when the **Category** widget is realized.

If no page is marked as the default, the Menu will have no default and the first child created will be the first page displayed. If more than one page is marked as the default, the first marked is made the default.

Category (3Olit)

XtNpaneGravity
Range of values:

```
AllGravity/"all"
NorthSouthEastWestGravity/"northsoutheastwest"
SouthEastWestGravity/"southeastwest"
NorthEastWestGravity/"northeastwest"
NorthSouthWestGravity/"northsouthwest"
NorthSouthEastGravity/"northsoutheast"
EastWestGravity/"eastwest"
NorthSouthGravity/"northsouth"
CenterGravity/"center"
NorthGravity/"north"
SouthGravity/"south"
EastGravity/"east"
WestGravity/"west"
NorthWestGravity/"northwest"
NorthEastGravity/"northeast"
SouthWestGravity/"southwest"
SouthEastGravity/"southeast"
```

This resource suggests Page placement within the suggested space. The names suggest the positioning and perhaps sizing imposed on the page; because north, south, east, and west mean the top, bottom, right, and left edges of the Pane, the gravity tells which edges of the Page are forced to touch the named edges of the Pane. For instance, **NorthGravity** means the current page is positioned with its top edge at the top of the Pane and centered left and right, **NorthEastGravity** means the page is positioned in the upper-right corner of the Pane, **CenterGravity** means the page is centered in the pane. The traditional gravity values have a meaning similar to the values for window and bit gravity. The new "gravity" values like **North-SouthGravity** allow stretching the page to fit the suggested size. For instance, **NorthSouthGravity** means the page is sized to span the height of the Pane and positioned so that it is centered left and right.

To minimize the amount of graphics redrawing that has to be done when a new page is selected, the **Category** widget sets the bit gravity of the child's window to be the same as this resource (except for **AllGravity**, **NorthSouthEastWestGravity**, **SouthEastWestGravity**, **NorthEastWestGravity**, **NorthSouthWestGravity**, **NorthSouthEastGravity**, **EastWestGravity**, and **NorthSouthGravity**).

Note that **AllGravity** is a synonym for **NorthSouthEastWestGravity**.

The gravity has no effect when the layout policy is **OL_MINIMIZE**.

XtNpageLabel
This resource gives the Page Label for the child. This label is displayed in the Menu, and as the Page Label when the page is displayed.

SEE ALSO
Manager(3Olit)

NAME

      CheckBox – create a label button with a check box

SYNOPSIS

```
#include <X11/Intrinsic.h>
#include <X11/StringDefs.h>
#include <Xol/OpenLook.h>
#include <Xol/CheckBox.h>

widget = XtCreateWidget(name, checkBoxWidgetClass, . . .);
```

DESCRIPTION

      The **CheckBox** widget implements one of the OPEN LOOK button widgets.

CheckBox Components

      It consists of a Label next to a Check Box; the Check Box will have a Check Mark, if selected.

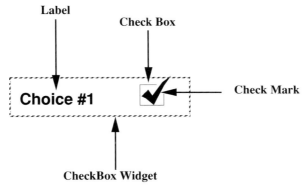

Figure 1. CheckBox Widget

Figure 2 shows several buttons, in unselected and selected, as well as normal and dim states.

Figure 2. CheckBoxes

CheckBox (3Olit)

Typical Use of Check Boxes

Check Boxes may be used alone, but are usually used in the **Nonexclusives** composite widget, where they are used to implement a several-of-many selection. Making the **CheckBox** widget a child of a different composite widget will not produce an error, but proper layout is not guaranteed.

Operating on Check Boxes

A **CheckBox** widget has two states: "set" and "not set". When set, the Check Mark is visible. Toggling this state alternates a resource (**XtNset**) between "true" and "false" and starts an action associated with the check box. Clicking SELECT on a check box toggles the state associated with it. Pressing SELECT, or moving the pointer into the check box while SELECT is pressed, adds or removes the Check Mark to reflect the state the check box would be in if SELECT was released. Releasing SELECT toggles the state. Moving the pointer off the check box before releasing SELECT restores the original CheckBox, but does not toggle the state. Clicking or pressing MENU does not do anything in the **CheckBox** widget; the event is passed up to an ancestor widget.

Bounds on SELECT

Only the CheckBox box and Check Mark respond to SELECT, as shown in Figure 3.

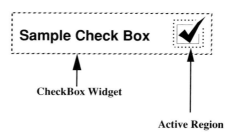

Figure 3. Active Region for a CheckBox

CheckBox Coloration

On a monochrome display, the **CheckBox** widget indicates that it has input focus by inverting the foreground color and parent's background colors within the bounding box of the widget.

On color displays, when the **CheckBox** widget receives the input focus, the background color within the bounding box of the widget is changed to the input focus color set in the **XtNinputFocusColor** resource. When the **CheckBox** widget loses the input focus, the background color reverts to its parent's **XtNbackground** color or **XtNbackgroundPixmap**.

EXCEPTIONS:

— If the input focus color is the same as the parent's background color, then the **CheckBox** widget inverts the foreground and background colors when it has input focus.

— If the input focus color is the same as the font color or foreground color, then the **CheckBox** widget inverts the foreground and background colors when it has input focus.

Figure 4 illustrates the resources that affect the coloration of the **CheckBox** widget.

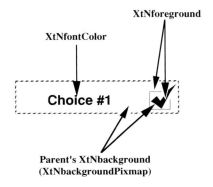

Figure 4. CheckBox Coloration

Keyboard Traversal

The default value of the **XtNtraversalOn** resource is **TRUE**.

The **CheckBox** widget responds to the following keyboard navigation keys:

NEXT_FIELD	NEXT_FIELD moves to the next traversable widget in the window
PREV_FIELD	moves to the previous traversable widget in the window
MOVEUP	moves to the CheckBox above the current widget in the Nonexclusives composite
MOVEDOWN	moves to the CheckBox below the current widget in the Nonexclusives composite
MOVELEFT	moves to the CheckBox to the left of the current widget in the Nonexclusives composite
MOVERIGHT	moves to the CheckBox to the right of the current widget in the Nonexclusives composite
NEXTWINDOW	moves to the next window in the application
PREVWINDOW	moves to the previous window in the application
NEXTAPP	moves to the first window in the next application
PREVAPP	moves to the first window in the previous application

CheckBox (3Olit)

CheckBox Widget Activation Types	
Activation Type	Expected Results
OL_SELECTKEY	Update its visual to reflect the new state and call the appropriate callback list

Display of Keyboard Mnemonic

The `CheckBox` widget displays the mnemonic accelerator as part of its label. If the mnemonic character is in the label, then that character is highlighted according to the value returned by `OlQueryMnemonicDisplay`. If the mnemonic character is not in the label, it is displayed to the right of the label in parenthesis and highlighted according to the value returned by `OlQueryMnemonicDisplay`.

If truncation is necessary, the mnemonic displayed in parenthesis is truncated as a unit.

Display of Keyboard Accelerators

The `CheckBox` widget displays the keyboard accelerator as part of its label. The string in the `XtNacceleratorText` resource is displayed to the right of the label (or mnemonic) separated by at least one space. The acceleratorText is right justified.

If truncation is necessary, the accelerator is truncated as a unit. The accelerator is truncated before the mnemonic or the label.

RESOURCES

CheckBox Resource Set					
Name	Class	Type	Default	Acc	Inherit
XtNaccelerator	XtCAccelerator	String	NULL	SGI	
XtNacceleratorText	XtCAcceleratorText	String	(calculated)	SGI	
XtNancestorSensitive	XtCSensitive	Boolean	(calculated)	G[1]	Core
XtNbackground	XtCBackground	Pixel	"XtDefaultBackground"	SGI	Core
XtNbackgroundPixmap	XtCPixmap	Pixmap	XtUnspecifiedPixmap	SGI	Core
XtNcolormap	XtCColormap	Colormap	(parent's)	GI	Core
XtNconsumeEvent	XtCCallback	XtCallbackList	NULL	SGI	Manager
XtNdepth	XtCDepth	Cardinal	(parent's)	GI	Core
XtNdestroyCallback	XtCCallback	XtCallbackList	NULL	SGI	Object
XtNdim	XtCDim	Boolean	FALSE	SGI	
XtNfont	XtCFont	XFontStruct *	"OlDefaultFont"	SGI	
XtNfontColor	XtCFontColor	Pixel	"XtDefaultForeground"	SGI	
XtNforeground	XtCForeground	Pixel	"XtDefaultForeground"	SGI	
XtNheight	XtCHeight	Dimension	(calculated)	SGI	Core
XtNinputFocusColor	XtCInputFocusColor	Pixel	"Red"	SGI	Manager
XtNlabel	XtCLabel	String	(widget name)	SGI	
XtNlabelImage	XtCLabelImage	XImage *	NULL	SGI	
XtNlabelJustify	XtCLabelJustify	OlDefine	OL_LEFT	SGI	
XtNlabelTile	XtCLabelTile	Boolean	FALSE	SGI	

CheckBox Resource Set (cont'd)					
Name	Class	Type	Default	Acc	Inherit
XtNlabelType	XtCLabelType	OlDefine	OL_STRING	SGI	
XtNmappedWhenManaged	XtCMappedWhenManaged	Boolean	TRUE	SGI	Core
XtNmnemonic	XtCMnemonic	char	NULL	SGI	
XtNposition	XtCPosition	OlDefine	OL_LEFT	SGI	
XtNrecomputeSize	XtCRecomputeSize	Boolean	TRUE	SGI	
XtNreferenceName	XtCReferenceName	String	NULL	SGI	Manager
XtNreferenceWidget	XtCReferenceWidget	Widget	NULL	SGI	Manager
XtNscreen	XtCScreen	Screen *	(parent's)	GI	Core
XtNselect	XtCCallback	XtCallbackList	NULL	SGI	
XtNsensitive	XtCSensitive	Boolean	TRUE	G[1]	Core
XtNset	XtCSet	Boolean	FALSE	SGI	
XtNtranslations	XtCTranslations	XtTranslations	NULL	SGI	Core
XtNtraversalOn	XtCTraversalOn	Boolean	TRUE	SGI	Manager
XtNunselect	XtCCallback	XtCallbackList	NULL	SGI	
XtNuserData	XtCUserData	XtPointer	NULL	SGI	Manager
XtNwidth	XtCWidth	Dimension	(calculated)	SGI	Core
XtNx	XtCPosition	Position	0	SGI	Core
XtNy	XtCPosition	Position	0	SGI	Core

[1] Use `XtSetSensitive` to set this resource.

XtNdim

Range of values:

> TRUE/"true"
> FALSE/"false"

If this resource is **TRUE**, the check box border is dimmed to show that the check box represents the state of one or more of several objects that, as a group, are in different states.

XtNlabel

This resource is a pointer to the text for the Label. This resource is ignored if the **XtNlabelType** resource has the value **OL_IMAGE**.

XtNlabelImage

This resource is a pointer to the image for the Label of the **CheckBox** widget. This resource is ignored unless the **XtNlabelType** resource has the value **OL_IMAGE**.

If the image is smaller than the space available for it next to the Check Box, it is centered vertically and either centered or left-justified horizontally depending on the value of the **XtNlabelJustify** resource. If the image is larger than the space available for it, it is clipped so that it does not stray outside the space.

XtNlabelJustify

Range of values:

> OL_LEFT/"left"
> OL_RIGHT/"right"

CheckBox (3Olit)

This resource dictates whether the Label should be left- or right-justified within the space left before or after the Check Box, if the **XtNwidth** resource gives more space than needed.

XtNlabelTile
Range of values:

TRUE/"true"
FALSE/"false"

This resource augments the **XtNlabelImage** resource to allow tiling of the sub-object's background. For an image that is smaller than the sub-object's background, the label area is tiled with the image to fill the sub-object's background if this resource is **TRUE**; otherwise, the label is placed as described by the **XtNlabelImage** resource.

The **XtNlabelTile** resource is ignored for text labels.

XtNlabelType
Range of values:

OL_STRING/"string"
OL_IMAGE/"image"

This resource identifies the form that the Label takes. It can have the value **OL_STRING** or **OL_IMAGE** for text or image, respectively.

XtNposition
Range of values:

OL_LEFT/"left"
OL_RIGHT/"right"

This resource determines on which side of the Check Box the Label is to be placed. The value may be one of **OL_LEFT** or **OL_RIGHT** to indicate that the Label is to be placed to the left or to the right of the Check Box, respectively.

XtNrecomputeSize
Range of values:

TRUE/"true"
FALSE/"false"

This resource indicates whether the **CheckBox** widget should calculate its size and automatically set the **XtNheight** and **XtNwidth** resources. If set to **TRUE**, the **CheckBox** widget will do normal size calculations that may cause its geometry to change. If set to **FALSE**, the **CheckBox** widget will leave its size alone; this may cause truncation of the visible image being shown by the **CheckBox** widget if the fixed size is too small, or may cause padding if the fixed size is too large. The location of the padding is determined by the **XtNlabelJustify** resource.

XtNselect
This is the list of callbacks invoked when the widget is selected.

XtNset
Range of values:

TRUE/"true"
FALSE/"false"

This resource reflects the current state of the check box. The Check Mark is present if **XtNset** is **TRUE** and is absent otherwise.

XtNunselect

This is the list of callbacks invoked when a **CheckBox** widget is toggled into the "unset" mode by the end user to make **XtNset** be **FALSE**. Note that simply setting **XtNset** to **FALSE** with a call to **XtSetValues** does not issue the **XtNunselect** callbacks.

XtNdim and XtNset Interaction

The **XtNdim** and **XtNset** resources can be set independently, as the state table in Figure 5 shows.

XtNset	XtNdim	Check Box Appearance
TRUE	TRUE	
TRUE	FALSE	
FALSE	TRUE	
FALSE	FALSE	

Figure 5. Check Box Appearance with Set/Default/Dim

Label and Check Box Appearance

The **XtNwidth**, **XtNheight**, **XtNrecomputeSize**, and **XtNlabelJustify** resources interact to produce a truncated, clipped, centered, left-justified, or right-justified Label and Check Box as shown in Figure 6.

XtNwidth	XtNrecomputeSize	XtNlabelJustify	Result
any value	TRUE	any	Just Fits
> needed for label	FALSE	OL-LEFT	Left Justified
> needed for label	FALSE	OL-RIGHT	Right Justified
< needed for label	FALSE	any	Truncated
XtNheight	**XtNrecomputeSize**	**XtNlabelJustify**	**Result**
any value	TRUE	any	Just Fits
> needed for label	FALSE	any	Centered
< needed for label	FALSE	any	Clipped

Figure 6. Label and Check Box Appearance

When the label is left-justified, right-justified, or centered the extra space is filled with the background color of the **CheckBox** widget's parent, as determined by the **XtNbackground** and **XtNbackgroundPixmap** resources of the parent.

Also the discussion under **XtNlabelTile** resource for how it affects the appearance of a label.

NOTES

The **CheckBox** widget does not support the MOTIF look and feel. For a MOTIF look and feel version, see **FlatButtons**(3Olit).

SEE ALSO

FlatButtons(3Olit), **OlQueryMnemonicDisplay**(3Olit)

NAME

ControlArea – manage a number of child widgets in rows or columns

SYNOPSIS

```
#include <X11/Intrinsic.h>
#include <X11/StringDefs.h>
#include <Xol/OpenLook.h>
#include <Xol/ControlAre.h>

widget = XtCreateWidget(name, controlAreaWidgetClass, . . .);
```

DESCRIPTION

The ControlArea widget manages a number of child widgets in rows or columns. It supports both the MOTIF and the OPEN LOOK look and feel.

ControlArea Components

The ControlArea widget has zero or more Child widgets and an optional Border. The Border may be shadowed.

Layout Control

The ControlArea composite widget arranges its child widgets, presenting them to the end-user as a group of "controls." The application can choose one of four simple layout schemes: Fixed number of columns in the control pane, fixed number of rows, fixed overall width of the control area, and fixed overall height. The application can also specify the inter-control spacing and the size of the margin around the children.

Equal Height Rows

The children in each row align at the top of the row. The distance between the top of one row and the next is the height of the tallest control in the row plus the application specified inter-row spacing.

ControlArea Coloration

Figure 1 illustrates the resources that affect the coloration of the ControlArea widget without the shadowed border. If the border is shadowed, the shadow color is calculated from **XtNbackground**.

ControlArea (3Olit)

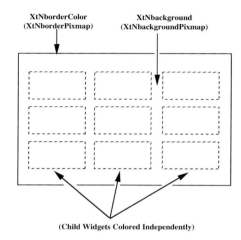

Figure 1. Control Area Coloration

RESOURCES

ControlArea Resource Set					
Name	Class	Type	Default	Acc	Inherit
XtNalignCaptions	XtCAlignCaptions	Boolean	FALSE	SGI	
XtNancestorSensitive	XtCSensitive	Boolean	(calculated)	G[1]	Core
XtNbackground	XtCBackground	Pixel	"XtDefaultBackground"	SGI	Core
XtNbackgroundPixmap	XtCPixmap	Pixmap	XtUnspecifiedPixmap	SGI	Core
XtNborderColor	XtCBorderColor	Pixel	"XtDefaultForeground"	SGI	Core
XtNborderPixmap	XtCPixmap	Pixmap	XtUnspecifiedPixmap	SGI	Core
XtNborderWidth	XtCBorderWidth	Dimension	0	SGI	Core
XtNcenter	XtCCenter	Boolean	FALSE	SGI	
XtNchildren	XtCReadOnly	WidgetList	NULL	G	Composite
XtNcolormap	XtCColormap	Colormap	(parent's)	GI	Core
XtNconsumeEvent	XtCCallback	XtCallbackList	NULL	SGI	Manager
XtNdepth	XtCDepth	Cardinal	(parent's)	GI	Core
XtNdestroyCallback	XtCCallback	XtCallbackList	NULL	SGI	Object
XtNhPad	XtCHPad	Dimension	4	SGI	
XtNhSpace	XtCHSpace	Dimension	4	SGI	
XtNheight	XtCHeight	Dimension	(calculated)	SGI	Core
XtNinsertPosition	XtCInsertPosition	XtWidgetProc	NULL	SGI	Composite
XtNlayoutType	XtCLayoutType	OlDefine	OL_FIXEDROWS	SGI	
XtNmappedWhenManaged	XtCMappedWhenManaged	Boolean	TRUE	SGI	Core

ControlArea Resource Set (cont'd)					
Name	Class	Type	Default	Acc	Inherit
XtNmeasure	XtCMeasure	int	1	SGI	
XtNnumChildren	XtCReadOnly	Cardinal	0	G	Composite
XtNreferenceName	XtCReferenceName	String	NULL	SGI	Manager
XtNreferenceWidget	XtCReferenceWidget	Widget	NULL	SGI	Manager
XtNsameSize	XtCSameSize	OlDefine	OL_COLUMNS	SGI	
XtNscreen	XtCScreen	Screen *	(parent's)	GI	Core
XtNsensitive	XtCSensitive	Boolean	TRUE	G[1]	Core
XtNshadowThickness	XtCShadowThickness	Dimension	"0 points"[3]	SGI	Manager
XtNshadowType	XtCShadowType	OlDefine	OL_SHADOW_OUT	SGI	Manager
XtNtranslations	XtCTranslations	XtTranslations	NULL	SGI	Core
XtNtraversalOn	XtCTraversalOn	Boolean	TRUE	SGI	Manager
XtNuserData	XtCUserData	XtPointer	NULL	SGI	Manager
XtNvPad	XtCVPad	Dimension	4	SGI	
XtNvSpace	XtCVSpace	Dimension	4	SGI	
XtNwidth	XtCWidth	Dimension	(calculated)	SGI	Core
XtNx	XtCPosition	Position	0	SGI	Core
XtNy	XtCPosition	Position	0	SGI	Core

[1] Use **XtSetSensitive** to set this resource.

[3] **"2 points"** in MOTIF look and feel.

XtNalignCaptions

Range of values:

> **TRUE**/"true"
> **FALSE**/"false"

This resource controls how the **ControlArea** widget aligns widgets of the **Caption** class. If set to **TRUE**, the **ControlArea** will align all **Caption** widgets in each column so that their captions are right justified. This may affect the width calculation for a column: The effective width for the **Caption** widgets in a column becomes the sum of the width of the widest caption, plus the largest caption/child widget separation and child widget width.

This alignment is only for groups of **Caption** widgets with all their captions on the left or the right. Mixed orientation, or captions above or below, cannot be aligned well.

ControlArea (3Olit)

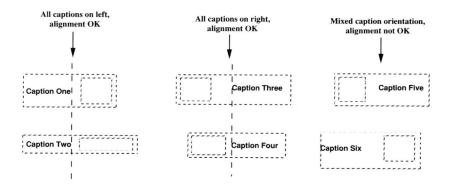

Figure 2. Aligning Captions

If the **XtNalignCaption** resource is set to **FALSE**, the **ControlArea** will align all **Caption** widgets the same as other widgets — by their overall width.

This resource takes precedence over the **XtNcenter** resource, but only for **Caption** widgets.

XtNcenter

Range of values:

> TRUE/**"true"**
> FALSE/**"false"**

This resource controls how the **ControlArea** widget orients each widget within a column [although see also **XtNalignCaptions** above]. If set to **TRUE**, the **ControlArea** will center each widget with each column; if set to **FALSE**, the **ControlArea** will left justify each widget within each column, unless the **XtNalignCaptions** resource is **TRUE**.

XtNvPad
XtNhPad

Range of values:

> $0 \leq$ **XtNhPad**
> $0 \leq$ **XtNvPad**

These resources give the amount of padding, in pixels, to leave around the edges of the control area, left and right, and top and bottom, respectively, as suggested by Figure 3.

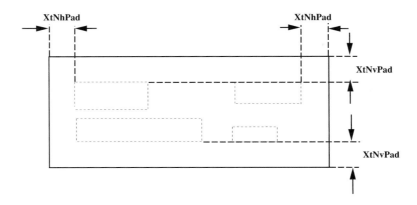

Figure 3. Padding Around Controls

XtNhSpace
XtNvSpace

Range of values:

$0 \leq$ `XtNhSpace`
$0 \leq$ `XtNvSpace`

These resources give the amount of space, in pixels, to leave between controls horizontally and vertically, respectively. If the controls are of different sizes in a row or column, the spacing applies to the widest or tallest dimension of all the controls.

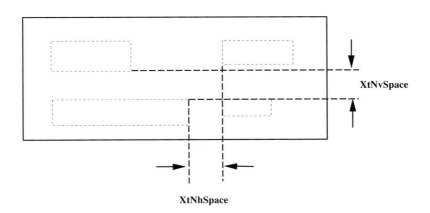

Figure 4. Spacing Between Controls

XtNlayoutType
Range of values:

> OL_FIXEDROWS/"fixedrows"
> OL_FIXEDCOLS/"fixedcols"
> OL_FIXEDWIDTH/"fixedwidth"
> OL_FIXEDHEIGHT/"fixedheight"

This resource controls the layout of the child widgets by the **ControlArea** composite. The choices are to specify the number of rows or columns, or to specify the overall height or width of the layout area. Only one of these dimensions can be specified directly; the other is determined by the number of controls added. For instance, if the application specifies that the control area should have four columns, the number of rows will be the number of controls divided by four.

The values of the **XtNlayoutType** resource can be:

OL_FIXEDROWS   if the layout should have a fixed number of rows and enough columns to hold all the controls;

OL_FIXEDCOLS   if the layout should have a fixed number of columns and enough rows to hold all the controls;

OL_FIXEDWIDTH   if the layout should be of a fixed width but tall enough to hold all the controls;

OL_FIXEDHEIGHT   if the layout should be of a fixed height but wide enough to hold all the controls.

The **XtNmeasure** resource gives the number of rows or columns or the fixed height or width.

XtNmeasure
Range of values:

> 0 < XtNmeasure

Default:

> If **XtNlayoutType** is **OL_FIXEDROWS** or **OL_FIXEDCOLS**: 1

> If **XtNlayoutType** is **OL_FIXEDWIDTH** or **OL_FIXEDHEIGHT**:

> > width or height of widest or tallest widget, depending on **XtNlayoutType**.

This resource gives the number of rows or columns in the layout of the child widgets, or the fixed width or height of the control area. When **XtNlayoutType** is **OL_FIXEDWIDTH** or **OL_FIXEDHEIGHT**, the measure includes the padding on both edges and the inter-control spacing, as suggested by Figure 5.

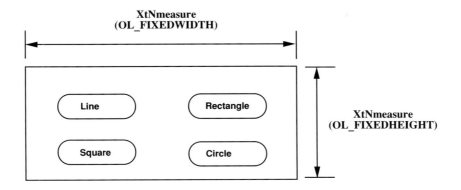

Figure 5. XtNmeasure

XtNsameSize
Range of values:
> OL_NONE/"none"
> OL_COLUMNS/"columns"
> OL_ALL/"all"

This resource controls which controls, if any, are forced to be the same width within the `ControlArea` widget:

OL_NONE   The controls are placed in fixed-width columns, but the size of each control is left alone. The width of each column is the width of the widest control in the column.

OL_COLUMNS   Controls of the same class in each column are made the same width as the widest of them. The width of each column is thus the width of the widest control in the column.

OL_ALL   All controls are made the same width, the width of the widest control in the `ControlArea` widget.

SEE ALSO
> Manager(3Olit)

Core(3Olit)

NAME

Core – **Core** widget superclass

SYNOPSIS

```
#include <X11/Intrinsic.h>
#include <X11/StringDefs.h>
#include <Xol/OpenLook.h>
```

DESCRIPTION

These are the resources of the **Core** superclass, of which all widget classes are subclasses. They are described here to avoid repeating their descriptions for each widget.

RESOURCES

<table>
<tr><th colspan="5">Core Resource Set</th></tr>
<tr><th>Name</th><th>Class</th><th>Type</th><th>Default</th><th>Acc</th></tr>
<tr><td>XtNancestorSensitive</td><td>XtCSensitive</td><td>Boolean</td><td>(calculated)</td><td>G[1]</td></tr>
<tr><td>XtNbackground</td><td>XtCBackground</td><td>Pixel</td><td>"XtDefaultBackground"</td><td>SGI</td></tr>
<tr><td>XtNbackgroundPixmap</td><td>XtCPixmap</td><td>Pixmap</td><td>XtUnspecifiedPixmap</td><td>SGI</td></tr>
<tr><td>XtNborderColor</td><td>XtCBorderColor</td><td>Pixel</td><td>"XtDefaultForeground"</td><td>SGI</td></tr>
<tr><td>XtNborderPixmap</td><td>XtCPixmap</td><td>Pixmap</td><td>XtUnspecifiedPixmap</td><td>SGI</td></tr>
<tr><td>XtNborderWidth</td><td>XtCBorderWidth</td><td>Dimension</td><td>1</td><td>SGI</td></tr>
<tr><td>XtNcolormap</td><td>XtCColormap</td><td>Colormap</td><td>(parent's)</td><td>GI</td></tr>
<tr><td>XtNdepth</td><td>XtCDepth</td><td>Cardinal</td><td>(parent's)</td><td>GI</td></tr>
<tr><td>XtNdestroyCallback</td><td>XtCCallback</td><td>XtCallbackList</td><td>NULL</td><td>SGI</td></tr>
<tr><td>XtNheight</td><td>XtCHeight</td><td>Dimension</td><td>0</td><td>SGI</td></tr>
<tr><td>XtNmappedWhenManaged</td><td>XtCMappedWhenManaged</td><td>Boolean</td><td>TRUE</td><td>SGI</td></tr>
<tr><td>XtNscreen</td><td>XtCScreen</td><td>Screen *</td><td>(parent's)</td><td>GI</td></tr>
<tr><td>XtNsensitive</td><td>XtCSensitive</td><td>Boolean</td><td>TRUE</td><td>G[1]</td></tr>
<tr><td>XtNtranslations</td><td>XtCTranslations</td><td>XtTranslations</td><td>NULL</td><td>SGI</td></tr>
<tr><td>XtNwidth</td><td>XtCWidth</td><td>Dimension</td><td>0</td><td>SGI</td></tr>
<tr><td>XtNx</td><td>XtCPosition</td><td>Position</td><td>0</td><td>SGI</td></tr>
<tr><td>XtNy</td><td>XtCPosition</td><td>Position</td><td>0</td><td>SGI</td></tr>
</table>

[1] Use **XtSetSensitive** to set this resource.

XtNaccelerators

This resource should not be set by an application.

XtNancestorSensitive

Range of values:

> TRUE/''true''
> FALSE/''false''

This resource specifies whether the immediate parent of the widget will receive input events. To preserve data integrity, the application should use the **XtSetSensitive** routine if it wants to change the resource (see **XtNsensitive** below).

XtNbackground

Range of values:

(any valid current display **Pixel** value)

This resource specifies the background color for the widget.

Note that the workspace manager arranges for a "normal video" (or "reverse video") effect on monochrome displays by setting the **XtNbackground** resource to white (black) and the **XtNforeground**, **XtNfontColor**, and **XtNborderColor** resources to black (white) where appropriate. The workspace manager also provides end user access to some of these resources on color displays. However, any color set by the application when a widget is created or in a later call to **XtSetValues** will override the colors set by the user. Applications should consider this and avoid setting these resources directly, letting the user have control over them.

XtNbackgroundPixmap

This resource specifies a pixmap for tiling the background. It can be set by the application. The first tile is placed at the upper left hand corner of the widget's window.

This resource takes precedence over the **XtNbackground** resource.

See the note about the interaction of this resource with other color resources under the description of the **XtNbackground** resource above.

XtNborderColor

Range of values:

(any valid current display **Pixel** value)/(any name from the **rgb.txt** file)

This resource specifies the color of the border.

See the note about the interaction of this resource with other color resources under the description of the **XtNbackground** resource above.

XtNborderPixmap

This resource specifies a pixmap for tiling the border. An application can set this resource. The first tile is placed at the upper left hand corner of the border.

This resource takes precedence over the **XtNborderColor** resource.

See the note about the interaction of this resource with other color resources under the description of the **XtNbackground** resource above.

XtNborderWidth

Range of values:

0 ≤ **XtNborderWidth**

This resource sets the width of the border for a widget. The width is specified in pixels, and a width of zero means no border will show.

XtNcolormap

Range of values:

StaticGray
GrayScale
StaticColor
PseudoColor
TRUEColor
DirectColor

This is the colormap to be used for the widget. While the range of values listed here is the entire list recognized, the actual valid values depend on the X server being used.

By default, a widget inherits its parent widget's colormap. If the widget is a top level shell, the default is the default colormap for the screen (see the **XtNscreen** resource).

XtNdepth

Range of values:

0 or (any value supported by the current display)

Determines how many bits should be used for each pixel in the widget's window. The value of this resource is used by the X Toolkit Intrinsics to set the depth of the widget's window when the widget is created. A value of zero causes a normal widget to inherit the depth of its parent, or a pop-up widget to inherit the default depth of the screen.

XtNdestroyCallback

This is a pointer to a callback list containing routines to be called when the widget is destroyed.

XtNheight

Range of values:

0 ≤ **XtNheight**

This resource contains the height of the widget's window in pixels, not including the border area. Programs may request a value at creation or through later calls to **XtSetValues**, but the request may not always succeed because of layout requirements of the parent widget.

The visual representations for some widgets have a fixed height for a given scale. For these widgets, the **XtNheight** resource gives the height of the space that contains the widget's representation; the representation is centered vertically in this space unless otherwise specified.

XtNmappedWhenManaged

Range of values:

TRUE/''true''
FALSE/''false''

If set to **TRUE**, the widget will be mapped (made visible) as soon as it is both realized and managed. If set to **FALSE**, the program is responsible for mapping and unmapping the widget. If the value is changed from **TRUE** to **FALSE** after the widget has been realized and managed, the widget is unmapped.

XtNscreen

This resource should not be set by an application.

XtNsensitive

Range of values:

TRUE/''true''
FALSE/''false''

This resource determines whether a widget will receive input events. If a widget is sensitive, the X Toolkit Intrinsic's event manager will dispatch to the widget all keyboard, mouse button, motion, window enter/leave, and focus events. Insensitive widgets do not receive these events. Also, insensitive widgets that appear on the screen are stippled with a 50% gray pattern to show that they are inactive, as a visual indication that the user can't interact with the widget. The 50% gray pattern is one that makes every other pixel of the widget the background color, in a checkerboard pattern.

An application should use the **XtSetSensitive** routine if it wants to change this resource. This ensures that if a parent widget has **XtNsensitive** set to **FALSE**, the **XtNancestorSensitive** flag of all its descendants will be appropriately set.

XtNtranslations

This resource should not be set by an application.

XtNwidth

Range of values:

    $0 \leq$ **XtNwidth**

This resource contains the width of the widget's window in pixels, not including the border area. Programs may request a value at creation or through later calls to **XtSetValues**, but the request may not always succeed because of layout requirements of the parent widget.

The visual representations for some widgets have a fixed width for a given scale. For these widgets, the **XtNwidth** resource gives the width of the space that contains the widget's representation; the representation is centered horizontally in this space unless otherwise specified.

XtNx

Range of values:

    $0 \leq$ **XtNx**

This argument contains the x-coordinate of the widget's upper left hand corner (excluding the border) relative to its parent widget. Programs may request a value at creation or through later calls to **XtSetValues**, but the request may not always succeed because of layout requirements of the parent widget.

XtNy

Range of values:

    $0 \leq$ **XtNy**

This resource contains the y-coordinate of the widget's upper left hand corner (excluding the border) relative to its parent widget. Programs may request a value at creation or through later calls to **XtSetValues**, but the request may not always succeed because of layout requirements of the parent widget.

Exclusives (3Olit)

NAME

      `Exclusives` – select one of a set of choices

SYNOPSIS

```
#include <X11/Intrinsic.h>
#include <X11/StringDefs.h>
#include <Xol/OpenLook.h>
#include <Xol/Exclusives.h>

widget = XtCreateWidget(name, exclusivesWidgetClass, . . .);
```

DESCRIPTION

The **Exclusives** widget provides a simple way to build a one-of-many button selection object in the OPEN LOOK look and feel. It manages a set of rectangular buttons, providing layout management.

Grid Layout and Button Labels

The **Exclusives** widget lays out the rectangular buttons in a grid in the order they were created. The number of rows or columns in this grid can be controlled by the application. If the grid has more than one row, the **Exclusives** widget forces the buttons in each column to be the same size as the widest in the column, and forces their labels to be left-justified. (Note that if the grid has a single row, each button will be only as wide as necessary to display the label.)

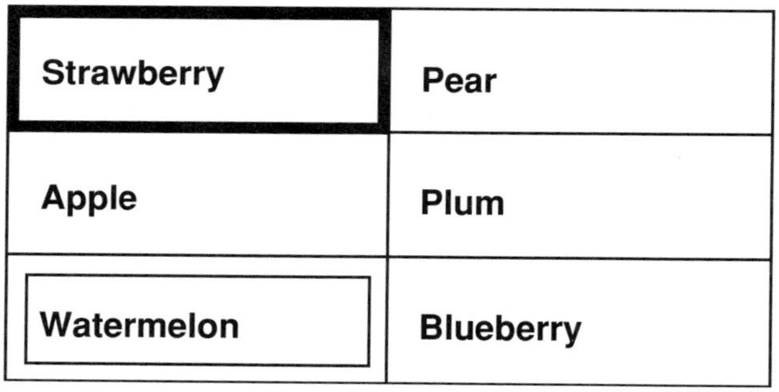

Figure 1. Example of Exclusive Buttons

Selection Control—One Set

In one mode of operation (for example, **XtNnoneSet** is **FALSE**), exactly one button in an **Exclusives** widget must be "set" (for example, the **XtNset** resource set to **TRUE**). An error is generated if an **Exclusives** is configured with two or more rectangular buttons set or with no button set. The **Exclusives** widget maintains this condition by ensuring that when a button is set by the user clicking SELECT over it, the button that was set is cleared and its **XtNunselect** callbacks are invoked. However, clicking SELECT over a button that was already set does nothing.

Selection Control—None Set

In the other mode of operation (for example, **XtNnoneSet** is **TRUE**), at most one button in an **Exclusives** widget can be set. An error is generated if an **Exclusives** is configured with two or more rectangular buttons set, but not if configured with no button set. The **Exclusives** widget maintains this condition by ensuring that when a button is set by the user clicking SELECT over it, or by the application programmer with the **XtNset** resource, any button that was previously set is cleared. Also, clicking SELECT over a button that was already set will unset it. Clearing a button in either case invokes its **XtNunselect** callbacks.

Use in a Menu

The **Exclusives** widget can be added as a single child to a menu pane to implement a one-of-many menu choice.

Child Constraint

The **Exclusives** widget constrains its child widgets to be of the class **rectButtonWidgetClass**.

Exclusives Coloration

When the **Exclusives** widget manages a number of children that is not a multiple of the **XtNmeasure** resource, the empty space is colored according to the **XtNbackground** or **XtNbackgroundPixmap** resource.

Keyboard Traversal

The Exclusives widget manages the traversal between a set of RectButtons. When the user traverses to a Exclusives widget, the first RectButton in the set will receive input focus. The MOVEUP, MOVEDOWN, MOVERIGHT, and MOVELEFT keys move the input focus between the RectButtons. To traverse out of the Exclusives widget, the following keys can be used:

NEXT_FIELD   moves to the next traversable widget in the window

PREV_FIELD   moves to the previous traversable widget in the window

NEXTWINDOW   moves to the next window in the application.

PREVWINDOW   moves to the previous window in the application.

NEXTAPP   moves to the first window in the next application.

PREVAPP   moves to the first window in the previous application.

The SELECTKEY acts as if the SELECT button had been clicked on the **RectButton** with input focus. The MENUKEY acts as if the MENU button had been clicked on the **RectButton** with input focus.

RESOURCES

Exclusives Resource Set					
Name	Class	Type	Default	Acc	Inherit
XtNancestorSensitive	XtCSensitive	Boolean	(calculated)	G[1]	Core
XtNbackground	XtCBackground	Pixel	"XtDefaultBackground"	SGI	Core
XtNbackgroundPixmap	XtCPixmap	Pixmap	XtUnspecifiedPixmap	SGI	Core
XtNchildren	XtCReadOnly	WidgetList	NULL	G	Composite
XtNcolormap	XtCColormap	Colormap	(parent's)	GI	Core
XtNconsumeEvent	XtCCallback	XtCallbackList	NULL	SGI	Manager
XtNdepth	XtCDepth	Cardinal	(parent's)	GI	Core
XtNdestroyCallback	XtCCallback	XtCallbackList	NULL	SGI	Object

Exclusives (3Olit)

\multicolumn{6}{c}{**Exclusives** Resource Set (cont'd)}
Name	Class	Type	Default	Acc	Inherit
XtNheight	XtCHeight	Dimension	(calculated)	SGI	Core
XtNinsertPosition	XtCInsertPosition	XtWidgetProc	NULL	SGI	Composite
XtNlayoutType	XtCLayoutType	OlDefine	OL_FIXEDROWS	SGI	
XtNmappedWhenManaged	XtCMappedWhenManaged	Boolean	TRUE	SGI	Core
XtNmeasure	XtCMeasure	int	1	SGI	
XtNnoneSet	XtCNoneSet	Boolean	FALSE	SGI	
XtNnumChildren	XtCReadOnly	Cardinal	0	G	Composite
XtNrecomputeSize	XtCRecomputeSize	Boolean	TRUE	SGI	
XtNreferenceName	XtCReferenceName	String	NULL	SGI	Manager
XtNreferenceWidget	XtCReferenceWidget	Widget	NULL	SGI	Manager
XtNscreen	XtCScreen	Screen *	(parent's)	GI	Core
XtNsensitive	XtCSensitive	Boolean	TRUE	G[1]	Core
XtNtranslations	XtCTranslations	XtTranslations	NULL	SGI	Core
XtNtraversalOn	XtCTraversalOn	Boolean	TRUE	SGI	Manager
XtNuserData	XtCUserData	XtPointer	NULL	SGI	Manager
XtNwidth	XtCWidth	Dimension	(calculated)	SGI	Core
XtNx	XtCPosition	Position	0	SGI	Core
XtNy	XtCPosition	Position	0	SGI	Core

[1]   Use XtSetSensitive to set this resource. lin +.2i

XtNlayoutType
Range of values:

>   OL_FIXEDROWS/"fixedrows"
>   OL_FIXEDCOLS/"fixedcols"

This resource controls the type of layout of the child widgets by the **Exclusives** composite. The choices are to specify the number of rows or the number of columns. Only one of these dimensions can be specified directly; the other is determined by the number of child widgets added, and will always be enough to show all the child widgets.

The values of the **XtNlayoutType** resource can be

OL_FIXEDROWS   if the layout should have a fixed number of rows;

OL_FIXEDCOLS   if the layout should have a fixed number of columns.

XtNmeasure
Range of values:

>   0 < XtNmeasure

This resource gives the number of rows or columns in the layout of the child widgets. If there are not enough child widgets to fill a row or column, the remaining space is left blank.

XtNnoneSet
Range of values:
    TRUE/''true''
    FALSE/''false''

This resource controls whether the buttons controlled by the **Exclusives** composite can be toggled into an unset mode directly. If set to **FALSE**, at all times exactly one button must be set. Attempting to select the currently set button does nothing. If set to **TRUE**, at all times no more than one button can be set. However, the user can select the currently set button again to toggle it back into an unset mode.

NOTES

To obtain a MOTIF look and feel for an **Exclusives** widget, use the **FlatButtons** widget.

SEE ALSO

FlatButtons(3Olit), **FlatExclusives**(3Olit), **Nonexclusives**(3Olit), **RectButton**(3Olit)

Flat (3Olit)

NAME

Flat - Flat widget superclass

SYNOPSIS

```
#include <X11/Intrinsic.h>
#include <X11/StringDefs.h>
#include <Xol/OpenLook.h>
```

DESCRIPTION

Flattened widgets give the visual appearance and functionality of many discrete windowed widgets, but are implemented as one widget with a single associated window created with one, convenient toolkit request. Flattened widgets consume a fraction of the memory that a similar non-flattened widget would require.

In general, flattened widgets have the following attributes:

1. They are container objects, responsible for managing the look and feel of one or more sub-objects.

2. The sub-objects classes are limited to one or a select few.

3. After the container is populated, minimal or no manipulation of the sub-objects is typically desired.

4. Each container is simply a region that contains zero or more sub-objects of a certain type.

5. The sub-objects within the container do not have an associated window or widget structure.

All of the flattened containers have the same layout characteristics. The superclass of all flattened widgets is a generic row/column manager. Though each column has its own width and each row has its own height, all columns can have the same width and all rows can have the same height, if desired.

The **Flat** manager lays out each managed sub-object in row-major order or in column-major order depending on the attributes of the container, starting with the NorthWest corner of the container.

Sub-objects of flattened containers are placed within the grid. If the sub-object's width (or height) is less than the column's width (or row's height), the sub-object is positioned in accordance to the **XtNitemGravity** resource.

RESOURCES

Flat Resource Set				
Name	Class	Type	Default	Access
XtNgravity	XtCGravity	int	CenterGravity	SGI
XtNhPad	XtCHPad	Dimension	0	SGI
XtNhSpace	XtCHSpace	Dimension	0	SGI
XtNitemField	XtCItemFields	String *	NULL	SGI
XtNitemGravity	XtCItemGravity	int	NorthWestGravity	SGI
XtNitemMaxHeight	XtCItemMaxHeight	Dimension	OL_IGNORE	SGI
XtNitemMaxWidth	XtCItemMaxWidth	Dimension	OL_IGNORE	SGI

Flat Resource Set (cont'd)				
Name	Class	Type	Default	Access
XtNitemMinHeight	XtCItemMinHeight	Dimension	OL_IGNORE	SGI
XtNitemMinWidth	XtCItemMinWidth	Dimension	OL_IGNORE	SGI
XtNitems	XtCItems	XtPointer	NULL	SGI
XtNlayoutHeight	XtCLayoutHeight	OlDefine	OL_MINIMIZE	SGI
XtNlayoutType	XtCLayoutType	OlDefine	OL_FIXEDROWS	SGI
XtNlayoutWidth	XtCLayoutWidth	OlDefine	OL_MINIMIZE	SGI
XtNmeasure	XtCMeasure	int	1	SGI
XtNnumItemFields	XtCNumItemFields	Cardinal	0	SGI
XtNnumItems	XtCNumItems	Cardinal	0	SGI
XtNsameHeight	XtCSameHeight	OlDefine	OL_ALL	SGI
XtNsameWidth	XtCSameWidth	OlDefine	OL_COLUMNS	SGI
XtNvPad	XtCVPad	Dimension	0	SGI
XtNvSpace	XtCVSpace	Dimension	0	SGI

XtNgravity

Range of values:

```
EastGravity/"east"
WestGravity/"west"
CenterGravity/"center"
NorthGravity/"north"
NorthEastGravity/"northEast"
NorthWestGravity/"northWest"
SouthGravity/"south"
SouthEastGravity/"southEast"
SouthWestGravity/"southWest"
```

The gravity resource specifies the position of all sub-objects (that is, as a group) whenever a tight-fitting bounding box that surrounds the sub-objects has a width, or height, less than the container's width or height, respectively. Essentially, this resource specifies how the sub-objects, as a group, float within its container.

XtNhPad
XtNvPad

Range of values:

$0 \le$ XtNhPad

$0 \le$ XtNvPad

These resources specify the minimum spacing to leave round the edges of the container, left and right, and top and bottom, respectively.

XtNhSpace
XtNvSpace

Range of values:

$0 \le$ XtNhSpace

$0 \le$ XtNvSpace

These resource specify the amount of space to leave between sub-objects horizontally and vertically, respectively. If the sub-objects are of different sizes in a row or column, the spacing applies to the widest or tallest dimension all sub-objects in the row or column.

XtNitemFields

This resource contains the list of resource names used to parse the records in the `XtNitems` list.

Although the flattened container does not reference this resource's value after initialization, it holds onto it for responding to an `XtGetValues` request and supplies it in the `OlFlatCallData` structure during callbacks. If the application plans on querying this resource, it should make this resources information static.

Applications should re-supply a new item list when `XtNitemFields` is changed, whether or not a new item resource is required. Failure to do so will cause a mismatch between the item list and the item field list.

XtNitemGravity

Range of values:

```
EastGravity/"east"
WestGravity/"west"
CenterGravity/"center"
NorthGravity/"north"
NorthEastGravity/"northEast"
NorthWestGravity/"northWest"
SouthGravity/"south"
SouthEastGravity/"southEast"
SouthWestGravity/"southWest"
```

This resource specifies how an item fits into its row or column whenever the item's width or height is less than the column's width or the row's height. The values of `XtNsameWidth` and `XtNsameHeight` govern the column's width and the row's height.

XtNitemMaxHeight
XtNitemMaxWidth

Range of values:

```
OL_IGNORE != XtNitemMaxHeight
OL_IGNORE != XtNitemMaxWidth
```

These resources specify the maximum allowable width and height (respectively) of all sub-objects. If either of these resources have a value of `OL_IGNORE`, the maximum size constraint is ignored.

XtNitemMinHeight
XtNitemMinWidth

Range of values:

```
OL_IGNORE != XtNitemMinHeight
OL_IGNORE != XtNitemMinWidth
```

These resources specify the minimum allowable width and height (respectively) of all sub-objects. If either resource has a value of `OL_IGNORE`, it is ignored.

XtNitems

This is the list of sub-object items.

This value must point to a static list because flattened containers reference this list after initialization, but do not cache its information.

XtNlayoutHeight
XtNlayoutWidth

Range of values:

```
OL_MINIMIZE/"minimize"
OL_MAXIMIZE/"maximize"
OL_IGNORE/"ignore"
```

These resources specify the resize policy of flattened containers whenever a sub-object is added, removed or altered. These resources have no affect when an external force applies a size change to the container, for example, if the application resizes a container. The explanation of the values are:

OL_MINIMIZE   The container will modify its width (or height) to be just large enough to tightly wrap around its sub-objects regardless of its current width (or height). Thus the container will grow and shrink depending on the size needs of its sub-objects.

OL_MAXIMIZE   The container will increase its width (or height) to be just large enough to tightly wrap around its sub-objects regardless of its current width (or height), but will not give up extra space. Thus the container will grow but never shrink depending on the size needs of its sub-objects.

OL_IGNORE   The container will honor its own width and height, for example, it will not grow or shrink in response to the addition, deletion or altering of its sub-objects.

XtNlayoutType

Range of values:

```
OL_FIXEDCOLS/"fixedcols"
OL_FIXEDROWS/"fixedrows"
```

This resource controls the number of rows and columns used to layout the sub-objects.

OL_FIXEDCOLS

The layout should have a maximum number of columns equal to the value specified by the **XtNmeasure** resource, and there will be enough rows to hold all sub-objects. Sub-objects are placed in row-major order, for example, the columns of the current row are filled before filling any columns in the next row.

OL_FIXEDROWS

The layout should have a maximum number of rows equal to the value specified by the **XtNmeasure** resource, and there will be enough columns to hold all sub-objects. Sub-objects are placed in column-major order, for example, the rows of the current column are filled before filling any rows in the next column.

XtNmeasure

Range of values:

```
0 < XtNmeasure
```

This resource gives the number of rows or columns requested from the **XtNlayout-Type** resource.

XtNnumItemFields

This resource specifies the number of resource names contained in **XtNitemFields**.

XtNnumItems

This resource specifies the number of sub-object items.

XtNsameHeight

Range of values:

```
OL_ALL/"all"
OL_ROWS/"rows"
OL_NONE/"none"
```

This resource defines which sub-objects are forced to be the same height within the container:

OL_ALL   All sub-objects are to be the same height.

OL_ROWS   All sub-objects appearing in the same row should be the same height.

OL_NONE   The sub-objects are placed in fixed-height rows but the height of each item is left alone. The height of each row is the height of the tallest sub-object.

XtNsameWidth

Range of values:

```
OL_ALL/"all"
OL_COLUMNS/"columns"
OL_NONE/"none"
```

This resource defines which sub-objects are forced to be the same width within the container:

OL_ALL   All sub-objects are to be the same width.

OL_COLUMNS   All sub-objects appearing in the same column should be the same width.

OL_NONE   The sub-objects are placed in fixed-width columns but the width of each item is left alone. The width of each column is the width of the widest sub-object.

USAGE

Layout Efficiency

As a programming note, the efficiency in both processing steps and data requirements increases as the grid becomes more regular in shape. For example, a grid specifying that all rows must have the same height and all columns must have the same width is the most efficient configuration.

Row-major order implies every column in the current row is filled before filling any columns in the next row. Column-major order implies every row in the current column is filled before filling any rows in the next column.

USAGE

Although there is no user distinguishable difference between a flattened widget and a traditional widget, flattened widgets have a different programming interface. A single toolkit request can specify an arbitrary number of primitive graphical user interface components (that is, the sub-objects), achieving a substantial reduction in the lines of code required to produce a complex graphical interface component.

List-specified Sub-Objects and Allowable resources

Sub-objects of a flattened container are specified in list format and both the flattened container and the application share the same list. Each list is an array of application-defined records, typically, in a 'C' structure format or as an array. Each record describes a particular sub-object. For efficiency, all records in an array must have the same form, that is, each structure in the list has identical fields. This restriction applies per list, because, if the application desires different attributes, each list may have a different set of fields. For data alignment and parsing, the fields of each record must use the `XtArgVal` type (see the code example).

The fields of each record are resource values describing the state of the sub-object. Allowable sub-object resources are a subset of its container's resource set.

Because all sub-object resources are part of a container, sub-objects inherit any non-specified resource from the container. For example, if the application wants a particular font color for all sub-objects, set the `XtNfontColor` resource on the container and all sub-objects will use that font color. The converse is not true, none of a sub-object's resources have any direct effect on the container.

The container must be given information about the record form in a resource name list so that it can parse the supplied list, because the form of the record is defined within the application's domain. While the field ordering in each record is not important, the application must provide the resource names in the same sequence as in the record. For example, if the records specifying sub-objects of a flattened exclusives container had a "label" field followed by the "selectProc" callback field, the application must supply the container with the `XtNlabel` resource name followed by the `XtNselectProc` resource name. Inconsistent ordering of the fields results in undefined behavior when the sub-objects are instantiated.

Specifying Sub-Objects

Sub-objects of flattened widget containers are specified in list format, each list having a corresponding set of resource names describing how to parse the list. The four common resources are used by each container class to describe the necessary sub-object information are `XtNitems`, `XtNnumItems`, `XtNitemFields`, and `XtNnumItemFields`.

Callbacks and Flattened Widgets

There are two differences in the way callbacks are handled for flattened widgets verses traditional widgets. The first difference is that sub-objects do not use `XtCallback` lists; instead, they use a single `XtCallbackProc` procedure.

(Remember a callback procedure has

```
typedef void (*XtCallbackProc)(
    Widget    widget,
    XtPointer client_data,
    XtPointer call_data
);
```

form.)

Second, because the sub-objects of flattened widget containers are not true widget instances, the widget argument supplied to an application's callback procedure shows the flattened container widget that is ultimately responsible for managing the sub-object. For example, the **flatExclusivesWidget** ID would be supplied as the widget ID to callback procedure for all sub-objects within the flattened exclusives container. By maintaining this rule, the application always has the correct widget handy in the event the application wants to modify the item or its list from within the callback procedure. The value of the **XtNclientData** resource is supplied as the *client_data* field to the callback procedure.

The *call_data* field is a structure the application can use to determine information about the sub-object associated with the current callback. The **OlFlatCallData** structure includes the following members:

```
Cardinal  item_index;       /* sub-object initiating callback */
XtPointer items;            /* Sub-object list head */
Cardinal  num_items;        /* number of items */
String *  item_fields;      /* key of fields for list */
Cardinal  num_item_fields;  /* number of fields per item */
XtPointer user_data;        /* widget's user_data value */
XtPointer item_user_data;   /* item's user_data value */
```

where:

item_index	index of the item responsible for the callback
items	head of item list containing the sub-object initiating the callback
num_items	total number of items in the sub-object list
item_fields	list of resource names used to parse the records in the **items** list
num_item_fields	number of resource names contained in **item_fields**
user_data	value of the widget's user_data
item_user_data	value of the item's user_data

Setting the State of a Sub-Object

Applications can use two methods to change the state of an item: use the **OlFlatSetValues** procedure to modify one or more attributes of a sub-object, or directly modify the item list that the container and the application share.

The first approach is very similar to doing an **XtSetValues** request on a widget, except that the **OlFlatSetValues** routine requires the item index as well as *widget*, *args* and *num_args* arguments [see **OlFlatSetValues**(3Olit)].

If the application does not use the above approach and modifies the item list directly, the application must ensure that all items within the list have valid states, because the container literally treats this type of modification as if the container was given a new list. For example, if an application wished to change a currently-set exclusive item, the application would have to unset the currently-set item and set the new item. If the application only set the new item, the container would generate a warning because the item list contains more than one set item.

Getting the State of a Sub-Object

Obtaining the state of a sub-object can be achieved in two ways: using the **OlFlat-GetValues** routine, specifying the index of the item to be queried, or looking directly into the sub-object list.

If the **OlFlatGetValues** routine is used, the application can query any sub-object resource even though it does not appear in the item fields. Take the font color example, the application can query the **XtNfontColor** resource from any sub-object even though it does not appear in the **FlatExclusives** structure.

Obtaining Help on a Sub-Object

The application can specify a unique help message for each sub-object just as for widgets, through the **OlRegisterHelp** routine. Since sub-objects are not real widgets, but are extensions of the flattened widget container, the help registration routine has a complex ID structure, **OlFlatHelpId**, which includes the following members:

```
Widget   widget;        /* Flattened Widget ID     */
Cardinal item_index;    /* item to register help on */
```

Examples

The following examples illustrate aspects of using **Flat** widgets.

If an application wanted to specify an "unselect" callback procedure for one group of exclusives but not for another, for example, the application would specify an **XtNunselectProc** field as an element field for the first list but not for the second list.

The following code example illustrates how to create a flattened exclusives settings. Notice that all the fields in the application defined structure, **FlatExclusives**, have the type **XtArgVal**. (Note that an alternate form for specifying the **FlatExclusives** type is:

```
typedef XtArgVal FlatExclusives[#];
```

where # is the number fields per record.)

Since each item has the same client data for the select callback procedure, the **XtNclientData** resource is specified for the container only, which allows each sub-object to inherit this value. If each sub-object needed a different client data, the **XtNclientData** resource should be added to the other sub-object resources, which would disable inheriting the container's client data value.

To improve the readability of this example, required type casts of the fields in the
`FlatExclusives` structure initialization deliberately have been omitted.

```
                      /* Application Defined Structure */
typedef struct {
    XtArgVal    label;              /* pointer to a string */
} FlatExclusives;
String exc_fields[] = { XtNlabel, XtNselectProc };
static void cb()
{ /* something interesting in here */ }
CreateObjects(Widget parent);
{
    Arg             args[6];
    static FlatExclusives exc_items[] = {
        { "Choice 1" },
        { "Choice 2" },
        { "Choice 3" }
    };

    XtSetArg(args[0], XtNitems, exc_items);
    XtSetArg(args[1], XtNnumItems, XtNumber(exc_items));
    XtSetArg(args[2], XtNitemFields, exc_fields);
    XtSetArg(args[3], XtNnumItemFields, XtNumber(exc_fields));
    XtSetArg(args[4], XtNselectProc, cb,);
    XtSetArg(args[5], XtNclientData, "test case");

    XtCreateManagedWidget("exclusives", flatExclusivesWidgetClass,
        parent, args, 6);
} /* END OF CreateObjects() */
```

The following code example illustrates how to change an item's label from within a
callback procedure. The example assumes the new label was specified as the client
data.

```
Callback(
    Widget      widget,          /* FlatExclusives Widget ID */
    XtPointer client_data,       /* the new static label */
    XtPointer call_data)         /* OlFlatCallData structure ptr */
{
    OlFlatCallData * fcd = (OlFlatCallData *)call_data;
    Arg    args[1];

        /* Set the label to be the new one passed in
         * with the client data field.
         */

        XtSetArg(args[0], XtNlabel, client_data);

        OlFlatSetValues(widget, fcp->item_index, args, 1);
} /* END OF Callback() */
```

Notice that the callback procedure need not know the number or order of the item fields. The only requirement was that the **XtNlabel** resource be among the application-specified item fields, because if it was not, the above request would be ignored. (Note that there are some exceptions to this rule. For instance, flattened containers maintain the set item and the default item even if the application did not specify **XtNset** or **XtNdefault** in the item fields. If the exceptions were not made, the application must always specify a minimum set of item fields, an undesirable requirement. See the individual manual pages for each widget for a better description of the exceptions.)

The following example shows how a callback procedure changes the set item by modifying the item list. This example makes the first item be the set item whenever the last item is selected. Notice that once the list has been touched, the application must "inform" the container of the modification. Also notice in this example the application needs to know the "structure" of the application to directly change its contents.

```
                /* Application Defined Structure From Previous Example */

typedef struct {
    XtArgVal  label;          /* pointer to a string */
    XtArgVal  select_proc;    /* pointer to a callback procedure */
    XtArgVal  set;            /* this item is currently set */
    XtArgVal  sensitive;      /* this item is sensitive */
} FlatExclusives;

Callback(
    Widget    widget,         /* FlatExclusives Widget ID */
    XtPointer client_data,    /* application's client data */
    XtPointer call_data)      /* OlFlatCallData structure ptr */
{
    OlFlatCallData * fcd = (OlFlatCallData *) call_data;

    if (fcd->num_items == (fcd->item_index + 1))
    {
        FlatExclusives * fexc_items = (FlatExclusives *) fcd->items;
        Arg     args[1];

            /* Unset this item and set the first one */

        fexc_items[fcd->item_index].set = FALSE;
        fexc_items[0].set               = TRUE;

            /* Inform the container that the list was modified */

        XtSetArg(args[0], XtNitemsTouched, TRUE);
        XtSetValues(widget, args, 1);
    }
} /* END OF Callback() */
```

Flat (3Olit)

The following example registers help on item #8.

```
static String    tag = "Item 8";
static String    source = "Item 8's help";
OlFlatHelpId     help_id;

help_id.widget     = flat_widget;
help_id.item_index = 8;

OlRegisterHelp((XtPointer) &help_id, OL_FLAT_HELP, tag,
    OL_STRING_SOURCE, source);
```

SEE ALSO

FlatButtons(3Olit), FlatCheckBox(3Olit), FlatExclusives(3Olit),
FlatList(3Olit), FlatNonexclusives(3Olit), OlFlatGetValues(3Olit),
OlFlatSetValues(3Olit), OlRegisterHelp(3Olit)

NAME

    `FlatButtons` – provide flat buttons

SYNOPSIS

    `#include <X11/Intrinsic.h>`
    `#include <X11/StringDefs.h>`
    `#include <Xol/OpenLook.h>`
    `#include <Xol/FButtons.h>`

    `Widget flatButtons;`

    `flatButtons = XtCreateWidget(`*name*`, flatButtonsWidgetClass, ...);`

DESCRIPTION

    The `FlatButtons` widget provides all of the various button types, and supports both the OPEN LOOK and MOTIF look and feel.

    Based on the settings of the `XtNbuttonType` and `XtNexclusives` resources the `FlatButton` widget produces any of the three basic types of buttons: CheckBox, Exclusive/Nonexclusive, and Menu.

    The resources `XtNexclusives`, `XtNnoneSet`, and `XtNpopupMenu` specify the appearance and behavior of the `FlatButtons` widget. The table below defines the possible configurations of the `FlatButtons` widget:

Configurations of the `FlatButtons` Widget

XtNbuttonType	XtNexclusives	XtNnoneSet	XtNpopupMenu	Effect
OL_OBLONG_BTN	N/A	N/A	NULL	Oblong Button
OL_OBLONG_BTN	N/A	N/A	Widget	Menu Button
OL_RECT_BTN	TRUE	FALSE	N/A	1-of-many
OL_RECT_BTN	TRUE	TRUE	N/A	at most 1-of-many
OL_RECT_BTN	FALSE	TRUE	N/A	n-of-many
OL_CHECKBOX	TRUE	FALSE	N/A	1-of-many
OL_CHECKBOX	TRUE	TRUE	N/A	at most 1-of-many
OL_CHECKBOX	FALSE	TRUE	N/A	n-of-many

    The `FlatButtons` widget can be used to emulate many of the MOTIF style buttons. The following table shows the correspondence of button types in both OPEN LOOK and MOTIF look and feel.

Look and Feel Button Correspondence

OPEN LOOK look and feel	MOTIF look and feel
OblongButton	PushButton
Exclusive	RadioButton (diamond)
NonExclusive	ToggleButton (square)
CheckBox	ToggleButton (square)
MenuButton	CascadeButton (in a menu)
MenuButton	OptionButton (not in menu)

FlatButtons (3Olit)

In the MOTIF look and feel

> the MOTIF style limits menu buttons to a menu bar across the top of base windows,
>
> the button will appear as a MOTIF style OptionButton if `XtNbuttonType` is `OL_OBLONG_BTN`, `XtNlayoutTYpe` is `OL_FIXEDROWS`, and the button is not inside a Menu,
>
> buttons will indicate receipt of focus by showing a location cursor, a solid border (of the input focus color) surrounding the button.

In the OPEN LOOK look and feel

> menu buttons preview the default action of the menu when the user presses the SELECT button. The normal previewing action in the OPEN LOOK look and feel is the same as the MENU action in the MOTIF look and feel. Because of this, the functionality has been removed from the MOTIF look and feel (even though its style guidelines allow this functionality).

Keyboard Traversal

If `XtNbuttonType` is `OL_RECT_RTN` or `OL_CHECKBOX`, keyboard traversal functionality is identical to `FlatCheckBox`, `FlatExclusives`, and `FlatNonexclusives`. If `XtNbuttonType` is `OL_OBLONG_BTN` then the NEXT_FIELD and PREV_FIELD keys can be used to traverse between sub-objects. The NEXT_FIELD key will traverse out of the `FlatButtons` if the last sub-object has the input focus and the PREV_FIELD key will traverse out of the `FlatButtons` if the first sub-object has the input focus.

Keyboard Operation

If `XtNbuttonType` is `OL_RECT_RTN` or `OL_CHECKBOX`, keyboard traversal functionality is identical to `FlatCheckBox`, `FlatExclusives`, and `FlatNonexclusives` The following activation types are available if `XtNbuttonType` is `OL_OBLONG_BTN`:

`FlatButtons` Activation Types	
Activation Type	Expected Results
OL_MENUDEFAULTKEY	Set the sub-object as the shell's default object (if on a menu).
OL_SELECTKEY	If `XtNpopupMenu` is NULL then simply call its callbacks. If `XtNpopupMenu` is not NULL, the action depends on whether the user has selected the power-user option, that is, act as `OL_MENUKEY` or activate the default menu item. [See `Application`(3Olit) or `MenuButton`(3Olit)].
OL_MENUKEY	If `XtNpopupMenu` is not NULL then Popup the menu and set focus to the menu's default item.
OL_DEFAULTACTIONKEY	activate the default control in the menu (that is, `XtNpopupMenu`) as if the user clicked the SELECT button on the control.
OL_CANCEL	dismiss a MenuButton's menu (that is, `XtNpopupMenu`).

Coloration

If `XtNbuttonType` is `OL_RECT_RTN` or `OL_CHECKBOX`, coloration is identical to `FlatCheckBox`, `FlatExclusives`, and `FlatNonexclusives`. If `XtNbuttonType` is `OL_OBLONG_BTN` coloration is identical to `OblongButton` and `MenuButton`.

RESOURCES

The table lists the resources for **FlatButtons**. Resources that have a bullet (•) in the Access column denote sub-object resources. If these resources are not included in the `XtNitemFields` list, they are inherited from the container widget. An application can change the default values for sub-object resources by setting them directly on the container. Even though a sub-subject resource is not included in the `XtNitemFields` list, the application can query the value of any sub-object resource with `OlFlatGetValues`.

FlatButtons Resource Set					
Name	Class	Type	Default	Acc	Inherit
XtNaccelerator	XtCAccelerator	String	NULL	SGI•	Primitive
XtNacceleratorText	XtCAcceleratorText	String	(calculated)	SGI•	Primitive
XtNancestorSensitive	XtCSensitive	Boolean	(calculated)	G[1]	Core
XtNbackground	XtCBackground	Pixel	"XtDefaultBackground"	SGI•	Core
XtNbackgroundPixmap	XtCPixmap	Pixmap	XtUnspecifiedPixmap	SGI•	Core
XtNborderColor	XtCBorderColor	Pixel	"XtDefaultForeground"	SGI	Core
XtNborderPixmap	XtCPixmap	Pixmap	XtUnspecifiedPixmap	SGI	Core
XtNborderWidth	XtCBorderWidth	Dimension	0	SGI	Core
XtNbusy	XtCBusy	Boolean	FALSE	SGI•	
XtNbuttonType	XtCButtonType	OlDefine	OL_OBLONG_BTN	GI	
XtNclientData	XtCClientData	XtPointer	NULL	SGI•	
XtNcolormap	XtCColormap	Colormap	(parent's)	GI	Core
XtNconsumeEvent	XtCCallback	XtCallbackList	NULL	SGI	Primitive
XtNdefault	XtCDefault	Boolean	FALSE	SGI•	
XtNdepth	XtCDepth	Cardinal	(parent's)	GI	Core
XtNdestroyCallback	XtCCallback	XtCallbackList	NULL	SGI	Object
XtNdim	XtCDim	Boolean	FALSE	SGI	
XtNexclusives	XtCExclusives	Boolean	FALSE	GI	
XtNfillOnSelect	XtCFillOnSelect	Boolean	FALSE	SGI	
XtNfocusOnSelect	XtCFocusOnSelect	Boolean	FALSE[4]	SGI	
XtNfont	XtCFont	XFontStruct *	"OlDefaultFont"	SGI•	Primitive
XtNfontColor	XtCFontColor	Pixel	"XtDefaultForeground"	SGI•	Primitive
XtNfontGroup	XtCFontGroup	OlFontList *	NULL	SGI	Primitive
XtNforeground	XtCForeground	Pixel	"XtDefaultForeground"	SGI•	Primitive
XtNgravity	XtCGravity	int	CenterGravity	SGI	
XtNhPad	XtCHPad	Dimension	0	SGI	
XtNhSpace	XtCHSpace	Dimension	(calculated)	SGI	
XtNheight	XtCHeight	Dimension	(calculated)	SGI•	Core
XtNhighlightThickness	XtCHighlightThickness	Dimension	"2 points"[2]	SGI	Primitive

FlatButtons (3Olit)

			FlatButtons Resource Set (cont'd)			
Name	Class	Type	Default	Acc	Inherit
XtNinputFocusColor	XtCInputFocusColor	Pixel	"Red"	SGI•	Primitive
XtNitemFields	XtCItemFields	String*	NULL	GI	
XtNitemGravity	XtCItemGravity	int	NorthWestGravity	SGI	
XtNitemMaxHeight	XtCItemMaxHeight	Dimension	OL_IGNORE	SGI	
XtNitemMaxWidth	XtCItemMaxWidth	Dimension	OL_IGNORE	SGI	
XtNitemMinHeight	XtCItemMinHeight	Dimension	OL_IGNORE	SGI	
XtNitemMinWidth	XtCItemMinWidth	Dimension	OL_IGNORE	SGI	
XtNitems	XtCItems	XtPointer	NULL	SGI	
XtNitemsTouched	XtCItemsTouched	Boolean	FALSE	SG	
XtNlabel	XtCLabel	String	NULL	SGI•	
XtNlabelImage	XtCLabelImage	XImage*	NULL	SGI•	
XtNlabelJustify	XtCLabelJustify	OlDefine	OL_LEFT	SGI•	
XtNlabelTile	XtCLabelTile	Boolean	FALSE	SGI•	
XtNlayoutHeight	XtCLayout	OlDefine	OL_MINIMIZE	SGI	
XtNlayoutType	XtCLayoutType	OlDefine	OL_FIXEDROWS	SGI	
XtNlayoutWidth	XtCLayout	OlDefine	OL_MINIMIZE	SGI	
XtNmanaged	XtCManaged	Boolean	TRUE	SGI•	
XtNmappedWhenManaged	XtCMappedWhenManaged	Boolean	TRUE	SGI•	Core
XtNmeasure	XtCMeasure	int	1	SGI	
XtNmenubarBehavior	XtCMenubarBehavior	Boolean	FALSE	GI	
XtNmnemonic	XtCMnemonic	char	NULL	SGI•	Primitive
XtNnoneSet	XtCNoneSet	Boolean	FALSE	SGI	
XtNnumItemFields	XtCNumItemFields	Cardinal	0	SGI	
XtNnumItems	XtCNumItems	Cardinal	0	SGI	
XtNpopupMenu	XtCPopupMenu	Widget	NULL	SGI•	
XtNposition	XtCPosition	OlDefine	OL_LEFT[5]	SGI	
XtNpreview	XtCPreview	Widget	NULL	SGI	
XtNpreviewItem	XtCPreviewItem	Cardinal	OL_NO_ITEM	SGI	
XtNreferenceName	XtCReferenceName	String	NULL	SGI	Primitive
XtNreferenceWidget	XtCReferenceWidget	Widget	NULL	SGI	Primitive
XtNsameHeight	XtCSameHeight	OlDefine	OL_ALL	SGI	
XtNsameWidth	XtCSameWidth	OlDefine	OL_COLUMNS	SGI	
XtNscreen	XtCScreen	Screen*	(parent's)	GI	Core
XtNselectColor	XtCSelectColor	Pixel	(input focus color)	SGI	
XtNselectProc	XtCCallbackProc	XtCallbackProc	NULL	SGI•	
XtNsensitive	XtCSensitive	Boolean	TRUE	G[1]•	Core
XtNset	XtCSet	Boolean	FALSE	SGI•	
XtNshadowThickness	XtCShadowThickness	Dimension	"0 points"[3]	SGI•	Primitive
XtNshadowType	XtCShadowType	OlDefine	OL_SHADOW_OUT	SGI	Primitive
XtNtranslations	XtCTranslations	XtTranslations	NULL	SGI	Core

FlatButtons Resource Set (cont'd)					
Name	Class	Type	Default	Acc	Inherit
XtNtraversalOn	XtCTraversalOn	Boolean	TRUE	SGI•	Primitive
XtNunselectProc	XtCCallbackProc	XtCallbackProc	NULL	SGI•	
XtNuserData	XtCUserData	XtPointer	NULL	SGI•	Primitive
XtNvPad	XtCVPad	Dimension	0	SGI	
XtNvSpace	XtCVSpace	Dimension	(calculated)	SGI	
XtNwidth	XtCWidth	Dimension	(calculated)	SGI•	Core
XtNx	XtCPosition	Position	0	SGI	Core
XtNy	XtCPosition	Position	0	SGI	Core

[1] Use XtSetSensitive to set this resource.
[2] Not used in OPEN LOOK look and feel.
[3] "2 points" in MOTIF look and feel.
[4] TRUE in MOTIF look and feel.
[5] OL_RIGHT in MOTIF look and feel.

XtNbusy

Range of values:

          TRUE/''true''
          FALSE/''false''

This resource controls whether the button interior should be stippled to show that the action associated with the button is ''busy''. This resource on has effect if XtNbuttonType is OL_OBLONG_BTN

XtNbuttonType

Range of values:

          OL_OBLONG_BTN/''oblongbtn''
          OL_RECT_BTN/''rectbtn''
          OL_CHECKBOX/''checkbox''

This resource is used to set the type of button. When set to OL_OBLONG_BTN, the buttons will be drawn as either oblong buttons or menu buttons.

When set to OL_RECT_BTN, the items will be drawn as an exclusive set or a non-exclusive set. Exclusivity is determined by the setting of the XtNexclusives resource.

When set to OL_CHECKBOX, then items are drawn as checkbox choices.

XtNdefault

Range of values:

          TRUE/''true''
          FALSE/''false''

When used on the sub-object, this resource specifies whether or not the sub-object is a default item. If more than one item is set as a default item, a warning is generated and all but the first default item is unselected.

When used on the container, this resource indicates whether or not one of the sub-objects is a default item. If a sub-object is a default item, XtNdefault has a value of TRUE; else it has a value of FALSE. Setting this resource on the container widget indicates whether or not one of the sub-objects should be a default item. If the application sets this value to **TRUE** on the container, the container will set the first managed and mapped sub-object as the default item if a default item does not exist. If the application sets this value to **FALSE**, the container will unset its default item if one exists.

Even if the application does not use **XtNdefault** in its item fields list, the container will correctly maintain the default item and the application can change the default item via **OlFlatSetValues**.

XtNdim

Range of values:

> **TRUE**/"true"
> **FALSE**/"false"

If **TRUE**, the sub-object shows a dimmed visual indicating that the item represents the state of one or more objects, that as a group, are in different states.

XtNexclusives

Range of values:

> **TRUE**/"true"
> **FALSE**/"false"

This resource is used to determine the exclusivity of the settings of the buttons in the container. When set to **TRUE**, the container will maintain a one-of-many state. When set to **FALSE**, the container will maintain an N-of-many state.

The exclusivity of the container is further governed by the **XtNnoneSet** resource.

XtNfillOnSelect

Range of values:

> **TRUE**/"true"
> **FALSE**/"false"

This resource determines whether the background of the button of type **OL_RECT_BTN** or **OL_CHECKBOX** should be filled with **XtNselectColor** when the user presses the SELECT mouse button while the pointer is inside the button or when the exclusive or checkbox item is set. This resource only has an effect in the MOTIF look and feel.

XtNfocusOnSelect

Range of values:

> **TRUE**/"true"
> **FALSE**/"false"

This resource shows whether a **FlatButtons** should follow toolkit wide focus policy. If **TRUE**, the default behavior is assumed (that is, Focus follow SELECT button Press). If **FALSE**, this widget does not follow "Focus follow SELECT button Press".

This resource only has effect if **XtNbuttonType** is **OL_OBLONG_BTN**.

XtNmenubarBehavior

This resource allows a **FlatButtons** widget to behave like a MOTIF style menubar. Setting **XtNmenubarBehavior** to **TRUE** enables the menuBarKey, multiUp, multi-Down, multiRight and multiLeft keys. MultiUp and multiLeft act as PrevMenu keys, and multiDown and MultiRight are NextMenu keys. This means that with **menubarBehavior** turned on, hitting Down (or MultiDown) in a horizontal menubar will bring up a menu, then hitting MultiRight will pop down the current menu, traverse to the next item to the right and bring up its menu.

In addition, if using the regular Up, Down, Left, and Right keys, traversal moves off of a menu, the keys function as their corresponding Multi keys. That is, after the above actions, hitting Right will bring up the next menu.

XtNnoneSet

Range of values:

> **TRUE**/"true"
> **FALSE**/"false"

This resource is used to determine the whether of not the container will support a state where none of the buttons are set.

When set to **TRUE**, the container will allow a zero-of-many state. When set to **FALSE**, the container will enforce at least one-of-many.

The exclusivity of the container is further governed by the **XtNexclusives** resource.

XtNpreview

This resource is used to specify the widget in which the current default is to be previewed.

XtNpreviewItem

This resource identifies the item to preview in the **XtNpreview** widget. When Select-Does-Preview mode is in effect and the user presses the SELECT button in the **FlatButtons**, the default menu preview item is displayed in the preview widget's window. The default item is drawn using the preview widget's size and location. If the **XtNpreview** resource is not set, or if the preview widget is not mapped, previewing does not take place.

XtNselectColor

Range of values:

> (Valid Pixel value for the display)/(Valid color name)

This resource specifies the background of the indicator of the exclusive or checkbox item when it is set or the background of the button when the user presses the SELECT mouse button while the pointer is inside the button. **XtNfillOnSelect** must be set to **TRUE** for this resource to have an effect. This resource only has an effect in the MOTIF look and feel.

XtNshadowThickness

This resource, when used on a container, shows the number of pixels in the width of the shadow border around the container.

When used on a sub-object, it shows the number of pixels in the width of the shadow border around the sub-object.

SEE ALSO

Flat(3Olit), **FlatCheckBox**(3Olit), **FlatExclusives**(3Olit), **FlatNonExclusives**(3Olit), **MenuButton**(3Olit), **OblongButton**(3Olit), **OlFlatGetValues**(3Olit), **OlFlatSetValues**(3Olit)

FlatCheckBox (3Olit)

NAME

FlatCheckBox – create a high performance **NonExclusives** with **CheckBox** widget

SYNOPSIS

```
#include <X11/Intrinsic.h>
#include <X11/StringDefs.h>
#include <Xol/OpenLook.h>
#include <Xol/FCheckBox.h>

widget = XtCreateWidget(name, flatCheckBoxWidgetClass, . . .);
```

DESCRIPTION

The **FlatCheckBox** widget is a Primitive widget that manages the traversal between a set of OPEN LOOK sub-objects.

Keyboard Traversal

When the user traverses to a **FlatCheckBox** widget, the first sub-object in the set will display itself as having input focus (see the **CheckBox** widget for a description of this appearance). The MOVEUP, MOVEDOWN, MOVERIGHT, and MOVELEFT keys move the input focus between the sub-objects. To traverse out of the **FlatCheckBox** widget, the following keys can be used:

NEXT_FIELD   moves to the next traversable widget in the window

PREV_FIELD   moves to the previous traversable widget in the window

NEXTWINDOW   moves to the next window in the application.

PREVWINDOW   moves to the previous window in the application.

NEXTAPP   moves to the first window in the next application.

PREVAPP   moves to the first window in the previous application.

Keyboard Operation

OL_SELECTKEY, the **FlatCheckBox** activation type, controls have two states: "set" and "not set." (When set, its border is thickened.) Pressing the SELECTKEY while a flat checkbox item has focus will toggle the checkbox's current state. If the control is "set," then toggling the control will call the **XtNunselect** callback list. If the control is "not set," then toggling the control will call the **XtNselect** callback list.

Display of Keyboard Mnemonic

The **FlatCheckBox** widget displays the mnemonic accelerator of a sub-object as part of the sub-object's label. If the mnemonic character is in the label, then that character is highlighted according to the value of the application resource **XtNshowMneumonics**. If the mnemonic character is not in the label, it is displayed to the right of the label in parenthesis and highlighted according to the value of the application resource **XtNshowMneumonics**.

If truncation is necessary, the mnemonic displayed in parenthesis is truncated as a unit.

Display of Keyboard Accelerators

The **FlatCheckBox** widget displays the keyboard accelerator as part of the sub-object's label. The string in the **XtNacceleratorText** resource is displayed to the right of the label (or mnemonic) separated by at least one space. The accelerator-Text is right justified.

If truncation is necessary, the accelerator is truncated as a unit. The accelerator is truncated before the mnemonic or the label.

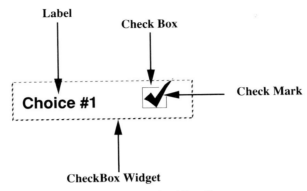

Figure 1. Flat CheckBox Item

FlatCheckbox Coloration

The **FlatCheckBox** container inherits its background color from the container's parent widget. Setting the background color affects only the sub-objects' background.

On a monochrome display, the **FlatCheckBox** widget indicates that it has input focus by inverting the foreground color and parent's background colors within the bounding box of the first sub-object.

On color displays, when the **FlatCheckBox** widget receives the input focus, the background color within the bounding box of the first sub-object is changed to the input focus color set in the **XtNinputFocusColor** resource. When the **FlatCheckBox** sub-object loses the input focus, the background color reverts to its parent's **XtNbackground** color or **XtNbackgroundPixmap**.

EXCEPTIONS:

— If the input focus color is the same as the parent's background color, then the **FlatCheckBox** widget inverts the foreground and background colors of the sub-object when it has input focus.

— If the input focus color is the same as the font color or foreground color, then the **FlatCheckBox** widget inverts the foreground and background colors of the sub-object when it has input focus.

RESOURCES

The following table lists the resources for the **FlatCheckBox**. Resources that have a bullet (•) in the Access column denote sub-object resources. If these resources are not included in the **XtNitemFields** list, they are inherited from the container widget. An application can change the default values for sub-object resources by setting them directly on the container. Even though a sub-object resource is not included in the **XtNitemFields** list, the application can query the value of any sub-object resource with **OlFlatGetValues**.

FlatCheckBox (3Olit)

This resource indicates the sensitivity of the sub-object's ancestors. If **TRUE**, all the sub-object's ancestors are sensitive and the sub-object is sensitive to user input. If **FALSE**, one or more of the sub-object's ancestors are insensitive, so the sub-object displays an inactive visual and is not sensitive to user input.

XtNbackground

This is the pixel color used to fill in the background of the check box.

XtNbackgroundPixmap

This resource specifies the pixmap that is displayed as the sub-object's label. Any supplied pixmap must have the same depth as the flat widget's depth. Pixmaps of **None** and **ParentRelative** are not considered valid values. If either **XtNlabel** or **XtNlabelImage** has a non-NULL value, this resource is ignored.

XtNclientData

This is the client data supplied to all callback procedures.

XtNitems

This is the list of sub-object items. This value must point to a static list since flat containers reference this list after initialization but do not cache its information.

XtNitemFields

This is the list of resource names used to parse the records in the **XtNitems** list. This resource does not have to point to static information since the flat container does not use this information after initialization. Though the flat container does not reference this resource's value after initialization, it holds onto it for responding to an **XtGetValues** request and supplying it in the **OlFlatCallData** structure during callbacks. Therefore, if the application plans on querying this resource, it's recommended that the application make this resource point to static information.

XtNitemsTouched

Range of values:

> TRUE/"true"
> FALSE/"false"

Whenever the application modifies an item list directly, it must supply this resource (with a value of **TRUE**) to the flat widget container so that the container can update the visual. If the resource value is supplied, the flat widget container treats its current item list as a new list and hence, updates its entire visual. Since the list is treated as a new list, the flat container may request a change in geometry from its parent.

Note that it is not necessary to use this resource if the application modifies the list with the **OlFlatSetValues** procedure; nor is it necessary to use this resource whenever the application supplies a new list to the flat container.

XtNlabel

This is the text string that appears in the sub-object.

XtNlabelImage

This is an **XImage** pointer that can appear in a sub-object. This resource is ignored if **XtNlabel** is non-NULL.

XtNlabelJustify
Range of values:

```
OL_LEFT/"left"
OL_CENTER/"center"
OL_RIGHT/"right"
```

This resource specifies the justification of the label or **XImage** that appears within a sub-object.

XtNlabelTile
Range of values:

```
TRUE/"true"
FALSE/"false"
```

This resource augments the **XtNlabelImage/XtNlabelPixmap** resource to allow tiling of the sub-object's background. For an image/pixmap that is smaller than the sub-object's background, the label area is tiled with the image/pixmap to fill the sub-object's background if this resource is **TRUE**; otherwise, the label is placed as described by the **XtNlabelJustify** resource.

The **XtNlabelTile** resource is ignored for text labels.

XtNmappedWhenManaged
Range of values:

```
TRUE/"true"
FALSE/"false"
```

This resource specifies whether or not a managed sub-object is displayed. Regardless of this resource's value, all managed sub-objects will be included when determining the layout.

Note that this resource is never inherited from the container, so its default value is always **TRUE**.

XtNnumItems
This resource specifies the number of sub-object items.

XtNnumItemFields
This resource indicates the number of resource names contained in **XtNitemFields**.

XtNposition
Range of values:

```
OL_LEFT/"left"
OL_RIGHT/"right"
```

This resource determines on which side of the check box the label is to be placed. The value of **OL_LEFT** or **OL_RIGHT** indicates the label is placed to the left or to the right of the check box, respectively.

XtNsameHeight
Range of values:

```
OL_ALL/"all"
OL_ROWS/"rows"
OL_NONE/"none"
```

FlatCheckBox (3Olit)

This resource specifies the rows that are forced to the same height.

XtNsameWidth
Range of values:

    OL_ALL/"all"
    OL_COLUMNS/"columns"
    OL_NONE/"none"

This resource specifies the columns that are forced to the same width.

XtNselectProc
This callback procedure is called whenever the sub-object becomes selected by user input.

XtNsensitive
Range of values:

    TRUE/"true"
    FALSE/"false"

If **TRUE**, the sub-object is sensitive to user input. If **FALSE**, the sub-object is insensitive to user input and an inactive visual is displayed to indicate this state.

Note this resource is never inherited from the container, so its default value is always **TRUE**.

XtNset
Range of values:

    TRUE/"true"
    FALSE/"false"

This resource reflects the current state of the sub-object.

Note this resource is never inherited from the container, so its default value is always **FALSE**.

Even if the application does not use **XtNset** in its item fields list, the container will correctly maintain the set item and the application can change the set item via **OlFlatSetValues**.

XtNunselectProc
This callback procedure is called whenever the sub-object becomes unselected by user input.

NOTES
Use the **FlatButtons** widget to obtain a MOTIF look and feel.

SEE ALSO
CheckBox(3Olit), **Flat**(3Olit), **FlatButtons**(3Olit), **OlFlatGetValues**(3Olit)

NAME

FlatExclusives – create a choose one widget

SYNOPSIS

```
#include <X11/Intrinsic.h>
#include <X11/StringDefs.h>
#include <Xol/OpenLook.h>
#include <Xol/FExclusive.h>

widget = XtCreateWidget(name, flatExclusivesWidgetClass, ...);
```

DESCRIPTION

The **FlatExclusives** widget provides a way to build a one-of-many button selection object in the OPEN LOOK look and feel. It manages a set of rectangular buttons, providing layout management.

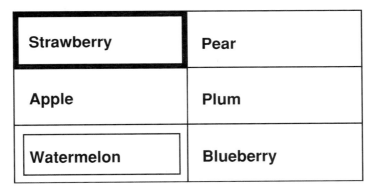

Figure 1. Flat Exclusives Widget

Selection Control - One Set

In one mode operation (that is, **XtNnoneSet** is **FALSE**), exactly one sub-object in a **FlatExclusives** widget must be "set," that is, the **XtNset** resource is **TRUE** for one of the sub-objects. A warning is generated if two or more sub-objects are set. If no items are set, the **FlatExclusives** makes the first sub-object that is both managed and mapped when managed be the set item. No warning is produced in this case. The **FlatExclusives** maintains this condition by ensuring that when a sub-object is set by the user clicking SELECT over it, the sub-object that was set is cleared and its **XtNunselectProc** procedure is called and the sub-object under the pointer is made to be set and its **XtNselectProc** procedure is called. However, clicking SELECT over a sub-object that is already set does nothing.

Selection Control - None Set

In the other mode of operation (that is, **XtNnoneSet** is **TRUE**), at most one sub-object in a **FlatExclusives** widget can be "set." A warning is generated if two or more sub-objects are set. The **FlatExclusives** maintains this condition by ensuring that when a sub-object is set by the user clicking SELECT over it, the sub-object that was set is cleared and its **XtNunselectProc** procedure is called and the sub-object

473

FlatExclusives (3Olit)

under the pointer is made to be set and its **XtNselectProc** procedure is called. Clicking SELECT over a sub-object that is already set clears it and its **XtNunselectProc** procedure is called.

Use in a Menu

The **FlatExclusives** widget can be added as child in a menu pane to implement a one-of-many menu choice.

FlatExclusives Coloration

The **FlatExclusives** container inherits its background color from the container's parent widget. Setting the background color affects only the sub-objects' background.

Keyboard Traversal

The FlatExclusives widget is a Primitive widget that manages the traversal between a set of sub-objects. When the user traverses to a FlatExclusives widget, the first sub-object in the set will display itself as having input focus (see the RectButton widget for a description of this appearance). The MOVEUP, MOVEDOWN, MOVERIGHT, and MOVELEFT keys move the input focus between the sub-objects. To traverse out of the FlatExclusives widget, the following keys can be used:

NEXT_FIELD	moves to the next traversable widget in the window
PREV_FIELD	moves to the previous traversable widget in the window
NEXTWINDOW	moves to the next window in the application.
PREVWINDOW	moves to the previous window in the application.
NEXTAPP	moves to the first window in the next application.
PREVAPP	moves to the first window in the previous application.

Keyboard Operation

Flat Exclusives Activation Types	
Activation Type	Expected Results
OL_MENUDEFAULTKEY	If the **FlatExclusives** is on a menu, this command will set the item with focus to be menu's default; otherwise, this command is ignored.
OL_SELECTKEY	This command acts as if the SELECT mouse button had been clicked on the **RectButton** with focus. See the "Selection Control" sections above.

Display of Keyboard Mnemonic

The **FlatExclusives** widget displays the mnemonic accelerator of a sub-object as part of the sub-object's label. If the mnemonic character is in the label, then that character is highlighted according to the value of the application resource **XtNshowMneumonics**. If the mnemonic character is not in the label, it is displayed to the right of the label in parenthesis and highlighted according to the value of the application resource **XtNshowMneumonics**.

If truncation is necessary, the mnemonic displayed in parenthesis is truncated as a unit.

Display of Keyboard Accelerators

The **FlatExclusives** widget displays the keyboard accelerator as part of the sub-object's label. The string in the **XtNacceleratorText** resource is displayed to the right of the label (or mnemonic) separated by at least one space. The accelerator-Text is right justified.

If truncation is necessary, the accelerator is truncated as a unit. The accelerator is truncated before the mnemonic or the label.

RESOURCES

The following table lists the resources for the **FlatExclusives**. Resources that have a bullet (•) in the Access column denote sub-object resources. If these resources are not included in the **XtNitemFields** list, they are inherited from the container widget. An application can change the default values for sub-object resources by setting them on the container directly. Even though a sub-object resource is not included in the **XtNitemFields** list, the application can query the value of any sub-object resource with **OlFlatGetValues**.

FlatExclusives Resource Set					
Name	Class	Type	Default	Acc	Inherit
XtNaccelerator	XtCAccelerator	String	NULL	SGI•	Primitive
XtNacceleratorText	XtCAcceleratorText	String	(calculated)	SGI•	Primitive
XtNancestorSensitive	XtCSensitive	Boolean	(calculated)	G[1]•	Core
XtNbackground	XtCBackground	Pixel	"XtDefaultBackground"	SGI•	Core
XtNbackgroundPixmap	XtCPixmap	Pixmap	XtUnspecifiedPixmap	SGI•	Core
XtNborderColor	XtCBorderColor	Pixel	"XtDefaultForeground"	SGI	Core
XtNborderPixmap	XtCPixmap	Pixmap	XtUnspecifiedPixmap	SGI	Core
XtNborderWidth	XtCBorderWidth	Dimension	0	SGI	Core
XtNclientData	XtCClientData	XtPointer	NULL	SGI•	FlatButtons
XtNcolormap	XtCColormap	Colormap	(parent's)	GI	Core
XtNconsumeEvent	XtCCallback	XtCallbackList	NULL	SGI	Primitive
XtNdefault	XtCDefault	Boolean	FALSE	SGI•	FlatButtons
XtNdepth	XtCDepth	Cardinal	(parent's)	GI	Core
XtNdestroyCallback	XtCCallback	XtCallbackList	NULL	SGI	Object
XtNdim	XtCDim	Boolean	FALSE	SGI	FlatButtons
XtNfillOnSelect	XtCFillOnSelect	Boolean	FALSE	SGI	FlatButtons
XtNfocusOnSelect	XtCFocusOnSelect	Boolean	FALSE[4]	SGI	FlatButtons
XtNfont	XtCFont	XFontStruct *	"OlDefaultFont"	SGI•	Primitive
XtNfontColor	XtCFontColor	Pixel	"XtDefaultForeground"	SGI•	Primitive
XtNfontGroup	XtCFontGroup	OlFontList *	NULL	SGI	Primitive
XtNforeground	XtCForeground	Pixel	"XtDefaultForeground"	SGI•	Primitive
XtNgravity	XtCGravity	int	CenterGravity	SGI	FlatButtons
XtNhPad	XtCHPad	Dimension	0	SGI	FlatButtons

FlatExclusives (3Olit)

Name	Class	Type	Default	Acc	Inherit
FlatExclusives Resource Set (cont'd)					
XtNhSpace	XtCHSpace	Dimension	(calculated)	SGI	FlatButtons
XtNheight	XtCHeight	Dimension	(calculated)	SGI•	Core
XtNhighlightThickness	XtCHighlightThickness	Dimension	"2 points"[2]	SGI	Primitive
XtNinputFocusColor	XtCInputFocusColor	Pixel	"Red"	SGI•	Primitive
XtNitemFields	XtCItemFields	String *	NULL	GI	FlatButtons
XtNitemGravity	XtCItemGravity	int	NorthWestGravity	SGI	FlatButtons
XtNitemMaxHeight	XtCItemMaxHeight	Dimension	OL_IGNORE	SGI	FlatButtons
XtNitemMaxWidth	XtCItemMaxWidth	Dimension	OL_IGNORE	SGI	FlatButtons
XtNitemMinHeight	XtCItemMinHeight	Dimension	OL_IGNORE	SGI	FlatButtons
XtNitemMinWidth	XtCItemMinWidth	Dimension	OL_IGNORE	SGI	FlatButtons
XtNitems	XtCItems	XtPointer	NULL	SGI	FlatButtons
XtNitemsTouched	XtCItemsTouched	Boolean	FALSE	SG	FlatButtons
XtNlabel	XtCLabel	String	NULL	SGI•	FlatButtons
XtNlabelImage	XtCLabelImage	XImage *	NULL	SGI•	FlatButtons
XtNlabelJustify	XtCLabelJustify	OlDefine	OL_LEFT	SGI•	FlatButtons
XtNlabelTile	XtCLabelTile	Boolean	FALSE	SGI•	FlatButtons
XtNlayoutHeight	XtCLayout	OlDefine	OL_MINIMIZE	SGI	FlatButtons
XtNlayoutType	XtCLayoutType	OlDefine	OL_FIXEDROWS	SGI	FlatButtons
XtNlayoutWidth	XtCLayout	OlDefine	OL_MINIMIZE	SGI	FlatButtons
XtNmanaged	XtCManaged	Boolean	TRUE	SGI•	FlatButtons
XtNmappedWhenManaged	XtCMappedWhenManaged	Boolean	TRUE	SGI•	Core
XtNmeasure	XtCMeasure	int	1	SGI	FlatButtons
XtNmnemonic	XtCMnemonic	char	NULL	SGI•	Primitive
XtNnoneSet	XtCNoneSet	Boolean	FALSE	SGI	FlatButtons
XtNnumItemFields	XtCNumItemFields	Cardinal	0	SGI	FlatButtons
XtNnumItems	XtCNumItems	Cardinal	0	SGI	FlatButtons
XtNreferenceName	XtCReferenceName	String	NULL	SGI	Primitive
XtNreferenceWidget	XtCReferenceWidget	Widget	NULL	SGI	Primitive
XtNsameHeight	XtCSameHeight	OlDefine	OL_ALL	SGI	FlatButtons
XtNsameWidth	XtCSameWidth	OlDefine	OL_COLUMNS	SGI	FlatButtons
XtNscreen	XtCScreen	Screen *	(parent's)	GI	Core
XtNselectColor	XtCSelectColor	Pixel	(input focus color)	SGI	FlatButtons
XtNselectProc	XtCCallbackProc	XtCallbackProc	NULL	SGI•	FlatButtons
XtNsensitive	XtCSensitive	Boolean	TRUE	G[1]•	Core
XtNset	XtCSet	Boolean	FALSE	SGI•	FlatButtons
XtNshadowThickness	XtCShadowThickness	Dimension	"0 points"[3]	SGI•	Primitive
XtNshadowType	XtCShadowType	OlDefine	OL_SHADOW_OUT	SGI	Primitive
XtNtranslations	XtCTranslations	XtTranslations	NULL	SGI	Core
XtNtraversalOn	XtCTraversalOn	Boolean	TRUE	SGI•	Primitive
XtNunselectProc	XtCCallbackProc	XtCallbackProc	NULL	SGI•	FlatButtons

FlatExclusives Resource Set (cont'd)					
Name	Class	Type	Default	Acc	Inherit
XtNuserData	XtCUserData	XtPointer	NULL	SGI•	Primitive
XtNvPad	XtCVPad	Dimension	0	SGI	FlatButtons
XtNvSpace	XtCVSpace	Dimension	(calculated)	SGI	FlatButtons
XtNwidth	XtCWidth	Dimension	(calculated)	SGI•	Core
XtNx	XtCPosition	Position	0	SGI	Core
XtNy	XtCPosition	Position	0	SGI	Core

[1]   Use **XtSetSensitive** to set this resource.
[2]   Not used in OPEN LOOK look and feel.
[3]   **"2 points"** in MOTIF look and feel.
[4]   **TRUE** in MOTIF look and feel.

XtNancestorSensitive

Range of values:

> TRUE/''true''
> FALSE/''false''

This resource indicates the sensitivity of the sub-object's ancestors. If **TRUE**, all the sub-object's ancestors are sensitive and the sub-object is sensitive to user input. If **FALSE**, one or more of the sub-object's ancestors are insensitive, so the sub-object displays an inactive visual and is not sensitive to user input.

XtNbackground

This is the pixel color used to fill in the background of the sub-object.

XtNbackgroundPixmap

This resource specifies the pixmap that is displayed as the sub-object's label. Any supplied pixmap must have the same depth as the flat widget's depth. Pixmaps of **None** and **ParentRelative** are not considered valid values. If either **XtNlabel** or **XtNlabelImage** has a non-NULL value, this resource is ignored.

XtNclientData

This is the client data supplied to all callback procedures.

XtNdefault

Range of values:

> TRUE/''true''
> FALSE/''false''

When used on the sub-object, this resource specifies whether or not the sub-object is a default item. If more than one item is a set as a default item, a warning is generated and all but the first default item is unselected.

When used on the container, this resource indicates whether or not one of the sub-objects is a default item. If a sub-object is a default item, **XtNdefault** has a value of **TRUE**; else it has a value of **FALSE**. Setting this resource on the container widget indicates whether or not one of the sub-objects should be a default item. If the application sets this value to **TRUE** on the container, the container will set the first managed and mapped sub-object as the default item if a default item does not exist. If the application sets this value to **FALSE**, the container will unset its default item if one exists.

FlatExclusives (3Olit)

Even if the application does not use **XtNdefault** in its item fields list, the container will correctly maintain the default item and the application can change the default item via **OlFlatSetValues**.

XtNdim

Range of values:

```
TRUE/"true"
FALSE/"false"
```

If **TRUE**, the sub-object shows a dimmed visual indicating that the item represents the state of one or more objects, that as a group, are in different states.

XtNitemFields

This is the list of resource names used to parse the records in the **XtNitems** list. This resource does not have to point to static information since the flat container does not use this information after initialization. Though the flat container does not reference this resource's value after initialization, it holds onto it for responding to an **XtGetValues** request and supplying it in the **OlFlatCallData** structure during callbacks. Therefore, if the application plans on querying this resource, it's recommended that the application make this resource point to static information.

XtNitemsTouched

Range of values:

```
TRUE/"true"
FALSE/"false"
```

Whenever the application modifies an item list directly, it must supply this resource (with a value of **TRUE**) to the flat widget container so that the container can update the visual. If the resource value is supplied, the flat widget container treats its current item list as a new list and hence, updates its entire visual. Since the list is treated as a new list, the flat container may request a change in geometry from its parent.

Note that it is not necessary to use this resource if the application modifies the list with the **OlFlatSetValues** procedure; nor is it necessary to use this resource whenever the application supplies a new list to the flat container.

XtNlabel

This is the text string that appears in the sub-object.

XtNlabelImage

This is an **XImage** pointer that can appear in a sub-object. This resource is ignored if **XtNlabel** is non-NULL.

XtNlabelJustify

Range of values:

```
OL_LEFT/"left"
OL_CENTER/"center"
OL_RIGHT/"right"
```

This resource specifies the justification of the label or **XImage** that appears within a sub-object.

XtNlabelTile
Range of values:
```
TRUE/"true"
FALSE/"false"
```

This resource augments the **XtNlabelImage/XtNlabelPixmap** resource to allow tiling of the sub-object's background. For an image/pixmap that is smaller than the sub-object's background, the label area is tiled with the image/pixmap to fill the sub-object's background if this resource is **TRUE**; otherwise, the label is placed as described by the **XtNlabelJustify** resource.

The **XtNlabelTile** resource is ignored for text labels.

XtNmappedWhenManaged
Range of values:
```
TRUE/"true"
FALSE/"false"
```

This resource specifies whether or not a managed sub-object is displayed. Regardless of this resource's value, all managed sub-objects will be including when determining the layout.

Note that this resource is never inherited from the container, so its default value is always **TRUE**.

XtNnoneSet
Range of values:
```
TRUE/"true"
FALSE/"false"
```

This resource controls whether the settings can be toggled into an unset mode directly. If set to **FALSE**, exactly one sub-object must be in the set state always. Attempting to select the currently set sub-object does nothing. If set to **TRUE**, no more than one sub-object can be set at any time. However, the user can select the currently set sub-object and toggle it back to an unset state.

XtNnumItems
This resource specifies the number of sub-object items.

XtNnumItemFields
This resource indicates the number of resource names contained in **XtNitemFields**.

XtNsameHeight
Range of values:
```
OL_ALL/"all"
OL_ROWS/"rows"
```

This resource specifies the rows that are forced to the same height.

XtNsameWidth
Range of values:
```
OL_ALL/"all"
OL_COLUMNS/"columns"
```

FlatExclusives (3Olit)

This resource specifies the columns that are forced to the same width.

XtNselectProc

This callback procedure is called whenever the sub-object becomes selected by user input.

XtNsensitive

Range of values:

> TRUE/"true"
> FALSE/"false"

If **TRUE**, the sub-object is sensitive to user input. If **FALSE**, the sub-object is insensitive to user input and an inactive visual is displayed to indicate this state.

Note that this resource is never inherited from the container, so its default value is always **TRUE**.

XtNset

Range of values:

> TRUE/"true"
> FALSE/"false"

This resource reflects the current state of the sub-object.

Note that this resource is never inherited from the container, so its default value is always **FALSE**.

Even if the application does not use **XtNset** in its item fields list, the container will correctly maintain the set item and the application can change the set item via **OlFlatSetValues**.

XtNunselectProc

This callback procedure is called whenever the sub-object becomes unselected by user input.

NOTES

Use the **FlatButtons** widget to obtain a MOTIF look and feel.

SEE ALSO

Exclusives(3Olit), Flat(3Olit), FlatButtons(3Olit), OlFlatGetValues(3Olit), OlFlatSetValues(3Olit), RectButton(3Olit)

NAME

FlatList - provide a scrollable view into a list of items

SYNOPSIS

```
#include <X11/Intrinsic.h>
#include <X11/StringDefs.h>
#include <Xol/OpenLook.h>
#include <Xol/FList.h>

widget = XtCreateWidget(name, flatListWidgetClass, . . .);
```

DESCRIPTION

The **FlatList** widget is a Flat widget which maintains a view into an array of List items. Scrolling is achieved by placing the widget in a **ScrolledWindow** widget. It supports both the OPEN LOOK and the MOTIF look and feel.

The "look" of the **FlatList** widget is made up of the visual associated with the view and scrolling, location cursor, and list items themselves.

scrolling the view

> In both the MOTIF and the OPEN LOOK look and feel, the list is made scrollable by making it the child of a **ScrolledWindow** widget. Vertical and horizontal scrollbars can be individually fixed (that is, always present) or can appear on an as needed basis. The view height is controlled by the resource, **XtNviewHeight**.

location cursor

> In the OPEN LOOK look and feel, the location cursor is the focus item — the item with focus is drawn with the input focus color.

> In the MOTIF look and feel, the location cursor is shown with a solid (Normal mode) or dashed (Add mode) border around the item with focus, and it moves with the selection policy (see below).

list items

> The FlatList supports multi-field list items. Items are made up of one or more fields containing text or an image. This is a a superset of MOTIF style list items which can only be a single field of text.

The "feel" of the **FlatList** widget is defined by the selection policies.

Selection Policies	
MOTIF feel	OPEN LOOK feel
Browse Select	Exclusives with wipe-through selection
Extended Select	Nonexclusives with wipe-through selection

In the MOTIF look and feel, selection policies Single Select and Multiple Select are superceded by Browse Select and Extended Select, respectively. The selection policy Browse Select forces the **XtNnoneSet** to be **FALSE** and unavailable, and **XtNexclusives** to be **TRUE**.

A callback is issued when the user double-clicks on an item.

FlatList (3Olit)

Exclusive or Nonexclusive Behavior

The **FlatList** can maintain the List items as a collection of exclusive settings where at most one item can be set or non-exclusive settings where any number of items can be set. This behavior is determined by widget resources. The table below shows the result of clicking SELECT over an item while the widget is in exclusive mode, exclusive mode with **XtNnoneSet TRUE** and while in non-exclusive mode:

Mode	Clicking SELECT over an item that is	
	Selected	Unselected
Exclusive	No effect	Selected item is unselected and new item is selected
Exclusive and **XtnoneSet TRUE**	Item is unselected	Any currently selected item is unselected and new item is selected
Nonexclusive	Item is unselected	Item is selected

Scrolling

Scrolling is achieved by placing the **FlatList** in a **ScrolledWindow** widget (that is, when the parent of the **FlatList** is a **ScrolledWindow** widget). With the **FlatList** in a ScrolledWindow, the list can be scrolled vertically and horizontally using the scrollbars provided by the ScrolledWindow. When the **FlatList** has focus, the keyboard may be used to scroll the list using the OPEN LOOK-defined scrolling keys (Scroll Up, Page Down, and so on). Key bindings for keys, including scrolling keys are listed in on **OlLookupInputEvent**(3Olit).

Keyboard Traversal and Mouseless Operation

In the MOTIF look and feel, the focus item is identified by the location cursor (typically a border the color of the **XtNinputFocusColor**).

In the OPEN LOOK look and feel, the **FlatList** can accept keyboard focus, typically by traversing to it. When the **FlatList** has focus, one list item, the "focus item" is assigned to receive keyboard input. The focus item is displayed using the input focus color (**XtNinputFocusColor**) as its background color.

The **FlatList** can be traversed to and the focus item can be activated from the keyboard. [See **OlLookupInputEvent**(3Olit) for key bindings.] The following traversal keys are defined for the **FlatList**:

MOTIF look and feel Traversal Keys

Virtual Name	Traversal
OLM_KBeginData	to the first item in the list
OLM_KBeginLine	to the left most edge, or as KBeginData
OLM_KEndData	to the last item in the list
OLM_KEndLine	to the right most edge, or as KEndData
OLM_KUp	move between List items, up
OLM_KDown	move between List items, down
OLM_KNextField	to the next traversable widget in the window
OLM_KPrevField	to the previous traversable widget in the window
OLM_KNextWindow	to the next window in the application

OLM_KPrevWindow	to the previous window in the application
OLM_KNextFamilyWindow	to the first window in the next application
OLM_KPrevFamilyWindow	to the first window in the previous application

OPEN LOOK look and feel Traversal Keys

Virtual Name	Traversal
OL_DOCSTART	to the first item in the list
OL_LINESTART	to the left most edge, or as KBeginData
OL_DOCEND	to the last item in the list
OL_LINEEND	to the right most edge, or as KEndData
OL_MOVEUP	move between List items, up
OL_MOVEDOWN	move between List items, down
OL_NEXT_FIELD	to the next traversable widget in the window
OL_PREV_FIELD	to the previous traversable widget in the window
OL_NEXTWINDOW	to the next window in the application
OL_PREVWINDOW	to the previous window in the application
OL_NEXTAPP	to the first window in the next application
OL_PREVAPP	to the first window in the previous application

When the **FlatList** has focus, the focus item can be activated with the SELECT-KEY. Pressing the SELECTKEY is equivalent to clicking the SELECT button over the focus item.

Coloration

The background color of the **FlatList** is inherited from its parent. Setting the background color affects only the item's background.

The background color for each item and for all items is settable and encompasses the background of all fields in the items and any space between fields; that is, the item's background pertains to the entire item (fields are described in the List Item description below).

In the OPEN LOOK look and feel, the input focus color is used for the background color of the focus item.

3D Visual

When running on a color server, the **FlatList** can be displayed with a 3D appearance: The List items appear in a pane with a chiseled border. Selected items appear "pressed-into" the screen, unselected items appear "flush" with the screen.

The appearance of the 3D visual is controlled by a user-settable application resource.

List Items

List items consist of one or more *fields*. Items are laid out in a single column, corresponding fields within the items are aligned vertically. Fields are formatted according to a **printf**-style format string:

format → field_description field_description[*]

That is, the format is specified by one or more field descriptions. Spaces may be used between field descriptions to affect inter-field spacing.

Each field description is introduced by the character %, followed by optional elements and terminated by a conversion character:

field_description → %[−][*width*][.*max*] *conv*

Where:

−   (minus) specifies right-justification of the converted argument in its field.

width   (a number) specifies the *field width*. The converted argument is placed in a field this wide. For fields which contain images (%*i* conversions), the pixel width of the field is simply the pixel width of the image. For fields which contain text (%*s* conversions), *width* refers to a character width; that is, the pixel width of the field is *width* multiplied by the width of the ´n´ (en) character in the font. If the converted argument is narrower than the pixel width of the field, it is left-justified unless right-justification is specified.

max   (a number, the precision) for string conversions, specifies the maximum number of characters to be printed from a string. If *max* is absent, it is treated as zero; that is, `%10.s` is equivalent to `%10.0s`.

conv   The table below shows the possible conversion characters:

conv	Argument Type	Conversion
s	`char *`	String
w	`char *`	Wrapped string
b	`Pixmap` (single plane)	Bitmap
i	`XImage *`	Image
p	`Pixmap`	Pixmap

The format string is specified by the resource `XtNformat`. The data corresponding to the format string (the equivalent of the `printf` arguments) is specified by the resource `XtNformatData`. This resource is a pointer to a vector of `XtPointer`'s, one argument for each conversion (%) in the format string.

Selection

Items are selected using the SELECT mouse button or its keyboard equivalent, the SELECTKEY. The result of clicking SELECT over an item depends on whether the `FlatList` is in the exclusive or nonexclusive mode (refer to the description of Exclusive or Nonexclusive Behavior above). The client can be notified via a callback when a user action results in an item becoming selected or unselected.

double-click selection

> The client can be notified when the user double-clicks SELECT over an item. Mouse damping and multi-click timeout are user-settable.

wipe-through selection

> When a SELECT is pressed and dragged over items, the items are selected accordingly. If the pointer moves above or below the view, the view scrolls additional items into the view, selecting them as well. The rate at which items scroll into the view is equivalent to the scrollbar repeat-rate. The pointer can move out of the view horizontally without interrupting the selection.

Drag and Drop

Drag and Drop is supported via a callback. A client-registered procedure is called when a user drags item(s) in the list and drops them outside of the list. Drag and Drop is initiated by pressing SELECT over a selected item and moving the pointer outside of the list, and is completed by releasing the mouse button while the pointer is outside of the list.

Visibility Notification

The client can be notified via a callback when selected items enter or leave the view. This is only meaningful when the list is scrollable; that is, when the **FlatList** is in a ScrolledWindow and the view is shorter than the total height of the list. For each scroll operation, the set of selected items in the current view is compared against the set of selected items in the previous view. If one or more selected items have entered the new view and/or one or more selected items have left the previous view, the callback will be called. Note that this can be a computationally expensive operation while dragging the scrollbar elevator depending on the mode of the drag callback [see **Scrollbar**(3Olit)] especially for nonexclusives settings where there may be many selected items.

RESOURCES

The following table lists the resources for the **FlatList**. Resources that have a bullet (•) in the Access column denote item resources. If these resources are not included in the **XtNitemFields** list, they are inherited from the container widget. An application can change the default values for item resources by setting them on the container directly. Even though an item resource is not included in the **XtNitemFields** list, the application can query the value of any item resource with **OlFlatGetValues**.

FlatList Resource Set					
Name	Class	Type	Default	Acc	Inherit
XtNancestorSensitive	XtCSensitive	Boolean	(calculated)	G[1]	Core
XtNbackground	XtCBackground	Pixel	"XtDefaultBackground"	SGI•	Core
XtNbackgroundPixmap	XtCPixmap	Pixmap	XtUnspecifiedPixmap	SGI•	Core
XtNborderColor	XtCBorderColor	Pixel	"XtDefaultForeground"	SGI	Core
XtNborderPixmap	XtCPixmap	Pixmap	XtUnspecifiedPixmap	SGI	Core
XtNborderWidth	XtCBorderWidth	Dimension	0	SGI	Core
XtNclientData	XtCClientData	XtPointer	NULL	SGI•	
XtNcolormap	XtCColormap	Colormap	(parent's)	GI	Core
XtNconsumeEvent	XtCCallback	XtCallbackList	NULL	SGI	Primitive
XtNdblSelectProc	XtCCallbackProc	XtCallbackProc	NULL	SGI•	
XtNdepth	XtCDepth	Cardinal	(parent's)	GI	Core
XtNdestroyCallback	XtCCallback	XtCallbackList	NULL	SGI	Object
XtNdragCursorProc	XtCCallbackProc	XtCallbackProc	NULL	SGI•	
XtNdropProc	XtCCallbackProc	XtCallbackProc	NULL	SGI•	
XtNexclusives	XtCExclusives	Boolean	TRUE	GI	
XtNfont	XtCFont	XFontStruct *	"OlDefaultFont"	SGI•	Primitive

FlatList Resource Set (cont'd)					
Name	Class	Type	Default	Acc	Inherit
XtNfontColor	XtCFontColor	Pixel	"XtDefaultForeground"	SGI•	Primitive
XtNfontGroup	XtCFontGroup	OlFontList *	NULL	SGI	Primitive
XtNforeground	XtCForeground	Pixel	"XtDefaultForeground"	SGI•	Primitive
XtNformat	XtCFormat	String	"%s"	SGI	
XtNformatData	XtCFormatData	XtPointer	NULL	SGI•	
XtNheight	XtCHeight	Dimension	(calculated)	SGI•	Core
XtNhighlightThickness	XtCHighlightThickness	Dimension	"2 points"[2]	SGI	Primitive
XtNinputFocusColor	XtCInputFocusColor	Pixel	"Red"	SGI•	Primitive
XtNitemFields	XtCItemFields	String *	NULL	GI	FlatButtons
XtNitemVisibility	XtCCallback	XtCallbackList	NULL	SGI	
XtNitems	XtCItems	XtPointer	NULL	SGI	FlatButtons
XtNitemsTouched	XtCItemsTouched	Boolean	FALSE	SG	FlatButtons
XtNlabel	XtCLabel	String	NULL	SGI•	FlatButtons
XtNlabelImage	XtCLabelImage	XImage *	NULL	SGI•	FlatButtons
XtNmaintainView	XtCMaintainView	Boolean	FALSE	SGI	
XtNmanaged	XtCManaged	Boolean	TRUE	SGI•	FlatButtons
XtNmappedWhenManaged	XtCMappedWhenManaged	Boolean	TRUE	SGI•	Core
XtNmnemonic	XtCMnemonic	char	NULL	SGI•	Primitive
XtNnoneSet	XtCNoneSet	Boolean	FALSE	SGI	
XtNnumItemFields	XtCNumItemFields	Cardinal	0	SGI	FlatButtons
XtNnumItems	XtCNumItems	Cardinal	0	SGI	FlatButtons
XtNreferenceName	XtCReferenceName	String	NULL	SGI	Primitive
XtNreferenceWidget	XtCReferenceWidget	Widget	NULL	SGI	Primitive
XtNscreen	XtCScreen	Screen *	(parent's)	GI	Core
XtNselectProc	XtCCallbackProc	XtCallbackProc	NULL	SGI•	
XtNsensitive	XtCSensitive	Boolean	TRUE	G[1]	Core
XtNset	XtCSet	Boolean	FALSE	SGI•	
XtNshadowThickness	XtCShadowThickness	Dimension	"0 points"[3]	SGI	Primitive
XtNshadowType	XtCShadowType	OlDefine	OL_SHADOW_IN	SGI	Primitive
XtNtranslations	XtCTranslations	XtTranslations	NULL	SGI	Core
XtNtraversalOn	XtCTraversalOn	Boolean	TRUE	SGI•	Primitive
XtNunselectProc	XtCCallbackProc	XtCallbackProc	NULL	SGI•	
XtNuserData	XtCUserData	XtPointer	NULL	SGI•	Primitive
XtNviewHeight	XtCViewHeight	Cardinal	4	SGI	
XtNviewItemIndex	XtCViewItemIndex	Cardinal	none	S	
XtNwidth	XtCWidth	Dimension	(calculated)	SGI•	Core
XtNx	XtCPosition	Position	0	SGI	Core
XtNy	XtCPosition	Position	0	SGI	Core

[1] Use XtSetSensitive to set this resource.
[2] Not used in OPEN LOOK look and feel.
[3] "2 points" in the MOTIF look and feel.

XtNancestorSensitive

Range of values:

>   TRUE/"true"
>   FALSE/"false"

This resource indicates the sensitivity of the item's ancestors. If **TRUE**, all the item's ancestors are sensitive and the item is sensitive to user input. If **FALSE**, one or more of the item's ancestors are insensitive. In this case, the item displays an inactive visual and is not sensitive to user input.

XtNbackground

This is the pixel color used to fill in the background of the item.

XtNbackgroundPixmap

This resource specifies the pixmap that is displayed for all items. Any supplied pixmap must have the same depth as the widget's depth. Pixmaps of **None** and **ParentRelative** are not considered valid values.

XtNclientData

This is the client data supplied to all callback procedures.

XtNdblSelectProc

This callback procedure is called when the user double-clicks SELECT over a list item. The *call_data* parameter for this procedure is a pointer to an **OlFlatCallData** structure. The **OlFlatCallData** structure includes the following members:

```
Cardinal  item_index;       /* sub-object initiating callback */
XtPointer items;            /* sub-object list */
Cardinal  num_items;        /* number of sub-objects */
String    *item_fields;     /* key of fields for list */
Cardinal  num_item_fields;  /* number of item fields */
XtPointer user_data;        /* widget's user_data value */
XtPointer item_user_data;   /* item's user_data value */
```

XtNdragCursorProc

This callback is invoked whenever a drag and drop operation starts. The **OlFlatDragCursorCallData** pointer will be passed in as *call_data* This callback is called to create the mouse cursor for dragging whenever an item is being dragged. The fields **x_hot** and **y_hot** should be the relative position from the hotspot of the cursor to the upper left corner of the item. The callback structure, **OlFlatDragCursorCallData**, includes the following members:

```
OlFlatCallData item_data;
OlVirtualEvent ve;          /* virtual event */
Cursor yes_cursor;          /* YES cursor in DnD, default None */
Cursor no_cursor;           /* NO cursor in DnD, default None */
Position x_hot;             /* hot spot position of YES cursor */
Position y_hot;             /* hot spot position of YES cursor */
Boolean static_cursor;      /* free cursor after operation */
```

If the **yes_cursor** is **None**, the cursor will use the default yes cursor depending on the drag and drop gesture. If the **no_cursor** is **None**, the default no cursor is used. The **static_cursor** member specifies whether application supplied yes and no cursors should be freed after the drag and drop operation by the widget. The default is **TRUE**.

XtNdropProc

This callback procedure is called when the user drags item(s) in the list and drops them outside the list. The *call_data* parameter for this procedure is a pointer to an `OlFlatDropCallData` structure including the following members:

```
OlFlatCallData item_data;
OlVirtualEvent ve;                      /* virtual event */
OlDnDDestinationInfoPtr dst_info;       /* destination window info */
OlDnDDragDropInfoPtr root_into;         /* drag-n-drop info */
OlDnDDropStatus drop_status;            /* drop status */
```

XtNexclusives

Range of values:

```
TRUE/"true"
FALSE/"false"
```

This resource determines the selection mode of the List. A value of **TRUE** results in exclusive behavior where, in conjunction with **XtNnoneSet**, at most one item can be set by the user. A value of **FALSE** results in nonexclusive behavior where any number of items may be set by the user.

XtNformat

This resource is the format string that specifies the format of the items' fields. Refer to the description of List Items in the DESCRIPTION section for a discussion of the format specification.

XtNformatData

This resource points to the format data which corresponds to the format string (**XtNformat**). Refer to the description of List Items in the DESCRIPTION section.

Note that this resource is never inherited from the container, so its default value is always NULL.

XtNitems

This is the list of items. This value must point to a static list since the widget references this list after initialization but does not cache its information.

XtNitemFields

This is the list of resource names used to parse the records in the **XtNitems** list. This resource does not have to point to static information since the widget does not use this information after initialization. Though the widget does not reference this resource's value after initialization, it holds onto it for responding to an **XtGet-Values** request and supplying it in the **OlFlatCallData** structure during callbacks. Therefore, if the application plans on querying this resource, it's recommended that the application make this resource point to static information.

XtNitemsTouched

Range of values:

```
TRUE/"true"
FALSE/"false"
```

Whenever the application modifies an item list directly, it must supply this resource (with a value of **TRUE**) so that the widget can update the visual. If the resource value is supplied, the current item list is considered a new list and the visual is updated as a result and a change in geometry may result.

Note that it is not necessary to use this resource if the application modifies the list with the `OlFlatSetValues` procedure; nor is it necessary to use this resource whenever the application supplies a new list (via `XtNitems`).

XtNitemVisibility

This callback list is called whenever one or more selected items enters or leaves the view. The *call_data* parameter for this procedure is a pointer to a `OlFListItemVisibilityCD` structure which includes the following members:

```
OlFlatCallData item_data;
Cardinal *enters;
Cardinal num_enters;
Cardinal *leaves;
Cardinal num_leaves;
```

where:

item_data	is a structure containing list information The `item_index` and `item_user_data` fields in the `OlFlatCallData` structure are unused for this callback.
enters	vector of indexes of selected items which have entered the view
num_enters	number of indexes in `enters`
leaves	vector of indexes of selected items which have left the view
num_leaves	number of indexes in `leaves`

Callbacks are called after scrolling is performed. For each scroll operation, the set of selected items in the current view is compared against the set of selected items in the previous view and the callbacks are called if one or more selected items have entered the new view and/or one or more selected items have left the previous view.

Note that this can be a computationally expensive operation while dragging the scrollbar elevator depending on the mode of the drag callback [see `Scrollbar`(3Olit)] especially for nonexclusives settings where there may be many selected items.

XtNlabel/XtNlabelImage

These resources are provided as a convenience for simple list; that is, for lists whose items consist of a single field. One of these resources can be specified instead of `XtNformatData`. For simple lists with text items ("%s" format), `XtNlabel` may be specified instead of `XtNformatData`. For simple lists with images, `XtNlabelImage` may be specified instead of `XtNformatData`.

Using `XtNlabel` or `XtNlabelImage` instead of `XtNformatData` alleviates the inconvenience of additional indirection necessary with the `XtNformatData` resource and allows static lists to be built. Also, for text items, it may not be necessary to specify the format (`XtNformat`) if its default value ("%s") is satisfactory.

XtNmaintainView

Range of values:

```
TRUE/"true"
FALSE/"false"
```

This resource maintains the current view when updating (that is, additions or deletions) an existing list.

When **TRUE**, **FlatList** will try to maintain the same view as before (although a refresh will still occur) when a list is touched (that is, **XtNitemTouched** is **TRUE** or **XtNformat** is changed), otherwise, the view starts with item "0".

XtNmappedWhenManaged

Range of values:

> TRUE/"true"
> FALSE/"false"

This resource specifies whether or not a managed item is displayed. Regardless of this resource's value, all items will be included when determining the layout.

Note that this resource is never inherited from the container, so its default value is always **TRUE**.

XtNnoneSet

Range of values:

> TRUE/"true"
> FALSE/"false"

This resource controls whether the settings can be toggled into an unset mode directly. In the MOTIF look and feel, if **XtNexclusives** is **TRUE**, **XtNnoneSet** is **FALSE** and is read only. If set to **FALSE**, exactly one item must always be in the set state. Attempting to select the currently set item has no effect. If set to **TRUE**, no more than one item can be set at any time. However, the user can select the currently set item and toggle it back to an unset state.

XtNnumItems

This resource specifies the number of items.

XtNnumItemFields

This resource indicates the number of resource names contained in **XtNitemFields**.

XtNselectProc

This callback procedure is called whenever an item becomes selected as a result of a user action (selecting an item, for example). The *call_data* parameter is a pointer to a **OlFlatCallData** structure.

XtNsensitive

Range of values:

> TRUE/"true"
> FALSE/"false"

If **TRUE**, the item is sensitive to user input. If **FALSE**, the item is insensitive to user input and is displayed with an inactive visual.

Note that this resource is never inherited from the container, so its default value is always **TRUE**.

XtNset

Range of values:

> TRUE/"true"
> FALSE/"false"

This resource reflects the current state of the item. Even if the application does not use **XtNset** in its item fields list, the container will correctly maintain the set item and the application can change the set item via **OlFlatSetValues**.

Note that this resource is never inherited from the container, so its default value is always **FALSE**.

XtNunselectProc
This callback procedure is called whenever an item becomes unselected as a result of a user action (unselecting an item, for example). The *call_data* parameter is a pointer to a **OlFlatCallData** structure.

XtNviewHeight
This resource specifies the height of the view in terms of how many items should be viewable. For fixed-height items, the resulting height is calculated by multiplying the value of this resource by the item height. When item heights vary, the value of this resource is multiplied by the height of the shortest item. This resource is ignored if the **FlatList** is not in a **ScrolledWindow** widget.

XtNviewItemIndex
This is a *settable*-only resource which facilitates viewing an item. The value supplied with this resource is the index of an item to be viewed. If the item is not already in view, the view is scrolled up or down: if the item is above the view, the view is scrolled so that the item appears at the top of the view; if the item is below the view, the view is scrolled so that the item appears at the bottom of the view. If the item is already in view, no action is taken. A warning is issued when an invalid index is supplied. The results of reading this resource via **XtGetValues** is undefined.

NOTES
The **FlatList** widget supports internationalized text strings, it draws EUC strings in their specified font groups.

Because the Xt Intrinsics define **Position** as a **short** and **Dimension** as an **unsigned short**, the total number of items is limited, depending on the total item heights and the screen resolution. When scrolling the list, the display may look strange if the number of total items is exceeded.

BSelect and **BDrag** in the MOTIF look and feel, and **OL_SELECT** in the OPEN LOOK look and feel, behave identically.

There are several MOTIF look and feel specifications not supported by the **FlatList** widget:

Normal mode
> In Normal mode, navigation keys move the location cursor and select the item. The FlatList navigation keys move the location cursor, but do not affect the selection.

Single Select selection policy
> use Browse Select

Multiple Select selection policy
> use Extended Select

FlatList (3Olit)

```
BToggle
BExtend   button events for toggling the state of a control
```

SEE ALSO

`Flat`(3Olit), `OlDnDTrackDragCursor`(3DnD), `OlDnDDragAndDrop`(3DnD),
`OlFlatGetValues`(3Olit), `Scrollbar`(3Olit), `ScrolledWindow`(3Olit)

NAME

`FlatNonexclusives` – create a choose one or more widget

SYNOPSIS

```
#include <X11/Intrinsic.h>
#include <X11/StringDefs.h>
#include <Xol/OpenLook.h>
#include <Xol/FNonexclus.h>

widget = XtCreateWidget(name, flatNonexclusivesWidgetClass, ...);
```

DESCRIPTION

The `FlatNonexclusives` widget provides a way to build a several-of-many OPEN LOOK look and feel button selection object. It manages a set of rectangular buttons or check boxes, providing layout management and selection control.

Default Spacing

The default spacing between items is 50% of the prevailing point size for the container's font.

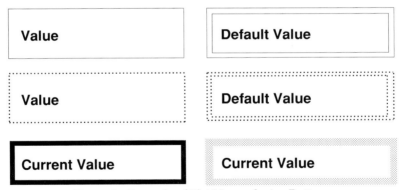

Figure 1. Example of Flat Nonexclusive Buttons

Selection Control

Clicking the SELECT mouse button over an object that is set will cause the object to become unset and its `XtNunselectProc` procedure is called. If the object is unset, clicking the SELECT mouse button over it causes it to become set and its `XtNselectProc` procedure is called.

Use in a Menu

The `FlatNonexclusives` can be added as a child in a menu pane to implement a several-of-many menu choice.

FlatNonexclusives Coloration

The `FlatNonexclusives` container inherits its background color from the container's parent widget. Setting the background color affects only the sub-objects' background.

FlatNonexclusives (3Olit)

Keyboard Traversal

The **FlatNonexclusives** widget is a Primitive widget that manages the traversal between a set of sub-objects. When the user traverses to a **FlatNonexclusives** widget, the first sub-object in the set will display itself as having input focus (see the **RectButton** widget for a description of this appearance). The MOVEUP, MOVE-DOWN, MOVERIGHT, and MOVELEFT keys move the input focus between the sub-objects. To traverse out of the **FlatNonexclusives** widget, the following keys can be used:

NEXT_FIELD	moves to the next traversable widget in the window.
PREV_FIELD	moves to the previous traversable widget in the window.
NEXTWINDOW	moves to the next window in the application.
PREVWINDOW	moves to the previous window in the application.
NEXTAPP	moves to the first window in the next application.
PREVAPP	moves to the first window in the previous application.

Keyboard Operation

FlatNonexclusives Activation Types	
Activation Type	Expected Results
OL_MENUDEFAULTKEY	If the **FlatNonexclusives** is on a menu, this command will set the item with focus to be menu's default; otherwise, this command is ignored.
OL_SELECTKEY	This command acts as if the SELECT mouse button had been clicked on the **RectButton** with focus. See "**Selection Control**"" section above.

Display of Keyboard Mnemonic

The **FlatNonexclusives** widget displays the mnemonic accelerator of a sub-object as part of the sub-object's label. If the mnemonic character is in the label, then that character is highlighted according to the value of the application resource **XtNshowMneumonics**. If the mnemonic character is not in the label, it is displayed to the right of the label in parenthesis and highlighted according to the value of the application resource **XtNshowMneumonics**.

If truncation is necessary, the mnemonic displayed in parenthesis is truncated as a unit.

Display of Keyboard Accelerators

The **FlatNonexclusives** widget displays the keyboard accelerator as part of the sub-object's label. The string in the **XtNacceleratorText** resource is displayed to the right of the label (or mnemonic) separated by at least one space. The accelerator Text is right justified.

If truncation is necessary, the accelerator is truncated as a unit. The accelerator is truncated before the mnemonic or the label.

RESOURCES

The following table lists the resources for the **FlatNonexclusives**. Resources that have a bullet (•) in the Access column denote sub-object resources. If these resources are not included in the **XtNitemFields** list, they are inherited from the container widget. An application can change the default values for sub-object resources by setting them directly on the container. Even though a sub-object resource is not included in the **XtNitemFields** list, the application can query the value of any sub-object resource with **OlFlatGetValues**.

\multicolumn{6}{l}{FlatNonexclusives Resource Set}
Name	Class	Type	Default	Acc	Inherit
XtNaccelerator	XtCAccelerator	String	NULL	SGI•	Primitive
XtNacceleratorText	XtCAcceleratorText	String	(calculated)	SGI•	Primitive
XtNancestorSensitive	XtCSensitive	Boolean	(calculated)	G[1]•	Core
XtNbackground	XtCBackground	Pixel	"XtDefaultBackground"	SGI•	Core
XtNbackgroundPixmap	XtCPixmap	Pixmap	XtUnspecifiedPixmap	SGI•	Core
XtNborderColor	XtCBorderColor	Pixel	"XtDefaultForeground"	SGI	Core
XtNborderPixmap	XtCPixmap	Pixmap	XtUnspecifiedPixmap	SGI	Core
XtNborderWidth	XtCBorderWidth	Dimension	0	SGI	Core
XtNclientData	XtCClientData	XtPointer	NULL	SGI•	FlatButtons
XtNcolormap	XtCColormap	Colormap	(parent's)	GI	Core
XtNconsumeEvent	XtCCallback	XtCallbackList	NULL	SGI	Primitive
XtNdefault	XtCDefault	Boolean	FALSE	SGI•	FlatButtons
XtNdepth	XtCDepth	Cardinal	(parent's)	GI	Core
XtNdestroyCallback	XtCCallback	XtCallbackList	NULL	SGI	Object
XtNdim	XtCDim	Boolean	FALSE	SGI	FlatButtons
XtNfillOnSelect	XtCFillOnSelect	Boolean	FALSE	SGI	FlatButtons
XtNfocusOnSelect	XtCFocusOnSelect	Boolean	FALSE[4]	SGI	FlatButtons
XtNfont	XtCFont	XFontStruct *	"OlDefaultFont"	SGI•	Primitive
XtNfontColor	XtCFontColor	Pixel	"XtDefaultForeground"	SGI•	Primitive
XtNfontGroup	XtCFontGroup	OlFontList *	NULL	SGI	Primitive
XtNforeground	XtCForeground	Pixel	"XtDefaultForeground"	SGI•	Primitive
XtNgravity	XtCGravity	int	CenterGravity	SGI	FlatButtons
XtNhPad	XtCHPad	Dimension	0	SGI	FlatButtons
XtNhSpace	XtCHSpace	Dimension	(calculated)	SGI	FlatButtons
XtNheight	XtCHeight	Dimension	(calculated)	SGI•	Core
XtNhighlightThickness	XtCHighlightThickness	Dimension	"2 points"[2]	SGI	Primitive
XtNinputFocusColor	XtCInputFocusColor	Pixel	"Red"	SGI•	Primitive
XtNitemFields	XtCItemFields	String *	NULL	GI	FlatButtons
XtNitemGravity	XtCItemGravity	int	NorthWestGravity	SGI	FlatButtons
XtNitemMaxHeight	XtCItemMaxHeight	Dimension	OL_IGNORE	SGI	FlatButtons
XtNitemMaxWidth	XtCItemMaxWidth	Dimension	OL_IGNORE	SGI	FlatButtons
XtNitemMinHeight	XtCItemMinHeight	Dimension	OL_IGNORE	SGI	FlatButtons

FlatNonexclusives (3Olit)

Name	Class	Type	Default	Acc	Inherit
FlatNonexclusives Resource Set (cont'd)					
XtNitemMinWidth	XtCItemMinWidth	Dimension	OL_IGNORE	SGI	FlatButtons
XtNitems	XtCItems	XtPointer	NULL	SGI	FlatButtons
XtNitemsTouched	XtCItemsTouched	Boolean	FALSE	SG	FlatButtons
XtNlabel	XtCLabel	String	NULL	SGI•	FlatButtons
XtNlabelImage	XtCLabelImage	XImage *	NULL	SGI•	FlatButtons
XtNlabelJustify	XtCLabelJustify	OlDefine	OL_LEFT	SGI•	FlatButtons
XtNlabelTile	XtCLabelTile	Boolean	FALSE	SGI•	FlatButtons
XtNlayoutHeight	XtCLayout	OlDefine	OL_MINIMIZE	SGI	FlatButtons
XtNlayoutType	XtCLayoutType	OlDefine	OL_FIXEDROWS	SGI	FlatButtons
XtNlayoutWidth	XtCLayout	OlDefine	OL_MINIMIZE	SGI	FlatButtons
XtNmanaged	XtCManaged	Boolean	TRUE	SGI•	FlatButtons
XtNmappedWhenManaged	XtCMappedWhenManaged	Boolean	TRUE	SGI•	Core
XtNmeasure	XtCMeasure	int	1	SGI	FlatButtons
XtNmnemonic	XtCMnemonic	char	NULL	SGI•	Primitive
XtNnumItemFields	XtCNumItemFields	Cardinal	0	SGI	FlatButtons
XtNnumItems	XtCNumItems	Cardinal	0	SGI	FlatButtons
XtNreferenceName	XtCReferenceName	String	NULL	SGI	Primitive
XtNreferenceWidget	XtCReferenceWidget	Widget	NULL	SGI	Primitive
XtNsameHeight	XtCSameHeight	OlDefine	OL_ALL	SGI	FlatButtons
XtNsameWidth	XtCSameWidth	OlDefine	OL_COLUMNS	SGI	FlatButtons
XtNscreen	XtCScreen	Screen *	(parent's)	GI	Core
XtNselectColor	XtCSelectColor	Pixel	(input focus color)	SGI	FlatButtons
XtNselectProc	XtCCallbackProc	XtCallbackProc	NULL	SGI•	FlatButtons
XtNsensitive	XtCSensitive	Boolean	TRUE	G[1]•	Core
XtNset	XtCSet	Boolean	FALSE	SGI•	FlatButtons
XtNshadowThickness	XtCShadowThickness	Dimension	"0 points"[3]	SGI•	Primitive
XtNshadowType	XtCShadowType	OlDefine	OL_SHADOW_OUT	SGI	Primitive
XtNtranslations	XtCTranslations	XtTranslations	NULL	SGI	Core
XtNtraversalOn	XtCTraversalOn	Boolean	TRUE	SGI•	Primitive
XtNunselectProc	XtCCallbackProc	XtCallbackProc	NULL	SGI•	FlatButtons
XtNuserData	XtCUserData	XtPointer	NULL	SGI•	Primitive
XtNvPad	XtCVPad	Dimension	0	SGI	FlatButtons
XtNvSpace	XtCVSpace	Dimension	(calculated)	SGI	FlatButtons
XtNwidth	XtCWidth	Dimension	(calculated)	SGI•	Core
XtNx	XtCPosition	Position	0	SGI	Core
XtNy	XtCPosition	Position	0	SGI	Core

[1] Use XtSetSensitive to set this resource.
[2] Not used in OPEN LOOK look and feel.
[3] "2 points" in MOTIF look and feel.
[4] TRUE in MOTIF look and feel.

XtNancestorSensitive

Range of values:

```
TRUE/"true"
FALSE/"false"
```

This resource indicates the sensitivity of the sub-object's ancestors. If **TRUE**, all the sub-object's ancestors are sensitive and the sub-object is sensitive to user input. If **FALSE**, one or more of the sub-object's ancestors are insensitive, so the sub-object displays an inactive visual and is not sensitive to user input.

XtNbackground

This is the pixel color used to fill in the background of the sub-object.

XtNbackgroundPixmap

This resource specifies the pixmap that is displayed as the sub-object's label. Any supplied pixmap must have the same depth as the flat widget's depth. Pixmaps of **None** and **ParentRelative** are not considered valid values. If either **XtNlabel** or **XtNlabelImage** has a non-NULL value, this resource is ignored.

XtNclientData

This is the client data supplied to all callback procedures.

XtNdefault

Range of values:

```
TRUE/"true"
FALSE/"false"
```

When used on the sub-object, this resource specifies whether or not the sub-object is a default item. If more than one item is a set as a default item, a warning is generated and all but the first default item is unselected.

When used on the container, this resource indicates whether or not one of the sub-objects is a default item. If a sub-object is a default item, **XtNdefault** has a value of **TRUE**; else it has a value of **FALSE**. Setting this resource on the container widget indicates whether or not one of the sub-objects should be a default item. If the application sets this value to **TRUE** on the container, the container will set the first managed and mapped sub-object as the default item if a default item does not exist. If the application sets this value to **FALSE**, the container will unset its default item if one exists.

Even if the application does not use **XtNdefault** in its item fields list, the container will correctly maintain the default item and the application can change the default item via **OlFlatSetValues**.

XtNdim

Range of values:

```
TRUE/"true"
FALSE/"false"
```

If **TRUE**, the sub-object shows a dimmed visual indicating that the item represents the state of one or more objects, that as a group, are in different states.

XtNitems

This is the list of sub-object items. This value must point to a static list since flat containers reference this list after initialization but do not cache its information.

FlatNonexclusives (3Olit)

XtNitemFields

This is the list of resource names used to parse the records in the **XtNitems** list. This resource does not have to point to static information since the flat container does not use this information after initialization. Though the flat container does not reference this resource's value after initialization, it holds onto it for responding to an **XtGetValues** request and supplying it in the **OlFlatCallData** structure during callbacks. Therefore, if the application plans on querying this resource, it's recommended that the application make this resource point to static information.

XtNitemsTouched

Range of values:

> TRUE/"true"
> FALSE/"false"

Whenever the application modifies an item list directly, it must supply this resource (with a value of **TRUE**) to the flat widget container so that the container can update the visual. If the resource value is supplied, the flat widget container treats its current item list as a new list and hence, updates its entire visual. Since the list is treated as a new list, the flat container may request a change in geometry from its parent.

Note that it is not necessary to use this resource if the application modifies the list with the **OlFlatSetValues** procedure, nor is it necessary to use this resource whenever the application supplies a new list to the flat container.

XtNlabel

This is the text string that appears in the sub-object.

XtNlabelImage

This is an **XImage** pointer that can appear in a sub-object. This resource is ignored if **XtNlabel** is non-NULL.

XtNlabelJustify

Range of values:

> OL_LEFT/"left"
> OL_CENTER/"center"
> OL_RIGHT/"right"

This resource specifies the justification of the label or **XImage** that appears within a sub-object.

XtNlabelTile

Range of values:

> TRUE/"true"
> FALSE/"false"

This resource augments the **XtNlabelImage/XtNlabelPixmap** resource to allow tiling of the sub-object's background. For an image/pixmap that is smaller than the sub-object's background, the label area is tiled with the image/pixmap to fill the sub-object's background if this resource is **TRUE**; otherwise, the label is placed as described by the **XtNlabelJustify** resource.

The `XtNlabelTile` resource is ignored for text labels.

XtNmappedWhenManaged
Range of values:
> `TRUE/"true"`
> `FALSE/"false"`

This resource specifies whether or not a managed sub-object is displayed. Regardless of this resource's value, all managed sub-objects will be including when determining the layout.

Note that this resource is never inherited from the container, so its default value is always `TRUE`.

XtNnumItems
This resource specifies the number of sub-object items.

XtNnumItemFields
This resource indicates the number of resource names contained in `XtNitemFields`.

XtNsameHeight
Range of values:
> `OL_ALL/"all"`
> `OL_ROWS/"rows"`
> `OL_NONE/"none"`

This resource specifies the rows that are forced to the same height.

XtNsameWidth
Range of values:
> `OL_ALL/"all"`
> `OL_COLUMNS/"columns"`
> `OL_NONE/"none"`

This resource specifies the columns that are forced to the same width.

XtNselectProc
This callback procedure is called whenever the sub-object becomes selected by user input.

XtNsensitive
Range of values:
> `TRUE/"true"`
> `FALSE/"false"`

If `TRUE`, the sub-object is sensitive to user input If `FALSE`, the sub-object is insensitive to user input and an inactive visual is displayed to indicate this state.

Note that this resource is never inherited from the container, so its default value is always `TRUE`.

XtNset
Range of values:
> `TRUE/"true"`
> `FALSE/"false"`

FlatNonexclusives (3Olit)

This resource reflects the current state of the sub-object.

Note that this resource is never inherited from the container, so its default value is always **FALSE**.

Even if the application does not use **XtNset** in its item fields list, the container will correctly maintain the set item and the application can change the set item via **OlFlatSetValues**.

XtNunselectProc

This callback procedure is called whenever the sub-object becomes unselected by user input.

NOTES

Use the **FlatButtons** widget to obtain a MOTIF look and feel.

SEE ALSO

Flat(3Olit), **FlatButtons**(3Olit), **OlFlatGetValues**(3Olit), **OlFlatSetValues**(3Olit), **RectButton**(3Olit)

NAME

Footer – display messages

DESCRIPTION

The **Footer** widget provides a convenient way to display status, error, and state messages in both the MOTIF and OPEN LOOK look and feel.

Components

Each **Footer** widget has two parts:

Left Footer

Right Footer

The Left Footer, typically used for status and error messages, occupies the left side of the **Footer** widget. The Right Footer, typically used for short state messages, occupies the right side of the **Footer** widget. The amount of space allocated for the Left and Right Footers is 3/4 and 1/4, respectively.

If only one of these parts is provided by a client, it occupies the entire widget. A client can provide a blank Left or Right Footer to prevent the other footer from occupying the entire space.

Geometry

If the client does not set the width of the **Footer** widget, the initial width is made just large enough to fit the Left and Right Footers, if given. If the client does not set the height (and typically it should not), the initial height is made large enough for the font at hand, subject to a minimum limit. Thereafter, changes in the Left or Right Footer do not cause a change in geometry; instead, where a message is too long for the space allocated it is truncated and a ''more'' arrow is shown. By resizing the widget larger a user can see the full message.

The **Footer** widget does not shrink to zero height when both the Left and Right Footers are null; if a client wishes to get this effect, it needs to unmanage (or destroy) the Footer.

RESOURCES

Footer Resource Set					
Name	Class	Type	Default	Acc	Inherit
XtNancestorSensitive	XtCSensitive	Boolean	(calculated)	G[1]	Core
XtNbackground	XtCBackground	Pixel	"XtDefaultBackground"	SGI	Core
XtNbackgroundPixmap	XtCPixmap	Pixmap	XtUnspecifiedPixmap	SGI	Core
XtNborderColor	XtCBorderColor	Pixel	"XtDefaultForeground"	SGI	Core
XtNborderPixmap	XtCPixmap	Pixmap	XtUnspecifiedPixmap	SGI	Core
XtNborderWidth	XtCBorderWidth	Dimension	0	SGI	Core
XtNcolormap	XtCColormap	Colormap	(parent's)	GI	Core
XtNconsumeEvent	XtCCallback	XtCallbackList	NULL	SGI	Primitive
XtNdepth	XtCDepth	Cardinal	(parent's)	GI	Core
XtNdestroyCallback	XtCCallback	XtCallbackList	NULL	SGI	Object
XtNfont	XtCFont	XFontStruct *	"OlDefaultFont"	SGI	Primitive

Footer (3Olit)

Footer Resource Set (cont'd)					
Name	Class	Type	Default	Acc	Inherit
XtNfontColor	XtCFontColor	Pixel	"XtDefaultForeground"	SGI	Primitive
XtNfontGroup	XtCFontGroup	OlFontList *	NULL	SGI	Primitive
XtNforeground	XtCForeground	Pixel	"XtDefaultForeground"	SGI	Primitive
XtNheight	XtCHeight	Dimension	(calculated)	SGI	Core
XtNhighlightThickness	XtCReadOnly	Dimension	"2 points"[2]	G	Primitive
XtNleftFoot	XtCFoot	String	NULL	SGI	
XtNleftWeight	XtCWeight	Dimension	3	SGI	
XtNmappedWhenManaged	XtCMappedWhenManaged	Boolean	TRUE	SGI	Core
XtNrightFoot	XtCFoot	String	NULL	SGI	
XtNrightWeight	XtCWeight	Dimension	1	SGI	
XtNscreen	XtCScreen	Screen *	(parent's)	GI	Core
XtNsensitive	XtCSensitive	Boolean	TRUE	G[1]	Core
XtNshadowThickness	XtCShadowThickness	Dimension	"0 points"[3]	SGI	Primitive
XtNshadowType	XtCShadowType	OlDefine	OL_SHADOW_IN	SGI	Primitive
XtNtranslations	XtCTranslations	XtTranslations	NULL	SGI	Core
XtNuserData	XtCUserData	XtPointer	NULL	SGI	Primitive
XtNwidth	XtCWidth	Dimension	(calculated)	SGI	Core
XtNx	XtCPosition	Position	0	SGI	Core
XtNy	XtCPosition	Position	0	SGI	Core

[1] Use **XtSetSensitive** to set this resource.
[2] Not used in OPEN LOOK look and feel.
[3] **"2 points"** in MOTIF look and feel.

XtNleftFoot
XtNrightFoot

These resources identify the Left and Right Footers, respectively. If only one is given (and the other is null), then the one message can occupy the entire widget's width, except for fixed margins at either end. If both are given, then each message occupies a fixed fraction of the widget's width, except for the margins and a fixed inter-message space.

The margins, inter-message space, and (default) fractions are designed to ensure the **Footer** widget displays a pair of messages compliant to the appropriate style guidelines.

XtNleftWeight
XtNrightWeight

These resources can be used to change the default fractions allocated for the Left and Right Footers. One should note that changing the default fractions will result in a deviation from the appropriate style guidelines.

The value of each resource gives the "weight", or number of units of width, to allocate to each message. The ratio of one value to the sum of both values gives the fraction of the width.

EXAMPLES

For example, to get default 3/4 and 1/4 OPEN LOOK-compliant fractions the weights are 3 and 1, for **XtNleftFoot** and **XtNrightFoot** respectively.

FooterPanel (3Olit)

NAME

FooterPanel – put a footer at the bottom of a window

SYNOPSIS

```
#include <X11/Intrinsic.h>
#include <X11/StringDefs.h>
#include <Xol/OpenLook.h>
#include <Xol/FooterPane.h>

widget = XtCreateWidget(name, footerPanelWidgetClass, . . .);
```

DESCRIPTION

The **FooterPanel** widget is a simple subclass of the **RubberTile** widget, providing an easy interface for attaching a footer message to the bottom of a base window. This widget supports both the OPEN LOOK and the MOTIF look and feel.

The **FooterPanel** expects the last of its managed children to be the footer. By default, it will keep that child from being resized when the FooterPanel itself is resized — any resize is given to (or taken from) the other children. A client can override this layout policy by explicitly setting the **XtNweight** constraints on its children.

RESOURCES

FooterPanel Resource Set					
Name	Class	Type	Default	Acc	Inherit
XtNancestorSensitive	XtCSensitive	Boolean	(calculated)	G[1]	Core
XtNbackground	XtCBackground	Pixel	"XtDefaultBackground"	SGI	Core
XtNbackgroundPixmap	XtCPixmap	Pixmap	XtUnspecifiedPixmap	SGI	Core
XtNborderColor	XtCBorderColor	Pixel	"XtDefaultForeground"	SGI	Core
XtNborderPixmap	XtCPixmap	Pixmap	XtUnspecifiedPixmap	SGI	Core
XtNborderWidth	XtCBorderWidth	Dimension	0	SGI	Core
XtNbottomMargin	XtCMargin	Dimension	0	SGI	Panes
XtNchildren	XtCReadOnly	WidgetList	NULL	G	Composite
XtNcolormap	XtCColormap	Colormap	(parent's)	GI	Core
XtNconsumeEvent	XtCCallback	XtCallbackList	NULL	SGI	Manager
XtNdepth	XtCDepth	Cardinal	(parent's)	GI	Core
XtNdestroyCallback	XtCCallback	XtCallbackList	NULL	SGI	Object
XtNheight	XtCHeight	Dimension	(calculated)	SGI	Core
XtNinsertPosition	XtCInsertPosition	XtWidgetProc	NULL	SGI	Composite
XtNlayoutHeight	XtCLayout	OlDefine	OL_MINIMIZE	SGI	Panes
XtNlayoutWidth	XtCLayout	OlDefine	OL_MINIMIZE	SGI	Panes
XtNleftMargin	XtCMargin	Dimension	0	SGI	Panes
XtNmappedWhenManaged	XtCMappedWhenManaged	Boolean	TRUE	SGI	Core
XtNnumChildren	XtCReadOnly	Cardinal	0	G	Composite
XtNorientation	XtCOrientation	OlDefine	OL_VERTICAL	SGI	RubberTile
XtNreferenceName	XtCReferenceName	String	NULL	SGI	Manager
XtNreferenceWidget	XtCReferenceWidget	Widget	NULL	SGI	Manager

FooterPanel Resource Set (cont'd)					
Name	Class	Type	Default	Acc	Inherit
XtNrightMargin	XtCMargin	Dimension	0	SGI	Panes
XtNscreen	XtCScreen	Screen *	(parent's)	GI	Core
XtNsensitive	XtCSensitive	Boolean	TRUE	G[1]	Core
XtNsetMinHints	XtCSetMinHints	Boolean	TRUE	SGI	Panes
XtNshadowThickness	XtCShadowThickness	Dimension	"0 points"[3]	SGI	Manager
XtNshadowType	XtCShadowType	OlDefine	OL_SHADOW_OUT	SGI	Manager
XtNtopMargin	XtCMargin	Dimension	0	SGI	Panes
XtNtranslations	XtCTranslations	XtTranslations	NULL	SGI	Core
XtNtraversalOn	XtCTraversalOn	Boolean	TRUE	SGI	Manager
XtNuserData	XtCUserData	XtPointer	NULL	SGI	Manager
XtNwidth	XtCWidth	Dimension	(calculated)	SGI	Core
XtNx	XtCPosition	Position	0	SGI	Core
XtNy	XtCPosition	Position	0	SGI	Core

[1]   Use **XtSetSensitive** to set this resource.

[3]   **"2 points"** in MOTIF look and feel.

SEE ALSO

   Footer(3Olit), **RubberTile**(3Olit)

Form (3Olit)

NAME

Form – provide sophisticated management of other widgets

SYNOPSIS

```
#include <X11/Intrinsic.h>
#include <X11/StringDefs.h>
#include <Xol/OpenLook.h>
#include <Xol/Form.h>
widget = XtCreateWidget(name, formWidgetClass, . . .);
```

DESCRIPTION

The **Form** widget is a constraint-based manager that provides a layout language used to establish spatial relationships between its children in both the OPEN LOOK and MOTIF look and feel. It then manipulates these relationships when the Form is resized, new children are added to the Form, or its children are moved, resized, unmanaged, remanaged, rearranged, or destroyed.

Spanning Constraints

A widget can be created with a set of constraints in such a manner that it spans the width or height of a form. Constraints that cause a widget to span both the width and height of a form can also be specified.

Row Constraints

Sets of widgets can be set up as a row so that resizing a form may increase or decrease the spacing between the widgets. The form may also make the widgets smaller if desired.

Column Constraints

Sets of widgets can be displayed in a single column or in multiple columns. The form may increase or decrease the spacing between widgets or resize the widgets.

Automatic Form Resizing

The form calculates new sizes or positions for its children whenever they change size or position. The new form size thus generated is passed as a geometry request to the parent of the form. Once resized, the form attempts to rearrange its children using the constraints of its children.

Managing, Unmanaging and Destroying Children

When a widget within a form is unmanaged or destroyed, it is removed from the constraint processing and the constraints are reprocessed to reposition and/or resize the form and its contents. Any widgets that referenced it are rereferenced to the widget that it had been referencing. For the unmanaged case, if the widget is remanaged, the widgets that were previously referencing it are rereferenced to it, thereby reestablishing the original layout.

Form Coloration

Figure 1 illustrates the resources that affect the coloration of the **Form** widget without a shadowed border. If a shadowed border is used, the shadow color is calculated from **XtNbackground**.

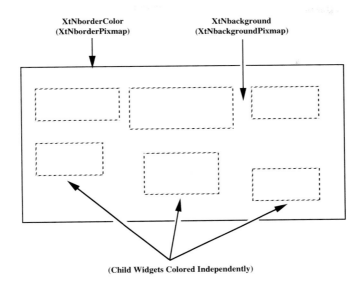

XtNborderColor
(XtNborderPixmap)

XtNbackground
(XtNbackgroundPixmap)

(Child Widgets Colored Independently)

Figure 1. Form Coloration

RESOURCES

Form Resource Set					
Name	Class	Type	Default	Acc	Inherit
XtNancestorSensitive	XtCSensitive	Boolean	(calculated)	G[1]	Core
XtNbackground	XtCBackground	Pixel	"XtDefaultBackground"	SGI	Core
XtNbackgroundPixmap	XtCPixmap	Pixmap	XtUnspecifiedPixmap	SGI	Core
XtNborderColor	XtCBorderColor	Pixel	"XtDefaultForeground"	SGI	Core
XtNborderPixmap	XtCPixmap	Pixmap	XtUnspecifiedPixmap	SGI	Core
XtNborderWidth	XtCBorderWidth	Dimension	0	SGI	Core
XtNchildren	XtCReadOnly	WidgetList	NULL	G	Composite
XtNcolormap	XtCColormap	Colormap	(parent's)	GI	Core
XtNconsumeEvent	XtCCallback	XtCallbackList	NULL	SGI	Manager
XtNdepth	XtCDepth	Cardinal	(parent's)	GI	Core
XtNdestroyCallback	XtCCallback	XtCallbackList	NULL	SGI	Object
XtNheight	XtCHeight	Dimension	(calculated)	SGI	Core
XtNinsertPosition	XtCInsertPosition	XtWidgetProc	NULL	SGI	Composite
XtNmappedWhenManaged	XtCMappedWhenManaged	Boolean	TRUE	SGI	Core
XtNnumChildren	XtCReadOnly	Cardinal	0	G	Composite
XtNreferenceName	XtCReferenceName	String	NULL	SGI	Manager

Form (3Olit)

<table>
<tr><td colspan="6" align="center">Form Resource Set (cont'd)</td></tr>
<tr><td>Name</td><td>Class</td><td>Type</td><td>Default</td><td>Acc</td><td>Inherit</td></tr>
<tr><td>XtNreferenceWidget</td><td>XtCReferenceWidget</td><td>Widget</td><td>NULL</td><td>SGI</td><td>Manager</td></tr>
<tr><td>XtNscreen</td><td>XtCScreen</td><td>Screen *</td><td>(parent's)</td><td>GI</td><td>Core</td></tr>
<tr><td>XtNsensitive</td><td>XtCSensitive</td><td>Boolean</td><td>TRUE</td><td>G[1]</td><td>Core</td></tr>
<tr><td>XtNshadowThickness</td><td>XtCShadowThickness</td><td>Dimension</td><td>"0 points"[3]</td><td>SGI</td><td>Manager</td></tr>
<tr><td>XtNshadowType</td><td>XtCShadowType</td><td>OlDefine</td><td>OL_SHADOW_OUT</td><td>SGI</td><td>Manager</td></tr>
<tr><td>XtNtranslations</td><td>XtCTranslations</td><td>XtTranslations</td><td>NULL</td><td>SGI</td><td>Core</td></tr>
<tr><td>XtNtraversalOn</td><td>XtCTraversalOn</td><td>Boolean</td><td>TRUE</td><td>SGI</td><td>Manager</td></tr>
<tr><td>XtNuserData</td><td>XtCUserData</td><td>XtPointer</td><td>NULL</td><td>SGI</td><td>Manager</td></tr>
<tr><td>XtNwidth</td><td>XtCWidth</td><td>Dimension</td><td>(calculated)</td><td>SGI</td><td>Core</td></tr>
<tr><td>XtNx</td><td>XtCPosition</td><td>Position</td><td>0</td><td>SGI</td><td>Core</td></tr>
<tr><td>XtNy</td><td>XtCPosition</td><td>Position</td><td>0</td><td>SGI</td><td>Core</td></tr>
</table>

[1] Use **XtSetSensitive** to set this resource.

[3] **"2 points"** in MOTIF look and feel.

Constraint Resources

Each child widget attached to the **Form** composite widget is constrained by the following resources: (In essence, these resources become resources for each child widget and can be set and read just like any other resources defined for the child.)

<table>
<tr><td colspan="5" align="center">Form Constraint Resource Set</td></tr>
<tr><td>Name</td><td>Class</td><td>Type</td><td>Default</td><td>Access</td></tr>
<tr><td>XtNxAddWidth</td><td>XtCXAddWidth</td><td>Boolean</td><td>FALSE</td><td>SGI</td></tr>
<tr><td>XtNxAttachOffset</td><td>XtCXAttachOffset</td><td>int</td><td>0</td><td>SGI</td></tr>
<tr><td>XtNxAttachRight</td><td>XtCXAttachRight</td><td>Boolean</td><td>FALSE</td><td>SGI</td></tr>
<tr><td>XtNxOffset</td><td>XtCXOffset</td><td>int</td><td>0</td><td>SGI</td></tr>
<tr><td>XtNxRefName</td><td>XtCXRefName</td><td>String</td><td>NULL</td><td>SGI</td></tr>
<tr><td>XtNxRefWidget</td><td>XtCXRefWidget</td><td>Widget</td><td>(form)</td><td>SGI</td></tr>
<tr><td>XtNxResizable</td><td>XtCXResizable</td><td>Boolean</td><td>FALSE</td><td>SGI</td></tr>
<tr><td>XtNxVaryOffset</td><td>XtCXVaryOffset</td><td>Boolean</td><td>FALSE</td><td>SGI</td></tr>
<tr><td>XtNyAddHeight</td><td>XtCYAddHeight</td><td>Boolean</td><td>FALSE</td><td>SGI</td></tr>
<tr><td>XtNyAttachBottom</td><td>XtCYAttachBottom</td><td>Boolean</td><td>FALSE</td><td>SGI</td></tr>
<tr><td>XtNyAttachOffset</td><td>XtCYAttachOffset</td><td>int</td><td>0</td><td>SGI</td></tr>
<tr><td>XtNyOffset</td><td>XtCYOffset</td><td>int</td><td>0</td><td>SGI</td></tr>
<tr><td>XtNyRefName</td><td>XtCYRefName</td><td>String</td><td>NULL</td><td>SGI</td></tr>
<tr><td>XtNyRefWidget</td><td>XtCYRefWidget</td><td>Widget</td><td>(form)</td><td>SGI</td></tr>
<tr><td>XtNyResizable</td><td>XtCYResizable</td><td>Boolean</td><td>FALSE</td><td>SGI</td></tr>
<tr><td>XtNyVaryOffset</td><td>XtCYVaryOffset</td><td>Boolean</td><td>FALSE</td><td>SGI</td></tr>
</table>

XtNxAddWidth
XtNyAddHeight

Range of values:

TRUE/"true"

FALSE/"false"

These resources indicate whether to add the width or height of the corresponding reference widget to a widget's location when determining the widget's position.

XtNxAttachOffset
XtNyAttachOffset
Range of values:

    0 ≤ XtNxAttachOffset
    0 ≤ XtNyAttachOffset

When a widget is attached to the right or bottom edge of the form, the separation between the widget and the form defaults to zero pixels. These resources allow that separation to be set to some other value. Also, for widgets that are not attached to the right or bottom edge of the form, these resources specify the minimum spacing between the widget and the form.

XtNxAttachRight
XtNyAttachBottom
Range of values:

    TRUE/"true"
    FALSE/"false"

Widgets are normally referenced from "form left" to "form right" or from "form top" to "form bottom." These resources allow this reference to occur on the opposite edges of the form. When used with the XtNxVaryOffset and XtNyVaryOffset resources, they allow a widget to float along the right or bottom edge of the form. This is done by setting both the XtNxAttachRight (XtNyAttachBottom) and XtNxVaryOffset (XtNyVaryOffset) resources to TRUE. A widget can also span the width (height) of the form by setting the XtNxAttachRight (XtNyAttachBottom) resource to TRUE and the XtNxVaryOffset (XtNyVaryOffset) resource to FALSE.

XtNxOffset
XtNyOffset
Range of values:

    0 ≤ XtNxOffset
    0 ≤ XtNyOffset

The location of a widget is determined by the widget it references. As the default, a widget's position on the form exactly matches its reference widget's location. There are two additional data used to determine the location. These resources define integer values representing the number of pixels to add to the reference widget's location when calculating the widget's location.

XtNxRefName
XtNyRefName
Range of values:
(the name of a widget already created as a child of the form)

When a widget is added as a child of the form, its position is determined by the widget it references. These resources allow the name of the reference widget to be given. The form converts this name to a widget to use for the referencing. Any widget that is a direct child of the form or the form widget itself can be used as a reference widget.

If one of these resources is set and the corresponding resource, **XtNxRefWidget** or **XtNyRefWidget**, is also set, they must agree: the name given in **XtNxRefName** or **XtNyRefName** must match the name of the identified widget. The advantage of using these resources rather than **XtNxRefWidget** and **XtNyRefWidget** is that the references can be used before the widget instances are made.

XtNxRefWidget
XtNyRefWidget
Range of values:

    (the ID of a widget already created as a child)

Instead of naming the reference widget, an application can give the reference widget's ID using these resources.

If both a widget ID and a widget name is given for a reference in the same dimension (x or y), they must refer to the same widget. If not, a warning is made and the widget ID is used.

XtNxResizable
XtNyResizable
Range of values:

    TRUE/"true"
    FALSE/"false"

These resources specify whether the form can resize (expand or shrink) a widget. When a form's size becomes smaller, the form will resize its children only after resizing all the inter-widget spacing of widgets with their **XtNxVaryOffset** (**XtNyVaryOffset**) resource set to **TRUE**. The form keeps track of a widget's initial size or its size generated through calls to **XtSetValues**, so that when the form then becomes larger, the widget will grow to its original size and no larger.

XtNxVaryOffset
XtNyVaryOffset
Range of values:

    TRUE/"true"
    FALSE/"false"

When a form is resized, it processes the constraints contained within its children. These resources allow the spacing between a widget and the widget it references to vary (either increase or decrease) when a form's size changes. The spacing between a widget and its reference widget can decrease to zero pixels if the **XtNxAddWidth** (**XtNyAddHeight**) resource is **FALSE** or to one pixel if **XtNxAddWidth** (**XtNyAddHeight**) is **TRUE**.

SEE ALSO
MenuShell(3Olit)

NAME

Gauge – provide a graphical read only analog control

SYNOPSIS

```
#include <X11/Intrinsic.h>
#include <X11/StringDefs.h>
#include <Xol/OpenLook.h>
#include <Xol/Gauge.h>

widget = XtCreateWidget(name, gaugeWidgetClass, . . .);
```

DESCRIPTION

Gauge Components

The **Gauge** widget is an indicator of amount of space available in any container it is measuring. It supports both the MOTIF and the OPEN LOOK look and feel.

In the MOTIF look and feel, a **Gauge** widget consists of the following elements:

— Slider

— Trough

— Location Cursor

— Current Value (optional)

In the OPEN LOOK look and feel, a **Gauge** widget consists of the following elements:

— Bar (typically)

— Shaded Bar (typically)

— Current Value (not visible)

— Minimum Value (not visible)

— Maximum Value (not visible)

— Tick Marks (optional)

Figure 1. MOTIF Style Horizontal Gauge Widget with Current Value

Gauge (3Olit)

Figure 2. OPEN LOOK Style Horizontal Gauge Widget

Application Notification

The application is responsible for providing any feedback to the end user deemed appropriate, such as updating the Current Value in a text field.

RESOURCES

The table lists the resources for **FlatButtons**. Resources that have a asterisk (*) in the Access column are set in other ways. See the individual description of the resource for more information.

Resources that have a dagger (†) in the Access column have conditional access. See the individual description of the resource for more information.

Gauge Resource Set					
Name	Class	Type	Default	Acc	Inherit
XtNancestorSensitive	XtCSensitive	Boolean	(calculated)	G^I	Core
XtNbackground	XtCBackground	Pixel	"XtDefaultBackground"	SGI	Core
XtNbackgroundPixmap	XtCPixmap	Pixmap	XtUnspecifiedPixmap	SGI	Core
XtNborderColor	XtCBorderColor	Pixel	"XtDefaultForeground"	SGI	Core
XtNborderPixmap	XtCPixmap	Pixmap	XtUnspecifiedPixmap	SGI	Core
XtNborderWidth	XtCBorderWidth	Dimension	0	SGI	Core
XtNcolormap	XtCColormap	Colormap	(parent's)	GI	Core
XtNconsumeEvent	XtCCallback	XtCallbackList	NULL	SGI	Primitive
XtNdepth	XtCDepth	Cardinal	(parent's)	GI	Core
XtNdestroyCallback	XtCCallback	XtCallbackList	NULL	SGI	Object
XtNfont	XtCFont	XFontStruct *	"OlDefaultFont"	SGI	Primitive
XtNfontColor	XtCFontColor	Pixel	"XtDefaultForeground"	SGI	Primitive
XtNfontGroup	XtCFontGroup	OlFontList *	NULL	SGI	Primitive
XtNforeground	XtCForeground	Pixel	"XtDefaultForeground"	SGI	Primitive
XtNheight	XtCHeight	Dimension	(calculated)	SGI	Core
XtNhighlightThickness	XtCHighlightThickness	Dimension	"2 points"^{2}	SGI	Primitive
XtNinputFocusColor	XtCInputFocusColor	Pixel	"Red"	SGI	Primitive
XtNmappedWhenManaged	XtCMappedWhenManaged	Boolean	TRUE	SGI	Core

Gauge Resource Set (cont'd)					
Name	Class	Type	Default	Acc	Inherit
XtNmaxLabel	XtCLabel	String	NULL	SGI	
XtNminLabel	XtCLabel	String	NULL	SGI	
XtNorientation	XtCOrientation	OlDefine	OL_VERTICAL	GI	
XtNrecomputeSize	XtCRecomputeSize	Boolean	FALSE	SGI	
XtNreferenceName	XtCReferenceName	String	NULL	SGI	Primitive
XtNreferenceWidget	XtCReferenceWidget	Widget	NULL	SGI	Primitive
XtNscreen	XtCScreen	Screen *	(parent's)	GI	Core
XtNsensitive	XtCSensitive	Boolean	TRUE	G[1]	Core
XtNshadowThickness	XtCShadowThickness	Dimension	"0 points"[3]	GI	Primitive
XtNshadowType	XtCShadowType	OlDefine	OL_SHADOW_IN	SGI	Primitive
XtNshowValue	XtCShowValue	Boolean	TRUE	SGI	
XtNsliderMax	XtCSliderMax	int	100	SGI	
XtNsliderMin	XtCSliderMin	int	0	SGI	
XtNsliderValue	XtCSliderValue	int	0	SGI	
XtNspan	XtCSpan	Dimension	OL_IGNORE	SGI	
XtNtickUnit	XtCTickUnit	OlDefine	OL_NONE	SGI	
XtNticks	XtCTicks	int	0	SGI	
XtNtranslations	XtCTranslations	XtTranslations	NULL	SGI	Core
XtNtraversalOn	XtCTraversalOn	Boolean	TRUE	SGI	Primitive
XtNuserData	XtCUserData	XtPointer	NULL	SGI	Primitive
XtNwidth	XtCWidth	Dimension	(calculated)	SGI	Core
XtNx	XtCPosition	Position	0	SGI	Core
XtNy	XtCPosition	Position	0	SGI	Core

[1]   Use **XtSetSensitive** to set this resource.
[2]   Not used in the OPEN LOOK look and feel.
[3]   **"2 points"** in the MOTIF look and feel.

XtNmaxLabel

This resource is only available in the OPEN LOOK look and feel. If specified in the MOTIF look and feel, this resource is ignored. This is the label to be placed next to the maximum value position. For a vertical Gauge, the label is placed to the right of the minimum value position. If there is not enough space for the entire label and **XtNrecomputeSize** is **FALSE**, the label will be truncated from the end. If there is not enough space for the entire label and **XtNrecomputeSize** is **TRUE**, then the widget will request for more space to show the entire label.

For an horizontal Gauge, the label is placed centered and below the maximum value position. If there is not enough room to center the label and **XtNrecompu- teSize** is set to **FALSE**, the end of the label will be aligned with the left anchor. If this label collides with the min label, some part of the labels will overlap. If there is not enough room to center the label and **XtNrecomputeSize** is set to **TRUE**, the widget will request for more space to center the label below the maximum value position.

Gauge (3Olit)

XtNminLabel

This resource is only available in the OPEN LOOK look and feel. If specified in the MOTIF look and feel, this resource is ignored. This is the label to be placed next to the minimum value position. For a vertical Gauge, the label is placed to the right of the minimum value position. If there is not enough space for the entire label and `XtNrecomputeSize` is `FALSE`, the label will be truncated from the end. If there is not enough space for the entire label and `XtNrecomputeSize` is `TRUE`, then the widget will request for more space to show the entire label.

For an horizontal Gauge, the label is placed centered and below the minimum value position. If there is not enough room to center the label and `XtNrecomputeSize` is set to `FALSE`, the beginning of the label will be aligned with the left anchor and is drawn to the right. If this label collides with the max label, some part of the labels will overlap. If there is not enough room to center the label and `XtNrecomputeSize` is set to `TRUE`, the widget will request for more space to center the label below the minimum value position.

XtNorientation

Range of values:

```
OL_HORIZONTAL/"horizontal"
OL_VERTICAL/"vertical"
```

This resource defines the direction for the visual presentation of the widget.

XtNrecomputeSize

This resource, if set to `TRUE`, allows the `Gauge` widget to resize itself whenever needed, to compensate for the space needed to show tick marks (OPEN LOOK look and feel only) and labels. The `Gauge` widget uses the `XtNspan`, the sizes of the labels, and `XtNtickUnit` to determine the preferred size.

XtNsliderMax
XtNsliderMin

Range of values:

```
XtNsliderMin < XtNsliderMax
```

These two resources give the range of values tracked by the `Gauge` widget. Mathematically, the range is open on the right; that is, the range is the following subset of the set of integers:

$$XtNsliderMin \le range \le XtNsliderMax$$

XtNsliderValue

Range of values:

$$XtNsliderMin \le XtNsliderValue \le XtNsliderMax$$

This resource gives the current position of the Slider or Drag Box, in the range [`XtNsliderMin` , `XtNsliderMax`]. The `Gauge` widget keeps this resource up to date.

XtNshowValue

```
TRUE/"true"
FALSE/"false"
```

This resource is only available in the MOTIF look and feel. If specified in the OPEN LOOK look and feel, this resource is ignored. Setting this resource to **TRUE** causes a label to show the current value of the Gauge. Based on orientation, the label will be to the left or below the Gauge. Setting this resource to **FALSE** prevents a label from drawing.

XtNspan

If **XtNrecomputeSize** is set to **TRUE**, then **XtNspan** should be set to reflect the preferred length of the Gauge, not counting the space needed for the labels. The **Gauge** widget uses the span value, the sizes of the labels, and **XtNtickUnit** to determine the preferred size.

XtNticks

This resource is only available in the OPEN LOOK look and feel. If specified in the MOTIF look and feel, this resource is ignored. This is the interval between tick marks. The unit of the interval value is determined by **XtNtickUnit**.

XtNtickUnit

Range of values:

      OL_NONE/"none"
      OL_SLIDERVALUE/"slidervalue"
      OL_PERCENT/"percent"

This resource is only available in the OPEN LOOK look and feel. If specified in the MOTIF look and feel, this resource is ignored. This resource can have one of the values: **OL_NONE**, **OL_SLIDERVALUE**, and **OL_PERCENT**. If it is **OL_NONE**, then no tick marks will be displayed and **XtNticks** is ignored. If it is **OL_PERCENT**, then **XtNticks** is interpreted as the percent of the Gauge value range. If it is **OL_SLIDERVALUE**, the **XtNticks** is interpreted as the same unit as Gauge value.

Note that to be consistent with the scrollbar widget, the effective spacing between tick marks, designated in **XtNticks** and **XtNtickUnit**, should be less than or equal to the spacing in **XtNgranularity**.

Figure 2. OPEN LOOK Vertical Gauge Widget with Tick Marks

Gauge (3Olit)

SEE ALSO

Primitive(3Olit), Slider(3Olit)

NAME

    `IntegerField` – provide an integer numeric input field

SYNOPSIS

```
#include <X11/Intrinsic.h>
#include <X11/StringDefs.h>
#include <Xol/OpenLook.h>
#include <Xol/IntegerFie.h>

widget = XtCreateWidget(name, integerFieldWidgetClass, . . .);
```

DESCRIPTION

The `IntegerField` widget provides a simple interface for clients to get a integer-valued numeric input field. It provides a step class proceedure, so that the **Text-Field** class will display stepping arrows on the right side of the widget. When the user clicks SELECT on the arrows or uses the keyboard to increment or decrement the integer value, the `IntegerField` widget updates the value and issues a callback to the client. If the user types a number and then presses RETURN, NEXT_FIELD, or PREV_FIELD, `IntegerField` verifies that the number is within a client specified range of integers; if it is not within range `IntegerField` sets the integer to the closest limit.

Figure 1 shows a MOTIF look and feel integer field in the middle of its range with a location cursor. Figure 2 shows an OPEN LOOK look and feel integer field at the low end of its range in 3D mode.

Figure 1. MOTIF Style Integer Field

Figure 2. OPEN LOOK Style Integer Field

IntegerField (3Olit)

RESOURCES

<table>
<tr><td colspan="6" align="center">IntegerField Resource Set</td></tr>
<tr><th>Name</th><th>Class</th><th>Type</th><th>Default</th><th>Acc</th><th>Inherit</th></tr>
<tr><td>XtNancestorSensitive</td><td>XtCSensitive</td><td>Boolean</td><td>(calculated)</td><td>G[1]</td><td>Core</td></tr>
<tr><td>XtNbackground</td><td>XtCBackground</td><td>Pixel</td><td>"XtDefaultBackground"</td><td>SGI</td><td>Core</td></tr>
<tr><td>XtNbackgroundPixmap</td><td>XtCPixmap</td><td>Pixmap</td><td>XtUnspecifiedPixmap</td><td>SGI</td><td>Core</td></tr>
<tr><td>XtNblinkRate</td><td>XtCBlinkRate</td><td>int</td><td>1000^{10}</td><td>SGI</td><td>TextEdit</td></tr>
<tr><td>XtNborderColor</td><td>XtCBorderColor</td><td>Pixel</td><td>"XtDefaultForeground"</td><td>SGI</td><td>Core</td></tr>
<tr><td>XtNborderPixmap</td><td>XtCPixmap</td><td>Pixmap</td><td>XtUnspecifiedPixmap</td><td>SGI</td><td>Core</td></tr>
<tr><td>XtNborderWidth</td><td>XtCBorderWidth</td><td>Dimension</td><td>0</td><td>SGI</td><td>Core</td></tr>
<tr><td>XtNbottomMargin</td><td>XtCMargin</td><td>Dimension</td><td>(calculated)</td><td>SGI</td><td>TextEdit</td></tr>
<tr><td>XtNcanDecrement</td><td>XtCCanStep</td><td>Boolean</td><td>TRUE</td><td>SGI</td><td>TextField</td></tr>
<tr><td>XtNcanIncrement</td><td>XtCCanStep</td><td>Boolean</td><td>TRUE</td><td>SGI</td><td>TextField</td></tr>
<tr><td>XtNcanScroll</td><td>XtCCanScroll</td><td>Boolean</td><td>FALSE</td><td>SGI</td><td>TextField</td></tr>
<tr><td>XtNcharsVisible</td><td>XtCCharsVisible</td><td>Cardinal</td><td>XtUnspecifiedCardinal</td><td>GI</td><td>TextEdit</td></tr>
<tr><td>XtNcolormap</td><td>XtCColormap</td><td>Colormap</td><td>(parent's)</td><td>GI</td><td>Core</td></tr>
<tr><td>XtNconsumeEvent</td><td>XtCCallback</td><td>XtCallbackList</td><td>NULL</td><td>SGI</td><td>Primitive</td></tr>
<tr><td>XtNcontrolCaret</td><td>XtCControlCaret</td><td>Boolean</td><td>TRUE</td><td>GI</td><td>TextEdit</td></tr>
<tr><td>XtNcursorPosition</td><td>XtCTextPosition</td><td>int</td><td>"0"</td><td>SGI</td><td>TextEdit</td></tr>
<tr><td>XtNdepth</td><td>XtCDepth</td><td>Cardinal</td><td>(parent's)</td><td>GI</td><td>Core</td></tr>
<tr><td>XtNdestroyCallback</td><td>XtCCallback</td><td>XtCallbackList</td><td>NULL</td><td>SGI</td><td>Object</td></tr>
<tr><td>XtNdisplayPosition</td><td>XtCTextPosition</td><td>int</td><td>"0"</td><td>SGI</td><td>TextEdit</td></tr>
<tr><td>XtNdragCursor</td><td>XtCCursor</td><td>Cursor</td><td>NULL</td><td>SGI</td><td>TextEdit</td></tr>
<tr><td>XtNdropSiteID</td><td>XtCReadOnly</td><td>OlDnDDropSiteID</td><td>NULL</td><td>G</td><td>TextEdit</td></tr>
<tr><td>XtNeditType</td><td>XtCEditType</td><td>OlEditMode</td><td>"textedit"</td><td>SGI</td><td>TextEdit</td></tr>
<tr><td>XtNfont</td><td>XtCFont</td><td>XFontStruct *</td><td>"OlDefaultFont"</td><td>SGI</td><td>Primitive</td></tr>
<tr><td>XtNfontColor</td><td>XtCTextFontColor</td><td>Pixel</td><td>"XtDefaultForeground"</td><td>SGI</td><td>Primitive</td></tr>
<tr><td>XtNfontGroup</td><td>XtCFontGroup</td><td>OlFontList *</td><td>NULL</td><td>SGI</td><td>Primitive</td></tr>
<tr><td>XtNforeground</td><td>XtCForeground</td><td>Pixel</td><td>"XtDefaultForeground"</td><td>SGI</td><td>Primitive</td></tr>
<tr><td>XtNheight</td><td>XtCHeight</td><td>Dimension</td><td>(calculated)</td><td>SGI</td><td>Core</td></tr>
<tr><td>XtNhighlightThickness</td><td>XtCHighlightThickness</td><td>Dimension</td><td>"2 points"[2]</td><td>SGI</td><td>Primitive</td></tr>
<tr><td>XtNinitialDelay</td><td>XtCInitialDelay</td><td>int</td><td>500</td><td>SGI</td><td>TextField</td></tr>
<tr><td>XtNinputFocusColor</td><td>XtCInputFocusColor</td><td>Pixel</td><td>"Red"</td><td>SGI</td><td>Primitive</td></tr>
<tr><td>XtNinsertReturn</td><td>XtCInsertReturn</td><td>Boolean</td><td>FALSE</td><td>SGI</td><td>TextEdit</td></tr>
<tr><td>XtNinsertTab</td><td>XtCInsertTab</td><td>Boolean</td><td>FALSE</td><td>SGI</td><td>TextEdit</td></tr>
<tr><td>XtNleftMargin</td><td>XtCMargin</td><td>Dimension</td><td>(calculated)</td><td>SGI</td><td>TextEdit</td></tr>
<tr><td>XtNlinesVisible</td><td>XtCLinesVisible</td><td>int</td><td>0</td><td>G</td><td>TextEdit</td></tr>
<tr><td>XtNmappedWhenManaged</td><td>XtCMappedWhenManaged</td><td>Boolean</td><td>TRUE</td><td>SGI</td><td>Core</td></tr>
<tr><td>XtNmargin</td><td>XtCCallback</td><td>XtCallbackList</td><td>NULL</td><td>SGI</td><td>TextEdit</td></tr>
<tr><td>XtNmaximumSize</td><td>XtCMaximumSize</td><td>Cardinal</td><td>0</td><td>SGI</td><td>TextField</td></tr>
<tr><td>XtNmodifyVerification</td><td>XtCCallback</td><td>XtCallbackList</td><td>NULL</td><td>SGI</td><td>TextEdit</td></tr>
<tr><td>XtNmotionVerification</td><td>XtCCallback</td><td>XtCallbackList</td><td>NULL</td><td>SGI</td><td>TextEdit</td></tr>
</table>

Name	Class	Type	Default	Acc	Inherit
IntegerField Resource Set (cont'd)					
XtNpostModifyNotification	XtCCallback	XtCallbackList	NULL	SGI	TextEdit
XtNpreselect	XtCPreselect	Boolean	TRUE	SGI	TextEdit
XtNreferenceName	XtCReferenceName	String	NULL	SGI	Primitive
XtNreferenceWidget	XtCReferenceWidget	Widget	NULL	SGI	Primitive
XtNrepeatRate	XtCRepeatRate	int	100	SGI	TextField
XtNrightMargin	XtCMargin	Dimension	(calculated)	SGI	TextEdit
XtNscreen	XtCScreen	Screen *	(parent's)	GI	Core
XtNselectEnd	XtCTextPosition	int	"0"	SGI	TextEdit
XtNselectStart	XtCTextPosition	int	"0"	SGI	TextEdit
XtNsensitive	XtCSensitive	Boolean	TRUE	G[1]	Core
XtNshadowThickness	XtCShadowThickness	Dimension	"0 points"[3]	SGI	Primitive
XtNshadowType	XtCShadowType	OlDefine	OL_SHADOW_IN	SGI	Primitive
XtNsourceType	XtCSourceType	OlSourceType	NULL	SGI	TextEdit
XtNstring	XtCString	String	NULL	SGI	TextField
XtNtabTable	XtCTabTable	XtPointer	NULL	SGI	TextEdit
XtNtextEditWidget	XtCReadOnly	Widget	(self)	G	TextField
XtNtopMargin	XtCMargin	Dimension	4	SGI	TextEdit
XtNtranslations	XtCTranslations	XtTranslations	NULL	SGI	Core
XtNtraversalOn	XtCTraversalOn	Boolean	TRUE	SGI	Primitive
XtNuserData	XtCUserData	XtPointer	NULL	SGI	Primitive
XtNvalue	XtCValue	int	(calculated)	SGI	
XtNvalueChanged	XtCCallback	XtCallbackList	NULL	SGI	
XtNvalueGranularity	XtCValueGranularity	int	1	SGI	
XtNvalueMax	XtCValueMax	int	100	SGI	
XtNvalueMin	XtCValueMin	int	0	SGI	
XtNverification	XtCCallback	XtCallbackList	NULL	SGI	TextField
XtNwidth	XtCWidth	Dimension	(calculated)	SGI	Core
XtNwrapMode	XtCWrapMode	OlWrapMode	NULL	SGI	TextEdit
XtNx	XtCPosition	Position	0	SGI	Core
XtNy	XtCPosition	Position	0	SGI	Core

[1] Use XtSetSensitive to set this resource.
[2] Not used in the OPEN LOOK look and feel.
[3] "2 points" in the MOTIF look and feel.
[10] 500 msec. in the MOTIF look and feel.

XtNvalue

Range of values:

XtNvalueMin $\leq$ XtNvalue $\leq$ XtNvalueMax

Default:

(derived from initial value of XtNstring resource of TextField or, if that is not set, the default is XtNvalueMin)

IntegerField (3Olit)

This resource gives the integer representation of the text buffer. **IntegerField** restricts the characters that the user may type to digits and a minus sign. At any time the client can change the value by setting this resource, and can conveniently fetch the value with **XtGetValues**. A client can still use the **TextField XtNstring** resources to fetch the character representation of the value. If the client attempts to initialize or change the text buffer to include characters other than digits or minus sign, **IntegerField** will refuse the change.

XtNvalueMin
XtNvalueMax

Range of values:

> XtNvalueMin ≤ XtNvalueMax

These resources specify the range to which the integer value of the numeric field is constrained. The range is inclusive.

When the user steps the value or enters a number that reaches one of these limits, the corresponding stepping arrow is dimmed and the **TextField XtNcanIncrement** or **XtNcanDecrement** resource is set to **FALSE**. When the value moves away from the limit the stepping arrow is enabled again.

IntegerField will complain if these resources describe a degenerate range, that is, if **XtNvalueMax** is less than **XtNvalueMin**.

XtNvalueGranularity

Range of values:

> XtNvalueGranularity ≤ (XtNvalueMax - XtNvalueMin)

This resource controls how much to step the integer value each time the user presses SELECT over a stepping arrow. If the user presses a keyboard equivalent that has a multi-count attribute, the increment or decrement is that multi-count times this granularity.

Note that this resource is not sufficient to constrain the numeric input to certain integers between **XtNvalueMin** and **XtNvalueMax**. One reason this is insufficient is that the user can enter any integer "by hand" and then press SELECT over a stepping arrow; the increment or decrement will be from the number entered by the user. Another reason is that if the (**XtNvalueMax** - **XtNvalueMin**) is not a whole multiple of the granularity, then when a limit would be exceeded by a step the numeric value is set to the limit. Steps back from that limit will be the size of **XtNgranularity**. This resource, then, should be seen as a way for the user to quickly step through a (probably large) range of numbers, not as a way to further restrict the set of possible input numbers.

XtNvalueChanged

This callback is issued when the user increments or decrements the numeric value with a stepping arrow, or types in a number and presses RETURN, NEXT_FIELD, or PREV_FIELD.

The *call_data* is a pointer to an **OlIntegerFieldChanged** structure which includes the following members:

```
int value;
Boolean changed;
OlChangedReason reason;
```

value the current numeric value of the text buffer; this is provided as a fast way to get the **XtNvalue** resource. The client can not change this value to cause the **XtNvalue** resource to change, rather it must use **XtSetValues** to effect a change.

changed
> **TRUE** if the value has changed since the last callback was issued or from the value the client last set, whichever was more recent

reason
> the reason **value** changed, one of **OlTextFieldReturn**, **OlTextFieldPrevious**, **OlTextFieldNext**, or **OlTextFieldStep**. The first three values are used when the user presses RETURN, NEXT, or PREVIOUS to move focus to another widget. The last is used when the user clicks on one of the stepping arrows. Future versions of this widget may provide additional values for **reason**; clients should be programmed accordingly.

SEE ALSO
> **StepField**(3Olit), **TextEdit**(3Olit), **TextField**(3Olit)

Manager (3Olit)

NAME

Manager – **Manager** widget superclass

SYNOPSIS

```
#include <X11/Intrinsic.h>
#include <X11/StringDefs.h>
#include <Xol/OpenLook.h>
```

DESCRIPTION

The following resources are available to the widgets that are a subclass of the **Manager** class.

RESOURCES

Manager Resource Set				
Name	Class	Type	Default	Acc
XtNconsumeEvent	XtCCallback	XtCallbackList	NULL	SGI
XtNinputFocusColor	XtCInputFocusColor	Pixel	"Red"	SGI
XtNreferenceName	XtCReferenceName	String	NULL	SGI
XtNreferenceWidget	XtCReferenceWidget	Widget	NULL	SGI
XtNshadowThickness	XtCShadowThickness	Dimension	0	SGI
XtNshadowType	XtCShadowType	OlDefine	OL_SHADOW_OUT	SGI
XtNtraversalOn	XtCTraversalOn	Boolean	TRUE	SGI
XtNuserData	XtCUserData	XtPointer	NULL	SGI

XtNconsumeEvent

This resource overrides the handling of events. Whenever an event is processed by the standard translation table, the **XtNConsumeEvent** list is called for the widget in question allowing the application to consume the **XEvent**. To consume an event, the application should turn on (set to **TRUE**) the consumed field in the *call_data* argument when a given event is processed. If the **XEvent** is consumed, the widget doesn't use it. If it is not consumed the widget uses it. The **OlVirtualEventRec** structure, and the pointer to the structure, *OlVirtualEvent*, includes the following members:

```
Boolean        consumed;
XEvent         xevent;
Modifiers      dont_care;
OlVirtualName  virtual_name;
KeySym         keysym;
String         buffer;
Cardinal       length;
Cardinal       item_index;
```

XtNinputFocusColor

Range of values:
> (valid **Pixel** value for the display)/(valid color name)

This resource specifies the color used to show that the widget has input focus. Normally, this color is derived from the value of **XtNinputFocusColor** resource and is dynamically maintained. This dynamic behavior is abandoned if the application explicitly sets this resource either at initialization or through a call to **XtSetValues**.

Note that setting this resource to manage subclasses usually has no effect. The **Manager** subclass should enable this functionality.

XtNreferenceName
Range of values:
> valid name of a widget

This resource specifies a position for inserting this widget in its managing ancestor's traversal list. If the named widget exists in the managing ancestor's traversal list, this widget will be inserted in front of it. Otherwise, this widget will be inserted at the end of the list.

If both the **XtNreferenceName** and **XtNreferenceWidget** resources are set, they must refer to the same widget. If not, a warning is issued and the widget referred to by name is used.

Note that setting this resource to manage subclasses usually has no effect. The **Manager** subclass should enable this functionality.

XtNreferenceWidget
This resource specifies a position for inserting this widget in its managing ancestor's traversal list. If the reference widget is non-null and exists in the managing ancestor's traversal list, this widget will be inserted in front of it. Otherwise, this widget will be inserted at the end of the list.

If both the **XtNreferenceName** and **XtNreferenceWidget** resources are set, they must refer to the same widget. If not, a warning is issued and the widget referred to by name is used.

Note that setting this resource to manage subclasses usually has no effect. The **Manager** subclass should enable this functionality.

XtNtraversalOn
This resource specifies whether this widget is accessible through keyboard traversal.

Note that setting this resource to manage subclasses usually has no effect. The **Manager** subclass should enable this functionality.

XtNuserData
This resource provides storage for application-specific data. It is not used or set by the widget.

SEE ALSO
> **Primitive**(3Olit)

MenuButton (3Olit)

NAME

    `MenuButton` – provide a button with a `MenuShell` attached

SYNOPSIS

```
#include <X11/Intrinsic.h>
#include <X11/StringDefs.h>
#include <Xol/OpenLook.h>
#include <Xol/MenuButton.h>

static Widget button, menupane, w;

Arg args[1];

button = XtCreateWidget(name, MenuButtonWidgetClass, . . .);
```
OR
```
button = XtCreateWidget(name, menubuttonGadgetClass, . . .);
XtSetArg(args[0], XtNmenuPane, &menupane);
XtGetValues(button, args, 1);

w = XtCreateWidget(name, widget-class, menupane, . . .);
```

DESCRIPTION

    The `MenuButton` widget provides the features of menu default selection and menu previewing as well as the features of the `MenuShell` widget in the OPEN LOOK look and feel.

MenuButton Components

    Each menu button has the following elements:

Label

Border

Menu

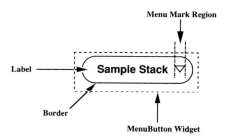

Figure 1. Menu Button

Each menu button also has the components of a `MenuShell` widget. These are not shown in Figure 1.

All Features of the Menu Widget

The **MenuButton** widget includes all the features of the **Menu** widget; the features of that widget apply here.

Selecting the Default Item

As trigger of a menu, each **MenuButton** widget has a Default Item. If the power-user option is on, this Default Item is selected by clicking SELECT over the **Menu-Button** widget. If the Default Item is inactive (its **XtNsensitive** resource is **FALSE**), or busy (its **XtNbusy** resource is **TRUE**), the system beeps. (If the power-user option is off, clicking SELECT brings up a pop-up menu. The power-user option is set in the property sheet of the desktop manager.)

Because the Default Item may be the **MenuButton** widget itself, selecting it really selects its Default Item; this recurses through the menu tree until a non-**MenuButton** widget is found as the Default Item. The Default Item may be the pushpin in a menu. If a pushpin is the Default Item, the menu is brought up as a pinned menu.

Previewing the Default Item

If the menu button is not in a pop-up menu and the power-user option is on, pressing SELECT, or moving the pointer into the menu button while SELECT is pressed, displays the highlighted label of the Default Item in place of the menu button's label. Releasing SELECT restores the original colors and label, and selects the Default Item as described above. Moving the pointer off the menu button before releasing also restores the original colors and label, but does not select the Default Item. (If the power-user option is off, pressing SELECT and releasing it displays a stayup menu. See Selecting the Default Item above for comments about the power-user option.)

This Default Item is the one in the menu directly under the menu button, not necessarily the Default Item at the end of the menu tree, that is activated when the Default Item is selected (see above).

Note that the previewing feature is not accessible with keyboard only operation. This feature functions only when using a mouse to SELECT an item.

Popping Up the Menu — Menu Button in Control Area

When the **MenuButton** widget is in a control area, pressing or clicking MENU when the pointer is within or on the Border pops up the menu button's menu in the direction of the menu mark.

Popping Up the Menu — Menu Button in Menu

When the **MenuButton** widget is in a stay-up menu, pressing or clicking MENU when the pointer is within or on the Border pops up the menu button's menu in the direction of the menu mark.

When the **MenuButton** widget is in a pop-up menu, moving the pointer into the menu mark region pops up the menu in the direction of the menu mark. The position is computed when the movement into the menu mark region is first detected.

Moving the pointer out of the **MenuButton** widget, but not directly into the newly popped up menu, causes that menu to be popped down. This occurs even if the pointer is moved into and out of the newly popped up menu in the interim.

MenuButton (3Olit)

Menu Placement When There is No Room

If the right or bottom edge of the screen is too close to allow the menu placement described above, the menu pops up aligned with the edge of the screen and the pointer is shifted horizontally to keep it four points from the left edge of the menu items. If the left edge of the screen is too close, the menu pops up four points from the edge and the pointer is shifted to lie on the edge. The pointer does not jump back after the menu is dismissed.

MenuButton Coloration

On a monochrome display, the **MenuButton** widget indicates that it has input focus by inverting the foreground and background colors of the control.

On color displays, when the **MenuButton** widget receives the input focus, the background color is changed to the input focus color set in the **XtNinputFocusColor** resource.

EXCEPTIONS:

— If the input focus color is the same as the font color for the control labels, then the coloration of the active control is inverted.

— If the input focus color is the same as the Input Window Header Color and the active control is in the window header, then invert the colors.

— If the input focus color is the same as the window background color, then the **MenuButton** widget inverts the foreground and background colors when it has input focus.

Figure 2 illustrates the resources that affect the coloration of the **MenuButton** widget. Events that occur outside the Border (but within the **MenuButton** widget) are still in the domain of the menu button.

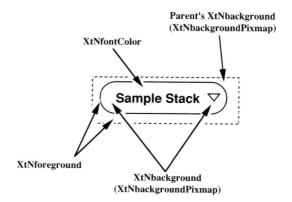

Figure 2. Menu Button Coloration

Label Appearance

The **XtNwidth**, **XtNheight**, **XtNrecomputeSize**, and **XtNlabelJustify** resources interact to produce a truncated, clipped, centered, or left-justified label as shown in Figure 3.

XtNwidth	XtNrecomputeSize	XtNlabelJustify	Result
any value	TRUE	any	Just Fits ▽
> needed for label	FALSE	OL_LEFT	Left Justified ▽
> needed for label	FALSE	OL_CENTER	Centered ▽
< needed for label	FALSE	any	Trunc▷ ▽
XtNheight	XtNrecomputeSize	XtNlabelJustify	Result
any value	TRUE	any	Just Fits ▽
> needed for label	FALSE	any	Centered▽
< needed for label	FALSE	any	**Clipped** ▽

Figure 3. Label Appearance

When the label is centered or left-justified, the extra space is filled with the background color of the **MenuButton** widget, as determined by the **XtNbackground** and **XtNbackgroundPixmap** resources.

When a text label is truncated, the truncation occurs at a character boundary and a solid-white triangle is inserted to show that part of the label is missing. The triangle, of course, requires that more of the label be truncated than would otherwise be necessary. If the width of the button is too small to show even one character with the triangle, only the triangle is shown. If the width is so small that the entire triangle cannot be shown, the triangle is clipped on the right.

Keyboard Traversal

The default value of the **XtNtraversalOn** resource is **TRUE**.

Keyboard traversal within a menu can be done using the PREV_FIELD, NEXT_FIELD, MOVEUP, MOVEDOWN, MOVELEFT, and MOVERIGHT keys. The semantics of these keys depends on the position of input focus within the menu pane.

The PREV_FIELD and MOVEUP keys move the input focus to the previous menu item with keyboard traversal enabled. If the input focus is on the first item of the menu, then pressing one of these keys wraps to the last item of the menu with keyboard traversal enabled. The NEXT_FIELD, MOVEDOWN, and MOVERIGHT keys move the input focus to the next menu item with keyboard traversal enabled. If the input focus is on the last item of the menu, then pressing one of these keys wraps to the first item of the menu with keyboard traversal enabled. One exception to the action of MOVERIGHT is when input focus is on a MenuButton with **XtNmenuMark OL_RIGHT**. In this case, the MOVERIGHT key posts the MenuButton's menu. One exception to the action of MOVEDOWN is when input focus is on a MenuButton with **XtNmenuMark OL_DOWN**. In this case, the MOVEDOWN key posts the MenuButton's menu.

To traverse out of the menu, the following keys can be used:

NEXTWINDOW	moves to the next window in the application
PREVWINDOW	moves to the previous window in the application
NEXTAPP	moves to the first window in the next application
PREVAPP	moves to the first window in the previous application

Keyboard Operation

The DEFAULTACTION key will activate the default control in the **MenuButton** widget as if the user clicked the SELECT button on the control.

The MENUDEFAULTKEY can be used by the user to change the default control in the **MenuButton** widget. When the user presses the MENUDEFAULTKEY, the control which has input focus will become the default control.

Abbreviated MenuButton Activation Types

Activation Type	Expected Results
OL_DEFAULTACTION	icall **OlActivateWidget** for the default item with the **activation_type** as **OL_SELECTKEY**
OL_MENUDEFAULTKEY	if the MenuButton is on a menu, this sets the MenuButton to be the menu's default
OL_MENUKEY	popup the MenuButton's submenu and set focus to the menu's default item
OL_SELECTKEY	see discussion above

Display of Keyboard Mnemonic

The **MenuButton** widget displays the mnemonic accelerator as part of its label. If the mnemonic character is in the label, then that character is highlighted according to the value of the application resource **XtNshowMnemonics**. If the mnemonic character is not in the label, it is displayed to the right of the label in parenthesis and highlighted according to the value of the application resource **XtNshowMnemonics**.

If truncation is necessary, the mnemonic displayed in parenthesis is truncated as a unit.

Display of Keyboard Accelerators

The **MenuButton** widget displays the keyboard accelerator as part of its label. The string in the **XtNacceleratorText** resource is displayed to the right of the label (or mnemonic) separated by at least one space. The accelerator text is right justified.

If truncation is necessary, the accelerator is truncated as a unit. The accelerator is truncated before the mnemonic or the label.

MenuButton Gadgets

MenuButton gadgets cannot be parents (that is, cannot be used as the parent parameter when creating a widget or other gadget.

Gadgets share some core fields. But since they are not subclasses of **Core**, they do not have all **Core** fields. In particular, they don't have a name field or a translation field (so translations cannot be specified/overridden).

SUBSTRUCTURE
Menu Component

Name: menu
Class: Menu

Application Resources				
Name	Class	Type	Default	Access
XtNcenter*	XtCCenter	Boolean	TRUE	I
XtNhPad*	XtCHPad	Dimension	4	I
XtNhSpace*	XtCHSpace	Dimension	4	I
XtNlayoutType*	XtCLayoutType	OlDefine	OL_FIXEDROWS	I
XtNmeasure*	XtCMeasure	int	1	I
XtNpushpin	XtCPushpin	OlDefine	OL_NONE	I
XtNpushpinDefault	XtCPushpinDefault	Boolean	FALSE	I
XtNsameSize*	XtCSameSize	OlDefine	OL_COLUMNS	I
XtNtitle	XtCTitle	String	(widget's name)	I
XtNvPad*	XtCVPad	Dimension	4	I
XtNvSpace*	XtCVSpace	Dimension	4	I

* See the **Menu** and **ControlArea** widgets for more information on these resources.

RESOURCES

MenuButton Resource Set					
Name	Class	Type	Default	Acc	Inherit
XtNaccelerator	XtCAccelerator	String	NULL	SGI	Event
XtNacceleratorText	XtCAcceleratorText	String	(calculated)	SGI	Event
XtNancestorSensitive	XtCSensitive	Boolean	(calculated)	G[1]	Core
XtNbackground	XtCBackground	Pixel	"XtDefaultBackground"	SGI	Button
XtNbusy	XtCBusy	Boolean	FALSE	SGI	Button
XtNconsumeEvent	XtCCallback	XtCallbackList	NULL	SGI	Event
XtNdefault	XtCDefault	Boolean	FALSE	SGI	Button
XtNdestroyCallback	XtCCallback	XtCallbackList	NULL	SGI	Object
XtNfont	XtCFont	XFontStruct *	"OlDefaultFont"	SGI	Event
XtNfontColor	XtCFontColor	Pixel	"XtDefaultForeground"	SGI	Event
XtNfontGroup	XtCFontGroup	OlFontList *	NULL	SGI	Event
XtNforeground	XtCForeground	Pixel	"XtDefaultForeground"	SGI	Event
XtNheight	XtCHeight	Dimension	(calculated)	SGI	Core

MenuButton(3Olit)

MenuButton Resource Set (cont'd)					
Name	Class	Type	Default	Acc	Inherit
XtNinputFocusColor	XtCInputFocusColor	Pixel	"Red"	SGI	Event
XtNlabel	XtCLabel	String	(widget name)	SGI	Button
XtNlabelJustify	XtCLabelJustify	OlDefine	OL_LEFT	SGI	Button
XtNmenuMark	XtCMenuMark	OlDefine	(calculated)	SGI	Button
XtNmenuPane	XtCMenuPane	Widget	(n/a)	G	
XtNmnemonic	XtCMnemonic	char	NULL	SGI	Event
XtNrecomputeSize	XtCRecomputeSize	Boolean	TRUE	SGI	Button
XtNreferenceName	XtCReferenceName	String	NULL	SGI	Event
XtNreferenceWidget	XtCReferenceWidget	Widget	NULL	SGI	Event
XtNsensitive	XtCSensitive	Boolean	TRUE	G[1]	Core
XtNtraversalOn	XtCTraversalOn	Boolean	TRUE	SGI	Event
XtNuserData	XtCUserData	XtPointer	NULL	SGI	Event
XtNwidth	XtCWidth	Dimension	(calculated)	SGI	Core
XtNx	XtCPosition	Position	0	SGI	Core
XtNy	XtCPosition	Position	0	SGI	Core

[1]   Use XtSetSensitive to set this resource.

XtNdefault

Range of values:

> TRUE/"true"
> FALSE/"false"

If this resource is **TRUE**, the Border is doubled to two lines to show that the menu button contains the default choice of several buttons.

XtNlabel

This resource is a pointer to the text for the Label of the **MenuButton** widget.

XtNlabelJustify

Range of values:

> OL_LEFT/"left"
> OL_CENTER/"center"

This resource dictates whether the Label should be left-justified or centered within the widget width.

XtNmenuMark

Range of values:

> OL_DOWN/"down"
> OL_RIGHT/"right"

This resource specifies the direction of the menu arrow.

XtNmenuPane

This is the widget where menu items can be attached; its value is available once the **MenuButton** widget has been created.

XtNrecomputeSize
Range of values:
        TRUE/"true"
        FALSE/"false"

This resource indicates whether the **MenuButton** widget should calculate its size and automatically set the **XtNheight** and **XtNwidth** resources. If set to **TRUE**, the **MenuButton** widget will do normal size calculations that may cause its geometry to change. If set to **FALSE**, the **MenuButton** widget will leave its size alone; this may cause truncation of the visible image being shown by the **MenuButton** widget if the fixed size is too small, or may cause padding if the fixed size is too large. The location of the padding is determined by the **XtNlabelJustify** resource.

NOTES
The **MenuButton** widget does not support the MOTIF look and feel. To obtain a MOTIF look and feel, use **FlatButtons**(3Olit).

SEE ALSO
ControlArea(3Olit), **FlatButtons**(3Olit), **MenuShell**(3Olit)

MenuShell (3Olit)

NAME

MenuShell – create a menu not associated with a menu button

SYNOPSIS

```
#include <X11/Intrinsic.h>
#include <X11/StringDefs.h>
#include <Xol/OpenLook.h>
#include <Xol/Menu.h>

static Widget menu, menupane, w;

Arg args[1];

menu = XtCreatePopupShell(name, menuShellWidgetClass, . . .);
XtSetArg(args[0], XtNmenuPane, &menupane);
XtGetValues(menu, args, 1);

w = XtCreateWidget(name, widget-class, menupane, . . .);
```

DESCRIPTION

MenuShell versus MenuButton

The **MenuShell** widget is used to create an OPEN LOOK look and feel menu not associated with either a menu button or an abbreviated menu button. For example, a **MenuShell** widget can be attached to a button, such as an **OblongButton** widget, but this does not make the button into a menu button. However, all the features of the **MenuShell** widget (except those related to menu creation) also pertain to the MenuButton menu.

MenuShell Components

A menu contains a set of Items that are presented to the end user for selection. These are specified by the application as widgets attached to the menu. One of these Items is a Default Item. (A menu always has exactly one Default Item.) The Items are laid out in a Control Area. A menu also has a Title, a Title Separator, a Border or Window Border, and an optional Pushpin. Sometimes it also has a Drop Shadow. See Figure 1.

The application chooses the label for the Title and whether a menu has a Pushpin.

Sub-class of the Shell Widget

The **MenuShell** widget is a sub-class of the **Shell** widget. Therefore, as the SYNOPSIS shows, the **XtCreatePopupShell** routine is used to create a menu instead of the normal **XtCreateWidget**.

The following table lists the **VendorShell** resources and defaults for the OPEN LOOK Menu Shell. **MenuShell** is also a subclass of **VendorShell**.

Default Window Decorations

Resource	Type	Default
XtNmenuButton	Boolean	FALSE
XtNpushpin	OlDefine	OL_NONE
XtNresizeCorners	Boolean	FALSE
XtNwindowHeader	Boolean	TRUE

Menu Pane

The Menu Pane is not described as a separate widget in these requirements; the only interface to it for the application programmer is as a parent widget to which the widgets comprising the menu items are attached. The menu items are not attached directly to the **MenuShell** widget, since a shell widget can take only one child.

The SYNOPSIS shows how the widget ID of the Menu Pane is obtained from the **MenuShell** widget.

Connecting a Menu to a Widget

A menu can be connected to any widget, including primitive widgets. The connection is made by creating the **MenuShell** widget as a child of the other widget. Of course, being a shell widget, the **MenuShell** widget is not a normal widget-child of its parent, but a pop-up child. If the application allows it, the menu augments the parent's event list so that the popping-up of the menu is handled automatically.

Popup Control

Pressing MENU when the pointer is over the parent of the **MenuShell** widget causes the menu to be popped up. The menu is presented as a pop-up menu, where the Items are available for a press-drag-release type of selection (see below). Clicking MENU when the pointer is over the parent of the **MenuShell** widget also causes the menu to be popped up, but the menu is presented as a stay-up menu, where the Items are available for a click-move-click type of selection, instead (see below). A "slow click" (a press with a noticeable delay before the release) may show the menu as a pop-up on the press, then as a stay-up on the release.

Use of the Pushpin

The Pushpin is presented to the end user like any of the items to be selected from the menu, except that it is always the top-most item, and is presented visually as an "adornment" of the header, next to the Title (if present). The end user selects the Pushpin, pushing it in to cause the menu to remain on the display as an OPEN LOOK window or pinned menu, and pulling it out to make the menu a stay-up menu. To the end user, a pinned menu behaves indistinguishably from a command window.

The Default Item

If none of the menu items are explicitly set as the default item, the menu picks the first menu item to be the default item. If the menu contains a pushpin and no other menu item is explicitly set as the default item, the pushpin is chosen as the default item.

Components Shown when Popped Up

A pop-up or stay-up menu shows the Title, Border, Pushpin (if available), Items, and Drop Shadow. The Title is left out if the menu is from either a menu button or an abbreviated menu button. A pinned menu shows the Window Border, Title, Pushpin, Items, but no Drop Shadow.

MenuShell (3Olit)

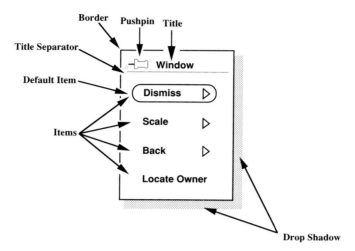

Figure 1. OPEN LOOK 2D Menu Components

Popup Position

If the menu is not from a menu button, the menu pops up so that the Default Item is vertically centered four points to the right of the pointer. If the right or bottom edge of the screen is too close to allow this placement, the menu pops up with the Drop Shadow aligned with the edge of the screen, and the mouse pointer is shifted horizontally to keep it four points from the left edge of the Default Item.

For the pop-up position when the menu is from a menu button, [see **MenuButton**(3Olit)].

Programmatic Menu Popup and Popdown

Four convenience routines are provided to programmatically control the mapping and unmapping of menus, **OlMenuPopup**, **OlMenuPositionProc**, **OlMenuPost**, and **OlMenuUnpost**.

```
void OlMenuPopup(
        Widget              menu,
        Widget              emanate,
        Cardinal            item_index,
        OlDefine            state,
        Boolean             set_position,
        Position            x,
        Position            y,
        OlMenuPositionProc  position_proc
);
```

      menu   A **MenuShell** widget ID obtained by creating a menu explicitly.

emanate   This field specifies the object that the menu is currently associated with and it is supplied to the *position_proc* when the menu positioning is done. If this field is NULL, the menu's parent object is used as the emanate object for later positioning calculations.

item_index   If emanate is a flattened widget this parameter specifies the particular item.

state   Range of values:

> `OL_PINNED_MENU`
> `OL_PRESS_DRAG_MENU`
> `OL_STAYUP_MENU`

This specifies the state the menu should be in when it visibly appears on the screen.

set_position   A Flag indicating whether the following two arguments (*x* and *y*) are used to help position the menu. If the flag is NULL the current Pointer Location is used to initialize *x* and *y*.

x y   These coordinates are used by the positioning routine. Typically, these values represent the pointer with respect to the RootWindow. For example, **xevent->xbutton.x_root** and **xevent->xbutton.y_root**. However, if the menu's state is **OL_PINNED_MENU**, these coordinates represent the desired upper-left hand corner of the pinned menu.

position_proc   Procedure called to determine the menu's position if the menu's state is either **OL_PINNED_MENU** or **OL_STAYUP_MENU**. If the menu's state is **OL_PINNED_MENU**, the position_proc value is ignored. If this procedure is NULL, the default positioning routine (that is, the one associated with the emanate widget or the menu's parent) is used.

```
void (*OlMenuPositionProc)(
        Widget    menu,
        Widget    emanate,
        Cardinal  item_index,
        OlDefine  state,
        Position  *mx,
        Position  *my,
        Position  *px,
        Position  *px
);
```

menu   **MenuShell** widget ID to be positioned.

emanate   Menu's emanate widget.

item_index   Emanate *item_index* or **OL_NO_ITEM**

state	menu's state, either **OL_PRESS_DRAG_MENU** or **OL_STAYUP_MENU**
mx	Pointer containing the menu's current x location. If the position routine wants to move the menu, it should change this value. The position routine should not move the menu explicitly.
my	Pointer containing the menu's current y location. If the position routine wants to move the menu, it should change this value. The position routine should not move the menu explicitly.
px	Represents the x location supplied to the **OlMenuPopup** routine. If the position routine changes this value, the pointer is warped to the new x location.
py	Represents the y location supplied to the **OlMenuPopup** routine. If the position routine changes this value, the pointer is warped to the new y location.

void OlMenuPost(Widget *menu***);**

This is a convenience routine that is equivalent to

```
OlMenuPopup(menu, NULL, OL_PRESS_DRAG_MENU, FALSE,
    0, 0, (OlMenuPositionProc)NULL);
```

```
void OlMenuPopdown(
    Widget      menu,
    Boolean     dismiss_pinned
);
```

This routine pops down a menu. If a menu is pinned, a value of **TRUE** for *dismiss_pinned* is required to dismiss it. If a menu does not have a pushpin or the menu is not pinned, the *dismiss_pinned* field is ignored.

void OlMenuUnpost(Widget *menu***);**

A convenience routine that is equivalent to **OlMenuPopdown(menu, TRUE)**.

Press-Drag-Release vs Click-Move-Click Selection Control

The **MenuShell** arranges for its children to respond to either the press-drag-release or the click-move-click type of selection. With the press-drag-release type of control, the user keeps MENU pressed and moves the pointer to the Item of choice; releasing MENU selects the Item and pops the menu down. If the pointer is not over an Item when MENU is released, the menu simply pops down. With the click-move-click type of control, the user moves the pointer to the Item of choice (MENU has already been released to end a click); clicking SELECT or MENU selects the Item and pops the menu down. If the pointer is not over an Item when SELECT or MENU is clicked, the menu simply pops down.

These selection methods apply to all menu items except menu buttons. For example, in Figure 1 above, Locate Owner can be selected using the methods described here. For the other items in Figure 1 (which are menu buttons), see **MenuButton**(3Olit) for the explanation of menu button selection behavior.

Converting a Stay-up Menu to a Pop-up Menu

Pressing MENU in a stay-up menu converts it to a pop-up menu. Thus the click-move-click selection control becomes a press-drag-release selection control.

Highlighting of Menu Items

In the press-drag-release type of selection control, each menu Item highlights while the pointer is over it. The form of the highlighting depends on the type of widget making up the Item. Again, the **MenuShell** widget arranges for its children to respond in this way. No highlighting occurs when the click-move-click type of selection control is used.

MenuShell Coloration

Figure 2 illustrates the resources that affect the coloration of the **MenuShell** widget.

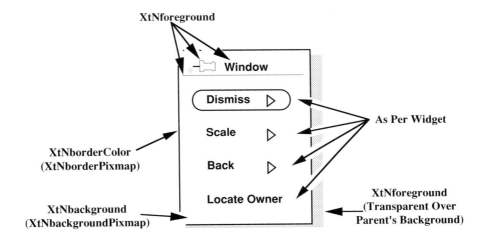

Figure 2. Menu Coloration

Keyboard Traversal

By default, all MenuShells will allow traversal among the traversable controls added to the widget.

Popping up a Menu via the keyboard is done by traversing to a MenuButton, using NEXT_FIELD, PREV_FIELD, MOVEUP, MOVEDOWN, MOVERIGHT, or LEFT, and pressing the MENUKEY key. If a Menu is attached to a control besides a MenuButton, it can be popped up by traversing to that control and pressing the MENUKEY.

Keyboard traversal within a menu can be done using the PREV_FIELD, NEXT_FIELD, MOVEUP, MOVEDOWN, MOVELEFT, and MOVERIGHT keys. The semantics of these keys depends on the position of input focus within the menu pane.

The PREV_FIELD and MOVEUP keys move the input focus to the previous menu item with keyboard traversal enabled. If the input focus is on the first item of the menu, then pressing one of these keys wraps to the last item of the menu with keyboard traversal enabled. The NEXT_FIELD, MOVEDOWN, and MOVERIGHT keys move the input focus to the next menu item with keyboard traversal enabled. If the input focus is on the last item of the menu, then pressing one of these keys wraps to the first item of the menu with keyboard traversal enabled. One exception to the action of MOVERIGHT is when input focus is on a MenuButton with **XtNmenuMark** **OL_RIGHT**. In this case, the MOVERIGHT key posts the MenuButton's menu. One exception to the action of MOVEDOWN is when input focus is on a MenuButton with **XtNmenuMark OL_DOWN**. In this case, the MOVEDOWN key posts the MenuButton's menu.

To traverse out of the menu, the following keys can be used:

CANCEL	dismisses the menu and returns focus to the originating control
NEXTWINDOW	moves to the next window in the application
PREVWINDOW	moves to the previous window in the application
NEXTAPP	moves to the first window in the next application
PREVAPP	moves to the first window in the previous application

Keyboard Operation

If input focus is on a MenuButton with in a Menu, pressing the MENUKEY will post the cascading Menu associated with the MenuButton, and input focus will be on the first Menu item with traversal enabled.

The DEFAULTACTION key will activate the default control in the **MenuShell** widget as if the user clicked the SELECT button on the control.

The MENUDEFAULTKEY can be used by the user to change the default control in the **MenuShell** widget. When the user presses the MENUDEFAULTKEY, the control which has input focus will become the default control.

The TOGGLEPUSHPIN key changes the state of the pushpin in the window header. If the pushpin is in, TOGGLEPUSHPIN will pull the pin out and dismiss the window. If the pushpin is out, TOGGLEPUSHPIN will stick the pin in.

MenuShell Activation Types

Activation Type	Expected Results
OL_CANCEL	Dismiss this menu and any other menus cascading off of it.
OL_DEFAULTACTION	Calls **OlActivateWidget** for the default item with the **activation_type** as **OL_SELECTKEY**.
OL_TOGGLEPUSHPIN	Same semantics as TOGGLEPUSHPIN above.

SUBSTRUCTURE

Menu Pane component

Application Resources				
Name	Class	Type	Default	Access
XtNcenter	XtCCenter	Boolean	TRUE	I
XtNhPad	XtCHPad	Dimension	4	I
XtNhSpace	XtCHSpace	Dimension	4	I
XtNlayoutType	XtCLayoutType	OlDefine	OL_FIXEDROWS	I
XtNmeasure	XtCMeasure	int	1	I
XtNsameSize	XtCSameSize	OlDefine	OL_COLUMNS	I
XtNvPad	XtCVPad	Dimension	4	I
XtNvSpace	XtCVSpace	Dimension	4	I

RESOURCES

MenuShell Resource Set (cont'd)					
Name	Class	Type	Default	Acc	Inherit
XtNallowShellResize	XtCAllowShellResize	Boolean	TRUE	SGI	Shell
XtNbaseHeight	XtCBaseHeight	int	XtUnspecifiedShellInt	SGI	WMShell
XtNbaseWidth	XtCBaseWidth	int	XtUnspecifiedShellInt	SGI	WMShell
XtNconsumeEvent	XtCCallback	XtCallbackList	NULL	SGI	
XtNcreatePopupChildProc	XtCCreatePopupChildProc	XtCreatePopupChildProc	NULL	SGI	Shell
XtNfocusWidget	XtCFocusWidget	Widget	NULL	SGI	VendorShell
XtNforeground	XtCForeground	Pixel	"XtDefaultForeground"	SGI	
XtNgeometry	XtCGeometry	String	NULL	GI	Shell
XtNheightInc	XtCHeightInc	int	XtUnspecifiedShellInt	SGI	WMShell
XtNinput	XtCInput	Boolean	FALSE	G	WMShell
XtNmaxAspectX	XtCMaxAspectX	int	XtUnspecifiedShellInt	SGI	WMShell
XtNmaxAspectY	XtCMaxAspectY	int	XtUnspecifiedShellInt	SGI	WMShell
XtNmaxHeight	XtCMaxHeight	int	XtUnspecifiedShellInt	SGI	WMShell
XtNmaxWidth	XtCMaxWidth	int	XtUnspecifiedShellInt	SGI	WMShell
XtNmenuAugment	XtCMenuAugment	Boolean	TRUE	GI	
XtNmenuPane	XtCMenuPane	Widget	(n/a)	G	
XtNminAspectX	XtCMinAspectX	int	XtUnspecifiedShellInt	SGI	WMShell
XtNminAspectY	XtCMinAspectY	int	XtUnspecifiedShellInt	SGI	WMShell
XtNminHeight	XtCMinHeight	int	XtUnspecifiedShellInt	SGI	WMShell
XtNminWidth	XtCMinWidth	int	XtUnspecifiedShellInt	SGI	WMShell
XtNoverrideRedirect	XtCOverrideRedirect	Boolean	TRUE	SGI	Shell
XtNpopdownCallback	XtCCallback	XtCallbackList	NULL	SGI	Shell
XtNpopupCallback	XtCCallback	XtCallbackList	NULL	SGI	Shell

<table>
<tr><th colspan="6">MenuShell Resource Set (cont'd)</th></tr>
<tr><th>Name</th><th>Class</th><th>Type</th><th>Default</th><th>Acc</th><th>Inherit</th></tr>
<tr><td>XtNpushpin</td><td>XtCPushpin</td><td>OlDefine</td><td>OL_NONE</td><td>SGI</td><td>VendorShell</td></tr>
<tr><td>XtNpushpinDefault</td><td>XtCPushpinDefault</td><td>Boolean</td><td>FALSE</td><td>SGI</td><td></td></tr>
<tr><td>XtNsaveUnder</td><td>XtCSaveUnder</td><td>Boolean</td><td>TRUE</td><td>SGI</td><td>Shell</td></tr>
<tr><td>XtNtitle</td><td>XtCTitle</td><td>String</td><td>NULL</td><td>SGI</td><td>WMShell</td></tr>
<tr><td>XtNtitleEncoding</td><td>XtCTitleEncoding</td><td>Atom</td><td>(calculated)</td><td>SGI</td><td>WMShell</td></tr>
<tr><td>XtNtransient</td><td>XtCTransient</td><td>Boolean</td><td>TRUE</td><td>SGI</td><td>WMShell</td></tr>
<tr><td>XtNtransientFor</td><td>XtCTransientFor</td><td>Widget</td><td>NULL</td><td>SGI</td><td>TransientShell</td></tr>
<tr><td>XtNuserData</td><td>XtCUserData</td><td>XtPointer</td><td>NULL</td><td>SGI</td><td>VendorShell</td></tr>
<tr><td>XtNvisual</td><td>XtCVisual</td><td>Visual *</td><td>NULL</td><td>GI</td><td>Shell</td></tr>
<tr><td>XtNwaitforwm</td><td>XtCWaitforwm</td><td>Boolean</td><td>TRUE</td><td>SGI</td><td>WMShell</td></tr>
<tr><td>XtNwidthInc</td><td>XtCWidthInc</td><td>int</td><td>XtUnspecifiedShellInt</td><td>SGI</td><td>WMShell</td></tr>
<tr><td>XtNwinGravity</td><td>XtCWinGravity</td><td>int</td><td>XtUnspecifiedShellInt</td><td>SGI</td><td>WMShell</td></tr>
<tr><td>XtNwindowGroup</td><td>XtCWindowGroup</td><td>Window</td><td>XtUnspecifiedWindow</td><td>SGI</td><td>WMShell</td></tr>
<tr><td>XtNwmProtocol</td><td>XtCCallback</td><td>XtCallbackList</td><td>NULL</td><td>SGI</td><td></td></tr>
<tr><td>XtNwmProtocolInterested</td><td>XtCWMProtocolInterested</td><td>int</td><td>(see note[9])</td><td>GI</td><td>VendorShell</td></tr>
<tr><td>XtNwmTimeout</td><td>XtCWmTimeout</td><td>int</td><td>5000</td><td>SGI</td><td>WMShell</td></tr>
</table>

[9]   Default is combination of OL_WM_DELETE_WINDOW and OL_WM_TAKE_FOCUS.

XtNfocusWidget

This is the ID of the widget to get focus the next time this shell takes focus. There-fore, as a user traverses objects via the keyboard or explicitly sets focus to an object (for example, clicking SELECT), the value of the **XtNfocusWidget** resource is updated to reflect this as the object with focus.

XtNmenuAugment

Range of values:

> TRUE/''true''
> FALSE/''false''

If this resource is **TRUE**, the **MenuShell** widget will augment its parent's event han-dling so that the pressing or clicking of MENU automatically pops up the menu. If **FALSE**, the application is responsible for detecting when the menu should be popped up. (Please see the earlier section on ''Programmatic Menu Popup and Popdown.'')

XtNmenuPane

This is the widget where menu items can be attached; its value is available once the **MenuShell** widget has been created.

XtNpushpin

Range of values:

> OL_NONE/''none''
> OL_OUT/''out''

This resource controls whether the **MenuShell** widget has a pushpin. If set to **OL_NONE**, no pushpin will be included in the list of menu items, which means the user cannot pin the menu to keep it around. If set to **OL_OUT**, a pushpin will be included as an item the user can select; if the end user selects the pushpin, the menu will be made into an OPEN LOOK window. Note that the pushpin item is always at the top of the menu list. (This resource is also available in other widgets, but with three allowed values, including **OL_IN**. This third value is not allowed for the **MenuShell** widget.)

XtNpushpinDefault
Range of values:
> **TRUE**/"**true**"
> **FALSE**/"**false**"

Setting this resource to **TRUE** makes the Pushpin the Default Item.

Note that if a menu has a pushpin and none of the menu pane items have been designated as the default, the pushpin automatically becomes the menu's Default Item.

XtNtitle
This resource gives the Title of the **MenuShell** widget.

NOTES
The **MenuShell** widget does not support the MOTIF look and feel and it does not work with Flat widgets. To obtain the MOTIF look and feel or when working with Flat widgets use **PopupMenuShell**(3Olit).

SEE ALSO
MenuButton(3Olit), **PopupMenuShell**(3Olit),
Widget_Activation/Association(3Olit)

ModalShell (3Olit)

NAME

ModalShell – create a modal window

SYNOPSIS

```
#include <X11/Intrinsic.h>
#include <X11/StringDefs.h>
#include <Xol/OpenLook.h>
#include <Xol/ModalShell.h>

#include <Xol/StaticText.h>
#include <Xol/FlatButtons.h>

Widget modal_shell, text, buttons;

modal_shell = XtCreatePopupShell("notice",
    modalShellWidgetClass, parent, NULL, 0);

text = XtVaCreateManagedWidget("text", staticTextWidgetClass,
    modal_shell, XtNstring, "File exists.  Overwrite it?",
    (String) NULL);

buttons = XtCreateManagedWidget("buttons", flatButtonsWidgetClass,
    modal_shell, NULL, 0);

XtPopup(modal_shell, XtGrabExculsive);
```

DESCRIPTION

The **ModalShell** widget is a shell widget that provides a look and feel for modal windows. A modal window is used to block all input to the rest of the application and hence create a *mode* in the application. **ModalShell** supports both the MOTIF and the OPEN LOOK look and feel.

OPEN LOOK Look and Feel

The **ModalShell** enforces the layout and size specified for the OPEN LOOK Notice window. The window is 390 points wide with 20 point margins on either side of the text. A 36 point vertical margin is used above and below the text. The controls are centered in a 390 by 36 point rectangle placed below the text area.

The **ModalShell** widget manages two children. The first child is used as the text area. Typically, this will be a **StaticText** widget, but other widgets such as a **ScrolledWindow** will allow longer messages. The second child is used as the control area and placed at the bottom of the window. Typically, this will be a **ControlArea** widget with gadget children. Use **FlatButtons** as the second child for improved performance.

MOTIF Look and Feel

In the MOTIF look and feel, the **ModalShell** widget has an additional resource to show the severity of the message.

The ModalShell lays out the children differently in the MOTIF look and feel. The maximum width of the ModalShell is 400 points. The width of the ModalShell is the greater of the width of the text and control area. The text is placed next to the glyph that indicates which type of notice is being used. The control area is centered.

Sub-class of the Transient Shell Widget

Because the **ModalShell** widget is a sub-class of the **TransientShell** widget, the **XtCreatePopupShell** routine is used to create the widget rather than the normal **XtCreateWidget**.

Popping the ModalShell Up and Down

Applications control when the ModalShell is to be displayed, or popped up. The Intrinsics function **XtPopup** is used to display the **ModalShell** widget (as shown in the SYNOPSIS). Use the **XtGrabExclusive** grab kind as the second argument to **XtPopup**. Note that the Intrinsics convenience callbacks **XtCallbackNone**, **XtCallbackNonexclusive**, and **XtCallbackExclusive** should not be used to pop-up a **ModalShell** because these callbacks set the originating button's **XtNsensitive** resource rather than **XtNbusy**.

Applications also control when the **ModalShell** widget is popped down. The callbacks for the buttons in the ModalShell must call **XtPopdown**. Popping down the ModalShell is particularly important since the ModalShell window type does not have a window header or window manager menu that is used to dismiss other types of popup windows.

Default ModalShell Action

Applications are responsible for setting a default button in the control area widget. The default action of the ModalShell is to activate the control area child.

Popup Position

The ModalShell is positioned relative to the position of the **XtNemanateWidget** and **XtNemanateItem**. When possible, the **ModalShell** does not obscure the emanate object.

Busy Button, Busy Application

When the **ModalShell** widget pops up, it "freezes" the entire application except the Modal to prevent the end user from interacting with any other part of the application. As feedback of this to the user, the **ModalShell** causes the headers of all the base windows and pop-up windows to be stippled in the "busy" pattern, and causes a stipple pattern in the **Emanate** widget. The latter stipple pattern is caused by setting the **XtNbusy** resource to **TRUE** in the **Emanate** widget. If the widget does not recognize this resource, nothing will happen.

On popping down, the **ModalShell** widget clears all stipple patterns and "unfreezes" the application.

ModalShell Appearance

The **ModalShell** is a sub-class of the **VendorShell** and sets **VendorShell** resources to obtain the appropriate style.

ModalShell (3Olit)

Default Window Decorations

Resource	Type	OPEN LOOK look Default	MOTIF look Default
XtNmenuButton	Boolean	FALSE	TRUE
XtNpushpin	OlDefine	OL_NONE	OL_NONE
XtNresizeCorners	Boolean	FALSE	TRUE
XtNwindowHeader	Boolean	FALSE	TRUE

RESOURCES

ModalShell Resource Set					
Name	Class	Type	Default	Acc	Inherit
XtNallowShellResize	XtCAllowShellResize	Boolean	TRUE	SGI	Shell
XtNbaseHeight	XtCBaseHeight	int	XtUnspecifiedShellInt	SGI	WMShell
XtNbaseWidth	XtCBaseWidth	int	XtUnspecifiedShellInt	SGI	WMShell
XtNconsumeEvent	XtCCallback	XtCallbackList	NULL	SGI	
XtNcreatePopupChildProc	XtCCreatePopupChildProc	XtCreatePopupChildProc	NULL	SGI	Shell
XtNemanateItem	XtCEmanateItem	Cardinal	OL_NO_ITEM	SGI	
XtNemanateWidget	XtCEmanateWidget	Widget	NULL	SGI	
XtNfocusWidget	XtCFocusWidget	Widget	NULL	SGI	VendorShell
XtNgeometry	XtCGeometry	String	NULL	GI	Shell
XtNheightInc	XtCHeightInc	int	XtUnspecifiedShellInt	SGI	WMShell
XtNinput	XtCInput	Boolean	FALSE	G	WMShell
XtNmaxAspectX	XtCMaxAspectX	int	XtUnspecifiedShellInt	SGI	WMShell
XtNmaxAspectY	XtCMaxAspectY	int	XtUnspecifiedShellInt	SGI	WMShell
XtNmaxHeight	XtCMaxHeight	int	XtUnspecifiedShellInt	SGI	WMShell
XtNmaxWidth	XtCMaxWidth	int	XtUnspecifiedShellInt	SGI	WMShell
XtNmenuButton	XtCMenuButton	Boolean	FALSE	GI	VendorShell
XtNmenuType	XtCMenuType	OlDefine	OL_NONE	SGI	VendorShell
XtNminAspectX	XtCMinAspectX	int	XtUnspecifiedShellInt	SGI	WMShell
XtNminAspectY	XtCMinAspectY	int	XtUnspecifiedShellInt	SGI	WMShell
XtNminHeight	XtCMinHeight	int	XtUnspecifiedShellInt	SGI	WMShell
XtNminWidth	XtCMinWidth	int	XtUnspecifiedShellInt	SGI	WMShell
XtNnoticeType	XtCNoticeType	OlDefine	OL_ERROR	SGI	
XtNoverrideRedirect	XtCOverrideRedirect	Boolean	FALSE	SGI	Shell
XtNpopdownCallback	XtCCallback	XtCallbackList	NULL	SGI	Shell
XtNpopupCallback	XtCCallback	XtCallbackList	NULL	SGI	Shell
XtNpushpin	XtCPushpin	OlDefine	OL_NONE	SGI	VendorShell
XtNresizeCorners	XtCResizeCorners	Boolean	FALSE	SGI	VendorShell
XtNsaveUnder	XtCSaveUnder	Boolean	TRUE	SGI	Shell
XtNtitle	XtCTitle	String	NULL	SGI	WMShell

ModalShell Resource Set (cont'd)					
Name	Class	Type	Default	Acc	Inherit
XtNtitleEncoding	XtCTitleEncoding	Atom	(calculated)	SGI	WMShell
XtNtransient	XtCTransient	Boolean	TRUE	SGI	WMShell
XtNtransientFor	XtCTransientFor	Widget	NULL	SGI	TransientShell
XtNuserData	XtCUserData	XtPointer	NULL	SGI	VendorShell
XtNvisual	XtCVisual	Visual *	NULL	GI	Shell
XtNwaitforwm	XtCWaitforwm	Boolean	TRUE	SGI	WMShell
XtNwidthInc	XtCWidthInc	int	XtUnspecifiedShellInt	SGI	WMShell
XtNwinGravity	XtCWinGravity	int	XtUnspecifiedShellInt	SGI	WMShell
XtNwindowGroup	XtCWindowGroup	Window	XtUnspecifiedWindow	SGI	WMShell
XtNwindowHeader	XtCWindowHeader	Boolean	FALSE	GI	VendorShell
XtNwmProtocol	XtCCallback	XtCallbackList	NULL	SGI	
XtNwmProtocolInterested	XtCWMProtocolInterested	int	(see note[9])	GI	VendorShell
XtNwmTimeout	XtCWmTimeout	int	5000	SGI	WMShell

[9]   Default is combination of **OL_WM_DELETE_WINDOW** and **OL_WM_TAKE_FOCUS**.

XtNemanateWidget
Range of values:
> (ID of existing widget)

This resource identifies the emanate widget. The emanate widget is used to position the ModalShell so that it does not obscure this widget.

XtNemanateItem
Range of values:
> $0 <=$ **XtNemanateItem** $<=$ **XtNemanateWidget**'s **XtNnumItems**

> or

> **OL_NO_ITEM**

This resource is used when the **XtNemanateWidget** is a **Flat** widget. The position of the ModalShell is calculated based on the geometry of the given emanate widget and emanate item so that the ModalShell does not obscure the item.

XtNnoticeType
Range of values:
> OL_ERROR/''error''
> OL_INFORMATION/''information''
> OL_QUESTION/''question''
> OL_WARNING/''warning''
> OL_WORKING/''working''

This resource affects the appearance of the ModalShell in the MOTIF look and feel. The specifies the symbol, window title (set via the **XtNtitle** resource), and buttons that should be created for each type of message. The ModalShell will take care of drawing the appropriate symbol to the left of the first child of the ModalShell. The ModalShell buttons and title must be created/set by the application. The following table gives the guidelines.

ModalShell (3Olit)

Dialog Type	Symbol	Title	Buttons
OL_ERROR	error symbol	"Error Dialog"	OK, Cancel
OL_INFORMATION	information symbol	"Information Dialog"	OK
OL_QUESTION	question mark	"Question Dialog"	Yes, No (*or* OK, Cancel) (*or* OK, Cancel)
OL_WARNING	exclamation point	"Warning Dialog"	OK, Cancel
OL_WORKING	timer	"Work-in-progress Dialog"	OK, Cancel

SEE ALSO

ControlArea(3Olit), FlatButtons(3Olit), Notice(3Olit), ScrolledWindow(3Olit), StaticText(3Olit), Shell(3Olit)

NAME

Nonexclusives – allow selection of one or more choices

SYNOPSIS

```
#include <X11/Intrinsic.h>
#include <X11/StringDefs.h>
#include <Xol/OpenLook.h>
#include <Xol/Nonexclusi.h>

widget = XtCreateWidget(name, nonexclusivesWidgetClass, ...);
```

DESCRIPTION

The Nonexclusives widget provides a simple way to build a several-of-many button selection object. It manages a set of rectangular buttons or check boxes, providing layout management and selection control.

Grid Layout and Button Labels

The Nonexclusives widget lays out the rectangular buttons or check boxes in a grid in the order they created. The number of rows or columns in this grid can be controlled by the application. If the grid has more than one row, the Nonexclusives widget forces the rectangular buttons or check boxes in each column to be the same size as the widest in the column. (Note: If the grid is a single row, each button will be only as wide as necessary to display the label.)

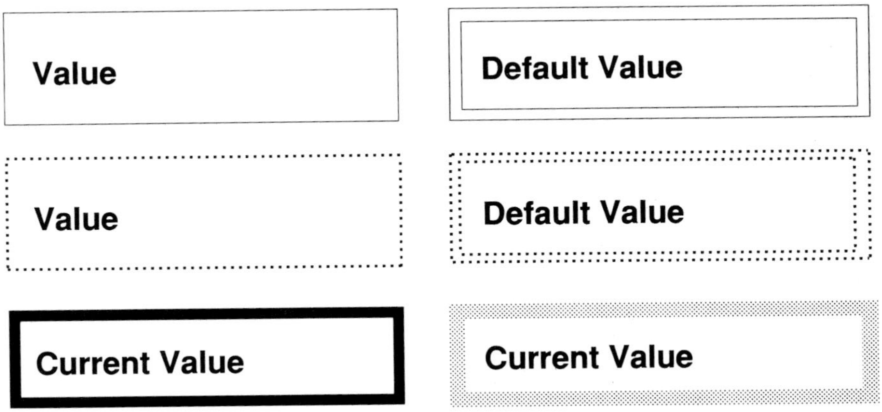

Figure 1. Example of Nonexclusive Buttons

Use in a Menu

The Nonexclusives widget can be added as a single child to a menu pane to implement a several-of-many menu choice. Only RectButton widgets can be used in a Nonexclusives widget in a menu.

Nonexclusives (3Olit)

Child Constraint

The **Nonexclusives** widget constrains its child widgets to be of class **rectButtonWidgetClass** or **checkBoxWidgetClass**. Additionally, all the child widgets must be of the same class.

Nonexclusives Coloration

Any space not colored by the Nonexclusives's children is colored according to the **XtNbackground** or **XtNbackgroundPixmap** resources.

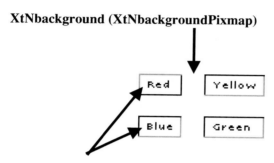

XtNbackground (XtNbackgroundPixmap)

Child Widgets Colored Independently

Figure 2. 3D Nonexclusive Buttons Coloration

Keyboard Traversal

The **Nonexclusives** widget manages the traversal between a set of RectButtons or Checkboxes. When the user traverses to a **Nonexclusives** widget, the first child in the set will receive input focus. The MOVEUP, MOVEDOWN, MOVERIGHT, and MOVELEFT keys move the input focus between the children. To traverse out of the Nonexclusives widget, the following keys can be used:

NEXT_FIELD	moves to the next traversable widget in the window
PREV_FIELD	moves to the previous traversable widget in the window
NEXTWINDOW	moves to the next window in the application.
PREVWINDOW	moves to the previous window in the application.
NEXTAPP	moves to the first window in the next application.
PREVAPP	moves to the first window in the previous application.

These controls have two states: "set" and "not set". Pressing the SELECTKEY on a nonexclusive control will toggle the current state. If the control is in a Menu, then the MENUKEY will also toggle the current state. If the control is "set", then toggling the control will call the **XtNunselect** callback list. If the control is "not set", then toggling the control will call the **XtNselect** callback list.

RESOURCES

Nonexclusives Resource Set					
Name	Class	Type	Default	Acc	Inherit
XtNancestorSensitive	XtCSensitive	Boolean	(calculated)	G[1]	Core
XtNbackground	XtCBackground	Pixel	"XtDefaultBackground"	SGI	Core
XtNbackgroundPixmap	XtCPixmap	Pixmap	XtUnspecifiedPixmap	SGI	Core
XtNchildren	XtCReadOnly	WidgetList	NULL	G	Composite
XtNcolormap	XtCColormap	Colormap	(parent's)	GI	Core
XtNconsumeEvent	XtCCallback	XtCallbackList	NULL	SGI	Manager
XtNdepth	XtCDepth	Cardinal	(parent's)	GI	Core
XtNdestroyCallback	XtCCallback	XtCallbackList	NULL	SGI	Object
XtNheight	XtCHeight	Dimension	(calculated)	SGI	Core
XtNinsertPosition	XtCInsertPosition	XtWidgetProc	NULL	SGI	Composite
XtNlayoutType	XtCLayoutType	OlDefine	OL_FIXEDROWS	SGI	
XtNmappedWhenManaged	XtCMappedWhenManaged	Boolean	TRUE	SGI	Core
XtNmeasure	XtCMeasure	int	1	SGI	
XtNnumChildren	XtCReadOnly	Cardinal	0	G	Composite
XtNrecomputeSize	XtCRecomputeSize	Boolean	TRUE	SGI	
XtNreferenceName	XtCReferenceName	String	NULL	SGI	Manager
XtNreferenceWidget	XtCReferenceWidget	Widget	NULL	SGI	Manager
XtNscreen	XtCScreen	Screen *	(parent's)	GI	Core
XtNsensitive	XtCSensitive	Boolean	TRUE	G[1]	Core
XtNtranslations	XtCTranslations	XtTranslations	NULL	SGI	Core
XtNtraversalOn	XtCTraversalOn	Boolean	TRUE	SGI	Manager
XtNuserData	XtCUserData	XtPointer	NULL	SGI	Manager
XtNwidth	XtCWidth	Dimension	(calculated)	SGI	Core
XtNx	XtCPosition	Position	0	SGI	Core
XtNy	XtCPosition	Position	0	SGI	Core

[1]   Use XtSetSensitive to set this resource.

XtNlayoutType

Range of values:

        OL_FIXEDROWS/''fixedrows''
        OL_FIXEDCOLS/''fixedcols''

This resource controls the type of layout of the child widgets by the **Nonexclusives** composite. The choices are to specify the number of rows or the number of columns. Only one of these dimensions can be specified directly; the other is determined by the number of child widgets added, and will always be enough to show all the child widgets.

The values of the **XtNlayoutType** resource can be

OL_FIXEDROWS   if the layout should have a fixed number of rows;

OL_FIXEDCOLS   if the layout should have a fixed number of columns.

XtNmeasure

Range of values:

$0 <$ XtNmeasure

This resource gives the number of rows or columns in the layout of the child widgets. If there are not enough child widgets to fill a row or column, the remaining space is left blank.

NOTES

To obtain a MOTIF look and feel, use **FlatNonexclusives** widgets.

SEE ALSO

FlatNonexclusives(3Olit), **RectButton**(3Olit)

NAME

NoticeShell – create a message area for user confirmation

SYNOPSIS

```
#include <X11/Intrinsic.h>
#include <X11/StringDefs.h>
#include <Xol/OpenLook.h>
#include <Xol/Notice.h>

static Widget notice, textarea, controlarea, w;

Arg args[2];

notice = XtCreatePopupShell(name, noticeShellWidgetClass, . . .);
XtSetArg(args[0], XtNtextArea, &textarea);
XtSetArg(args[1], XtNcontrolArea, &controlarea);
XtGetValues(notice, args, 2);

w = XtCreateWidget(name, widget-class, controlarea, . . .);
   .
   .
   .
XtPopup(notice, XtGrabExclusive);
```

DESCRIPTION

The **NoticeShell** widget creates a message area for user confirmation in both the MOTIF and the OPEN LOOK look and feel. When in the MOTIF look and feel, the Notice box has an additional resource to indicate the severity of the message.

Notice Components

The **Notice** widget has three components:

> Text Area where the message to the end user is displayed;

> Control Area containing one or more widgets that the end user uses to control how to continue with an application; and

> Default Button.

Another important element is the **Emanate** widget, which is typically the control activated by the end user that requires immediate attention. The application identifies the **Emanate** widget to the **Notice** widget.

NoticeShell (3Olit)

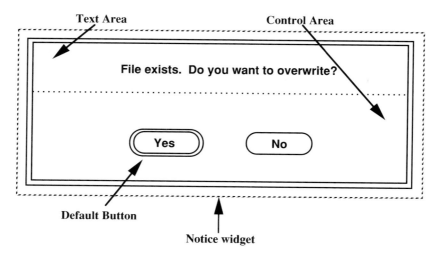

Figure 1. Notice Widget

Sub-class of the Shell Widget

The **Notice** widget is a sub-class of the **Shell** widget. Therefore, as the SYNOPSIS shows, the **XtCreatePopupShell** routine is used to create a notice instead of the normal **XtCreateWidget**.

The following table lists the **VendorShell** resources and defaults for the **Notice**. The **Notice** is a subclass of the **VendorShell**.

Default Window Decorations

Resource	Type	OPEN LOOK style Default	MOTIF style Default
XtNmenuButton	Boolean	FALSE	TRUE
XtNpushpin	OlDefine	OL_NONE	OL_NONE
XtNresizeCorners	Boolean	FALSE	TRUE
XtNwindowHeader	Boolean	FALSE	TRUE

Popping the Notice Up/Down

The application controls when the **Notice** widget is to be displayed or popped up. As shown in the SYNOPSIS, the **XtPopup** routine can be used for this. However, the application does not need to control when the **Notice** widget is to be popped down. The widget itself detects when to pop down: the end user clicks SELECT on an **OblongButton** widget in the Control Area. This behavior requires that there be at least one **OblongButton** widget in the Control Area. If other types of controls are used instead, the application can "manually" pop the notice down using a routine such as **XtPopdown**.

Busy Button, Busy Application

When the **Notice** widget pops up, it "freezes" the entire application except the Notice to prevent the end user from interacting with any other part of the application. As feedback of this to the user, the **Notice** causes the headers of all the base windows and pop-up windows to be stippled in the "busy" pattern, and causes a stipple pattern in the **Emanate** widget. The latter stipple pattern is caused by setting the **XtNbusy** resource to **TRUE** in the **Emanate** widget. If the widget does not recognize this resource, nothing will happen.

On popping down, the **Notice** widget clears all stipple patterns and "unfreezes" the application.

Text and Control Areas

The Text and Control Areas are handled by separate widget interfaces. The SYNOPSIS shows how the widget IDs of the Text Area (**textarea**) and the Control Area (**controlarea**) are obtained from the **Notice** widget.

The Text and Control Areas abut so that there is no space between the two. An application can control the distance between the text and the controls by setting margins in the Control Area.

Notice Coloration

Figure 2 illustrates the resources that affect the coloration of the **Notice** widget.

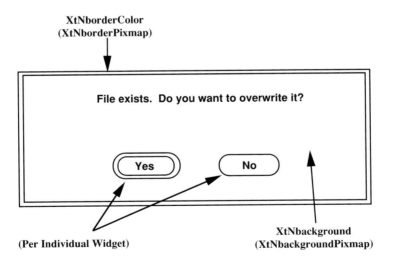

Figure 2. Notice Coloration

NoticeShell (3Olit)

Keyboard Traversal

The **Notice** widget limits keyboard traversal of the application to the buttons within the Control Area. The user can traverse between the controls in the Control Area using the NEXT_FIELD, PREV_FIELD, MOVEUP, MOVEDOWN, MOVERIGHT, and MOVELEFT keys. The NEXTAPP key will traverse to the next application, and the PREVAPP key will traverse to the the previous application, but the NEXTWINDOW and PREVWINDOW keys are disabled within the **Notice**'s application. When keyboard traversal is used to move back to the Notice's application, focus goes to the Notice.

Notice Activation Types

Activation Type	Expected Results
OL_CANCEL	Beep
OL_DEFAULTACTION	Call **OlActivateWidget** for the default widget with parameter **OL_SELECTKEY**

SUBSTRUCTURE

Control Area component

Name: controlarea
Class: **ControlArea**

Application Resources				
Name	Class	Type	Default	Access
XtNhPad	XtCHPad	Dimension	0	I
XtNhSpace	XtCHSpace	Dimension	4	I
XtNlayoutType	XtCLayoutType	OlDefine	OL_FIXEDROWS	I
XtNmeasure	XtCMeasure	int	1	I
XtNsameSize	XtCSameSize	OlDefine	OL_COLUMNS	I
XtNvPad	XtCVPad	Dimension	0	I
XtNvSpace	XtCVSpace	Dimension	4	I

See the **ControlArea** widget for the descriptions of these resources.

Text Area component

Name: **textarea**
Class: **StaticText**

<table>
<tr><th colspan="5" align="center">Application Resources</th></tr>
<tr><th>Name</th><th>Class</th><th>Type</th><th>Default</th><th>Access</th></tr>
<tr><td>XtNalignment</td><td>XtCAlignment</td><td>OlDefine</td><td>OL_LEFT</td><td>I</td></tr>
<tr><td>XtNfont</td><td>XtCFont</td><td>XFontStruct *</td><td>(OPEN LOOK font)</td><td>SGI</td></tr>
<tr><td>XtNfontColor</td><td>XtCFontColor</td><td>Pixel</td><td>XtDefaultForeground</td><td>SGI</td></tr>
<tr><td>XtNfontGroup</td><td>XtCFontGroup</td><td>OlFontList</td><td>NULL</td><td>GI</td></tr>
<tr><td>XtNlineSpace</td><td>XtCLineSpace</td><td>int</td><td>0</td><td>I</td></tr>
<tr><td>XtNstring</td><td>XtCString</td><td>String</td><td>NULL</td><td>I</td></tr>
<tr><td>XtNstrip</td><td>XtCStrip</td><td>Boolean</td><td>TRUE</td><td>I</td></tr>
<tr><td>XtNwrap</td><td>XtCWrap</td><td>Boolean</td><td>TRUE</td><td>I</td></tr>
</table>

See the **StaticText** widget for the descriptions of these resources.

RESOURCES

<table>
<tr><th colspan="6" align="center">NoticeShell Resource Set</th></tr>
<tr><th>Name</th><th>Class</th><th>Type</th><th>Default</th><th>Acc</th><th>Inherit</th></tr>
<tr><td>XtNallowShellResize</td><td>XtCAllowShellResize</td><td>Boolean</td><td>TRUE</td><td>SGI</td><td>Shell</td></tr>
<tr><td>XtNbaseHeight</td><td>XtCBaseHeight</td><td>int</td><td>XtUnspecifiedShellInt</td><td>SGI</td><td>WMShell</td></tr>
<tr><td>XtNbaseWidth</td><td>XtCBaseWidth</td><td>int</td><td>XtUnspecifiedShellInt</td><td>SGI</td><td>WMShell</td></tr>
<tr><td>XtNconsumeEvent</td><td>XtCCallback</td><td>XtCallbackList</td><td>NULL</td><td>SGI</td><td></td></tr>
<tr><td>XtNcontrolArea</td><td>XtCControlArea</td><td>Widget</td><td>NULL</td><td>G</td><td></td></tr>
<tr><td>XtNcreatePopupChildProc</td><td>XtCCreatePopupChildProc</td><td>XtCreatePopupChildProc</td><td>NULL</td><td>SGI</td><td>Shell</td></tr>
<tr><td>XtNemanateItem</td><td>XtCEmanateItem</td><td>Cardinal</td><td>OL_NO_ITEM</td><td>SGI</td><td></td></tr>
<tr><td>XtNemanateWidget</td><td>XtCEmanateWidget</td><td>Widget</td><td>NULL</td><td>SGI</td><td>ModalShell</td></tr>
<tr><td>XtNfocusWidget</td><td>XtCFocusWidget</td><td>Widget</td><td>NULL</td><td>SGI</td><td>VendorShell</td></tr>
<tr><td>XtNgeometry</td><td>XtCGeometry</td><td>String</td><td>NULL</td><td>GI</td><td>Shell</td></tr>
<tr><td>XtNheightInc</td><td>XtCHeightInc</td><td>int</td><td>XtUnspecifiedShellInt</td><td>SGI</td><td>WMShell</td></tr>
<tr><td>XtNinput</td><td>XtCInput</td><td>Boolean</td><td>FALSE</td><td>G</td><td>WMShell</td></tr>
<tr><td>XtNmaxAspectX</td><td>XtCMaxAspectX</td><td>int</td><td>XtUnspecifiedShellInt</td><td>SGI</td><td>WMShell</td></tr>
<tr><td>XtNmaxAspectY</td><td>XtCMaxAspectY</td><td>int</td><td>XtUnspecifiedShellInt</td><td>SGI</td><td>WMShell</td></tr>
<tr><td>XtNmaxHeight</td><td>XtCMaxHeight</td><td>int</td><td>XtUnspecifiedShellInt</td><td>SGI</td><td>WMShell</td></tr>
<tr><td>XtNmaxWidth</td><td>XtCMaxWidth</td><td>int</td><td>XtUnspecifiedShellInt</td><td>SGI</td><td>WMShell</td></tr>
<tr><td>XtNmenuButton</td><td>XtCMenuButton</td><td>Boolean</td><td>FALSE</td><td>GI</td><td>VendorShell</td></tr>
<tr><td>XtNmenuType</td><td>XtCMenuType</td><td>OlDefine</td><td>OL_NONE</td><td>SGI</td><td>VendorShell</td></tr>
<tr><td>XtNminAspectX</td><td>XtCMinAspectX</td><td>int</td><td>XtUnspecifiedShellInt</td><td>SGI</td><td>WMShell</td></tr>
<tr><td>XtNminAspectY</td><td>XtCMinAspectY</td><td>int</td><td>XtUnspecifiedShellInt</td><td>SGI</td><td>WMShell</td></tr>
<tr><td>XtNminHeight</td><td>XtCMinHeight</td><td>int</td><td>XtUnspecifiedShellInt</td><td>SGI</td><td>WMShell</td></tr>
<tr><td>XtNminWidth</td><td>XtCMinWidth</td><td>int</td><td>XtUnspecifiedShellInt</td><td>SGI</td><td>WMShell</td></tr>
<tr><td>XtNnoticeType</td><td>XtCNoticeType</td><td>OlDefine</td><td>OL_ERROR</td><td>SGI</td><td>ModalShell</td></tr>
<tr><td>XtNoverrideRedirect</td><td>XtCOverrideRedirect</td><td>Boolean</td><td>FALSE</td><td>SGI</td><td>Shell</td></tr>
<tr><td>XtNpopdownCallback</td><td>XtCCallback</td><td>XtCallbackList</td><td>NULL</td><td>SGI</td><td>Shell</td></tr>
</table>

NoticeShell (3Olit)

NoticeShell Resource Set (cont'd)					
Name	Class	Type	Default	Acc	Inherit
XtNpopupCallback	XtCCallback	XtCallbackList	NULL	SGI	Shell
XtNpushpin	XtCPushpin	OlDefine	OL_NONE	SGI	VendorShell
XtNresizeCorners	XtCResizeCorners	Boolean	FALSE	SGI	VendorShell
XtNsaveUnder	XtCSaveUnder	Boolean	TRUE	SGI	Shell
XtNtextArea	XtCTextArea	Widget	NULL	G	
XtNtitle	XtCTitle	String	NULL	SGI	WMShell
XtNtitleEncoding	XtCTitleEncoding	Atom	(calculated)	SGI	WMShell
XtNtransient	XtCTransient	Boolean	TRUE	SGI	WMShell
XtNtransientFor	XtCTransientFor	Widget	NULL	SGI	TransientShell
XtNuserData	XtCUserData	XtPointer	NULL	SGI	VendorShell
XtNvisual	XtCVisual	Visual *	NULL	GI	Shell
XtNwaitforwm	XtCWaitforwm	Boolean	TRUE	SGI	WMShell
XtNwidthInc	XtCWidthInc	int	XtUnspecifiedShellInt	SGI	WMShell
XtNwinGravity	XtCWinGravity	int	XtUnspecifiedShellInt	SGI	WMShell
XtNwindowGroup	XtCWindowGroup	Window	XtUnspecifiedWindow	SGI	WMShell
XtNwindowHeader	XtCWindowHeader	Boolean	FALSE	GI	VendorShell
XtNwmProtocol	XtCCallback	XtCallbackList	NULL	SGI	
XtNwmProtocolInterested	XtCWMProtocolInterested	int	(see note[9])	GI	VendorShell
XtNwmTimeout	XtCWmTimeout	int	5000	SGI	WMShell

[9]   Default is combination of OL_WM_DELETE_WINDOW and OL_WM_TAKE_FOCUS.

XtNcontrolArea

This is the widget ID of the **ControlArea** class composite child widget where controls can be attached; its value is available once the **Notice** widget has been created.

Any widgets of the class **OblongButton** added to the Control Area are assumed to be window disposition controls; that is, when the end user activates one of them, the **Notice** widget pops itself down.

XtNemanateItem

Range of values:

        0 <= **XtNemanateItem** <= **XtNemanateWidget**'s **XtNnumItems**

    or

    OL_NO_ITEM

This resource is used when the **XtNemanateWidget** is a **Flat** widget. The position of the Notice is calculated based on the geometry of the given emanate widget and emanate item so that the Notice does not obscure the item.

XtNemanateWidget

Range of values:

    (ID of existing widget)

This resource identifies the **Emanate** widget. On popping up, the **Notice** widget attempts to set this widget to be busy, by making its **XtNbusy** resource **TRUE**; if the widget doesn't recognize the resource, nothing happens. On popping down, the **Notice** widget clears the **XtNbusy** resource.

When the **Notice** widget pops up, it tries not to cover this widget; this may fail depending on its location and the size of the **Notice** widget.

The default for this resource is the parent. The parent, however, cannot be a Gadget (OblongButtonGadget, for instance). To emanate a Notice from a Gadget, specify another widget as the parent and set **XtNemanateWidget** to the Gadget.

XtNnoticeType
Range of values:
```
OL_ERROR/"error"
OL_INFORMATION/"information"
OL_QUESTION/"question"
OL_WARNING/"warning"
OL_WORKING/"working"
```

This resource affects the appearance of the Notice when in the MOTIF look and feel. The specifies the symbol, window title (set via the **XtNtitle** resource), and buttons that should be created for each type of message. The Notice will take care of drawing the appropriate symbol to the left of the **XtNtextArea** widget of the Notice. The Notice buttons and title must be created/set by the application. The following table gives the guidelines.

Dialog Type	Symbol	Title	Buttons
OL_ERRORerror	symbol	"Error Dialog"	OK, Cancel
OL_INFORMATION	information symbol	"Information Dialog"	OK
OL_QUESTION	question mark	"Question Dialog"	Yes, No (*or* OK, Cancel)
OL_WARNING	exclamation point	"Warning Dialog"	OK, Cancel
OL_WORKING	timer	"Work-in-progress Dialog"	OK, Cancel

XtNtextArea
This is the widget ID of the **StaticText** class child widget that controls the Text Area; its value is available once the **Notice** widget has been created.

SEE ALSO
ControlArea(3Olit), **OblongButton**(3Olit), **ModalShell**(3Olit), **StaticText**(3Olit)

OblongButton (3Olit)

NAME

OblongButton – execute a command with a one-choice element or button

SYNOPSIS

```
#include <X11/Intrinsic.h>
#include <X11/OpenLook.h>
#include <Xol/StringDefs.h>
#include <Xol/OblongButt.h>

widget = XtCreateWidget(name, oblongButtonWidgetClass, . . .);
```

OR

```
widget = XtCreateWidget(name, oblongButtonGadgetClass, . . .);
```

DESCRIPTION

The OblongButton widget creates an OPEN LOOK look and feel oblong button.

OblongButton Components

The OblongButton consists of a Label surrounded by a rounded oblong Border.

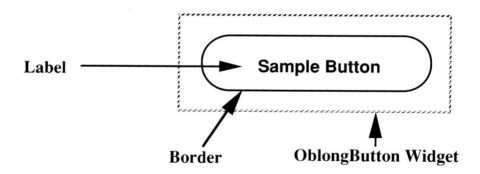

Figure 1. Oblong Buttons

Busy Button while Action Takes Place

Each OblongButton is associated with an application-defined action implemented as a list of callbacks. To let the end user know that an action is still taking place, the OblongButton stipples the area inside the border before issuing the callbacks. When the last callback returns, the OblongButton restores its original appearance. If the application's action continues to be "busy" after the callbacks return, the application should set the XtNbusy resource to TRUE before returning from the callbacks, then reset it to FALSE when the action is no longer taking place.

The "busy" stipple pattern is designed to show enough dots to gray the button noticeably, while still leaving a text label legible.

Oblong Buttons in a Pop-up Menu

Entering an oblong button while MENU is depressed previews the set appearance of the button. Releasing MENU then restores the original appearance and invokes the action for the button as described above. Leaving the button before releasing MENU restores the appearance but does not invoke the action.

Oblong Buttons not in a Pop-up Menu

Clicking SELECT on an oblong button starts the action associated with the button. Pressing SELECT, or moving the pointer into the button while SELECT is pressed, previews the set appearance of the button. Releasing SELECT restores the appearance and invokes the action for the button as described above. Moving the pointer off the button before releasing SELECT also restores the appearance, but does not invoke the action.

If the oblong button is in a stay-up menu, clicking or pressing MENU works the same as SELECT. If the oblong button is not in a stay-up (or pop-up) menu, clicking or pressing MENU does not do anything.

OblongButton Gadgets

`OblongButton` gadgets cannot be parents (that is, be used as the parent parameter when creating a widget or other gadget).

Correct button behavior is not guaranteed if gadgets are positioned so that they overlap.

Gadgets share some core fields but, since they are not subclasses of Core, do not have all Core fields. In particular, they don't have a name field or a translation field (so translations cannot be

Note that events that occur outside the Border (but within the `OblongButton` widget) are still in the domain of the button. specified/overriden).

Event Handlers cannot be added to gadgets using `XtAddEventHandler`.

Label Appearance

The `XtNwidth`, `XtNheight`, `XtNrecomputeSize`, and `XtNlabelJustify` resources interact to produce a truncated, clipped, centered, or left-justified label as shown in Figure 3.

XtNwidth	XtNrecomputeSize	XtNlabelJustify	Result
any value	TRUE	any	Just Fits
> needed for label	FALSE	OL_LEFT	Left Justified
> needed for label	FALSE	OL_CENTER	Centered
< needed for label	FALSE	any	Trunc

XtNheight	XtNrecomputeSize	XtNlabelJustify	Result
any value	TRUE	any	Just Fits
> needed for label	FALSE	any	Centered
< needed for label	FALSE	any	**Clipped**

Figure 3. Label Appearance

When the label is centered or left-justified, the extra space is filled with the background color of the **OblongButton** widget, as determined by the **XtNbackground** and **XtNbackgroundPixmap** resources.

When a text label is truncated, the truncation occurs at a character boundary and a solid triangle is inserted to show that part of the label is missing. The triangle requires that more of the label be truncated than would otherwise be necessary. If the width of the button is too small to show even one character with the triangle, only the triangle is shown. If the width is so small that the entire triangle cannot be shown, the triangle is clipped on the right.

An image label is simply truncated; no triangle is shown.

Also see the **XtNlabelTile** resource for how it affects the appearance of a label image.

OblongButton Coloration

Figure 2 illustrates the resources that affect the coloration of the **OblongButton** widget.

On a monochrome display, the **OblongButton** widget indicates that it has input focus by inverting the foreground and background colors of the control.

On color displays, when the **OblongButton** widget receives the input focus, the background color is changed to the input focus color set in the **XtNinput-FocusColor** resource.

EXCEPTIONS:

If the input focus color is the same as the font color for the control labels, then the coloration of the active control and fonts is inverted.

If the input focus color is the same as the Input Window Header Color and the active control is in the window header, then the colors are inverted.

If the input focus color is the same as the window background color, then the **OblongButton** widget inverts the foreground and background colors when it has input focus.

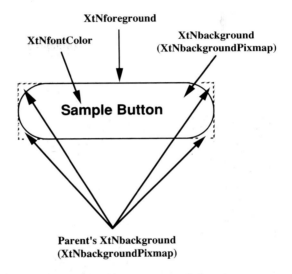

Figure 2. Oblong Button Coloration

Keyboard Traversal

The default value of the **XtNtraversalOn** resource is **TRUE**.

The **OblongButton** widget responds to the following keyboard navigation keys:

NEXT_FIELD MOVEDOWN MOVERIGHT	move to the next traversable widget in the window
PREV_FIELD MOVEUP MOVELEFT	move to the previous traversable widget in the window
NEXTWINDOW	moves to the next window in the application

OblongButton (3Olit)

PREVWINDOW	moves to the previous window in the application
NEXTAPP	moves to the first window in the next application
PREVAPP	moves to the first window in the previous application

The **OblongButton** will respond to the SELECTKEY by acting as if the SELECT buttons had been clicked.

Oblong Button/Gadget Activation Types

Activation Type	Expected Results
OL_MENUDEFAULTKEY	Set the sub-object as the shell's default object (if on a menu)
OL_SELECTKEY	Call its callbacks

Display of Keyboard Mnemonic

The **OblongButton** widget displays the mnemonic accelerator as part of its label. If the mnemonic character is in the label, then that character is displayed or highlighted according to the If the mnemonic character is not in the label, value of the application resource **XtNshowMneumonics**. it is displayed to the right of the label in parenthesis and displayed or highlighted according to the value of the application resource **XtNshowMneumonics**.

If truncation is necessary, the mnemonic displayed in parenthesis is truncated as a unit.

Display of Keyboard Accelerators

The **OblongButton** widget displays the keyboard accelerator as part of its label. The string in the **XtNacceleratorText** resource is displayed to the right of the label (or mnemonic) separated by at least one space. The acceleratorText is right justified.

If truncation is necessary, the accelerator is truncated as a unit. The accelerator is truncated before the mnemonic or the label.

RESOURCES

OblongButton Resource Set

Name	Class	Type	Default	Acc	Inherit
XtNaccelerator	XtCAccelerator	String	NULL	SGI	Event
XtNacceleratorText	XtCAcceleratorText	String	(calculated)	SGI	Event
XtNancestorSensitive	XtCSensitive	Boolean	(calculated)	G[1]	Core
XtNbackground	XtCBackground	Pixel	"XtDefaultBackground"	SGI	Button
XtNbusy	XtCBusy	Boolean	FALSE	SGI	Button
XtNconsumeEvent	XtCCallback	XtCallbackList	NULL	SGI	Event
XtNdefault	XtCDefault	Boolean	FALSE	SGI	Button
XtNdestroyCallback	XtCCallback	XtCallbackList	NULL	SGI	Object
XtNfont	XtCFont	XFontStruct *	"OlDefaultFont"	SGI	Event
XtNfontColor	XtCFontColor	Pixel	"XtDefaultForeground"	SGI	Event
XtNfontGroup	XtCFontGroup	OlFontList *	NULL	SGI	Event

OblongButton Resource Set (cont'd)					
Name	Class	Type	Default	Acc	Inherit
XtNforeground	XtCForeground	Pixel	"XtDefaultForeground"	SGI	Event
XtNheight	XtCHeight	Dimension	(calculated)	SGI	Core
XtNinputFocusColor	XtCInputFocusColor	Pixel	"Red"	SGI	Event
XtNlabel	XtCLabel	String	(widget name)	SGI	Button
XtNlabelImage	XtCLabelImage	XImage *	NULL	SGI	Button
XtNlabelJustify	XtCLabelJustify	OlDefine	OL_LEFT	SGI	Button
XtNlabelTile	XtCLabelTile	Boolean	FALSE	SGI	Button
XtNlabelType	XtCLabelType	OlDefine	OL_STRING	SGI	Button
XtNmnemonic	XtCMnemonic	char	NULL	SGI	Event
XtNrecomputeSize	XtCRecomputeSize	Boolean	TRUE	SGI	Button
XtNreferenceName	XtCReferenceName	String	NULL	SGI	Event
XtNreferenceWidget	XtCReferenceWidget	Widget	NULL	SGI	Event
XtNselect	XtCCallback	XtCallbackList	NULL	SGI	Button
XtNsensitive	XtCSensitive	Boolean	TRUE	G[1]	Core
XtNtraversalOn	XtCTraversalOn	Boolean	TRUE	SGI	Event
XtNuserData	XtCUserData	XtPointer	NULL	SGI	Event
XtNwidth	XtCWidth	Dimension	(calculated)	SGI	Core
XtNx	XtCPosition	Position	0	SGI	Core
XtNy	XtCPosition	Position	0	SGI	Core

[1]   Use XtSetSensitive to set this resource.

XtNbusy
Range of values:
> TRUE/"true"
> FALSE/"false"

This resource controls whether the button interior should be stippled to show that the action associated with the button is "busy." While **XtNbusy** is **TRUE**, the system will beep if the end user attempts to select the button; the attempt is refused and no callbacks are invoked.

XtNdefault
Range of values:
> TRUE/"true"
> FALSE/"false"

If this resource is **TRUE**, and the button is in a menu, an oval ring is drawn around the button to show that the button is the default choice of one or more buttons.

XtNlabel
This resource is a pointer to the text for the Label. This resource is ignored if the **XtNlabelType** resource has the value **OL_IMAGE**.

XtNlabelImage
This resource is a pointer to the image for the Label. This resource is ignored unless the **XtNlabelType** resource has the value **OL_IMAGE**.

If the image is of type **XYBitmap**, the image is highlighted when appropriate by reversing the 0 and 1 values of each pixel (that is, by "'xor'ing" the image data). If the image is of type **XYPixmap** or **ZPixmap**, the image is not highlighted, although the space around the image inside the Border is highlighted.

If the image is smaller than the space available for it inside the Border and **XtNlabelTile** is **FALSE**, the image is centered vertically and either centered or left-justified horizontally, depending on the value of the **XtNlabelJustify** resource. If the image is larger than the space available for it, it is clipped so that it does not stray outside the Border. If the **XtNdefault** resource is **TRUE** so that the Border is doubled, the space available is that inside the inner line of the Border.

XtNlabelJustify
Range of values:

    OL_LEFT/"left"
    OL_CENTER/"center"

This resource dictates whether the Label should be left-justified or centered within the widget width.

XtNlabelTile
Range of values:

    TRUE/"true"
    FALSE/"false"

This resource augments the **XtNlabelImage/XtNlabelPixmap** resource to allow tiling the sub-object's background. For an image/pixmap that is smaller than the sub-object's background, the label area is tiled with the image/pixmap to fill the sub-object's background if this resource is **TRUE**; otherwise, the label is placed as described by the **XtNlabelJustify** resource.

The **XtNlabelTile** resource is ignored for text labels.

XtNlabelType
Range of values:

    OL_STRING/"string"
    OL_IMAGE/"image"
    OL_POPUP/"popup"

This resource identifies the form that the Label takes. It can have the value **OL_STRING** for text, **OL_IMAGE** for an image, or **OL_POPUP** for text followed by an ellipsis (such as **label...**).

XtNrecomputeSize
Range of values:

    TRUE/"true"
    FALSE/"false"

This resource indicates whether the **OblongButton** widget should calculate its size and automatically set the **XtNheight** and **XtNwidth** resources. If set to **TRUE**, the **OblongButton** widget will do normal size calculations that may cause its geometry to change. If set to **FALSE**, the **OblongButton** widget will leave its size alone; this may cause truncation of the visible image being shown by the **OblongButton** widget if the fixed size is too small, or may cause padding if the fixed size is too large. The location of the padding is determined by the `XtNlabelJustify` resource.

XtNselect

This is the list of callbacks invoked when the widget is selected.

NOTES

To obtain a MOTIF look and feel, use `FlatButtons` widgets.

SEE ALSO

`FlatButtons`(3Olit)

NAME

Panes – tiling geometry manager

SYNOPSIS

```
#include <X11/Intrinsic.h>
#include <X11/StringDefs.h>
#include <Xol/OpenLook.h>
#include <Xol/Panes.h>

widget = XtCreateWidget(name, panesWidgetClass, . . .);
```

DESCRIPTION

The **Panes** widget is a two-dimensional, tiling geometry manager that also offers extremely flexible subclassing options.

Panes and Decorations

There are two classes of children that the **Panes** widget manages, "panes" and "decorations", and a client has full control over which children are which. The **Panes** widget primarily manages the panes, and considers the decorations to be subordinate to the panes. Each decoration is associated with a single pane, though a pane may have an arbitrary number of decorations.

Decorations are simple, spanning, or constraining.

simple   the **Panes** widget will not resize a simple decoration (the decoration is assumed to have fixed size)

spanning   the **Panes** widget will resize a spanning decoration to match the length of the pane (the decoration is assumed to span, in one dimension, the length of its pane)

constraining

the **Panes** widget will resize a constraining decoration to match the pane, but a constraining decoration may have a limited range of sizes that constrain the length of the pane.

A **Scrollbar** widget in the OPEN LOOK look and feel is a typical example of a constraining decoration – the OPEN LOOK specification dictates certain minimum sizes of a scrollbar.

Geometry Management

The **Panes** widget lays out the panes and their decorations in a two-dimensional tiling pattern: each pane is considered to belong to a "family" of panes, where each member of the family is laid out in a linear fashion with no overlap. A family can contain another family, whose members are laid out perpendicular to the first family. This nesting of families can be carried to an arbitrary level.

The following diagram shows a set of seven panes, organized into three families:

The members of the first family are panes A, B, and the second family.

The members of the second family are C, D, and the third family.

The members of the third family are panes E, F, and G.

A client specifies the geometric (or familial) relations of the panes by referencing each pane (except the first) to another and giving the position (left, right, top, bottom) of the pane relative to its reference. One way to achieve the above geometric organization would be as follows:

Pane	Reference	Position
A	(none)	(n/a)
C	A	right
B	A	right
D	C	bottom
E	D	bottom
F	E	right
G	F	right

When two or more panes have the same reference, the geometric order is the order they are managed, or if managed at the same time, the order they are inserted by the client. The default insertion order is the creation order, but a client can change this.

Decorations are attached to a pane and positioned relative to the pane in the same way, by referencing the pane and giving the position.

As the **Panes** widget is resized, it "partitions" the available space among the families of panes. The default partitioning is to reallocate the space uniformly among the families of panes. At the top level family, the change in overall size is distributed evenly across all the members of the family. This partitioning recurses through families, the newly allocated space for a family member is partitioned among its members, and if one of its members is another family the space allocated to that family is partitioned among its members, and so on. The partitioning procedure can also be changed by a subclass.

A client can change the partitioning by assigning different weights to each pane; the **Panes** widget will allocate more of the change in size to panes with higher weights.

Finally, each pane can be assigned a "gravity", that dictates how the pane should be positioned within its allocated space, if it doesn't expand to fill that space.

Panes (3Olit)

RESOURCES

Panes Resource Set					
Name	Class	Type	Default	Acc	Inherit
XtNancestorSensitive	XtCSensitive	Boolean	(calculated)	G[1]	Core
XtNbackground	XtCBackground	Pixel	"XtDefaultBackground"	SGI	Core
XtNbackgroundPixmap	XtCPixmap	Pixmap	XtUnspecifiedPixmap	SGI	Core
XtNborderColor	XtCBorderColor	Pixel	"XtDefaultForeground"	SGI	Core
XtNborderPixmap	XtCPixmap	Pixmap	XtUnspecifiedPixmap	SGI	Core
XtNborderWidth	XtCBorderWidth	Dimension	0	SGI	Core
XtNbottomMargin	XtCMargin	Dimension	0	SGI	
XtNchildren	XtCReadOnly	WidgetList	NULL	G	Composite
XtNcolormap	XtCColormap	Colormap	(parent's)	GI	Core
XtNconsumeEvent	XtCCallback	XtCallbackList	NULL	SGI	Manager
XtNdepth	XtCDepth	Cardinal	(parent's)	GI	Core
XtNdestroyCallback	XtCCallback	XtCallbackList	NULL	SGI	Object
XtNheight	XtCHeight	Dimension	(calculated)	SGI	Core
XtNinsertPosition	XtCInsertPosition	XtWidgetProc	NULL	SGI	Composite
XtNlayoutHeight	XtCLayout	OlDefine	OL_MINIMIZE	SGI	
XtNlayoutWidth	XtCLayout	OlDefine	OL_MINIMIZE	SGI	
XtNleftMargin	XtCMargin	Dimension	0	SGI	
XtNmappedWhenManaged	XtCMappedWhenManaged	Boolean	TRUE	SGI	Core
XtNnumChildren	XtCReadOnly	Cardinal	0	G	Composite
XtNreferenceName	XtCReferenceName	String	NULL	SGI	Manager
XtNreferenceWidget	XtCReferenceWidget	Widget	NULL	SGI	Manager
XtNrightMargin	XtCMargin	Dimension	0	SGI	
XtNscreen	XtCScreen	Screen *	(parent's)	GI	Core
XtNsensitive	XtCSensitive	Boolean	TRUE	G[1]	Core
XtNsetMinHints	XtCSetMinHints	Boolean	TRUE	SGI	
XtNshadowThickness	XtCShadowThickness	Dimension	"0 points"[3]	SGI	Manager
XtNshadowType	XtCShadowType	OlDefine	OL_SHADOW_OUT	SGI	Manager
XtNtopMargin	XtCMargin	Dimension	0	SGI	
XtNtranslations	XtCTranslations	XtTranslations	NULL	SGI	Core
XtNtraversalOn	XtCTraversalOn	Boolean	TRUE	SGI	Manager
XtNuserData	XtCUserData	XtPointer	NULL	SGI	Manager
XtNwidth	XtCWidth	Dimension	(calculated)	SGI	Core
XtNx	XtCPosition	Position	0	SGI	Core
XtNy	XtCPosition	Position	0	SGI	Core

[1] Use XtSetSensitive to set this resource.

[3] "2 points" in the MOTIF look and feel.

XtNinsertPosition

A client can provide an **XtNinsertPosition** procedure. However, the **Panes** class constrains the positions returned by this procedure to lie between 0 and *n* for children of type **OL_PANE** (see **XtNpaneType**); and between *n* and the total number of children, for decorations; where *n* is the number of panes.

XtNlayoutWidth
XtNlayoutHeight

> Range of values:
>
>> `OL_MINIMIZE`/`"minimize"`
>> `OL_MAXIMIZE`/`"maximize"`
>> `OL_IGNORE`/`"ignore"`

These resources identify the layout policy for each of the horizontal and vertical dimensions:

`OL_MINIMIZE`

> The **Panes** widget will always be just large enough to contain its children, regardless of any dimension set by the client. Thus the **Panes** widget will grow and shrink with its children.

`OL_MAXIMIZE`

> The **Panes** widget will grow as needed to accommodate its children but will not try to shrink.

`OL_IGNORE`

> The **Panes** widget will honor its set width or height and will not try to grow or shrink when its children change size. When the width or height is not set by the client, the size will be large enough to exactly fit the children at their initial sizes.

For the `OL_MAXIMIZE` and `OL_MINIMIZE` layout policies the **Panes** widget will always go through its parent to negotiate a new size.

The `OL_IGNORE` layout policy has an important effect: If a child pane attempts to grow or shrink, the change in size is at the expense of the pane's family siblings. This effect includes leftward or upward growth or shrinkage attempted by moving the x or y position while also changing the width or height. If the change in size is extensive enough, more than just the immediate siblings can be affected. Each affected sibling is queried to ensure that it can accommodate the change; where a sibling is another family, the query is recursively pushed down to the lowest panes in the family tree.

XtNsetMinHints

> Range of values:
>
>> `TRUE`/`"true"`
>> `FALSE`/`"false"`

This resource controls whether the **Panes** widget will attempt to set its **WMShell**-class parent's **XtNminWidth** and **XtNminHeight** resources. The **Panes** widget determines its minimum geometry by querying itself with a suggested size of (0,0). The resource is ignored if the **Panes** widget is not a child of a **WMShell** or **WMShell**-subclass widget.

XtNleftMargin
XtNrightMargin
XtNtopMargin
XtNbottomMargin

> These resources define the sizes of blank margins around the panes.

Panes (3Olit)

Constraint Resources
XtNpaneGravity
Range of values:

```
AllGravity/"all"
NorthSouthEastWestGravity/"northsoutheastwest"
SouthEastWestGravity/"southeastwest"
NorthEastWestGravity/"northeastwest"
NorthSouthWestGravity/"northsouthwest"
NorthSouthEastGravity/"northsoutheast"
EastWestGravity/"eastwest"
NorthSouthGravity/"northsouth"
CenterGravity/"center"
NorthGravity/"north"
SouthGravity/"south"
EastGravity/"east"
WestGravity/"west"
NorthWestGravity/"northwest"
NorthEastGravity/"northeast"
SouthWestGravity/"southwest"
SouthEastGravity/"southeast"
```

This resource affects the position and perhaps size of the pane and its decorations within the partitioned space. The names suggest the positioning and perhaps sizing imposed on the pane. Considering that north, south, east, and west mean the top, bottom, left, and right edges of the partitioned space, then the gravity tells which edges are forced to touch the named edges of the space. For instance, **NorthGravity** means the pane is positioned with its top edge (or the top edge of a decoration that lies above the pane) at the top of the partitioned space and centered left and right, **NorthEastGravity** means the pane and its decorations are positioned in the upper-right corner of the partitioned space, and and **CenterGravity** means the pane and its decorations are centered within the space.

The traditional gravities have a meaning similar to the values for window and bit gravity. New gravity values like **NorthSouthGravity** stretch the pane to fit the partitioned space. For instance, **NorthSouthGravity** means the pane is sized to span the height of the partitioned space (minus any space needed for decorations above and below the pane), and positioned so that it is centered left and right.

Note that **AllGravity** is a synonym for **NorthSouthEastWestGravity**.

XtNrefName
XtNrefWidget
These resources specify the reference for a pane or decoration. Only one needs to be given, but if both are given they must reference the same widget. The reference must be a child of the same **Panes** widget.

The named references are left unresolved until the last possible moment (typically when the **Panes** widget is realized and its children managed). This allows a client to construct "forward" references, that is, references to siblings that have not yet been created.

XtNrefPosition
>
> Range of values:
> OL_LEFT/"left"
> OL_RIGHT/"right"
> OL_TOP/"top"
> OL_BOTTOM/"bottom"

This resource identifies where a pane or decoration is to be placed relative to the referenced widget.

XtNpaneType
>
> Range of values:
> OL_PANE/"pane"
> OL_HANDLES/"handles"
> OL_DECORATION/"decoration"
> OL_SPANNING_DECORATION/"spanning"
> OL_CONSTRAINING_DECORATION/"constraining"
> OL_OTHER/"other"

This resource defines the type of a child, typically either a pane (OL_PANE) or a decoration. A decoration of type

OL_DECORATION
> has a fixed size, that is, its size will not be changed by the **Panes** widget

OL_SPANNING_DECORATION
> means the decoration spans its pane, that is, the **Panes** widget ensures that the decoration's dimension is the same as the similar dimension of the pane including the pane's border

OL_CONSTRAINING_DECORATION
> means the decoration not only spans its pane but constrains it, that is, the **Panes** widget will attempt to keep the decoration the same length as the pane, but will query the decoration to make sure it can take the new size.

The spanning dimension for OL_SPANNING_DECORATION or OL_CONSTRAINING_DECORATION is determined by the **XtNrefPosition** constraint resource of the decoration:

OL_RIGHT

OL_LEFT

OL_TOP   span the height

OL_BOTTOM   span the width

XtNrefSpace

This resource gives the separation between a child and its referenced widget. Note that the effect of a non-zero value for this resource may not be intuitive if the references are not carefully ordered. Always referencing panes and decorations in the same way (for example, OL_RIGHT for horizontally oriented children and OL_BOTTOM for vertically oriented children) ensures that the interwidget space is obvious. Mixed referencing, such as the following, may give surprising results:

Pane	Reference	Position	Space
A	(none)	(n/a)	(n/a)
B	A	left	5
C	B	right	5

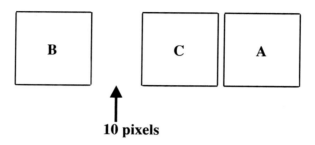

10 pixels

USAGE

Subclassing

The **Panes** widget is subclassed from the **Manager** widget.

In addition to the **Manager** and superior class fields, **Panes** widgets have the class fields listed below, members of the **PanesClassPart** structure. See **Xol/PanesP.h** for the exact listing and ordering of the class fields.

Class fields:

```
Cardinal                       node_size;
OlPanesNodeProc                node_initialize;
OlPanesNodeProc                node_destroy;
Cardinal                       state_size;
OlPanesPartitionInit           partition_initialize;
OlPanesPartitionProc           partition;
OlPanesPartitionProc           partition_accept;
OlPanesPartitionDestroyProc    partition_destroy;
OlPanesStealProc               steal_geometry;
OlPanesNodeProc                recover_geometry;
OlPanesGeometryProc            pane_geometry;
OlPanesConfigureProc           configure_pane;
OlPanesAccumulateSizeProc      accumulate_size;
XtPointer                      extension;
```

Class fields that are inheritable:

node_size	XtInheritNodeSize
state_size	XtInheritStateSize
partition_initialize	XtInheritInitialize
partition	XtInheritPartition
partition_accept	XtInheritPartitionAccept
partition_destroy	XtInheritPartitionDestroy
steal_geometry	XtInheritStealGeometry
recover_geometry	XtInheritRecoverGeometry
pane_geometry	XtInheritPaneGeometry
configure_pane	XtInheritConfigurePane
accumulate_size	XtInheritAccumulateSize

Class fields that are chained downward:

```
node_initialize
```

Class fields that are chained upward:

```
node_destroy
```

Data Structures

The data structure used to represent the families of panes is a tree structure. Each branch or leaf of the tree is a node; these nodes are created when panes are managed and are destroyed when panes are unmanaged or destroyed. For the **Panes** class each node is a **PanesNode** structure, but subclasses may extend the structure fields in each node. See **Xol/PanesP.h** for the exact listing and ordering of the data structures.

The enumeration **OlPanesNodeType** includes the following elements:

```
OlPanesTreeNode
OlPanesLeafNode
OlPanesAnyNode
```

The **OlPanesNodeAny** structure includes the following elements:

```
OlPanesNodeType type;
XRectangle geometry;
Position space;
```

The **OlPanesNodeLeaf** structure includes the following elements:

```
OlPanesNodeType type;
XRectangle geometry;
Position space;
Widget w;
Widget *decorations;
Cardinal num_decorations;
```

The **OlPanesNodeTree** structure includes the following elements:

```
OlPanesNodeType type;
XRectangle geometry;
Position space;
Cardinal num_nodes;
OlDefine orientation;
```

The `PanesNodePart` union includes the following elements:

```
OlPanesNodeAny any;
OlPanesNodeLeaf leaf;
OlPanesNodeTree tree;
```

The `PanesNode` structure includes the following elements:

```
PanesNodePart panes;
```

A `PanesNode` structure, then, is similar to a widget structure: each class defines the node fields it needs and appends them to a new structure. A subclass extends a node much the same way it defines new widget class fields and widget instance fields, by defining the new subclass part and defining a new node structure that includes the `PanesNodePart` structure first, followed by the new part structure. The subclass identifies the new size of the node in the `node_size` class field; this is typically initialized using `sizeof`.

Initializing and Destroying a Node

A subclass manages the data in its part of a node with the `node_initialize` and `node_destroy` class procedures. These procedures are of type `OlPanesNodeProc`:

```
typedef void (*OlPanesNodeProc)(
    Widget w,
    PanesNode *node,
    PanesNode *parent
);
```

A `node_initialize` procedure is expected to compute values for all its fields, typically from constraint resources. It should also allocate space for any extended values such as strings. The `Panes` class will have already initialized its part of the node structure; in particular, a subclass can determine the type of node via the `type` field, and — if the node is a leaf node — can determine the pane's widget ID from the `w` field. The `geometry` field will not have any meaningful data at this point, nor will the list of decorations be available yet.

A `node_destroy` procedure is expected to free any space allocated by the `node_initialize` procedure, and do any bookkeeping or clean up necessary for the subclass.

Creating New Nodes

A branch node is created when the `Panes` widget determines that a new pane references a pane in an existing family of nodes, but the new pane is positioned at a right angle to the family. The new (sub)family of nodes will contain the referenced pane and the new pane, and the new family replaces the referenced node as a member of the original family. In terms of a tree structure, an example of this process is represented by the following picture:

Before:

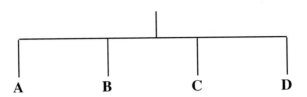

After:

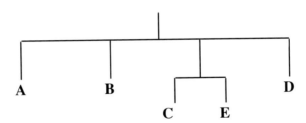

In this example, starting with, say, a horizontally oriented family of panes A,B,C,D, a new pane E is created. It references pane C but is to be positioned below it. The new family of panes C,E is created as a subfamily with siblings A,B,D.

When a new subfamily is created, the order of node creation and initialization is this: The referenced node will exist first, the branch node is created and initialized, then the new node is created and initialized. Thus, when the `node_initialize` procedure is called for the branch node it will already have one child node.

External Access to Nodes

The way the nodes are collected together in a tree structure should be considered opaque to a subclass. It is important to note that the structure is grown and shrunk as nodes are created and destroyed, and node pointers should be considered volatile. Several external routines are available to peruse the tree structure and search for nodes.

The **OlPanesWalkTree** procedure will walk the tree structure and call a subclass-specified routine for each node:

```
void OlPanesWalkTree (
    Widget w,
    OlPanesNodeType type,
    OlPanesWalkType walk,
    OlPanesWalkProc func,
    XtPointer client_data
);
```

w   **Panes** widget

type   identifies whether branch nodes, leaf nodes, or either are visited. It is one of **OlPanesTreeNode**, **OlPanesLeafNode**, or **OlPanesAnyNode**.

walk   identifies when branch nodes are visited. Is it one of **PreOrder**, **PostOrder**, or **NoOrder**.

func   subclass-specified procedure to be called for each visit

client_data value passed to *func*

PreOrder and **PostOrder** only apply to branch nodes (**NoOrder** is typically used as a "filler" value for *walk* when *type* is **OlPanesLeafNode**). **PreOrder** means the branch node is visited (that is, *func* is called) before the branches of the node are descended, while **PostOrder** means the branch node is visited after branches are descended. **PreOrder** and **PostOrder** may be ORed together to cause a visit both before and after.

The **OlPanesWalkAncestors** procedure calls a subclass-specified routine for each ancestor of a node.

```
void OlPanesWalkAncestors (
    Widget w,
    PanesNode *node,
    OlPanesWalkType walk,
    OlPanesWalkProc func,
    XtPointer client_data
);
```

w   **Panes** widget

node   pointer to the node whose ancestors are to be visited

walk   when to visit the ancestors, either **PreOrder** or **PostOrder**

func   subclass-specified routine to be called for each visit

client_data value passed to *func*

This procedure will walk up the tree from *node* to the root, visiting each node and calling *func*. A **PreOrder** walk visits an older ancestor before a younger ancestor (that is, an ancestor closer to the root before an ancestor further from the root), ending with *node* itself. A **PostOrder** walk visits the ancestors in the opposite order, starting with *node*. (This meaning of **PreOrder** and **PostOrder** is consistent with **OlPanesWalkTree**, though it may seem odd for an ancestor traversal. **PreOrder** always means a node should be visited before any of its descendents.)

For both of the above procedures, the subclass-specified procedure, *func*, is of type
OlPanesWalkProc:

```
typedef Boolean (*OlPanesWalkProc)(
    Widget w,
    PanesNode *node,
    PanesNode *parent,
    Cardinal n,
    OlPanesWalkType walk,
    XtPointer client_data
);
```

w   **Panes** widget ID

node   pointer to the node being visited

parent   pointer to the parent of *node*, or NULL if *node* is the initial (or only) node in the tree

n   ordinal of this node in its parents list of children

walk   either **PreOrder** or **PostOrder**, and identifies which visit is being made for branch nodes

client_data value passed by the subclass

This procedure should return **TRUE** if the walk should continue for the current branch, or **FALSE** if it should stop. Note that returning **TRUE** does not stop the entire walk; other branches will continue to be walked.

The **OlPanesFindNode** procedure can be used to find the leaf node for a particular pane:

```
void OlPanesFindNode(
    Widget w,
    Widget child,
    PanesNode **node,
    PanesNode **parent
);
```

w   **Panes** widget ID

child   pane to find. The pointers to the node and its parent are returned in **node** and **parent**.

node   return a pointer to the node. It will be NULL if *child* is not a managed pane.

parent   return a pointer to the parent node. It will be NULL if *child* is the only managed pane.

The **OlPanesFindSiblings** function can be used to find the adjacent "siblings" of a node:

```
void OlPanesFindSiblings(
    Widget w,
    PanesNode *node,
    PanesNode *parent,
    PanesNode **fore,
    PanesNode **aft
);
```

w   **Panes** widget

node   pointer to the node whose siblings need to be found

parent   pointer to the parent of *node*; this must not be NULL (it does not make sense to look for the siblings of the top node of a tree, or the siblings of a sole pane).

fore
aft
                 pointers to the sibling nodes, where *fore* points to the node geometrically positioned left-of or above, and *aft* points to the node positioned right-of or below. (Note that neither *node* nor either of its siblings need to be leaf nodes.) The pointers returned in *fore* or *aft* may be NULL if no sibling on that side exists.

The **OlPanesFindParent** function can be used to find the parent node of another node:

```
PanesNode *OlPanesFindParent (
    Widget w,
    PanesNode *node
);
```

w   **Panes** widget

node   node whose parent is to be found

This function will return the pointer to the parent of node, or NULL if *node* is the root node.

Partitioning Geometry Across Nodes

When the **Panes** class needs to rearrange the panes in response to some external change, it walks the node tree and partitions the available space over the nodes. In this process it will identify the space available for a branch node, then visit each of that branch's children to partition that space. As it descends the tree the space is further divided up until individual panes are reached; at that point each pane and its decorations are laid out in the space available for the leaf node.

A subclass can change the method that space is partitioned over the panes. For each node the **Panes** class calls a class procedure to compute the space available for that node. Since the partitioning process involves stepping through each branch and leaf node, a subclass may need to retain some state information across a family of nodes. Before dealing with the child nodes of a branch, the **Panes** class will allow a subclass to initialize this state information for the branch.

The state information is controlled completely by the subclass; there is no state information kept by the **Panes** class if the **partition** class procedure is not inherited by the subclass. The subclass identifies the size of the structure that will contain the state information in the **state_size** class field; typically this is set using **sizeof**.

A subclass should initialize the state information for each branch node with the **partition_initialize** procedure; this procedure is of type **OlPanesPartitionInit**:

```
typedef void (*OlPanesPartitionInit)(
    Widget w,
    XtPointer state,
    PanesNode *node,
    XtWidgetGeometry *current,
    XtWidgetGeometry *new
);
```

w   **Panes** widget.

state   area of size **state_size** allocated by the **Panes** class

node   branch node

current   current geometry of the branch node. This is the aggregate geometry for all the panes in the family and subfamilies of this branch

new   aggregate geometry available for all the panes in the family and subfamilies

The subclass is expected to use the **new** and **current** geometries, and any other information it can glean from the branch node, to initialize the state information in the space pointed to by **state**.

A subclass should destroy the state information with the **partition_destroy** procedure; this procedure is of type **OlPanesPartitionDestroyProc**:

```
typedef void (*OlPanesPartitionDestroyProc)(
    Widget w,
    XtPointer state
);
```

w   **Panes** widget

state   space allocated by the **Panes** class

The subclass is expected to clean up as necessary, but it should not free the space pointer to by **state** (the **Panes** class will do this).

As it visits each child node of a branch node, the **Panes** class will call the **partition** class procedure to determine the space available for the child node. This procedure is of type **OlPanesPartitionProc**:

```
typedef void (*OlPanesPartitionProc)(
    Widget w,
    XtPointer state,
    PanesNode *node,
    XtWidgetGeometry *partition
);
```

Panes (3Olit)

w	**Panes** widget
state	state information initialized by the **partition_initialize** procedure
node	node whose geometry is needed
partition	return the geometry that the subclass makes available to the node

It is expected that the subclass will compute *partition* from the aggregate geometry available for the entire family of nodes, as passed to the **partition_initialize** procedure. If the geometry returned in **partition** is not wholly contained within the new geometry passed to the **partition_initialize** procedure, the layout is unpredictable.

Once the **Panes** class is given the geometry available for a child node, it recursively repeats the above process with that node. When it reaches a leaf node, it applies the available geometry to the pane and its decorations. It will query the pane and the constraining decorations to see if they can handle the available geometry, and will honor any alternative geometry the pane or constraining decorations ask for. On backing up through the node tree, the **Panes** class will keep track of the aggregate geometry actually used by the nodes. When it gets back to the original child node, it will call the **partition_accept** class procedure to allow the subclass to readjust its state information. This procedure is also of type **OlPanesPartitionProc**.

Stealing and Recovering Geometry

When a new pane is created, a subclass may want to "steal" some or all of its required geometry from another pane. After creating and initializing the pane's node (and the parent branch node, if any), the **steal_geometry** procedure is called. This procedure is of type **OlPanesStealProc**:

```
typedef void (*OlPanesStealProc)(
    Widget w,
    PanesNode *new,
    PanesNode *old
);
```

w	**Panes** widget
new	node for the new pane
old	node for the pane referenced by the new pane

The subclass is expected to adjust the cached geometry of the old node or any other nodes, but it should not (re)configure the panes. The **Panes** class will call its layout procedure after the nodes for all newly managed panes have been created, and at that time the panes will be configured.

When a pane becomes unmanaged or destroyed, a subclass may want to return its geometry to one or more panes. Before destroying the pane's node, the **recover_geometry** class procedure is called. This procedure is of type **OlPanesNodeProc**. The subclass is expected to adjust the cached geometry of any of the node's siblings or any other nodes, but it should not (re)configure the panes. The **Panes** class will call its layout procedure after the nodes for all newly unmanaged or destroyed panes have been destroyed, and at that time the other panes will be configured.

Identifying the Core Pane Geometry

A subclass may have a different idea of the "core" geometry of a pane. For instance, a subclass that allows the scrolling of panes may place a smaller "viewer" widget in front of the pane so that the pane is clipped by the viewer widget. The viewer widget, then, really provides the geometry for the pane as the user sees it. When it needs to fetch the core geometry of a pane, the **Panes** class calls the **pane_geometry** class procedure. This procedure is of type **OlPanesGeometryProc**:

```
typedef void (*OlPanesGeometryProc)(
    Widget w,
    PanesNode *node,
    XtWidgetGeometry *geometry
);
```

w   **Panes** widget

node   node for the pane whose core geometry is needed

geometry   returns the core geometry

Configuring a Pane

A subclass may need to adjust the position and size of a pane within the space available for it when the pane is laid out. The **Panes** class will call the **configure_pane** class procedure when it has to lay out a pane. This procedure is of type **OlPanesConfigureProc**:

```
typedef XtGeometryResult (*OlPanesConfigureProc)(
    Widget w,
    PanesNode *node,
    XtWidgetGeometry *available,
    XtWidgetGeometry *aggregate,
    XtWidgetGeometry *allocated,
    XtWidgetGeometry *preferred,
    Boolean query_only,
    Widget who_asking,
    XtWidgetGeometry *request,
    XtWidgetGeometry *response
);
```

w   **Panes** widget

node   pointer to the node for the pane to be configured

available   total geometry available for the pane and its decorations

aggregate   total geometry available, reduced, if necessary, to meet the needs of constraining decorations

allocated   nominal size of just the pane, computed from *aggregate* and the sizes of the panes decorations

preferred   returns the geometry for just the pane

query_only   **TRUE** if this is just a query

who_asking widget requesting a geometry change, or NULL

request geometry change requested by *who_asking*, or NULL

response returns the geometry for the requesting pane, if *who_asking* is the pane at hand

The subclass is expected to compute the preferred geometry for the pane returning *preferred*, and if appropriate, *response*. The subclass is free to do other work at this point, including creating new decorations (but not new panes). For example, a subclass that allows scrolling of panes may have to create a scrollbar if a pane (or its viewer) becomes too small.

allocated is the largest size the pane can be within *available* if the needs of the panes constraining decorations are to be honored. *aggregate* reflects the total space used by the pane and its decorations, reduced from *available* as necessary for the constraining decorations, The **configure_pane** prodcdure should update *aggregate* to reflect the total space actually used by the pane and its decorations.

If the subclass computes the geometry and does no other substantial work, it should return **XtGeometryYes**. If the subclass also configures the pane, it should return **XtGeometryDone**. If the subclass does something that may affect the geometry of the pane, such as creating a decoration, it should return **XtGeometryAlmost**. In the latter case, the **Panes** class will recomput the available geometry and call the **configure_pane** class procedure again. To avoid an endless loop the subclass is expected to return **XtGeometryYes** or **XtGeometryDone** on the subsequent call.

The subclass should at most configure only the pane. The subclass should not configure the decorations (even newly created decorations); the **Panes** class will do this. The **Panes** class will configure the pane if the subclass does not. Also, if **query_only** is **TRUE** the subclass should not configure the pane.

Note: The **change_managed** class procedure will be called if new decorations are created by the subclass. This may be a reentrant call (that is, the layout procedure which spawned the **configure_pane** call may itself have been called from **change_managed**). The subclass should be prepared for this. The layout class procedure, though, will not be reentered.

Computing Required Geometry

Before beginning to lay out any panes, the **Panes** class may need to recompute the aggregate size of each node and the overall size of the entire set of panes. It will use this overall size in its initial calculations of how a geometry change should be effected. Each individual branch node aggregate size is also passed to the **partition_initialize** procedure. A subclass can override the **Panes** class' method of computing the geometries. When the **Panes**' layout class procedure is called, the **Panes** class will call the **accumulate_size** class procedure. This procedure is of type **OlPanesAccumulateSizeProc**:

```
typedef void (*OlPanesAccumulateSizeProc)(
    Widget w,
    Boolean cached_best_fit_ok_hint,
    Boolean query_only,
    Widget who_asking,
    XtWidgetGeometry *request,
    XtWidgetGeometry *result
);
```

w   **Panes** widget

cached_best_fit_ok_hint
                 TRUE if the geometry stored in the nodes might be correct. A subclass
                 can ignore this flag if it has evidence that the stored geometry may be
                 wrong.

query_only   **TRUE** if the layout is a query

who_asking   widget requesting a geometry change, or NULL

request   geometry change requested by *who_asking*, or NULL

result   overall geometry of the entire set of panes

The subclass is expected to walk the node tree and compute the geometry for each
branch and leaf node, and store this geometry in the **PanesNode** structure of each
node. It should also return the aggregate geometry for whole set of panes in *result*.

Other Public Procedures

Some additional public functions are described below.

The **OlPanesChangeConstraints** function will reconstruct the tree when constraint resources have changed:

```
Boolean OlPanesChangeConstraints(
    Widget new,
    Widget current
);
```

new   widget ID of the pane for the changed constraint resources

current   copy of the current (unchanged) widget

The new constraint resources are used to reconstruct the tree. Typically *new* and
current are the parameters passed to the constraint **set_values** function.

The **OlPanesReconstructTree** procedure can be used to reconstruct the entire
node tree.

```
void OlPanesReconstructTree(Widget w);
```

w   **Panes** widget

This function first walks the tree to call the **node_destroy** class function for each
node, in a **PostOrder** walk so that children nodes are destroyed before branch
nodes. It then reconstructs the tree. A subclass should use this function when layout changes are so extensive that the **OlPanesChangeConstraints** function would
be too costly or difficult to use.

Panes (3Olit)

The `OlPanesQueryGeometry` function can be used to find the possible overall size of a pane:

```
void OlPanesQueryGeometry(
     Widget w,
     PanesNode *node,
     XtWidgetGeometry *available,
     XtWidgetGeometry *aggregate,
     XtWidgetGeometry *pane
);
```

w   **Panes** widget

node   leaf node whose geometry is of interest

available   geometry the caller has made available to the pane

aggregate   returns overall size of the node, including the space for all decorations and borders

pane   returns size of just the pane (not including borders)

This function computes the acceptable geometry for the node as a whole (that is, the geometry of the pane and its decorations), returning this in *aggregate*. It will query the decorations to find a size they can accept. Thus the geometry returned in **aggregate** may be less than the geometry passed in **available**. The part of the geometry needed for just the pane is returned in *pane*.

The pane itself is not queried by `OlPanesQueryGeometry`, instead the caller is expected to do this if necessary, using the geometry returned in *pane*.

The `OlPanesLeafGeometry` function can be used to fetch the current geometry of a pane:

```
void OlPanesLeafGeometry(
     Widget w,
     PanesNode *node,
     Widget who_asking,
     XtWidgetGeometry *request,
     XtWidgetGeometry *aggregate,
     XtWidgetGeometry *pane
);
```

w   **Panes** widget

node   leaf node whose geometry is of interest

who_asking   pane of interest, one of its decorations, or NULL

request   requested geometry of the pane or its decoration, as identified by *who_asking*, or NULL

aggregate   returns the overall geometry of the pane, including the space for all the pane decorations and borders

pane   returns the size of just the pane (not including its borders)

This function calculates the geometry of the pane, using the current widget geometries of the pane and its decorations, returning the aggregate geometry in *aggregate* and the pane's geometry in *pane*. The caller can specify in *request* an alternate geometry for the pane or one of its decorations, as identified by *who_asking*.

PopupMenuShell (3Olit)

NAME

PopupMenuShell – create a popup menu

SYNOPSIS

```
#include <X11/Intrinsic.h>
#include <X11/StringDefs.h>
#include <Xol/OpenLook.h>
#include <Xol/PopupMenu.h>

Widget popupMenu;

popupMenu = XtCreatePopupShell(name, popupMenuShellWidgetClass, ...);
```

DESCRIPTION

The **PopupMenuShell** widget is a popup shell widget that supports the creation of popup menus in both the MOTIF and the OPEN LOOK look and feel. **PopupMenu-Shell** widgets can be attached to **AbbreviatedButton** widgets, or to the items of a **FlatButtons** widget through the **XtNpopupWidget** and **XtNpopupMenu** resources, or to arbitrary widgets using the **OlAddDefaultPopupMenuEH** event handler. In these cases, the posting and unposting of the **PopupMenuShell** is automatically managed. The **PopupMenuShell** can also be attached to arbitrary widgets by explicitly posting the menu using the **OlPostPopupMenu** and **OlUnpostPopupMenu** procedures. **PopupMenuShell** supports both the MOTIF and the OPEN LOOK look and feel.

PopupMenuShell Children

The **PopupMenuShell** widget accepts one or more children. The layout of children is single column and in creation order.

Sub-class of the Shell Widget

The **PopupMenuShell** widget is a sub-class of the **Shell** widget. Therefore, as the SYNOPSIS shows, the **XtCreatePopupShell** routine is used to create a menu instead of the normal **XtCreateWidget**.

The following table lists the **VendorShell** resources and defaults for the **Popup-MenuShell**. The **PopupMenuShell** is also a subclass of **VendorShell**.

Default Window Decorations		
Resource	Type	Default
XtNmenuButton	Boolean	FALSE
XtNpushpin	OlDefine	OL_NONE
XtNresizeCorners	Boolean	FALSE
XtNwindowHeader	Boolean	TRUE

Use of the Pushpin

The **PopupMenuShell** provides the functionality of the OPEN LOOK pushbin in both the MOTIF and the OPEN LOOK look and feel.

In the OPEN LOOK look and feel, the Pushpin is presented to the end user like any of the items to be selected from the menu, except that it is always the top-most item, and is presented visually as an "adornment" of the header, next to the Title (if present). The end user selects the Pushpin, pushing it in to cause the menu to remain on the display as an OPEN LOOK window or pinned menu, and pulling it out to make the menu a pop down. To the end user, a pinned menu behaves indistinguishably from a command window.

In the MOTIF look and feel, an additional button is added to the `PopupMenuShell`. Its label toggles from Stay Up to Dismiss. Pressing the Stay Up button causes the menu to remain on the display with window manager decorations, and pressing the Dismiss button makes the menu pop down.

The Default Item

If none of the menu items are explicitly set as the default item, the menu picks the first menu item to be the default item. If the menu contains a pushpin or Stay Up/Dismiss button and no other menu item is explicitly set as the default item, the pushpin or Stay Up/Dismiss button is chosen as the default item.

Components Shown when Popped Up

The `PopupMenuShell` widget may display a title and/or pushpin, or Stay Up/Dismiss button, when posted. The display of these components is governed by the `XtNtitle` and `XtNpushpin` resources. When `XtNTitle` is set to a string, the `PopupMenuShell` widget will display this string as its title. When the `XtNpushpin` resource is set to `OL_OUT` the widget will display a pushpin.

Press-Drag-Release vs Click-Move-Click Selection Control

The `PopupMenuShell` arranges for its children to respond to either the press-drag-release or the click-move-click type of selection. With the press-drag-release type of control, the user keeps MENU pressed and moves the pointer to the Item of choice; releasing MENU selects the Item and pops the menu down. If the pointer is not over an Item when MENU is released, the menu simply pops down. With the click-move-click type of control, the user moves the pointer to the Item of choice (MENU has already been released to end a click); clicking SELECT or MENU selects the Item and pops the menu down. If the pointer is not over an Item when SELECT or MENU is clicked, the menu simply pops down.

Converting a Stay-up Menu to a Pop-up Menu

Pressing MENU in a stay-up menu converts it to a pop-up menu. Thus the click-move-click selection control becomes a press-drag-release selection control.

Keyboard Traversal

By default, all `PopupMenuShell`s will allow traversal among the traversable controls added to the widget.

Popping up a Menu via the keyboard is done by traversing to a MenuButton, using NEXT_FIELD, PREV_FIELD, MOVEUP, MOVEDOWN, and pressing the MENU-KEY key. If a Menu is attached to a control besides a MenuButton, it can be popped up by traversing to that control and pressing the MENUKEY.

Keyboard traversal within a Menu is done using the PREV_FIELD, NEXT_FIELD, MOVEUP, MOVEDOWN, MOVELEFT and MOVERIGHT keys. The PREV_FIELD and MOVEUP keys move the input focus to the previous Menu item with keyboard traversal enabled. If the input focus is on the first item of the Menu, then pressing one of these keys will wrap to the last item of the Menu with keyboard traversal enabled. The NEXT_FIELD and MOVEDOWN keys move the input focus to the next Menu item with keyboard traversal enabled. If the input focus is on the last item of the Menu, then pressing one of these keys will wrap to the first item of the Menu with keyboard traversal enabled.

PopupMenuShell (3Olit)

To traverse out of the menu, the following keys can be used:

CANCEL	dismisses the menu and returns focus to the originating control
NEXTWINDOW	moves to the next window in the application
PREVWINDOW	moves to the previous window in the application
NEXTAPP	moves to the first window in the next application
PREVAPP	moves to the first window in the previous application
MOVERIGHT	when focus is on a menu button, posts the menu button's **PopupMenuShell**. Otherwise, dismisses the Menu and posts tht menu to the right.
MOVELEFT	dismisses the Menu and post the menu to the left

Keyboard Operation

If input focus is on a MenuButton within a Menu, pressing the MENUKEY will post the cascading Menu associated with the MenuButton, and input focus will be on the first Menu item with traversal enabled.

The DEFAULTACTION key will activate the default control in the **PopupMenuShell** widget as if the user clicked the SELECT button on the control.

The MENUDEFAULTKEY can be used by the user to change the default control in the **PopupMenuShell** widget. When the user presses the MENUDEFAULTKEY, the control which has input focus will become the default control.

In the OPEN LOOK look and feel, the TOGGLEPUSHPIN key changes the state of the pushpin in the window header. If the pushpin is in, TOGGLEPUSHPIN will pull the pin out and dismiss the window. If the pushpin is out, TOGGLEPUSHPIN will stick the pin in.

In the MOTIF look and feel, the TOGGLEPUSHPIN key changes the state of the Stay Up/Dismiss button in the **PopupMenuShell**. If the button label is "Stay Up", TOGGLEPUSHPIN causes the menu to become a window manager decorated window and the button label changes to Dismiss. When the button label is "Dismiss", TOGGLEPUSHPIN dismisses the menu window.

PopupMenuShell Activation Types	
Activation Type	Expected Results
OL_CANCEL	Dismiss this menu and any other menus cascading off of it.
OL_DEFAULTACTION	Calls **OlActivateWidget** for the default item with the **activation_type** as **OL_SELECTKEY**.
OL_TOGGLEPUSHPIN	Same semantics as TOGGLEPUSHPIN above.

RESOURCES

PopupMenuShell Resource Set					
Name	Class	Type	Default	Acc	Inherit
XtNallowShellResize	XtCAllowShellResize	Boolean	TRUE	SGI	Shell
XtNbaseHeight	XtCBaseHeight	int	XtUnspecifiedShellInt	SGI	WMShell
XtNbaseWidth	XtCBaseWidth	int	XtUnspecifiedShellInt	SGI	WMShell
XtNconsumeEvent	XtCCallback	XtCallbackList	NULL	SGI	
XtNcreatePopupChildProc	XtCCreatePopupChildProc	XtCreatePopupChildProc	NULL	SGI	Shell
XtNdefault	XtCDefault	Boolean	FALSE	SGI	
XtNfocusWidget	XtCFocusWidget	Widget	NULL	SGI	VendorShell
XtNfont	XtCFont	XFontStruct *	"OlDefaultBoldFont"	SGI	
XtNfontColor	XtCFontColor	Pixel	"XtDefaultForeground"	SGI	
XtNfontGroup	XtCFontGroup	OlFontList *	NULL	SGI	
XtNforeground	XtCForeground	Pixel	"XtDefaultForeground"	SGI	
XtNgeometry	XtCGeometry	String	NULL	GI	Shell
XtNheightInc	XtCHeightInc	int	XtUnspecifiedShellInt	SGI	WMShell
XtNinput	XtCInput	Boolean	FALSE	G	WMShell
XtNmaxAspectX	XtCMaxAspectX	int	XtUnspecifiedShellInt	SGI	WMShell
XtNmaxAspectY	XtCMaxAspectY	int	XtUnspecifiedShellInt	SGI	WMShell
XtNmaxHeight	XtCMaxHeight	int	XtUnspecifiedShellInt	SGI	WMShell
XtNmaxWidth	XtCMaxWidth	int	XtUnspecifiedShellInt	SGI	WMShell
XtNmenuButton	XtCMenuButton	Boolean	FALSE	GI	VendorShell
XtNminAspectX	XtCMinAspectX	int	XtUnspecifiedShellInt	SGI	WMShell
XtNminAspectY	XtCMinAspectY	int	XtUnspecifiedShellInt	SGI	WMShell
XtNminHeight	XtCMinHeight	int	XtUnspecifiedShellInt	SGI	WMShell
XtNminWidth	XtCMinWidth	int	XtUnspecifiedShellInt	SGI	WMShell
XtNoptionMenu	XtCOptionMenu	Boolean	FALSE	SGI	
XtNoverrideRedirect	XtCOverrideRedirect	Boolean	TRUE	SGI	Shell
XtNpopdownCallback	XtCCallback	XtCallbackList	NULL	SGI	Shell
XtNpopupCallback	XtCCallback	XtCallbackList	NULL	SGI	Shell
XtNpushpin	XtCPushpin	OlDefine	OL_NONE	SGI	VendorShell
XtNresizeCorners	XtCResizeCorners	Boolean	FALSE	SGI	VendorShell
XtNsaveUnder	XtCSaveUnder	Boolean	TRUE	SGI	Shell
XtNshadowThickness	XtCShadowThickness	Dimension	"0 points"[3]	SGI	
XtNtitle	XtCTitle	String	NULL	SGI	WMShell
XtNtitleEncoding	XtCTitleEncoding	Atom	(calculated)	SGI	WMShell
XtNtransient	XtCTransient	Boolean	TRUE	SGI	WMShell
XtNtransientFor	XtCTransientFor	Widget	NULL	SGI	TransientShell
XtNuserData	XtCUserData	XtPointer	NULL	SGI	VendorShell

PopupMenuShell (3Olit)

PopupMenuShell Resource Set (cont'd)					
Name	Class	Type	Default	Acc	Inherit
XtNvisual	XtCVisual	Visual *	NULL	GI	Shell
XtNwaitforwm	XtCWaitforwm	Boolean	TRUE	SGI	WMShell
XtNwidthInc	XtCWidthInc	int	XtUnspecifiedShellInt	SGI	WMShell
XtNwinGravity	XtCWinGravity	int	XtUnspecifiedShellInt	SGI	WMShell
XtNwindowGroup	XtCWindowGroup	Window	XtUnspecifiedWindow	SGI	WMShell
XtNwindowHeader	XtCWindowHeader	Boolean	TRUE	GI	VendorShell
XtNwmProtocol	XtCCallback	XtCallbackList	NULL	SGI	
XtNwmProtocolInterested	XtCWMProtocolInterested	int	(see note[9])	GI	VendorShell
XtNwmTimeout	XtCWmTimeout	int	5000	SGI	WMShell

[3] "2 points" in the MOTIF look and feel.

[9] Default is combination of OL_WM_DELETE_WINDOW and OL_WM_TAKE_FOCUS.

XtNfont
> Range of values:
>> (any valid return from XLoadQueryFont)
>
> Default:
>> (a bold font chosen to match the scale and screen resolution)

This resource identifies the font to be used to display the menu's title.

The default value points to a cached font structure; an application should not expect to get this value with a call to XtGetValues and use it reliably thereafter.

XtNfontColor
> Range of values:
>> (any Pixel value valid for the current display)/
>> (any name from the rgb.txt file)

This resource specifies the color of the font. If not set, the color from the XtNforeground resource, if available, is used for the font.

XtNfocusWidget
This is the ID of the widget to get focus the next time this shell takes focus. Therefore, as a user traverses objects via the keyboard or explicitly sets focus to an object (for example, clicking SELECT), the value of the XtNfocusWidget resource is updated to reflect this as the object with focus.

XtNforeground
> Range of values:
>> (any Pixel value valid for the current display)/
>> (any name from the rgb.txt file)

This resource specifies the foreground color for the widget.

XtNpushpin
> Range of values:
>> OL_IN/"in"
>> OL_OUT/"out"
>> OL_NONE/"none"

This resource is used to specify whether or not a pushpin should be included in the **PopupMenuShell** display. When set to **OL_NONE** no pushpin will appear. When set to **OL_IN**, the pin will appear and be in the pinned state. When set to **OL_OUT**, the pin will appear and be in the unpinned state.

XtNDefault

Range of values:

> **TRUE**/"**true**"
> **FALSE**/"**false**"

This resource is used to specify whether or not the pushpin is the default for the menu. When set to **TRUE**, the pushpin is set to the menu's default. When set to **FALSE**, the pushpin is not set to the default. Note that adding a child which has a default set will unset the shell's default.

XtNshadowThickness

This resource, when used on a container, shows the number of pixels in the width of the shadow border around the container.

When used on a sub-object, it shows the number of pixels in the width of the shadow border around the sub-object.

XtNtitle

This resource gives the title of the **PopupMenu** widget.

NOTES

The **PopupMenuShell** widget eliminates the use of internal widgets by managing the geometry and display of the title and pushpin. Using **PopupMenuShell** rather than **MenuShell** improves performance of applications.

SEE ALSO

AbbreviatedButton(3Olit), **FlatButtons**(3Olit),
OlAddDefaultPopupMenuEH(3Olit), **OlPostPopupMenu**(3Olit),
OlUnpostPopupMenu(3Olit), **Shell**(3Olit)

NAME

PopupWindowShell – create a property or command window

SYNOPSIS

```
#include <X11/Intrinsic.h>
#include <X11/StringDefs.h>
#include <Xol/OpenLook.h>
#include <Xol/PopupWindo.h>

static void Apply(
    Widget w,
    XtPointer client_data,
    XtPointer call_data
)
{
    printf("Apply callback!\n");
}

Arg     args[3];
Widget      popupwindow, parent;
Widget      upper, lower, panel;

static XtCallbackRec applycalls[] = {
    { Apply, NULL },
    { NULL, NULL },
};

XtSetArg(args[0], XtNapply, (XtArgVal) applycalls);

popupwindow = XtCreatePopupShell(name, popupWindowShellWidgetClass,
    parent, args, 1);

XtSetArg(args[0], XtNupperControlArea, &upper);
XtSetArg(args[1], XtNlowerControlArea, &lower);
XtSetArg(args[2], XtNfooterPanel, &panel);

XtGetValues(popupshell, args, 3);

w = XtCreateWidget(name, widget-class, upper, ...);
w = XtCreateWidget(name, widget-class, lower, ...);
w = XtCreateWidget(name, widget-class, panel, ...);
.
.
.

XtPopup(popupwindow, XtGrabNone);
```

DESCRIPTION

The `PopupWindowShell` provides a popup window in both the MOTIF and the OPEN LOOK look and feel.

Controls not Automatically Related to Selected Objects

The `PopupWindow` widget manages the creation of a property window and provides a simple interface for populating the window with controls. However, it has no innate semantics to relate the controls with a selected object; this must be handled by the application. For example, the application must dim all the controls if an object selected by the end user is incompatible with a displayed property window.

PopupWindow Components

The `PopupWindow` widget has the following parts:

— Upper Control Area

— Lower Control Area

— Window Border

— Popup Window Menu (provided by the window manager)

— Settings Menu (Conditional)

— OK Button (Conditional, MOTIF look and feel only)

— Apply Button (Conditional)

— Reset Button (Conditional)

— Reset to Factory Button (Conditional)

— Set Defaults Button (Conditional)

— Cancel Button (Conditional)

— Title

— Window Mark

— Pushpin (Optional)

— Resize Corners (Optional)

— Footer (Optional, added by the application)

The Window Border, Popup Window Menu, Header, Window Mark, and Pushpin provide end user window management control over the `PopupWindow` widget. The OK, Apply, Reset, Reset to Factory, Set Defaults, and Cancel Buttons are automatically created, if needed, to help create a standard layout of a property window. The application controls which of these, if any, appear in the pop-up window.

The OK button appears only in the MOTIF look and feel and if and only if the Apply button is added. Selecting the OK button will call the Apply callback list and dismiss the PopupWindow unless the `XtNverify` callback prevents this by returning **FALSE**.

The Cancel button appears only if the `XtNCancel` callback resource is non-NULL at initialization. Selecting Cancel dismisses the PopupWindow unless the `XtNverify` callback prevents it by returning **FALSE**. In the MOTIF look and feel only, if present, the Apply, Reset, Reset to Factory, and Set Defaults buttons only invoke their callback lists when selected; they will not dismiss the PopupWindow.

PopupWindowShell (3Olit)

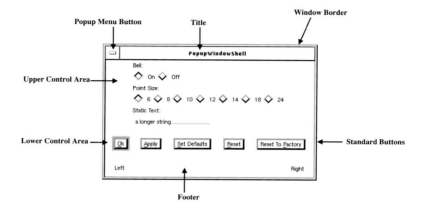

Figure 1. MOTIF Style Popup Window

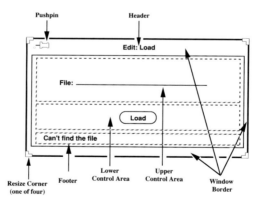

Figure 2. OPEN LOOK Style Popup Window

Automatic Addition of Buttons, Settings Menu

To aid the creation of a property window, the **PopupWindow** widget has several callbacks, set in the application argument list, used for creating the PopupWindow; for example, applying, resetting, and so on. For each of these callbacks, the **PopupWindow** widget automatically creates a button in the Lower Control Area, and the same button in the Settings Menu. If no callbacks are defined, no buttons and no Settings Menu are created.

If the application is building a command window, it has to create whatever buttons and menus are needed.

Sub-class of the Shell Widget

The **PopupWindow** widget is a sub-class of the **Shell** widget. Therefore, as the SYNOPSIS shows, the **XtCreatePopupShell** routine is used to create a pop-up window instead of the normal **XtCreateWidget**.

The following table lists the **VendorShell** resources and defaults for the **PopupWindowShell**. The **PopupWindowShell** is also a subclass of the **VendorShell**.

Default Window Decorations

Resource	Type	Default
XtNmenuButton	Boolean	FALSE
XtNpushpin	OlDefine	OL_OUT
XtNresizeCorners	Boolean	FALSE
XtNwindowHeader	Boolean	TRUE

Popping the Pop-up Window Up/Down

The application controls when the **PopupWindow** widget should displayed or popped up. As shown in the SYNOPSIS, the **XtPopup** routine can be used for this.

The application is also responsible for raising a mapped pop-up window to the front if the user attempts to pop up an already popped up window. This can be accomplished using the **XRaiseWindow** function, or with X11R5, **XtPopup** raises the window if it is already popped up.

The application cannot, however, control when the **PopupWindow** widget should be popped down, since the end user may have pinned it up, intending it stay up until dismissed. The widget itself detects when to pop down:

> MOTIF look and feel

> > the end user clicks SELECT on OK or Cancel

> > the end user dismisses it via pushpin

> > the end user dismisses it via window menu

> OPEN LOOK look and feel

> > the end user clicks SELECT on a button

> > the end user dismisses it via pushpin

> > the end user dismisses it via window menu

Upper and Lower Control Areas

The Upper and Lower Control Areas are handled by separate widget interfaces. The SYNOPSIS shows how the widget IDs of the control areas (**upper** and **lower**) and footer container (**panel**) are obtained from the **PopupWindow** widget.

The two Control Areas and the Footer abut so that there is no space between them. An application can control the distance between the controls in the Control Areas by setting margins in each area.

PopupWindowShell (3Olit)

If the **PopupWindow** widget automatically creates the OK, Apply, Reset, Reset to Factory, Set Defaults, or Cancel Buttons, it puts them in that order in the Lower Control Area. No space is left for a missing button.

PopupWindow Coloration

Figures 3 and 4 illustrate the resources that affect the coloration of the **PopupWindow** widget.

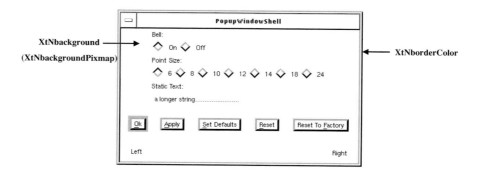

Figure 3. MOTIF Style Popup Window Coloration

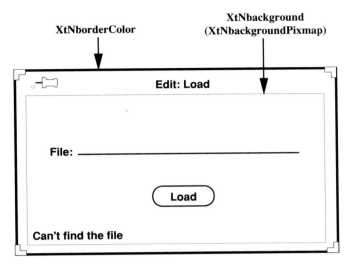

Figure 4. OPEN LOOK Style Popup Window Coloration

Keyboard Traversal

The **PopupWindow** widget has a number of components the user can traverse. The buttons in the Lower Control Area and in the Settings Menu have the following mnemonics.

Button Name	Mnemonic
Apply	A
Cancel	C
OK	O (MOTIF look only)
Reset	R
Reset to Factory	F
Set Defaults	S

These mnemonics are displayed in the button labels according to the value returned by **OlQueryMnemonicDisplay**.

The TOGGLEPUSHPIN key changes the state of the pushpin in the window header. If the pushpin is in, TOGGLEPUSHPIN will pull the pin out and pop down the window. If the pushpin is out, TOGGLEPUSHPIN will stick the pin in.

PopupWindowShell (3Olit)

PopupWindow Activation Types

Activation Type	Expected Results
OL_CANCEL	Popdown window
OL_DEFAULTACTION	Call OlActivateWidget for the default widget with parameter OL_SELECTKEY
OL_TOGGLEPUSHPIN	Toggle pushpin state

SUBSTRUCTURE

Lower Control Area and Upper Control Area components

Names: lower, upper
Class: ControlArea

The following resources are directed to both Control Area components. To set different values for the same resources in the different Control Areas, the application must access the resources using the appropriate Control Area widget IDs.

Application Resources				
Name	Class	Type	Default	Access
XtNalignCaptions	XtCAlignCaptions	Boolean	†	I
XtNcenter	XtCCenter	Boolean	FALSE	I
XtNhPad	XtCHPad	Dimension	4	I
XtNhSpace	XtCHSpace	Dimension	4	I
XtNlayoutType	XtCLayoutType	OlDefine	‡	I
XtNmeasure	XtCMeasure	int	1	I
XtNsameSize	XtCSameSize	OlDefine	OL_COLUMNS	I
XtNuserData	XtCUserData	XtPointer	NULL	SGI
XtNvPad	XtCVPad	Dimension	4	I
XtNvSpace	XtCVSpace	Dimension	4	I

† The default is TRUE for the Upper Control Area and FALSE for the Lower Control Area.

‡ The default is OL_FIXEDCOLS for the Upper Control Area and OL_FIXEDROWS for the Lower Control Area.

Footer

Names: panel
Class: FooterPanel

When using an input method that requires a status window, **TextEdit** and **Text-Field** widgets contained in a Popup Window will create the status window as the second (lower) child of the footer panel.

To add a footer, retrieve the widget ID of the **FooterPanel** via **XtGetValues** on **XtNfooterPanel** and then create a **Footer** as a child of the **FooterPanel**.

PopupWindowShell (3Olit)

RESOURCES

Name	Class	Type	Default	Acc	Inherit
	PopupWindowShell Resource Set				
XtNallowShellResize	XtCAllowShellResize	Boolean	TRUE	SGI	Shell
XtNapply	XtCCallback	XtCallbackList	NULL	I	
XtNbaseHeight	XtCBaseHeight	int	XtUnspecifiedShellInt	SGI	WMShell
XtNbaseWidth	XtCBaseWidth	int	XtUnspecifiedShellInt	SGI	WMShell
XtNbusy	XtCBusy	Boolean	FALSE	SGI	VendorShell
XtNcancel	XtCCallback	XtCallbackList	NULL	I	
XtNconsumeEvent	XtCCallback	XtCallbackList	NULL	SGI	
XtNcreatePopupChildProc	XtCCreatePopupChildProc	XtCreatePopupChildProc	NULL	SGI	Shell
XtNfocusWidget	XtCFocusWidget	Widget	NULL	SGI	VendorShell
XtNfooterPanel	XtCFooterPanel	XtPointer	NULL	G	
XtNgeometry	XtCGeometry	String	NULL	GI	Shell
XtNheightInc	XtCHeightInc	int	XtUnspecifiedShellInt	SGI	WMShell
XtNinput	XtCInput	Boolean	FALSE	G	WMShell
XtNlowerControlArea	XtCLowerControlArea	Widget	NULL	G	
XtNmaxAspectX	XtCMaxAspectX	int	XtUnspecifiedShellInt	SGI	WMShell
XtNmaxAspectY	XtCMaxAspectY	int	XtUnspecifiedShellInt	SGI	WMShell
XtNmaxHeight	XtCMaxHeight	int	XtUnspecifiedShellInt	SGI	WMShell
XtNmaxWidth	XtCMaxWidth	int	XtUnspecifiedShellInt	SGI	WMShell
XtNmenuButton	XtCMenuButton	Boolean	FALSE	GI	VendorShell
XtNminAspectX	XtCMinAspectX	int	XtUnspecifiedShellInt	SGI	WMShell
XtNminAspectY	XtCMinAspectY	int	XtUnspecifiedShellInt	SGI	WMShell
XtNminHeight	XtCMinHeight	int	XtUnspecifiedShellInt	SGI	WMShell
XtNminWidth	XtCMinWidth	int	XtUnspecifiedShellInt	SGI	WMShell
XtNoverrideRedirect	XtCOverrideRedirect	Boolean	FALSE	SGI	Shell
XtNpopdownCallback	XtCCallback	XtCallbackList	NULL	SGI	Shell
XtNpopupCallback	XtCCallback	XtCallbackList	NULL	SGI	Shell
XtNpushpin	XtCPushpin	OlDefine	OL_OUT	SGI	VendorShell
XtNreset	XtCCallback	XtCallbackList	NULL	I	
XtNresetFactory	XtCCallback	XtCallbackList	NULL	I	
XtNresizeCorners	XtCResizeCorners	Boolean	TRUE	SGI	VendorShell
XtNsaveUnder	XtCSaveUnder	Boolean	TRUE	SGI	Shell
XtNsetDefaults	XtCCallback	XtCallbackList	NULL	I	
XtNtitle	XtCTitle	String	NULL	SGI	WMShell
XtNtitleEncoding	XtCTitleEncoding	Atom	(calculated)	SGI	WMShell
XtNtransient	XtCTransient	Boolean	TRUE	SGI	WMShell
XtNtransientFor	XtCTransientFor	Widget	NULL	SGI	TransientShell

PopupWindowShell (3Olit)

	PopupWindowShell Resource Set (cont'd)					
Name	Class	Type	Default	Acc	Inherit	
XtNupperControlArea	XtCUpperControlArea	Widget	NULL	G		
XtNuserData	XtCUserData	XtPointer	NULL	SGI	VendorShell	
XtNverify	XtCCallback	XtCallbackList	NULL	I		
XtNvisual	XtCVisual	Visual *	NULL	GI	Shell	
XtNwaitforwm	XtCWaitforwm	Boolean	TRUE	SGI	WMShell	
XtNwidthInc	XtCWidthInc	int	XtUnspecifiedShellInt	SGI	WMShell	
XtNwinGravity	XtCWinGravity	int	XtUnspecifiedShellInt	SGI	WMShell	
XtNwindowGroup	XtCWindowGroup	Window	XtUnspecifiedWindow	SGI	WMShell	
XtNwindowHeader	XtCWindowHeader	Boolean	TRUE	GI	VendorShell	
XtNwmProtocol	XtCCallback	XtCallbackList	NULL	SGI		
XtNwmProtocolInterested	XtCWMProtocolInterested	int	(see note[9])	GI	VendorShell	
XtNwmTimeout	XtCWmTimeout	int	5000	SGI	WMShell	

[9]   Default is combination of OL_WM_DELETE_WINDOW and OL_WM_TAKE_FOCUS.

XtNfooterPanel

This is the widget ID of the **FooterPanel** class composite child widget that handles the Footer; its value is available once the **PopupWindow** widget has been created. If the application wants a footer, it can add one to the composite identified by this resource.

XtNlowerControlArea
XtNupperControlArea

These are the widget IDs of the **ControlArea** class composite child widgets that handle the Lower Control Area and Upper Control Area, respectively. The application can use each widget ID to populate the **PopupWindow** with controls. These widget IDs are available once the **PopupWindow** widget has been created.

In the OPEN LOOK look and feel, all controls (that is, buttons) added to the lower control area are considered window disposition controls. That is, after they have been activated with SELECT, the **PopupWindow** pops itself down, if allowed by the application and the state of the pushpin.

XtNverify

This resource defines the callbacks to be invoked when the **PopupWindow** attempts to pop itself down. The **call_data** parameter is a pointer to a variable of type **Boolean**. It is initially set to **TRUE**, and the application should set a value that reflects whether the pop-down is allowed. Typically, the application will use this to prevent a pop-down so that an error message can be displayed.

Since more than one callback routine may be registered for this resource, each callback routine can first check the value pointed to by the **call_data** parameter to see if a previous callback in the list has already rejected the pop-down attempt. If one has, the subsequent callback need not continue evaluating whether a pop-down is allowed. If the value is still **TRUE** after the last callback returns, the pop-down continues.

Since these callbacks are issued before the `PopupWindow` checks the state of the pushpin, the application should not assume that the pop-down will occur even though it has allowed it.

USAGE

The automatically created buttons in the lower control area cannot be augmented by the application. If an application needs different or additional buttons in the lower control area, it must provide all buttons.

SEE ALSO

`FlatButtons`(3Olit), `FooterPanel`(3Olit), `PopupMenuShell`(3Olit), `OblongButton`(3Olit), `OlQueryAcceleratorDisplay`(3Olit), `OlQueryMnemonicDisplay`(3Olit), `TransientShell`(3Olit)

Primitive (3Olit)

NAME

Primitive – **Primitive** widget superclass

SYNOPSIS

```
#include <X11/Intrinsic.h>
#include <X11/StringDefs.h>
#include <Xol/OpenLook.h>
```

DESCRIPTION

The following resources are available to the widgets that are a subclass of the **Primitive** class.

RESOURCES

<table>
<tr><th colspan="5">Primitive Resource Set</th></tr>
<tr><th>Name</th><th>Class</th><th>Type</th><th>Default</th><th>Acc</th></tr>
<tr><td>XtNaccelerator</td><td>XtCAccelerator</td><td>String</td><td>NULL</td><td>SGI</td></tr>
<tr><td>XtNacceleratorText</td><td>XtCAcceleratorText</td><td>String</td><td>(calculated)</td><td>SGI</td></tr>
<tr><td>XtNconsumeEvent</td><td>XtCCallback</td><td>XtCallbackList</td><td>NULL</td><td>SGI</td></tr>
<tr><td>XtNfont</td><td>XtCFont</td><td>XFontStruct *</td><td>"OlDefaultFont"</td><td>SGI</td></tr>
<tr><td>XtNfontColor</td><td>XtCFontColor</td><td>Pixel</td><td>"XtDefaultForeground"</td><td>SGI</td></tr>
<tr><td>XtNfontGroup</td><td>XtCFontGroup</td><td>OlFontList *</td><td>NULL</td><td>SGI</td></tr>
<tr><td>XtNforeground</td><td>XtCForeground</td><td>Pixel</td><td>"XtDefaultForeground"</td><td>SGI</td></tr>
<tr><td>XtNhighlightThickness</td><td>XtCHighlightThickness</td><td>Dimension</td><td>"2 points"</td><td>SGI</td></tr>
<tr><td>XtNinputFocusColor</td><td>XtCInputFocusColor</td><td>Pixel</td><td>"Red"</td><td>SGI</td></tr>
<tr><td>XtNmnemonic</td><td>XtCMnemonic</td><td>char</td><td>NULL</td><td>SGI</td></tr>
<tr><td>XtNreferenceName</td><td>XtCReferenceName</td><td>String</td><td>NULL</td><td>SGI</td></tr>
<tr><td>XtNreferenceWidget</td><td>XtCReferenceWidget</td><td>Widget</td><td>NULL</td><td>SGI</td></tr>
<tr><td>XtNshadowThickness</td><td>XtCShadowThickness</td><td>Dimension</td><td>0</td><td>SGI</td></tr>
<tr><td>XtNshadowType</td><td>XtCShadowType</td><td>OlDefine</td><td>OL_SHADOW_IN</td><td>SGI</td></tr>
<tr><td>XtNtraversalOn</td><td>XtCTraversalOn</td><td>Boolean</td><td>TRUE</td><td>SGI</td></tr>
<tr><td>XtNuserData</td><td>XtCUserData</td><td>XtPointer</td><td>NULL</td><td>SGI</td></tr>
</table>

XtNaccelerator

This resource is used to define a single KeyPress event that will select a **Primitive** widget. The format of this string is identical to the translation manager syntax. Virtual Keys can be used in this translation.

XtNacceleratorText

This resource specifies a string that describes the **Primitive**'s accelerator. For example, a HELP button may set the resource to the string "F1" to remind the users that function key 1 is the HELP button. This text will be displayed to the right of the **Primitive**'s label or image if the return from **OlQueryAcceleratorDisplay** is **OL_DISPLAY**.

This resource defaults to the **XtNaccelerator** string with "+"s inserted between multiple key sequences.

XtNconsumeEvent

The resource overrides the toolkit's handling of events. Whenever an event is processed by the standard translation table, the **XtNConsumeEvent** list is called for the widget in question allowing the application to consume the **XEvent**. To consume an event, the application should turn on (set to **TRUE**) the consumed field in the **call_data** argument when a given event is processed. If the **XEvent** is consumed, the widget doesn't use it. If it is not consumed the widget uses it. The structure, **OlVirtualEventRec**, and the corresponding pointer to it, *OlVirtualEvent, includes the following members:

```
Boolean        consumed;
XEvent         xevent;
Modifiers      dont_care;
OlVirtual Name virtual_name;
KeySym         keysym;
String         buffer;
Cardinal       length;
Cardinal       item_index;
```

XtNfont

Range of values:

(valid **XFontStruct** *)/(valid font name)

This resource specifies the font used to display text within the widget. If a font group is specified, the font is ignored.

XtNfontGroup

Range of values:

(**OlFontList** *)/(valid fontlist name)

This resource specified the font group used to display text in the widget. A font group consists of a set of fonts (up to 4) corresponding to the code sets used for text encoding in the current locale [see **OlDrawString**(3Olit)]. **XtNfontGroup** overrides the **XtNfont** resource. **XtNfontGroup**

XtNfontcolor
XtNforeground
XtNinputFocusColor

Range of values:

(valid **Pixel** value for the display)/(valid color name)

This resource specifies the color used to show that the widget has input focus. Normally, this color is derived from the value of **XtNinputFocusColor** resource and is dynamically maintained. This dynamic behavior is abandoned if the application explicitly sets this resource either at initialization or through a call to **XtSetValues**.

XtNmnemonic

This resource is a single character that is used as a mnemonic accelerator for keyboard operation. Typing this character modified with the **XtNmnemonicPrefix** will be equivalent to clicking select on the **Primitive** widget. Note that in a Menu shell, the **mnemonicPrefix** modifier is not needed. The **Primitive** widget may visually display this character.

Primitive (3Olit)

XtNreferenceName

Range of values:

(the name of a widget already created in the traversal list)

This resource specifies a position for inserting this widget in its managing ancestor's traversal list. If the the named widget exists in the managing ancestor's traversal list, this widget will be inserted in front of it. Otherwise, this widget will be inserted at the end of the list.

If both the **XtNreferenceName** and **XtNreferenceWidget** resources are set, they must refer to the same widget. If not, a warning is issued and the widget referred to by name is used.

XtNreferenceWidget

This resource specifies a position for inserting this widget in its managing ancestor's traversal list. If the reference widget is non-null and exists in the managing ancestor's traversal list, this widget will be inserted in front of it. Otherwise, this widget will be inserted at the end of the list.

If both the **XtNreferenceName** and **XtNreferenceWidget** resources are set, they must refer to the same widget. If not, a warning is issued and the widget referred to by name is used.

XtNtraversalOn

This resource specifies whether this widget is accessible through keyboard traversal.

XtNuserData

This resource provides storage for application-specific data. It is not used or set by the widget.

USAGE

Setting the widget traversal order using **XtNreferenceName** or **XtNreferenceWidget** should be done in reverse order.

Examples

This is an example of setting widget traversal order. If there are 8 **TextField** widgets, in order, 1, 2, 3, 4, 5, 6, 7, 8, and the desired traversal order is 1, 3, 5, 7, 2, 4, 6, 8, then the reference widgets should be set in the following order:

make 8 the reference widget for 6
make 6 the reference widget for 4
make 4 the reference widget for 2
make 2 the reference widget for 7
make 7 the reference widget for 5
make 5 the reference widget for 3
make 3 the reference widget for 1

SEE ALSO

OlDrawString(3Olit), OlQueryAcceleratorDisplay(3Olit)

NAME

RectButton – create a rectangular border enclosed label primitive widget

SYNOPSIS

```
#include <X11/Intrinsic.h>
#include <X11/StringDefs.h>
#include <Xol/OpenLook.h>
#include <Xol/RectButton.h>

widget = XtCreateWidget(name, rectButtonWidgetClass, . . .);
```

DESCRIPTION

The **RectButton** widget implements one of the OPEN LOOK button widgets.

RectButton Components

RectButton consists of a Label surrounded by a rectangular Border. The Border can change to reflect that the button may be a default of several buttons (double border), or represents a current state of an object (thick border), or represents a current state of one of several objects with different states (dimmed border).

Figure 1 shows several buttons, in normal, default, and current states (two versions).

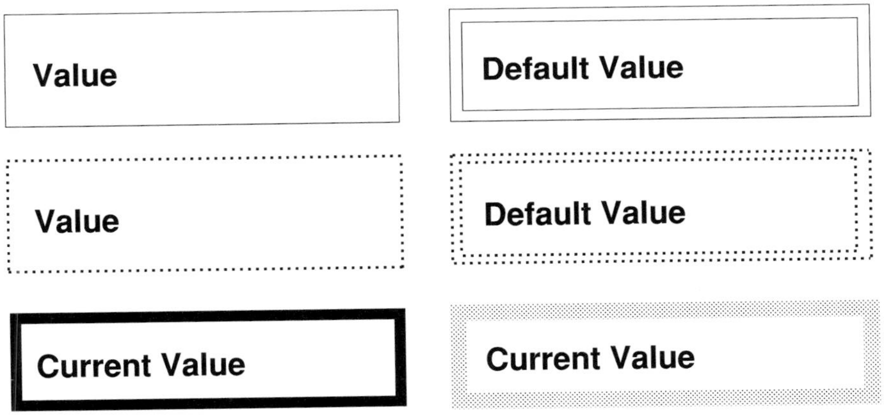

Figure 1. Rectangular Buttons

Use of Rectangular Buttons

Rectangular buttons are not used alone but in one of the **Exclusives** or **Non-exclusives** composite widgets for implementing a one-of-many or several-of-

RectButton (3Olit)

many selection. Making this widget a child of a different composite widget will not produce an error message, but proper behavior is not guaranteed.

Toggling the State

A `RectButton` widget has two states: "set" and "not set". (When set, its border is thickened.) Toggling this state alternates a resource (**XtNset**) between **TRUE** and **FALSE** and starts an action associated with the button. The `RectButton` widget is typically toggled by the user using SELECT or MENU, except that it is possible to disable user toggling of a button that is already set.

Work in Exclusives/Nonexclusives Only

If a `RectButton` widget is not the child of an **Exclusives** or **NonExclusives** widget, it will toggle between set and unset status, as in **Nonexclusives**.

Rectangular Buttons in a Pop-up Menu

Entering a rectangular button while MENU is depressed changes the appearance of the button from unset to set state or vice versa, to reflect the state the button would be in if MENU were released. Releasing MENU toggles the state associated with the button. Leaving the button before releasing MENU restore the original state appearance and does not toggle the button.

Rectangular Buttons Not in a Pop-up Menu

Clicking SELECT on a rectangular button toggles the state associated with it. Pressing SELECT, or moving the pointer into the button while SELECT is pressed, changes the border from unset to set state or vice versa, to reflect the state the button would be in if SELECT were released. Releasing SELECT toggles the state. Moving the pointer off the button before releasing SELECT restores the state appearance and does not toggle the button. but does not toggle the state.

If the button is in a stay-up menu, clicking or pressing MENU works the same as SELECT. If the button is not in a stay-up (or pop-up) menu, clicking or pressing MENU does not do anything; the event is passed up to an ancestor widget.

RectButton Border Resource Interactions

The **XtNdim**, **XtNdefault**, and **XtNset** resources can be set independently; however, all these states cannot be reflected in the visual appearance of the rectangular button, as the state table in Figure 3 shows.

XtNset	XtNdefault	XtNdim	Border appearance
TRUE	TRUE/FALSE	TRUE	Dimmed
TRUE	TRUE/FALSE	FALSE	Thickened
FALSE	TRUE	TRUE	Open
FALSE	TRUE	FALSE	Open
FALSE	FALSE	TRUE	Normal
FALSE	FALSE	FALSE	Normal

Figure 3. Rectangular Button Appearance when Set/Default/Dim

Label Appearance

The `XtNwidth`, `XtNheight`, `XtNrecomputeSize`, and `XtNlabelJustify` resources interact to produce a truncated, clipped, centered, or left-justified label as shown in Figure 4.

XtNwidth	XtNrecomputeSize	XtNlabelJustify	Result
any value	TRUE	any	Just Fits
needed for label	FALSE	OL_LEFT	Left Justified
needed for label	FALSE	OL_CENTER	Centered
needed for label	FALSE	any	Trunc
XtNheight	XtNrecomputeSize	XtNlabelJustify	Result
any value	TRUE	any	Just Fits
needed for label	FALSE	any	Centered
needed for label	FALSE	any	**Clipped**

Figure 4. Label Appearance

When the label is centered or left-justified, the extra space is filled with the background color of the **RectButton** widget, as determined by the **XtNbackground** and **XtNbackgroundPixmap** resources.

When the label is truncated, a solid-black triangle is inserted to show that part of the label is missing. The triangle requires that more of the label be truncated than would otherwise be necessary. If the width of the button is too small to show even one character with the triangle, only the triangle is shown. If the width is so small that the entire triangle cannot be shown, the triangle is clipped on the right.

See also the **XtNlabelTile** resource for how it affects the appearance of a label.

RectButton Coloration

Figure 2 illustrates the resources that affect the coloration of the **RectButton** widget.

On a monochrome display, the **RectButton** widget indicates that it has input focus by inverting the foreground and background colors of the control.

On color displays, when the **RectButton** widget receives the input focus, the background color is changed to the input focus color set in the **XtNinputFocusColor** resource.

EXCEPTIONS:

— If the input focus color is the same as the font color for the control labels, then the coloration of the active control is inverted.

— If the input focus color is the same as the Input Window Header Color and the active control is in the window header, then invert the colors.

— If the input focus color is the same as the window background color, then the **RectButton** widget inverts the foreground and background colors when it has input focus.

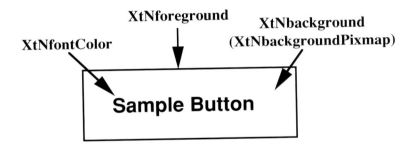

Figure 2. Rectangular Button Coloration

Keyboard Traversal

The default value of the **XtNtraversalOn** resource is **TRUE**.

The **RectButton** widget responds to the following keyboard navigation keys:

NEXT_FIELD	moves to the next traversable widget in the window
PREV_FIELD	moves to the previous traversable widget in the window
MOVEUP	moves to the **RectButton** above the current widget in the **Nonexclusives** or **Exclusives** composite
MOVEDOWN	moves to the **RectButton** below the current widget in the **Nonexclusives** or **Exclusives** composite

RectButton (3Olit)

MOVELEFT	moves to the **RectButton** to the left of the current widget in the **Nonexclusives** or **Exclusives** composite
MOVERIGHT	moves to the **RectButton** to the right of the current widget in the **Nonexclusives** or **Exclusives** composite
NEXTWINDOW	moves to the next window in the application
PREVWINDOW	moves to the previous window in the application
NEXTAPP	moves to the first window in the next application
PREVAPP	moves to the first window in the previous application

The **RectButton** will respond to the SELECTKEY by acting as if the SELECT buttons had been clicked.

RectButton Activation Types

Activation Type	Expected Results
OL_MENUDEFAULTKEY	Set the sub-object as the shell's default object (if on a menu)
OL_SELECTKEY	Update its visual to reflect the new state and call the appropriate callback list.

Display of Keyboard Mnemonic

The **RectButton** widget displays the mnemonic accelerator as part of its label. If the mnemonic character is in the label, then that character is highlighted according to the value of the application resource **XtNshowMnemonic**. If the mnemonic character is not in the label, it is displayed to the right of the label in parenthesis and highlighted according to the value of the application resource **XtNshowMnemonic**.

If truncation is necessary, the mnemonic displayed in parenthesis is truncated as a unit.

Display of Keyboard Accelerators

The display of keyboard accelerators is controlled by the application resource **XtNshowAccelerators**. When the value of **XtNshowAccelerators** is **OL_DISPLAY**, the **RectButton** widget displays the keyboard accelerator as part of its label. The string in the **XtNacceleratorText** resource is displayed to the right of the label (or mnemonic) separated by at least one space. The accelerator text is right justified.

If truncation is necessary, the accelerator is truncated as a unit. The accelerator is truncated before the mnemonic or the label.

RESOURCES

		RectButton Resource Set			
Name	Class	Type	Default	Acc	Inherit
XtNaccelerator	XtCAccelerator	String	NULL	SGI	Primitive
XtNacceleratorText	XtCAcceleratorText	String	(calculated)	SGI	Primitive
XtNancestorSensitive	XtCSensitive	Boolean	(calculated)	G[1]	Core
XtNbackground	XtCBackground	Pixel	"XtDefaultBackground"	SGI	Core
XtNbackgroundPixmap	XtCPixmap	Pixmap	XtUnspecifiedPixmap	SGI	Core
XtNcolormap	XtCColormap	Colormap	(parent's)	GI	Core
XtNconsumeEvent	XtCCallback	XtCallbackList	NULL	SGI	Primitive
XtNdefault	XtCDefault	Boolean	FALSE	SGI	Button
XtNdepth	XtCDepth	Cardinal	(parent's)	GI	Core
XtNdestroyCallback	XtCCallback	XtCallbackList	NULL	SGI	Object
XtNdim	XtCDim	Boolean	FALSE	SGI	Button
XtNfont	XtCFont	XFontStruct *	"OlDefaultFont"	SGI	Primitive
XtNfontColor	XtCFontColor	Pixel	"XtDefaultForeground"	SGI	Primitive
XtNfontGroup	XtCFontGroup	OlFontList *	NULL	SGI	Primitive
XtNforeground	XtCForeground	Pixel	"XtDefaultForeground"	SGI	Primitive
XtNheight	XtCHeight	Dimension	(calculated)	SGI	Core
XtNinputFocusColor	XtCInputFocusColor	Pixel	"Red"	SGI	Primitive
XtNlabel	XtCLabel	String	(widget name)	SGI	Button
XtNlabelImage	XtCLabelImage	XImage *	NULL	SGI	Button
XtNlabelJustify	XtCLabelJustify	OlDefine	OL_LEFT	SGI	Button
XtNlabelTile	XtCLabelTile	Boolean	FALSE	SGI	Button
XtNlabelType	XtCLabelType	OlDefine	OL_STRING	SGI	Button
XtNmappedWhenManaged	XtCMappedWhenManaged	Boolean	TRUE	SGI	Core
XtNmnemonic	XtCMnemonic	char	NULL	SGI	Primitive
XtNrecomputeSize	XtCRecomputeSize	Boolean	TRUE	SGI	Button
XtNreferenceName	XtCReferenceName	String	NULL	SGI	Primitive
XtNreferenceWidget	XtCReferenceWidget	Widget	NULL	SGI	Primitive
XtNscreen	XtCScreen	Screen *	(parent's)	GI	Core
XtNselect	XtCCallback	XtCallbackList	NULL	SGI	Button
XtNsensitive	XtCSensitive	Boolean	TRUE	G[1]	Core
XtNset	XtCSet	Boolean	FALSE	SGI	Button
XtNtranslations	XtCTranslations	XtTranslations	NULL	SGI	Core
XtNtraversalOn	XtCTraversalOn	Boolean	TRUE	SGI	Primitive
XtNunselect	XtCCallback	XtCallbackList	NULL	SGI	Button
XtNuserData	XtCUserData	XtPointer	NULL	SGI	Primitive
XtNwidth	XtCWidth	Dimension	(calculated)	SGI	Core
XtNx	XtCPosition	Position	0	SGI	Core
XtNy	XtCPosition	Position	0	SGI	Core

[1]   Use XtSetSensitive to set this resource.

XtNdefault

Range of values:

    TRUE/"true"
    FALSE/"false"

If this resource is **TRUE**, the Border is doubled to two lines, to show that the button is the default choice of one or more buttons.

XtNdim

Range of values:

    TRUE/"true"
    FALSE/"false"

If this resource is **TRUE**, then the button border is dimmed to show that the button represents the state of one or more of several objects that, as a group, are in different states.

XtNlabel

This resource is a pointer to the text for the Label. This resource is ignored if the **XtNlabelType** resource has the value **OL_IMAGE**.

XtNlabelImage

This resource is a pointer to the image for the Label. This resource is ignored unless the **XtNlabelType** resource has the value **OL_IMAGE**.

If the image is of type **XYBitmap**, the image is highlighted when appropriate by reversing the 0 and 1 values of each pixel (for example, by "'xor'ing" the image data). If the image is of type **XYPixmap** or **ZPixmap**, the image is not highlighted, although the space around the image inside the Border is highlighted.

If the image is smaller than the space available for it inside the Border and **XtNlabelTile** is **FALSE**, the image is centered vertically and either centered or left-justified horizontally, depending on the value of the **XtNlabelJustify** resource. If the image is larger than the space available for it, it is clipped so that it does not stray outside the Border. If the **XtNdefault** resource is **TRUE** so that the Border is doubled, the space available is that inside the inner line of the Border.

XtNlabelJustify

Range of values:

    OL_LEFT/"left"
    OL_CENTER/"center"

This resource dictates whether the Label should be left-justified or centered within the widget width.

XtNlabelTile

Range of values:

    TRUE/"true"
    FALSE/"false"

This resource augments the **XtNlabelImage/XtNlabelPixmap** resource to allow tiling of the object's background. For an image/pixmap that is smaller than the object's background, the label area is tiled with the image/pixmap to fill the object's background if this resource is **TRUE**; otherwise, the label is placed as described by the **XtNlabelJustify** resource.

The **XtNlabelTile** resource is ignored for text labels.

XtNlabelType
Range of values:
> **OL_STRING**/"**string**"
> **OL_IMAGE**/"**image**"

This resource identifies the form that the Label takes. It can have the value **OL_STRING** or **OL_IMAGE** for text or image, respectively.

XtNrecomputeSize
Range of values:
> **TRUE**/"**true**"
> **FALSE**/"**false**"

This resource indicates whether the **RectButton** widget should calculate its size and automatically set the **XtNheight** and **XtNwidth** resources. If set to **TRUE**, the **RectButton** widget will do normal size calculations that may cause its geometry to change. If set to **FALSE**, the **RectButton** widget will leave its size alone; this may cause truncation of the visible image being shown by the **RectButton** widget if the fixed size is too small, or may cause padding if the fixed size is too large. The location of the padding is determined by the **XtNlabelJustify** resource.

XtNselect
This is the list of callbacks invoked when the widget is selected.

XtNset
Range of values:
> **TRUE**/"**true**"
> **FALSE**/"**false**"

This resource reflects the current state of the button. The button's border is thickened to show a **TRUE** state.

XtNunselect
This is the list of callbacks invoked when a **RectButton** widget is toggled into the "unset" mode by the end user to make **XtNset** be **FALSE**. Note that simply setting **XtNset** to **FALSE** with a call to **XtSetValues** does not issue the **XtNunselect** callbacks.

NOTES
To obtain a MOTIF look and feel, use **FlatExclusives** or **FlatNonexclusives** widgets.

SEE ALSO
FlatExclusives(3Olit), **FlatNonexclusives**(3Olit)

RubberTile (3Olit)

NAME

RubberTile – create a one dimensional **Panes** widget

SYNOPSIS

```
#include <X11/Intrinsic.h>
#include <X11/StringDefs.h>
#include <Xol/OpenLook.h>
#include <Xol/RubberTile.h>
```

widget = XtCreateWidget(*name*, **rubberTilewidgetClass**, . . .);

DESCRIPTION

The **RubberTile** widget is a one-dimensional, simplified subclass of the **Panes** widget for either the MOTIF or OPEN LOOK look and feel.

One-Dimensional Orientation

Where the **Panes** widget allows a two-dimensional tiling of its panes, the **Rubber-Tile** widget simplifies the client interface with a one-dimensional tiling of panes. The client specifies the orientation, horizontal or vertical, for each **RubberTile** widget instance; the widget's children are arranged accordingly.

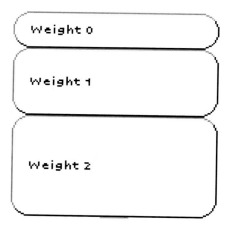

Figure 1. Rubber Tile widget

Layout Policy

The layout policy is inherited from the **Panes** class. With the layout constrained to a single dimension, this means that all pane children are tiled in a horizontal or vertical arrangement. For a horizontal layout, the initial width of the **RubberTile** widget is the sum of the widths of the panes, and the initial height is the height of the tallest pane. On resize, the difference in the **RubberTile** widget's width is distributed over the panes, using a weighting system to allow some panes to absorb more of the difference than other panes. The difference in the **RubberTile** widget's height is applied to all the panes. For a vertical layout, the initial height is the sum of the individual heights and the width is the width of the widest pane. On resize, the difference in the **RubberTile** widget's height is distributed over the panes using the same weighting system as above, and the difference in the **RubberTile** widget's width is applied to all the panes.

This is the default behavior, which a client can change using the resources of the **Panes** class.

RESOURCES

	RubberTile Resource Set				
Name	Class	Type	Default	Acc	Inherit
XtNancestorSensitive	XtCSensitive	Boolean	(calculated)	G^I	Core
XtNbackground	XtCBackground	Pixel	"XtDefaultBackground"	SGI	Core
XtNbackgroundPixmap	XtCPixmap	Pixmap	XtUnspecifiedPixmap	SGI	Core
XtNborderColor	XtCBorderColor	Pixel	"XtDefaultForeground"	SGI	Core
XtNborderPixmap	XtCPixmap	Pixmap	XtUnspecifiedPixmap	SGI	Core
XtNborderWidth	XtCBorderWidth	Dimension	0	SGI	Core
XtNbottomMargin	XtCMargin	Dimension	0	SGI	Panes
XtNchildren	XtCReadOnly	WidgetList	NULL	G	Composite
XtNcolormap	XtCColormap	Colormap	(parent's)	GI	Core
XtNconsumeEvent	XtCCallback	XtCallbackList	NULL	SGI	Manager
XtNdepth	XtCDepth	Cardinal	(parent's)	GI	Core
XtNdestroyCallback	XtCCallback	XtCallbackList	NULL	SGI	Object
XtNheight	XtCHeight	Dimension	(calculated)	SGI	Core
XtNinsertPosition	XtCInsertPosition	XtWidgetProc	NULL	SGI	Composite
XtNlayoutHeight	XtCLayout	OlDefine	OL_MINIMIZE	SGI	Panes
XtNlayoutWidth	XtCLayout	OlDefine	OL_MINIMIZE	SGI	Panes
XtNleftMargin	XtCMargin	Dimension	0	SGI	Panes
XtNmappedWhenManaged	XtCMappedWhenManaged	Boolean	TRUE	SGI	Core
XtNnumChildren	XtCReadOnly	Cardinal	0	G	Composite
XtNorientation	XtCOrientation	OlDefine	OL_VERTICAL	SGI	
XtNreferenceName	XtCReferenceName	String	NULL	SGI	Manager
XtNreferenceWidget	XtCReferenceWidget	Widget	NULL	SGI	Manager
XtNrightMargin	XtCMargin	Dimension	0	SGI	Panes
XtNscreen	XtCScreen	Screen *	(parent's)	GI	Core
XtNsensitive	XtCSensitive	Boolean	TRUE	G^I	Core
XtNsetMinHints	XtCSetMinHints	Boolean	TRUE	SGI	Panes
XtNshadowThickness	XtCShadowThickness	Dimension	"0 points"^{3}	SGI	Manager
XtNshadowType	XtCShadowType	OlDefine	OL_SHADOW_OUT	SGI	Manager
XtNtopMargin	XtCMargin	Dimension	0	SGI	Panes
XtNtranslations	XtCTranslations	XtTranslations	NULL	SGI	Core
XtNtraversalOn	XtCTraversalOn	Boolean	TRUE	SGI	Manager
XtNuserData	XtCUserData	XtPointer	NULL	SGI	Manager
XtNwidth	XtCWidth	Dimension	(calculated)	SGI	Core

RubberTile Resource Set (cont'd)					
Name	Class	Type	Default	Acc	Inherit
XtNx	XtCPosition	Position	0	SGI	Core
XtNy	XtCPosition	Position	0	SGI	Core

[1] Use XtSetSensitive to set this resource.

[3] "2 points" in the MOTIF look and feel.

XtNorientation

Range of values:

        OL_HORIZONTAL/"horizontal"
        OL_VERTICAL/"vertical"

This resource identifies the direction for laying out the panes of the RubberTile widget. Setting an orientation of OL_HORIZONTAL is equivalent to setting the Panes' XtNposition constraint resource to OL_RIGHT for each pane. Setting an orientation of OL_VERTICAL is equivalent to setting the constraint to OL_BOTTOM for each pane. The default order of the panes is their order of being managed (typically this is the same as their creation order); a client can change this with the XtNrefName and XtNrefWidget constraint resources [see Panes(3Olit)].

A client should not attempt to set the XtNposition constraint resource directly.

Constraint Resources

The RubberTile widget has the following constraint resources:

RubberTile Constraint Resource					
Name	Class	Type	Default	Acc	Inherit
XtNpaneGravity	XtCGravity	int	AllGravity	SGI	Panes
XtNpaneType	XtCPaneType	OlDefine	OL_PANE	SGI	Panes
XtNrefName	XtCRefName	String	NULL	SGI	Panes
XtNrefPosition	XtCReadOnly	OlDefine	OL_BOTTOM	G	Panes
XtNrefSpace	XtCRefSpace	Position	0	SGI	Panes
XtNrefWidget	XtCRefWidget	Widget	NULL	SGI	Panes
XtNweight	XtCWeight	short	1	SGI	Panes

XtNposition

The value of this resource is computed from the XtNorientation resource, as described above. This resource is marked "read-only" (class XtCReadOnly), to prevent a client from trying to set a different value. Any attempt to set a value directly will cause a warning message to be printed.

USAGE

Subclassing

The RubberTile widget is subclassed from the Panes widget. It adds no new class procedures, and inherits all its class procedures from the Panes class.

SEE ALSO

Panes(3Olit)

NAME

Scrollbar – move or scroll the view of an associated pane

SYNOPSIS

```
#include <X11/Intrinsic.h>
#include <X11/StringDefs.h>
#include <Xol/OpenLook.h>
#include <Xol/Scrollbar.h>

static Widget scrollbar, menupane, w;

Arg args[1];

scrollbar = XtCreateWidget(name, scrollbarWidgetClass, . . .);

    /*use the following instruction to add a button to the
     scrollbar menu*/

XtSetArg(args[0], XtNmenuPane, &menupane);
XtGetValues(scrollbar, args, 1)
w = XtCreateWidget(name, widget-class, menupane, . . .);
```

DESCRIPTION

The Scrollbar widget supports both the MOTIF and the OPEN LOOK look and feel.

MOTIF Look
Scrollbar Components

Each full MOTIF style scrollbar has the following parts:

— Top (Left) Arrow

— Bottom (Right) Arrow

— Slider

— Trough

A scrollbar consists of a Slider, a Trough, and two Arrows. The Arrows are located at both ends of the Trough, which shows the full size of the of the scrolled component, and move the view in the direction of the arrow by one unit of granularity. The Slider, which shows the position and size of the scrolled component visible relative to the Trough and slides along the Trough, is used to drag the view. A location cursor is shown when the scrollbar has focus (the location cursor takes the form of a box surrounding the scrollbar).

Scrollbar (3Olit)

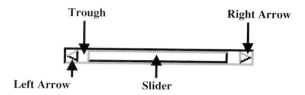

Figure 1. MOTIF Style Horizontal Scrollbar

Figure 2. MOTIF Style Vertical Scrollbar

Each scrollbar is associated with a Content, as defined by the application. The Content is composed of Units (for example, lines of text) that are visible in a viewing area. For a scrollbar to be useful, the Content typically has more Units than can fit in the viewing area. Hence, "scrolling" the Content brings Units into view as other Units move out of view. The amount of the Content that is visible at one time is called a pane in the descriptions below.

Abbreviated Scrollbar

The `Scrollbar` widget responds to a parent's request to resize smaller.

In the MOTIF look and feel, this is done by shortening the Slider and Trough.

Figure 3. MOTIF Style Abbreviated Scrollbars

Minimum Scrollbar

If necessary, the **Scrollbar** widget will eliminate both the Slider and Trough to meet a resize request to form a minimum scrollbar.

Scrolling Several Units

Dragging SELECT on the Slider moves the Slider along the Trough. The Content scrolls in the opposite direction, bringing one or more Units into view as other Units move out of view.

If granularity is enforced and the Slider is moved to a position that represents a non-integral number of Units, the closest integral number of Units is considered instead. If granularity is not enforced, the Slider is moved by the non-integral number of Units. The **XtNsliderMoved** callback allows the application to enforce granularity.

When the application reaches the limit that it can scroll, the view no longer changes and the Slider stops moving.

While dragging SELECT, the pointer is not constrained to stay within the Slider, window, or pane.

Scrolling to Limits

Clicking SELECT BDrag (Paste) on the Top, Bottom, Left or Right arrow causes the view of the Content to change to the top-most, bottom-most, left-most, or right-most pane, respectively, and moves the Slider to the limit in that direction. If the Slider is already at the limit, nothing happens.

Scrolling a Pane of Units

Clicking SELECT on the Trough above/left-of or below/right-of the Slider causes the view of the Content to change to the previous or next pane, respectively. The pointer is moved along the direction of the Slider travel to keep it off the Slider. If only a partial pane remains before the limit of the Content is reached, the effect is as if the user clicked SELECT on the corresponding Anchor. If the application cannot move to another pane, the view does not change and the Slider and pointer do not move.

Pressing SELECT on the Trough repeats the action described above.

Scrollbar Coloration

When the **Scrollbar** widget receives the input focus, the location cursor, a box surrounding the scrollbar, is shown. The box color is defined by the resource **XtNinputFocusColor**. If the user traverses out of the **Scrollbar** widget, the box disappears.

EXCEPTION: If the input focus color is the same as either the foreground or background color, then the widget shows input focus by switching the background and foreground colors.

OPEN LOOK Feel
OPEN LOOK Scrollbar Components

Each full OPEN LOOK scrollbar has the following parts:

— Top (Left) Anchor

Scrollbar (3Olit)

— Bottom (Right) Anchor
— Up (Left) Arrow
— Down (Right) Arrow
— Drag Area
— Elevator
— Cable
— Proportion Indicator
— Scrollbar Menu
— Page Indicator (optional)

A scrollbar consists of two Anchors, an Elevator, a Cable, a Proportion Indicator, a Menu, and optionally a Page Indicator. The Anchors are located at both ends of the cable, and move the view to the corresponding extreme of the item or list of items being viewed. The Elevator, which slides along the length of the cable, consists of the Up Arrow, Down Arrow, and a Drag Area in the middle for moving the view. The arrow boxes are used to move the view in the direction of the arrow by one unit of granularity. The Drag Area is used to move the view by tracking the position of the mouse pointer relative to the scrollbar. The Proportion Indicator moves along with the Elevator to indicate the size of the view and its position relative to the entire item or list of items being viewed. The optional Page Indicator located next to the Drag Area indicates the page number of the content being viewed. The Page Indicator will be displayed only when the SELECT button is pressed in the Drag Area.

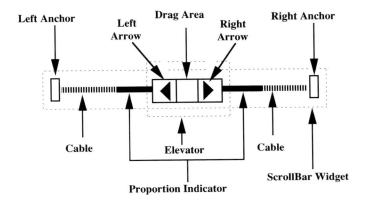

Figure 1. OPEN LOOK Horizontal Scroll Bar

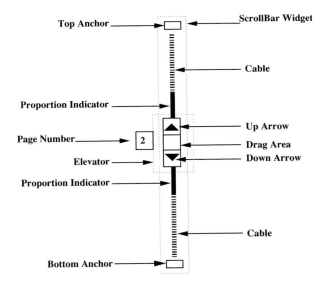

Figure 2. OPEN LOOK Vertical Scroll Bar

Scrollbar (3Olit)

Because a scrollbar can be seen and used horizontally as well as vertically, the parts Top Anchor and Bottom Anchor have the aliases Left Anchor and Right Anchor, respectively.

Each scrollbar is associated with a Content, as defined by the application. The Content is composed of Units (for example, lines of text) that are visible in a viewing area. For a scrollbar to be useful, the Content typically has more Units than can fit in the viewing area. Hence, "scrolling" the Content brings Units into view as other Units move out of view. The amount of the Content that is visible at one time is called a pane in the descriptions below.

OPEN LOOK Abbreviated Scrollbar

The **Scrollbar** widget responds to a parent's request to resize smaller.

In the OPEN LOOK look and feel, this is done by shortening the Cable (and Proportion Indicator) but leaving the other elements full-sized. The **Scrollbar** widget will eliminate the Cable and drag area entirely, if necessary, to meet a resize request. These abbreviated scrollbars are shown in Figure 3.

Figure 3. OPEN LOOK Abbreviated Scroll Bars

OPEN LOOK Minimum Scrollbar

If necessary, the Scrollbar widget will eliminate the anchors (in addition to the Cable and drag area) to meet a resize request to form a minimum scrollbar.

MOTIF Feel
Slider Motion

As visual feedback to the user, the Slider moves up and down (or left and right) along the Trough as the Content scrolls or changes panes. The range of motion of the Slider is not necessarily the full distance between Arrows. The application decides how far the Slider can be moved by evaluating each attempt to move it.

Scrolling One Unit

Clicking SELECT on one of the Up, Down, Left, or Right Arrows moves the Slider in the direction of the arrow, moves the pointer to stay on the Arrow, and changes the Content to move one Unit out of view and another Unit into view, such that the view scrolls in the opposite direction of the Slider motion. If the application cannot scroll this time, the Slider and pointer do not move, and the view does not change.

Pressing SELECT on an Arrow repeats the action described above.

When SELECT is clicked or pressed, the Arrow highlights while the scrolling action takes place. If SELECT is pressed, the highlighting stays until SELECT is released.

OPEN LOOK Look
Elevator Motion

As visual feedback to the user, the Elevator moves up and down (or left and right) along the line of the Cable as the Content scrolls or changes panes. The range of motion of the Elevator is not necessarily the full distance between the Anchors. The application decides how far the Elevator can be moved by evaluating each attempt to move it.

The user manipulates the scrollbar by pressing or clicking SELECT. The action performed depends on the position of the pointer and whether the application is willing to scroll the Content.

Scrolling One Unit

Clicking SELECT on one of the Up, Down, Left, or Right Arrows moves the Elevator in the direction of the arrow, moves the pointer to stay on the Arrow, and changes the Content to move one Unit out of view and another Unit into view, such that the view scrolls in the opposite direction of the Elevator motion. If the application cannot scroll this time, the Elevator and pointer do not move, and the view does not change.

Pressing SELECT on an Arrow repeats the action described above.

When SELECT is clicked or pressed, the Arrow highlights while the scrolling action takes place. If SELECT is pressed, the highlighting stays until SELECT is released.

When the Elevator has reached the end of a Cable, the Arrow in that direction is made inactive.

Scrolling Several Units

Dragging SELECT on the Drag Area moves the Elevator along the Cable, to track the component of the pointer motion parallel to the Cable. The Content scrolls in the opposite direction, bringing one or more Units into view as other Units move out of view.

If granularity is enforced and the Elevator is moved to a position that represents a non-integral number of Units, the closest integral number of Units is considered instead. If granularity is not enforced, the Elevator is moved by the non-integral number of Units. The **XtNsliderMoved** callback allows the application to enforce granularity.

When the application reaches the limit that it can scroll, the view no longer changes and the Elevator stops moving.

While dragging SELECT, the Drag Area highlights. The pointer is constrained to stay within the Drag Area as the Elevator moves.

Scrolling to Limits

Clicking SELECT on one of the Top, Bottom, Left, or Right Anchors causes the view of the Content to change to the top-most, bottom-most, left-most, or right-most pane, respectively, and moves the Elevator to the limit in the direction of the Anchor. If the Elevator is already at the limit, nothing happens.

Clicking SELECT on an Anchor highlights the Anchor while the scrolling action takes place.

Scrollbar (3Olit)

Scrolling a Pane of Units

Clicking SELECT on the Cable above/left-of or below/right-of the Elevator causes the view of the Content to change to the previous or next pane, respectively. The pointer is moved along the direction of the Elevator travel to keep it off the Elevator. If only a partial pane remains before the limit of the Content is reached, the effect is as if the user clicked SELECT on the corresponding Anchor. If the application cannot move to another pane, the view does not change and the Elevator and pointer do not move.

Pressing SELECT on the Cable repeats the action described above.

Elevator Approaching Limits

The application calibrates the scrollbar so that the position of the elevator on the scrollbar is in units useful to the application. In general, these units will not be pixels or points. If the scrollbar is close enough to an Anchor, the separation in application units may equate to zero pixels, because of the discrete nature of pixels. Here, the elevator is kept away from the Anchor so that two points of the Cable length are visible. The Elevator is placed at the limit of motion only when the user explicitly moves the elevator to an Anchor by clicking SELECT on the Anchor, or drags the Elevator until it reaches the limit.

Indicating View Proportion

The Proportion Indicator gives a gross measure of what part of the Content is in view. Its size relative to the length of the Cable is the same as the size of the pane relative to the size of the Content. However, the scrollbar widget does not maintain this relation but relies on the application to provide the length of the Proportion Indicator.

The Proportion Indicator moves with the Elevator such that both reach the limits together. When the Content is scrolled to the beginning, the proportion indicator and the elevator align at the left or top end of the scrollbar, as in Figure 4. When the Content is scrolled to the end, the proportion indicator and the elevator align at the right or bottom end of the scrollbar, as in Figure 5. For intermediate positions, the Elevator is positioned proportionally between the ends of the Proportion Indicator. Thus, as the Content is scrolled at a constant rate (for example, by dragging SELECT), the Elevator creeps from one end of the Proportion Indicator to the other at a constant rate.

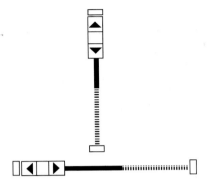

Figure 4. OPEN LOOK Elevator and Proportion Indicator at Left/Top Limits

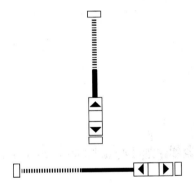

Figure 5. OPEN LOOK Elevator and Proportion Indicator at Right/Bottom Limits

Scrollbar Menu

The Scrollbar Menu (not shown in the figures) pops up when the user presses MENU anywhere over the scrollbar widget. The menu has three default choices depending on the scrollbar orientation.

Here to Top
Here to Left This choice scrolls the Content so that the Unit next to the pointer is placed at the top or left of the viewing area.

Top to Here
Left to Here This choice scrolls the Content so that the Unit at the top or left of the viewing area is placed next to the pointer.

Scrollbar (3Olit)

Previous   This choice scrolls the Content to restore the previous view. The scrollbar widget remembers only the last two scroll positions, so repeated access to this choice alternates the Content between two views. Note that if the Scrollbar menu was invoked from the keyboard, then only the "Previous" button is usable. In this case, the "Here To" button and the "To Here" button are not sensitive.

An application can add choices to this menu, using the same technique for populating other menus [see **MenuShell**(3Olit)]. The ID of the menu widget is available as a resource of the scrollbar.

Scrollbar Coloration

When the **Scrollbar** widget receives the input focus through keyboard traversal, the background color of the widget changes to the input focus color, found in the resource **XtNinputFocusColor**. If the user traverses out of the **Scrollbar** widget, the background of the widget reverts to its original background color.

In 2D mode, the Arrows, Cable, Elevator, and outline of the Anchors are determined by the **XtNforeground** resource. In 3D mode, they are related to the **XtNbackground** resource.

EXCEPTION: If the input focus color is the same as either the foreground or background color, then the widget shows input focus by switching the background and foreground colors.

Figure 6 illustrates the resources that affect the coloration of the **Scrollbar** widget.

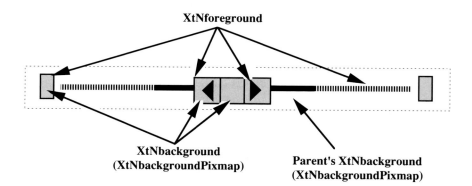

Figure 6. OPEN LOOK 2D Scrollbar Coloration

MOTIF and OPEN LOOK Keyboard Traversal

The **Scrollbar**'s default values of the **XtNtraversalOn** resource is **TRUE**.

The user can operate the Scrollbar by using the keyboard to move the Slider (MOTIF look and feel) or Elevator (OPEN LOOK look and feel) and access the Arrows (MOTIF look and feel) or Anchors (OPEN LOOK look and feel). The following keys manipulate the Scrollbar:

— SCROLLUP and SCROLLDOWN (SCROLLLEFT and SCROLLRIGHT for horizontal Scrollbars) move the Slider or Elevator one Unit in the given direction. The Content changes to move one Unit out of view and another Unit into view, such that the view scrolls in the opposite direction of the Slider or Elevator motion. If the application cannot scroll at this time, the Slider or Elevator does not move and the view does not change.

The appropriate Arrow or Anchor highlights while the scrolling action takes place.

— SCROLLTOP and SCROLLBOTTOM (SCROLLLEFTEDGE and SCROLLRIGHTEDGE for horizontal Scrollbars) cause the view of the Content to change to the top-most, bottom-most, left-most, or right-most pane respectively. The Slider or Elevator moves to the limit in the direction of the Anchor.

These keys cause the appropriate Arrow or Anchor to highlight while the scrolling action takes place.

— PAGEUP and PAGEDOWN (PAGELEFT and PAGERIGHT for horizontal Scrollbars) cause the view of the Content to change to the previous or next pane, respectively.

— MENUKEY posts the Scrollbar's Menu.

Vertical Scrollbar Activation Types

Activation Type	Expected Results	Look and Feel
OL_MENUKEY, or		OPEN LOOK only
OL_VSBMENU	Popup the scrollbar menu	OPEN LOOK only
OL_PAGEUP	Scrolls up one view	
OL_PAGEDOWN	Scrolls down one view	
OL_SCROLLUP	Scrolls up one Unit	
OL_SCROLLDOWN	Scrolls down one Unit	
OL_SCROLLTOP	Scrolls to top edge of pane	
OL_SCROLLBOTTOM	Scrolls to bottom edge of pane	

Horizontal Scrollbar Activation Types

Activation Type	Expected Results	Look and Feel
OL_MENUKEY, or		OPEN LOOK only
OL_HSBMENU	Popup the scrollbar menu	OPEN LOOK only
OL_PAGELEFT	Scrolls left one view	
OL_PAGERIGHT	Scrolls right one view	
OL_SCROLLRIGHT	Scrolls right one Unit	
OL_SCROLLLEFT	Scrolls left one Unit	
OL_SCROLLRIGHTEDGE	Scrolls to right edge of pane	
OL_SCROLLLEFTEDGE	Scrolls to left edge of pane	

Scrollbar (3Olit)

The **Scrollbar** widget responds to the following keyboard navigation keys:

— NEXT_FIELD, MOVEDOWN, and MOVERIGHT move to the next traversable widget in the window

— PREV_FIELD, MOVEUP, and MOVELEFT move to the previous traversable widget in the window

— NEXTWINDOW moves to the next window in the application

— PREVWINDOW moves to the previous window in the application

— NEXTAPP moves to the first window in the next application

— PREVAPP moves to the first window in the previous application

Operating the Scrollbar with keyboard disables any pointer warping.

OPEN LOOK Scrollbar Menu

In the OPEN LOOK look and feel, the default choices in the Scrollbar Menu are created with **XtNtraversalOn** set to **TRUE** and **XtNmnemonic** set to the first character of their label.

When the Scrollbar Menu is posted via keyboard traversal, the "Here to Top" and "Top to Here" buttons are not sensitive. These buttons depend on the position of the pointer when the menu is posted, and so they are not applicable when the menu is posted from the keyboard.

Display of Keyboard Mnemonic

The **Scrollbar** does not display the mnemonic accelerator. If the **Scrollbar** is the child of a **Caption** widget, the **Caption** widget can be used to display the **Scrollbar**'s mnemonic.

Display of Keyboard Accelerators

The **Scrollbar** does not respond to a keyboard accelerator because clicking the SELECT button on a Scrollbar activates depending on the pointer position. So, the **Scrollbar** does not display a keyboard accelerator.

OPEN LOOK SUBSTRUCTURE

In the OPEN LOOK look and feel, the Scrollbar Menu component is defined as follows.

Name: **ScrollMenu**
Class: **Menu**

Application Resources				
Name	Class	Type	Default	Access
*XtNcenter	XtCCenter	Boolean	TRUE	I
*XtNhPad	XtCHPad	Dimension	4	I
*XtNhSpace	XtCHSpace	Dimension	4	I
*XtNlayoutType	XtCLayoutType	OlDefine	OL_FIXEDROWS	I
*XtNmeasure	XtCMeasure	int	1	I
XtNpushpin	XtCPushpin	OlDefine	OL_NONE	I
XtNpushpinDefault	XtCPushpinDefault	Boolean	FALSE	I

<table>
<tr><td colspan="5" align="center">Application Resources (cont'd)</td></tr>
<tr><th>Name</th><th>Class</th><th>Type</th><th>Default</th><th>Access</th></tr>
<tr><td>*XtNsameSize</td><td>XtCSameSize</td><td>OlDefine</td><td>OL_COLUMNS</td><td>I</td></tr>
<tr><td>XtNtitle</td><td>XtCTitle</td><td>String</td><td>"Scrollbar"</td><td>I</td></tr>
<tr><td>*XtNvPad</td><td>XtCVPad</td><td>Dimension</td><td>4</td><td>I</td></tr>
<tr><td>*XtNvSpace</td><td>XtCVSpace</td><td>Dimension</td><td>4</td><td>I</td></tr>
</table>

*See the **MenuShell** and **ControlArea** widgets for the descriptions of these resources.

RESOURCES

			Scrollbar Resource Set			
Name	Class	Type	Default	Acc	Inherit
XtNancestorSensitive	XtCSensitive	Boolean	(calculated)	G[1]	Core
XtNbackground	XtCBackground	Pixel	"XtDefaultBackground"	SGI	Core
XtNbackgroundPixmap	XtCPixmap	Pixmap	XtUnspecifiedPixmap	SGI	Core
XtNborderColor	XtCBorderColor	Pixel	"XtDefaultForeground"	SGI	Core
XtNborderPixmap	XtCPixmap	Pixmap	XtUnspecifiedPixmap	SGI	Core
XtNborderWidth	XtCBorderWidth	Dimension	0	SGI	Core
XtNcolormap	XtCColormap	Colormap	(parent's)	GI	Core
XtNconsumeEvent	XtCCallback	XtCallbackList	NULL	SGI	Primitive
XtNcurrentPage	XtCCurrentPage	int	1	SGI	
XtNdepth	XtCDepth	Cardinal	(parent's)	GI	Core
XtNdestroyCallback	XtCCallback	XtCallbackList	NULL	SGI	Object
XtNdragCBType	XtCDragCBType	OlDefine	OL_CONTINUOUS	SGI	
XtNforeground	XtCForeground	Pixel	"XtDefaultForeground"	SGI	Primitive
XtNgranularity	XtCGranularity	int	1	SGI	
XtNheight	XtCHeight	Dimension	(calculated)	SGI	Core
XtNhighlightThickness	XtCHighlightThickness	Dimension	"2 points"[2]	SGI	Primitive
XtNinitialDelay	XtCInitialDelay	int	500[6]	SGI	
XtNinputFocusColor	XtCInputFocusColor	Pixel	"Red"	SGI	Primitive
XtNmappedWhenManaged	XtCMappedWhenManaged	Boolean	TRUE	SGI	Core
XtNmenuPane	XtCMenuPane	Widget	NULL	G	
XtNorientation	XtCOrientation	OlDefine	OL_VERTICAL	GI	
XtNproportionLength	XtCProportionLength	int	100	SGI	
XtNreferenceName	XtCReferenceName	String	NULL	SGI	Primitive
XtNreferenceWidget	XtCReferenceWidget	Widget	NULL	SGI	Primitive
XtNrepeatRate	XtCRepeatRate	int	100[7]	SGI	
XtNscreen	XtCScreen	Screen *	(parent's)	GI	Core
XtNsensitive	XtCSensitive	Boolean	TRUE	G[1]	Core
XtNshadowThickness	XtCShadowThickness	Dimension	"0 points"[3]	GI	Primitive
XtNshadowType	XtCShadowType	OlDefine	OL_SHADOW_IN	SGI	Primitive
XtNshowPage	XtCShowPage	OlDefine	OL_NONE	SGI	
XtNsliderMax	XtCSliderMax	int	100	SGI	

Scrollbar (3Olit)

Scrollbar Resource Set (cont'd)					
Name	Class	Type	Default	Acc	Inherit
XtNsliderMin	XtCSliderMin	int	0	SGI	
XtNsliderMoved	XtCSliderMoved	XtCallbackList	NULL	SGI	
XtNsliderValue	XtCSliderValue	int	0	SGI	
XtNstopPosition	XtCStopPosition	OlDefine	OL_ALL	SGI	
XtNtranslations	XtCTranslations	XtTranslations	NULL	SGI	Core
XtNtraversalOn	XtCTraversalOn	Boolean	FALSE	SGI	Primitive
XtNuserData	XtCUserData	XtPointer	NULL	SGI	Primitive
XtNwidth	XtCWidth	Dimension	(calculated)	SGI	Core
XtNx	XtCPosition	Position	0	SGI	Core
XtNy	XtCPosition	Position	0	SGI	Core

1   Use **XtSetSensitive** to set this resource.
2   Not used in the OPEN LOOK look and feel.
3   **"2 points"** in the MOTIF look and feel.
6   250 msec. in the MOTIF look and feel.
7   50 msec. in the MOTIF look and feel.

XtNbackground
Whenever this resource is changed, the Anchors, the Elevator, and the Proportion Indicator will be redisplayed with the new color.

XtNcurrentPage
This resource allows an arbitrary number to be displayed in a popup window. It is used in conjunction with **XtNshowPage**.

XtNdragCBType
Range of values:

> OL_CONTINUOUS/"continuous"
> OL_GRANULARITY/"granularity"
> OL_RELEASE/"release"

This resource determines the frequency of issuing **XtNsliderMoved** callbacks. If set to **OL_CONTINUOUS**, callbacks will be issued continuously (just like in Xt+ 2.0). If set to **OL_GRANULARITY**, callbacks will only be issued when the drag box crosses any granularity positions. If set to **OL_RELEASE**, callback will only be issued once when the SELECT button is released.

XtNgranularity
Range of values:

> $1 \le$ XtNgranularity $\le$ XtNsliderMax - XtNsliderMin

Clicking or pressing SELECT on an Up, Left, Down, or Right Arrow attempts to change the position of the Elevator by the distance given in this resource. Normally, the drag operation does not honor granularity unless enforcement is set in the **XtNsliderMoved** callback procedure.

XtNinitialDelay
Range of values:

> $0 <$ XtNinitialDelay

This resource gives the time, in milliseconds, before the first action occurs when SELECT is pressed on the Cables or Arrows. Note that millisecond timing precision may not be possible for all implementations, so the value may be rounded up to the nearest available unit by the toolkit.

XtNmenuPane

This resource is only available in the OPEN LOOK look and feel. If specified in the MOTIF look and feel, this resource is ignored. This is the widget where scrollbar menu items can be attached; its value is set once the scrollbar is created. Menu items can be added to this widget just as they are to a menu pane for a **Menu** or **MenuButton** widget.

The menu initially contains the items

— Here to Top (Here to Left)

— Top to Here (Left to Here)

— Previous

If these items are removed from the menu by the application, a warning is generated [see **Error**(3Olit)].

XtNorientation

Range of values:

> OL_HORIZONTAL/"horizontal"
> OL_VERTICAL/"vertical"

This resource defines the direction for the visual presentation of the widget. This resource cannot be changed via **SetValues**.

XtNproportionLength

Range of values:

> $1 \leq$ **XtNproportionLength** $\leq$ (**XtNsliderMax** - **XtNsliderMin**)

Default:

> (**XtNsliderMax** - **XtNsliderMin**)

This resource gives the size of the Proportion Indicator. The application uses the **XtNsliderMax** and **XtNsliderMin** resources to calibrate the scrollbar, making its overall length correspond to the overall length of the Content, and uses the **XtNproportionLength** resource to indicate how much of the Content is visible.

While this resource gives the overall length of the Proportion Indicator, the Elevator always covers part of it. If the Elevator would completely hide the Proportion Indicator, 3-point sections of it are shown above and below (or left of and right of) the Elevator. If the Elevator is too close to an Anchor to show all of a 3-point section, as much as possible of the section is shown on that side (this may be a zero-length section).

For example, if you have 100 items to be displayed and only one item is viewable in the pane at a time, then set **XtNsliderMin** to 0, **XtNsliderMax** to 100, and **XtNproportionLength** to 1. The possible **sliderValues** are from 0 to 99, inclusive. If, on the other hand, you have 100 items to be displayed, but 25 items are viewable at a time, then set **XtNsliderMin** to 0, **XtNsliderMax** to 100, and **XtNproportionLength** to 25. The possible **sliderValues** are from 0 to 75, inclusive.

XtNrepeatRate
Range of values:

> $0 <$ `XtNrepeatRate`

This resource gives the time, in milliseconds, between repeated actions when SELECT is pressed on the Cables or Arrows. Note that millisecond timing precision may not be possible for all implementations, so the value may be rounded up to the nearest available unit by the toolkit.

XtNshowPage
Range of values:

> `OL_NONE`/"none"
> `OL_LEFT`/"left"
> `OL_RIGHT`/"right"

This resource is only available in the OPEN LOOK look and feel. If specified in the MOTIF look and feel, this resource is ignored. If **XtNshowPage** changes from **OL_NONE** to one of the other values, a pop-up window for the page indicator is created. If the value changes to **OL_NONE**, then the pop-up is destroyed.

This value is checked when dragging is initiated. If it is not set to **OL_NONE**, the page indicator will be popped to the screen. While dragging, the page number in the indicator is constantly updated.

Note that the page indicator feature is not popped to the screen when using the keyboard rather than the mouse for drag operations.

XtNsliderMax
XtNsliderMin
Range of values:

> `XtNsliderMin` $<$ `XtNsliderMax`

These two resources are used to calibrate the **Scrollbar** widget. An application should set their values to correspond to the range of the Content, and should set the value of the **XtNproportionLength** resource to the length of the view into the Content. This calibrates the scrollbar.

The **Scrollbar** uses the calibration to convert the pixel location of the Elevator into a value in the range

> `XtNsliderMin` $\leq$ range $\leq$ `XtNsliderMax` - `XtNproportionLength`

The reason for this range relation is that an application calibrates the scrollbar so that **XtNsliderMin** and **XtNsliderMax** span the length of the Content and **XtNproportionLength** gives the length of the view of the Content. This is because when the Elevator tracks a fixed position in the view, the position is arbitrary, but remains the same as the view is scrolled over the Content. This can be the first line in the view. As Figure 7 shows, when the view is at the top of the Content, the Elevator is at the top of the scrollbar and the calibrated position of the first line is **XtNsliderMin**. However, when the view is at the bottom of the content, the Elevator is at the bottom of the scrollbar and the calibrated position of the first line is **XtNsliderMax** − **XtNproportionLength**.

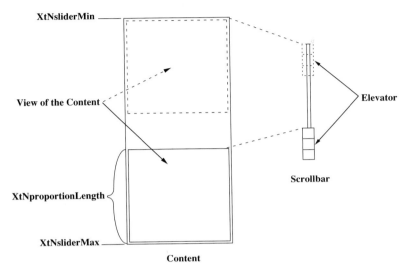

Figure 7. Elevator Range of Movement

XtNsliderMoved

This resource defines the callback lists used when the scrollbar is manipulated in various ways. The **Scrollbar** widget passes the final location of the Elevator, as an integer between **XtNsliderMin** and **XtNsliderMax** inclusive, in a structure pointed to by the **call_data** parameter. The structure, **OlScrollbarVerify**, includes the following elements:

```
int new_location;
int new_page;
Boolean ok;
int slider_min;
int slider_max;
int delta;
Boolean more_cb_pending;
```

new_location

When the **XtNsliderMoved** callbacks are made, the **new_location** member gives the position of the attempted scroll. This will be the new value of the **XtNsliderValue** resource if the scroll attempt is successful; however, the **XtNsliderValue** resource is not updated until after the callbacks return.

new_page

This will be the new value of the **XtNcurrentPage** resource if the scroll attempt is succssful. **new_page** is used to set the page number. To see the page number, you have to set **XtNshowPage** to **OL_LEFT** or **OL_RIGHT**.

ok   The **ok** member of this structure is initially set to **TRUE**; the application should set a value that reflects whether the scroll attempt is allowed. Since more than one callback routine may be registered for these resources, each callback routine can first check the **ok** member to see if a previous callback routine in the list has already rejected the scroll attempt. The scrollbar will complete the scroll attempt only if, after the last callback has returned, the **ok** member is still **TRUE**.

If the **ok** member is **FALSE** after the last callback returns, the **Scrollbar** restores the Elevator to the position it was in before the user attempted to move it. This is required only when the Elevator has been dragged. The **Scrollbar** does not move the Elevator for other scrollbar manipulations until the scroll attempt has been verified.

slider_min
slider_max

These are the same values as in the **XtNsliderMin** and **XtNsliderMax** resources.

delta   This is the distance between the new scroll position and the old, as a signed value:

delta = **new_location** - old location

A callback can change the **new_location** value to reflect a partial scroll. For example, if the scrolling granularity causes a scroll attempt past the end of an application's partially full buffer, the application should adjust **new_location** to a value representing the end of the buffer. The adjusted value must lie between the values present before the attempted scroll and the new values given in the **OlScrollbarVerify** structure.

more_cb_pending

The boolean, **more_cb_pending**, is set to **TRUE** if more callbacks are pending. If an application received a callback with this set to **TRUE**, a callback with **more_cb_pending** set to **FALSE** is guaranteed to follow shortly, before or when an operation is completed. Currently, **more_cb_pending** is set to **TRUE** only during a drag operation.

The **XtNsliderMoved** callbacks are issued when the Elevator position has been conditionally changed by the user

— clicking or pressing SELECT on the Up/Left or Down/Right arrow buttons;

— moving the Elevator to a new position by dragging SELECT on the Drag Area;

— clicking SELECT on the Top/Left or Bottom/Right Anchors;

— clicking or pressing SELECT on the Cable.

XtNsliderValue

Range of values:

$$XtNsliderMin \leq range \leq XtNsliderMax - XtNproportionLength$$
$$XtNsliderValue = range$$

This resource gives the current position of the Elevator. The **Scrollbar** widget keeps this resource up to date.

XtNstopPosition

Range of values:

`OL_ALL`/"`all`"
`OL_GRANULARITY`/"`granularity`"

This resource determines the disposition of the drag box at the end of an drag operation. If set to `OL_ALL`, upon the release of the SELECT button in a drag operation, the drag box will be positioned at where it stops. If set to `OL_GRANULARITY`, the drag box will snap to the nearest granularity position.

SEE ALSO

`Caption`(3Olit), `ControlArea`(3Olit), `Error`(3Olit), `MenuButton`(3Olit), `MenuShell`(3Olit)

ScrolledWindow (3Olit)

NAME

      `ScrolledWindow` – create a scrollable pane

SYNOPSIS

```
#include <X11/Intrinsic.h>
#include <X11/StringDefs.h>
#include <Xol/OpenLook.h>
#include <Xol/ScrolledWi.h>

static Widget scrolledwindow, controlarea1, controlarea2, w;

Arg args[2];

scrolledwindow = XtCreateWidget(name, scrolledWindowWidgetClass, . . .);

    /*Use the following instructions to add two buttons to the
            scrolling window. */

XtSetArg(args[0], XtNhMenuPane, &controlarea1);
XtSetArg(args[1], XtNvMenuPane, &controlarea2);
XtGetValues(scrolledwindow, args, 2);
w = XtCreateWidget(name, widget-class, controlarea1, . . .);
w = XtCreateWidget(name, widget-class, controlarea2, . . .);
```

DESCRIPTION

      The `ScrolledWindow` widget creates a scrollable pane in either the OPEN LOOK or the MOTIF look and feel.

No Text or Graphics Semantics

      The `ScrolledWindow` can be used as the basis for implementing a scrollable text or graphics pane. However, it has no innate text or graphics semantics.

      "Window" does not refer to an pop-up window; it is a general term used because the `ScrolledWindow` widget provides a "window" onto a larger widget.

ScrolledWindow Components

      The `ScrolledWindow` widget has the following components:

          Vertical Scrollbar (typically)

          Horizontal Scrollbar (typically)

          Content (not all visible)

          View of the Content (visible part of Content)

          View Border

      Figure 1 shows the various components of a typical scrolled window with OPEN LOOK look and feel scrollbars. In the MOTIF look and feel, the scrollbars will be in the MOTIF style.

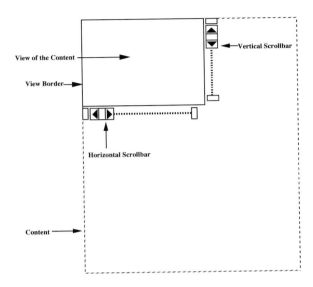

Figure 1. Scrolled Window with OPEN LOOK scrollbars

View Border

The View Border is a 1-point outline around the View of the Content.

View onto Larger Data Display

The **ScrolledWindow** widget incorporates the features of the **ScrollBar** class of widgets to implement a visible window (the View of the Content) onto another, typically larger, data display (the Content). The View of the Content can be scrolled through the Content using the scroll bars.

Child Widget as Content

To use the **ScrollWindow**, the application creates a widget capable of displaying the entire Content as a child of the **ScrolledWindow** widget. The **ScrolledWindow** widget positions the child widget "within" the View of the Content, and creates scroll bars for the horizontal and/or vertical dimensions, as needed. When the end user performs some action on the scroll bars, the child widget will be repositioned accordingly within the View of the Content.

The word "within" is used strictly in the widget sense: the larger child widget is positioned within the smaller View of the Content part of the **ScrolledWindow** widget, which necessarily forces the child widget to display only the visible part of itself. The protocol for this is through normal widget geometry interactions.

Upper Left Corner Fixed on Resize

If the **ScrolledWindow** widget is resized, the upper left corner of the View stays fixed over the same spot in the Content, unless this would cause the View to extend past the right or bottom edge of the Content. If necessary, the upper left corner will shift left or up only enough to keep the View from extending past the right or bottom edge.

View Never Larger than Content

The View of the Content is never made larger than needed to show the Content. Unless forced to appear, a scrollbar is removed from the side where it is no longer needed. Remaining scrollbars stay a fixed distance from the View.

Scrolling Sensitivity

The scrollbars are configured to scroll integer values, in pixels, through the width and length of the Content. This allows the finest degree of control of the positioning of the View of the Content. However, the application can set the step rate through these values to avoid a large number of view updates as the end user scrolls through the Content.

ScrolledWindow Coloration

Figures 2 and 3 illustrate which resources affect the coloration of the **Scrolled-Window** widget.

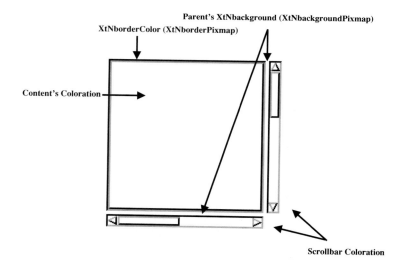

Figure 2. MOTIF Scrolled Window Coloration

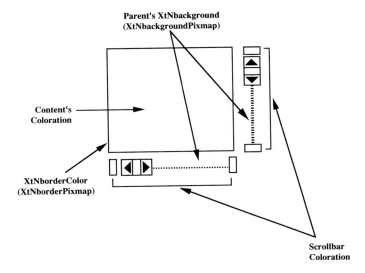

Figure 3. OPEN LOOK Scrolled Window Coloration

Application Controlled Scrolling

The **ScrolledWindow** widget also provides support for the application to control the scrolling of the content data within the view. In this mode of operation, the application creates a content window no larger than the view window. The application monitors user interaction with the Scrollbars and displays the appropriate data in the content window.

This mode of operation supports the scrolling of large amounts of data such as text.

The application specifies this mode of operation by setting the **XtNvAutoScroll** and/or **XtNhAutoScroll** resources to **FALSE**. Normally, these settings are combined with the setting of the **XtNvSliderMoved** and/or **XtNhSliderMoved** callbacks. Also, the application will specify an **XtNcomputeGeometries** callback which is used to layout the **ScrolledWindow**.

Keyboard Traversal

The **ScrolledWindow** controls the keyboard traversal between the Content, the Horizontal Scrollbar, and the Vertical Scrollbar. The Scrollbars that are created by the ScrolledWindow have the **XtNtraversalOn** resource set to **FALSE**. A Content widget added to the ScrolledWindow with traversal enabled will be added to the traversalable widgets in the window with the Scrollbars so that the user can move between them with the NEXT_FIELD (or MOVEUP or MOVELEFT) and PREV_FIELD (or MOVEDOWN or MOVERIGHT) keys.

ScrolledWindow (3Olit)

ScrolledWindow Activation Types
(if it has a Vertical Scrollbar)

Activation Type	Expected Results	Look and Feel
OL_VSBMENU	Popup the vertical scrollbar menu	OPEN LOOK only
OL_PAGEUP	Scrolls up one view	OPEN LOOK only
OL_PAGEDOWN	Scrolls down one view	
OL_SCROLLUP	Scrolls up one Unit	
OL_SCROLLDOWN	Scrolls down one Unit	
OL_SCROLLTOP	Scrolls to top edge of pane	
OL_SCROLLBOTTOM	Scrolls to bottom edge of pane	

ScrolledWindow Activation Types
(if it has a Horizontal Scrollbar)

Activation Type	Expected Results	Look and Feel
OL_HSBMENU	Popup the horizontal scrollbar menu	OPEN LOOK only
OL_PAGELEFT	Scrolls left one view	OPEN LOOK only
OL_PAGERIGHT	Scrolls right one view	
OL_SCROLLRIGHT	Scrolls right one Unit	
OL_SCROLLLEFT	Scrolls left one Unit	
OL_SCROLLRIGHTEDGE	Scrolls to right edge of pane	
OL_SCROLLLEFTEDGE	Scrolls to left edge of pane	

SUBSTRUCTURE

Vertical Scrollbar and Horizontal Scrollbar components

Names: **HScrollbar, VScrollbar**

Class: **Scrollbar**

See the regular resource list for alternate names used for some key **Scrollbar** resources.

RESOURCES

ScrolledWindow Resource Set					
Name	Class	Type	Default	Acc	Inherit
XtNalignHorizontal	XtCAlignHorizontal	int	5	SGI	
XtNalignVertical	XtCAlignVertical	int	58	SGI	
XtNancestorSensitive	XtCSensitive	Boolean	(calculated)	G[I]	Core
XtNbackground	XtCBackground	Pixel	"XtDefaultBackground"	SGI	Core
XtNbackgroundPixmap	XtCPixmap	Pixmap	XtUnspecifiedPixmap	SGI	Core
XtNborderColor	XtCBorderColor	Pixel	"XtDefaultForeground"	SGI	Core
XtNborderPixmap	XtCPixmap	Pixmap	XtUnspecifiedPixmap	SGI	Core
XtNborderWidth	XtCBorderWidth	Dimension	0	SGI	Core
XtNchildren	XtCReadOnly	WidgetList	NULL	G	Composite
XtNcolormap	XtCColormap	Colormap	(parent's)	GI	Core
XtNcomputeGeometries	XtCComputeGeometries	XtWidgetProc	NULL	SGI	
XtNconsumeEvent	XtCCallback	XtCallbackList	NULL	SGI	Manager

	ScrolledWindow Resource Set (cont'd)				
Name	Class	Type	Default	Acc	Inherit
XtNcurrentPage	XtCCurrentPage	int	1	SGI	
XtNdepth	XtCDepth	Cardinal	(parent's)	GI	Core
XtNdestroyCallback	XtCCallback	XtCallbackList	NULL	SGI	Object
XtNforceHorizontalSB	XtCForceHorizontalSB	Boolean	FALSE	SGI	
XtNforceVerticalSB	XtCForceVerticalSB	Boolean	FALSE	SGI	
XtNforeground	XtCForeground	Pixel	"Black"	SGI	
XtNhAutoScroll	XtCHAutoScroll	Boolean	TRUE	SGI	
XtNhInitialDelay	XtCHInitialDelay	int	500^6	SGI	
XtNhMenuPane	XtNHMenuPane	Widget	NULL	G	
XtNhRepeatRate	XtCHRepeatRate	int	100^7	SGI	
XtNhScrollbar	XtCHScrollbar	Widget	NULL	G	
XtNhSliderMoved	XtCHSliderMoved	XtCallbackList	NULL	SI	
XtNhStepSize	XtCHStepSize	int	1	SGI	
XtNheight	XtCHeight	Dimension	(calculated)	SGI	Core
XtNinitialX	XtCInitialX	int	0	GI	
XtNinitialY	XtCInitialY	int	0	GI	
XtNinsertPosition	XtCInsertPosition	XtWidgetProc	NULL	SGI	Composite
XtNmappedWhenManaged	XtCMappedWhenManaged	Boolean	TRUE	SGI	Core
XtNnumChildren	XtCReadOnly	Cardinal	0	G	Composite
XtNrecomputeHeight	XtCRecomputeHeight	Boolean	TRUE	SGI	
XtNrecomputeWidth	XtCRecomputeWidth	Boolean	TRUE	SGI	
XtNreferenceName	XtCReferenceName	String	NULL	SGI	Manager
XtNreferenceWidget	XtCReferenceWidget	Widget	NULL	SGI	Manager
XtNscreen	XtCScreen	Screen *	(parent's)	GI	Core
XtNsensitive	XtCSensitive	Boolean	TRUE	G^1	Core
XtNshadowThickness	XtCShadowThickness	Dimension	"0 points"[3]	SGI	Manager
XtNshadowType	XtCShadowType	OlDefine	OL_SHADOW_ETCHED_IN	SGI	Manager
XtNshowPage	XtCShowPage	OlDefine	OL_NONE	SGI	
XtNtranslations	XtCTranslations	XtTranslations	NULL	SGI	Core
XtNtraversalOn	XtCTraversalOn	Boolean	TRUE	SGI	Manager
XtNuserData	XtCUserData	XtPointer	NULL	SGI	Manager
XtNvAutoScroll	XtCVAutoScroll	Boolean	TRUE	SGI	
XtNvInitialDelay	XtCVInitialDelay	int	500^6	SGI	
XtNvMenuPane	XtNVMenuPane	Widget	NULL	G	
XtNvRepeatRate	XtCVRepeatRate	int	100^7	SGI	
XtNvScrollbar	XtCVScrollbar	Widget	NULL	G	
XtNvSliderMoved	XtCVSliderMoved	XtCallbackList	NULL	SI	
XtNvStepSize	XtCVStepSize	int	1	SGI	
XtNviewHeight	XtCViewHeight	Dimension	0	SGI	
XtNviewWidth	XtCViewWidth	Dimension	0	SGI	

ScrolledWindow (3Olit)

Name	Class	Type	Default	Acc	Inherit
	**ScrolledWindow** Resource Set (cont'd)				
XtNwidth	XtCWidth	Dimension	(calculated)	SGI	Core
XtNx	XtCPosition	Position	0	SGI	Core
XtNy	XtCPosition	Position	0	SGI	Core

1   Use `XtSetSensitive` to set this resource.
3   "`2 points`" in MOTIF look and feel.
6   250 msec. in MOTIF look and feel.
7   50 msec. in MOTIF look and feel.

XtNalignHorizontal

Range of values:

```
OL_BOTTOM/''bottom''
OL_TOP/''top''
```

This resource is used to specify whether the horizontal scrollbar should be placed at the top or bottom of the **ScrolledWindow**. The default placement is at the bottom.

XtNalignVertical

Range of values:

```
OL_RIGHT/''right''
OL_LEFT/''left''
```

This resource is used to specify whether the vertical scrollbar should be placed at the left or right of the **ScrolledWindow**. The default placement is at the right.

XtNcomputeGeometries

This resource is used to allow intelligent cooperation during the layout stage between the **ScrolledWindow** and its content widget. The content widget sets this resource to a pointer to a function which is to be called whenever the **ScrolledWindow** needs to layout its children. The function is called as:

```
(*function)(Widget content_widget_id, OlSWGeometries *geometries);
```

Where the `OlSWGeometries` structure contains the following elements:

```
Widget      sw;                 /* ScrolledWindow widget      */
Widget      vsb;                /* vertical scrollbar widget  */
Widget      hsb;                /* horiz scrollbar widget     */
Dimension   bb_border_width;    /* bboard border width        */
Dimension   vsb_width;          /* vert scrollbar min width   */
Dimension   vsb_min_height;     /*  "    scrollbar min height */
Dimension   hsb_min_width;      /* horiz scrollbar min width  */
Dimension   hsb_height;         /*  "    scrollbar min height */
Dimension   sw_view_width;      /* scrollwindow view width    */
Dimension   sw_view_height;     /* scrollwindow view height   */
Dimension   bbc_width;          /* bulletin board width       */
Dimension   bbc_height;         /* bulletin board height      */
Dimension   bbc_real_width;     /* bboard real width          */
Dimension   bbc_real_height;    /* bboard real height         */
Boolean     force_hsb;          /* force horiz scrollbar      */
Boolean     force_vsb;          /* force vertical scrollbar   */
```

The `ScrolledWindow` widget populates the values in this structure prior to the call and examines them after the call to perform the layout operation.

The callback function is responsible for populating the **bbc_width** and **bbc_height** elements of this structure with the desired size of its window; the **bbc_real_width** and **bbc_real_height** elements with the logical size of the data; and the **force_hsb** and **force_vsb** flags to indicate which scrollbars the `ScrolledWindow` should include in the layout.

XtNcurrentPage

The value of this resource is passed through to the vertical scrollbar of the `ScrolledWindow` [see `Scrollbar`(3Olit)].

XtNshowPage

This resource is only available in the OPEN LOOK look and feel. If specified in the MOTIF look and feel, this resource is ignored. It is directed to the vertical scrollbar in the `ScrolledWindow` widget. See `Scrollbar`(3Olit) for more detail.

XtNforceHorizontalSB
XtNforceVerticalSB

Range of values:

> TRUE/"true"
> FALSE/"false"

When the child widget is created and positioned within the `ScrolledWindow`, its width and height are examined. If the entire child widget will fit within the width (length) of the `ScrolledWindow`, the horizontal (vertical) scrollbar will not be created, since there is no need to scroll in that direction. Setting these resources to **TRUE** disables this checking and will force a horizontal (vertical) scrollbar to be attached to the window regardless of the dimension of the child widget. If a scrollbar is forced but not needed because the Content fits within the View, the scrollbar is made insensitive.

XtNhAutoScroll
XtNvAutoScroll

This resource is used to set the scrolling mode in the horizontal (vertical) direction. When set to **TRUE**, the `ScrolledWindow` widget is responsible for all interaction with the scrollbar and the positioning of the content window within the view. When set to **FALSE**, the application is responsible for all scrollbar interaction and scrolling of the data within the content window.

XtNhInitialDelay
XtNvInitialDelay

These resources are used to specify the time in milliseconds of the initial repeat delay to be used when the scrolling arrows of the horizontal (vertical) scrollbar component of the `ScrolledWindow` are pressed.

XtNhMenuPane
XtNvMenuPane

These resources are only available in the OPEN LOOK look and feel. If specified in the MOTIF look and feel, they are ignored. These resources mimic the **XtNmenuPane** resources for the horizontal and vertical scrollbars, respectively. See `Scrollbar`(3Olit) for more details.

XtNhRepeatRate
XtNvRepeatRate

These resources are used to specify the time in milliseconds of the repeat delay to be used when the scrolling arrows of the horizontal (vertical) scrollbar component of the `ScrolledWindow` are pressed.

XtNhScrollbar
XtNvScrollbar

These resources provide the widget ID's of the horizontal and vertical scrollbars. An application can use these values to set scrollbar characteristics, such as coloration.

XtNhSliderMoved
XtNvSliderMoved

An application may track the position of the child within the `ScrolledWindow` by linking into these callbacks. They mimic the `XtNsliderMoved` resources of the horizontal and vertical scrollbars, respectively.

The `call_data` parameter for these callbacks is a pointer to an `OlScrollBar-Verify` structure, as in the `Scrollbar` widget. The application can validate a scroll attempt before the `ScrolledWindow` widget will reposition the View of the Content, and can update the page number and adjust the scrollbar elevator position. See `Scrollbar`(3Olit) for more details.

XtNhStepSize
XtNvStepSize

Range of values:

    0 < XtNhStepSize
    0 < XtNStepSize

These resources are related to the `XtNgranularity` resource for horizontal and vertical scrollbars, respectively, but have an important distinction: their values are the size in pixels of the minimum scrollable unit in the Content. For instance, to allow the end user to scroll a single pixel in either direction, these values would be 1. Or, to allow the end user to scroll a character at a time horizontally and a line at a time vertically, these values would be the width of a character and the height of a line, respectively. (Scrolling a character at a time requires a constant width font, of course.) The `ScrolledWindow` widget uses these values to calibrate the minimum scrolling step, `XtNgranularity`, of the scrollbars.

XtNinitialX
XtNinitialY

Range of values:

    XtNinitialX ≤ 0
    XtNinitialY ≤ 0

The child widget is initially positioned at the upper left corner (x,y coordinates 0,0). This positioning can be changed by specifying a new x,y location. The scrollbars are adjusted to give a visual indication of the offset specified in these resources. Note that the Content is positioned within the View of the Content, so as the View of the Content moves progressively further through the Content, the coordinates of the position become more negative. Thus the initial coordinates given in these resources should be zero or negative to assure proper operation of the scrolled window.

XtNrecomputeHeight
XtNrecomputeWidth

Range of values:

>   TRUE/"true"
>   FALSE/"false"

These resources control how the **ScrolledWindow** widget should respond to requests to resize itself. Where one of these resources is **TRUE**, the **ScrolledWindow** shrinks the View of the Content in the corresponding direction to absorb the change in the **ScrolledWindow** widget's size. Where one of these resources is **FALSE**, the **ScrolledWindow** does not shrink the View in that direction.

These resources, together with the **XtNviewWidth** and **XtNviewHeight** resources, are typically used to set a preferred dimension in a direction that should not be scrolled.

XtNviewHeight
XtNviewWidth

Range of values:

>   0 ≤ XtNviewHeight
>   0 ≤ XtNviewWidth

These resources define the preferred size of the View of the Content in pixels. For each, if a nonzero value is given, the corresponding **XtNheight** or **XtNwidth** resource is computed by adding the thickness of any scrollbar that appears. Any value in the **XtNheight** or **XtNwidth** resource is overwritten. If a zero value is given in the **XtNviewHeight** or **XtNviewWidth** resource, the corresponding **XtNheight** or **XtNwidth** resource is used instead.

Regardless of which resources identify the preferred height or width, the height or width of the View is never smaller than any scrollbar next to it.

These resources also represent the maximum size of the View. While the **ScrolledWindow** may resize the View smaller than indicated in these resources (as compared to **XtNrecomputeHeight** and **XtNrecomputeWidth**), it will never resize the View larger than indicated.

SEE ALSO

Scrollbar(3Olit)

ScrollingList (3Olit)

NAME

    `ScrollingList` – create an OPEN LOOK pane with a scrollable list of text items

SYNOPSIS

```
#include <X11/Intrinsic.h>
#include <X11/StringDefs.h>
#include <Xol/OpenLook.h>
#include <Xol/ScrollingL.h>

static Widget scrollinglist, textfield;

Args args[1];

scrollinglist = XtCreateWidget(name, scrollingListWidgetClass, . . .);
XtSetArg(args[0], XtNtextField, &textfield);
XtGetValues(scrollinglist, args, 1);
```

DESCRIPTION

    `ScrollingList` creates an OPEN LOOK style pane with a scrollable list of text items.

ScrollingList Components

    Each `ScrollingList` widget has the following parts:

— Border

— Current Item

— Current Item Border

— Items

— Scrollbar

— View

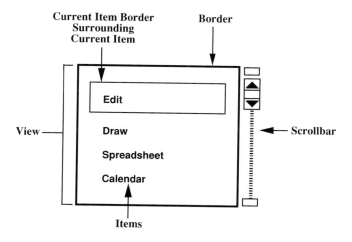

Figure 1. Common Scrolling List Components

If the application allows the list to be edited in place (in the View), the **Scrolling-List** widget uses the following components:

— Editable Text Field

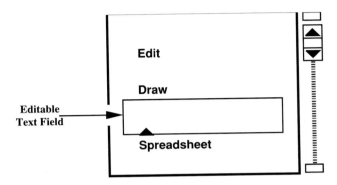

Figure 2. Editable Scrolling List Additional Components

Editable Scrolling List

The application can choose whether to allow the end user to add, change, and/or delete the items in a scrolling list. The Editable Text Field is the interface for entering, or changing the Item, and is described later. Other aspects of the user interface for editing are controlled by the application. For example, the application can attach a menu to the scrolling list to allow the end user to select where a new Item is to be inserted, and can employ pop-up windows to gather additional information about a new Item.

Editing Directly in the List—the Editable Text Field

The application can request that the **ScrollingList** widget manage part of the visual aspect of changing an existing Item in the View. The **ScrollingList** widget automatically creates a widget of class **TextField** that implements the Editable Text Field. The **ScrollingList** widget manages the Editable Text Field widget as follows:

- The application asks the **ScrollingList** widget to "open" and "close" the Editable Text Field. Opening the Editable Text Field widget maps it and positions it so that, as the end user types in the name of a new or changed Item, the name lines up with the existing Item names. Closing the Editable Text Field widget unmaps it. (As described below, there may be times when the widget is unmapped yet still open.) If an existing Item is being edited, the application requests the Editable Text Field to overlay the Item. If a new Item is being inserted, the application requests Items to be scrolled down in the View to accommodate the Editable Text Field.

- The **ScrollingList** widget maps and unmaps the Editable Text Field widget; the application does not.

- If the end user scrolls the list while the Editable Text Field is still open, the `ScrollingList` widget scrolls it with the rest of the Items. If it has to be scrolled out of the View, it is scrolled out entirely, causing it to be unmapped but not closed. The application should not try to remap the child since it will be remapped when the list is scrolled back again.

- If the end user attempts to make a selection or set a Current Item, the Editable Text Field is automatically closed.

The application is responsible for handling the verification callbacks of the Editable Text Field and for telling the `ScrollingList` widget to add a new Item or change an existing Item as a result of the user input.

Selectable Scrolling List

The application can choose whether to allow the end user to select Items from a scrolling list. If Items can be selected, they can be copied elsewhere as text, and may be deletable ("cut"); see below for details.

Deleting Selected Items

The end user can delete selected Items. The `ScrollingList` widget provides some deletion capabilities through the selection mechanisms (see the discussion under "Selecting and Operating on the Items" below), and the application can provide other capabilities, such as with a pop-up menu choice. The application verifies that each selected Item can be deleted; it is responsible for providing feedback to the end user for any Items it will not delete. The `ScrollingList` widget updates the View to remove any deleted Items.

Virtual List

The `ScrollingList` widget "virtualizes" the list to allow the application to use list data structures best suited to its needs. The `ScrollingList` widget provides routines the application uses to build and maintain a version of the list for the `ScrollingList` widget to use. With these routines, the application:

— adds new Items to the list;

— deletes Items from the list;

— edit items and mark them as changed;

— shifts the View to show a particular Item;

— and opens and closes the Editable Text Field for a new or changed Item.

The application is responsible for defining callbacks that the `ScrollingList` widgets invoke when the end user attempts to change a Current Item, or cuts Items from the list. Each Item is identified by the Item name that is shown in the View for the end user, a token assigned by the `ScrollingList` widget that uniquely identifies the Item, and an attributes bit-vector that identifies if the Item is a Current Item.

Order of Items in the Virtual List

The list is assumed to have an order defined by the application. As it adds Items, the application tells the `ScrollingList` widget where to insert them: either before or after an Item already in the list.

Changeable List

The application may change the content of a list at any time, including while it is displayed. The widget updates the View, if necessary, to reflect the changed list. To avoid unnecessary updates to the View when several changes need to be made, the application can tell the **ScrollingList** widget to avoid updates until the changes are finished.

Setting a Current Item

The end user can make one or more of the Items a Current Item, as determined by the application, by

— clicking or pressing SELECT over it,

— or moving the input focus inside the Border and typing the first letter of the Item's name.

Either of these actions causes a callback to the application, which can decide if the Item should be made a Current Item, remain a Current Item, or be changed to a regular Item, depending on the current state of the Item and the needs of the application. Thus, the application can make the scrolling list behave as a set of exclusive or nonexclusive Items.

Clicking or pressing SELECT also starts a selection, as described below.

Selecting and Operating on the Items

The **ScrollingList** widget allows selection operations on the Items. Items that are moved or copied from the View are treated as a newline-separated list of text items, in the order they appear in the scrolling list, with no leading or trailing blanks on any Item.

selecting a single Item
> Clicking SELECT on an Item selects it and unselects any other active selection on the screen.

selecting other Items
> Clicking ADJUST on an Item toggles its state, making an unselected Item selected and a selected Item unselected.

wipe-through selection, with SELECT
> Pressing and dragging SELECT over Items selects them and unselects any other active selection on the screen. The selection starts with the Item where SELECT is pressed and extends to the Item where SELECT is released. If the pointer moves above or below the View, the View scrolls additional Items into the View, selecting them as well. The rate at which Items scroll into the View is the same as when pressing SELECT on the up or down arrows of the Scrollbar. The pointer can move out of the View to the left or right without interrupting the selection.

wipe-through selection, with ADJUST
> Pressing and dragging ADJUST marks the bounds of a selection the same way as pressing and dragging SELECT, except that the Items covered are "toggled." (Previously selected Items are unselected and previously unselected Items are selected.)

copying Items
> Pressing COPY copies any selected Items to the clipboard and unselects them.

cutting Items
> Pressing CUT moves any selected Items to the clipboard and deletes them from the list. This operation is allowed only if the scrolling list is editable.

Coloration

On a monochrome display, the `ScrollingList` widget indicates that it has input focus by inverting foreground and background colors. When an editable Text Field has input focus, it shows that it has input focus by showing an active caret.

On color displays, the `ScrollingList` widget shows that the Current Item has input focus by filling the background of the Current Item with the input focus color set in the `XtNinputFocusColor` resource. When a selected item has input focus, the label is drawn with the input focus color. When an item is both Selected and Current, it shows that it has input focus by drawing the text of the label in the input focus color. When an editable Text Field has input focus, it shows that it has input focus by showing an active caret in the input focus color.

EXCEPTIONS: If the input focus color is the same as either the background, foreground, or font color, then revert to the monochrome coloration scheme.

Figures 3 and 4 illustrate the resources that affect the coloration of the `Scrolling-List` widget.

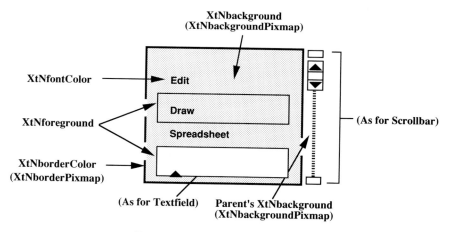

Figure 3. Scrolling List Coloration

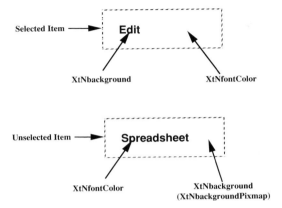

Figure 4. Selected Item and Unselected Item Coloration

Keyboard Traversal

The default value of the **XtNtraversalOn** resource is **TRUE**.

The **ScrollingList** widget responds to the following keyboard navigation keys:

NEXT_FIELD	moves to the next traversable widget in the window
PREV_FIELD	moves to the previous traversable widget in the window
NEXTWINDOW	moves to the next window in the application
PREVWINDOW	moves to the previous window in the application
NEXTAPP	moves to the first window in the next application
PREVAPP	moves to the first window in the previous application
MOVEUP	moves the input focus up one line
MOVEDOWN	moves the input focus down one line
PANESTART	moves the input focus to the first item in the pane
PANEEND	moves the input focus to the last item in the pane
SCROLLUP	scrolls up one item in the list
SCROLLDOWN	scrolls down one item in the list
SCROLLTOP	scrolls to the first item in the list
SCROLLBOTTOM	scrolls to the last item in the list
PAGEUP	scrolls up one page so that the first item visible is the last item visible in the pane

ScrollingList (3Olit)

PAGEDOWN scrolls down one page so that the last item visible is the first item visible in the pane

When an Editable Text Field is in the **ScrollingList**, the keyboard traversal keys defined for **TextField** widgets apply.

The SELECTKEY selects the Current Item and unselects any other active selection on the screen. The ADJUSTKEY toggles the Current Item's state, making an unselected Item selected and a selected Item unselected.

Note that the scrolling keys of interest are defined within the ScrollingList and traversal to the Scrollbar is not necessary to manipulate the ScrollingList.

Scrolling List Activation Types

Activation Type	Expected Results
OL_MENUKEY	Popup scrolling List menu

Display of Keyboard Mnemonic

The **ScrollingList** widget displays the mnemonic accelerator for each item as part of its label. If the mnemonic character is in the label, then that character is displayed/highlighted according to the value of the application resource **XtNshowMneumonics**. If the mnemonic character is not in the label, it is displayed to the right of the label in parenthesis and highlighted according to the value of the application resource **XtNshowMneumonics**.

If truncation is necessary, the mnemonic displayed in parenthesis is truncated as a unit.

SUBSTRUCTURE

Scrollbar component

Name: **scrollbar**
Class: **Scrollbar**

Editable Text Field component

Name: **textfield**
Class: **TextField**

Application Resources				
Name	Class	Type	Default	Access
XtNfont	XtCFont	XFontStruct *	‡	SGI
XtNfontColor	XtCFontColor	Pixel	‡	I
XtNfontGroup	XtCFontGroup	Pixel	‡	GI
XtNforeground	XtCForeground	Pixel	‡	I
XtNmaximumSize	XtCMaximumSize	int	(none)	I
XtNstring	XtCString	String	NULL	I
XtNverification	XtCCallback	XtCallbackList	NULL	I

‡ The defaults are set to agree with the values of these resources for the **ScrollingList** widget itself.

RESOURCES

ScrollingList Resource Set					
Name	Class	Type	Default	Acc	Inherit
XtNancestorSensitive	XtCSensitive	Boolean	(calculated)	G[1]	Core
XtNapplAddItem	XtCApplAddItem	OlListToken(*)()	(n/a)	G	
XtNapplDeleteItem	XtCApplDeleteItem	void(*)()	(n/a)	G	
XtNapplEditClose	XtCApplEditClose	void(*)()	(n/a)	G	
XtNapplEditOpen	XtCApplEditClose	void(*)()	(n/a)	G	
XtNapplTouchItem	XtCApplTouchItem	void(*)()	(n/a)	G	
XtNapplUpdateView	XtCApplUpdateView	void(*)()	(n/a)	G	
XtNapplViewItem	XtCApplViewItem	void(*)()	(n/a)	G	
XtNbackground	XtCBackground	Pixel	"XtDefaultBackground"	SGI	Core
XtNbackgroundPixmap	XtCPixmap	Pixmap	XtUnspecifiedPixmap	SGI	Core
XtNborderColor	XtCBorderColor	Pixel	"XtDefaultForeground"	SGI	Core
XtNborderPixmap	XtCPixmap	Pixmap	XtUnspecifiedPixmap	SGI	Core
XtNborderWidth	XtCBorderWidth	Dimension	0	SGI	Core
XtNchildren	XtCReadOnly	WidgetList	NULL	G	Composite
XtNcolormap	XtCColormap	Colormap	(parent's)	GI	Core
XtNconsumeEvent	XtCCallback	XtCallbackList	NULL	SGI	Manager
XtNdepth	XtCDepth	Cardinal	(parent's)	GI	Core
XtNdestroyCallback	XtCCallback	XtCallbackList	NULL	SGI	Object
XtNfont	XtCFont	XFontStruct *	OlDefaultFont	SGI	
XtNfontColor	XtCFontColor	Pixel	XtDefaultForeground	SGI	
XtNfontGroup	XtCFontGroup	OlFontList *	NULL	SGI	
XtNforeground	XtCForeground	Pixel	XtDefaultForeground	SGI	
XtNheight	XtCHeight	Dimension	(calculated)	SGI	Core
XtNinputFocusColor	XtCInputFocusColor	Pixel	"Red"	SGI	Manager
XtNinsertPosition	XtCInsertPosition	XtWidgetProc	NULL	SGI	Composite
XtNmappedWhenManaged	XtCMappedWhenManaged	Boolean	TRUE	SGI	Core
XtNnumChildren	XtCReadOnly	Cardinal	0	G	Composite
XtNrecomputeWidth	XtCRecomputeWidth	Boolean	TRUE	SGI	
XtNreferenceName	XtCReferenceName	String	NULL	SGI	Manager
XtNreferenceWidget	XtCReferenceWidget	Widget	NULL	SGI	Manager
XtNscreen	XtCScreen	Screen *	(parent's)	GI	Core
XtNselectable	XtCSelectable	Boolean	TRUE	SGI	
XtNsensitive	XtCSensitive	Boolean	TRUE	G[1]	Core
XtNshadowThickness	XtCShadowThickness	Dimension	"0 points"[3]	SGI	Manager
XtNshadowType	XtCShadowType	OlDefine	OL_SHADOW_OUT	SGI	Manager
XtNtextField	XtCTextField	Widget	NULL	G	
XtNtranslations	XtCTranslations	XtTranslations	NULL	SGI	Core
XtNtraversalOn	XtCTraversalOn	Boolean	TRUE	SGI	Manager
XtNuserData	XtCUserData	XtPointer	NULL	SGI	Manager

ScrollingList (3Olit)

ScrollingList Resource Set (cont'd)					
Name	Class	Type	Default	Acc	Inherit
XtNuserDeleteItems	XtCCallback	XtCallbackList	NULL	SGI	
XtNuserMakeCurrent	XtCCallback	XtCallbackList	NULL	SGI	
XtNviewHeight	XtCViewHeight	Cardinal	0	SI	
XtNwidth	XtCWidth	Dimension	(calculated)	SGI	Core
XtNx	XtCPosition	Position	0	SGI	Core
XtNy	XtCPosition	Position	0	SGI	Core

[1]   Use **XtSetSensitive** to set this resource.

[3]   "**2 points**" in the MOTIF look and feel.

OlListItem Structure

Several of the resources defined below use the **OlListItem** structure, which includes the following members:

```
OlDefine label_type;
XtPointer label;
XImage *glyph;
OlBitMask attr;
XtPointer user_data;
unsigned char mnemonic;
```

label_type

    identifies the type of label to display for the Item in the View. It can have one of the values

    OL_STRING   for a text label;

    OL_IMAGE   for an image label.

    Note that only text labels are supported in this version of the **Scrolling-List** widget, so the only value allowed is **OL_STRING**. Any other legal values generate an error message that tells the application programmer that the value is not yet supported. Any illegal values generate a different error message.

label   is what to display for the Item in the View. The type of the value of this member depends on the value of the **label_type** member:

    OL_STRING **String**

    OL_IMAGE   **XImage***

glyph   is currently unused.

attr   defines attributes of the Item. It is a bit vector with the bit references:

    OL_LIST_ATTR_APPL

        for application use. This is a mask of 16 contiguous bits that can be subdivided as the application sees fit. These are the low 16 bits of the value, so no shifting is necessary to access the bits as an integer value.

`OL_LIST_ATTR_CURRENT`
> if the Item is a Current Item.

Other bit values are undefined but should not be used by the application.

`mnemonic`
> is a single character that is used as a mnemonic accelerator for keyboard traversal.

OlListToken Structure

The `ScrollingList` widget identifies each Item with a "token" of type `OlList-Token`. The `ScrollingList` widget assigns the token when an Item is added by the application, and the application uses the token in later references to the Item. A zero value is allowed in some contexts where an `OlListToken` is expected, as a way to refer to no Item.

As a convenience to the application, the function `OlListItemPointer`(*token*) converts an `OlListToken` value into a pointer to the corresponding `OlListItem`. The application can change the values of the `OlListItem` members, but should let the `ScrollingList` widget know that they have changed, using the `XtNapplTouchItem` routine. No checking is done for incorrect `OlListToken` arguments to the `OlListItemPointer` function.

The `OlListToken` value can be coerced into the type `XtPointer` and back without loss of precision.

XtNapplAddItem

This resource gives a pointer to a routine the application can call when it adds a new Item to the list. This routine is also used to build the list from scratch.

Synopsis:

```
OlListToken (*applAddItem)(), token;

static Arg query[] = {
        { XtNapplAddItem, (XtArgVal)&applAddItem }
};
XtGetValues(widget, query, XtNumber(query));

token = (*applAddItem)(
    Widget widget,
    OlListToken parent,
    OlListToken reference,
    OlListItem item
);
```

widget   identifies the `ScrollingList` widget instance.

parent   should be set to 0, for compatibility with future changes.

reference
> identifies an Item before which to insert the new Item. This value can be zero to append the new Item to the list.

item   describes the new Item. The content of the `OlListItem` structure is copied by the `ScrollingList` widget into space that it maintains; however, the data pointed to by the *label* and *glyph* members are not copied. The application can access the copied data directly, using the `OlListItemPointer` function to get a pointer to the `OlListItem` structure for the Item. If it changes the data, the application should use the `XtNapplTouchItem` routine to let the `ScrollingList` widget know the data has changed.

If mapped and if allowed by the application (see `XtNapplUpdateView`), the `ScrollingList` widget updates the View if the new Item will be in the View. The View is changed as little as possible: if the new Item is in the upper half of the View, the Items above it are scrolled up and the top Item is scrolled off; if the new Item is in the lower half of the View, the Items below it are scrolled down and the bottom Item is scrolled off.

XtNapplDeleteItem

This resource gives a pointer to a routine the application can call when it deletes an Item from the list.

Synopsis:

```
void (*applDeleteItem)();

static Arg query[] = {
        { XtNapplDeleteItem, (XtArgVal)&applDeleteItem }
};
XtGetValues(widget, query, XtNumber(query));

(*applDeleteItem)(
    Widget widget,
    OlListToken token
);
```

widget   identifies the `ScrollingList` widget instance.

token   identifies the deleted Item.

If mapped and if allowed by the application (see `XtNapplUpdateView`), the `ScrollingList` widget updates the View if the deleted Item was visible. The View is changed as little as possible: if the deleted Item was in the upper half of the View, Items above it are scrolled down and an Item is scrolled in from the top; if the deleted Item was in the lower half of the View, Items below it are scrolled up and an Item is scrolled in from the bottom. If the View is already at the top or bottom, the additional Item is scrolled in from the other end, if possible.

XtNapplEditClose

This resource gives a pointer to a routine the application can call when the user has finished editing an Item in the View.

Synopsis:

```
void (*applEditClose)();

static Arg query[] = {
        { XtNapplEditClose, (XtArgVal)&applEditClose }
};
XtGetValues(widget, query, XtNumber(query));

(*applEditClose)(
    Widget widget
);
```

widget   identifies the **ScrollingList** widget instance.

When this routine is called, the **ScrollingList** widget unmaps the Editable Text Field widget, scrolling up the Items below it if they had been scrolled down to allow an insert. The application is responsible for calling the **XtNapplAddItem** routine to add the new Item, or calling the **XtNapplTouchItem** routine to mark the Item as changed. To avoid unnecessary updates to the View, the application should add the new Item (using **XtNapplAddItem**) or mark the changed Item (using **XtNapplTouchItem**) before closing the Editable Text Field.

A later call to the **XtNapplEditClose** routine without an intervening call to the **XtNapplEditOpen** routine is ignored.

If mapped, the **ScrollingList** widget updates the View, even if the application had halted updates (see **XtNapplUpdateView**). If the application had halted updates, they will continue to be halted afterwards.

XtNapplEditOpen

This resource gives a pointer to a routine the application can call when it wants to allow the end user to insert a new Item or change an existing Item in the View.

Synopsis:

```
void (*applEditOpen)();

static Arg query[] = {
        { XtNapplEditOpen, (XtArgVal)&applEditOpen }
};
XtGetValues(widget, query, XtNumber(query));

(*applEditOpen)(
    Widget widget,
    Boolean insert,
    OlListToken reference
);
```

widget   identifies the **ScrollingList** widget instance.

insert   tells whether Items should be scrolled down to make room for inserting a new Item. A value of **FALSE** implies that an Item is being edited in place and no Items are to be scrolled.

reference

identifies an Item before which a new Item is to be inserted (**insert** is **TRUE**) or identifies the Item that is being changed (**insert** is **FALSE**). If **insert** is **TRUE**, this value can be zero to append a new Item at the end of the list. If **insert** is **FALSE**, this value must refer to an existing Item. The referenced Item does not have to be in the View — see below.

If a new Item is being inserted, the **ScrollingList** widget makes room for the Editable Text Field by scrolling down the referenced Item and any Items below it. If the referenced Item is not in the View, it is automatically made visible just as if the application had called the **XtNapplViewItem** routine first.

ScrollingList (3Olit)

The **XtNapplEditOpen** routine can be called again before an intervening call to the **XtNapplEditClose** routine. The effect is as if the **XtNapplEditClose** routine was called, but without multiple updates to the View. For example, this allows the application to let the end user insert several new Items in succession: the Editable Text Field moves down as each Item is inserted, but is never removed from the View.

If mapped, the **ScrollingList** widget updates the View, even if the application had halted updates (see **XtNapplUpdateView**). If the application had halted updates, they will continue to be halted afterwards.

XtNapplTouchItem

This resource gives a pointer to a routine the application can call when it changes an Item in the list.

Synopsis:

```
void (*applTouchItem)();

static Arg query[] = {
        { XtNapplTouchItem, (XtArgVal)&applTouchItem }
};
XtGetValues(widget, query, XtNumber(query));

(*applTouchItem)(
    Widget widget,
    OlListToken token
);
```

widget identifies the **ScrollingList** widget instance.

token identifies the Item that has changed.

If mapped and if allowed by the application (see **XtNapplUpdateView**), the **ScrollingList** widget updates the View if the changed Item is visible.

XtNapplUpdateView

This resource gives a pointer to a routine the application can call to keep the **ScrollingList** widget from updating the View, or to let it update the View again.

Synopsis:

```
void (*applUpdateView)();

static Arg query[] = {
        { XtNapplUpdateView, (XtArgVal)&applUpdateView }
};
XtGetValues(widget, query, XtNumber(query));

(*applUpdateView)(
    Widget widget,
    Boolean ok
);
```

ok is either **TRUE** or **FALSE**, depending on whether the **ScrollingList** can update the View as it changes, or not, respectively.

From the time the **XtNapplUpdateView** routine is called with a **FALSE** argument until it is called with a **TRUE** argument, the **ScrollingList** does not update the View in response to application-made changes, except:

— if the application opens or closes the Editable Text Field (compared to **Xt-NapplEditOpen** and **XtNapplEditClose**);

— if the end user manipulates the list by scrolling it, selecting an Item, cutting, etc.

The **ScrollingList** widget updates the View once for each of these exceptions, each time an exception occurs.

An application should use this routine to bracket a set of changes to avoid spurious changes to the View. This routine is not needed if only one change is made to the list. The following example illustrates the use of the **XtNapplUpdateView** routine.

```
/*
 * Stop View updates.
 */
(*applUpdateView)(widget, FALSE);

/*
 * Make some changes.
 */
(*applDeleteItem)(widget, . . .);
(*applDeleteItem)(widget, . . .);
(*applDeleteItem)(widget, . . .);
(*applAddItem)(widget, . . .);
(*applTouchItem)(widget, . . .);

/*
 * Allow the View to be updated again.
 */
(*applUpdateView)(widget, TRUE);
```

XtNapplViewItem

This resource gives a pointer to a routine the application can call when it wants a particular Item placed in the View.

Synopsis:

```
void (*applViewItem)();

static Arg query[] = {
        { XtNapplViewItem, (XtArgVal)&applViewItem }
};
XtGetValues(widget, query, XtNumber(query));

(*applViewItem)(
    Widget widget,
    OlListToken token
);
```

widget   identifies the `ScrollingList` widget instance.

token   identifies the Item to move into the View.

The Item is moved into the View in a way that minimizes the change to the View. If the Item is currently in the View, nothing is changed. If scrolling the list up or down brings the Item into the View while keeping at least one previously viewed Item in the View, the list is scrolled. Otherwise, the Item is placed at the top of the View, or as close to the top as possible if there aren't enough Items in the current Level to fill the View below it.

If mapped and if allowed by the application (see `XtNapplUpdateView`), the `ScrollingList` widget updates the View.

XtNrecomputeWidth
Range of values:

    TRUE/"true"
    FALSE/"false"

This resource controls how the `ScrollingList` widget should respond to requests to resize itself. If this resource is `TRUE`, the `ScrollingList` shrinks the View of the Content in the corresponding direction to absorb the change in the `ScrollingList` widget's size. If this resource is `FALSE`, the `ScrollingList` does not shrink the View in that direction.

This resource, together with the `XtNviewHeight` resource, are typically used to set a preferred dimension in a direction that should not be scrolled.

XtNselectable
Range of values:

    TRUE/"true"
    FALSE/"false"

This resource controls whether the end user can select Items in the scrolling list. If set to `TRUE`, then Items can be selected with SELECT and ADJUST and copied with the COPY key. Items may be deleted with the CUT key, although the application can stop some or all selected Items from being deleted. If set to `FALSE`, then Items cannot be selected and the COPY and CUT keys have no effect.

XtNtextField
This is the widget ID of the Editable `TextField` widget; its value is available once the `ScrollingList` widget has been created.

The `ScrollingList` widget resets the following values before returning from each invocation of the `XtNapplEditOpen` routine:

Editable Text Field Reset Values

Name	Class	Value
XtNwidth	XtCWidth	(width available in View)
XtNstring	XtCString	(name of Item to be changed)

XtNtraversalOn
This resource specifies whether this widget is selectable during traversal.

XtNuserDeleteItems

This resource defines the callbacks issued when the end user tries to delete Items from the list. (Currently, the only way the **ScrollingList** widget handles deletions is through a cut operation.)

The **call_data** parameter points to a structure **OlListDelete** that includes the following members:

```
OlListToken *tokens;
Cardinal num_tokens;
```

tokens is a list identifying the Items to be deleted. The application is expected to act on each Item separately, calling the **XtNapplDeleteItem** routine to delete each from the list. The application may refuse to delete some or all of the Items, and is responsible for providing any feedback to the end-user.

num_tokens
is the number of Items to delete.

XtNuserMakeCurrent

This resource defines the callbacks issued when the end user presses SELECT over an Item.

The **call_data** parameter is the **OlListToken** value that identifies the Item. The application is expected to decide if the Current Item status of this Item should change. The *attr* member of the **OlListItem** structure for this Item is not automatically changed by the **ScrollingList** widget.

XtNviewHeight

Range of values:

$$0 \leq \text{XtNviewHeight}$$

This resource gives the preferred height of the View as the number of Items to show. If a nonzero value is given, the corresponding **XtNheight** resource is computed by converting this number to pixels and adding any padding or border thickness. In this case, any value given in the **XtNheight** resource is overwritten.

If a zero value is given in the **XtNviewHeight** resource, the **XtNheight** resource is used as an estimate. The View is sized to show an integral number of Items, such that the overall height of the **ScrollingList** widget is less than or equal to **XtNheight**, if possible. However, the View is always large enough to show at least one Item, and is no shorter than the minimum scrollbar size.

If neither the **XtNviewHeight** resource nor the **XtNheight** resource is set, or both are set to zero, the View is made as small as possible, limited as described above.

SEE ALSO

FlatList(3Olit)

NOTES

For a MOTIF look and feel, use the **FlatList** widget.

Shell (3Olit)

NAME

    Shell – **Shell** widget superclass

SYNOPSIS

```
#include <X11/Intrinsic.h>
#include <X11/StringDefs.h>
#include <Xol/OpenLook.h>
```

DESCRIPTION

    These are resources that are common to all widget classes that are subclasses of **Shell**. They are described here to avoid repeating their descriptions for each shell widget.

RESOURCES

<table>
<tr><th colspan="5">Shell Resource Set</th></tr>
<tr><th>Name</th><th>Class</th><th>Type</th><th>Default</th><th>Acc</th></tr>
<tr><td>XtNallowShellResize</td><td>XtCAllowShellResize</td><td>Boolean</td><td>TRUE</td><td>SGI</td></tr>
<tr><td>XtNargc</td><td>XtCArgc</td><td>int</td><td>0</td><td>SGI</td></tr>
<tr><td>XtNargv</td><td>XtCArgv</td><td>String *</td><td>NULL</td><td>SGI</td></tr>
<tr><td>XtNbaseHeight</td><td>XtCBaseHeight</td><td>int</td><td>XtUnspecifiedShellInt</td><td>SGI</td></tr>
<tr><td>XtNbaseWidth</td><td>XtCBaseWidth</td><td>int</td><td>XtUnspecifiedShellInt</td><td>SGI</td></tr>
<tr><td>XtNbusy</td><td>XtCBusy</td><td>Boolean</td><td>FALSE</td><td>SGI</td></tr>
<tr><td>XtNconsumeEvent</td><td>XtCCallback</td><td>XtCallbackList</td><td>NULL</td><td>SGI</td></tr>
<tr><td>XtNcreatePopupChildProc</td><td>XtCCreatePopupChildProc</td><td>XtCreatePopupChildProc</td><td>NULL</td><td>SGI</td></tr>
<tr><td>XtNfocusModel</td><td>XtCFocusModel</td><td>OlDefine</td><td>OL_CLICK_TO_TYPE</td><td>SGI</td></tr>
<tr><td>XtNfocusWidget</td><td>XtCFocusWidget</td><td>Widget</td><td>NULL</td><td>SGI</td></tr>
<tr><td>XtNgeometry</td><td>XtCGeometry</td><td>String</td><td>NULL</td><td>GI</td></tr>
<tr><td>XtNheightInc</td><td>XtCHeightInc</td><td>int</td><td>XtUnspecifiedShellInt</td><td>SGI</td></tr>
<tr><td>XtNiconMask</td><td>XtCIconMask</td><td>Bitmap</td><td>None</td><td>SGI</td></tr>
<tr><td>XtNiconName</td><td>XtCIconName</td><td>String</td><td>NULL</td><td>SGI</td></tr>
<tr><td>XtNiconNameEncoding</td><td>XtCIconNameEncoding</td><td>Atom</td><td>(calculated)</td><td>SGI</td></tr>
<tr><td>XtNiconPixmap</td><td>XtCIconPixmap</td><td>Bitmap</td><td>None</td><td>SGI</td></tr>
<tr><td>XtNiconWindow</td><td>XtCIconWindow</td><td>Window</td><td>None</td><td>SGI</td></tr>
<tr><td>XtNiconX</td><td>XtCIconX</td><td>int</td><td>XtUnspecifiedShellInt</td><td>SGI</td></tr>
<tr><td>XtNiconY</td><td>XtCIconY</td><td>int</td><td>XtUnspecifiedShellInt</td><td>SGI</td></tr>
<tr><td>XtNiconic</td><td>XtCIconic</td><td>Boolean</td><td>FALSE</td><td>SGI</td></tr>
<tr><td>XtNinitialState</td><td>XtCInitialState</td><td>int</td><td>NormalState</td><td>GI</td></tr>
<tr><td>XtNinput</td><td>XtCInput</td><td>Boolean</td><td>FALSE</td><td>G</td></tr>
<tr><td>XtNmaxAspectX</td><td>XtCMaxAspectX</td><td>int</td><td>XtUnspecifiedShellInt</td><td>SGI</td></tr>
<tr><td>XtNmaxAspectY</td><td>XtCMaxAspectY</td><td>int</td><td>XtUnspecifiedShellInt</td><td>SGI</td></tr>
<tr><td>XtNmaxHeight</td><td>XtCMaxHeight</td><td>int</td><td>XtUnspecifiedShellInt</td><td>SGI</td></tr>
<tr><td>XtNmaxWidth</td><td>XtCMaxWidth</td><td>int</td><td>XtUnspecifiedShellInt</td><td>SGI</td></tr>
<tr><td>XtNmenuButton</td><td>XtCMenuButton</td><td>Boolean</td><td>TRUE</td><td>GI</td></tr>
<tr><td>XtNmenuType</td><td>XtCMenuType</td><td>OlDefine</td><td>OL_MENU_FULL</td><td>SGI</td></tr>
<tr><td>XtNminAspectX</td><td>XtCMinAspectX</td><td>int</td><td>XtUnspecifiedShellInt</td><td>SGI</td></tr>
</table>

Shell Resource Set (cont'd)				
Name	Class	Type	Default	Acc
XtNminAspectY	XtCMinAspectY	int	XtUnspecifiedShellInt	SGI
XtNminHeight	XtCMinHeight	int	XtUnspecifiedShellInt	SGI
XtNminWidth	XtCMinWidth	int	XtUnspecifiedShellInt	SGI
XtNoverrideRedirect	XtCOverrideRedirect	Boolean	FALSE	SGI
XtNpopdownCallback	XtCCallback	XtCallbackList	NULL	SGI
XtNpopupCallback	XtCCallback	XtCallbackList	NULL	SGI
XtNpushpin	XtCPushpin	OlDefine	OL_NONE	SGI
XtNresizeCorners	XtCResizeCorners	Boolean	TRUE	SGI
XtNsaveUnder	XtCSaveUnder	Boolean	FALSE	SGI
XtNstatusAreaGeometry	XtCStatusAreaGeometry	XtWidgetGeometry	NULL	SGI
XtNtitle	XtCTitle	String	NULL	SGI
XtNtitleEncoding	XtCTitleEncoding	Atom	(calculated)	SGI
XtNtransient	XtCTransient	Boolean	FALSE	SGI
XtNuserData	XtCUserData	XtPointer	NULL	SGI
XtNvisual	XtCVisual	Visual *	NULL	GI
XtNwaitforwm	XtCWaitforwm	Boolean	TRUE	SGI
XtNwidthInc	XtCWidthInc	int	XtUnspecifiedShellInt	SGI
XtNwinGravity	XtCWinGravity	int	XtUnspecifiedShellInt	SGI
XtNwinType	XtCWinType	OlDefine	OL_WT_BASE	SGI
XtNwindowGroup	XtCWindowGroup	Window	XtUnspecifiedWindow	SGI
XtNwindowHeader	XtCWindowHeader	Boolean	TRUE	GI
XtNwmProtocol	XtCCallback	XtCallbackList	NULL	SGI
XtNwmProtocolInterested	XtCWMProtocolInterested	int	(see note[9])	GI
XtNwmTimeout	XtCWmTimeout	int	5000	SGI

[9] Default is combination of OL_WM_DELETE_WINDOW and OL_WM_TAKE_FOCUS.

XtNallowShellResize

Range of values:

> TRUE/"true"
> FALSE/"false"

This resource controls whether the shell widget is allowed to resize itself in response to a geometry request from its child. If set to **TRUE**, it will attempt to resize itself as requested by the child. The attempt may be refused by the window manager, which will cause the shell widget to refuse the geometry management request of its child. Otherwise, it accepts the request. If the **XtNallowShellResize** request is set to **FALSE**, the shell widget will immediately refuse the geometry management request.

XtNbusy

Setting this resource to **TRUE** makes the application window associated with this shell busy. When a window becomes busy, the window manager grays the window header (if there is one). Setting the **XtNbusy** resource back to **FALSE** causes the window to return to its normal appearance and event processing.

NOTE: Neither the window manager or the toolkit grabs mouse or keyboard events when an application window becomes busy.

XtNconsumeEvent

The resource overrides the handling of events. Whenever an event is processed by the standard translation table, the **XtNConsumeEvent** list is called for the widget in question allowing the application to consume the **XEvent**. To consume an event, the application should turn on (set to **TRUE**) the consumed field in the `call_data` argument when a given event is processed.

NOTE: **OlAddCallback** must be used instead of **XtAddCallback** when adding callbacks to the **XtNconsumeEvent** callback list.

XtNcreatePopupChildProc

This resource defines a pointer to a single function (not a callback list) that is called during the process of popping up the shell widget. It is called after the **XtNpopup-Callback** callbacks are issued but before the shell widget is realized and mapped. The function is passed a single argument, the ID of the shell widget.

XtNfocusWidget

This resource controls which widget gets the input focus when a pop-up or base window gains input focus. If this resource is non-NULL, focus is set it. If this resource is NULL or the widget to which it refers is unwilling to accept input focus, the pop-up or base window sets focus to either the default widget in the window or the first widget willing to accept focus. As focus changes within the shell, this resource is updated to reflect the last widget with focus.

A resource converter will translate widget names specified in a resource file to a widget ID for this resource.

XtNgeometry

Range of values:

(any syntactically correct argument to the **XParseGeometry** function)

This resource can be used to specify the size and position of the shell widget when it pops up.

XtNheightInc/XtNwidthInc

Range of values:

0 ≤ **XtNheightInc**
0 ≤ **XtNwidthInc**

These resources define an arithmetic progression of sizes, from **XtNminHeight** and **XtNminWidth** to **XtNmaxHeight** and **XtNmaxWidth**, into which the shell widget prefers to be resized by the window manager.

XtNiconic

Range of values:

TRUE/"true"
FALSE/"false"

This resource provides an equivalent method of setting the **XtNinitialState** resource to **IconicState**.

XtNiconMask

This resource defines an image that specifies which pixels of the `XtNiconPixmap` resource should be used for the base window's icon. This image must be a single plane pixmap.

XtNiconName

This resource defines a name that the window manager will display in the shell widget's icon. If the `XtNtitle` resource is not defined or is NULL, this resource is used instead. If this resource is NULL, the name of the application is used in its place.

XtNiconPixmap

This resource defines the image to be used as the base window's icon. It must be a single plane pixmap.

XtNiconWindow

Range of values:

(ID of any existing window)

This resource defines the ID of a window that the window manager should use for the base window's icon, in place of `XtNiconPixmap`. The `XtNiconWindow` takes precedence over the `XtNiconPixmap` resource.

XtNiconX/XtNiconY

Range of values:

$-1 \leq$ `XtNiconX`
$-1 \leq$ `XtNiconY`

These resources define the location where the base window's icon should appear. If the value of one of these resources is -1, the window manager automatically picks a value, according to its icon placement requirements.

XtNinitialState

Range of values:

`NormalState`/"1"
`IconicState`/"3"

This resource defines how the base window (and associated pop-up windows) appears when the application starts up.

`NormalState`

When set to this value, the application starts up with its base window open.

`IconicState`

When set to this value, the application starts up with its base window closed into an icon.

NOTE: Other values are defined by the X Window System for this resource, but the window manager recognizes only the iconic and normal states.

XtNinput

This resource controls the type of input focus behavior of the application. It should not be set by an application.

XtNmenuButton

This Boolean resource determines if the menu button decoration should be drawn in the upper left corner of the shell window's header The default, **TRUE**, indicates that it should be drawn. If the **XtNpushpin** resource is not **OL_NONE**, this resource is ignored.

XtNmenuType

Range of values:

> OL_MENU_FULL/"full"
> OL_MENU_LIMITED/"limited"
> OL_MENU_CANCEL/"cancel"
> OL_NONE/"none"

This resource provides the application access to the type of window menu that the window manager creates. The default value is **OL_MENU_FULL** for a base shell. This full menu contains the following entries: Close, Full Size, Properties, Back, Refresh, and Quit. Setting this resource to **OL_MENU_LIMITED** results in a window menu with the following buttons: Dismiss (a MenuButton), Back, Refresh, and Owner?. PopupWindow and Help shells set this resource to **OL_MENU_LIMITED**. The menu type **OL_MENU_CANCEL** provides the same menu as the **OL_MENU_LIMITED** with the exception that the Dismiss button is replaced with a Cancel button. When the **XtNmenuType** resource is **OL_NONE**, the window manager does not create a menu or a menu mark.

XtNmaxAspectX/XtNmaxAspectY
XtNminAspectX/XtNminAspectY

Range of values:

> $-1 = $ XtNmaxAspectX, $1 \leq$ XtNmaxAspectX
> $-1 = $ XtNmaxAspectY, $1 \leq$ XtNmaxAspectY
> $-1 = $ XtNminAspectX, $1 \leq$ XtNminAspectX
> $-1 = $ XtNminAspectY, $1 \leq$ XtNminAspectY

$$\frac{\text{XtNminAspectX}}{\text{XtNminAspectY}} \leq \frac{\text{XtNmaxAspectX}}{\text{XtNmaxAspectY}}$$

These resources define the range of aspect ratios allowed for the size of the shell widget's window. Assuming the width and height of the window are given by *width* and *height*, the following relation shows how the window size is constrained:

$$\frac{\text{XtNminAspectX}}{\text{XtNminAspectY}} \leq \frac{width}{height} \leq \frac{\text{XtNmaxAspectX}}{\text{XtNmaxAspectY}}$$

If the end user tries to resize the window to a narrower or wider aspect ratio than allowed by these resources, the window manager adjusts the window to the closest allowed aspect ratio. If possible, it will do this by increasing the width or height to compensate. The **XtNmaxHeight** and **XtNmaxWidth** resources may force the window manager to reduce the width or height instead.

If the values of these resources are -1, the window manager does not constrain the size of the window to any aspect ratio.

NOTE: An application should either set all values to -1 (the default) or should set all to a positive value. An application should never set a value of zero to any of these resources.

XtNmaxHeight/XtNmaxWidth/XtNminHeight/XtNminWidth

Range of values:

$$XtNminHeight \leq XtNmaxHeight$$
$$XtNminWidth \leq XtNmaxWidth$$

(or OL_IGNORE for any of these resources)

These resources define the range allowed for the size of the shell widget's window. If the end user tries to resize the window smaller or larger than these values allow, the window manager adjusts the width and/or height to compensate.

The default value of OL_IGNORE keeps the window manager from constraining the window's size.

XtNoverrideRedirect

Range of values:

TRUE/"true"
FALSE/"false"

This resource controls whether the shell widget's window is managed by the window manager. Since this toolkit is designed to have a certain pop-up window behavior, this resource should not be set by an application for the shell widgets defined in this toolkit (**Menu, Notice**, and **PopupWindow**).

XtNpopdownCallback

This resource defines callbacks automatically issued right after the shell widget's window has been unmapped (that is, popped down.)

XtNpopupCallback

This resource defines callbacks automatically issued right before the shell widget is realized and mapped (that is, popped up.)

XtNpushpin

Range of values:

OL_NONE/"none"
OL_OUT/"out"
OL_IN/"in"

This resource controls whether the pushpin is included in the window's decorations. The default for the base shell type is OL_NONE, indicating that the pushpin is not included in the window's decorations. Setting this resource to OL_OUT adds the pushpin to the window's decorations, and sets its state to be unpinned. OL_OUT is the default value for this resource in PopupWindow shells. Setting this resource to OL_IN adds the pushpin to the window's decorations, and sets its state to be pinned. OL_IN is the default value for this resource in Help shells. Applications can query the state of the pushpin by getting the value of this resource, since it is updated when the pushpin's state changes.

If the shell does not have an header (**XtNwindowHeader** set to **FALSE**), then **XtNpushpin** is always OL_NONE, and attempts to change the value are ignored.

XtNresizeCorners

This Boolean resource determines if the resize corners should be part of the window decorations. The default for the base shell is **TRUE**, that resize corners are present. PopupWindow also defaults to having resize corners, but Notice, Help and Menu shells do not have resize corners.

XtNsaveUnder

Range of values:

> TRUE/"true"
> FALSE/"false"

This resource directs the shell widget to instruct the server to attempt to save the contents of windows obscured by the shell when it is mapped, and to restore the contents when the shell widget is unmapped.

XtNtitle

This resource gives the title to include in the header of the base or pop-up window. Widgets of other classes besides **Shell** may have a resource with the same name.

XtNtransient

Range of values:

> TRUE/"true"
> FALSE/"false"

This resource controls whether the shell widget's window is "transient" and is to be unmapped when the associated base window is iconified (see **XtNwindowGroup**). Since this toolkit is designed to have a certain pop-up window behavior, this resource should not be set by an application for the shell widgets defined in this toolkit (**Menu**, **Notice**, and **PopupWindow**).

XtNuserData

This resource provides storage for application-specific data. It is not used or set by the widget. Its default value is NULL.

XtNwaitForWm

This resource should not be set by an application.

XtNwindowGroup

Range of values:

> (ID of any existing window)

This resource identifies the base window associated with this shell widget's window. When the end user closes the base window, all its associated windows are unmapped (pop-up windows or other shell widget windows with **XtNtransient** set to **TRUE**) or closed (base windows with **XtNtransient** set to **FALSE**).

XtNwindowHeader

This Boolean resource determines if the window manager should provide a header for the window. The header is the area of the window that contains the pushpin, title, and window mark. The default for the base shell is **TRUE**, that the window does have a header. The PopupWindow and Help shells also have default headers, but the Notice shell would default to **FALSE**. This resource can only be set at initialization.

XtNwmProtocol

Range of values:

> OL_WM_TAKE_FOCUS
> OL_WM_SAVE_YOURSELF
> OL_WM_DELETE_WINDOW

This resource controls the action that is taken whenever a shell widget (which is a subclass of a **VendorShell** widget class) receives **WM_PROTOCOL** messages. If no callback list is specified, the shell performs its default action(s). If a callback list is specified, it is invoked and no default action(s) is taken. The application can, however, simulate the default action(s) at its convenience by calling `OlWMProtocolAction` with the `action` parameter set to `OL_DEFAULTACTION`. (See `OlWMProtocolAction`(3Olit) for more information on this routine.)

When the application's callback procedure is invoked, the `call_data` field is a pointer to a `OlWMProtocolVerify` structure, which includes the following members:

```
int        msgtype;         /* type of WM msg */
XEvent *   xevent;
```

The field `msgtype` is an integer constant indicating the type of protocol message which invoked the callback and has a range of values of:

```
OL_WM_TAKE_FOCUS
OL_WM_SAVE_YOURSELF
OL_WM_DELETE_WINDOW
```

Note that `OlAddCallback` must be used instead of `XtAddCallback` when adding callbacks to the `XtNwmProtocol` callback list.

XtNwmProtocolInterested

This specifies the types of protocol messages that interest the application. By default, it is both `OL_WM_DELETE_WINDOW` and `OL_WM_TAKE_FOCUS`. Furthermore, these two types are always turned on and cannot be turned off. Thus, setting `XtNwmProtocolInterested` to `OL_WM_SAVE_YOURSELF` will get all three types.

SEE ALSO

`OlToolkitInitialize`(3Olit)

Slider (3Olit)

NAME

Slider – create a visual and numeric setting range

SYNOPSIS

```
#include <X11/Intrinsic.h>
#include <X11/StringDefs.h>
#include <Xol/OpenLook.h>
#include <Xol/Slider.h>

widget = XtCreateWidget(name, sliderWidgetClass, . . .);
```

DESCRIPTION

The Slider widget implements a simple control used to change a numeric value. The Slider widget supports both the MOTIF and the OPEN LOOK look and feel.

MOTIF Slider Components

The MOTIF look and feel Slider widget consists of the following elements:

— Slider

— Trough

— Current Value (optional)

— Location Cursor (a box surrounding the Trough, when the slider has focus)

Figures 1 and 2 show a MOTIF look and feel Slider in 3D.

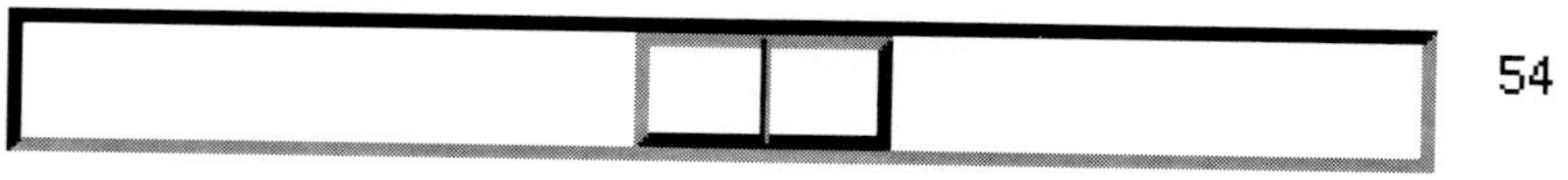

Figure 1. MOTIF Style Horizontal Slider with Current Value

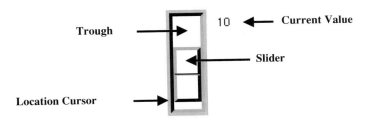

Figure 2. MOTIF Style Vertical Slider with Current Value and Location Cursor

OPEN LOOK Slider Components
The OPEN LOOK look and feel **Slider** widget consists of the following elements:

— Top (Left) Anchor (optional)

— Bottom (Right) Anchor (optional)

— Drag Box

— Bar (typically)

— Shaded Bar (typically)

— Current Value (not visible)

— Minimum Value (not visible)

— Minimum Value Label (optional)

— Maximum Value (not visible)

— Maximum Value Label (optional)

— Tick Marks (optional)

The Current Value is the numeric value a user attempts to change with the **Slider** widget.

Figures 3 and 4 show an OPEN LOOK look and feel Slider in 2D.

Slider (3Olit)

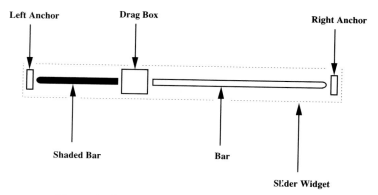

Figure 3. OPEN LOOK Style Horizontal Slider

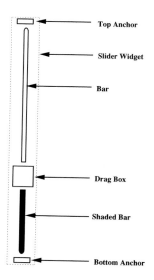

Figure 4. OPEN LOOK Style Vertical Slider

Slider Motion

As visual feedback to the user, the Slider (MOTIF look and feel) or Drag Box (OPEN LOOK look and feel) moves up or down (or left or right) along the Trough (MOTIF look and feel) or Bar (OPEN LOOK look and feel) as the Current Value changes.

Dragging SELECT

The user can change the Current Value by dragging the Slider or Drag Box with SELECT. The pressing of SELECT must start with the pointer in the Slider or Drag Box, but the Slider or Drag Box (and the Current Value) track the pointer motion regardless of where it goes while SELECT is pressed. This means it is not possible for the user to change the Current Value by first pressing SELECT outside the Slider or Drag Box and then moving the pointer into it. Only the component of the pointer motion parallel to the Bar is tracked, and the motion of the Slider or Drag Box (and change in the Current Value) are limited by the length of the Trough or Bar.

Clicking SELECT

Clicking SELECT above the Slider or Drag Box for a vertical slider, or to the right for a horizontal slider, increases the Current Value by an application-specified amount, moves the Slider or Drag Box to correspond to the new Current Value, and moves the pointer to keep it on the Slider or Drag Box. Clicking SELECT to the other side of the Slider or Drag Box decreases the value by the same amount and moves the Slider or Drag Box and pointer accordingly. Pressing SELECT repeats this action.

Moving to Limits

In the MOTIF look and feel, clicking Btoggle in the Trough on either side of the slider causes the Slider to move to the end on which the button was pressed.

In the OPEN LOOK look and feel, clicking SELECT on one of the Bottom/Left or Top/Right Anchors causes the Current Value to take on the Minimum Value or Maximum Value, respectively, and moves the Drag Box to the limit in the direction of the Anchor. If the Drag Box is already at the limit, nothing happens.

Clicking SELECT on an Anchor highlights the Anchor while the Current Value is changed.

Application Notification

The application finds out about a change in the Current Value on the release of SELECT for either the drag or click. It is responsible for providing any feedback to the end user deemed appropriate, such as updating the Current Value in a text field.

Coloration

In the MOTIF look and feel, when the **Slider** widget receives the input focus through keyboard traversal, the Location Cursor takes on the **inputFocusColor**. If the background color and the **inputFocusColor** are the same, the Location Cursor is "invisible".

In the OPEN LOOK look and feel, when the **Slider** widget receives the input focus through keyboard traversal, the background color of the widget changes to the input focus color, found in the resource **XtNinputFocusColor**. If the user traverses out of the **Slider** widget, the background of the widget reverts to its original background color. If the input focus color is the same as either the foreground or background color, then the widget shows input focus by switching the background and foreground colors.

Figures 5 and 6 illustrate the resources that affect the coloration of the **Slider** widget in both 3D and 2D modes.

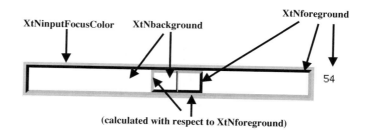

Figure 5. 3D MOTIF Slider Coloration

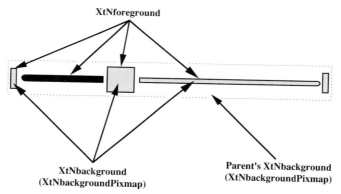

Figure 6. 2D OPEN LOOK Slider Coloration

Keyboard Traversal

The **Slider**'s default values of the **XtNtraversalOn** resource is **TRUE**.

The user can operate the Slider by using the keyboard to move the Slider and access the Trough, or move the Drag Box and access the Anchors. The following keys manipulate the Current Value:

— SCROLLUP and SCROLLRIGHT increase the Current Value by an application-specified amount, and move the Slider or Drag Box to correspond to the new Current Value.

— SCROLLDOWN and SCROLLLEFT decrease the Current Value by an application-specified amount, and move the Slider or Drag Box to correspond to the new Current Value.

— SCROLLTOP and SCROLLRIGHTEDGE have effect only in the OPEN LOOK look and feel, cause the Current Value to take on the Maximum Value, and move the Drag Box to a vertical slider's top anchor or a horizontal slider's right anchor. The anchor is briefly highlighted while the Current Value is changed and the Drag Box is moved.

— SCROLLBOTTOM and SCROLLLEFTEDGE have effect only in the OPEN LOOK look and feel, cause the Current Value to take on the Minimum Value, and move the Drag Box to a vertical slider's bottom anchor or a horizontal slider's left anchor. The anchor is briefly highlighted while the Current Value is changed and the Drag Box is moved.

Vertical Slider Activation Types

Activation Type	Expected Results	Look and Feel
OL_SCROLLUP	Drag Box moves up one Unit	
OL_SCROLLDOWN	Drag Box moves down one Unit	
OL_SCROLLTOP	Drag Box moves to top anchor	OPEN LOOK only
OL_SCROLLBOTTOM	Drag Box moves to bottom anchor	OPEN LOOK only

Horizontal Slider Activation Types

Activation Type	Expected Results	Look and Feel
OL_SCROLLRIGHT	Drag Box moves right one Unit	
OL_SCROLLLEFT	Drag Box moves left one Unit	
OL_SCROLLRIGHTEDGE	Drag Box moves to right anchor	OPEN LOOK only
OL_SCROLLLEFTEDGE	Drag Box moves to left anchor	OPEN LOOK only

The **Slider** widget responds to the following keyboard navigation keys:

— NEXT_FIELD, MOVEDOWN, and MOVERIGHT move to the next traversable widget in the window

— PREV_FIELD, MOVEUP, and MOVELEFT move to the previous traversable widget in the window

— NEXTWINDOW moves to the next window in the application

— PREVWINDOW moves to the previous window in the application

— NEXTAPP moves to the first window in the next application

— PREVAPP moves to the first window in the previous application

Display of Keyboard Mnemonic

The **Slider** does not display the mnemonic accelerator. If the **Slider** is the child of a **Caption** widget, the **Caption** widget will display the mnemonic as part of the label.

Slider (3Olit)

Display of Keyboard Accelerators

The `Slider` does not respond to a keyboard accelerator because clicking the SELECT button on a Slider activates depending on the pointer position. So, the `Slider` does not display a keyboard accelerator.

RESOURCES

<table>
<tr><td colspan="6" align="center">Slider Resource Set</td></tr>
<tr>
<th>Name</th>
<th>Class</th>
<th>Type</th>
<th>Default</th>
<th>Acc</th>
<th>Inherit</th>
</tr>
<tr><td>XtNancestorSensitive</td><td>XtCSensitive</td><td>Boolean</td><td>(calculated)</td><td>G[1]</td><td>Core</td></tr>
<tr><td>XtNbackground</td><td>XtCBackground</td><td>Pixel</td><td>"XtDefaultBackground"</td><td>SGI</td><td>Core</td></tr>
<tr><td>XtNbackgroundPixmap</td><td>XtCPixmap</td><td>Pixmap</td><td>XtUnspecifiedPixmap</td><td>SGI</td><td>Core</td></tr>
<tr><td>XtNborderColor</td><td>XtCBorderColor</td><td>Pixel</td><td>"XtDefaultForeground"</td><td>SGI</td><td>Core</td></tr>
<tr><td>XtNborderPixmap</td><td>XtCPixmap</td><td>Pixmap</td><td>XtUnspecifiedPixmap</td><td>SGI</td><td>Core</td></tr>
<tr><td>XtNborderWidth</td><td>XtCBorderWidth</td><td>Dimension</td><td>0</td><td>SGI</td><td>Core</td></tr>
<tr><td>XtNcolormap</td><td>XtCColormap</td><td>Colormap</td><td>(parent's)</td><td>GI</td><td>Core</td></tr>
<tr><td>XtNconsumeEvent</td><td>XtCCallback</td><td>XtCallbackList</td><td>NULL</td><td>SGI</td><td>Primitive</td></tr>
<tr><td>XtNdepth</td><td>XtCDepth</td><td>Cardinal</td><td>(parent's)</td><td>GI</td><td>Core</td></tr>
<tr><td>XtNdestroyCallback</td><td>XtCCallback</td><td>XtCallbackList</td><td>NULL</td><td>SGI</td><td>Object</td></tr>
<tr><td>XtNdragCBType</td><td>XtCDragCBType</td><td>OlDefine</td><td>OL_CONTINUOUS</td><td>SGI</td><td></td></tr>
<tr><td>XtNendBoxes</td><td>XtCEndBoxes</td><td>Boolean</td><td>TRUE[11]</td><td>SGI</td><td></td></tr>
<tr><td>XtNfont</td><td>XtCFont</td><td>XFontStruct *</td><td>"OlDefaultFont"</td><td>SGI</td><td>Primitive</td></tr>
<tr><td>XtNfontColor</td><td>XtCFontColor</td><td>Pixel</td><td>"XtDefaultForeground"</td><td>SGI</td><td>Primitive</td></tr>
<tr><td>XtNfontGroup</td><td>XtCFontGroup</td><td>OlFontList *</td><td>NULL</td><td>SGI</td><td>Primitive</td></tr>
<tr><td>XtNforeground</td><td>XtCForeground</td><td>Pixel</td><td>"XtDefaultForeground"</td><td>SGI</td><td>Primitive</td></tr>
<tr><td>XtNgranularity</td><td>XtCGranularity</td><td>int</td><td>0</td><td>SGI</td><td></td></tr>
<tr><td>XtNheight</td><td>XtCHeight</td><td>Dimension</td><td>(calculated)</td><td>SGI</td><td>Core</td></tr>
<tr><td>XtNhighlightThickness</td><td>XtCHighlightThickness</td><td>Dimension</td><td>"2 points"[2]</td><td>SGI</td><td>Primitive</td></tr>
<tr><td>XtNinitialDelay</td><td>XtCInitialDelay</td><td>int</td><td>500[6]</td><td>SGI</td><td></td></tr>
<tr><td>XtNinputFocusColor</td><td>XtCInputFocusColor</td><td>Pixel</td><td>"Red"</td><td>SGI</td><td>Primitive</td></tr>
<tr><td>XtNmappedWhenManaged</td><td>XtCMappedWhenManaged</td><td>Boolean</td><td>TRUE</td><td>SGI</td><td>Core</td></tr>
<tr><td>XtNmaxLabel</td><td>XtCLabel</td><td>String</td><td>NULL</td><td>SGI</td><td></td></tr>
<tr><td>XtNminLabel</td><td>XtCLabel</td><td>String</td><td>NULL</td><td>SGI</td><td></td></tr>
<tr><td>XtNorientation</td><td>XtCOrientation</td><td>OlDefine</td><td>OL_VERTICAL</td><td>GI</td><td></td></tr>
<tr><td>XtNrecomputeSize</td><td>XtCRecomputeSize</td><td>Boolean</td><td>FALSE</td><td>SGI</td><td></td></tr>
<tr><td>XtNreferenceName</td><td>XtCReferenceName</td><td>String</td><td>NULL</td><td>SGI</td><td>Primitive</td></tr>
<tr><td>XtNreferenceWidget</td><td>XtCReferenceWidget</td><td>Widget</td><td>NULL</td><td>SGI</td><td>Primitive</td></tr>
<tr><td>XtNrepeatRate</td><td>XtCRepeatRate</td><td>int</td><td>100[7]</td><td>SGI</td><td></td></tr>
</table>

Slider Resource Set (cont'd)					
Name	Class	Type	Default	Acc	Inherit
XtNscreen	XtCScreen	Screen*	(parent's)	GI	Core
XtNsensitive	XtCSensitive	Boolean	TRUE	G[1]	Core
XtNshadowThickness	XtCShadowThickness	Dimension	"0 points"[3]	GI	Primitive
XtNshadowType	XtCShadowType	OlDefine	OL_SHADOW_IN	SGI	Primitive
XtNshowValue	XtCShowValue	Boolean	TRUE	SGI	
XtNsliderMax	XtCSliderMax	int	100	SGI	
XtNsliderMin	XtCSliderMin	int	0	SGI	
XtNsliderMoved	XtCSliderMoved	XtCallbackList	NULL	SGI	
XtNsliderValue	XtCSliderValue	int	0	SGI	
XtNspan	XtCSpan	Dimension	OL_IGNORE	SGI	
XtNstopPosition	XtCStopPosition	OlDefine	OL_ALL	SGI	
XtNtickUnit	XtCTickUnit	OlDefine	OL_NONE	SGI	
XtNticks	XtCTicks	int	0	SGI	
XtNtranslations	XtCTranslations	XtTranslations	NULL	SGI	Core
XtNtraversalOn	XtCTraversalOn	Boolean	TRUE	SGI	Primitive
XtNuserData	XtCUserData	XtPointer	NULL	SGI	Primitive
XtNwidth	XtCWidth	Dimension	(calculated)	SGI	Core
XtNx	XtCPosition	Position	0	SGI	Core
XtNy	XtCPosition	Position	0	SGI	Core

[1]   Use **XtSetSensitive** to set this resource.
[2]   Not used in the OPEN LOOK look and feel.
[3]   **"2 points"** in the MOTIF look and feel.
[6]   250 msec. in the MOTIF look and feel.
[7]   50 msec. in the MOTIF look and feel.
[11] **FALSE** in the MOTIF look and feel.

XtNendBoxes

In the OPEN LOOK look and feel, this resource selects the display of the end boxes. In the MOTIF look and feel, this resource is always **FALSE**.

XtNgranularity

Range of values:

$$1 \leq \texttt{XtNgranularity} \leq (\texttt{XtNsliderMax} - \texttt{XtNsliderMin})$$

Clicking SELECT on the Trough (MOTIF look and feel) Bar or Shaded Bar (OPEN LOOK look and feel) attempts to change the Current Value by the amount given in this resource. Dragging the Slider or Drag Box with SELECT changes the Current Value by this amount before the **XtNsliderMoved** callbacks are issued.

XtNinitialDelay

Range of values:

$0 <$ XtNinitialDelay

This resource gives the time, in milliseconds, before the first action occurs when SELECT is pressed on the Trough, Bar or Shaded Bar.

XtNminLabel

This resource is only available in the OPEN LOOK look and feel. If specified in the MOTIF look and feel, this resource is ignored. It is the label to be placed next to the minimum value position.

For a vertical slider, the label is placed to the right of the minimum value position. If there is not enough space for the entire label and XtNrecomputeSize is FALSE, the label will be truncated from the end. If there is not enough space for the entire label and XtNrecomputeSize is TRUE, then the widget will request for more space to show the entire label.

For an horizontal slider, the label is placed centered and below the minimum value position. If there is not enough room to center the label and XtNrecomputeSize is set to FALSE, the beginning of the label will be aligned with the left anchor and is drawn to the right. If this label collides with the max label, some part of the labels will overlap. If there is not enough room to center the label and XtNrecomputeSize is set to TRUE, the widget will request for more space to center the label below the minimum value position.

XtNmaxLabel

This resource is only available in the OPEN LOOK look and feel. If specified in the MOTIF look and feel, this resource is ignored. It is the label to be placed next to the maximum value position.

For a vertical slider, the label is placed to the right of the maximum value position. If there is not enough space for the entire label and XtNrecomputeSize is FALSE, the label will be truncated from the end. If there is not enough space for the entire label and XtNrecomputeSize is TRUE, then the widget will request for more space to show the entire label.

For a horizontal slider, the label is placed centered and below the maximum value position. If there is not enough room to center the label and XtNrecomputeSize is set to FALSE, the end of the label will be aligned with the right anchor. If this label collides with the min label, some part of the labels will overlap. If there is not enough room to center the label and XtNrecomputeSize is set to TRUE, the widget will request for more space to center the label below the maximum value position.

XtNorientation

Range of values:

OL_HORIZONTAL/"horizontal"
OL_VERTICAL/"vertical"

This resource defines the direction for the visual presentation of the widget.

XtNrepeatRate

Range of values:

$0 <$ XtNrepeatRate

This resource gives the time, in milliseconds, between repeated actions when SELECT is pressed on the Trough, Bar or Shaded Bar.

XtNshowValue

This resource is only available in the MOTIF look and feel. If specified in the OPEN LOOK look and feel, this resource is ignored. The MOTIF look and feel Slider has the ability to display a label next to the Slider's slider. Setting this resource to **TRUE** causes the label to show the current value of the Slider. Setting this resource to **FALSE** prevents a label from showing.

XtNsliderMax
XtNsliderMin

Range of values:

XtNsliderMin < **XtNsliderMax**

These two resources give the range of values tracked by the **Slider** widget. Mathematically, the range is open on the right; that is, the range is the following subset of the set of integers:

XtNsliderMin ≤ range ≤ **XtNsliderMax**

This is independent of the Slider or Drag Box displayed in the **Slider** widget. The **Slider** widget is responsible for taking into account the size of the Slider or Drag Box when relating the physical range of movement to the range of values.

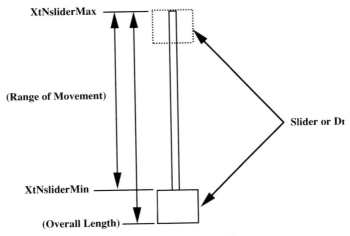

Figure 7. Drag Box Range of Movement

XtNsliderMoved

This resource defines the callback list used when the **Slider** widget is manipulated. The **call_data** parameter is a pointer to a structure containing **new_location** and **more_cb_pending** [see **Scrollbar**(3Olit)]. An **XtGetValue** inside the callback will return the previous value.

XtNsliderValue

Range of values:

$$XtNsliderMin \leq XtNsliderValue \leq XtNsliderMax$$

This resource gives the current position of the Slider or Drag Box, in the range [XtNsliderMin, XtNsliderMax]. The Slider widget keeps this resource up to date.

XtNticks

This resource is only available in the OPEN LOOK look and feel. If specified in the MOTIF look and feel, this resource is ignored. It is the interval between tick marks. The unit of the interval value is determined by XtNtickUnit.

XtNtickUnit

Range of values:

```
OL_NONE/"none"
OL_SLIDERVALUE/"slidervalue"
OL_PERCENT/"percent"
```

This resource is only available in the OPEN LOOK look and feel. If specified in the MOTIF look and feel, this resource is ignored. This resource can have one of the values: OL_NONE, OL_SLIDERVALUE, and OL_PERCENT. If it is OL_NONE, then no tick marks will be displayed and XtNticks is ignored. If it is OL_PERCENT, then XtNticks is interpreted as the percent of the slider value range. If it is OL_SLIDERVALUE, the XtNticks is interpreted as the same unit as slider value.

XtNdragCBType

Range of values:

```
OL_CONTINUOUS/"continuous"
OL_GRANULARITY/"granularity"
OL_RELEASE/"release"
```

This resource determines the frequency of issuing XtNsliderMoved callbacks during a drag operation. If set to OL_CONTINUOUS, callbacks will be issued continuously. If set to OL_GRANULARITY, callbacks will only be issued when the Slider or Drag Box crosses any granularity positions. If set to OL_RELEASE, callback will only be issued once when the SELECT button is released.

XtNstopPosition

Range of values:

```
OL_ALL/"all"
OL_TICKMARK/"tickmark"
OL_GRANULARITY/"granularity"
```

This resource determines the behavior of the Slider or Drag Box at the end of an drag operation. If set to OL_ALL, upon the release of the SELECT button in a drag operation, the drag box will be positioned at where it stops. If set to OL_TICKMARK, the drag box will snap to the nearest tickmark position. If set to OL_GRANULARITY, the drag box will snap to the nearest granularity position.

XtNrecomputeSize

This resource, if set to TRUE, allows the slider widget to resize itself whenever needed, to compensate for the space needed to show the tick marks and the labels. The slider widget uses the XtNspan, the sizes of the labels, and XtNtickUnit to determine the preferred size.

XtNspan

If **XtNrecomputeSize** is set to **TRUE**, then **XtNspan** should be set to reflect the preferred length of the slider, not counting the space needed for the labels. The **Slider** widget uses the span value, the sizes of the labels, and **XtNtickUnit** to determine the preferred size.

NOTES

Note that for **XtNinitialDelay** and **XtNrepeatRate**, millisecond timing precision may not be possible for all implementations, so values may be rounded up to the nearest available unit by the toolkit.

SEE ALSO

Gauge(3Olit), **Primitive**(3Olit), **Scrollbar**(3Olit)

StaticText (3Olit)

NAME

StaticText – display read-only text

SYNOPSIS

```
#include <X11/Intrinsic.h>
#include <X11/StringDefs.h>
#include <Xol/OpenLook.h>
#include <Xol/StaticText.h>

widget = XtCreateWidget(name, staticTextWidgetClass, . . .);
```

DESCRIPTION

The **StaticText** widget provides a way to present an uneditable block of text using a few simple layout controls.

The ability to select text for copying is not allowed by the MOTIF look and feel, and that the **shadowThickness** is always 0.

Word Wrapping

If the text is too long to fit in the width provided by the **StaticText** widget, the text may be "wrapped" if the application requests it. The wrapping occurs at a space between words, if possible, leaving as many words on a line as will fit. If a word is too long for the width, it will be truncated. An embedded newline will always cause a wrap.

Text Clipping—In Width

If the text is not wrapped, it will be truncated if it cannot fit in the width of the **StaticText** widget. The application can choose whether the truncation occurs on the left, right, or evenly on both sides of each line of the text.

Text Clipping—In Height

If the text is too large to fit in the height provided by the **StaticText** widget, the text is clipped on the bottom. The clipping falls on a pixel boundary, not between lines, so that it is possible that only the upper part of the last line of text may be visible.

Stripping of Spaces

The application can choose to have leading spaces, trailing spaces, or both leading and trailing space stripped from the text before display, or can choose to have no stripping done.

Selecting and Operating on the Text

In the OPEN LOOK look and feel only, the **StaticText** widget allows text to be selected in several ways and then copied. See **Text Selection** earlier in this manual for the description of these operations.

Coloration

Figure 1 illustrates the resources that affect the coloration of the **StaticText** widget.

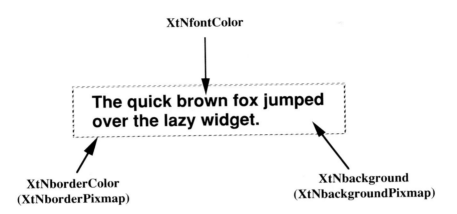

Figure 1. Static Text Coloration

Keyboard Traversal

The default value of the **XtNtraversalOn** resource is **FALSE**.

The widget responds to the following keyboard navigation keys:

NEXT_FIELD	moves to the next traversable widget in the window
PREV_FIELD	moves to the previous traversable widget in the window
NEXTWINDOW	moves to the next window in the application
PREVWINDOW	moves to the previous window in the application
NEXTAPP	moves to the first window in the next application
PREVAPP	moves to the first window in the previous application

Display of Keyboard Mnemonic And Accelerator

The **StaticText** does not have keyboard mnemonic or keyboard accelerator capabilities.

StaticText (3Olit)

RESOURCES

<table>
<tr><th colspan="6">StaticText Resource Set</th></tr>
<tr><th>Name</th><th>Class</th><th>Type</th><th>Default</th><th>Acc</th><th>Inherit</th></tr>
<tr><td>XtNalignment</td><td>XtCAlignment</td><td>OlDefine</td><td>OL_LEFT</td><td>SGI</td><td></td></tr>
<tr><td>XtNancestorSensitive</td><td>XtCSensitive</td><td>Boolean</td><td>(calculated)</td><td>G[1]</td><td>Core</td></tr>
<tr><td>XtNbackground</td><td>XtCBackground</td><td>Pixel</td><td>"XtDefaultBackground"</td><td>SGI</td><td>Core</td></tr>
<tr><td>XtNbackgroundPixmap</td><td>XtCPixmap</td><td>Pixmap</td><td>XtUnspecifiedPixmap</td><td>SGI</td><td>Core</td></tr>
<tr><td>XtNborderColor</td><td>XtCBorderColor</td><td>Pixel</td><td>"XtDefaultForeground"</td><td>SGI</td><td>Core</td></tr>
<tr><td>XtNborderPixmap</td><td>XtCPixmap</td><td>Pixmap</td><td>XtUnspecifiedPixmap</td><td>SGI</td><td>Core</td></tr>
<tr><td>XtNborderWidth</td><td>XtCBorderWidth</td><td>Dimension</td><td>0</td><td>SGI</td><td>Core</td></tr>
<tr><td>XtNcolormap</td><td>XtCColormap</td><td>Colormap</td><td>(parent's)</td><td>GI</td><td>Core</td></tr>
<tr><td>XtNconsumeEvent</td><td>XtCCallback</td><td>XtCallbackList</td><td>NULL</td><td>SGI</td><td>Primitive</td></tr>
<tr><td>XtNdepth</td><td>XtCDepth</td><td>Cardinal</td><td>(parent's)</td><td>GI</td><td>Core</td></tr>
<tr><td>XtNdestroyCallback</td><td>XtCCallback</td><td>XtCallbackList</td><td>NULL</td><td>SGI</td><td>Object</td></tr>
<tr><td>XtNdragCursor</td><td>XtCCursor</td><td>Cursor</td><td>NULL</td><td>SGI</td><td></td></tr>
<tr><td>XtNfont</td><td>XtCFont</td><td>XFontStruct *</td><td>"OlDefaultFont"</td><td>SGI</td><td>Primitive</td></tr>
<tr><td>XtNfontColor</td><td>XtCFontColor</td><td>Pixel</td><td>"XtDefaultForeground"</td><td>SGI</td><td>Primitive</td></tr>
<tr><td>XtNfontGroup</td><td>XtCFontGroup</td><td>OlFontList *</td><td>NULL</td><td>SGI</td><td>Primitive</td></tr>
<tr><td>XtNforeground</td><td>XtCForeground</td><td>Pixel</td><td>"XtDefaultForeground"</td><td>SGI</td><td>Primitive</td></tr>
<tr><td>XtNgravity</td><td>XtCGravity</td><td>int</td><td>CenterGravity</td><td>SGI</td><td></td></tr>
<tr><td>XtNhSpace</td><td>XtCHSpace</td><td>Dimension</td><td>"2 points"</td><td>SGI</td><td></td></tr>
<tr><td>XtNheight</td><td>XtCHeight</td><td>Dimension</td><td>(calculated)</td><td>SGI</td><td>Core</td></tr>
<tr><td>XtNlineSpace</td><td>XtCLineSpace</td><td>int</td><td>0</td><td>SGI</td><td></td></tr>
<tr><td>XtNmappedWhenManaged</td><td>XtCMappedWhenManaged</td><td>Boolean</td><td>TRUE</td><td>SGI</td><td>Core</td></tr>
<tr><td>XtNrecomputeSize</td><td>XtCRecomputeSize</td><td>Boolean</td><td>TRUE</td><td>SGI</td><td></td></tr>
<tr><td>XtNscreen</td><td>XtCScreen</td><td>Screen *</td><td>(parent's)</td><td>GI</td><td>Core</td></tr>
<tr><td>XtNsensitive</td><td>XtCSensitive</td><td>Boolean</td><td>TRUE</td><td>G[1]</td><td>Core</td></tr>
<tr><td>XtNstring</td><td>XtCString</td><td>String</td><td>NULL</td><td>SGI</td><td></td></tr>
<tr><td>XtNstrip</td><td>XtCStrip</td><td>Boolean</td><td>TRUE</td><td>SGI</td><td></td></tr>
<tr><td>XtNtranslations</td><td>XtCTranslations</td><td>XtTranslations</td><td>NULL</td><td>SGI</td><td>Core</td></tr>
<tr><td>XtNuserData</td><td>XtCUserData</td><td>XtPointer</td><td>NULL</td><td>SGI</td><td>Primitive</td></tr>
<tr><td>XtNvSpace</td><td>XtCVSpace</td><td>Dimension</td><td>"2 points"</td><td>SGI</td><td></td></tr>
<tr><td>XtNwidth</td><td>XtCWidth</td><td>Dimension</td><td>(calculated)</td><td>SGI</td><td>Core</td></tr>
<tr><td>XtNwrap</td><td>XtCWrap</td><td>Boolean</td><td>TRUE</td><td>SGI</td><td></td></tr>
<tr><td>XtNx</td><td>XtCPosition</td><td>Position</td><td>0</td><td>SGI</td><td>Core</td></tr>
<tr><td>XtNy</td><td>XtCPosition</td><td>Position</td><td>0</td><td>SGI</td><td>Core</td></tr>
</table>

[1] Use XtSetSensitive to set this resource.

XtNalignment

Range of values:

OL_LEFT/"left"
OL_CENTER/"center"
OL_RIGHT/"right"

This specifies the alignment to be applied when drawing the text, as described below:

OL_LEFT   causes the left sides of the lines to be vertically aligned

OL_CENTER   causes the centers of the lines to be vertically aligned

OL_RIGHT   causes the right sides of the lines to be vertically aligned

XtNdragCursor
This resource is only available in the OPEN LOOK look and feel. If specified in the MOTIF look and feel, this resource is ignored. It allows the cursor to animate dragging of selected text. When the Default is NULL, **StaticText** creates a bitmap containing the first three letters of the dragged text.

XtNgravity
Range of values:

          CenterGravity
          NorthGravity
          SouthGravity
          EastGravity
          WestGravity
          NorthWestGravity
          NorthEastGravity
          SouthWestGravity
          SouthEastGravity

The application can set a width and height to the **StaticText** widget that exceeds the size needed to display the string. This resource controls the use of any extra space with the **StaticText** widget:

CenterGravity
> The string is centered vertically and horizontally in the extra space.

NorthGravity
> The top edge of the string is aligned with the top edge of the space and centered horizontally.

SouthGravity
> The bottom edge of the string is aligned with the bottom edge of the space and centered horizontally.

EastGravity
> The right edge of the string is aligned with the right edge of the space and centered vertically.

WestGravity
> The left edge of the string is aligned with the left edge of the space and centered vertically.

NorthWestGravity
> The top and left edges of the string are aligned with the top and left edges of the space.

NorthEastGravity

> The top and right edges of the string are aligned with the top and right edges of the space.

SouthWestGravity

> The bottom and left edges of the string are aligned with the bottom and left edges of the space.

SouthEastGravity

> The bottom and right edges of the string are aligned with the bottom and right edges of the space.

XtNlineSpace

Range of values:

    -100 ≤ XtNlineSpace

This resource controls the amount of space between lines of text. It is specified as a percentage of the font height, and is the distance between the baseline of one text line and the top of the next font line. Thus, the distance between successive text baselines, in percentage of the font height, is

    XtNlineSpace+100

XtNrecomputeSize

Range of values:

    TRUE/"true"
    FALSE/"false"

This resource indicates whether the **StaticText** widget should calculate its size and automatically set the **XtNheight** and **XtNwidth** resources. If set to **TRUE**, the **StaticText** widget will do normal size calculations that may cause its geometry to change. If set to **FALSE**, the **StaticText** widget will leave its size alone; this may cause truncation of the visible image being shown by the **StaticText** widget if the fixed size is too small, or may cause centering if the fixed size is too large.

XtNstring

This resource is the string that will be drawn. The string must be null terminated.

XtNstrip

Range of values:

    TRUE/"true"
    FALSE/"false"

This resource controls the stripping of leading and trailing spaces during the layout of the text string.

XtNstrip	XtNalignment	Spaces stripped
	OL_LEFT	Leading spaces stripped
TRUE	OL_RIGHT	Trailing spaces stripped
	OL_CENTER	Both leading and trailing spaces stripped
FALSE	(any)	None

XtNwrap

Range of values:

      `TRUE`/`"true"`
      `FALSE`/`"false"`

This resource controls the wrapping of lines that are too long to fit in the width of the `StaticText` widget.

XtNwrap	XtNalignment	Wrap action
FALSE	OL_LEFT	Clipped on the right
	OL_RIGHT	Clipped on the left
	OL_CENTER	Clipped equally on both left and right
TRUE	(any)	Long text is broken at spaces between words so that each line of the displayed text has as many words as can fit.

StepField (3Olit)

NAME

StepField – build a numeric input field

SYNOPSIS

```
#include <X11/Intrinsic.h>
#include <X11/StringDefs.h>
#include <Xol/OpenLook.h>
#include <Xol/StepField.h>
```

widget = XtCreateWidget(*name*, stepFieldWidgetClass, . . .);

DESCRIPTION

The **StepField** widget is a simple subclass of **TextField** that provides a generic interface for clients to build a numeric input field. It provides a step method, so that the **TextField** widget will display stepping arrows on the right side of the widget. When the user clicks SELECT on the arrows or uses the keyboard to increment or decrement the text value, the **StepField** class issues a callback to the client. The client is expected to update the text field according to its meaning of increment or decrement.

Figure 1 shows a MOTIF look and feel step field with a location cursor. Figure 2 shows an OPEN LOOK look and feel step field in the middle of its range in 3D mode.

Figure 1. MOTIF Style Step Field

Figure 2. OPEN LOOK Style Step Field

RESOURCES

StepField Resource Set					
Name	Class	Type	Default	Acc	Inherit
XtNancestorSensitive	XtCSensitive	Boolean	(calculated)	G[1]	Core
XtNbackground	XtCBackground	Pixel	"XtDefaultBackground"	SGI	Core
XtNbackgroundPixmap	XtCPixmap	Pixmap	XtUnspecifiedPixmap	SGI	Core
XtNblinkRate	XtCBlinkRate	int	1000[10]	SGI	TextEdit
XtNborderColor	XtCBorderColor	Pixel	"XtDefaultForeground"	SGI	Core
XtNborderPixmap	XtCPixmap	Pixmap	XtUnspecifiedPixmap	SGI	Core
XtNborderWidth	XtCBorderWidth	Dimension	0	SGI	Core
XtNbottomMargin	XtCMargin	Dimension	(calculated)	SGI	TextEdit
XtNcanDecrement	XtCCanStep	Boolean	TRUE	SGI	TextField
XtNcanIncrement	XtCCanStep	Boolean	TRUE	SGI	TextField
XtNcanScroll	XtCCanScroll	Boolean	FALSE	SGI	TextField
XtNcharsVisible	XtCCharsVisible	Cardinal	XtUnspecifiedCardinal	GI	TextEdit
XtNcolormap	XtCColormap	Colormap	(parent's)	GI	Core
XtNconsumeEvent	XtCCallback	XtCallbackList	NULL	SGI	Primitive
XtNcontrolCaret	XtCControlCaret	Boolean	TRUE	GI	TextEdit
XtNcursorPosition	XtCTextPosition	int	"0"	SGI	TextEdit
XtNdepth	XtCDepth	Cardinal	(parent's)	GI	Core
XtNdestroyCallback	XtCCallback	XtCallbackList	NULL	SGI	Object
XtNdisplayPosition	XtCTextPosition	int	"0"	SGI	TextEdit
XtNdragCursor	XtCCursor	Cursor	NULL	SGI	TextEdit
XtNdropSiteID	XtCReadOnly	OlDnDDropSiteID	NULL	G	TextEdit
XtNeditType	XtCEditType	OlEditMode	"textedit"	SGI	TextEdit
XtNfont	XtCFont	XFontStruct *	"OlDefaultFont"	SGI	Primitive
XtNfontColor	XtCTextFontColor	Pixel	"XtDefaultForeground"	SGI	Primitive
XtNfontGroup	XtCFontGroup	OlFontList *	NULL	SGI	Primitive
XtNforeground	XtCForeground	Pixel	"XtDefaultForeground"	SGI	Primitive
XtNheight	XtCHeight	Dimension	(calculated)	SGI	Core
XtNhighlightThickness	XtCHighlightThickness	Dimension	"2 points"[2]	SGI	Primitive
XtNinitialDelay	XtCInitialDelay	int	500	SGI	TextField
XtNinputFocusColor	XtCInputFocusColor	Pixel	"Red"	SGI	Primitive
XtNinsertReturn	XtCInsertReturn	Boolean	FALSE	SGI	TextEdit
XtNinsertTab	XtCInsertTab	Boolean	FALSE	SGI	TextEdit
XtNleftMargin	XtCMargin	Dimension	(calculated)	SGI	TextEdit
XtNlinesVisible	XtCLinesVisible	int	0	G	TextEdit
XtNmappedWhenManaged	XtCMappedWhenManaged	Boolean	TRUE	SGI	Core
XtNmargin	XtCCallback	XtCallbackList	NULL	SGI	TextEdit
XtNmaximumSize	XtCMaximumSize	Cardinal	0	SGI	TextField
XtNmodifyVerification	XtCCallback	XtCallbackList	NULL	SGI	TextEdit
XtNmotionVerification	XtCCallback	XtCallbackList	NULL	SGI	TextEdit

StepField (3Olit)

StepField Resource Set (cont'd)					
Name	Class	Type	Default	Acc	Inherit
XtNpostModifyNotification	XtCCallback	XtCallbackList	NULL	SGI	TextEdit
XtNpreselect	XtCPreselect	Boolean	TRUE	SGI	TextEdit
XtNreferenceName	XtCReferenceName	String	NULL	SGI	Primitive
XtNreferenceWidget	XtCReferenceWidget	Widget	NULL	SGI	Primitive
XtNrepeatRate	XtCRepeatRate	int	100	SGI	TextField
XtNrightMargin	XtCMargin	Dimension	(calculated)	SGI	TextEdit
XtNscreen	XtCScreen	Screen *	(parent's)	GI	Core
XtNselectEnd	XtCTextPosition	int	"0"	SGI	TextEdit
XtNselectStart	XtCTextPosition	int	"0"	SGI	TextEdit
XtNsensitive	XtCSensitive	Boolean	TRUE	G[1]	Core
XtNshadowThickness	XtCShadowThickness	Dimension	"0 points"[3]	SGI	Primitive
XtNshadowType	XtCShadowType	OlDefine	OL_SHADOW_IN	SGI	Primitive
XtNsourceType	XtCSourceType	OlSourceType	NULL	SGI	TextEdit
XtNstepped	XtCCallback	XtCallbackList	NULL	SGI	
XtNstring	XtCString	String	NULL	SGI	TextField
XtNtabTable	XtCTabTable	XtPointer	NULL	SGI	TextEdit
XtNtextEditWidget	XtCReadOnly	Widget	(self)	G	TextField
XtNtopMargin	XtCMargin	Dimension	4	SGI	TextEdit
XtNtranslations	XtCTranslations	XtTranslations	NULL	SGI	Core
XtNtraversalOn	XtCTraversalOn	Boolean	TRUE	SGI	Primitive
XtNuserData	XtCUserData	XtPointer	NULL	SGI	Primitive
XtNverification	XtCCallback	XtCallbackList	NULL	SGI	TextField
XtNwidth	XtCWidth	Dimension	(calculated)	SGI	Core
XtNwrapMode	XtCWrapMode	OlWrapMode	NULL	SGI	TextEdit
XtNx	XtCPosition	Position	0	SGI	Core
XtNy	XtCPosition	Position	0	SGI	Core

[1]   Use XtSetSensitive to set this resource.
[2]   Not used in the OPEN LOOK look and feel.
[3]   "2 points" in the MOTIF look and feel.
[10]   500 msec. in the MOTIF look and feel.

XtNstepped

This callback is issued each time the user presses or clicks SELECT over one of the stepping arrows, or presses one of several keyboard equivalents. The *call_data* is a pointer to an **OlTextFieldStepped** structure which includes the following members:

```
OlSteppedReason reason;
Cardinal        count;
```

reason tells the client the direction and extent of the desired "numeric" change, and is one of **OlSteppedIncrement**, **OlSteppedDecrement**, **OlSteppedToMaximum**, and **OlSteppedToMinimum**. **count** modifies **OlSteppedIncrement** and **OlSteppedDecrement** reasons to indicate how far to step.

The client is responsible for updating the text buffer according to its needs. The user can press SELECT and hold it down to cause automatically repeated callbacks; the visual feedback during this time is a depressed arrow. If the client removes the callback during this period, the visual feedback changes to a regular arrow to let the user know that further stepping is impossible. The client can also change the **Text-Field XtNcanIncrement** or **XtNcanDecrement** resources during a callback; the visual feedback will change to dim the corresponding arrow to let the user know further stepping in that direction is impossible.

SEE ALSO

TextEdit(3Olit), **TextField**(3Olit)

Stub (3Olit)

NAME

Stub – create a stub for widget prototyping

SYNOPSIS

```
#include <X11/Intrinsic.h>
#include <X11/StringDefs.h>
#include <Xol/OpenLook.h>
#include <Xol/Stub.h>

Widget stub;

stub = XtCreateWidget(name, stubWidgetClass, . . .);
```

DESCRIPTION

The **Stub** widget is essentially a method-driven widget that allows the application to specify procedures at creation and/or **XtSetValues** time which normally are restricted to a widget's class part. Most class part procedures have been attached to the instance part. For example, with the **Stub** widget, it's possible to set the procedure that's called whenever an exposure occurs. It's also possible to set the SetValues and Initialize procedures.

Build Unique Widgets Within an Application

By allowing the application to specify procedures outside the widget class structure, applications can use the stub widget to build local widgets without having to go through the formal steps. For example, suppose an application wanted to create a menu separator widget that inherits its parent's background color at creation time. It would be wasteful to create a new widget to perform these trivial tasks. Instead, the application would use a stub widget and specify an Initialize procedure for it.

Graphics Applications

The stub widget also implements graphics applications. Since the application has direct access to the widget's internal expose procedure, the application can take advantage of the exposure compression provided with the *region* argument. This field is not accessible if the application used an Event Handler to trap exposures. Also, since the application has access to the SetValues and SetValuesHook procedures, the application can programmatically modify graphic-related resources of the stub widget.

Inheriting Procedures from Existing Widgets

Once a stub widget is created, other stub widgets can inherit its methods without the application having to specify them again. All the application has to do is specify a reference stub widget in the creation Arg list and the new stub widget will inherit all instance methods from the referenced stub widget.

Wrapping Widgets around an existing Window

The **Stub** widget also allows the application to give widget functionality to existing X windows. For example, if the application wanted to track button presses on the root window, the application would create a stub widget using the RootWindow ID as the **XtNwindow** resource. Once this has been done, the application can monitor events on the root window by attaching event handlers to the stub widget.

Keyboard Traversal

The **Stub** is a Primitive widget and it inherits the translations for traversal actions from the Primitive class. The user of a Stub widget should add translations for dealing with the navigation events listed in the section of VIRTUAL KEYS/BUTTONS that apply to the particular use of the Stub.

Display of Keyboard Mnemonic

The **Stub** does not display the mnemonic accelerator. If the **Stub** is the child of a **Caption** widget, the **Caption** widget can be used to display the **Stub**'s mnemonic.

Display of Keyboard Accelerators

The **Stub** does not display the keyboard accelerator. If the **Stub** is the child of a **Caption** widget, the **Caption** widget can be used to display the **Stub**'s accelerator as part of the label.

Coloration

The Stub widget should display a state which indicates that it has input focus. The general heuristic used for this display in widgets is that the background color is replaced with the input focus color found in the resource **XtNinputFocusColor**.

RESOURCES

	Stub Resource Set				
Name	Class	Type	Default	Acc	Inherit
XtNaccelerator	XtCAccelerator	String	NULL	SGI	Primitive
XtNacceleratorText	XtCAcceleratorText	String	(calculated)	SGI	Primitive
XtNacceptFocusFunc	XtCAcceptFocusFunc	XtWidgetProc	NULL	SGI	
XtNactivateFunc	XtCActivateFunc	OlActivateFunc	NULL	SGI	
XtNancestorSensitive	XtCSensitive	Boolean	(calculated)	G[1]	Core
XtNbackground	XtCBackground	Pixel	"XtDefaultBackground"	SGI	Core
XtNbackgroundPixmap	XtCPixmap	Pixmap	XtUnspecifiedPixmap	SGI	Core
XtNborderColor	XtCBorderColor	Pixel	"XtDefaultForeground"	SGI	Core
XtNborderPixmap	XtCPixmap	Pixmap	XtUnspecifiedPixmap	SGI	Core
XtNborderWidth	XtCBorderWidth	Dimension	0	SGI	Core
XtNcolormap	XtCColormap	Colormap	(parent's)	GI	Core
XtNconsumeEvent	XtCCallback	XtCallbackList	NULL	SGI	Primitive
XtNdepth	XtCDepth	Cardinal	(parent's)	GI	Core
XtNdestroy	XtCDestroy	XtWidgetProc	NULL	SGI	
XtNdestroyCallback	XtCCallback	XtCallbackList	NULL	SGI	Object
XtNexpose	XtCExpose	XtExposeProc	NULL	SGI	
XtNfont	XtCFont	XFontStruct *	"OlDefaultFont"	SGI	Primitive
XtNfontColor	XtCFontColor	Pixel	"XtDefaultForeground"	SGI	Primitive
XtNfontGroup	XtCFontGroup	OlFontList *	NULL	SGI	Primitive
XtNforeground	XtCForeground	Pixel	"XtDefaultForeground"	SGI	Primitive
XtNgetValuesHook	XtCGetValuesHook	XtArgsProc	NULL	SGI	

Stub (3Olit)

Stub Resource Set (cont'd)					
Name	Class	Type	Default	Acc	Inherit
XtNheight	XtCHeight	Dimension	(calculated)	SGI	Core
XtNhighlightHandlerProc	XtCHighlightHandlerProc	OlHighlightProc	NULL	SGI	
XtNhighlightThickness	XtCHighlightThickness	Dimension	"2 points"[2]	SGI	Primitive
XtNinitialize	XtCInitialize	XtInitProc	(internal function)	GI	
XtNinitializeHook	XtCInitializeHook	XtArgsProc	NULL	GI	
XtNinputFocusColor	XtCInputFocusColor	Pixel	"Red"	SGI	Primitive
XtNmappedWhenManaged	XtCMappedWhenManaged	Boolean	TRUE	SGI	Core
XtNmnemonic	XtCMnemonic	char	NULL	SGI	Primitive
XtNqueryGeometry	XtCQueryGeometry	XtGeometryHandler	NULL	SGI	
XtNrealize	XtCRealize	XtRealizeProc	(internal function)	SGI	
XtNreferenceName	XtCReferenceName	String	NULL	SGI	Primitive
XtNreferenceStub	XtCReferenceStub	Widget	NULL	GI	
XtNreferenceWidget	XtCReferenceWidget	Widget	NULL	SGI	Primitive
XtNregisterFocusFunc	XtCRegisterFocusFunc	OlRegisterFocusFunc	NULL	SGI	
XtNresize	XtCResize	XtWidgetProc	NULL	SGI	
XtNscreen	XtCScreen	Screen *	(parent's)	GI	Core
XtNsensitive	XtCSensitive	Boolean	TRUE	G[1]	Core
XtNsetValues	XtCSetValues	XtSetValuesFunc	NULL	SGI	
XtNsetValuesAlmost	XtCSetValuesAlmost	XtAlmostProc	(inherited)	SGI	
XtNsetValuesHook	XtCSetValuesHook	XtArgsFunc	NULL	SGI	
XtNshadowThickness	XtCShadowThickness	Dimension	"0 points"[3]	SGI	Primitive
XtNshadowType	XtCShadowType	OlDefine	OL_SHADOW_IN	SGI	Primitive
XtNtranslations	XtCTranslations	XtTranslations	NULL	SGI	Core
XtNtraversalHandlerFunc	XtCTraversalHandlerFunc	OlTraversalFunc	NULL	SGI	
XtNtraversalOn	XtCTraversalOn	Boolean	FALSE	SGI	Primitive
XtNuserData	XtCUserData	XtPointer	NULL	SGI	Primitive
XtNwidth	XtCWidth	Dimension	(calculated)	SGI	Core
XtNwindow	XtCWindow	Window	None	GI	
XtNx	XtCPosition	Position	0	SGI	Core
XtNy	XtCPosition	Position	0	SGI	Core

[1]   Use **XtSetSensitive** to set this resource.
[2]   Not used in the OPEN LOOK look and feel.
[3]   **"2 points"** in the MOTIF look and feel.

XtNacceptFocusFunc

This procedure has the same semantics as the **XtAcceptFocusFunc** Core Widget Class procedure and it's called by the Stub Widget Class's accept focus class procedure. Applications that want to override the default accept focus procedure should use this function. When overriding the default accept focus procedure, the convenience routine **OlCanAcceptFocus** can be used to check the widget's focus-taking eligibility. `OlSetInputFocus` should be used instead of `XSetInputFocus` when explicitly setting focus to a window. (See the section "Input Focus" for more on setting and accepting focus.)

XtNactivateFunc

```
void activateProc(
    Widget        w,
    OlVirtualName activation_type,
    XtPointer     data
);
```

This procedure is called whenever `OlActivateWidget` is called with the stub widget ID for which this routine was assigned. The procedure has the following declaration:

```
Boolean (*OlActivateFunc)(
    Widget        w,
    OlVirtualName activation_type,
    XtPointer     data
);
```

If the *activation_type* is valid, the routine should take the appropriate action and return `TRUE`; otherwise, the routine should return `FALSE`.

XtNdestroy

```
void destroy(
    Widget w
);
```

Specifies the procedure called when this stub instance is destroyed.

XtNexpose

```
void expose(
    Widget  w,
    XEvent  *xevent,
    Region  region
);
```

Procedure called whenever the a stub instance receives an exposure event. Since the Stub widget class has requested exposure compression, the region field is valid.

XtNgetValuesHook

```
void getValuesHook(
    Widget   w,
    ArgList  args,
    Cardinal *num_args
);
```

Procedure called whenever the application does an `XtGetValues` call on a stub widget instance.

XtNhighlightHandlerProc

This procedure has the same semantics as the `OlHighlightProc` class procedure and it is called by the Stub widget class's `HighlightProc` class procedure. Applications that have Stub widgets which accept focus should set this routine so that the Stub widget can display an appropriate visual whenever it gains or loses focus.

XtNinitialize

```
void initialize(
     Widget    request,
     Widget    new
);
```

Procedure called by **XtCreateWidget** for a stub widget instance. The default initialize procedure knows how to deal with the **XtNwindow** resource (see the section on **XtNwindow**). If the application supplies its own initialize procedure, it's the application's responsibility to deal with the **XtNwindow** resource.

When the **XtNwindow** resource is non-NULL, the default initialize procedure fills in **XtNx**, **XtNy**, **XtNwidth** and **XtNheight** with the attributes specified by the **XtNwindow** ID.

XtNinitializeHook

```
void initializeHook(
     Widget     w,
     ArgList    args,
     Cardinal  *num_args
);
```

This procedure is called by **XtCreateWidget** for a stub widget instance after the initialize procedure has been called. The application can access the creation arg list through this routine. The widget specified with the *w* argument is the *new* widget from the initialize procedure.

XtNqueryGeometry

```
XtGeometryResult queryGeometry(
     Widget              w,
     XtWidgetGeometry   *request,
     XtWidgetGeometry   *preferred_return
);
```

Procedure called whenever the application does an **XtQueryGeometry** request on a stub widget instance.

XtNrealize

```
void realize(w, value_mask, attributes)
     Widget                 w,
     XtValueMask           *value_mask,
     XSetWindowAttributes  *attributes
);
```

Procedure called to realize a stub widget instance. The default realize procedure knows how to deal with the **XtNwindow** resource (see the section on **XtNwindow**). If the application supplies its own realize procedure, it's the application's responsibility to deal with the **XtNwindow** resource.

When **XtNwindow** is non-NULL, the realize procedure uses this window for the widget instance instead of creating a new window. The default realize procedure gives an error message if another widget in its process space is referencing the window already. Note, the default realize procedure does not reparent the specified window, if one is supplied.

XtNreferenceStub

This is a pointer to an existing Stub widget. If this pointer is non-NULL, the new Stub will inherit all instance methods from the referenced stub widget. An **XtSet-Values** request on the new Stub widget should be used to change any inherited methods.

XtNresize

```
void resize(
    Widget w
);
```

Procedure called whenever a stub widget instance is resized.

XtNregisterFocusFunc

This is a Stub widget resource that points to a function of type

```
void (*OlRegisterFocusFunc) (
    Widget w
);
```

Whenever a stub widget gains focus this procedure is called and the stub's shell sets the "current focus widget" (see the input focus routines) to the value returned by it. If this function is NULL or returns NULL, the stub widget is set to the current focus widget. This is the typical case. If this procedure returns a widget ID other than the stub widget's, that ID is used to update the current focus widget so that a subsequent call to **OlGetCurrentFocusWidget** would return it. Note, returning a widget ID other than the stub widget's will not move the focus away from the stub widget.

XtNsetValues

```
Boolean setValues(
    Widget current,
    Widget request,
    Widget new
);
```

Procedure called whenever the application does an **XtSetValues** call on a stub widget instance.

XtNsetValuesAlmost

```
void setValuesAlmost(
    Widget              w,
    Widget              new_widget,
    XtWidgetGeometry *request,
    XtWidgetGeometry *reply
);
```

This procedure is called when the application attempts to set a stub widget's geometry via an **XtSetValues** call and the stub widget's parent did not accept the requested geometry. The default **setValuesAlmost** procedure simply accepts the suggested compromise.

XtNsetValuesHook

```
Boolean setValuesHook(
        Widget    w,
        ArgList   args,
        Cardinal *num_args
);
```

This procedure is called whenever the application does an **XtSetValues** on a stub widget instance. Since this procedure is called after the **setValues** procedure, the widget specified by the *w* argument is the *new* widget from the **setValues** procedure.

XtNtraversalHandlerFunc

If an application wants the stub widget to process traversal commands whenever the stub widget has focus, this resource is used to supply the traversal routine. An example of a case when this is desirable is when a stub widget is used to implement a spread-sheet. In this case the stub widget would trap the **OL_MOVERIGHT**, **OL_MOVELEFT**, and so on commands to move focus between the cells in the spread-sheet. The traversal handling routine has the following declaration:

```
Widget  (*OlTraversalFunc)(
        Widget         w,         /* Stub widget ID */
        Widget         start,     /* Stub widget ID */
        OlVirtualName  direction,
        Time           time
);
```

If the traversal routine can process the traversal command, it returns the ID of the widget which now has focus. (Note that the widget ID returned can be the stub widget's ID. This is the case when the traversal command was processed, but focus did not leave the stub widget.) If the traversal routine cannot process the given command, it should return NULL. (See the section "Input Focus" for a discussion on valid **direction** values and focus movement.)

XtNwindow

This resource specifies a window ID that the Stub widget should associate with its instance data at realization time. The **XtNwindow** resource can be specified at initialization time only. If a window ID is supplied, that stub widget instance will trap events on the given window. After the stub widget instance is realized, the function **XtWindow** will return this window ID.

If the stub widget is managed by its parent widget, the supplied window will be included in geometry calculations even though the stub widget (by default) does not reparent the supplied window to be a child of the parent widget's window.

Explicit calls to **XtMoveWidget**, **XtResizeWidget**, **XtConfigureWidget**, or **XtSetValues** can be used to modify the window's attributes.

Note: When the stub widget instance is destroyed, the window will be destroyed along with it.

   If the **Stub** widget is managed, the window ID supplied with **XtNwindow** will be included in the geometry calculation causing undesirable reconfiguration. This is an anomaly that exists only with this resource.

XtNwidth
XtNheight

If **XtNwindow** has a NULL value, the application must insure that the dimensions of **XtNwidth** and **XtNheight** are non-NULL. The application can specify the width and height with an Arg list or specify an *initialize* procedure that sets them with non-NULL values. If either of these dimensions are NULL when the application attempts to realize the stub widget, an error will result.

EXAMPLE

The following example illustrates how an application can use the stub widget to perform some particular type of exposure handling. Since an *initialize* procedure was not specified and the **XtNwindow** resource was not used, the initial Arg list includes non-NULL values for the widget's width and height.

```
static void
Redisplay(w, xevent, region)
        Widget    w;
        XEvent *  xevent;
        Region    region;
{
    /*
     * do something interesting here
     */
} /* END OF Redisplay() */

main(...)
{
    Widget    base;
    Widget    stub;
    static Arg args[] = {
            { XtNexpose,    (XtArgVal) Redisplay },
            { XtNwidth,     (XtArgVal) 1         },
            { XtNheight,    (XtArgVal) 1         }
    };

    base = OlInitialize(...);

    stub = XtCreateManagedWidget("graphics pane",
            stubWidgetClass, base, args, XtNumber(args));

    .......

} /* END OF main() */
```

SEE ALSO

Caption(3Olit), OlCallAcceptFocus(3Olit), OlCanAcceptFocus(3Olit), OlHasFocus(3Olit), OlGetCurrentFocusWidget(3Olit), OlMoveFocus(3Olit), OlSetInputFocus(3Olit)

NAME

TextEdit – provide multiple line editing

SYNOPSIS

```
#include <X11/Intrinsic.h>
#include <X11/StringDefs.h>
#include <Xol/OpenLook.h>
#include <Xol/TextEdit.h>

widget = XtCreateWidget(name, textEditWidgetClass, . . .);
```

DESCRIPTION

The **TextEdit** widget provides an n-line text editing facility that has both a customizable user interface and a programmatic interface. It can be used for single line string entry as well as full-window editing. It provides a consistent editing paradigm for textual data. Both the MOTIF and OPEN LOOK look and feel are supported.

In the MOTIF look and feel, **TextEdit** support includes

(clipboard) cut/copy/paste and primary cut/copy/paste

an I-beam text cursor when it has focus and an unfilled caret when it does not have focus

a location cursor and a shadow

helvetica default font

In the OPEN LOOK look and feel, **TextEdit** support includes

(clipboard) cut/copy/paste

a triangle cursor when it has focus and no cursor when it does not have focus

Lucida default font

The **TextEdit** widget provides three text wrap modes: wrapoff, wrapany, and wrapwhitespace. (See the **XtNwrapMode** resource for more information.)

The **TextEdit** widget provides several distinct callback lists used to monitor the state of the textual data: insertion cursor movement, modification of the text, and post modification notification. Each of these callbacks provide information to the application regarding the intended action. The application can simply examine this information to maintain its current state or can disallow the action and perform any of the programmatic manipulations instead. (See the **XtNmotionVerification**, **XtNmodifyVerification**, and **XtNpostModifyVerification** resources.)

The **TextEdit** widget also provides distinct callback lists for user input: mouse button down and key press. The call data for these callbacks decodes the input for the application. The application can examine the input and either consume the action and perform any of the programmatic manipulations, or allow the widget to act upon it. (See the **XtNconsumeEvent** resource.)

The **TextEdit** widget also provides the application with a callback list used when the widget is redisplayed. With this callback the application can add callbacks which can be used to display information in the margins of the **TextEdit** such as line numbers or update marks. (See the **XtNmargin** resource.)

Editing Capabilities

The **TextEdit** widget provides editing capabilities to move the insert point, select text, delete text, scroll the display, perform cut, copy, paste, and undo operations, and refresh the text display. All of these capabilities are bound to global resources stored in the X server. Many of these settings can be changed using the property windows available in the desktop manager. All of these settings dynamically change immediately after new settings are stored in the server. The key bindings used by the **TextEdit** widget are listed under "Keyboard Traversal".

Hierarchical Text

Text is considered to be hierarchically composed of white space, spans, lines, and paragraphs within a document. "Whitespace" is defined as any non-empty sequence of the ASCII characters space, tab, linefeed, or carriage return (decimal values 32, 9, 10, 13; respectively); a "span" is any non-empty sequence of characters bounded by whitespace. A "source line" is any (possibly empty) sequence of characters bounded by newline characters; a "display line" is any (possibly empty) sequence of characters appearing on a single screen display line. A "paragraph" is any sequence of characters bounded by sets of two or more adjacent newline characters. A "document" is the entire content of the text.

In all cases, the beginning or end of the text is an acceptable bounding element in the previous definitions.

Sizing the Display

When making display decisions during initialization, the **TextEdit** widget first will use either the application specified width and height or, if these values are not specified, calculate width and height by applying the values of the **XtNcharsVisible** and **XtNlinesVisible** resources. Once the width and height are determined the **TextEdit** widget will request an appropriate size from its parent (considering the margins). If the request is denied or only partially satisfied, no future growth requests will be made unless there is an intervening resize operation externally imposed.

Once the size of the display is settled, the **TextEdit** widget recalculates the display lines based on this size, the various margins, the font, tab table, and wrap mode.

Wrapping

If the wrap mode is **OL_WRAP_ANY**, as many characters from the source line as will entirely fit before the right margin are written to the current display line, then the next character starts at the left margin of the next display line, and so on. If the wrap mode is **OL_WRAP_WHITE_SPACE**, the line wrap occurs at the first whitespace character that follows the last full word that does fit on the current display line. If, however, under **OL_WRAP_WHITE_SPACE**, the first full word that does not fit is the first word on the display line, the wrap is made as if **OL_WRAP_ANY** were selected. If the wrap mode is **OL_WRAP_OFF** the lines are not wrapped but are clipped at the right margin. In this mode the text is horizontally scrollable.

ScrolledWindow

The application can place the **TextEdit** widget within a **ScrolledWindow** widget. When this arrangement is used, the text is easily scrollable using the Scrollbars provided by the **ScrolledWindow**.

TextEdit (3Olit)

The proportion indicators on the scrollbars show relatively how much of the text is currently in the display.

As the user enters text, the view automatically scrolls when the insert point moves beyond a margin boundary (right or bottom) to keep the insert point in view.

Application Access

The **TextEdit** widget provides complete programmatic control of the text and its display.

Keyboard Traversal

The **OlLookupInputEvent**(3Olit) manual page lists the complete set of virtual event translations. The default value of the **XtNtraversalOn** resource is **TRUE**.

The widget responds to the following keyboard navigation keys:

NEXT_FIELD	move to the first control in the next group
PREV_FIELD	move to the first control in the previous group
NEXTWINDOW	move to the next window in the application
PREVWINDOW	move to the previous window in the application
NEXTAPP	move to the first window in the next application
PREVAPP	move to the first window in the previous application
ROWUP	move the caret up one line in the current column
ROWDOWN	move the caret down one line in the current column
CHARBAK	move the caret backward one character
CHARFWD	move the caret forward one character
WORDFWD	move the caret forward one word
WORDBAK	move the caret back one word
LINESTART	move the caret to the beginning of the line
LINEEND	move the caret to the end of the line
PANESTART	move the caret to the first row and column on the display
PANEEND	move the caret to the last row and column on the display
DOCSTART	move the caret to the beginning of the document
DOCEND	move the caret to the end of the document

Note that it is expected that the user will use the alternate bindings for NEXT_FIELD and PREV_FIELD because the primary binding, TAB and SHIFT Tab, are valid characters in a Text pane. Also, in the MOTIF look and feel, if **XtNlinesVisible** is 1, ROWUP and ROWDOWN will act as interwidget navigation commands rather than cursor navigation commands.

The **TextEdit** widget responds to the following selection keys:

SELECTALL	select entire text
DESELECTALL	deselect entire text
SELCHARFWD	adjust the selection one character forward
SELWORDFWD	adjust the selection to the end of the current (or next) word
SELLINEFWD	adjust the selection to the end of the current (or next) line
SELCHARBAK	adjust the selection one character backward
SELWORDBAK	adjust the selection to the beginning of the current (or previous) word
SELLINEBAK	adjust the selection to the beginning of the current (or previous) line
SELLINE	adjust the selection to include the entire current line
SELFLIPENDS	reverse the "anchor" and cursor position of the selection

The **TextEdit** widget responds to the following scrolling keys:

SCROLLUP	scroll the view up one screen line
SCROLLDOWN	scroll the view down one screen line
PAGEUP	scroll to the next page up
PAGEDOWN	scroll to the next page down
PAGERIGHT	scroll to the next page to the right
PAGELEFT	scroll to the next page to the left
SCROLLLEFT	scroll the view one screen to the left
SCROLLRIGHT	scroll the view one screen to the right
SCROLLTOP	scroll to the beginning of the document
SCROLLBOTTOM	scroll to the end of the document
SCROLLLEFTEDGE	scroll to the left edge of the document
SCROLLRIGHTEDGE	scroll to the right edge of the document

The **TextEdit** widget responds to the following edit keys:

DELCHARFWD	delete the character to the right of the caret
DELCHARBAK	delete the character to the left of the caret
DELWORDFWD	delete the word to the right of the caret
DELWORDBAK	delete the word to the left of the caret
DELLINEFWD	delete to the end of the line from the caret

DELLINEBAK	delete from the beginning of the line to the caret
DELLINE	delete the line containing the caret
UNDO	undo the previous edit operation

The **TextEdit** widget also responds to the following miscellaneous keys:

| DRAG | initiate a drag and drop operation with the currently selected text |
| MENU | bring up the TextEdit menu |

The following activation types are valid in both the MOTIF and the OPEN LOOK look and feel:

TextEdit Activation Types

Activation Type	Expected Results
OL_CUTBTN	primary cut
OL_COPYBTN	primary copy
OL_PASTEBTN	primary paste

The following activation types are valid in the MOTIF look and feel:

TextEdit Activation Types

Activation Type	Expected Results
OL_PRIMARYCUTKEY	primary cut
OL_PRIMARYCOPYKEY	primary copy
OL_PRIMARYPASTEKEY	primary paste

Menu

The **TextEdit** widget has an edit menu that contains buttons for Undo, Cut, Copy, Paste, and Delete. Menu items which would have no effect are inactive.

Coloration

When this widget receives the input focus, it changes the text caret in the text field to the active caret and the color specified in **XtNfontColor**. In the MOTIF look and feel, it also changes the location cursor to **XtNinputFocusColor**.

Display of Keyboard Mnemonic

The **TextEdit** widget does not display the mnemonic. If the **TextEdit** widget is the child of a **Caption** widget, the **Caption** widget can be used to display the mnemonic.

TextEdit (3Olit)

RESOURCES

TextEdit Resource Set					
Name	Class	Type	Default	Acc	Inherit
XtNancestorSensitive	XtCSensitive	Boolean	(calculated)	G[1]	Core
XtNbackground	XtCTextBackground	Pixel	"XtDefaultBackground"	SGI	Core
XtNbackgroundPixmap	XtCPixmap	Pixmap	XtUnspecifiedPixmap	SGI	Core
XtNblinkRate	XtCBlinkRate	int	1000[10]	SGI	
XtNborderColor	XtCBorderColor	Pixel	"XtDefaultForeground"	SGI	Core
XtNborderPixmap	XtCPixmap	Pixmap	XtUnspecifiedPixmap	SGI	Core
XtNborderWidth	XtCBorderWidth	Dimension	0	SGI	Core
XtNbottomMargin	XtCMargin	Dimension	(calculated)	SGI	
XtNcharsVisible	XtCCharsVisible	int	"50"	GI	
XtNcolormap	XtCColormap	Colormap	(parent's)	GI	Core
XtNconsumeEvent	XtCCallback	XtCallbackList	NULL	SGI	Primitive
XtNcontrolCaret	XtCControlCaret	Boolean	TRUE	GI	
XtNcursorPosition	XtCTextPosition	int	"0"	SGI	
XtNdepth	XtCDepth	Cardinal	(parent's)	GI	Core
XtNdestroyCallback	XtCCallback	XtCallbackList	NULL	SGI	Object
XtNdisplayPosition	XtCTextPosition	int	"0"	SGI	
XtNdragCursor	XtCCursor	Cursor	NULL	SGI	
XtNdropSiteID	XtCReadOnly	OlDnDDropSiteID	NULL	G	
XtNeditType	XtCEditType	OlEditMode	"textedit"	SGI	
XtNfont	XtCFont	XFontStruct *	"OlDefaultFont"	SGI	Primitive
XtNfontColor	XtCTextFontColor	Pixel	"XtDefaultForeground"	SGI	Primitive
XtNfontGroup	XtCFontGroup	OlFontList *	NULL	SGI	Primitive
XtNforeground	XtCForeground	Pixel	"XtDefaultForeground"	SGI	Primitive
XtNheight	XtCHeight	Dimension	(calculated)	SGI	Core
XtNhighlightThickness	XtCHighlightThickness	Dimension	"2 points"[2]	SGI	Primitive
XtNinputFocusColor	XtCInputFocusColor	Pixel	"Red"	SGI	Primitive
XtNinsertReturn	XtCInsertReturn	Boolean	TRUE	SGI	
XtNinsertTab	XtCInsertTab	Boolean	TRUE	SGI	
XtNleftMargin	XtCMargin	Dimension	(calculated)	SGI	
XtNlinesVisible	XtCLinesVisible	int	"16"	GI	
XtNmappedWhenManaged	XtCMappedWhenManaged	Boolean	TRUE	SGI	Core
XtNmargin	XtCCallback	XtCallbackList	NULL	SGI	
XtNmodifyVerification	XtCCallback	XtCallbackList	NULL	SGI	
XtNmotionVerification	XtCCallback	XtCallbackList	NULL	SGI	
XtNpostModifyNotification	XtCCallback	XtCallbackList	NULL	SGI	
XtNpreselect	XtCPreselect	Boolean	FALSE	SGI	
XtNreferenceName	XtCReferenceName	String	NULL	SGI	Primitive
XtNreferenceWidget	XtCReferenceWidget	Widget	NULL	SGI	Primitive
XtNrightMargin	XtCMargin	Dimension	(calculated)	SGI	

Name	Class	Type	Default	Acc	Inherit
			TextEdit Resource Set (cont'd)		
XtNscreen	XtCScreen	Screen *	(parent's)	GI	Core
XtNselectEnd	XtCTextPosition	int	"0"	SGI	
XtNselectStart	XtCTextPosition	int	"0"	SGI	
XtNsensitive	XtCSensitive	Boolean	TRUE	G[1]	Core
XtNshadowThickness	XtCShadowThickness	Dimension	"0 points"[3]	SGI	Primitive
XtNshadowType	XtCShadowType	OlDefine	OL_SHADOW_IN	SGI	Primitive
XtNsource	XtCSource	String	NULL	SGI	
XtNsourceType	XtCSourceType	OlSourceType	"stringsource"	SGI	
XtNtabTable	XtCTabTable	XtPointer	NULL	SGI	
XtNtopMargin	XtCMargin	Dimension	4	SGI	
XtNtranslations	XtCTranslations	XtTranslations	NULL	SGI	Core
XtNtraversalOn	XtCTraversalOn	Boolean	TRUE	SGI	Primitive
XtNuserData	XtCUserData	XtPointer	NULL	SGI	Primitive
XtNwidth	XtCWidth	Dimension	(calculated)	SGI	Core
XtNwrapMode	XtCWrapMode	OlWrapMode	"wrapwhitespace"	SGI	
XtNx	XtCPosition	Position	0	SGI	Core
XtNy	XtCPosition	Position	0	SGI	Core

[1] Use XtSetSensitive to set this resource.
[2] Not used in the OPEN LOOK look and feel.
[3] "2 points" in the MOTIF look and feel.
[10] 500 msec. in the MOTIF look and feel.

XtNblinkRate

This resource is used to specify the rate that the "active" input caret blinks. The value of this resource is interpreted as the number of milliseconds between blinks. Setting this value to zero (0) turns the blink effect off.

XtNborderColor

This resource specifies the color of the window border. In the MOTIF look and feel, the border is used as the location cursor. It takes the input focus color when the widget has focus and the widget's background color when it loses focus.

XtNbottomMargin

Range of values:

$$0 <= \text{XtNbottomMargin} <= \text{height} - \text{XtNtopMargin} - \text{font\_height}$$

This resource specifies the number of pixels used for the bottom margin. The range is relative to the top margin value. The default is a maximum of 4 pixels or 1 + 1/3 the font height (maximum ascent + maximum descent). Note that in the MOTIF look and feel, the border shadow is drawn inside the margins.

XtNcharsVisible

This resource is used to specify the "initial" width of the text in terms of characters. It overrides the XtNwidth resource setting. The XtNwidth is recalculated to be the value of XtNcharsVisible multiplied by the width of the 'n' (en) character in the font plus the values for the left and right margins. The value of this resource changes to reflect the effects of geometry changes imposed by the widget tree and the user. `XtSetValues` for this resource is ignored.

XtNcontrolCaret
Range of values:

        TRUE/"true"
        FALSE/"false"

This resource controls the display of ASCII control characters. These characters are transformed to a printable ASCII character, by adding a constant value (0x40), and displayed with a preceding a caret. If **FALSE**, all characters are passed unmodified to the X drawing functions.

XtNcursorPosition
Range of values:

        0 <= `cursorPosition` < size of buffer

This resource is used to specify the relative character position in the text source of the insert cursor. Changing the value of this resource may affect the `XtNdisplay-Position` resource if the `cursorPosition` is not visible in the pane.

XtNdisplayPosition
Range of values:

        0 <= `displayPosition` < size of buffer

This resource contains the position in the text source that will be displayed at the top of the pane. A value of 0 indicates the beginning of the text source. When the position is near the end of the buffer, this position is recalculated to ensure that the last line in the buffer appears as the last line in the pane.

XtNdragCursor
This resource identifies the cursor used to animate dragging of selected text. If left null, **TextEdit** creates a bitmap containing the first three letters of the dragged text.

XtNdropSiteId
This resource is the ID of the drop site registered by **TextEdit** to receive drop operations [see `OlDnDRegisterWidgetDropSite`(3DnD)].

XtNeditType
Range of values:

        OL_TEXT_READ/"textread"
        OL_TEXT_EDIT/"textedit"

This resource controls the edit state of the source:

`OL_TEXT_READ`   The source is read-only; the end-user cannot edit it.

`OL_TEXT_EDIT`   The source is fully editable.

XtNinputFocusColor
Range of values:

        (Valid Pixel value for the display)/(Valid color name)

This resource specifies the color of the location cursor in the MOTIF look and feel. It has no effect in the OPEN LOOK look and feel.

XtNinsertTab

If this resource is set to **FALSE**, a TAB character is not insertable. Setting this resource to **FALSE** makes traversal of the controls easier if the TAB key is bound as **OL_NEXT_FIELD**; if set to **TRUE**, a TAB character is insertable.

XtNleftMargin

Range of values:

$$0 <= \texttt{XtNleftMargin} <= \texttt{width} - \texttt{XtNrightMargin} - \texttt{font\_width}$$

This resource specifies the number of pixels used for the left margin. The range is relative to the right margin value. The default is a maximum of 4 pixels or $1 + 1/3$ the font height (maximum ascent + maximum descent). Note that in the MOTIF look and feel, the border shadow is drawn inside the margins. The **XtNshadowTh-ickness** resource is forced to be smaller than the smallest margin (top, bottom, left, or right).

XtNlinesVisible

This resource specifies the initial height of the text in terms of lines. The height is calculate to be the value of **XtNlinesVisible** multiplied by the font height (maximum ascent + maximum descent) plus the values for the top and bottom margin. The value of the resource is updated to reflect the effects of geometry changes imposed by the widget tree and the user. **XtSetValues** for this resource is ignored.

XtNmargin

This is the NULL terminated callback list of **XtCallbackList** used when the pane is redisplayed. The *call_data* parameter is a pointer to a **OlTextMarginCallData** structure which includes the following members:

```
OlTextMarginHint    hint;
XRectangle *        rect;
```

Where **OlTextMarginHint** is one of:

```
OL_MARGIN_EXPOSED;
OL_MARGIN_CALCULATED;
```

OlTextMarginCallDataPointer is a pointer to a **OlTextMarginCallData**.

The **OlTextMarginHint** indicates whether the area to be redrawn was explicitly known because of an exposure event (**OL_MARGIN_EXPOSED**) or if the rectangle was calculated relative to the textual display (**OL_MARGIN_CALCULATED**). The margin callback should respond to the **OL_MARGIN_EXPOSED** hint by repainting the area defined by the **XRectangle rect**. The margin callback may wish to calculate its own rectangle in the **OL_MARGIN_CALCULATED** case. It can freely use the rectangle structure passed in with the call data for this purpose.

This callback can be used to repair the margins for the text. For example, this callback may be used to display line numbers for the text in the left margin.

XtNmodifyVerification

This is the NULL terminated callback list of type **XtCallbackList** used when a modification of the buffer is attempted. The *call_data* parameter is a pointer to an **OlTextModifyCallData** structure which includes the following members:

```
Boolean             ok;
TextPosition        current_cursor;
TextPosition        select_start;
TextPosition        select_end;
TextPosition        new_cursor;
TextPosition        new_select_start;
TextPosition        new_select_end;
char  *             text;
int                 text_length;
```

OlTextModifyCallDataPointer is a pointer to **OlTextModifyCallData**.

All of the fields in this structure, with the exception of the **ok** flag, are treated as read-only information. The application can return without changing the value of the **ok** flag, in which case the update will occur. The application can also set the **ok** flag to **FALSE**, perform any other operations it desires, and return, in which case the update will not be performed.

text_length will return the number of bytes in the returned string, not the number of characters. The distinction is important when, applications use (non-ASCII) multi-byte characters.

XtNmotionVerification

This NULL terminated callback list of type **XtCallbackList** is used whenever the cursor position moves within the widget. The *call_data* parameter is a pointer to an **OlTextMotionCallData** structure which includes the following members:

```
Boolean             ok;
TextPosition        current_cursor;
TextPosition        new_cursor;
TextPosition        select_start;
TextPosition        select_end;
```

OlTextMotionCallDataPointer is a pointer to **OlTextMotionCallData**.

This callback list is used whenever the cursor position changes due to cursor movement operations or by modification of the text.

The application can distinguish between a simple cursor movement and a modify operation by comparing the **current_cursor** and **new_cursor** values.

When these values are equal the callback is the result of a modify operation. In this case the **ok** field is ignored and the application should not attempt to perform updates to the text or its display during this callback.

If the values of **current_cursor** and **new_cursor** are different, the application is guaranteed that the operation is the result of a cursor movement. In this mode all of the fields in this structure, with the exception of the **ok** flag, are treated as read-only information. The application can return without changing the value of the **ok** flag, in which case the movement will occur. The application can also set the **ok** flag to **FALSE**, perform any other operations it desires, and return, in which case the movement will not be performed.

XtNpostModifyNotification

This is the NULL terminated callback list of type `XtCallbackList` used after a buffer update has completed. The *call_data* parameter is a pointer to an `OlTextPostModifyCallData` structure which includes the following members:

```
Boolean              requestor;
TextPosition         new_cursor;
TextPosition         new_select_start;
TextPosition         new_select_end;
char *               inserted;
char *               deleted;
TextLocation         delete_start;
TextLocation         delete_end;
TextLocation         insert_start;
TextLocation         insert_end;
TextLocation         cursor_position;
```

`OlTextPostModifyCallDataPointer` is a pointer to `OlTextPostModifyCall-Data`.

This callback is used to synchronize the application with the text once a modify operation is completed. For example, the application may record successful edit operations in an undo buffer to provide multi-level undo functionality. The data provided in this callback is considered read-only and volatile (for example, the application should copy what it needs from this structure before returning).

XtNpreselect

Range of values:

```
TRUE/"true"
FALSE/"false"
```

This resource controls text selection when **TextEdit** receives focus from other than the SELECT button (for example, when the user traverses to the **TextEdit** widget via the NEXT_FIELD key). If **TRUE**, **TextEdit** selects all its text. **XtNpreselect** is ignored if **XtNeditType** is **OL_TEXT_READ**.

XtNrightMargin

Range of values:

```
0 <= XtNrightMargin <= width - XtNleftMargin - font_width
```

This resource specifies the number of pixels used for the right margin. Note that the range is relative to the left margin value. The default is a maximum of 4 pixels or 1 + 1/3 the font height (maximum ascent + maximum descent). Also, in the MOTIF look and feel, the border shadow is drawn inside the margins.

XtNselectEnd

This resource is used to specify the last character position selected in the text. Its value is one greater than the position of the last selected character. It is used along with the **XtNselectStart** and **XtNcursorPosition** resources to specify a selection. To be effective, the **XtNselectStart** value must be less than or equal to **XtNselectEnd** and the **XtNcursorPosition** must be equal to either **XtNselectStart** or **XtNselectEnd**. If either of these tests fails then **XtNselectStart** and **XtNselectEnd** are set equal to the value of the **XtNcursorPosition**.

XtNselectStart

This resource is used to specify the first character position selected in the text. It is used along with the **XtNselectEnd** and **XtNcursorPosition** resources to specify a selection. To be effective, the **XtNselectStart** value must be less than or equal to **XtNselectEnd** and the **XtNcursorPosition** must be equal to either **XtNselectStart** or **XtNselectEnd**. If either of these tests fails then **XtNselectStart** and **XtNselectEnd** are set equal to the value of the **XtNcursorPosition**.

XtNsource

Range of values:

<string> for **OL_STRING_SOURCE**
<name of file> for **OL_DISK_SOURCE**
<pointer to an existing **TextBuffer**> for **OL_TEXT_BUFFER_SOURCE**

This resource is used in tandem with the **XtNsourceType** resource to specify the source. See the **XtNsourceType** resource for a full description of these resources.

Setting this resource via **XtSetValues** automatically resets **XtNcursorPosition**, **XtNdisplayPosition**, **selectStart**, and **selectEnd** resources to 0, unless otherwise specified by the application in the **XtSetValues** argument list.

XtNsource is replaced by a **TextBuffer**. Doing a **XtGetValues** will return a pointer to a **TextBuffer**, independent of the **XtNsource** or **XtNsourceType** resource setting. Note that **TextEdit** always internally converts **XtNsource** to a **TextBuffer**. When retrieving **XtNsource** via **XtGetValues**, applications should expect a (**TextBuffer** *) to be returned.

XtNsourceType

Range of values:

OL_STRING_SOURCE/''stringsource''
OL_DISK_SOURCE/''disksource''
OL_TEXT_BUFFER_SOURCE

This resource controls the interpretation of the **XtNsource** resource value. When set to **OL_STRING_SOURCE** the **XtNsource** value is interpreted as the string to be used as the source, when set to **OL_DISK_SOURCE** the **XtNsource** value is interpreted as the name of the file containing the source, when set to **OL_TEXT_BUFFER_SOURCE** the **XtNsource** value is interpreted as a pointer to a previously initialized **TextBuffer** (see the **TextBuffer Utilities** manual page for a description of **TextBuffers**).

XtNtabTable

This resource is used to specify a pointer to an array of tab positions. These tab positions are specified in terms of pixels and must be terminated by a zero (0) entry. The widget calculates tabs by finding the next tab table entry that exceeds the current x offset for the line. If no such entry exists in the table or if the pointer to the tab table is NULL, the tab is set to the next greater multiple of eight (8) times the size of the 'n' (en) character in the font.

XtNtopMargin

Range of values:

$0 <=$ **XtNtopMargin** $<=$ **height** - **XtNbottomMargin** - **font_height**

TextEdit (3Olit)

This resource specifies the number of pixels used for the top margin. The range is relative to the bottom margin value. Note that in the MOTIF look and feel, the border shadow is drawn inside the margins.

XtNwrapMode

Range of values:

> OL_WRAP_WHITE_SPACE/"wrapwhitespace"
> OL_WRAP_ANY/"wrapany"
> OL_WRAP_OFF/"wrapoff"

This resource is used to control how the source is wrapped in the pane. When OL_WRAP_ANY, lines are wrapped at the last character before the right margin; when set to OL_WRAP_WHITE_SPACE, lines are wrapped at the last white space before the right margin or as in OL_WRAP_ANY if the line does not contain any white space; when OL_WRAP_OFF, lines are not wrapped and the pane may horizontally scroll.

NOTES

The TextEdit widget does not support Reselect and Add Mode keys.

SEE ALSO

AllocateTextBuffer(3Olit) OlDnDRegisterWidgetDropSite(3DnD), OlLookupInputEvent(3Olit), OlTextEditClearBuffer(3Olit), OlTextEditCopyBuffer(3Olit), OlTextEditCopySelection(3Olit), OlTextEditGetCursorPosition(3Olit), OlTextEditGetLastPosition(3Olit), OlTextEditInsert(3Olit), OlTextEditPaste(3Olit), OlTextEditReadSubString(3Olit), OlTextEditRedraw(3Olit), OlTextEditSetCursorPosition(3Olit), OlTextEditTextBuffer(3Olit), OlTextEditUpdate(3Olit), ReadFileIntoTextBuffer(3Olit), ReadPipeIntoTextBuffer(3Olit), ReadStringIntoTextBuffer(3Olit), RegisterTextBufferScanFunctions(3Olit), RegisterTextBufferUpdate(3Olit), RegisterTextBufferWordDefinition(3Olit), TextBuffer_Macros(3Olit)

NAME

TextField – provide a one-line editable text field

SYNOPSIS

```
#include <X11/Intrinsic.h>
#include <X11/StringDefs.h>
#include <Xol/OpenLook.h>
#include <Xol/TextField.h>

widget = XtCreateWidget(name, textFieldWidgetClass, . . .);
```

DESCRIPTION

The **TextField** widget provides a one-line input field for text data.

In the OPEN LOOK look and feel it can display scrolling arrows on the left, right, or both sides, to allow the user to scroll the field left or right using the mouse.

In both the OPEN LOOK and the MOTIF look and feel it can be made to display "stepping" arrows on the right side, to allow the user to increment or decrement "numeric" values. In the OPEN LOOK look and feel these arrows present the OPEN LOOK numeric field feature. Because the standard MOTIF look and feel has no similar feature, the visuals are designed to integrate well into the MOTIF look and feel. The stepping arrows are presented only if a **TextField** class method is set by a subclass (the **TextField** class does not set this method).

TextField Components

The **TextField** widget contains the following elements:

Input Caret

Input Field

Left Scrolling Arrow (conditional)

Right Scrolling Arrow (conditional)

Up Stepping Arrows (optional)

Down Stepping Arrows (optional)

Figures 1 and 2 show examples of one-line text fields. For examples of text fields with Up/Down Arrows, see **IntegerField**(3Olit) and **StepField**(3Olit).

TextField (3Olit)

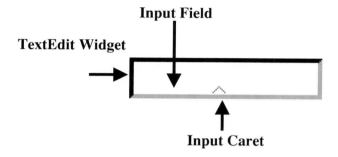

Figure 1. MOTIF Style One-Line Text Field

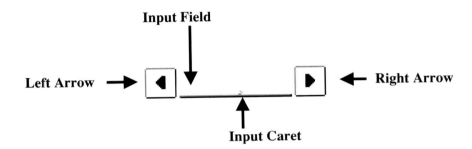

Figure 2. OPEN LOOK One-Line Text Field with Left/Right Scrolling Arrows

Keyboard Input

Once the input focus has been moved to the Input Field, keyboard entry is allowed. The **TextField** widget does not validate the input, leaving that up to the application.

Keyboard Traversal

The default value of the **XtNtraversalOn** resource is **TRUE**.

The **TextField** widget responds to the following keyboard navigation keys:

RETURN	
NEXT_FIELD	move to the next traversable widget in the window
PREV_FIELD	move to the previous traversable widget in the window
CHARBAK	move the caret backward one character
CHARFWD	move the caret forward one character
WORDFWD	move the caret forward one word
WORDBAK	move the caret back one word
LINESTART	move the caret to the beginning of the display
LINEEND	move the caret to the end of the display

TextField (3Olit)

The MENUKEY posts the menu attached to the TextField.

Selection Keys

The `TextField` widget responds to the following selection keys:

SELCHARFWD	adjust the selection one character forward
SELWORDFWD	adjust the selection to the end of the current (or next) word
SELLINEFWD	adjust the selection to the end of the current (or next) line
SELCHARBAK	adjust the selection one character backward
SELWORDBAK	adjust the selection to the beginning of the current (or previous) word
SELLINEBAK	adjust the selection to the beginning of the current (or previous) line
SELLINE	adjust the selection to include the entire current line
SELFLIPENDS	reverse the "anchor" and cursor position of the selection

Scrolling Keys

The `TextField` widget responds to the following scrolling keys:

SCROLLLEFT	scroll the view one screen to the left
SCROLLRIGHT	scroll the view one screen to the right
SCROLLLEFTEDGE	scroll to the left edge of the textfield
SCROLLRIGHTEDGE	scroll to the right edge of the textfield

Edit Keys

The `TextField` widget responds to the following edit keys:

DELCHARFWD	delete the character to the right of the caret
DELCHARBAK	delete the character to the left of the caret
DELWORDFWD	delete the word to the right of the caret
DELWORDBAK	delete the word to the left of the caret
DELLINEFWD	delete to the end of the line from the caret
DELLINEBAK	delete from the beginning of the line to the caret
DELLINE	delete the line containing the caret
UNDO	undo the last edit

Stepping Keys

The `TextField` widget responds to the following stepping keys:

SCROLLDOWN MOVEDOWN ROWDOWN PAGEDOWN	step down one unit

MULTIDOWN	step down *n* units
SCROLLUP	
MOVEUP	
ROWUP	step up one unit
PAGEUP	
MULTIUP	step up *n* units
SCROLLTOP	step up to limit
SCROLLBOTTOM	step down to limit

Display of Keyboard Mnemonic

The **TextField** does not display the mnemonic. If the **TextField** is the child of a **Caption** widget, the **Caption** widget can be used to display the mnemonic.

Display of Keyboard Accelerators

The **TextField** does not respond to a keyboard accelerator because clicking the SELECT button on a TextField activates depending on the pointer position. So, the **TextField** does not display a keyboard accelerator.

Scrolling Long Text Input

In the OPEN LOOK look and feel only, if an input value exceeds the length of the Input Field, the Left Arrow and/or Right Arrow appear and the input value is visually truncated on the left and/or the right to show only as many characters as can fit in the Input Field. Since the Arrows take up space that would otherwise be used for the input, the truncation is more severe than would be necessary if they were not visible. An Arrow is present only if characters are hidden in the direction expressed by the arrow.

The user can scroll to show the hidden parts of the input by clicking or pressing SELECT on the Left or Right Arrow. Clicking SELECT on the Left Arrow scrolls the input one character to the right to show the next character that was hidden to the left. Clicking SELECT on the Right Arrow scrolls the input one character to the left to show the next character that was hidden to the right. Pressing SELECT scrolls continuously, with a user-adjustable wait between changes.

Input Validation

A validation callback list can be used to perform limited per-field validation. This callback is used when the end-user hits the RETURN, PREV_FIELD, or NEXT_FIELD. It is not called if the user moves the focus to another input area.

Position of the Input Caret

As characters are entered from the keyboard, the Input Caret moves to the right until it reaches the right end of the Input Field. As additional characters are typed the text scrolls to the left (the Left Arrow appears as discussed above) and the Input Caret moves relative to the text but remains stationary on the screen.

Selecting and Operating on the Input Field

The **TextField** widget allows text to be copied or moved to and from the Input Field.

TextField (3Olit)

Coloration

Figures 3 and 4 illustrate the resources that affect the coloration of the **TextField** widget.

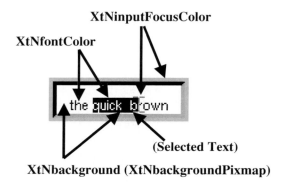

Figure 3. Text Field Coloration MOTIF Look

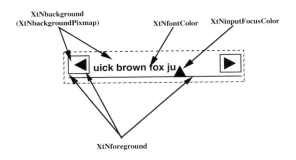

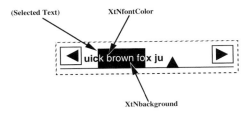

Figure 4. Text Field Coloration OPEN LOOK Look

RESOURCES

TextField Resource Set					
Name	Class	Type	Default	Acc	Inherit
XtNancestorSensitive	XtCSensitive	Boolean	(calculated)	G[1]	Core
XtNbackground	XtCBackground	Pixel	"XtDefaultBackground"	SGI	Core
XtNbackgroundPixmap	XtCPixmap	Pixmap	XtUnspecifiedPixmap	SGI	Core
XtNblinkRate	XtCBlinkRate	int	1000[10]	SGI	TextEdit
XtNborderColor	XtCBorderColor	Pixel	"XtDefaultForeground"	SGI	Core
XtNborderPixmap	XtCPixmap	Pixmap	XtUnspecifiedPixmap	SGI	Core
XtNborderWidth	XtCBorderWidth	Dimension	0	SGI	Core
XtNbottomMargin	XtCMargin	Dimension	(calculated)	SGI	TextEdit
XtNcanDecrement	XtCCanStep	Boolean	TRUE	SGI	
XtNcanIncrement	XtCCanStep	Boolean	TRUE	SGI	
XtNcanScroll	XtCCanScroll	Boolean	TRUE	SGI	
XtNcharsVisible	XtCCharsVisible	Cardinal	XtUnspecifiedCardinal	GI	TextEdit
XtNcolormap	XtCColormap	Colormap	(parent's)	GI	Core
XtNconsumeEvent	XtCCallback	XtCallbackList	NULL	SGI	Primitive
XtNcontrolCaret	XtCControlCaret	Boolean	TRUE	GI	TextEdit
XtNcursorPosition	XtCTextPosition	int	"0"	SGI	TextEdit

TextField (3Olit)

TextField Resource Set (cont'd)					
Name	Class	Type	Default	Acc	Inherit
XtNdepth	XtCDepth	Cardinal	(parent's)	GI	Core
XtNdestroyCallback	XtCCallback	XtCallbackList	NULL	SGI	Object
XtNdisplayPosition	XtCTextPosition	int	"0"	SGI	TextEdit
XtNdragCursor	XtCCursor	Cursor	NULL	SGI	TextEdit
XtNdropSiteID	XtCReadOnly	OlDnDDropSiteID	NULL	G	TextEdit
XtNeditType	XtCEditType	OlEditMode	"textedit"	SGI	TextEdit
XtNfont	XtCFont	XFontStruct *	"OlDefaultFont"	SGI	Primitive
XtNfontColor	XtCTextFontColor	Pixel	"XtDefaultForeground"	SGI	Primitive
XtNfontGroup	XtCFontGroup	OlFontList *	NULL	SGI	Primitive
XtNforeground	XtCForeground	Pixel	"XtDefaultForeground"	SGI	Primitive
XtNheight	XtCHeight	Dimension	(calculated)	SGI	Core
XtNhighlightThickness	XtCHighlightThickness	Dimension	"2 points"[2]	SGI	Primitive
XtNinitialDelay	XtCInitialDelay	int	500	SGI	
XtNinputFocusColor	XtCInputFocusColor	Pixel	"Red"	SGI	Primitive
XtNinsertReturn	XtCInsertReturn	Boolean	FALSE	SGI	TextEdit
XtNinsertTab	XtCInsertTab	Boolean	FALSE	SGI	TextEdit
XtNleftMargin	XtCMargin	Dimension	(calculated)	SGI	TextEdit
XtNlinesVisible	XtCLinesVisible	int	0	G	TextEdit
XtNmappedWhenManaged	XtCMappedWhenManaged	Boolean	TRUE	SGI	Core
XtNmargin	XtCCallback	XtCallbackList	NULL	SGI	TextEdit
XtNmaximumSize	XtCMaximumSize	Cardinal	0	SGI	
XtNmodifyVerification	XtCCallback	XtCallbackList	NULL	SGI	TextEdit
XtNmotionVerification	XtCCallback	XtCallbackList	NULL	SGI	TextEdit
XtNpostModifyNotification	XtCCallback	XtCallbackList	NULL	SGI	TextEdit
XtNpreselect	XtCPreselect	Boolean	TRUE	SGI	TextEdit
XtNreferenceName	XtCReferenceName	String	NULL	SGI	Primitive
XtNreferenceWidget	XtCReferenceWidget	Widget	NULL	SGI	Primitive
XtNrepeatRate	XtCRepeatRate	int	100	SGI	
XtNrightMargin	XtCMargin	Dimension	(calculated)	SGI	TextEdit
XtNscreen	XtCScreen	Screen *	(parent's)	GI	Core
XtNselectEnd	XtCTextPosition	int	"0"	SGI	TextEdit
XtNselectStart	XtCTextPosition	int	"0"	SGI	TextEdit
XtNsensitive	XtCSensitive	Boolean	TRUE	G[1]	Core
XtNshadowThickness	XtCShadowThickness	Dimension	"0 points"[3]	SGI	Primitive
XtNshadowType	XtCShadowType	OlDefine	OL_SHADOW_IN	SGI	Primitive
XtNsourceType	XtCSourceType	OlSourceType	NULL	SGI	TextEdit
XtNstring	XtCString	String	NULL	SGI	
XtNtabTable	XtCTabTable	XtPointer	NULL	SGI	TextEdit
XtNtextEditWidget	XtCReadOnly	Widget	(self)	G	
XtNtopMargin	XtCMargin	Dimension	4	SGI	TextEdit

	TextField Resource Set (cont'd)				
Name	Class	Type	Default	Acc	Inherit
XtNtranslations	XtCTranslations	XtTranslations	NULL	SGI	Core
XtNtraversalOn	XtCTraversalOn	Boolean	TRUE	SGI	Primitive
XtNuserData	XtCUserData	XtPointer	NULL	SGI	Primitive
XtNverification	XtCCallback	XtCallbackList	NULL	SGI	
XtNwidth	XtCWidth	Dimension	(calculated)	SGI	Core
XtNwrapMode	XtCWrapMode	OlWrapMode	NULL	SGI	TextEdit
XtNx	XtCPosition	Position	0	SGI	Core
XtNy	XtCPosition	Position	0	SGI	Core

[1]   Use **XtSetSensitive** to set this resource.
[2]   Not used in the OPEN LOOK look and feel.
[3]   **"2 points"** in the MOTIF look and feel.
[10]   500 msec. in the MOTIF look and feel.

XtNcanIncrement
XtNcanDecrement

When the stepping arrows are visible (see Subclassing under USAGE), these resources control whether the stepping arrows work. For each resource, if **TRUE**, the corresponding stepping arrow is shown in normal mode and the user can click SELECT over it to change the text; if **FALSE**, the arrow is dimmed to show that it is inactive, and clicking SELECT will not do anything.

XtNcanScroll

This resource controls whether the scrolling arrows can appear on the left and right. If **XtNcanScroll** is **TRUE**, the buttons will appear when the field has more text than can appear in the window; if **FALSE**, the buttons will not appear. This resource does not prevent the user from scrolling the text from the keyboard.

(The OPEN LOOK specification is not clear whether numeric fields can also have left-right scrolling buttons, but it seems that allowing both left-right scrolling and numeric stepping leads to much clutter and is not desirable. Clients or numeric field subclasses may set this resource to **FALSE** to avoid mixing the scrolling and stepping arrows.)

XtNcharsVisible

By default, this resource is set to the value of **XtNmaximumSize** or **20** if **XtNmaximumSize** is 0 or not set. Its behavior is the same as in the **TextEdit** class.

XtNinitialDelay

Range of values:

> 0 < **XtNinitialDelay**

This resource gives the time, in milliseconds, before the first action occurs when SELECT is pressed on an Arrow. Note that millisecond timing precision may not be possible for all implementations, so the value may be rounded up to the nearest available unit by the toolkit.

TextField (3Olit)

XtNinsertTab

If this resource is set to **FALSE**, a TAB character is not insertable; Setting this resource to **FALSE** makes traversal of controls easier if the TAB key is bound as `OL_NEXT_FIELD`. If set to **TRUE**, a TAB character is insertable.

XtNmaximumSize

Range of values:

$$0 \leq \texttt{XtNmaximumSize}$$

This resource is the maximum number of characters that can be entered into the internal buffer. If this value is not set or is zero, the internal buffer will increase its size as needed limited only by the space limitations of the process.

XtNrepeatRate

This resource is used to specify the time in milliseconds of the repeat delay to be used when the scrolling arrows are pressed.

XtNstring

For **XtSetValues** and widget initialization, this resource is an alias for the **XtNsource** resource of the **TextEdit** class. Setting a new **XtNstring** value will also zero the **TextEdit XtNcursorPosition**, **XtNselectStart**, and **XtNselectEnd** resources. For **XtGetValues**, this resource provides copy of the one-line text buffer, in allocated space that should be freed by the client.

XtNtextEditWidget

This resource is present for compatibility to an earlier version of the **TextField** widget. Its value can only be retrieved with **XtGetValues**, and is the widget ID of the **TextField** instance.

XtNtopMargin
XtNbottomMargin

These **TextEdit** resources are controlled by the **TextField** subclass; clients cannot change the values, though they can use **XtGetValues** to retrieve the values. **XtNtopMargin** is adjusted to hold the border shadow (in the MOTIF look and feel) and to absorb any increase in height offered the **TextField** widget. **XtNbottomMargin** is adjusted to allow space for the underline (in the OPEN LOOK look and feel) or border shadow (in the MOTIF look and feel).

XtNverification

This is the callback list used when the user hits the RETURN, PREV_FIELD, or NEXT_FIELD. The *call_data* parameter, *****OlTextFieldVerifyPointer**, is a pointer to an **OlTextFieldVerify** structure containing the following members:

```
OlTextVerifyReason reason;
String             string;
Boolean            ok;
```

Where **OlTextVerifyReason** is an **enum** including the following elements:

```
OlTextFieldReturn
OlTextFieldPrevious
OlTextFieldNext
```

This callback list can be used to perform per-field validation. The callback is called only when a key is used to traverse from the field; it is not called when the user mouses the focus to another input area, therefore applications will still need to perform per-form validation. Future version of this widget may provide other values for **reason**, so clients shoudl be programmed accordingly.

USAGE
Subclassing

The **TextField** widget is subclassed from the **TextEdit** widget. In addition to the **TextEdit** and its superclass fields, **TextField** widgets have the following class fields:

```
OlTextFieldScrollProc scroll;
OlTextFieldStepProc step;
XtPointer extension;
```

The **scroll** procedure is of type **OlTextFieldScrollProc**:

```
typedef Boolean (*OlTextFieldScrollProc)(
    Widget w,
    Arrow arrow
);
```

The **scroll** procedure is invoked whenever the user presses or clicks SELECT over a scrolling arrow, where

w   widget being scrolled

arrow   **ArrowLeft** or **ArrowRight**

Each time **scroll** is called it should shift the text left or right (according to *arrow*) in a subclass-specific manner.

The default scroll method changes the x-offset of where **TextEdit** displays the line and calls the **TextEdit** class to handle the redisplay. It also arranges to turn off the blinking input cursor when the insert point has moved out of view. Subclasses can inherit the scroll method by setting **XtInheritScrollProc** in their class records.

The **step** procedure is of type **OlTextFieldStepProc**:

```
typedef Boolean (*OlTextFieldStepProc)(
    Widget w,
    OlSteppedReason reason,
    Cardinal count
);
```

When a non-NULL method is provided by a subclass, **TextField** will display the Stepping Arrows on the right in the widget's window. The **step** procedure is invoked whenever the user presses or clicks SELECT over a stepping arrow, or uses a keyboard equivalent, where

w   widget involved

reason one of **OlSteppedIncrement**, **OlSteppedDecrement**, **OlSteppedToMaximum**, or **OlSteppedToMinimum** *count*   *reason* step-distance modifier (**OlSteppedIncrement** and **OlSteppedDecrement** only)

Each time **step** is called it should increment or decrement the text in a subclass-specific manner.

Subclasses can inherit the step method by setting **XtInheritStepProc** in their class records. There is no default step method.

Public Routines

A client can fetch the current value of the text using **XtGetValues** or the public routines **OlTextFieldCopyString** or **OlTextFieldGetString**:

```
Cardinal OlTextFieldCopyString(
    Widget w,
    String string
);

String OlTextFieldGetString(
    Widget w,
    Cardinal *size
);
```

OlTextFieldCopyString copies the text into the buffer pointed to by *string*, and returns the number of bytes copied. The client is expected to provide a buffer large enough to hold the entire text.

OlTextFieldGetString returns a copy of the one-line text buffer, and returns in *size* the length of this copy in bytes. The client is responsible for freeing the copy.

NOTES

Earlier versions of **TextField** were subclassed from **Manager** and automatically created a **TextEdit** child.

SEE ALSO

IntegerField(3Olit), **StepField**(3Olit), **TextEdit**(3Olit)

Reference Manual Index

The Permuted Index that follows is a list of keywords, alphabetized in the second of three columns, together with the context in which each keyword is found. The manual page that produced an entry is listed in the right column.

Entries are identified with their section numbers shown in parentheses. This is important because there is considerable duplication of names among the sections, arising principally from commands and functions that exist only to exercise a particular system call.

The index is produced by rotating the NAME section of each manual page to alphabetize each keyword in it. Words that cannot fit in the middle column are rotated into the left column. If the entry is still too long, some words are omitted, and their omission is indicated with a slash ("/").

How the Permuted Index Is Created

Many users find that understanding a few things about how the permuted index is created helps them to read it more effectively and clarifies what kind of information can and cannot be obtained from it.

The basic building block for the index is the one-line description given in the NAME line on the top of each manual page. For example, this is what the top of the `GetTextBufferBlock`(3Olit) manual page looks like:

GetTextBufferBlock(3Olit)   GetTextBufferBlock(3Olit)

NAME
         `GetTextBufferBlock` – retrieve a text block from a `TextBuffer`

Each NAME line includes:

- the library function for which the manual page is named (this is the primary function; `GetTextBufferBlock` is the primary function in the example) or the general name under which all functions on this page fall [for example, see `Error`(3Olit)].

- secondary functions, which are also described on that manual page and do not have a separate manual page of their own (this example does not have a secondary function)

- a brief description of the utility function(s)

For each manual page NAME line, the indexing software generates several index entries, generally one entry for each keyword in the phrase. The middle column of the index is alphabetized on these keywords.

For:

NAME

      `GetTextBufferBlock` – retrieve a text block from a `TextBuffer`

This is generated:

GetTextBufferBlock retrieve a text block from a TextBuffer	block from a TextBuffer	GetTextBufferBlock(3Olit)
	GetTextBufferBlock retrieve a text	
	....	GetTextBufferBlock(3Olit)
TextBuffer GetTextBufferBlock	retrieve a text block from a	GetTextBufferBlock(3Olit)
GetTextBufferBlock retrieve a	text block from a TextBuffer	GetTextBufferBlock(3Olit)
retrieve a text block from a	TextBuffer GetTextBufferBlock	GetTextBufferBlock(3Olit)

How to Use the Index

Look in the middle column of the index for the word of interest. Then read the complete phrase by starting with the utility name, which may appear in the left or middle column. Utility names are followed by a colon.

The NAME line phrase is contained in the two columns, with long phrases wrapping around to the beginning of the left column. The right column of the index provides the manual page name and section number.

A slash (/) sometimes appears in the index entry to indicate that space limitations were exceeded and one or more words from the phrase were deleted.

Permuted Index

Permuted Index

/scr_restore, scr_init, scr_set	read (write) a curses screen from/
	.... curs_scr_dump(3curses)
a Buffer	ReadFileIntoBuffer read a file into
	.... ReadFileIntoBuffer(3Olit)
into a TextBuffer	ReadFileIntoTextBuffer read a file
	.... ReadFileIntoTextBuffer(3Olit)
StaticText display	read-only text .... StaticText(3Olit)
into a TextBuffer	ReadPipeIntoTextBuffer read a pipe
	.... ReadPipeIntoTextBuffer(3Olit)
into a Buffer	ReadStringIntoBuffer read a string
	.... ReadStringIntoBuffer(3Olit)
string into a TextBuffer	ReadStringIntoTextBuffer read a
	.... ReadStringIntoTextBuffer(3Olit)
/notify Input Method that window	received keyboard focus .... OlSetIcFocus(3Olit)
extension record to vendor class	record /Desktop drag and drop class
	.... OlDnDVCXInitialize(3DnD)
/drag and drop class extension	record to vendor class record .... OlDnDVCXInitialize(3DnD)
primitive/ RectButton create a	rectangular border enclosed label .... RectButton(3Olit)
border enclosed label primitive/	RectButton create a rectangular .... RectButton(3Olit)
/wrefresh, wnoutrefresh, doupdate,	redrawwin, wredrawln refresh curses/
	.... curs_refresh(3curses)
/is_wintouched curses	refresh control routines .... curs_touch(3curses)
/doupdate, redrawwin, wredrawln	refresh curses windows and lines .... curs_refresh(3curses)
OlTextEditRedraw force a	refresh of a TextEdit display .... OlTextEditRedraw(3Olit)
update_panels panels virtual screen	refresh routine panel_update: .... panel_update(3curses)
doupdate, redrawwin,/ curs_refresh:	refresh, wrefresh, wnoutrefresh, ... curs_refresh(3curses)
/find drop site clipping	regions .... OlDnDWidgetConfiguredInHier(3DnD)
specific widget/ OlClassSearchIEDB	register a given database on a .... OlClassSearchIEDB(3Olit)
specific widget/ OlWidgetSearchIEDB	register a given database on a .... OlWidgetSearchIEDB(3Olit)
procedure OlDnDRegisterDragKeyProc	register a OlDnDDragKeyProc
	.... OlDnDRegisterDragKeyProc(3DnD)
/create an Input Context to	register a text insertion window .... OlCreateIc(3Olit)
OlClassSearchTextDB	register an OPEN LOOK TEXT database
	.... OlClassSearchTextDB(3Olit)
OlDnDRegisterDDI	register the Desktop drag-and-drop
	.... OlDnDRegisterDDI(3DnD)
database on a/ OlWidgetSearchTextDB	register the OPEN LOOK TEXT
	.... OlWidgetSearchTextDB(3Olit)
/list currently	registered widget drop sites
	.... OlDnDGetDropSitesOfWidget(3DnD)
/list currently	registered window drop sites
	.... OlDnDGetDropSitesOfWindow(3DnD)
replace functions for scanning/	RegisterTextBufferScanFunctions
	.... RegisterTextBufferScanFunctions(3Olit)
TextBuffer an update function and/	RegisterTextBufferUpdate assign
	.... RegisterTextBufferUpdate(3Olit)
replace word definition	RegisterTextBufferWordDefinition
	.... RegisterTextBufferWordDefinition(3Olit)
strexp forward scan a	regular expression .... strexp(3Olit)
OlUngrabDragPointer	release an active pointer grab
	.... OlUngrabDragPointer(3Olit)

Permuted Index